GUINNESS® WORLD RECORDS 2000

MILLENNIUM EDITION

British Library cataloguing-in-Publication Data
A catalogue record for this book is available from the British Library
ISBN 0-85112-098-9

Guinness World Records 2000

Managing Editor
Nic Kynaston

Design
Lesley Horowitz & Dominic Sinesio at Office, NYC

Editorial Manager
Rhonda Carrier

Picture Editor
Gregory King

Special Content Consultant
Brian Ford

Senior Editor
Tim Footman

Design and Production
Robert Hackett

Assistant Designers
Elliot Jarrett, Yahya El-Droubie

Editors
Emma Dixon, Heather Goetz, Phil Hunt

Cover Design
Lesley Horowitz & Dominic Sinesio at Office, NYC
Ron Callow at Design 23

Technical Consultant (Cover)
Esteve Font Canadell

Guinness World Records, London

Research Manager
Geoff Trotter

Research Co-ordinator
Shelley Flacks

Records Research
Duncan Flett, Della Howes, Lina Liu, Shazia Mirza, Manjushri Mitra, Stewart Newport, John Rattagan

Keeper of the Records
Clive Carpenter

Correspondence
Martin Downham, Amanda Brooks, Ann Collins

Guinness Media Inc., USA

CEO/Publisher
Mark C. Young

Research Manager
John W. Hansen

Special Projects Co-ordinator
Kim Stram

Researchers
Ellen Mosher, Andrew Myerberg

Correspondence
Helen Andrews, Carole Browne
Cindy Cominsky, Linda Sammis

Pre Production Manager
Patricia Langton

Production Co-ordinator
Clair Savage

Colour Origination
Colour Systems, UK

Production Director
Chris Lingard

Printing and Binding
Printer Industria Grafica, S.A., Barcelona

Fulfilment
Mary Hill and Cathryn Harker

Publishing Director
Ian Castello-Cortes

Managing Director
Christopher Irwin

Abbreviations and Measurements

Guinness World Records uses both metric and imperial measurements (imperial in brackets). The only exception to this rule is for some scientific data, where metric measurements only are universally accepted, and for some sports data.

All currency values are shown in dollars with the sterling equivalent in brackets except when transactions took place in the United Kingdom, when this is reversed. Where a specific date is given the exchange rate is calculated according to the currency values that were in operation at the time. Where only a year date is given the exchange rate is calculated from December of that year. The billion conversion is one thousand million.

'GDR' (the German Democratic Republic) refers to the East German state which unified with West Germany in 1990. The abbreviation is used for sporting records broken before 1990.

The Union of Soviet Socialist Republics split into a number of parts in 1991, the largest of these being Russia. The Commonwealth of Independent States replaced it and the abbreviation 'CIS' is used mainly for sporting records broken at the 1992 Olympic Games.

Accreditation

Guinness World Records Ltd has a very thorough accreditation system for records verification. However, whilst every effort is made to ensure accuracy, Guinness World Records Ltd cannot be held responsible for any errors contained in this work. Feedback from our readers on any points of accuracy is always welcomed.

General Warning

Attempting to break records or set new records can be dangerous. Appropriate advice should be taken first and all record attempts are undertaken entirely at the participant's risk. In no circumstances will Guinness World Records Ltd have any liability for death or injury suffered in any record attempts. Guinness World Records Ltd has complete discretion over whether or not to include any particular records in the book.

This book is printed on wood free, chlorine free and acid free paper

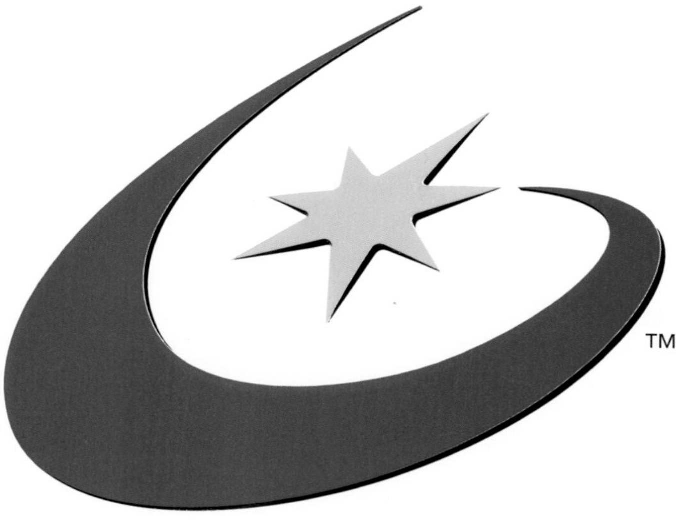

GUINNESS® WORLD RECORDS 2000

MILLENNIUM EDITION

introduction

The theme of our Year 2000 *Guinness Book of Records* is celebration.

It has been an extraordinary year for record-breakers worldwide and an amazing year for us too. We decided to celebrate with our silver memento cover, a brand new design and new records that define the limits of human achievement as we head into the new Millennium.

Which records spring to mind? One of the last great aviation journeys – the circumnavigation of the globe by balloon – was finally made by Bertrand Piccard and Brian Jones; Maurice Greene smashed the world 100-metre record by 0.05 seconds – the biggest margin to be taken off this record since electronic timing began in the 1960s; in music Lauryn Hill won a record-breaking five Grammys; in sport Pete Sampras won his 12th Grand Slam tournament at Wimbledon, equalling Roy Emerson's record

set in 1967; and at the cinema Mike Myers' *Austin Powers* sequel became the highest-grossing film comedy in the USA during its first weekend of release.

We broke records too. *The Guinness Book of Records* remains the world's biggest-selling copyright book and this year we achieved the highest print-run record for a colour hardback title. Millions are also watching our new TV shows on both sides of the Atlantic, so the fascinating world of records is reaching a bigger audience than ever.

We are sure you will enjoy what we believe is the most significant *Guinness Book of Records* ever.

contents

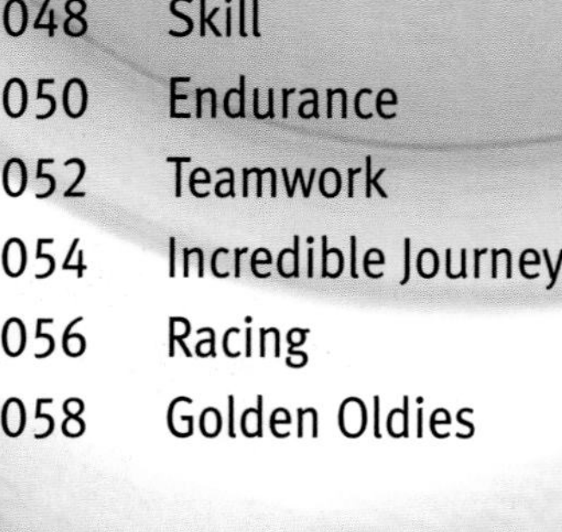

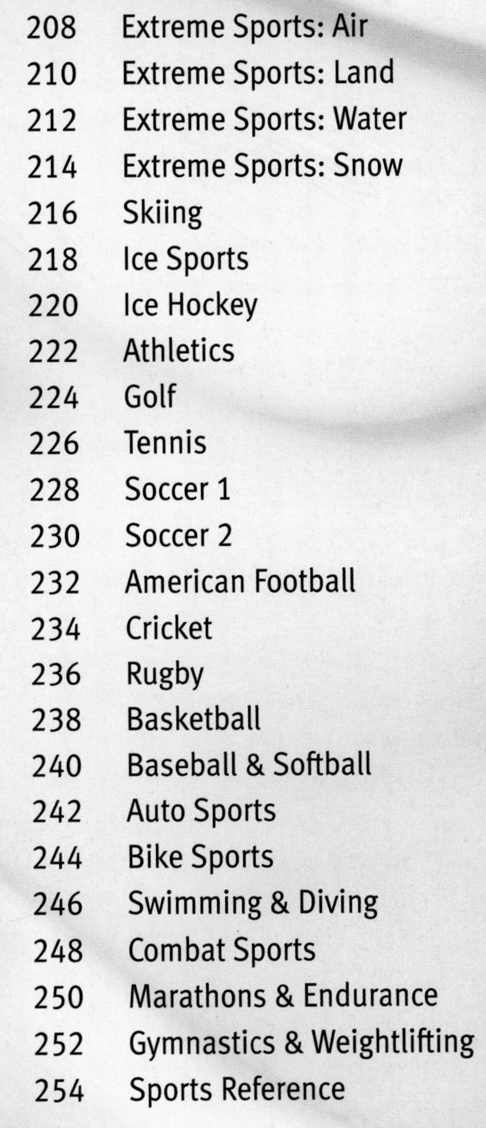

courage

space heroes

MOST SPACE JOURNEYS

Story Musgrave (USA) made six space shuttle missions between 1983 and 1996, giving him a total of 53 days' flight experience. He is pictured below alongside the space shuttle *Columbia*, in which he flew his last mission. On that occasion, from 19 Nov to 7 Dec 1996, the shuttle made a record 278 earth orbits and travelled over 11.27 million km (7 million miles) in 17 days 15 hr 53 min. Capt. John Young (USA) was the first person to make a total of six space flights, from 1965 to 1983. In doing so he acquired 34 days' flight experience. The only other astronaut to have made six space flights is Franklin Chang-Diaz (Costa Rica), who flew on six missions between 1986 and 1998 and has logged 52 days in Space.

FASTEST SPEEDS ATTAINED

The record for the greatest speed at which a human being has ever travelled is 39,897 km/h (24,791 mph), by the crew of the command module of *Apollo 10* (Col. Thomas Stafford, Cdr. Eugene Cernan and Cdr. John Young, all USA) on the craft's trans-Earth return flight in May 1969.

GREATEST ALTITUDE ATTAINED BY A WOMAN

Kathryn Thornton (USA) attained an altitude of 600 km (375 miles) after an orbital engine burn on 10 Dec 1993 during the *STS 61 Endeavour* mission.

MOST ISOLATED HUMAN BEING

The greatest distance that a person has ever been from a fellow human being is 3,596.4 km (2,234 miles 1,330 yd). This was experienced by command module pilot Alfred Worden during the US *Apollo 15* lunar mission, which lasted from 30 July to 1 Aug 1971. Fellow astronauts David Scott and James Irwin were at Hadley Base exploring the Moon's surface.

MOST EXPERIENCED SPACE TRAVELLER

Russian doctor Valeriy Poliyakov clocked up 678 days 16 hr 33 min 16 sec during two space missions.

MOST PEOPLE IN SPACE AT ONCE

On 14 March 1995 a record 13 people were in Space at the same time: seven Americans aboard the US *STS 67 Endeavour*, three CIS cosmonauts aboard the Russian *Mir* space station and two CIS cosmonauts and a US astronaut aboard the CIS *Soyuz TM21*.

MOST NATIONALITIES IN SPACE

Five countries had astronauts or cosmonauts in Space on 31 July 1992: four Russian cosmonauts and one Frenchman were aboard *Mir*, and one Swiss, one Italian and five US astronauts were on *STS 46 Atlantis*.

On 22 Feb 1996 there were four US, one Swiss and two Italian astronauts on *STS 75 Columbia* and one German and four Russian cosmonauts aboard the *Mir* space station.

BIGGEST SHUTTLE CREWS

Two shuttles have had a crew of eight: the *Challenger STS 61A*, which was launched on 30 Oct 1985, and *STS 71 Atlantis*, which docked with the *Mir* space station on 7 July 1995.

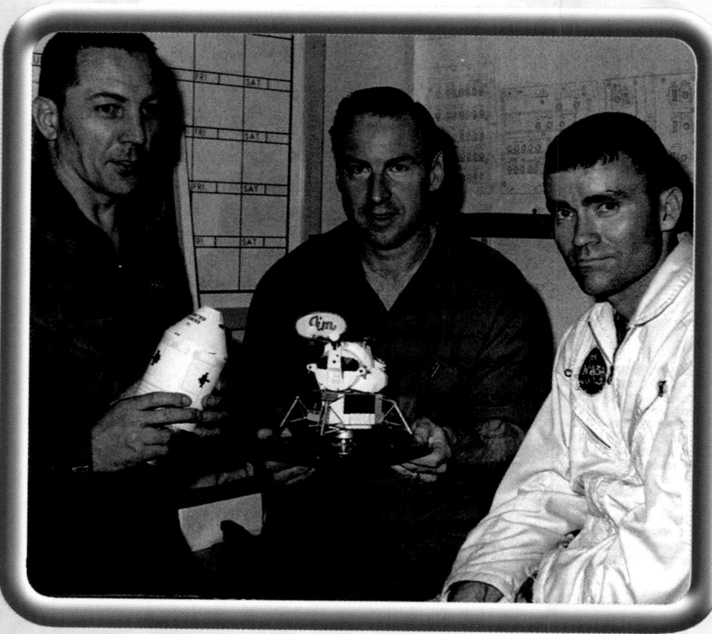

GREATEST ALTITUDE ATTAINED

The crew of Apollo 13 *(from left to right: Jack Swigert, Jim Lovell and Fred Haise, all USA) were a record distance of 254 km (158 miles) from the Moon's surface and 400,171 km (248,655 miles) from the Earth's surface on 15 April 1970. The mission was dramatized in the movie* Apollo 13 *(USA, 1995), which starred Tom Hanks as Lovell.*

MOST PEOPLE ABOARD A SPACECRAFT

In June 1995 a record 10 people (four Russians and six Americans) were aboard the *Mir* station.

LONGEST LUNAR MISSION

The crew of *Apollo 17* (Capt. Eugene Cernan and Dr Harrison Hagen Schmitt, all USA) were on the surface of the Moon for a record 74 hr 59 min during a lunar mission lasting 12 days 13 hr 51 min (7–19 Dec 1972).

LONGEST SHUTTLE FLIGHT

Columbia's 21st mission, *STS 80*, began on 19 Nov 1996 and lasted for 17 days 15 hr 53 min 26 sec (to main gear shutdown), beating its own previous record. Bad weather at the Kennedy Space Center, Florida, USA, meant that the landing had to be postponed for two days.

LONGEST MANNED SPACEFLIGHT

Valeriy Poliyakov was launched to the Russian *Mir* space station aboard *Soyuz TM18* on 8 Jan 1994 and landed aboard *Soyuz TM20* on 22 March 1995, after a spaceflight lasting 437 days 17 hr 58 min 16 sec.

MOST TRIPS AROUND THE EARTH BY A SPACE STATION

By 2 March 1999 *Mir* had completed more than 75,000 trips around the Earth. By the time of its scheduled landing the station will have been in orbit for 13 years.

BIGGEST SPACE FUNERAL

The ashes of 24 space pioneers and enthusiasts, including *Star Trek* creator Gene Roddenberry and counter-culture guru Dr Timothy Leary, were sent into orbit in April 1997 aboard Spain's *Pegasus* rocket, at a cost of $5,000 (£3,000) each. They will stay in orbit for anything between 3½ and 10 years.

FURTHEST FINAL RESTING PLACE

In Jan 1998, 28.35 g (1 oz) of the ashes of the celebrated geologist Dr Eugene Shoemaker (USA) were launched aboard NASA's *Lunar Prospector* as it set out on a one-year mapping mission above the Moon's surface. When its

LONGEST SPACEFLIGHT BY A WOMAN

The longest spaceflight by a woman lasted 188 days 4 hr 14 sec, when Shannon Lucid (USA) was launched to the Mir *space station aboard the US space shuttle* STS 76 Atlantis *on 22 March 1996 and landed aboard* STS 79 Atlantis *on 26 Sept of that year. Her stay is also the longest by any US astronaut. Upon returning to Earth she was awarded the Congressional Space Medal of Honour by President Clinton.*

power fails, the craft will crash to the Moon's surface, carrying Shoemaker's remains with it. He once said that never having been to the Moon was his greatest disappointment.

BIGGEST AUDIENCE FOR A SPACE EVENT

The broadcast of the first moonwalk by the *Apollo 11* astronauts (Neil Armstrong and Edwin 'Buzz' Aldrin) in July 1969 was watched by an estimated 600 million people worldwide (about one-fifth of the world's population at that time).

OLDEST ASTRONAUT

The oldest astronaut is John Glenn Jr (US), who was a record 77 years 103 days old when he was launched into Space as part of the crew of *Discovery STS-95* on 29 Oct 1998. The mission lasted 11 days, landing on 7 Nov 1998.

ASTRONAUT RESPONSIBLE FOR MOST LAPTOP COMPUTERS

Spanish astronaut Pedro Duque had to look after a total of 19 laptop computers aboard *Discovery* in Oct 1998.

SHORTEST SPACEFLIGHT

The shortest ever manned spaceflight was made on the first of the Mercury *missions by Cdr. Alan Shepard (USA) aboard* Freedom 7 *on 5 May 1961. The sub-orbital mission lasted 15 min 28 sec and made Shepard the second person to fly into Space — Yuri Gagarin (USSR) was the first, on 12 April 1961. Shepard is pictured here (back row, left) with the six other astronauts in the* Mercury *team.*

epic adventurers

BIGGEST ANCIENT CIVILIZATION DISCOVERY
In the late 1820s deserting soldier Charles Masson discovered the ruins of the world's biggest ancient civilization — the Indus Valley civilization at Harappa, India (now Pakistan). Extensive excavations carried out at the site by Rai Bahadur Daya Ram Sahni in 1920 indicated that the civilization dated back to 3300 BC. The discovery of a second site at Mohenjo-daro showed that the Harappans used the same sized bricks and standard weights for 1,600 km (1,000 miles), and that the civilization supported a population of 50,000 at certain periods. More recent excavations have shown that it extended even further than had been thought, stretching along and beyond the banks of the ancient Ghaggar-Hakra (Saraswati) River and covering an area of 570,000 km² (220,000 miles²) from Baluchistan, Pakistan, in the west to Uttar Pradesh, India, in the east and Bombay (Mumbai), India, in the south. The majority of the civilization's cities have still to be excavated, while its script has not yet been deciphered.

BIGGEST INCA DISCOVERY
The two Yale University Peruvian Expeditions of 1911–12 and 1914–15, both led by US historian Hiram Bingham, resulted in the discovery of the 'lost' Inca cities of Machu Picchu and Vitcos — two of the most important archeological finds in the Americas.

GREATEST DISTANCE TRAVELLED ON A MODERN-DAY ABORIGINAL RAFT
In 1947 Norwegian explorer and archeologist Thor Heyerdahl set out to convince the scientific community that ancient mariners regularly crossed the world's great oceans. He was particularly keen to show that migrants to Polynesia had not come from the east, as was generally believed, but from the west, with the Pacific's currents. To this end, Heyerdahl built a replica of an aboriginal balsa wood raft, which he named *Kon-Tiki,* and, together with five companions, crossed the 8,000 km (4,970 miles) from Callio, Peru, to Raroia Atoll, Polynesia, in 101 days. The success of the voyage proved that Polynesia's settlers could indeed have been Peruvians. Heyerdahl is pictured here with a model of *Kon-Tiki*.

MOST GENERATIONS OF ADVENTURERS IN ONE FAMILY
Jacques Piccard (left of picture) is seen saying goodbye to his son Bertrand before the latter set off on his successful attempt to circumnavigate the world in a balloon in Jan 1999. Jacques and Bertrand represent the second and third generations of a well-known family of adventurers. Jacques' father, August Piccard, made the first successful balloon flight into the stratosphere when he ascended to 15,785 m (51,790 ft) above Augsburg, Germany, in May 1931. He subsequently made a second successful ascent and went on to build a bathyscaphe, a revolutionary type of submarine that is capable of descending to the bottom of the ocean. In Jan 1960 Jacques realized his father's dream by manning the bathyscaphe to a record depth of 10,911 m (35,797 ft).

FASTEST DESERT CROSSING
In 1998 Moroccan adventurer Mohammed Ahansal completed the Marathon des Sables in a record time of 16 hr 22 min 29 sec. The marathon, which has been held every year since 1986, is a six-day event in which runners must cross 220 km (137 miles) of the Sahara Desert, where temperatures regularly reach 49°C (120°F). The runners carry food, clothes, a sleeping bag and a first-aid kit with them, and have to prepare their own meals. The youngest person to have competed in the marathon is a 16-year-old boy, and the oldest is a 76-year-old man. In April 1999, 584 people from 27 different countries took part in the marathon.

LONGEST JOURNEY IN A LEATHER BOAT
In 1976 British adventurer Tim Severin set out to prove that the voyage allegedly made by St Brendan to the New World could have been accomplished. Following instructions given in medieval writings, he built a boat by tanning ox hides with oak bark, stretching them across a wooden frame and then sewing them in place with leather thread. The resulting vessel, similar to the currachs still made today in Ireland, took him and his crew from Tralee Bay in Kerry, Republic of Ireland, to the coast of Newfoundland, Canada, after 13 months, 7,240 km (4,500 miles) and stopovers in the Hebrides, the Faroe Islands and Iceland.

FASTEST SOLAR-POWERED TRANSPACIFIC CROSSING

In 1996 Kenichi Horie (Japan) made the fastest ever crossing of the Pacific in a solar-powered boat when he travelled 16,000 km (10,000 miles) from Salinas, Ecuador, to Tokyo, Japan, in 148 days. His cigar-shaped vessel Malt's Mermaid *(seen left with Horie) was 8.7 m (9½ yd) long, weighed 369 kg (813 lb) and was powered by 12.08 m² (130 ft²) of solar panels. It was partly made from a quantity of recycled aluminium equivalent to more than 20,000 drink cans.*

FASTEST SOLO ROW ACROSS THE ATLANTIC (EAST TO WEST)

From Dec 1969 to July 1970 Sidney Genders (UK) rowed from Las Palmas, Canary Islands, to Antigua, W. Indies — a distance of 6,115 km (3,800 miles) — in 73 days 8 hours.

FIRST PEOPLE TO REACH THE NORTH POLE

The American Arctic explorer Robert Peary is widely regarded as the first person to have reached the North Pole. Peary set off on his expedition from Cape Columbia, Ellesmere Island, Canada, on 1 March 1909 with his close associate Matt Henson, seven other Americans, 17 Eskimos, 19 sledges and 133 dogs. The expedition reached a latitude of 88° N at the end of March and the final supporting party turned back, leaving Peary, Henson, four Eskimos and 40 dogs to make the final dash for 90° N — the location of the Pole. On 6 April Peary made observations indicating that he had reached his destination. Although Frederick Cook (also USA) challenged his claim and asserted that he had reached the pole first earlier that month, the US Congress acknowledged Peary's achievement in 1911.

FIRST PEOPLE TO REACH THE SOUTH POLE

On 14 Dec 1911 a party of five Norwegians led by Capt. Roald Amundsen reached the South Pole after a 53-day march with dog sledges from the Bay of Whales, Antarctica. They narrowly beat the five-man team of explorers led by British explorer Capt. Robert Falcon Scott.

LONGEST TREK IN ANTARCTICA

The longest unsupported trek ever made in Antarctica is 2,170 km (1,348 miles), by Sir Ranulph Fiennes (team leader) and Dr Michael Stroud. The pair set out from Gould Bay on 9 Nov 1992, reached the South Pole on 16 Jan 1993 and finally abandoned their walk on the Ross Ice Shelf on 11 Feb of the same year.

YOUNGEST PERSON TO WALK TO THE MAGNETIC NORTH POLE

On 7 May 1997 Giles Kershaw (UK) reached the magnetic North Pole after walking a distance of at least 580 km (360 miles). He was 22 years 351 days old.

FIRST SOLO TRANSATLANTIC FLIGHT

The first person to fly solo across the Atlantic was Capt. (later Brig. Gen.) Charles Lindbergh of Minnesota, USA. Lindbergh set out from Roosevelt Field, Long Island, New York, USA, at 12:52 pm GMT on 20 May 1927 and landed at Le Bourget airfield, Paris, France, at 10:21 pm GMT on 21 May 1927. The 5,810-km (3,610-mile) journey therefore took him a total of 33 hr 29 min. Lindbergh flew in the 165 kW (220-hp) Ryan monoplane *Spirit of St Louis.*

FIRST SOLO TRANSATLANTIC FLIGHT BY A WOMAN

On 20 May 1932 Amelia Earhart of Kansas, USA, became the first woman and second person to make a solo transatlantic flight when she piloted a single-engine Lockheed Vega from Harbour Grace, Newfoundland, Canada, to Londonderry, Republic of Ireland, in 13 hr 30 min. Earhart later became the first person to fly solo across the Pacific from Honolulu, Hawaii, USA, to Oakland, California, USA. She then went on to make two unsuccessful attempts to circumnavigate the world. On 2 July 1937, after completing 35,400 km (22,000 miles) of her second attempt, Earhart set off with her navigator from Lae, Papua New Guinea, for Howland Island in the Pacific. Neither was ever seen again.

FIRST PERSON TO COMPLETE THE ADVENTURER'S GRAND SLAM

British adventurer David Hempleman-Adams (pictured below) is the first person to have completed the Adventurer's Grand Slam, a gruelling challenge that involves climbing the highest peak on every continent and visiting all four poles. Hempleman-Adams began his quest in 1980 by climbing Mt McKinley in Alaska, USA. He completed it 18 years later when he and fellow adventurer Rune Gjeldnes walked to the North Pole from March to May 1998.

circumnavigators

LONGEST NON-STOP ROUND-THE-WORLD FLIGHT
The duration record is 64 days 22 hr 19 min 5 sec, by Robert Timm and John Cook in a Cessna 172 Hacienda. They took off from McCarran Airfield, Las Vegas, Nevada, USA, just before 3:53 pm local time on 4 Dec 1958 and landed at the same airfield just before 2:12 pm on 7 Feb 1959. They covered a distance equivalent to six times around the world, and were refuelled without making any landings.

FASTEST ROUND-THE-WORLD FLIGHT
The fastest flight under FAI (Fédération Aéronautique Internationale) rules, which define as circumnavigations flights that exceed the length of the tropics of Cancer or Capricorn (36,787.6 km or 22,858.8 miles), was 31 hr 27 min 49 sec, by an Air France Concorde (Capts. Michel Dupont and Claude Hetru) from JFK Airport in New York, USA, eastbound via Toulouse, Dubai, Bangkok, Guam, Honolulu and Acapulco from 15 to 16 Aug 1995. There were 80 passengers and 18 crew on board.

FASTEST ROUND-THE-WORLD JOURNEYS BY SCHEDULED FLIGHT
The fastest round-the-world journey taking in antipodal points was by David Sole (UK), who travelled 41,709 km (25,917 miles) in a time of 64 hr 2 min from 2 to 5 May 1995.

Brother Michael Bartlett of Sandy, Beds, UK, flew around the world on scheduled flights in a time of 58 hr 44 min in 1995, taking in the airports closest to antipodal points and covering 41,547 km (25,816 miles).

The world's fastest circumnavigation using scheduled flights under FAI regulations was 44 hr 6 min, by David J. Springbett (UK). He travelled a distance of 37,124 km (23,068 miles) from 8 to 10 Jan 1980.

OLDEST PERSON TO COMPLETE A ROUND-THE-WORLD FLIGHT
Fred Lasby (b. 1912) made a solo round-the-world flight at the age of 82 in his single-engined Piper Comanche. He left Fort Myers, Florida, USA, on 30 June 1994 and flew 37,366 km (23,218 miles) westwards with 21 stops, arriving back at Fort Myers on 20 Aug 1994.

FASTEST HELICOPTER CIRCUMNAVIGATION
In 1996 Ron Bower and John Williams (both USA) flew round the world in a Bell helicopter in 17 days 6 hr 14 min 25 sec. Bower also holds the eastbound record of 24 days 4 hr 36 min, which he set in a Bell JetRanger III in 1994.

FASTEST MICROLIGHT CIRCUMNAVIGATION
Brian Milton (UK) landed at Brooklands Airfield, Surrey, UK, on 21 July 1998, after circumnavigating the globe in a microlight aircraft. During his trip, which covered 38,623 km (24,000 miles) in 120 days, he was held for 27 days by the Russian authorities and made seven emergency landings in Saudi Arabia.

FASTEST ROUND-THE-WORLD DRIVE (CURRENT RULES)
Between 1 Oct and 11 Dec 1997 Garry Sowerby, Colin Bryant and Graham McGaw (UK) circumnavigated the globe in a Vauxhall Frontera in 21 days 2 hr 14 min, following current Guinness® Book of Records *regulations. They travelled 29,522 km (18,344 miles), starting and finishing their journey in Greenwich, London, UK.*

FASTEST MARINE CIRCUMNAVIGATIONS
The fastest marine circumnavigation was 74 days 22 hr 17 min, by the 28-m-long (92-ft) catamaran *Enza*, sailed by Peter Blake (NZ) and Robin Knox-Johnston (UK) from Ushant, France, between 16 Jan and 1 April 1994.

The record for the world's fastest ever solo non-stop marine circumnavigation is 109 days 8 hr 48 min, by the 18.3-m-long (60-ft) monohull *Ecureuil d'Aquitaine II*, sailed by Titouan Lamazou (France) from Les Sables d'Olonne, France, between Nov 1989 and March 1990.

FASTEST HELICOPTER CIRCUMNAVIGATION BY A WOMAN

The record for the first and fastest helicopter circumnavigation by a woman is held by 57-year-old British grandmother Jennifer Murray, who, with co-pilot Quentin Smith, flew a Robinson R44 57,448.7 km (35,698 miles) in 97 days in 1997. They crossed 26 countries, making 80 refuelling stops, and took time to visit the Monaco Grand Prix and the ceremonies marking the handover of Hong Kong to China. They also flew over one of the world's highest ice caps, at an altitude of 2,926 m (9,600 ft), in a temperature of −13°C (8.6°F). The journey raised £100,000 ($162,500) for the Save the Children Fund. Upon the pair's return to the starting-point of Denham, Bucks, UK, they were greeted by friends including the Duchess of York.

YOUNGEST SOLO MARINE CIRCUMNAVIGATOR
The youngest person to sail solo around the world was David Dicks (Australia), who was 18 years 41 days old when he arrived back in in Fremantle, Western Australia, after 264 days 16 hr 49 min on 16 Nov 1996.

FASTEST CIRCUMNAVIGATION IN A POWER VESSEL
On 3 July 1998 the *Cable & Wireless Adventurer* circumnavigated the world in 74 days 20 hr 58 min. The 35.05-m-long (115-ft) boat travelled more than 41,841 km (26,000 miles), breaking the 38-year-old record set by USS *Triton*, a submarine that circumnavigated the globe in 83 days 9 hr 54 min.

FASTEST MOTORBIKE CIRCUMNAVIGATION
Nick Sanders (UK) made a 32,074-km (19,930-mile) circumnavigation in a record riding time of 31 days 20 hr from 18 April to 9 June 1997, starting and finishing in Calais, France.

LONGEST CYCLE JOURNEYS
Jay Aldous and Matt DeWaal (USA) cycled 22,997 km (14,290 miles) in a time of 106 days on a round-the-world trip in 1984, starting and finishing in Salt Lake City, Utah, USA.

Tal Burt (Israel) circumnavigated the world from Place du Trocadéro, Paris, France, in 77 days 14 hr in 1992. He covered 21,329 km (13,253 miles).

Phil and Louise Shambrook (UK) travelled 38,143 km (23,701 miles) around the world on a tandem from 17 Dec 1994 to 1 Oct 1997.

FASTEST CIRCUMNAVIGATION BY CAR
The record for the first and fastest circumnavigation of the world by car, under the rules applicable in 1989 and 1991, embracing more than an equator's length of driving (40,750 km or 24,901.41 road miles), is held by Mohammed Salahuddin Choudhury and his wife Neena of Calcutta, India. The first circumnavigation took 69 days 19 hr 5 min from 9 Sept to 17 Nov 1989. The Choudhurys drove a Hindustan 'Contessa Classic' 1989 car, starting and finishing in Delhi, India.

LONGEST NON-STOP BALLOON JOURNEY
On 20 March 1999 the Breitling Orbiter 3, *piloted by Bertrand Piccard of Switzerland (left of picture) and Brian Jones of the UK (right of picture), reached Mauritania, having travelled a distance of 42,810 km (26,600 miles), and became the first ever balloon to circumnavigate the globe non-stop. The journey, which began in Château d'Oex, Switzerland, lasted 19 days 1 hr 49 min.*

mountaineers

FIRST PERSON TO CLIMB MT EVEREST

The summit of Mt Everest (8,848 m or 29,029 ft in altitude) was first reached in May 1953 by Edmund Hillary (New Zealand), shortly followed by Sherpa Tenzing Norgay (Nepal), in an expedition led by John Hunt (UK).

FIRST WOMAN TO CLIMB MT EVEREST SOLO

In May 1994, 33-year-old Alison Hargreaves (UK) became the first woman to reach the summit of Mt Everest alone and without oxygen supplies. Hargreaves was one of seven climbers who died during a descent from the summit of K2 in Aug 1995.

YOUNGEST PERSON TO CLIMB MT EVEREST

Shambu Tamang (Nepal) was the youngest ever person to ascend Mt Everest, reaching the summit at the age of 17 years 6 months 15 days on 5 May 1973.

OLDEST PERSON TO CLIMB MT EVEREST

Ler Sarkisor (Armenia, resident in Georgia) became the oldest person to reach the summit of Mt Everest on 12 May 1999, at the age of 60 years 161 days.

MOST ASCENTS OF MT EVEREST

Sherpa Ang Rita (Nepal) has scaled Mt Everest a record 10 times (in 1983, 1984, 1985, 1987, 1988, 1990, 1992, 1993, 1995 and 1996), each time without the use of bottled oxygen.

FASTEST ASCENT OF MT EVEREST FROM BASE CAMP TO SUMMIT

Kaji Sherpa (Nepal) became the fastest person to climb from base camp, which is located at an altitude of 5,350 m (17,552 ft), to the summit of Mt Everest when he made the ascent in 20 hr 24 min on 17 Oct 1998. Climbing on the Nepalese side, to the South Col, he knocked 2 hr 5 min off the record set by Marc Batard (France) 25 to 26 Sept 1988. Kaji Sherpa used oxygen on the descent; Batard went without oxygen on ascent and descent.

HIGHEST CLIMB BY AN AMPUTEE

On 27 May 1998 Tom Whittaker (UK; pictured above) became the first ever amputee to climb to the summit of Mt Everest. Whittaker, who lost a leg after a road accident in 1979, wears an artificial limb below the knee. Currently working as an outdoor pursuits instructor in Arizona, USA, he is soon to begin training as an astronaut with NASA, and if chosen for a flight will become the first amputee in Space.

MOST PEOPLE ON THE SUMMIT OF MT EVEREST IN ONE DAY

On 10 May 1993 40 climbers (32 men and eight women) from nine expeditions and 10 different countries reached the summit of Mt Everest.

MOST PEOPLE FROM ONE EXPEDITION TO CLIMB MT EVEREST

The Mount Everest International Peace Climb, a team of US, Soviet and Chinese climbers led by James Whittaker (USA), succeeded in putting a record 10 people on the summit of Mt Everest from 7 to 10 May 1990.

FASTEST SKI DOWN MT EVEREST

In Sept 1992 Pierre Tardivel (France) skied 3,200 m (10,500 ft) from the South Summit of Mt Everest to base camp in three hours of jump turns. Tardivel has notched up more than 60 first descents of mountains, mostly in the Alps.

OLDEST PERSON TO CLIMB MT KILIMANJARO

William Masheu (Tanzania) was born in 1929 and began working as a mountain guide at Mt Kilimanjaro

MOST SUCCESSFUL MOUNTAINEER

Italian climber Reinhold Messner (below) has scaled 14 of the world's mountains over 8,000 m (26,250 ft) in altitude, without oxygen. In 1982 he made a successful ascent of Kanchenjunga, which made him the first person ever to climb the world's three highest mountains — the others being Mt Everest and K2. Messner was also the first person to make the entire climb of Mt Everest solo, in Aug 1980.

in 1953. He was still climbing the mountain regularly in 1999.

FIRST PERSON TO CLIMB THE SEVEN SUMMITS

The first person to scale the highest peak on every continent (counting Puncak Jayakesuma on Irian Jaya, Indonesia, as the highest peak in Oceania) was Patrick Morrow (Canada), who completed his conquest on 7 May 1986.

FASTEST ASCENT OF THE SEVEN SUMMITS

In 1990 New Zealanders Gary Ball, Peter Hillary (son of Sir Edmund Hillary) and Andy Hall completed an ascent of the seven summits in a record time of seven months.

FIRST PERSON TO CLIMB THE TRANGO TOWERS

The main summit of the Trango Towers was first climbed by Glenn Rowell, John Roskelly, Kim Schmitz and Dennis Henner (all USA) in 1977. The Trango Towers, which are next to the Baltoro Glacier on the approach to K2, the Gasherbrums and Broad Peak in Kashmir, are home to the largest vertical faces in the world. Their three summits are all over 6,000 m (19,685 ft) high, with the main summit standing at 6,286 m (20,625 ft).

MOST EUROPEAN SUMMITS CLIMBED

British climber Eamon Fullen has climbed the highest mountains in 45 European countries — more than any other person. He began with Mt Elbrus in Russia, Europe's highest point, in Aug 1992, and by the end of May 1999 he only had the highest peaks in Georgia and Turkey to go.

FIRST ASCENT OF MT DROHMO

Doug Scott and Roger Mear (both UK) made the first ascent of Mt Drohmo, which is at an altitude of 6,855 m (22,490 ft), on 8 Oct 1998. Mt Drohmo, in eastern Nepal, was first attempted by a Swiss expedition in 1949.

FIRST ASCENT OF CROSS PEAK

Cross Peak, a 6,340-m (20,800-ft) mountain southwest of Mt Drohmo, was first climbed by Misako Miyazawa (Japan) and Pemba Lama, Gumba Sherpa and Kancha Sunwar (all Nepal) on 8 Oct 1998. The mountain is not currently on the Nepalese Tourism Ministry's list of peaks open to climbers, and had only been attempted once before, by a Japanese expedition in 1963.

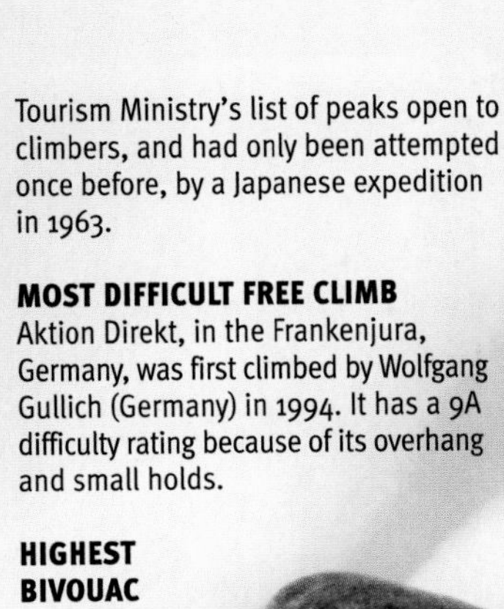

MOST DIFFICULT FREE CLIMB

Aktion Direkt, in the Frankenjura, Germany, was first climbed by Wolfgang Gullich (Germany) in 1994. It has a 9A difficulty rating because of its overhang and small holds.

HIGHEST BIVOUAC

Mark Whetu (New Zealand) and Michael Rheinberger (Australia) reached the summit of Mt Everest on 26 May 1994 and bivouacked 20 m (66 ft) below the summit. Rheinberger died the next day during the descent.

HIGHEST UNCLIMBED PEAK

At 8,410 m (27,600 ft), Lhotse Middle Peak is the highest peak yet to be climbed. It is the intermediate summit of Mt Lhotse, the world's fourth highest mountain, on the border of China and Nepal.

heroes of the deep

GREATEST OCEAN DESCENTS
In Jan 1960 the Swiss-built US Navy bathyscape *Trieste*, which was manned by Dr Jacques Piccard (Switzerland) and Lt. Donald Walsh (USA), reached a record depth of 10,911 m (35,797 ft) in the Challenger Deep of the Mariana Trench in the Pacific Ocean — the lowest point of the Earth's surface.

On 11 Aug 1989 the *Shinkai 6500* reached a depth of 6,527 m (21,414 ft) in the Japan Trench off Sanriku, Japan — the greatest descent by a manned vessel currently in commission. The vessel is capable of surveying about 96% of Japan's 321.9-km (200-mile) exclusion zone and about 98% of the oceans across the world.

LONGEST DEEP-DIVE
Richard Presley (USA) spent a record 69 days 19 min in an underwater module in a lagoon in Key Largo, Florida, USA, from 6 May to 14 July 1992. The test was carried out as part of Project Atlantis, which aimed to explore the human factors of life in an undersea environment.

LONGEST SIMULATED SATURATION DEEP-DIVE
Arnaud Denechaud de Feral (France) performed a record simulated saturation dive of 73 days from 9 Oct to 21 Dec 1989 in a hyperbaric chamber, simulating a depth of 300 m (985 ft), as part of the HYDRA 9 operation carried out by COMEX S.A. at Marseille, France. He was breathing 'hydrox', a mixture of hydrogen and oxygen.

MOST IMPORTANT DIVING INVENTION
French explorer and film-maker Jacques Cousteau is pictured with an aqualung. He invented the device, which provides a self-contained supply of compressed air, in collaboration with French engineer Emile Gagnan in 1943, freeing divers from the need to stay connected to their ships through air tubes. Cousteau, who ran his expeditions from the ship Calypso, *introduced millions to life under the sea with films such as* The Silent World *(France, 1952).*

LONGEST SIMULATED DEEP-DIVE
On 20 Nov 1992, during a 43-day dive, Théo Mavrostomos (France) dived to a depth of 701 m (2,300 ft) of seawater in a hyperbaric chamber, as part of the COMEX S.A. HYDRA 10 operation in Marseille, France, He was breathing 'hydreliox' (a mixture of hydrogen, oxygen and helium).

DEEPEST SCUBA DIVE
The record for the deepest dive made with scuba (self-contained underwater breathing apparatus) is held by Jim Bowden of the USA. In April 1994 Bowden dived to a depth of 305 m (1,000 ft) in the freshwater Zacatón Cave, Mexico.

GREATEST WRECK FINDER

Robert Ballard (USA) gained international fame in 1985 when he located the remains of the *Titanic*, which had been on the Atlantic sea bed since being sunk by an iceberg in 1912. This photograph shows him with a model of the ill-fated vessel. He was also responsible for finding the German battleship *Bismarck*, which was sunk by the Royal Navy in 1942, British ocean liner *Lusitania*, torpedoed by a German submarine in 1915, the *Andrea Doria* and the *Britannica*. In July 1997 he pinpointed the biggest concentration of Roman ships ever found in the deep sea. The eight vessels, some 2,000 years old, lay 762 m (2,500 ft) beneath the waves on an ancient Mediterranean trade route off the coast of Tunisia.

DEEPEST SALVAGE OPERATIONS
The greatest depth at which salvage has been successfully carried out is 5,258 m (17,251 ft). A helicopter had crashed into the Pacific Ocean in Aug 1991 with the loss of four lives; crew of the *USS Salvor* and personnel from Eastport International managed to raise the wreckage to the surface on 27 Feb 1992 so that authorities could try to determine the cause of the accident.

The deepest salvage operation ever achieved with divers was on the wreck of HM cruiser *Edinburgh*, which sank on 2 May 1942 in the Barents Sea off northern Norway, in 245 m (803 ft) of water. Over 31 days from 7 Sept to 7 Oct 1981, 12 divers worked on the wreck in pairs. A total of 460 gold ingots were recovered, making it the only totally successful marine salvage to date.

MOST VALUABLE SHIPWRECK
The late Mel Fisher (USA), one of the most famous 20th-century treasure-hunters, found the *Nuestra Señora de Atocha* off the Key West coast in Florida, USA, in 1985. The ship carried 40 tonnes of gold and silver and some 31.75 kg (70 lb) of emeralds when it went down in a hurricane in Sept 1622.

BIGGEST CARGO OF GOLD FOUND IN A SUBMARINE WRECK
In May 1995 Paul R. Tidwell (USA) discovered 2 tonnes of gold, 228 tonnes of tin, 54 tonnes of raw rubber and 3 tonnes of quinine in a 108.8-m-long (357-ft) Japanese submarine. The sub, which had also carried 109 men, had been destroyed by a 226.8-kg (500-lb) US bomb on 23 June 1944. Tidwell is now working to recover the vessel, which is submerged at a depth of 5,180 m (17,000 ft), 1,931 km (1,200 miles) west of the Cape Verde islands in the Atlantic Ocean.

BIGGEST DISCOVERY OF PORCELAIN
In 1994 treasure-hunter Dorian Ball and his company, Malaysia Historic Salvors (MHS), unearthed a record $5 million (£3.1 million) worth of Chinese Qing porcelain from the British trading ship *Diana*, which had sunk off the Straits of Malacca in 1817.

MOST PIRATE SHIPS DISCOVERED
Barry Clifford (USA) has discovered three authenticated wrecks of pirate vessels: in July 1998 he found the 18th-century Whydah *off Cape Cod, Massachusetts, USA, and in Nov of the same year he discovered two 17th-century vessels off the coast of Venezuela. He is pictured holding a cannonball from one of the latter ships.*

speed stars

FASTEST LAND SPEED

The one-mile (1.6-km) land speed record is 1,227.985 km/h (763.035 mph), by Andy Green (UK) in *Thrust SSC* in the Black Rock Desert, Nevada, USA, in Oct 1997. The car, designed by Richard Noble, is powered by two Rolls-Royce jet engines, which generate 22.68 tonnes of thrust. It is the first car to have exceeded the speed of sound.

HIGHEST SPEED REACHED IN A ROCKET CAR
The record for the highest speed attained in a rocket-engined car is 1,016.086 km/h (631.367 mph) over the first kilometre (1,094 yd) by *The Blue Flame*, driven by Gary Gabelich on the Bonneville Salt Flats, Utah, USA, on 23 Oct 1970. The car was powered by a rocket engine that could develop thrust up to 9,979 kg (22,000 lb).

HIGHEST SPEED REACHED IN A WHEEL-DRIVEN CAR
The highest speed reached in a wheel-driven car is 696.331 km/h (432.692 mph), by Al Teague (USA) in *Speed-O-Motive/Spirit of '76* over the final 40 m (132 ft) of a 1.6-km (one-mile) run at Bonneville Salt Flats, Utah, USA, on 21 Aug 1991. His speed over the mile was 684.322 km/h (425.230 mph).

FASTEST WOMAN ON LAND
The world's fastest woman is Kitty Hambleton, who reached a speed of 843.323 km/h (524.016 mph) in the rocket-powered *SM1 Motivator* in the Alvard Desert, Oregon, USA, on 6 Dec 1976.

FASTEST 'FUNNY CAR' DRAG RACER
John Force (USA) reached a speed of 518 km/h (323.89 mph) from a standing start over 402 m (440 yd) in his '98 Ford Mustang 'funny car' during a meet in Englishtown, New Jersey, USA, in May 1998.

HIGHEST SPEED REACHED IN A STEAM CAR
On 19 Aug 1985 Robert Barber broke the 79-year-old speed record for a steam car when *Steamin' Demon* reached 234.33 km/h (145.6 mph) at Bonneville Salt Flats, Utah, USA.

FASTEST HEARSE DRIVER
Rock Griffith (USA) covered 402 m (440 yd) in 16.058 seconds, reaching a speed of 141 km/h (85.47 mph) in a 1964 Pontiac hearse at Pomona, California, USA, on 25 Oct 1998.

FASTEST REVERSE DRIVER
The highest average speed attained in any non-stop reverse drive exceeding 805 km (500 miles) is 58.42 km/h (36.3 mph), by John Smith (USA). He drove a 1983 Chevrolet Caprice Classic 806.2 km (501 miles) in 13 hr 48 min at the I-94 Speedway, Fergus Falls, Minnesota, USA, on 11 Aug 1996.

FASTEST SIDE-WHEEL DRIVER
Göran Eliason (Sweden) set the world record for driving on two side wheels of a car when he attained a speed of 181.25 km/h (112.62 mph) over a 100-m (328-ft) flying start in a Volvo 850 Turbo at Såtenäs, Sweden, on 19 April 1997.

FASTEST GRAVITY FORMULA ONE DRIVER
Alternative International Sports, the sanctioning body for Gravity Formula One racing, recognizes Dwight Garland (USA) as the fastest driver

FASTEST 'TOP FUEL' DRAG RACER
The record for the fastest 'top fuel' drag racer — an extended car like the pictured racer driven by Jim Butler — is held by Gary Scelzi (USA), the 1998 National Hot Rod Association (NHRA) Winston Champion, who achieved a speed of 522.3 km/h (326.44 mph) from a standing start over 402 m (440 yd) during a meet in Houston, Texas, USA, in Nov 1998.

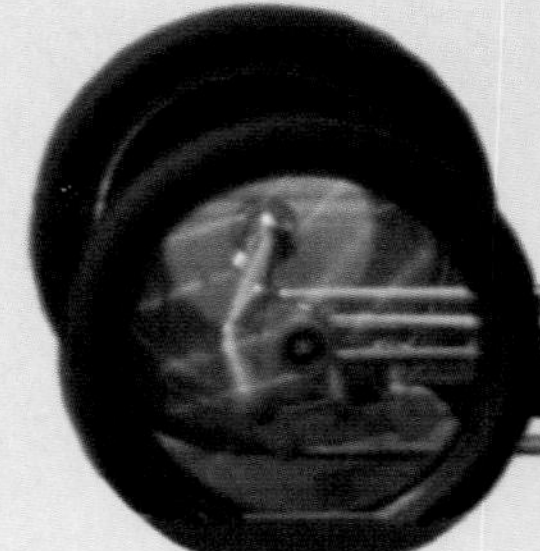

after he attained a speed of 103.3 km/h (64.2 mph) on 28 Sept 1998. A Gravity Formula One car has a tubular steel chassis and runs on pneumatic racing slicks. The rider is protected by a roll cage and roll bar, and is held in place by a five-point racing harness.

FASTEST PERSON ON ICE
The highest speed achieved on ice (without rails) is 399 km/h (247.93 mph), by Sammy Miller in the rocket-powered sled *Oxygen* on Lake George, New York, USA, on 15 Feb 1981.

FASTEST MOTORCYCLIST
On 14 July 1990 US rider Dave Campos set the world speed record on the 7-m-long (23-ft) streamline *Easyrider*, powered by two 1,491 cc Ruxton Harley-Davidson engines, at Bonneville Salt Flats, Utah, USA. Campos' overall average speed was 518.44 km/h (322.15 mph) and he completed the faster run at an average speed of 519.59 km/h (322.87 mph).

FASTEST WHEELIE
Patrick Furstenhoff (Sweden) reached a speed of 307.9 km/h (191.3 mph) on the back wheel of his motorcycle at Bruntingthorpe Proving Ground, Leics, UK, on 18 April 1999. The feat was shown on the TV show *Guinness® World Records*.

FASTEST CYCLIST
The highest speed ever achieved on a pedalled bicycle is 268.831 km/h (166.944 mph), by Fred Rompelberg (Netherlands) at Bonneville Salt Flats, Utah, USA, on 3 Oct 1995. His record attempt was greatly assisted by the slipstream from his lead vehicle.

FASTEST PEOPLE IN THE AIR
Capt. Eldon Joersz and Major George Morgan Jr attained a record speed of 3,529.56 km/h (2,193.17 mph) in a Lockheed SR-71A Blackbird over a 25-km (15-mile 941-yd) course near Beale Air Force Base, California, USA, on 28 July 1976.

FASTEST TRANSATLANTIC FLIGHTS
Major James Sullivan and Major Noel Widdifield flew a Lockheed SR-71A Blackbird from New York City, USA, to London, UK, in 1 hr 54 min 56.4 sec in 1974. The average speed for the 5,570.80-km (3,461.53-mile) journey was 2,908.02 km/h (1,806.96 mph); their time would have been faster if they had not refuelled in mid-air.

The fastest time in which a solo pilot has crossed the Atlantic is 8 hr 47 min 32 sec, at an average speed of 426.7 km/h (265.1 mph) — a record set by Capt. John Smith in a Rockwell Commander 685 twin-turboprop in 1978. He flew from Gander, Newfoundland, Canada, to Gatwick Airport, W Sussex, UK.

FASTEST HELICOPTER PILOT
The fastest average speed attained in a helicopter (under FAI rules) is 400.87 km/h (249.09 mph), by John Eggington and Derek Clews on 11 Aug 1986, in a Westland Lynx demonstrator over Glastonbury, Somerset, UK.

FASTEST AUTOGYRO PILOT
Wing Cdr Kenneth Wallis flew his WA-116/F/S gyrocopter, with a 45kW 60-hp Franklin aero-engine, at a speed of 193.6 km/h (120.3 mph) over a 3-km (1-mile 1,521-yd) course at Marham, Norfolk, UK, on 18 Sept 1986.

FASTEST PERSON ON WATER
The official water speed record is 275.8 knots (511.11 km/h or 317.6 mph) by Ken Warby (Australia) on Blowering Dam Lake, NSW, Australia, in his hydroplane, *Spirit of Australia*, on 8 Oct 1978. Warby had reached an estimated 300 knots (555 km/h or 345 mph) in the same craft and on the same lake on 20 Nov 1977, but the speed was not officially confirmed.

FASTEST CYCLIST ON A GLACIER
The fastest ever speed attained cycling down a glacier is 212.139 km/h (132 mph), by downhill mountain bike racer Christian Taillefer (France) on a Peugeot Cycle at the Speed Ski Slope in Vars, France, in March 1998.

stunt heroes

MOST STUNTS BY A LIVING ACTOR

Jackie Chan, the Hong Kong actor, director, producer, stunt co-ordinator and writer, has appeared in more than 65 films, including *The Big Brawl* (USA, 1980) and *Rumble In The Bronx* (USA, 1996). He made his debut in *Big And Little Wong Tin Bar* (Hong Kong, 1962) at the age of eight. No insurance company will underwrite Chan's productions, in which he performs all his own stunts. After a number of stuntmen were injured during the making of *Police Story* (Hong Kong, 1985), the star formed the Jackie Chan Stuntmen Association, training the stuntmen personally and paying their medical bills out of his own pocket.

MOST PROLIFIC MOVIE STUNTMEN

Vic Armstrong (UK) has doubled for every actor playing James Bond, and in a career spanning three decades has performed stunts in more than 200 films, including *Raiders Of The Lost Ark* (USA, 1981). He has co-ordinated stunts for movies such as *Tomorrow Never Dies* (UK/USA, 1997) and is married to stuntwoman Wendy Leech, whom he met when they doubled for the stars of *Superman* (USA, 1978).

Yakima Canutt (USA) performed stunts in more than 150 films in his 15-year career. In 1941 he broke his ankles and thereafter he devoted his time to creating stunts and handling the action scenes in Hollywood movies, including the chariot race in *Ben Hur* (USA, 1959). In 1966 he was awarded an Oscar for his stunt work.

MOST EXPENSIVE AERIAL STUNT

Simon Carne performed one of the most dangerous ever aerial stunts when he moved between two jets at an altitude of 4.752 km (2 miles 1,480 yd) for *Cliffhanger* (USA, 1993). The stunt, performed only once because it was so risky, cost a record $1 million (£568,000). Sylvester Stallone, the film's star, is said to have offered to reduce his fee by the same amount to ensure that the stunt was made.

BIGGEST FILM STUNT BUDGET

More than $3 million (£1.87 million) of the $200-million (£125-million) budget for *Titanic* (USA, 1997) went towards the movie's stunts. In the most complex scene, 100 stuntpeople leapt, fell and slid 229 m (70 ft) as the ship broke in half and rose out of the water to a 90° angle. The ship was docked in a tank filled with 77 million litres (17 million gallons) of water.

BIGGEST CO-ORDINATOR OF FILM AERIAL STUNTS

Flying Pictures of Surrey, UK, has planned and co-ordinated air stunts for more than 200 feature films, including *Cliffhanger* (USA, 1993), *GoldenEye* (UK/USA, 1995) and *Mission Impossible* (USA, 1996), and has co-ordinated the aerial stunts for hundreds of TV shows and ads.

HIGHEST DIVE INTO AN AIRBAG

Stig Günther (Denmark) jumped from a height of 104.55 m (343 ft) into a 12 x 15 x 4.5-m (39-ft 4½-in x 49-ft 2½-in x 14-ft 9-in) airbag on 7 Aug 1998.

LONGEST BLINDFOLD SKYWALK

Jay Cochrane (USA) walked between the towers of the Flamingo Hilton, Las Vegas, Nevada, USA, on 11 Nov 1998. Cochrane was blindfolded and traversed 182.88 m (600 ft) of tightrope between the two towers.

HIGHEST FREEFALL

The greatest height from which a stuntman has ever leapt in a freefall is 335 m (1,100 ft), by Dar Robinson from a ledge at the summit of the CN Tower in Toronto, Canada, for the movie *Highpoint* (Canada, 1979). Robinson's parachute opened just 91 m (300 ft) from the ground after a six-second freefall. He was paid $150,000 (£70,671) for the jump — the highest ever fee for a single stunt.

LONGEST FREEFALL SKYGLIDE

Adrian Nicholas (UK) made a freefall glide in the horizontal plane of 16.09 km (10 miles) over Yolo County, California, USA, on 12 March 1999. He exited the plane at 10,320 m (33,850 ft) and reached speeds in excess of 160 km/h (100 mph). His feat was made possible with a flying suit developed by his mentor Patrick de Gayardon (France), who died while practising the stunt in April 1998.

GREATEST HEIGHT RANGE PLAYED BY A STUNTMAN

Stuntman Riky Ash from Nottingham, UK, is pictured with a 1.07-m-tall (3-ft 6-in) boy for whom he doubled during the filming of the BBC TV show *Out Of The Blue* in Feb 1995. He also doubled for a 1.93-m (6-ft 4-in) adult in the ITV series *Heartbeat* in March 1998. Riky, who stands 1.6 m (5 ft 3 in) tall and is 31 years old, has been a stuntman for six years. He has doubled for over 150 children and for characters spanning an age range of six to 70 years.

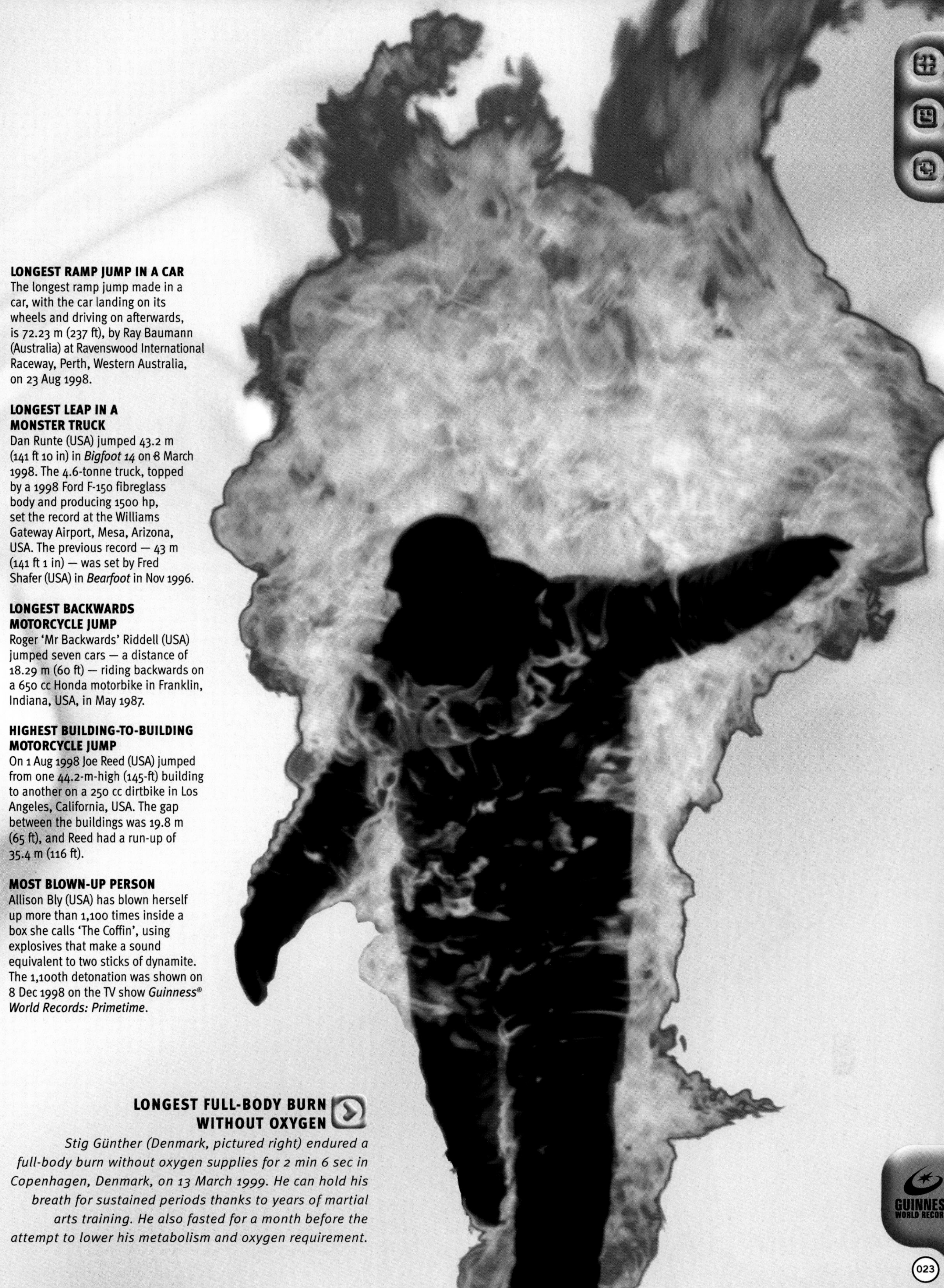

LONGEST RAMP JUMP IN A CAR
The longest ramp jump made in a car, with the car landing on its wheels and driving on afterwards, is 72.23 m (237 ft), by Ray Baumann (Australia) at Ravenswood International Raceway, Perth, Western Australia, on 23 Aug 1998.

LONGEST LEAP IN A MONSTER TRUCK
Dan Runte (USA) jumped 43.2 m (141 ft 10 in) in *Bigfoot 14* on 8 March 1998. The 4.6-tonne truck, topped by a 1998 Ford F-150 fibreglass body and producing 1500 hp, set the record at the Williams Gateway Airport, Mesa, Arizona, USA. The previous record — 43 m (141 ft 1 in) — was set by Fred Shafer (USA) in *Bearfoot* in Nov 1996.

LONGEST BACKWARDS MOTORCYCLE JUMP
Roger 'Mr Backwards' Riddell (USA) jumped seven cars — a distance of 18.29 m (60 ft) — riding backwards on a 650 cc Honda motorbike in Franklin, Indiana, USA, in May 1987.

HIGHEST BUILDING-TO-BUILDING MOTORCYCLE JUMP
On 1 Aug 1998 Joe Reed (USA) jumped from one 44.2-m-high (145-ft) building to another on a 250 cc dirtbike in Los Angeles, California, USA. The gap between the buildings was 19.8 m (65 ft), and Reed had a run-up of 35.4 m (116 ft).

MOST BLOWN-UP PERSON
Allison Bly (USA) has blown herself up more than 1,100 times inside a box she calls 'The Coffin', using explosives that make a sound equivalent to two sticks of dynamite. The 1,100th detonation was shown on 8 Dec 1998 on the TV show *Guinness® World Records: Primetime*.

LONGEST FULL-BODY BURN WITHOUT OXYGEN

Stig Günther (Denmark, pictured right) endured a full-body burn without oxygen supplies for 2 min 6 sec in Copenhagen, Denmark, on 13 March 1999. He can hold his breath for sustained periods thanks to years of martial arts training. He also fasted for a month before the attempt to lower his metabolism and oxygen requirement.

lifesavers

MOST ARTISTS SAVED

Varian Fry (pictured below), 'The Artists' Schindler', journeyed from the USA to France in 1940 with a list of 200 prominent artists and intellectuals known to be in parts of Nazi-occupied Europe. He subsequently helped to save around 4,000 people from the Gestapo, among them some of the most famous cultural figures of our age, including Max Ernst, Marc Chagall, André Breton and Nobel Prize-winning chemist Otto Meyerhof. Fry was arrested and deported in 1942. In 1997 the Israeli Yad Vashem Memorial Museum awarded the late hero their highest accolade, naming him one of the Righteous Among The Nations. He was the first US citizen to receive the tribute.

OLDEST LIFESAVING ORGANIZATION
The Royal National Lifeboat Institution (RNLI), a British lifesaving society, was formed by royal edict in March 1824 and celebrated its 175th anniversary in 1999. By April 1999, the organization had saved 132,500 lives. The RNLI currently has 223 lifeboat stations around the coasts of the UK and Ireland, with a total of 4,200 volunteer crew members.

MOST LIFESAVING AWARDS
The greatest number of awards won by a member of the British Royal Life Saving Society is 234, by Eric Deakin of Hightown, Merseyside, UK, since 1960.

YOUNGEST RECIPIENTS OF LIFESAVING AWARDS
Ryan Woods of Kent, UK, became the youngest ever person to receive a bravery award when he was presented with the Royal Humane Society's 'Testimonial on Parchment' at the age of 4 years 52 days. The award was made in recognition of his actions during an accident in Portugal in July 1997. Ryan had saved his grandmother's life by climbing for help when the car they were travelling in plunged down a steep cliff.

Kristina Stragauskaite of Skirmantiskis, Lithuania, was awarded a medal for 'Courage in Fire' when she was just 4 years 252 days old, making her the youngest ever female to earn such an honour. She had saved the lives of her younger brother and sister when a fire broke out in the family's home on 7 April 1989, while her parents were out. The award was decreed by the Presidium of the then Lithuanian Soviet Socialist Republic.

The youngest person to have received an official gallantry award is Julius Rosenberg of Winnipeg, Canada, who was given the Canadian Medal of Bravery in March 1994 for foiling the efforts of a black bear that had attacked his three-year-old sister in Sept 1992. Julius, who was five years old at the time of the incident, managed to save his sister by growling at the bear.

BIGGEST RESCUE WITHOUT LOSS OF LIFE
All 2,689 people aboard the *Susan B. Anthony* were rescued when the ship sank off the coast of Normandy, France, on 7 June 1944.

BIGGEST PRESENT-DAY WAR HOSPITAL
Staff and patients at the International Committee of the Red Cross (ICRC) hospital in Lopiding, Kenya, are seen with the Princess Royal, Princess Anne. Founded in 1987 with just 40 beds, it is now the world's biggest war hospital, with a capacity of 560 beds. It has treated approximately 17,000 victims of the long-running civil war in neighbouring Sudan since its establishment, fitting 1,500 with artificial limbs. Around 70% of patients admitted have gunshot wounds, and the vast majority are civilians.

OLDEST LIFEGUARD
Lee Wee Wong (Singapore) was born in 1929 and has been a voluntary lifeguard since 1966 and a professional since 1973. Although he reached the age of 70 in 1999, he still beats many younger guards in the annual fitness test required to renew his licence.

LONGEST HIATUS BEFORE BRAVERY AWARD
On 19 May 1997 Murphy, an Australian army donkey, was posthumously awarded the RSPCA Australia Purple Cross, an award for animal bravery, on behalf of all the donkeys that had served in the Gallipoli campaign in 1915–16. During the abortive offensive in the Dardanelles, Turkey, Murphy carried wounded servicemen from the front down rocky, exposed gullies to field hospitals.

MOST SUCCESSFUL FLYING DOCTOR SERVICE
The Australian Royal Flying Doctor Service was set up in 1928. In 1998 the service's 53 doctors, 103 nurses and 95 pilots treated 181,621 patients, performed 21,604 aerial evacuations and flew a total of 13.35 million km (8.3 million miles). The area covered by the Royal Flying Doctor Service measures 7.15 million km² (2.76 million miles²).

MOST LIVES SAVED BY A SEATBELT INNOVATION
The three-point safety belt, invented by Swedish engineer Nils Bohlin, was patented in 1959 by Volvo. Inertia-roll technology was developed by the same company in 1968. The US National Highway and Traffic Safety Administration estimates that seatbelts have prevented 55,600 deaths and 1.3 million injuries in the last decade in the USA alone, saving $105 billion (£63.4 billion) in medical costs.

MOST PEOPLE RESCUED BY ONE DOG
The most famous canine rescuer of all time is Barry, a St Bernard who saved more than 40 people during his 12-year career in the Swiss Alps. His best-

known rescue was that of a boy who lay half-frozen under an avalanche in which his mother had died. Barry spread himself across the boy's body to warm him up and licked the child's face to wake him, before carrying him to the nearest house.

LOWEST MID-AIR RESCUE BY A PARACHUTIST
On 16 Oct 1988 Eddie Turner saved the life of fellow parachutist Frank Farnan, who was unconscious after being injured in a collision while jumping out of an aircraft at 3,950 m (13,000 ft). Turner pulled Farnan's ripcord at 550 m (1,800 ft) over Clewiston, Florida, USA, less than 10 seconds from impact.

BIGGEST CPR TRAINING SESSION
On 19 May 1997 the American Heart Association, Dutchess Region, trained 1,320 people in Cardio-Pulmonary Resuscitation and Early Defibrillation Awareness at the Casperkill Conference Center, Dutchess County, New York, USA.

BIGGEST BLOOD DONATION
The Valle de Cauca, Colombia, branch of the Red Cross organised the world's biggest blood donor session in Cali, Colombia, on 13 Dec 1997. A total of 3,295 units of blood were taken from 3,403 donors in 12 hours.

MOST BLOOD PLATELET DONATIONS
Robert J. Watson of Sudbury, Massachusetts, USA, has been a platelet pheresis donor on a weekly basis at Children's Hospital in Boston, Massachusetts, since Nov 1986. He made his 500th platelet donation on 8 June 1999.

BIGGEST VOLUNTEER AMBULANCE ORGANIZATION
Abdul Sattar Edhi (Pakistan, pictured below) began his ambulance service in 1948 by ferrying injured people to hospital, and has since developed a service which attracts funds of $5 million (£3.02 million) per year, with no government assistance. His radio-linked network includes 500 ambulances throughout Pakistan, and he has also set up 300 relief centres, three air ambulances, 24 hospitals, three drug rehabilitation centres, women's centres, free dispensaries, adoption programmes and soup kitchens that feed 100,000 people a month. He has paid for and supervised the training of 17,000 nurses. The ambulance service even picks up corpses, and the organization arranges Muslim burials. Edhi has not taken a holiday in 45 years.

survivors

GREATEST AGE REACHED BY A *TITANIC* SURVIVOR
Edith Haisman, who died in a nursing home in Southampton, Hants, UK, at the age of 100 in Jan 1997, was 15 years old when the *Titanic* struck an iceberg and sank on the night of 14 April 1912. She could remember sitting in one of the ship's lifeboats watching her father, Thomas Brown, standing on deck holding a glass of brandy and a cigar and saying "I'll see you in New York!". He was taking his family from South Africa to Seattle, Washington, USA, where they intended to start a hotel business. Edith appeared in public in 1993 to accept her father's gold watch, which had been recovered from the wreckage.

LONGEST PERIOD SURVIVED WITHOUT FOOD AND WATER
Andreas Mihavecz of Bregenz, Austria, lived for 18 days without food and water after police in Höchst, Austria, put him into a holding cell in a local government building and then totally forgot about him. The 18-year-old, who had been a passenger in a crashed car, was discovered close to death.

LONGEST FALL SURVIVED BY AN INFANT
In Nov 1997 an 18-month-old baby named Alejandro fell 20 m (65 ft 7 in) from the seventh-floor kitchen window of his parents' flat in Murcia, Spain. Although no one witnessed the fall, the baby's bruises and a damaged clothes line below indicated that he hit the clothes line before landing on a street-level skylight. Doctors at the nearby Virgen de Arrixaca hospital confirmed that the only damage suffered by Alejandro, besides the bruises, was a broken tooth and a split lip.

LONGEST FALL SURVIVED WITHOUT A PARACHUTE

On 26 Jan 1972 Vesna Vulovic (pictured above), an air stewardess from Yugoslavia, survived a fall from a height of 10,160 m (33,330 ft) when the DC-9 airliner in which she was travelling blew up over Srbskă Kamenice, Czechoslovakia (now Czech Republic). The other 27 passengers on board the plane were killed.

YOUNGEST *TITANIC* SURVIVOR

Millvina Dean was just eight weeks old when she travelled third class on the *Titanic* with her parents and 18-month-old brother. She, her mother and brother all survived when the ship sank, but her father Bert was among the 1,517 passengers who were never seen again. Millvina is pictured here with Cdr. P.H. Nargeolet, who was with her on the *M.V. Royal Majesty* when it sailed to the site where the *Titanic* sank and watched research vessels try to raise part of the ship's hull. The attempt was unsuccessful.

MOST LIGHTNING STRIKES SURVIVED
Roy Sullivan, a park ranger from Virginia, USA, was struck by lightning a record seven times in the course of his life: in 1942, when he lost a big toenail; in 1969, when he lost his eyebrows; in 1970, when his left shoulder was seared; in 1972, when his hair caught fire; in 1973, when his hair caught fire and his legs were seared; in 1976, when his ankle was injured; and in 1977, when he received chest and stomach burns. Sullivan committed suicide in Sept 1983, reportedly after being rejected in love.

LONGEST PERIOD SURVIVED IN AN UNDERGROUND CAVERN
Speleologist George Du Prisne was exploring caves in Wisconsin, USA, in 1983 when he fell into an underground river and was sucked down a water siphon into a cavern. Rescuers abandoned their search after four days, but Du Prisne was alive, surviving on fish and algae scraped from the cavern's walls. Determined to escape, he unravelled orange yarn from his jersey and tied it to the legs of a dozen bats. Residents of a nearby town saw the bats and he was saved 13 days later.

LONGEST PERIODS SURVIVED ON RAFTS
Poon Lim of the British Merchant Navy survived on a raft for a record 133 days after his ship, the *SS Ben Lomond*, was torpedoed in the Atlantic 910 km (565 miles) west of St Paul's Rocks on 23 Nov 1942. He was picked up by a fishing boat off Salinópolis, Brazil, on 5 April 1943, and was able to walk ashore.

The longest period two people on a raft have survived is 177 days. Tabwai Mikaie and Arenta Tebeitabu from the island of Nikunau in Kiribati, together with a fellow fisherman, were caught in a cyclone shortly after setting out on a trip in their 4-m-long (13-ft) open

dinghy on 17 Nov 1991. The three were found washed ashore 1,800 km (1,100 miles) away in Western Samoa (now Samoa) on 11 May 1992. The third man had died a few days previously.

LONGEST TIME SURVIVED ADRIFT IN A FISHING BOAT

On 4 Jan 1999 a drifting Nicaraguan fishing boat with a crew of seven was found by Norwegian oil tanker *Joelm* 800 km (497 miles) southwest of the Nicaraguan port of San Juan del Sur. The fishermen had been lost at sea for a record 35 days after the engine of their vessel ceased working. They had survived by eating turtle flesh and drinking turtle blood.

DEEPEST UNDERWATER ESCAPES

The greatest depth from which anyone has been rescued is 480 m (1,575 ft). On 29 Aug 1973 Roger Chapman and Roger Mallinson became trapped in the mini-submarine *Pisces III* for 76 hours after it sank 240 km (150 miles) south-east of Cork, Republic of Ireland. The vessel was hauled to the surface on 1 Sept by the cable ship *John Cabot* after work by *Pisces V*, *Pisces II* and the remote-control recovery vessel *Curv*.

The greatest depth from which an escape has been made without any kind of equipment is 68.6 m (225 ft). Richard Slater escaped from the rammed submersible *Nekton Beta* off Catalina Island, California, USA, on 28 Sept 1970.

LONGEST PERIODS SURVIVED UNDERWATER WITHOUT EQUIPMENT

In 1991 Michael Proudfoot was investigating a sunken naval cruiser around Baja California, Mexico, when he smashed his scuba regulator and lost all his air. Unable to make it back to the ship's hull, Proudfoot found a big bubble of air trapped in the galley and a tea-urn almost full of fresh water. By rationing the water, breathing shallowly and eating sea urchins, he managed to stay alive for two days before being rescued.

In 1986 two-year-old Michelle Funk from Salt Lake City, Utah, USA, made a full recovery after spending 1 hr 6 min underwater. She had fallen into a creek.

HIGHEST PARACHUTE ESCAPE

Flight Lieutenant J. de Salis and Flying Officer P. Lowe (both UK) escaped at an altitude of 17,100 m (56,000 ft) over Derby, UK, on 9 April 1958.

LOWEST PARACHUTE ESCAPE

Squadron Leader Terence Spencer (UK) made the lowest ever parachute escape, at 9–12 m (30–40 ft) over Wismar Bay in the Baltic Sea on 19 April 1945.

MOST LABOUR CAMP ESCAPES

Tatyana Mikhailovna Russanova, a former Soviet citizen who now lives in Haifa, Israel, escaped from Stalinist labour camps in the former Soviet Union a total of 15 times between 1943 and 1954. She was recaptured and sentenced 14 times. All of her escapes have been judicially recognized by independent Russian lawyers, but only nine of them were recognized by Soviet Supreme Court officials.

YOUNGEST PERSON TO SURVIVE A CAR CRASH

On 25 Feb 1999 Virginia Rivero from Misiones, Argentina, went into labour at her home and walked to a nearby road in order to hitchhike to hospital. Offered a lift by two men, she then gave birth to a baby girl in the back seat of their car. When she told them she was about to have a second baby, the driver overtook the car in front, only to collide with a third vehicle. Virginia and her newborn daughter were ejected through the back door of the car, suffering minor injuries, but Virginia was able to stand up and flag down another car, which took them to the hospital. Once there, she gave birth to a baby boy.

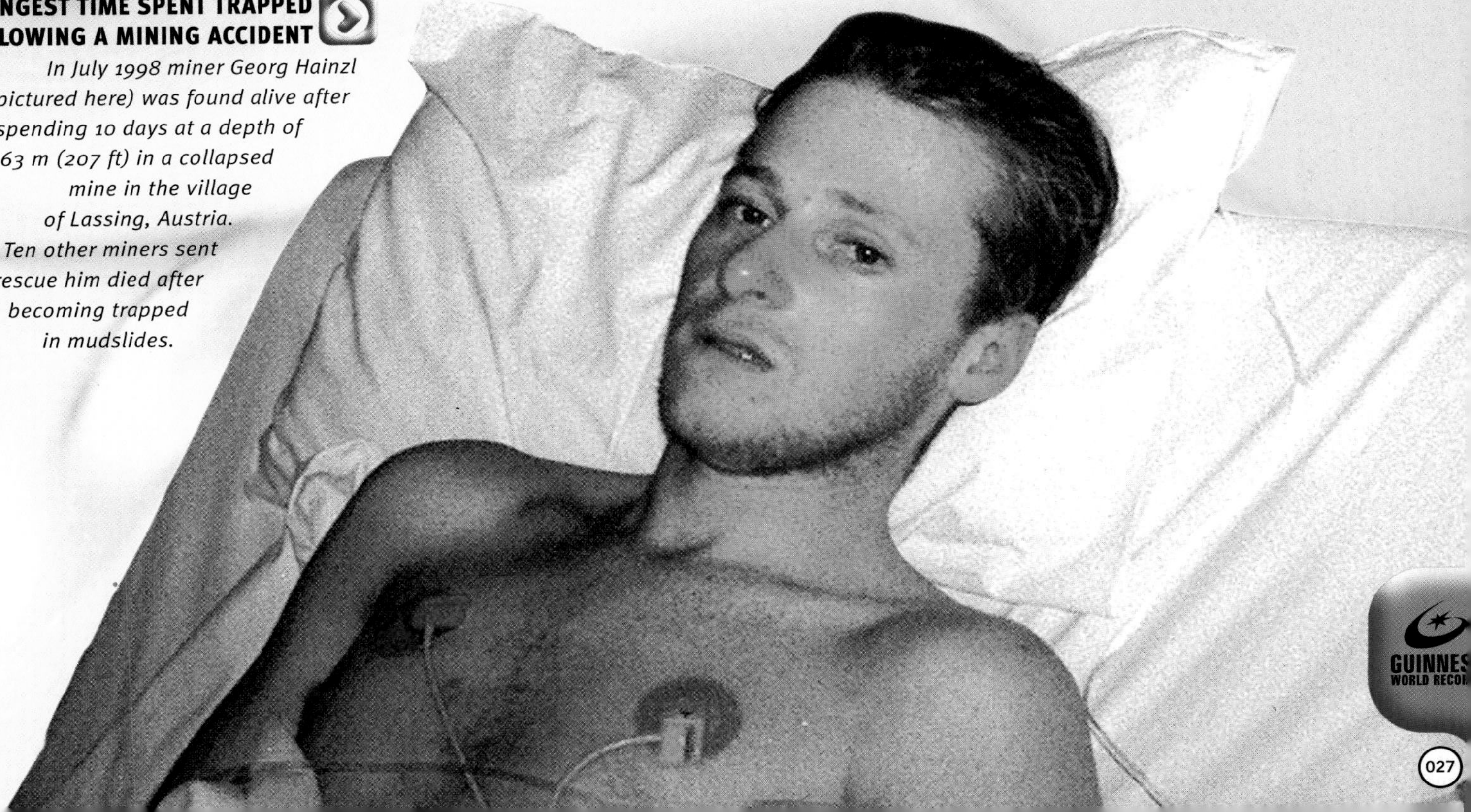

LONGEST TIME SPENT TRAPPED FOLLOWING A MINING ACCIDENT

In July 1998 miner Georg Hainzl (pictured here) was found alive after spending 10 days at a depth of 63 m (207 ft) in a collapsed mine in the village of Lassing, Austria. Ten other miners sent to rescue him died after becoming trapped in mudslides.

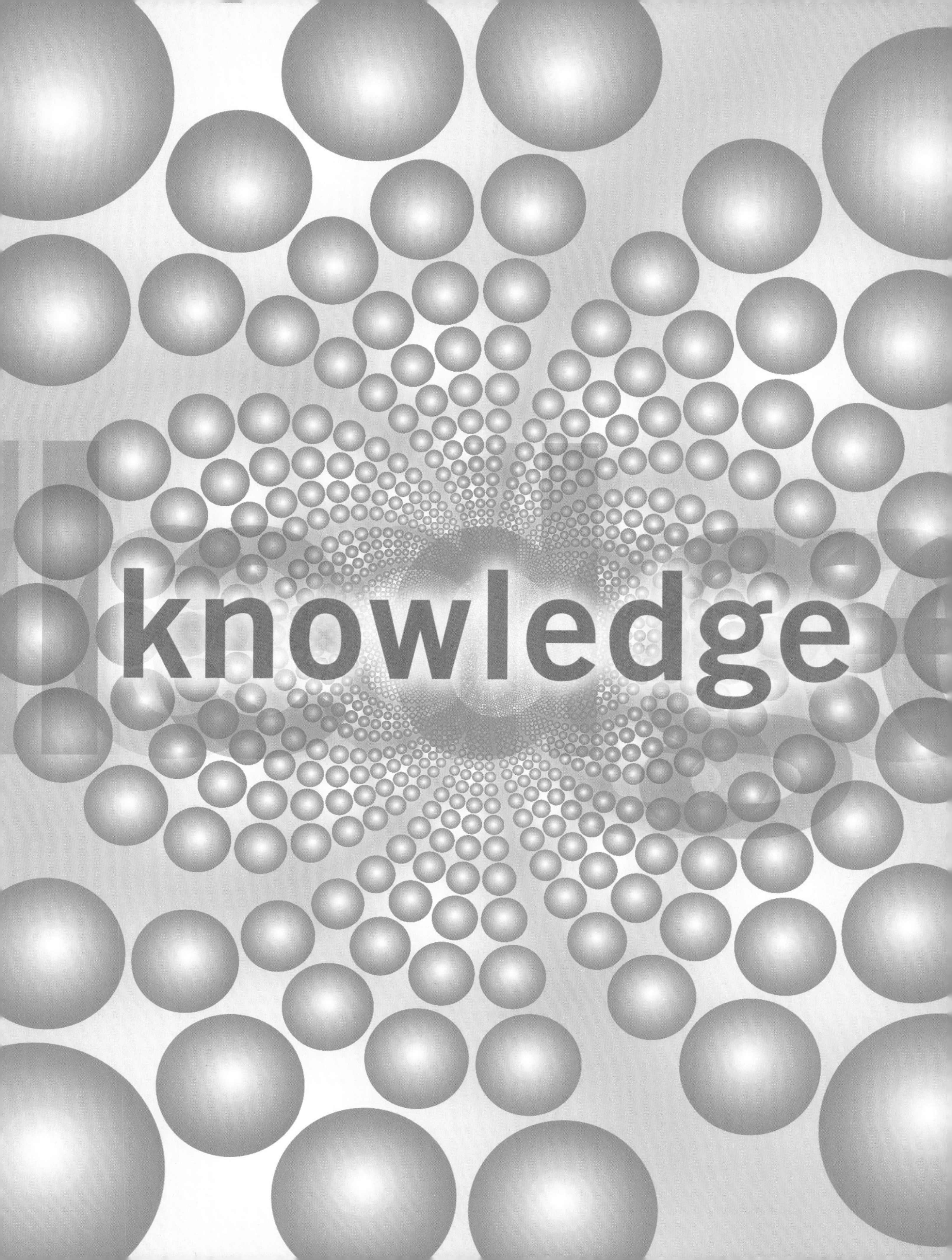
knowledge

science 1

NEWEST AND HEAVIEST ELEMENT

In Jan 1999 a team of scientists based at the Lawrence Livermore National Laboratory, California, USA, and the Joint Institute for Nuclear Research, Dubna, Russia, announced the creation of what may be the world's newest and heaviest element, element 114. It contains 114 protons, is claimed to be much more stable than other super-heavy atoms, and resulted from the bombardment of a neutron-enriched plutonium isotope by a calcium isotope.

STRONGEST ACID SOLUTION

Solutions of strong acids and alkalis tend towards pH values of 0 and 14 respectively, but this scale is inadequate for describing the 'superacids' — the strongest of which is an 80% solution of antimony pentafluoride in hydrofluoric acid (fluoro-antimonic acid $HF{:}SbF_5$). The HØ acidity function of this solution has not been measured, but even a weaker 50% solution is 1,018 times stronger than concentrated sulphuric acid.

MOST LETHAL ARTIFICIAL CHEMICAL

The compound 2, 3, 7, 8-tetrachlorodibenzo-*p*-dioxin, or TCDD, is the most deadly of the 75 known dioxins. It is 150,000 times more lethal than cyanide.

MOST MAGNETIC SUBSTANCE

Neodymium iron boride $Nd_2Fe_{14}B$ has a maximum energy product (defined as the greatest amount of energy that a magnet can supply when operating at a particular operating point) of up to 280 kJ/m^3.

MOST POWERFUL NERVE GAS

Ethyl S-2-diisopropylaminoethylmethyl phosphonothiolate, known as VX, which was developed at the Chemical Defence Experimental Establishment, Porton Down, Wilts, UK, in 1952, is 300 times more powerful than the phosgene ($COCl_2$) used in the First World War. A lethal dosage of VX is 10 mg/m^3 ($^1/_{93}$ oz/ft^3) airborne, or 0.3 mg ($^1/_{675,000}$ oz) administered orally.

MOST ABSORBENT SUBSTANCE

The US Department of Agriculture Research Service announced on 18 Aug 1974 that 'H-span' or Super Slurper, composed of 50% starch derivative and 25% each of acrylamide and acrylic acid, can, when treated with iron, hold 1,300 times its own weight in water. Its ability to maintain a constant temperature for a long time makes it ideal for reusable ice packs, as demonstrated by this 14-year-old baseball fan cooling off at a game in Detroit, Michigan, USA.

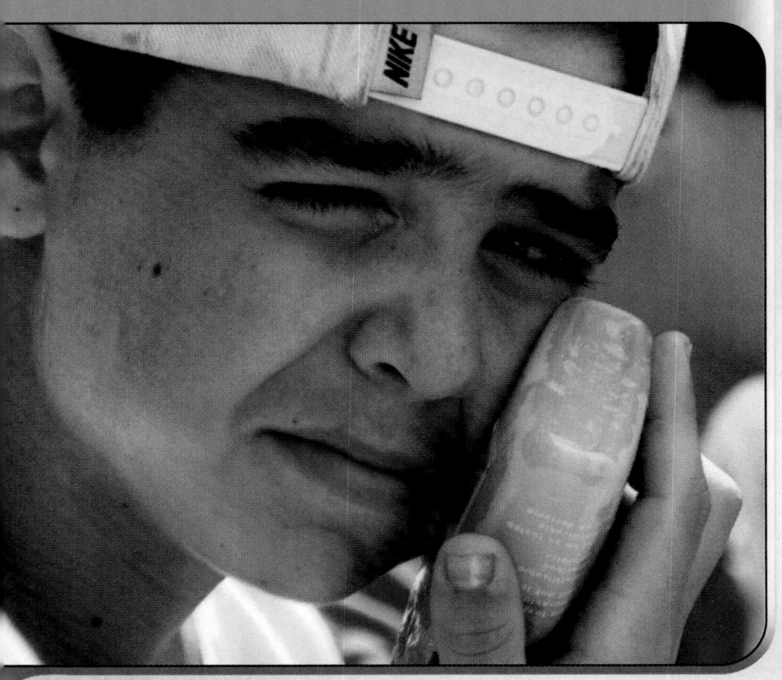

BITTEREST SUBSTANCE

The bitterest-tasting substances are based on the denatonium cation and produced commercially as benzoate and saccharide. Taste detection levels can be as low as one part in 500 million, and a dilution of one part in 100 million will leave a lingering taste.

SWEETEST SUBSTANCES

Talin, which is obtained from arils (appendages found on certain seeds) of the katemfe plant (*Thaumatococcus daniellii*), is 6,150 times as sweet as sucrose (table sugar). The plant is found in parts of west Africa.

DENSEST ELEMENT

The densest substance on Earth is the metal osmium (Os — element 76), at 22.8 g/cm^3 ($13^9/_{50}$ oz/in^3).

The singularities at the centre of black holes are calculated to have infinite density.

LEAST DENSE SOLID

The solid substances with the lowest density are silica aerogels, in which tiny spheres of bonded silicon and oxygen atoms are joined into long strands separated by pockets of air. The lightest of these aerogels, with a density of only 0.005 g/cm^3 (5 oz/ft^3), was produced at the Lawrence Livermore National Laboratory, California, USA. It will be used mainly in Space to collect micrometeoroids and the debris present in comets' tails.

HIGHEST TEMPERATURE

The highest temperature created by humans is 510 million°C (950 million°F) — 30 times hotter than the centre of the Sun — on 27 May 1994, at the Tokamak Fusion Test Reactor at the Princeton Plasma Physics Laboratory, New Jersey, USA, using a deuterium-tritium plasma mix.

HIGHEST SUPERCONDUCTING TEMPERATURE

In April 1993, at the Laboratorium für Festkörperphysik, Zürich, Switzerland, bulk superconductivity with a maximum transition temperature of

-140.7°C (-221.3°F) was achieved in a mixture of oxides of mercury, barium, calcium and copper, $HgBa_2Ca_{23}Cu_3O_1+x$ and $HgBa_2CaCu_2O_6+x$. Claims to higher temperatures are unsubstantiated.

HOTTEST FLAME
The hottest flame is produced by carbon subnitride (C_4N_2) which, at 1 atmosphere pressure, can generate a flame of 4,988°C (9,010°F).

LOWEST TEMPERATURE
The absolute zero of temperature — zero K on the Kelvin scale — corresponds to -273.15°C (-459.67°F), a point when all atomic and molecular thermal motion ceases. The lowest temperature reached is 280 picoKelvin (280 trillionths of a degree), in a nuclear demagnetization device at the Low Temperature Laboratory of the Helsinki University of Technology, Finland, and announced in Feb 1993.

MOST ELUSIVE PROTEIN
Biochemists at Harvard School of Medicine, Boston, Massachusetts, USA, made a major discovery relating to protein behaviour in 1990. It had been believed that blocks of proteins, made up of amino acids, could only be split and rejoined by other proteins called enzymes. The Harvard team monitored a type of tiny protein, known as an intein, separating from a longer protein chain and then rejoining the chain's two cut ends, removing any indication of its former presence within the chain. It is hoped that the unique capabilities of inteins may help in the fight against diseases such as TB and leprosy.

BIGGEST GALAXY
The central galaxy of the Abell 2029 galaxy cluster, 1,070 million light years from Earth, has a major diameter of 5.6 million light years — 80 times the diameter of the Milky Way.

BRIGHTEST GALAXY
The brightest galaxy appears to be AMP 08279+5255, a remote galaxy with a red shift (a measure of lengthening wavelengths of light) of 3.87 and a luminosity 5×10^{15} times that of the Sun.

REMOTEST OBJECT
The remotest known object is an unnamed galaxy of red shift 6.68, discovered by Hsiao Wen-chen, Kenneth Lanzetta and Sebastian Pascarelle (all USA) in 1998. The view that this gives us is of the universe when it was only 10% of its present age — the most distant view of prehistory ever obtained.

BIGGEST STAR
The M-class supergiant Betelgeuse has a diameter of 980 million km (610 million miles), making it 700 times bigger than the Sun.

BIGGEST SATELLITE
The biggest satellite of any planet in our solar system is Ganymede, in the orbit of Jupiter, with a diameter of 5,268 km (3,273 miles) and a mass of 1.48^{20} tonnes — 2.017 times that of the Moon.

BEST-HIDDEN STARS
In Feb 1999 Dr Rabindra Mohaptra of the University of Maryland, USA, announced that clumps of matter known as MACHOs (Massive Compact Halo Objects), at the edge of the Milky Way, may be stars from a 'mirror sector' of the galaxy. Invisible to us, but detectable because of their gravity's bending of light from background stars, they may have mirror planets orbiting them, populated by life-forms that can see their mirror stellar systems but are blind to ours in just the same manner as we are to theirs.

SMALLEST AMOUNT OF SUBSTANCE
In 1997 the chemistry of Seaborgium (Sg — element 106) was deduced from the production of only seven atoms. It was named in honour of Dr Glenn Seaborg (pictured), the late Nobel Prize-winning physicist who discovered plutonium.

science 2

SMALLEST ARTEFACT
The tips of probes on scanning tunnelling microscopes (STMs) have been shaped to end in a single atom — the last three layers form the world's smallest human-made pyramid, of seven, three and one atoms. In Jan 1990 it was announced that scientists at the IBM Almaden Research Center, San José, California, USA, had used an STM to move and reposition single atoms of xenon on a nickel surface in order to spell out the initials 'IBM'. Other laboratories have used similar techniques on single atoms of other elements.

MOST HEAT-RESISTANT SUBSTANCE
The existence of a complex material known as NFAAR, or Ultra Hightech Starlite, was announced in April 1993. Invented by Maurice Ward (UK), it can temporarily resist plasma temperatures (10,000°C or 18,032°F).

MOST POWERFUL LIGHT SOURCE
Of continuously burning light sources, the most powerful is a 313-kW high-pressure argon arc lamp of 1.2 million candles, completed by Vortek Industries Ltd of Vancouver, British Columbia, Canada, in March 1984.

MOST POWERFUL ELECTRIC CURRENT
The largest ever electrical current was achieved by scientists at Oak Ridge National Laboratory, USA, in April 1996. They sent a current of 2 million amperes/cm^3 down a superconducting wire. Household wires carry a current of less than 1,000 amperes/cm^3.

BIGGEST SOLAR POWER PLANT
In terms of nominal capacity, the largest solar electric power facility in the world is the Harper Lake Site (LSP 8 & 9) in the Mojave Desert, California, USA, operated by UC Operating Services. These two solar electric generating stations (SEGS) have a nominal capacity of 160 MW (80 MW each). The station site covers 518 hectares (1,280 acres).

BIGGEST DC GENERATOR
The largest DC generator with an overall capacity of 51,300 kW was developed by Mitsubishi Electric for use in nuclear fusion experiments. Installed in the Japan Atomic Energy Research Institute in May 1995, it is 16.5 m (54 ft) long and weighs 353 tonnes.

FASTEST CENTRIFUGE
The highest artificial rotary speed ever achieved by a centrifuge is 7,250 km/h (4,500 mph), by a tapered 15.2-cm (6-in) carbon fibre rod rotating in a vacuum at Birmingham University, UK, in 1975. Ultracentrifuges were invented by the Swedish chemist Theodor Svedberg in 1923 and are used to separate mixtures of organic substances. To allow them to go faster, friction is reduced by supporting the spinning rotor by a magnetic field and enclosing it in a vacuum.

FINEST BALANCE
The Sartorius Microbalance Model 4108, manufactured in Göttingen, Germany, can weigh objects of up to 0.5 g ($^{18}/_{1,000}$ oz) to an accuracy of 0.01µg, or 1×10^{-8} g (3.5×10^{-10} oz), which is equivalent to little more than one-sixtieth of the weight of the ink on one of the full stops on this page.

BIGGEST SCIENTIFIC INSTRUMENT
The largest scientific instrument is the Large Electron Positron (LEP) storage ring at CERN, Geneva, Switzerland, which is 27 km (17 miles) in circumference. The ring itself has a diameter of 3.8 m (12 ft 6 in). Over 60,000 tonnes of technical equipment have been installed in the tunnel and its eight working zones.

FINEST CUT
The Large Optics Diamond Turning Machine at the Lawrence Livermore National Laboratory in California, USA, was reported in June 1983 to be able to sever a human hair lengthways a total of 3,000 times.

FASTEST SIGNAL
In 1996 a team of physicists at Cologne University, Germany, announced that they had accomplished what Einstein's Special Theory of Relativity had considered to be impossible — they had sent a signal at a speed exceeding that of light. The signal was a portion of Mozart's 40th Symphony, sent to confirm the findings of an earlier experiment in which microwaves were split in two, one part being sent through a special filter and the other through air. Both should have been travelling at the speed of light, but the microwaves sent through the filter were found to be travelling 4.7 times faster than those sent through the air.

LONGEST ECLIPSES
The longest possible solar eclipse (when the Moon passes between the Sun and the Earth) is 7 min 31 sec. The longest in recent times lasted 7 min 8 sec, west of the Philippines in 1955, and one lasting 7 min 29 sec is predicted to occur in the mid-Atlantic in 2186. A mother and child are pictured in Bangkok, Thailand, on 24 Oct 1995, during an eclipse that was total in some areas of the country. The longest possible lunar eclipse (when the Moon passes into the shadow of the Earth) is 1 hr 47 min — this will be visible on the west coast of North America on 16 July 2000.

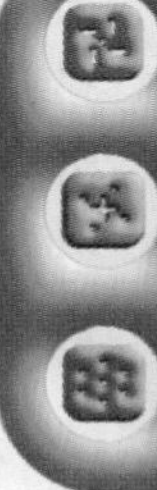

LONGEST SCIENTIFIC INDEX
The 12th collective *Index of Chemical Abstracts*, completed in Dec 1992, contains 35,137,626 entries in 215,880 pages and 115 volumes and weighs 246.7 kg (544 lb). It provides references to 3,052,700 published documents in the field of chemistry.

MOST COMPLETE SEQUENCING OF A MULTICELLULAR ANIMAL'S GENOME
The first multicellular animal whose entire genome (genetic code) has been sequenced is *Caenorhabditis elegans*, a 1-mm-long (3/100-in) soil-dwelling nematode worm. Although its entire adult body consists of only 959 cells (humans have trillions), it has 100 million genetic bases comprising at least 18,000 genes, and more than 50% of known human genes correspond with versions possessed by *C. elegans*. The task of mapping the worm's entire genome was the brainchild of Dr Sydney Brenner, who initiated the project in the 1960s at the Medical Research Council's Laboratory of Molecular Biology, UK, and began the actual sequencing in 1990.

EARLIEST MACHINE TO LEVITATE A LIVING CREATURE
Dr Andre Geim and colleagues at Nijmegen University, Amsterdam, Netherlands, used a superconducting magnet to enable a live frog to float in mid-air in 1997. They also performed the experiment with fish and grasshoppers.

EARLIEST TELEPORTATION
Researchers led by Anton Zeilinger at Innsbruck University, Austria, have teleported a single photon (a particle of light). Physical properties of the photon were transferred instantly to another photon without any connection or communication between them. The experiment requires three photons — the original and a pair of 'entangled' photons, whose quantum properties (or spin) are complementary. When the spin of the original photon and one of the other two is measured, the third takes on the spin of the first. Popular interest in the principle of teleportation was first kindled in the 1960s by the popular television sci-fi series *Star Trek*.

LONGEST-STANDING MATHS PUZZLE
Andrew Wiles (UK), who works at Princeton University, New Jersey, USA, is pictured in front of Fermat's Last Theorem. In 1998 Wiles was awarded the $200,000 (£120,671) King Faisal International Prize for proving the conjecture of the 17th-century French mathematician Pierre de Fermat. The problem had left the world's greatest mathematicians baffled for 350 years.

inventors

MOST PATENTS HELD BY ONE INVENTOR
The US inventor Thomas Alva Edison registered the most patents of any inventor in history: he held a total of 1,093, some jointly with other inventors. They included the carbon transmitter (which was used as a microphone in the production of Alexander Graham Bell's telephone), the motion-picture projector and the incandescent electric lamp.

EARLIEST RECORDED US PATENT
The first patent issued in the USA was to Samuel Hopkins for potash, a substance used in fertilizer, on 31 July 1790. The patent was countersigned by George Washington, who was president at the time.

YOUNGEST US PATENT-HOLDER
Sydney Dittman of Houston, Texas, USA, was two years old when she submitted an application to the US Patent Office. Her patent for an 'Aid for Grasping Round Door Knobs' was granted when she was four years old, on 3 Aug 1993.

BIGGEST DAMAGES IN A PATENT CASE
On 31 Aug 1993 Litton Industries Inc. of Los Angeles, California, USA, was awarded a record $1.2 billion (£804.66 million) in damages from Honeywell Inc. in a case involving a patent for airline navigation systems. Litton had filed a suit in March 1990, which was followed by a counterclaim from Honeywell nine months later.

EARLIEST CASH DISPENSER
One of the biggest developments in personal finance in the 20th century, the world's first cash dispenser was installed at Barclays Bank, Enfield, Middlesex, UK, on 27 June 1967. Invented by John Shepherd-Barron and developed by De La Rue, the machine operated on a voucher system. The maximum amount that could be withdrawn at one time was £10 ($28).

EARLIEST AIR CONDITIONER
US inventor Willis Haviland Carrier, later dubbed the 'Father of Cool', designed and built the first air conditioning system in 1902. It was devised for a printer in New York, USA, who had found that temperature fluctuations were causing his paper to warp, resulting in the misalignment of the coloured inks. Carrier's patent was granted in 1906.

EARLIEST BALLPOINT PEN
The Hungarian journalist László Biro created the first ballpoint pen in collaboration with his brother Georg in 1938. Biro took his inspiration from watching newspaper ink dry quickly, leaving the paper smudge-free. This thicker ink would not flow from a conventional nib, so he designed the ballpoint and in doing so revolutionized pen design. One of the first organizations to exploit Biro's idea was the British Royal Air Force, whose pilots needed a pen that would not leak at high altitudes, as the fountain pen did. The biro's success with the RAF brought it into the limelight.

MOST SUCCESSFUL CLOCKWORK RADIO

British inventor Trevor Bayliss devised the BayGen freeplay/freepower clockwork radio in 1993, and his Baygen factory in Cape Town, South Africa, currently produces 20,000 units a month. The radio is popular in Africa and other regions where electricity sources can be scarce.

MOST WIDESPREAD CONTACT LENS DESIGN
Czech researcher Otto Wichterle invented the soft contact lens in 1956. The development gave rise to a huge industry, with over 100 million people now wearing soft lenses worldwide.

EARLIEST FLOPPY DISK
In 1971 a team of IBM engineers led by Alan Shugart (USA) invented the floppy disk. The 20.32-cm² (8-in²) plastic disk was nicknamed 'floppy' because of its flexibility. Shugart went on to refine the design for Wang Computers, producing a 13.335-cm (5¹/₄-in) flexible disk and disk drive in 1976. In 1981 Sony were the first to introduce the 8.89-cm² (3¹/₂-in²) drives and diskettes which are standard in modern personal computer systems.

MOST SUCCESSFUL INSTANT CAMERA
Edwin Land (US), founder of the Polaroid Corporation in 1937, created a system of one-step photography that used the principle of diffusion transfer

MOST 'USELESS' INVENTIONS

Kenji Kawakami has popularized the concept of *chindogu*, which he defines as "inventions that seem like they're going to make life a lot easier, but don't". The Japanese journalist is the founder of the 10,000-member International *Chindogu* Society and has published two books on the subject, *101 Unuseless Japanese Inventions* and *99 More Unuseless Inventions: The Art Of Chindogu*. Examples of these inventions include: tiny dusters that slip onto a cat's paws and clean surfaces as it walks over them; a fish-face-cover, to spare the cook that traumatic stare into the dead fish's eyes; a backscratching T-shirt; and a chin-operated light switch. The books include membership forms for the *Chindogu* Society, and rules for creating prototypes.

to reproduce the image recorded by the camera lens directly onto a photosensitive surface, which functioned as both film and photo. Land first demonstrated the Polaroid Camera at a meeting of the Optical Society of America in February 1947. Colour Polaroids followed in 1963. In 1998, the Polaroid Corporation generated $1.86 billion (£1.12 billion). in revenue.

MOST SUCCESSFUL PORTABLE MUSIC SYSTEM
The Sony Corporation developed the Walkman in 1979, the first model on the market being the TPS-L2. Cassette Walkman sales to April 1999 total 195 million units, the CD Discman has sold 54 million and the MiniDisc Walkman has sold 6.9 million.

MOST WIDESPREAD VIDEO RECORDING SYSTEM
Charles Ginsburg of San Francisco, California, USA, led the research team at Ampex Corporation in developing the first practical videotape recorder (VTR). The system used a rapidly rotating recording head to apply high-frequency signals onto a reel of magnetic tape. VTR revolutionized television broadcasting, as recorded programmes that could be edited replaced most live broadcasts. In 1956, the US broadcaster CBS became the first network to employ VTR technology.

The VHS system was invented by JVC in 1976. By 1997 the market for blank VHS tape alone had reached $2.2 billion (£1.34 billion).

MOST WIDESPREAD HELICOPTER DESIGN
Igor Sikorsky, originally from Ukraine, designed the world's first successful multi-motor aeroplane and the world's first true production helicopter. Educated in Russia and Paris, Sikorsky emigrated to the USA after the Russian Revolution, establishing himself as an aircraft designer. Sikorsky's US Patent 1,994,488, filed on 27 June 1931, marked the crucial breakthrough in helicopter technology. In late 1938, the management of United Aircraft (now United Technologies) approved his experimental helicopter, and on 14 Sept 1939 the VS-300 made its first flight. His single-rotor design, a major breakthrough in helicopter technology, remains the dominant configuration today.

MOST WIDESPREAD FASTENING DEVICE
In 1893 Whitcomb Judson (USA) patented a 'Clasp Locker', the precursor of the modern zip fastener. Working with businessman Col. Lewis Walker, Judson launched the Universal Fastener Company to promote the device. Gideon Sundback (Sweden) rose to the position of head designer at Universal, and after years of refinement he came up with the zip we know today in Dec 1913, registering a patent in 1917. The name 'zipper' comes from the B.F. Goodrich company, which renamed the device when it was added to their rubber boot range.

MOST SUCCESSFUL SOFT DRINK
Pharmacist Dr. John Stith Pemberton introduced Coca-Cola in Atlanta, Georgia, USA, in, May 1886. For 5¢ (£0.01), consumers could enjoy a glass of Coca-Cola at the soda fountain at Jacobs' Pharmacy and sales averaged nine drinks per day. In 1998 the world's most popular soft drink had sales of more than 683 million drinks per day. The total sales for the company in 1998 were over $18.8 billion (£11.6 billion) and the worldwide market share was 51%.

MOST LIVES SAVED BY AIRBAG TECHNOLOGY
William R. Carey, a project engineer with the US firm Eaton, Yale and Town, was the first to develop the airbag for installation into automobiles and make it a practical safety feature. He registered his patent in 1969. To date, airbags, which deploy at 200 mph (321.87 kph), have been credited with saving more than 4,230 lives in the USA alone by May 1999.

FIRST HYPERTEXT BROWSER

In 1989 Tim Berners-Lee (UK) proposed a global hypertext project to allow people to combine their knowledge in a web of hypertext documents. He started work in October 1990 and WorldWideWeb — the first hypertext browser/editor — was made available on the internet in the summer of 1991.

architects & masterbuilders

TALLEST STRUCTURE
The world's tallest structure is a stayed television transmitting tower 629 m (2,064 ft) high, near Fargo, North Dakota, USA. It was built for KTHI-TV between 2 Oct and 1 Nov 1963 by Hamilton Erection, Inc. of York, South Carolina. A mast constructed at Konstantynow, Poland, took the record in July 1974, with a height of 645.38 m (2,117 ft 4 1/2 in), but following its collapse in Aug 1991 the record reverted to the KTHI tower.

TALLEST BUILDING
The CN Tower in Toronto, Canada, is the world's tallest self-supporting building. It is 553.34 m (1,815 ft 5 in) in height and was built between 1973 and 1975 at a cost of $63 million (£26.9 million). The tower was designed by architects John Andrews, Webb Zerafa, Menkes Housden and E.R. Baldwin.

TALLEST OFFICE BUILDINGS

In 1996 the Petronas Towers in Kuala Lumpur, Malaysia, became the world's tallest office buildings when 73.5-m-tall (241-ft) pinnacles were placed on top of the 88-storey towers, bringing their height to 451.9 m (1,482 ft 8 in). The Universal Financial Centre in the Pudong New Area of Shanghai, China, will be taller when it is completed in 2001, at a height of 454 m (1,490 ft).

TALLEST BLOCK OF FLATS
The John Hancock Center in Chicago, Illinois, USA, is 343.5 m (1,127 ft) tall and has 100 storeys, of which only floors 44–92 are residential. The remaining floors are used for offices. Engineer Fazlur Kahn worked with architect Bruce Graham to devise a 'braced tube' system that carries the load of the building downward so efficiently that the building requires one-third less steel per square metre than conventional buildings.

The tallest purely residential block of flats is the 70-storey Lake Point Tower in Chicago, Illinois, USA, which is 195 m (640 ft) high and has 879 apartments.

BIGGEST BLOCK OF FLATS
The largest aggregation of residential blocks is the Barbican Estate in the City of London, UK, which was designed in 1959 by architects Chamberlin, Powell & Bond. The site occupies a total of 16 ha (40 acres) and includes 2,014 flats and parking for 1,710 cars.

BIGGEST URBAN COMPLEX
Pudong New Area, which faces the Chinese city of Shanghai across the Huangpu River, covers an area of 520 km² (201 miles²) and had a population of 1.4 million in 1995. The New Area comprises the Lujiazui export-processing zone, the Waigaoqiao free trade zone and the Zhangjiang hi-tech zone. Construction began in April 1990 and by Feb 1999 a total of 5,548 projects had found foreign investors. More than 80 structures are currently being built in the finance and trade zone, including what will eventually become the world's tallest office building, the Universal Financial Centre.

BIGGEST RENTABLE OFFICE COMPLEX
The World Trade Center in New York City, USA, has a total of 1.115 million m² (12 million ft²) of rentable space available in its seven buildings, including 406,000 m² (4.37 million ft²) in each of the twin towers. Around 50,000 people work in some 500 companies and organizations located in the complex, and a further 70,000 tourists and business people visit it every day.

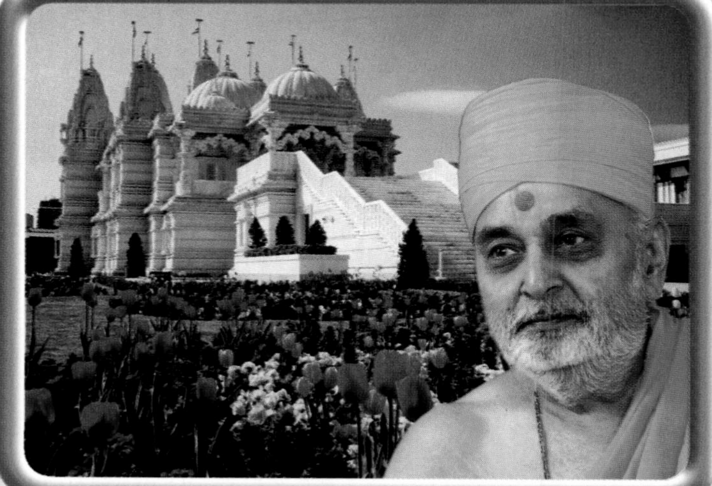

BIGGEST HINDU TEMPLE OUTSIDE INDIA
The Shri Swaminarayan Temple in Neasden, London, UK, is the largest Hindu temple outside India. It was built by His Holiness Pramukh Swami Maharaj (pictured), a 79-year-old Indian sadhu (holy man), and is made of 2,828 tonnes of Bulgarian limestone and 2,000 tonnes of Italian marble, which was first shipped to India to be carved by a team of 1,526 sculptors. The temple cost £12 million ($19.2 million) to build.

BIGGEST ADMINISTRATIVE BUILDING
The Pentagon in Arlington, Virginia, USA, designed by George Bergstrom, covers the largest ground area of any office building. Built to house the US Defense Department's offices, it was completed on 15 Jan 1943 and cost an estimated $83 million (£29.7 million). Its five storeys enclose a floor area of 60.4 ha (149.2 acres).

BIGGEST SINGLE CONSTRUCTION PROJECT
The Three Gorges Dam in China, which is due for completion in 2009, will span 2.31 km (1.44 miles), stand nearly 182.88 m (600 ft) high and boast 26 supersized turbines and generators. It will create a reservoir with a surface area equivalent to Singapore. It has been estimated that the project will cost $24.5 billion (£14.8 billion).

MOST EXPENSIVE STADIUM
The $466-million (£281-million) Stade de France in the Paris suburb of Saint-Denis, France, was built for the 1998 World Cup and was the venue for the home team's 3–0 victory over Brazil in the final. The stadium, which is able to seat 80,000 spectators, has a massive roof with little visible means of support, although it contains steelwork weighing as much as the Eiffel Tower. It was designed by architects Michel Macary, Aymeric Zublena, Michel Regembal and Claude Constantini in association with three leading French construction companies – Bouygues, GTM and SGE.

BIGGEST MUSEUM GALLERY
The biggest gallery in the Guggenheim Museum, Bilbao, Spain, is 137 m (450 ft) long and 30 m (98 ft) wide. The $100-million (£60.3-million) art museum was designed by American architect Frank Gehry and opened to the public on 10 Oct 1997.

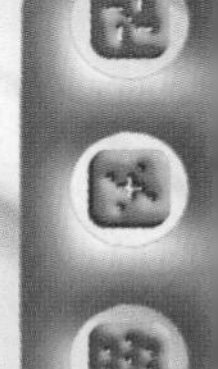

RECORD-BREAKING ARCHITECT

British architect Lord Foster is pictured outside the Reichstag, Berlin, Germany. He redesigned the old parliament building for the relocation of the government back to Berlin from Bonn. He is also the designer of the world's largest airport, Chep Lap Kok, Hong Kong, China, and Europe's tallest building, the Commerzbank, Frankfurt, Germany.

BIGGEST IGLOO
With a total floor area of 5,000 m^2 (53,821 ft^2) and the capacity to sleep up to 150 guests per night, the Ice Hotel in Jukkasjarvi, Sweden, is the world's biggest igloo. Rebuilt every December for the past five years, the igloo increases in size every year. It currently features ice sculptures, a cinema, saunas, an ice bar and the world's only ice chapel.

LONGEST BRIDGE
The Second Lake Pontchartrain Causeway, which joins Mandeville and Metrairie, Lousiana, USA, is 38.42 km (23 miles 1,538 yd) long. The bridge was completed in 1969.

LONGEST CABLE SUSPENSION BRIDGE
The Akashi-Kaikyo road bridge in Japan has a main span of 1,991 m (6,532 ft). It took eight years to build, and when it was finished in 1997 it also broke records for the highest bridge towers, at 297 m (974 ft 5 in) and the largest supporting cable diameter, at 1.122 m (3 ft 8 in).

LONGEST UNDERSEA TUNNEL
The £10-billion ($17-billion) Channel Tunnel, which runs underneath the English Channel between Folkestone, Kent, UK, and Calais, France, was constructed between Dec 1987 and Dec 1990. It was officially opened by Queen Elizabeth II of the United Kingdom and President François Mitterrand of France on 6 May 1994. Each of the twin rail tunnels is 49.94 km (31 miles 53 yd) long and has a diameter of 7.6 m (24 ft 11 in). Plans for a tunnel under the English Channel were first proposed during the Napoleonic Wars, at the beginning of the 19th century.

LONGEST ROAD TUNNEL
The two-land St Gottard road tunnel from Göschenen to Airlo, Switzerland, is 16.32 km (10 miles 246 yd) long and was opened to traffic in Sept 1980. Construction began in 1969 and cost $420 million (£175 million). During the tunnel's construction 19 workers lost their lives.

BIGGEST RAILWAY STATION
Grand Central Terminal, New York City, USA, was designed by two firms of US architects – Warren and Whetmore and Reed & Stem at the beginning of the 20th century with money provided by the millionaire William Vanderbilt. The station covers a record 19 ha (48 acres) on two levels, with 41 tracks on the upper level and 26 on the lower. On average more than 550 trains and 210,000 commuters use it every day.

medical heroes

LONGEST TIME A PATIENT HAS BEEN KEPT ALIVE WITHOUT A PULSE
In Aug 1998 Julie Mills, a student teacher, was kept alive without a pulse for six days by the AB180 Left Ventricular Assist Device. This gave her heart a chance to repair itself following a bout of viral myocarditis. The device, which was implanted by cardiac specialist Stephen Westaby at the John Radcliffe Hospital, Oxford, UK, circulated blood around Ms Mills' body in a continuous flow instead of mimicking the pumping action of the heart — hence the absence of a pulse. She was the fourth person to have the device implanted since its development in the USA, and the first to survive the procedure.

LONGEST TIME AFTER WHICH A SURGEON HAS RESTORED SPEECH
In Jan 1998 40-year-old Tim Heilder received a donor voice box and windpipe in an operation performed by Dr Marshall Strome at the Cleveland Clinic, Ohio, USA. Heilder had lost his voice following a motorbike accident at the age of 21, when doctors removed his voice box to save his life. Three days after the transplant, Heilder said his first words for 19 years.

MOST ORGANS TRANSPLANTED IN A SINGLE OPERATION
Dr Andreas Tzakis transplanted seven organs — a liver, pancreas, stomach, large and small intestines and two kidneys — into a 10-month old Italian girl during 16 hours of surgery at Jackson Children's Hospital in Miami, Florida, USA, on 23 March 1997. The girl suffered from megacystismicrocolon syndrome, a rare congenital defect that interferes with the body's ability to absorb nutrients.

EARLIEST HAND TRANSPLANT

On 24 Sept 1998 an international team of eight surgeons in Lyon, France, performed the world's first ever hand transplant when they stitched the hand of a dead man to the wrist of 48-year-old Australian Clint Hallam (pictured below). Hallam had lost his own hand in a chainsaw accident nine years previously. It takes around 12 months to establish whether or not such a transplant is successful.

MOST RECONSTRUCTIVE SURGERY BY A TRAVELLING TEAM
Operation Smile's 'World Journey of Hope '99' lasted from 5 Feb to 14 April 1999, during which time a team of volunteer doctors visited 18 countries and treated 5,139 patients. They repaired cleft lips and cleft palates, as well as performing surgery on facial tumours, burns and facial injuries. Operation Smile was founded in 1982 by Bill Magee, a plastic surgeon, and his wife Kathy, a nurse, in Norfolk, Virginia, USA.

YOUNGEST PATIENT TO UNDERGO A TRANSPLANT
On 8 Nov 1996 one-hour-old Cheyenne Pyle became the youngest ever patient to undergo a transplant when she received a donor heart at Jackson Children's Hospital, Miami, Florida, USA. The six-hour operation, performed by Dr Richard Perryman, involved draining Cheyenne's blood and cooling her body to 17°C (62.6°F), the temperature at which organs cease to function. Dr Perryman then had to complete the transplant within an hour to prevent damage to her other organs. Cheyenne's new heart was the size of a ping-pong ball.

YOUNGEST PATIENT TO UNDERGO A LIVER TRANSPLANT
The youngest patient to undergo a liver transplant was Baebhen Schuttke, who was just five days old when she received part of a 10-year-old child's liver in Aug 1997. Baebhen suffered liver failure 24 hours after her birth. She was flown to King's College Hospital, London, UK, where surgeon Mohammed Rela led the delicate seven-hour operation to transplant a single lobe from the donor liver into her body. For two weeks the surgical wound was left open, covered by a dressing, until the liver had shrunk to the correct size. She has now fully recovered.

LEAST BLOOD TRANSFUSED DURING A TRANSPLANT OPERATION
In June 1996 a transplant team led by surgeon Stephen Pollard from St James' University Hospital, Leeds, UK, performed a liver transplant on 47-year-old housewife Linda Pearson without any blood being transfused. Such an operation usually requires 2.3–3.4 litres (4–6 pints) of blood, but Pearson is a Jehovah's Witness and therefore cannot receive any blood that is not her own. The surgeons operated slowly, keeping incisions small to minimize blood loss. In addition, Pearson had been prepared for the operation by having daily injections of the hormone erythropoietin, which allowed her to sustain a greater blood loss than normal by stimulating the production of her red blood cells. The surgeons had agreed with a Jehovah's Witness liaison team that, even if the patient's life was under threat during the operation, no blood would be given to her.

YOUNGEST RECIPIENT OF TWO DONOR HEARTS
In 1992 Sophie Parker, then two years old, underwent a seven-hour operation at Harefield Hospital, London, UK, to give her a donor heart to complement her weak natural heart. The operation was performed by Dr Ashgar Khaghani, who arranged the two hearts in a 'piggyback' fashion. In March 1998 it became evident that Sophie's natural heart was no longer functioning properly, so it was replaced with a second donor heart in another operation at Harefield. Sophie thus became the youngest transplant patient to receive two donor hearts.

EARLIEST BRAIN CELL TRANSPLANT
The first ever brain cell transplant was performed by a team of doctors from the University of Pittsburgh Medical Center, Pennsylvania, USA, on 23 June 1998. The aim of the operation was to reverse the damage which had been caused by a stroke to 62-year-old Alma Cerasini, who had suffered paralysis of her right arm and leg as well as the loss of most of her speech. The team has subsequently performed a further 11 operations of this type.

EARLIEST ARTIFICIAL HEART TRANSPLANT
From 1 to 2 Dec 1982 Dr William DeVries performed the first ever artificial heart transplant, on Dr Barney Clark at the Utah Medical Center, Salt Lake City, Utah, USA. The new 'heart' was a Jarvik 7, which had been designed by Dr Robert Jarvik. Clark survived until 23 March 1983.

MOST SUCCESSFUL BIONIC ARM
In 1993 five bioengineers at the Margaret Rose Hospital, Edinburgh, UK, created a new arm for hotel owner Campbell Aird, who had had his right arm amputated in 1982 after he developed muscular cancer. Called the Edinburgh Modular Arm System, the limb is packed with microchips, position control circuits, miniature motors, gears and pulleys. It rotates at the shoulder and wrist, bends at the elbow and can grip using artificial fingers. When Aird wants to move the arm, an array of microsensors inside a special cap allow him to do so by picking up electrical pulses sent by his brain.

EARLIEST CYBER CLINIC
In March 1997 clinical psychologist Dr Kimberley Young (USA) established the Virtual Clinic, the world's first psychiatric cyber centre for internet addicts and those with related mental health problems. Dr Young aims, via the internet, to provide help for people experiencing such things as addiction to the web, troublesome e-mail affairs and Star Trek addiction, as well as more conventional mental health problems like depression and anxiety. Dr Young's clinic can be found at www.netaddiction.com/clinic.htm/.

GREATEST DISTANCE BETWEEN DOCTOR AND PATIENT
Dr Daniel Carlin of Boston, Massachusetts, USA, is pictured with a photograph of Russian yachtsman Victor Yazykov, whose life he saved with the help of the internet. Yazykov was taking part in a solo round-the-world yacht race in Nov 1998 when he developed an abscess under the skin of his elbow. Fearing that the abscess could burst and eventually kill him, Carlin sent him an e-mail telling him how to cut and drain it. Yazykov performed the operation successfully but the bleeding continued. Carlin discovered that Yazykov was taking aspirin, which acts as an anti-coagulant: when he stopped taking it the wound stopped bleeding. A few days later he sailed into Cape Town, South Africa, 12,400 km (9,906 miles) from Boston.

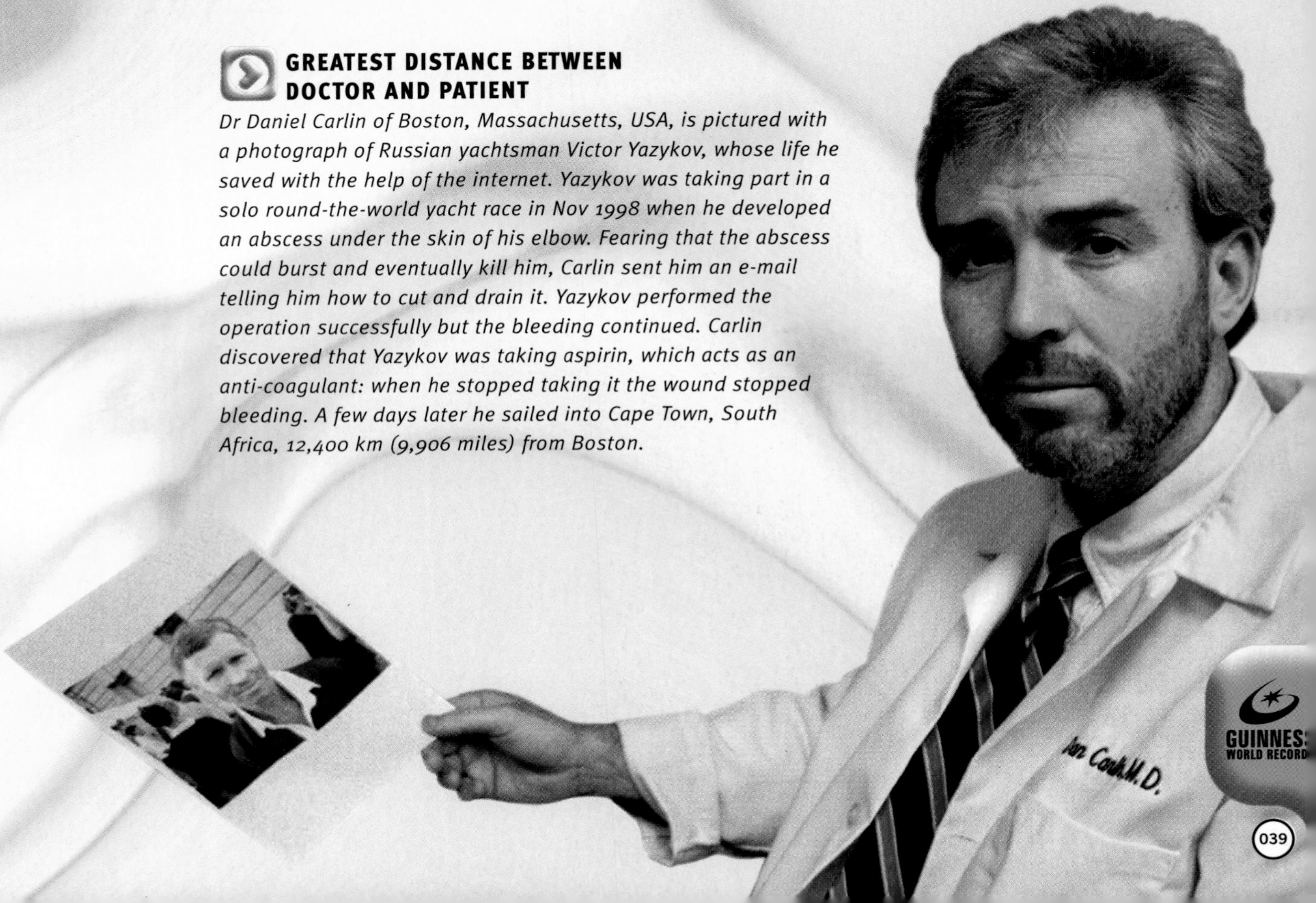

zoology 1

BIGGEST ANIMAL
The blue whale (*Balaenoptera musculus*) weighs 3 tonnes at birth and reaches an average weight of 26 tonnes by the age of 12 months. A record-breaking 190-tonne, 27.6-m-long (90-ft 6-in) female blue whale was caught in 1947.

TALLEST MAMMAL
Male giraffes (*Giraffa camelopardis*) grow to a height of around 5.5 m (18 ft). The tallest specimen on record was a 5.88-m-tall (19-ft) Masai bull (*G. camelopardis tippelskirchi*) named George, who died in Chester Zoo, UK, in 1969.

SMALLEST MAMMAL
The smallest specimens of the bumblebee or Kitti's hog-nosed bat (*Craesonycteris thonglongyai*), found in limestone caves on the Kwae Noi River, Kanchanaburi Province, Thailand, have a head–body length of 2.9 cm ($1\frac{7}{50}$ in) and a wingspan of about 13 cm ($5\frac{1}{10}$ in). They weigh 1.7 g ($\frac{3}{50}$ oz).

BIGGEST PRIMATE
The male eastern lowland gorilla (*Gorilla gorilla graueri*) found in the eastern Congo (formerly Zaïre) has a bipedal standing height of 1.75 m (5 ft 9 in) and weighs 163.4 kg (25 st 10 lb).

SMALLEST PRIMATE
The smallest true primate (excluding tree shrews, which are normally classified separately) is the pygmy mouse lemur (*Microcebus myoxinus*), which has recently been rediscovered in the deciduous forests of western Madagascar. It has a head–body length of about 6.2 cm ($2\frac{2}{5}$ in), a tail length of 13.6 cm ($5\frac{2}{5}$ in) and an average weight of 30.6 g ($1\frac{1}{10}$ oz).

LONGEST-LIVED PRIMATE
The greatest age recorded for a non-human primate is 59 years 5 months, for a chimpanzee (*Pan troglodytes*) named Gamma, who died at the Yerkes Primate Research Center in Atlanta, Georgia, USA, on 19 Feb 1992. Gamma was born at the Florida branch of the Yerkes Center in Sept 1932.

LONGEST-LIVED MONKEY
The world's oldest monkey, a male white-throated capuchin (*Cebus capucinus*) named Bobo, died on 10 July 1988 aged 53 years.

BIGGEST RODENT
The capybara (*Hydrochoerus hydrochaeris*) of northern South America has a head-and-body length of 1–1.3 m (3 ft 3 in–4 ft 3 in) and can weigh up to 79 kg (12 st 6 lb). One cage-fat specimen weighed 113 kg (17 st 12 lb).

SMALLEST RODENT
Several species vie for the title of smallest rodent in the world. The northern pygmy mouse (*Baiomys taylori*) of Mexico and of Arizona and Texas, USA, and the Baluchistan pygmy jerboa (*Salpingotulus michaelis*) of Pakistan, both have a head–body length of as little as 3.6 cm ($1\frac{2}{5}$ in) and a tail length of 7.2 cm ($2\frac{4}{5}$ in).

SLOWEST MAMMAL
*The three-toed sloth (*Bradypus tridactylus*) of tropical South America has an average ground speed of between 1.8 and 2.4 m (6 and 8 ft) per minute, or 0.1–0.16 km/h ($\frac{7}{100}$–$\frac{1}{10}$ mph). In the trees it can accelerate to 4.6 m (15 ft) per minute, or 0.27 km/h ($\frac{17}{100}$ mph).*

LONGEST-LIVED RODENT
The greatest age reported for a rodent is 27 years 3 months, for a Sumatran crested porcupine (*Hystrix brachyura*) that died in Washington DC, USA, on 12 Jan 1965.

LONGEST HIBERNATION BY A RODENT
Arctic ground squirrels (*Spermophilus parryi*) living in northern Canada and Alaska, USA, hibernate for nine months of the year.

BIGGEST PINNIPED
The largest of the 34 known species of pinniped is the southern elephant seal (*Mirounga leonina*) of the sub-Antarctic islands. Bulls average 5 m (16 ft 6 in) in length from the tip of the inflated snout to the tips of the outstretched tail flippers, have a maximum girth of 3.7 m (12 ft) and weigh about 2–3.5 tonnes. The largest accurately measured specimen of the elephant seal was a bull that weighed at least

MOST EXPENSIVE RETURN TO THE WILD
The return of the orca whale Keiko to a near-natural environment has cost the Free Willy Keiko Foundation over $22 million (£13.27 million). The star of the film *Free Willy* (USA, 1993) was captured off the coast of Iceland in the late 1970s and kept in a cramped tank in Mexico until 1996, when he was taken to a $7.3-million (£4.67-million) salt-water tank with a giant-screen colour television in Newport, Oregon, USA — an operation that cost $10 million (£6.4 million) overall. In Sept 1998 he was returned to a $12-million (£7.24-million) soccer-pitch-sized pen off the Westmann Islands, Iceland, with mesh sides to allow fish in, and a clear plastic bottom.

MOST ENDANGERED FELINE

*The most endangered feline is the Sumatran tiger (*Panthera tigris*) of which there are only about 20 specimens in the wild. The species is expected to become extinct in the near future, following the Caspian tiger, which died out in the 1970s, and the Bali tiger, which disappeared in the 1940s. As with most endangered mammals, the main threats to tigers' survival are hunting and loss of natural habitat.*

4 tonnes and measured 6.5 m (21 ft 4 in) after flensing (stripping of the blubber or skin). Its original length was estimated to be about 6.85 m (22 ft 6 in). It was killed at Possession Bay, South Georgia, on 28 Feb 1913.

SMALLEST PINNIPED
The smallest pinniped is the Galapagos fur seal (*Arctocephalus galapagoensis*). Adult females average 1.2 m (3 ft 11 in) in length and weigh about 27 kg (4 st 4 lb). Males are usually considerably larger, averaging 1.5 m (4 ft 11 in) in length and weighing around 64 kg (10 st 1 lb).

BIGGEST BIRD
The largest living bird is the ostrich (*Struthio camelus*). Male examples of this flightless sub-species can be up to 2.75 m (9 ft) tall and weigh 156.5 kg (24 st 9 lb).

SMALLEST BIRD
The smallest bird is the bee hummingbird (*Mellisuga helenae*) of Cuba and the Isle of Pines, South Carolina, USA. Males measure 5.7 cm (2¼ in) in total length — half of which is taken up by the bill and tail — and weigh 1.6 g (7/125 oz). Females are slightly larger.

RAREST BIRD
In the wild, Spix's macaw (*Cyanopsitta spixii*) is as rare as it is possible to be without actually becoming extinct. Ornithologists searching for the bird in 1990 managed to locate only one survivor, believed to be a male, living in a remote corner of north-eastern Brazil. The only hope for its survival now lies in one of the 31 or so individuals known to be in captivity.

LONGEST FEATHERS
The longest feathers grown by any bird are those of the Phoenix fowl or Yokohama chicken (a strain of the red junglefowl *Gallus gallus*), which has been bred in south-western Japan for ornamental purposes since the mid-17th century. In 1972 a tail covert measuring 10.6 m (34 ft 9½ in) was reported for a rooster owned by Masasha Kubota of Kochi, Shikoku, Japan.

MOST EXPERT TOOL-USER

*Chimpanzees (*Pan troglodytes*) can make and use tools with greater expertise than any other mammal except humans: they use straw and twigs to extract termites; branches to investigate out-of-reach objects; stones to hammer open hard-shelled nuts; pointed sticks to prise pieces of nut from shells; and leaves as cloths to remove dirt from their bodies and as sponges to obtain water.*

zoology 2

HEAVIEST INSECT

The heaviest insects are the Goliath beetles (family Scarabaeidae) of equatorial Africa. The largest are *Goliathus regius*, *G. meleagris*, *G. goliathus* (=*G. giganteus*) and *G. druryi*. In measurements of one series of males (females are smaller) the lengths from the tips of the small frontal horns to the end of the abdomen were 11 cm (4 1/3 in), with weights of 70–100 g (2 1/2–3 1/2 oz).

LONGEST INSECT

The longest recorded insect in the world is *Pharnacia kirbyi*, a stick insect from the rainforests of Borneo. The longest known specimen is in the Natural History Museum, London, UK. It has a body length of 32.8 cm (1 ft 9/10 in) and a total length, including the legs, of 54.6 cm (1 ft 9 1/2 in). In the wild this species is often found with some legs missing because they are so long and easily trapped when the insect sheds its skin.

OLDEST INSECTS

The longest-lived insects are the splendour beetles (family Buprestidae). A specimen of *Buprestis aurulenta* appeared in 1983 in a house in Prittlewell, Essex, UK, after at least 51 years as a larva.

FASTEST FLYING INSECT

The highest maintainable airspeed of any insect, including the deer bot-fly (*Cephenemyia pratti*), hawk moths (*Sphingidae*), horseflies (*Tabanus bovinus*) and some tropical butterflies (*Hesperiidae*), is 39 km/h (24 mph). The fastest flying insect is the Australian dragonfly (*Austrophlebia costalis*) which can reach 58 km/h (36 mph) in short bursts.

FASTEST LAND INSECT

The fastest insects on land are large tropical cockroaches of the family Dictyoptera. The record is 5.4 km/h (3.36 mph), or 50 body lengths per second, registered by *Periplaneta americana* at the University of California at Berkeley, USA , in 1991.

LOUDEST INSECT

At 7,400 pulses/min, the tymbal organs of the male cicada (family Cicadidae) produce a noise — officially described by the US Department of Agriculture as 'Tsh-ee-EEEE-e-ou' — detectable more than 400 m (437 yd) away.

BIGGEST BUTTERFLY

The largest butterfly is the Queen Alexandra's birdwing (*Ornithoptera alexandrae*) of Papua New Guinea. Females can have a wingspan exceeding 28 cm (11 in) and weigh over 25 g (9/10 oz).

BIGGEST FISH

The largest fish is the rare plankton-feeding whale shark (*Rhincodon typus*), found in the Atlantic, Pacific and Indian oceans. The largest recorded example was 12.65-m (41-ft 6-in) long, measured 7 m (23 ft) round the thickest part of the body and weighed an estimated 15–21 tonnes. It was captured off Baba Island, near Karachi, Pakistan, on 11 Nov 1949.

BIGGEST SPIDER

*The largest known spider is the goliath bird-eating spider (*Theraphosa leblondi*), mainly found in the coastal rainforests of north-east South America. Two specimens with leg-spans of 28 cm (11 in) have been reported: one found in Rio Cavro, Venezuela, in April 1965; and one bred by Robert Bustard of Alyth, Perthshire, UK, that was measured in Feb 1998.*

SHORTEST FISH

The shortest recorded marine fish — and the shortest vertebrate — is the dwarf goby (*Trimmatom nanus*) of the Indo-Pacific. Average lengths recorded during a 1978/79 expedition were 8.6 mm (1/3 in) for males and 8.9 mm (7/20 in) for females.

FASTEST FISH

The cosmopolitan sailfish (*Istiophorus platypterus*) is considered to be the fastest species of fish over short distances, although practical difficulties make measurements extremely difficult to secure. In a series of speed trials carried out at the Long Key Fishing Camp, Florida, USA, one sailfish took out 91 m (300 ft) of fishing line in three seconds, which is equivalent to a velocity of 109 km/h (68 mph).

BIGGEST STARFISH

The largest of the 1,600 known species of starfish is the very fragile brisingid *Midgardia xandaros*. A specimen collected by a team from Texas A&M University, USA, in the Gulf of Mexico in 1968 measured 1.38 m (4 ft 6 in) from tip to tip, but its disc was only 2.6 cm (1 in) in diameter.

SMALLEST STARFISH

The smallest known starfish is the asterinid sea star *Patiriella parvivipara* discovered by Wolfgang Zeidler on the west coast of the Eyre peninsula, South Australia, in 1975. It has a diameter of less than 9 mm (7/20 in).

MOST DESTRUCTIVE INSECT

The most destructive insect is the desert locust (*Schistocerca gregaria*) of Africa and western Asia. Certain weather conditions can induce swarms that devour almost all vegetation in their path. In one day 50 million locusts can eat food that would sustain 500 people for a year. Moroccan villagers are pictured with a day's catch of dead insects.

BIGGEST AMPHIBIANS
The largest amphibians are the giant salamanders (family Cryptobranchidae), of which there are three species. The record-holder is the Chinese giant salamander (*Andrias davidianus*), which lives in mountain streams in north-eastern, central and southern China. One record-breaking specimen collected in Hunan Province measured 1.8 m (5 ft 11 in) in length and weighed 65 kg (10 st 3 lb).

BIGGEST CHELONIAN
The largest chelonian is the leatherback turtle (*Dermochelys coriacea*), which averages 1.83–2.13 m (6–7 ft) from the tip of the beak to the end of the tail (carapace 1.52–1.67 m or 5–5 ft 6 in), about 2.13 m (7 ft) across the front flippers and weighs up to 450 kg (71 st 6 lb). The largest leatherback ever recorded is a male found dead on a beach in Gwynedd, UK, on 23 Sept 1988. It measured 2.91 m (9 ft 5½ in) over the carapace, 2.77 m (9 ft) across the front flippers and weighed 961.1 kg (151 st 6 lb).

BIGGEST MARINE CRUSTACEAN
The largest crustacean is the *taka-ashi-gani* or giant spider crab (*Macrocheira kaempferi*). The biggest specimen had a record claw-span of 3.7 m (12 ft 1½ in) and weighed 18.6 kg (2 st 12 lb).

BIGGEST FRESHWATER CRUSTACEAN
The largest freshwater crustacean is the crayfish or crawfish (*Astacopsis gouldi*), found in Tasmania, Australia. Specimens of up to 61 cm (2 ft) in length have been measured, possibly weighing as much as 4.1 kg (9 lb).

BIGGEST JELLYFISH
An Arctic giant (*Cyanea capillata arctica*) of the north-western Atlantic that washed up in Massachusetts Bay, USA, in 1870 had a bell diameter of 2.28 m (7 ft 6 in) and tentacles stretching 36.5 m (120 ft).

BIGGEST LAND GASTROPOD
The largest known land gastropod is the African giant snail (*Achatina achatina*), the largest recorded specimen of which measured 39.3 cm (15½ in) from snout to tail when fully extended (shell length 27.3 cm or 10¾ in) in Dec 1978 and weighed 907 g (2 lb). It was collected in Sierra Leone in June 1976 and was named Gee Geronimo by its owner Christopher Hudson (UK).

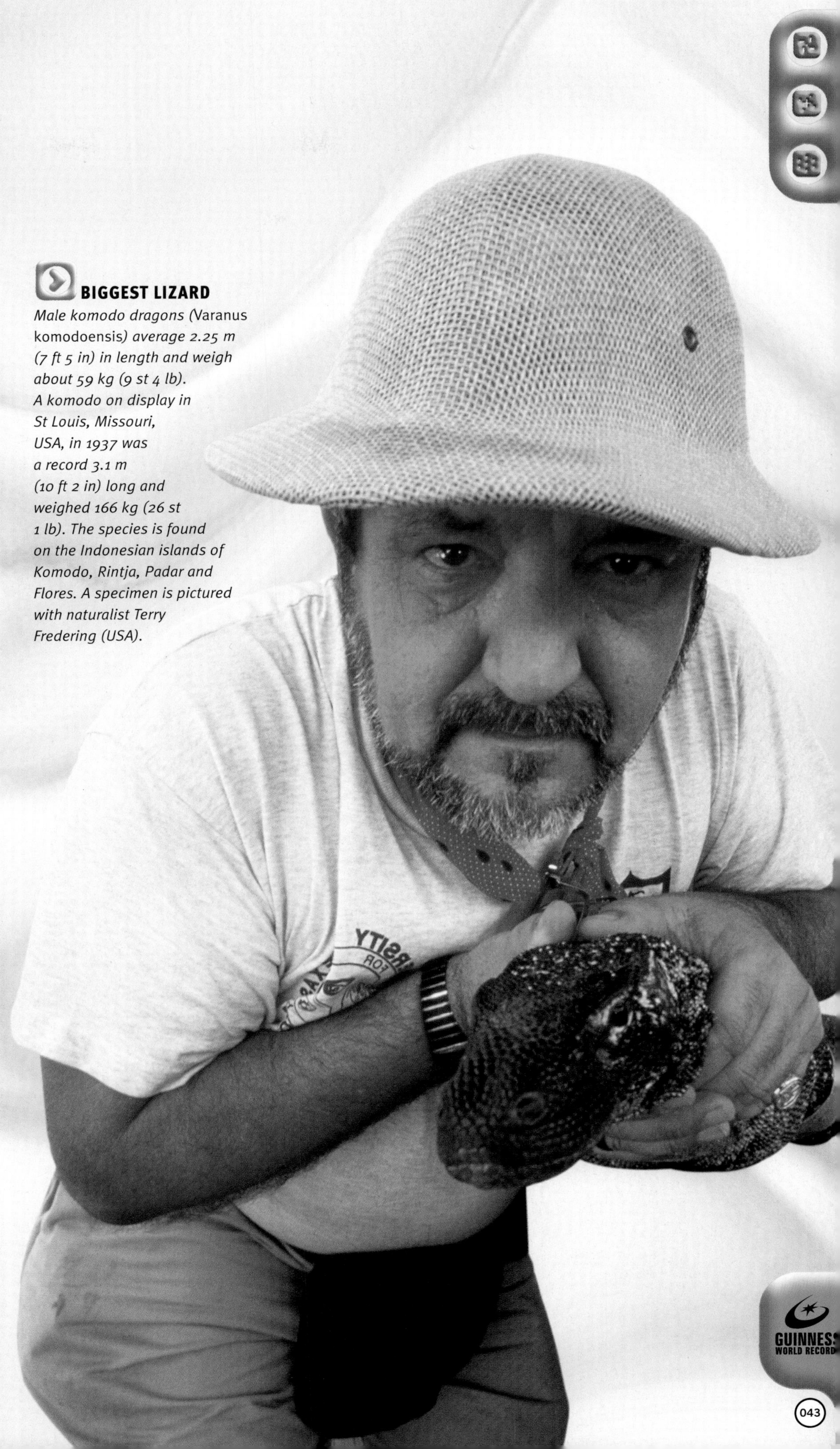

BIGGEST LIZARD
*Male komodo dragons (*Varanus komodoensis*) average 2.25 m (7 ft 5 in) in length and weigh about 59 kg (9 st 4 lb). A komodo on display in St Louis, Missouri, USA, in 1937 was a record 3.1 m (10 ft 2 in) long and weighed 166 kg (26 st 1 lb). The species is found on the Indonesian islands of Komodo, Rintja, Padar and Flores. A specimen is pictured with naturalist Terry Fredering (USA).*

achievement

strength

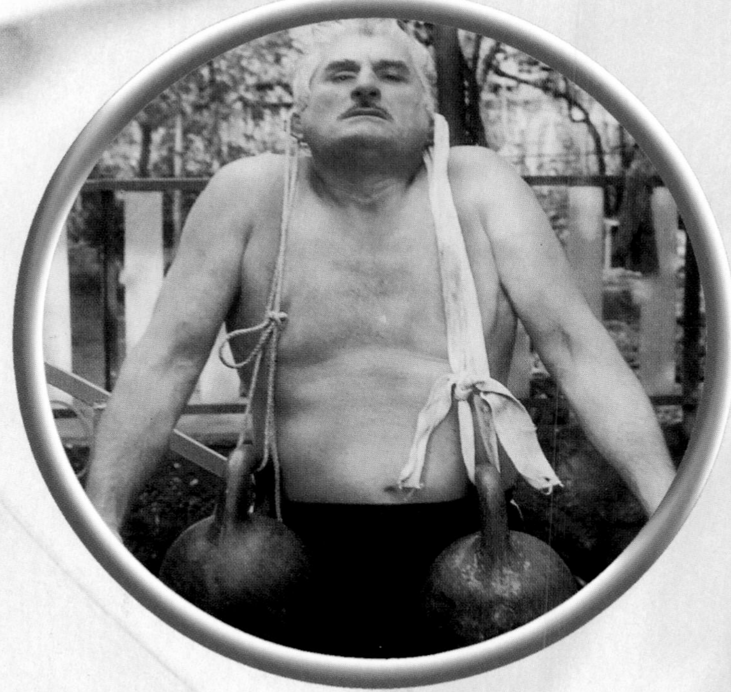

GREATEST DISPLAYS OF HUMAN STRENGTH

On 20 June 1997 Otto Acron stopped two Cessna 300-hp aeroplanes from taking off in opposite directions for more than 15 seconds at Hervey Bay, Queensland, Australia.

David Huxley single-handedly pulled a 187-tonne Qantas Boeing 747-400 a distance of 91 m (298 ft 6 in) across the tarmac at Sydney Airport, NSW, Australia, in Oct 1997.

Grant Edwards of Sydney, NSW, Australia, single-handedly pulled a 201-tonne train a distance of 36.8 m (120 ft 9 in) along a railway track at the NSW Rail Transport Museum, Thirlmere, Australia, on 4 April 1996.

Juraj Barbaric single-handedly pulled a 360-tonne train a record distance of 7.7 m (25 ft 3 in) along a rail track at Kosice, Slovakia, on 25 May 1996.

Maurice Catarcio (USA) became the oldest person to pull a passenger vessel on 12 Sept 1998, at the age of 69 years 6 months. He pulled the *Silver Bullet* (44 tonnes dwt) with a total of 125 people on board a distance of 91.44 m (300 ft), using only his feet for propulsion, in Sunset Lake, New Jersey, USA.

Yuri Scherbina, a powerjuggler from Ukraine, threw a 16-kg (35-lb 4½-oz) weightball from hand to hand 100 times on Mount Elbrus, at an altitude of 4,200 m (13,800 ft), in July 1995.

Khalil Oghaby (Iran) lifted an elephant weighing around 2 tonnes off the ground using a harness and platform at Gerry Cottle's Circus, UK, in 1975.

GREATEST LIFT USING TEETH

Walter Arfeuille of Ieper-Vlamertinge, Belgium, lifted weights totalling 281.5 kg (620 lb 10 oz) 17 cm (6¾ in) off the ground with his teeth in Paris, France, on 31 March 1990.

GREATEST PULL USING TEETH

Robert Galstyan of Masis, Armenia, pulled two railway wagons a distance of 7 m (23 ft) along a rail track with his teeth at Shcherbinka, Moscow, Russia, on 21 July 1992. The wagons weighed a total of 219 tonnes.

FASTEST BEER KEG LIFTER

Tom Gaskin lifted a 62.5-kg (137-lb 8-oz) keg of beer above his head 902 times in six hours at Liska House, Newry, Northern Ireland, on 26 Oct 1996.

GREATEST DISTANCE COVERED WHILE CARRYING BEER STEINS

Duane Osborn covered a record distance of 15 m (49 ft 2½ in) with five full steins of beer in each hand in a time of 3.65 seconds in a contest held at Cadillac, Michigan, USA, on 10 July 1992.

GREATEST DISTANCE COVERED WHILE CARRYING A BRICK

The greatest distance over which a brick weighing 4.5 kg (10 lb) has been carried in a nominated ungloved hand in an uncradled downward pincer grip is 124.72 km (77 miles 880 yd), by Paddy Doyle (UK), who travelled from Birmingham to Lower Shuckburgh, UK, and back from 11 to 12 Feb 1998.

STRONGEST EARS

Dimitry Kinkladze of Georgia lifted 48 kg (7 st 7 lb 13 oz) with his ears — a 32-kg (70-lb 9-oz) weight hung from the left ear and a 16-kg (35-lb 4-oz) weight from the right ear — for 10 minutes at Batumi, Georgia, on 2 Nov 1997.

GREATEST WEIGHT OF BRICKS LIFTED

Fred Burton of Cheadle, Staffs, UK, held 20 bricks weighing a record total of 102.73 kg (226 lb 7 oz) for two seconds on 5 June 1998.

MOST BRICKS LIFTED

In 1992 Russell Bradley of Worcester, UK, lifted a record 31 bricks — laid side by side — from a table and held them at chest height for two seconds.

MOST BRICKS BALANCED ON HEAD

John Evans (UK) balanced 101 bricks weighing 188.7 kg (416 lb) on his head for 10 seconds on the National Lottery programme on 24 Dec 1997.

HEAVIEST CAR BALANCED ON HEAD

John Evans (UK) is pictured here balancing a Nissan on his head at the Great World City Shopping Centre in Singapore. Evans is the current holder of the record for balancing a car on one's head, having balanced a Chevrolet weighing 158.76 kg (350 lb) for 12 seconds at the Master Locksmith public house in Derby, UK, on 4 Nov 1997. John is the holder of many strength-related Guinness records and makes regular appearances on *Guinness® World Records* TV shows. He claims to have the strongest neck in the world and has offered £2,000 ($3,315) to anybody who breaks one of his records.

MOST MILK CRATES BALANCED ON HEAD
In 1997 John Evans (UK) balanced 95 crates, each weighing 1.36 kg (3 lb), on his head for 10 seconds at Kerr Street Green, Co. Antrim, Northern Ireland.

STRONGEST HOD CARRIER
On 20 Nov 1993 Russell Bradley from Worcester, UK, carried bricks with a combined weight of 264 kg (582 lb) in a hod weighing 48 kg (105 lb 13 oz) for 5 m (16 ft 5 in), before climbing to a height of 2.49 m (8 ft 2 in). This gave a total weight of 312 kg (687 lb 13 oz).

MOST MILK CRATES BALANCED ON CHIN
Terry Cole (UK) balanced 29 milk crates on his chin for a specified minimum time of 10 seconds on 16 May 1994.

FASTEST COAL-CARRYING MARATHON
Brian Newton of Leicester, UK, covered 42.195 km (26 miles 385 yd) carrying a 50.8-kg (112-lb) open bag of household coal in 8 hr 26 min on 27 May 1983.

GREATEST FIELD GUN PULL
Three teams of eight men from the British Army's 72 Ordnance Company (V) RAOC pulled an 11.34-kg (25-lb) field gun 177.98 km (110 miles 1,041 yd) in 24 hours at Donnington, Shropshire, UK, from 2 to 3 April 1993. The field gun pull is a traditional military test of strength, discipline and teamwork.

HEAVIEST BARROW PUSHED
The heaviest loaded one-wheeled barrow pushed for a minimum distance of 71 level metres (200 ft) weighed 3.75 tonnes gross. It was pushed 74.1 m (243 ft) by John Sarich at London, Ontario, Canada, on 19 Feb 1987.

MOST TYRES SUPPORTED
Gary Windebank of Romsey, Hants, UK, supported 96 motor tyres weighing 653 kg (1,440 lb) in Feb 1984.

GREATEST DISPLAY OF LUNG POWER
In 1994 Nicholas Mason of Manchester, UK, inflated a balloon weighing 1 kg (2 lb 3 oz) to a diameter of 2.44 m (8 ft) in 45 min 2.5 sec.

HEAVIEST HARRIJASOKETA LIFT
Mieltxo Saralegi took 18 seconds to lift a rectangular stone weighing 327 kg (721 lb) at Anoeta sports arena, San Sebastián (Donostia), Spain, on 7 Feb 1998. Harrijasoketa is an ancient Basque sport.

GREATEST WEIGHT BENCH-PRESSED
James Henderson (USA) holds the world powerlifting record for the bench-press in the 125+ kg class, lifting 322.5 kg in 1997. Pictured is Anthony Clarke, the 1994 record-holder, who is also able to push a 3-tonne elephant around in a wheelbarrow and lift cars off their back wheels with ease.

skill

MOST SWORDS SWALLOWED

Bradley Byers of Idaho, USA, swallowed nine 68.5-cm (27-in) swords on the US TV show Guinness® World Records: Primetime *on 16 Oct 1998. The women's record is held by Amy Saunders (UK), who swallowed five swords between 35.5 cm and 51 cm (14 in and 20 in) in length on* Guinness® World Records *on 28 April 1999.*

MOST BOOMERANGS CAUGHT
Lawrence West from Basingstoke, Hants, UK, threw and caught a boomerang 20 times in one minute at the Indoor Boomerang Throwing Competition held on BBC TV's *Tomorrow's World* on 20 March 1998.

LONGEST NON-STOP SEPAK TAKRAW BALL JUGGLING
Ahmad Tajuddin from Malaysia juggled a sepak takraw ball (a ball made of cane) for three hours non-stop in Sept 1996. He juggled the ball 10,000 times with his right foot without letting it touch the ground.

MOST FLAMING TORCHES JUGGLED
Anthony Gatto (USA) juggled seven flaming torches at the International Jugglers Association Festival in Baltimore, Maryland, USA, in July 1989.

FASTEST POOL TABLE CLEARANCE
The fastest time for potting all 15 standard pool balls on a standard table is 26.5 seconds, by Dave Pearson (UK). He performed the feat at Pepper's Bar & Grill, Windsor, Ontario, Canada, on 4 April 1997.

TALLEST TOWER OF PLATES
On 9 Feb 1999 during *La Fiesta Magistral Ultra* at Mar del Plata, Buenos Aires, Argentina, a 59.7-m (195-ft 10-in) high tower of plates was constructed. It consisted of 10,038 plates and also holds the record for the most plates washed up at one time. Just one 750 ml (1 pint) bottle of washing-up liquid was used to clean all the plates.

MOST DOMINOES STACKED
Ralf Laue of Leipzig, Germany, successfully stacked 529 dominoes on a single supporting domino on 26 June 1997 at the Ramada Hotel, Linz, Austria.

MOST EGGS BALANCED
The most eggs balanced on end simultaneously on a flat surface by one person is 210, by Kenneth Epperson of Monroe, Georgia, USA, on 23 Sept 1990.

The most eggs simultaneously balanced by a group is 467, by a class at Bayfield School, Colorado, USA, on 20 March 1986.

LONGEST EGG THROW
Johnny Dell Foley threw a fresh hen's egg a distance of 98.51 m (323 ft 2 in) without breaking it on 12 Nov 1978 at Jewett, Texas, USA. The egg was caught by Keith Thomas.

LONGEST FLYING DISC THROWS
The World Flying Disc (frisbee) Federation distance record for men is 211.32 m (693 ft 4 in), by Scott Stokely (USA) on 5 April 1998 in Kingston, New Mexico, USA.

The official flying disc distance record for women is 136.31 m (447 ft 3 in), by Anni Kreml (USA) at Fort Collins, Colorado, USA, on 21 Aug 1994.

LONGEST COW PAT THROW
The greatest distance that a cow pat has been thrown under the 'non-sphericalization and 100% organic' rule is 81.1 m (266 ft), by Steve Urner at the Mountain Festival, Tehachapi, California, USA, on 14 Aug 1981.

LONGEST GUMBOOT THROWS
A size 8 (US size 8½) Challenger Dunlop boot was thrown a record distance of 63.98 m (209 ft 9 in) by Teppo Luoma in Hämeenlinna, Finland, on 12 Oct 1996.

The women's record is 40.87 m (134 ft 1 in), by Sari Tirkkonen at Turku, Finland, on 19 April 1996.

LONGEST SPEAR THROW
The furthest that a spear has been thrown using an atlatl, a hand-held device that fits onto it, is 258.63 m (848 ft 6½ in), by David Engvall at Aurora, Colorado, USA, on 15 July 1995.

GREATEST WEIGHT BALANCED ON TEETH

On 28 April 1999 Frank Simon from Key West, Florida, USA, balanced a motorbike weighing 61.2 kg (135 lb) on his teeth for 14.5 seconds on the TV show *Guinness® World Records*. He balanced the bike on its kickstand and did not use a special mouthguard — his only concession to protecting his mouth was a piece of cloth covering his teeth. In doing so he broke his own record, set on the US show *Guinness® World Records: Primetime* on 20 Nov 1998, when he balanced a motorbike weighing 58.3 kg (129 lb) for 15.25 seconds. He also balanced a number of other objects on his teeth during the show, including a cooker and a refrigerator.

YOUNGEST CIDER-POURING CHAMPION
Jorge Alberto Ramos became the youngest ever champion *escanciador* (cider pourer) at the age of 19 in 1998, when he won the annual Concurso de Escanciadores in Nava, Asturias, Spain. Each participant has to pour the contents of a cider bottle (70 cl or 23.7 fl oz) into five glasses, each of which has to contain 13 cl (4.4 fl oz) of cider. The competitor has to leave a maximum of 5 cl (1.7 fl oz) of cider in the bottle after pouring.

LONGEST BUBBLE
Alan McKay of Wellington, New Zealand, created a 32-m-long (105-ft) bubble on 9 Aug 1996. He used a bubble wand, washing-up liquid, glycerine and water.

LARGEST BUBBLE WALL
Fan-Yang of Mississauga, Ontario, Canada, created a 47.7-m (156-ft) bubble wall with an area of about 376.1 m² (4,000 ft²) at the Kingdome Pavilion, Seattle, Washington, USA, on 11 Aug 1997. The bubble stayed up continuously for between 5 and 10 seconds.

BIGGEST BUBBLE-GUM BUBBLE
The greatest reported diameter of a bubble-gum bubble is 58.4 cm (23 in). It was blown by Susan Montgomery Williams of Fresno, California, USA, at the ABC-TV studios in New York City, USA, on 19 July 1994.

FASTEST CUT-THROAT SHAVER
The record for the most people shaved with a cut-throat razor in 60 minutes is 278, by Tom Rodden of Chatham, Kent, UK, on 10 Nov 1993 for BBC TV's *Record Breakers* show. Averaging 12.9 seconds per face, he drew blood seven times.

FASTEST SAFETY-RAZOR SHAVER
The fastest barber using a retractor safety razor to shave is Denny Rowe (UK), who shaved 1,994 men in 60 minutes at Herne Bay, UK, on 19 June 1988. He took an average of 1.8 seconds to shave each person and drew blood just four times.

GREATEST GRAPE CATCH
The greatest ever distance at which a grape thrown from level ground has been caught in the mouth is 99.82 m (327 ft 6 in), by Paul Tavilla at East Boston, Massachusetts, USA, on 27 May 1991. The grape was thrown by James Deady.

LONGEST SPITS
The greatest recorded distance that a cherry stone has been spat is 28.98 m (95 ft 1 in), by Horst Ortmann at Langenthal, Germany, on 27 Aug 1994.

David O'Dell of Apple Valley, California, USA, spat a wad of tobacco a record distance of 16.23 m (53 ft 3 in) at the 22nd World Tobacco Spitting Championships at Calico Ghost Town, California, in March 1997.

The greatest distance that a watermelon seed has been spat is 22.91 m (75 ft 2 in), by Jason Schayot at De Leon, Texas, USA, on 12 Aug 1995.

FASTEST TALKERS
Sean Shannon (Canada) recited Hamlet's 'To be or not to be' soliloquy (260 words) in a time of 23.8 seconds (equivalent to 655 words per minute) in Edinburgh, UK, on 30 Aug 1995.

Steve Briers (UK), recited the lyrics of Queen's album *A Night at the Opera* backwards at Tenby, Dyfed, UK, in 9 min 58.44 sec on 6 Feb 1990.

MOST BEER MATS FLIPPED
Dean Gould (UK) flipped a pile of 111 beer mats (consisting of 1.2-mm-thick (0.04-in) wood pulp board) through an angle of 180° and caught them, at Edinburgh, UK, on 13 Jan 1993.

GREATEST WEIGHT BALANCED ON A KNIFE
Ali Bandbaz balanced his brother Massoud on two 37-cm (14½-in) daggers with a tip width of only 0.95 cm (⅜ in) on Guinness® World Records: Primetime *on 20 Nov 1998. The brothers, from Tehran, Iran, placed the daggers in their mouths and Massoud, who weighs 68 kg (150 lb), was balanced unaided for 29 seconds. The feat had never been attempted before.*

endurance

LONGEST BACKWARDS UNICYCLE
Ashrita Furman (USA) rode a unicycle backwards for a distance of 85.56 km (53 miles 299 yd) at Forest Park, New York, USA, on 16 Sept 1994.

LONGEST BARREL ROLL
A team of 10 people from Tecza sports club, Lódz, Poland, rolled a 63.5-kg (140-lb) barrel a distance of 200.11 km (124 miles 598 yd) in 24 hours from 1 to 2 Sept 1995.

GREATEST DISTANCE COVERED ON A POGO STICK
Ashrita Furman (USA) set a distance record of 37.18 km (23 miles 182 yd) in 12 hr 27 min at Queensborough Community College Track, New York, USA, on 22 June 1997.

LONGEST BATH TUB PUSH
The greatest distance covered in 24 hours pushing a wheeled bath tub with a passenger is 513.32 km (318 miles 1,689 yd), by a team of 25 from Tea Tree Gully Baptist Church, Westfield Shoppingtown Plaza, Australia, from 11 to 12 March 1995.

LONGEST CRAWL
The longest continuous voluntary crawl was 50.6 km (31 miles 778 yd), by Peter McKinlay and John Murrie, who covered 115 laps of an athletics track at Falkirk, UK, from 28 to 29 March 1992. *The Guinness® Book of Records* guidelines state that in a crawling record attempt, either knee must keep unbroken contact with the ground.

Over 15 months ending on 9 March 1985, Jagdish Chander (India) crawled 1,400 km (870 miles) from Aligarh to Jammu, India, to appease the Hindu goddess Mata.

LONGEST KISS
Mark and Roberta Griswold from Allen Park, Michigan, USA, kissed continuously for a record 29 hours at the 'Breath Savers Longest Kiss Challenge' in New York, from 24 to 25 March 1998. The couple remained standing without rest breaks throughout the attempt to capture the record.

MOST PEOPLE KISSED
Alfred Wolfram of Minnesota, USA, kissed 11,030 people in eight hours at the Minnesota Renaissance Festival on 12 Sept 1998 — approximately one every 2.6 seconds.

LONGEST DANCE MARATHON
The most taxing marathon dance staged as a public spectacle was performed by Mike Ritof and Edith Boudreaux, who logged 5,148 hr 28 min 30 sec to win $2,000 (£412) at the Merry Garden Ballroom, Chicago, Illinois, USA, from 29 Aug 1930 to 1 April 1931. Rest periods were progressively cut from 20 to 10 to five minutes per hour to none. They were permitted to shut their eyes for a maximum of 15 seconds at a time.

MOST STEP-UPS
Terry Heidt completed 3,967 step-ups in an hour at Penticton High School, British Columbia, Canada, on 18 April 1997, using a 38.1-cm-high (15-in) exercise bench.

MOST 'BLINDFOLD' CHESS WINS
In Jan 1947, in São Paulo, Brazil, Miguel Najdorf (Argentina) played 45 simultaneous chess games over 23 hr 25 min against some of the best players in Brazil. He sat in a separate room from his opponents and never saw the boards, communicating his moves through a microphone. He won 39, drew four and lost only two. Najdorf was at a chess tournament in Argentina when the Germans invaded his native Poland in 1939, and he subsequently became an Argentinian citizen. He died in July 1997 at the age of 87.

SNAKE SITTING
The record for sitting in a bath tub with the greatest number of poisonous snakes is currently held by Jackie Bibby of Fort Worth, Texas, USA, who sat with a total of 35 rattlesnakes on 17 June 1998. The record was broadcast on the television series *Guinness® World Records* (right). Bibby has competed at the American National Rattlesnake Sacking Championships, which are held every spring at the Taylor Chamber of Commerce, Texas. He has received numerous awards for his proficiency with snakes, including the Riled Rattlesnake Round-Up Safety Award.

LONGEST RADIO DJ MARATHON

The world's longest radio DJ marathon under The Guinness® Book of Records *guidelines was achieved by Simon Mayo of BBC Radio 1 in London, UK, for the charity Comic Relief. He played records for 37 hours, from 9 am on 11 March to 10 pm on 12 March 1999, with visits from comedians Dawn French and Jennifer Saunders (top left), fellow Radio 1 DJ Zoë Ball (top right) and TV star Terry Wogan (middle left).*

LONGEST CARDIOPULMONARY RESUSCITATION

Brent Shelton and John Ash completed a cardiopulmonary resuscitation (CPR) marathon (15 compressions alternating with two breaths) lasting 130 hours from 28 Oct to 2 Nov 1991 at Regina, Saskatchewan, Canada.

LONGEST CLAPPING SESSION

The record for continuous clapping (sustaining an average 160 claps per minute, audible at 110 m or 360 ft) is 58 hr 9 min, set by V. Jeyaraman of Tamil Nadu, India, from 12 to 15 Feb 1988.

MOST YO-YO LOOPS

'Fast' Eddy McDonald of Toronto, Canada, completed 21,663 loops with a yo-yo in three hours on 14 Oct 1990 at Boston, Massachusetts, USA, having previously set a one-hour speed record of 8,437 loops at Cavendish, Prince Edward Island, Canada, on 14 July 1990.

LONGEST TIME SPENT BALANCING ON ONE FOOT

Arulanantham Suresh Joachim (Sri Lanka) balanced on one foot for a record 76 hr 40 min at Uihara Maha Devi Park Open Air Stadium, Sri Lanka, from 22 to 25 May 1997.

LONGEST STATIC WALL SIT

Rajkumar Chakraborty (India) stayed in an unsupported sitting position against a wall for 11 hr 5 min at Panposh Sports Hostel, Rourkela, India, on 22 April 1994.

LONGEST TIME SPENT MOTIONLESS

Radhey Shyam Prajapati (India) stood motionless for 18 hr 5 min 50 sec at Gandhi Bhawan, Bhopal, India, from 25 to 26 Jan 1996.

LONGEST HAND RAISING

Amar Bharti of India claims to have kept his right hand raised for 26 years as a gesture of devotion to the Hindu god Shiva. In 1973 he decided to raise his right arm 90° in the air. His fingers have withered into the palm of his hand, his knuckles are white with rot and his nails have grown long and twisted.

teamwork

LOUDEST SCREAM BY A CROWD
A scream registering 126.3 dB was measured at the Party in the Park pop concert featuring Robbie Williams, Boyzone and All Saints in Hyde Park, London, UK, by Trevor Lewis of CEL Instruments on 5 July 1998.

BIGGEST PIANO ORCHESTRA
A total of 96 pianists on 96 pianos performed together at the Old Castle, Koldinghus, Kolding, Denmark, on 2 May 1996. They were conducted by José Ribera.

BIGGEST DRUM BAND
On 15 March 1998 a total of 1,700 musicians in Huesca, Spain, formed the largest ever drum band. The event was organized by the Certamen de Bandas de Huesca.

BIGGEST DRUM ENSEMBLE
On 9 Aug 1998, 1,850 people played the tune *Yamabiko* on 1,845 Japanese drums for 25 minutes at Ire Stadium, Muroran City, Hokkaido, Japan.

LONGEST HUMAN CHAIN
On 23 Aug 1989 an estimated 1 million people joined hands to form a chain 595 km (370 miles) long across Estonia, Latvia and Lithuania. It marked the 50th anniversary of the Russo-German pact that led to the Baltic States' annexation.

BIGGEST BREAKFAST
On 17 April 1998, 13,797 people ate a breakfast of Kellogg's cereals at Dubai Creekside Park, United Arab Emirates.

BIGGEST COFFEE MORNING
On 4 Oct 1996 a total of 513,659 people attended 14,652 coffee mornings held simultaneously throughout the United Kingdom as part of The Macmillan Cancer Fund Appeal, raising a total of £1.5 million ($2.34 million).

BIGGEST CHILDREN'S PARTY
The International Year of the Child party held in Hyde Park, London, UK, on 30 and 31 May 1979 was attended by members of the British royal family and a record 160,000 children.

MOST KISSING COUPLES
The greatest number of couples to have kissed in the same place at the same time was 1,543, at the Sarnia Sports and Entertainment Centre, Ontario, Canada, on 13 Feb 1999.

BIGGEST HUMAN CONVEYOR BELT
On 7 Sept 1998 a total of 1,000 students formed a human conveyor belt and carried a surfboard over the top at the University of Guelph, Ontario, Canada.

BIGGEST DANCE
An estimated 72,000 people took part in a Chicken Dance during the Canfield Fair, Ohio, USA, on 1 Sept 1996.

LONGEST CONGA
On 13 March 1988 the Miami Super Conga, held in conjunction with Calle Ocho — a Cuban-American celebration of life held in Miami, Florida, USA — consisted of a total of 119,986 people.

LONGEST PAPERCLIP CHAIN
A chain of 60,000 paperclips measuring 16.36 km (10 miles 303 yd) was put together by a team of 60 volunteers at Lympsham First School, Somerset, UK, between 2 and 3 May 1998.

BIGGEST TAP DANCE
A record-breaking 6,776 people tap danced outside Macy's department store in New York, USA, on 17 Aug 1997.

BIGGEST LINE DANCE
On 25 Jan 1997 a total of 5,502 people took part in a country line dance held in Tamworth, NSW, Australia. They danced to Brooks and Dunn's extended play version of *Bootscootin' Boogie*, which lasts for 6 min 28 sec.

BIGGEST 'YMCA' DANCE
On 1 Nov 1997, 6,907 students from Southwest Missouri State University, USA, danced to the song *YMCA* for five minutes while it was performed live by the group Village People at the University's Plaster Stadium.

BIGGEST HUMAN MOBILE
On 6 Aug 1998 the Circus of Horrors broke their own record when they created a human mobile consisting of 20 people in Edinburgh, UK.

MOST OBJECTS JUGGLED
On 7 Aug 1998 a total of 1,508 people juggled 4,524 objects at the European Juggling Convention, Edinburgh, UK.

MOST DOMINOS TOPPLED
Sixty students at Expo Centrum FEC, Leeuwarden, Netherlands, set up 2.3 million dominos over a seven-week period. Of these 1,605,757 were toppled by one push on 28 Aug 1998.

BIGGEST SAND CASTLES AND SAND SCULPTURES

The world's tallest sand castle (right) was made at Duquoin State Fairground, Illinois, USA, from 26 Aug to 2 Sept 1998 by the Totally In Sand team. It was 7.31 m (24 ft) tall. Under *The Guinness Book of Records* rules, sand sculptures can be built with mechanical assistance, but builders of sand castles are restricted to using hands, buckets and spades. The longest ever sand castle was made by staff and pupils of Ellon Academy, Aberdeenshire, UK, on 24 March 1988. It was 8.37 km (5 miles 352 yd) long. The world's longest sand sculpture was the GTE Directories Ultimate Sandcastle, built at Myrtle Beach, South Carolina, USA, on 31 May 1991. It stretched 26.376 km (16 miles 686 yd).

BIGGEST GAME OF PASS-THE-PARCEL
On 28 Feb 1998 a record 3,918 people (mainly secondary school students and students from Nanyang Technology University, Singapore) unwrapped 2,200 layers of a parcel that initially measured 1.5 x 1.5 x 0.5 m (4 ft 11 in x 4 ft 11 in x 1 ft 7½ in). The entire process took two and a half hours. The prize in the middle of the parcel was a voucher for a mobile telephone.

BIGGEST GAME OF MUSICAL CHAIRS
The biggest known game of musical chairs started with 8,238 participants and was held at the Anglo-Chinese School, Singapore, on 5 Aug 1989. Xu Chong Wei sat on the final chair.

LONGEST BUCKET CHAIN
On 5 Aug 1997 a total of 6,569 boys representing the Boy Scouts of America made a fire service bucket chain that stretched for a record length of 4.18 km (2 miles 59 yd) as part of the National Scout Jamboree, held in Fort A.P. Hills, Virginia, USA. The scouts started with 636.44 litres (140 gal) of water and only spilled 63.64 litres (14 gal), finishing with 572.8 litres (126 gal).

LONGEST DAISY CHAIN
The longest ever daisy chain measured 2.12 km (6,980 ft 7 in) and was made in seven hours by villagers of Good Easter, Chelmsford, Essex, UK, on 27 May 1985. The teams are limited to 16 members.

LONGEST DANCING DRAGON
On 21 Dec 1997 a Chinese dancing dragon measuring a record 2.47 km (1 mile 936 yd) was brought to life by 3,760 people at Happy Valley Racecourse, Hong Kong.

LONGEST HUMAN CENTIPEDE
On 2 Sept 1996, 1,665 students from the University of Guelph, Ontario, Canada, moved 30 m (98 ft 5 in) with their ankles tied together. They all remained upright.

LONGEST LEAP-FROG
The greatest distance covered by leap-froggers was 1,603.2 km (996 miles 292 yd), by 14 students from Stanford University, California, USA, who started leap-frogging on 16 May 1991 and stopped 244 hr 43 min later on 26 May.

MOST SHOES SHINED
The greatest number of shoes shined 'on the hoof' by four people in eight hours is 14,975, by members of the London Church of Christ at Leicester Square, London, UK, on 15 June 1996.

BIGGEST ORIGAMI MODEL
A paper crane with a wing-span of 63.33 m (207 ft 9 in) was folded by residents of Atika Prefecture, Odate, Japan, on 1 Aug 1998. Consisting of 4,195 m² (45,156 ft²) of paper, it took 200 people seven hours to create.

MOST BODIES PAINTED
On 9 Nov 1998 a total of 110 people had their bodies painted as part of the Living Bridges celebrations held in Rotterdam, Netherlands.

GUINNESS WORLD RECORDS

incredible journeys

LONGEST WALK IN THE WESTERN HEMISPHERE
George Meegan from Rainham, Essex, UK, walked 30,431 km (19,019 miles) from Ushuaia, the southern tip of South America, to Prudhoe Bay in northern Alaska, in 2,426 days from 26 Jan 1977 to 18 Sept 1983. He thus completed the first traverse of the Americas and the western hemisphere.

LONGEST BACKWARDS WALK
Plennie Wingo of Abilene, Texas, USA, made a 12,875-km (8,000-mile) transcontinental walk from Santa Monica, California, USA, to Istanbul, Turkey, from 15 April 1931 to 24 Oct 1932.

LONGEST BACKWARDS RUN
Arvind Pandya of India ran backwards from Los Angeles to New York, USA, in 107 days between 18 Aug and 3 Dec 1984, covering more than 5,000 km (3,100 miles). He also ran backwards from John O' Groats to Land's End, UK, in a time of 26 days 7 hr from 6 April to 2 May 1990, covering a total distance of 1,512 km (940 miles).

LONGEST HORSE-DRAWN JOURNEY
The Grant family from the United Kingdom covered a distance of more than 27,650 km (17,200 miles) during a round-the-world trip in a horse-drawn caravan. They began their journey at Vierhouten, Netherlands, on 25 Oct 1990 and returned to the UK early in 1998, after travelling through Belgium, France, Italy, Austria, northern Yugoslavia (which became Slovenia while they were there), Hungary, Russia, the Ukraine, Kazakhstan, Mongolia, China, Japan, the USA and Canada. They sold their house to finance the trip, which cost them £60,000 ($96,000) over seven years.

LONGEST UNICYCLE RIDE
Akira Matsushima from Japan unicycled 5,248 km (3,261 miles) across the USA from Newport, Oregon, to Washington DC between 10 July and 22 Aug 1992.

LONGEST ONE-WAY TANDEM RIDE
Laura Geoghean and Mark Tong travelled 32,248 km (20,155 miles) from London, UK, to Sydney, NSW, Australia, from 21 May 1994 to 11 Nov 1995.

LONGEST STILT-WALKS
The greatest distance ever covered on stilts is 4,804 km (3,008 miles), by Joe Bowen from Los Angeles, California, to Bowen, Kentucky, USA, from 20 Feb to 26 July 1980.

In 1891 Sylvain Dornon walked from Paris, France, to Moscow, Russia, on stilts in either 50 or 58 stages, covering a distance of 2,945 km (1,830 miles) at a much greater speed than Bowen's.

LONGEST WALK ON HANDS
The record for the greatest distance ever covered by a person walking on their hands is 1,400 km (870 miles), by Johann Hurlinger (Austria) in 1900. He walked from Vienna, Austria, to Paris, France, in a total of 55 daily 10-hour stints, averaging a speed of 2.54 km/h (1.58 mph).

LONGEST 'WALK ON WATER'
Rémy Bricka of Paris, France, holds the record for the longest 'walk on water', after covering 5,636 km (3,502 miles) from Tenerife, Canary Islands, to Trinidad in the Caribbean from 2 April to 31 May 1988. He 'walks' with 4.2-m-long (13-ft 9-in) ski-floats attached to his feet, moving in the same way as cross-country skiers but using a double-headed paddle instead of ski poles.

LONGEST LAND-ROW
Rob Bryant of Fort Worth, Texas, USA, covered a distance of 5,278.5 km (3,280 miles) on a land-rowing machine. He left Los Angeles, California, USA, on 2 April 1990 and reached Washington DC on 30 July.

LONGEST PIZZA DELIVERY ROUTE
Eagle Boys Dial-a-Pizza in Christchurch, New Zealand, regularly delivers pizzas to Scott Base, Antarctica, for the New Zealand Antarctic Programme. The pizzas are cooked, packed and shipped to a military airfield, where they are then loaded onto a C.130 Hercules. They arrive at the base nine hours later, complete with re-heating instructions.

MOST COUNTRIES TRAVELLED THROUGH BY TRAIN IN 24 HOURS
The most countries travelled through by train in 24 hours is 11, by Alison Bailey, Ian Bailey, John English and David Kellie from 1 to 2 May 1993. They started their journey in Hungary and continued through Slovakia, the Czech Republic, Austria, Germany, Switzerland, Liechtenstein, France, Luxembourg and Belgium, and arrived in the Netherlands 22 hr 10 min after setting off.

LONGEST JOURNEY BY CAR
Since 16 Oct 1984 Emil and Liliana Schmidt from Switzerland have travelled a record distance of 482,800 km (300,000 miles) through 125 countries in a Toyota Landcruiser.

LONGEST ROLLING JOURNEY
Lotan Baba (right) an Indian sadhu (holy man) rolled his body 4,000 km (2,485 miles 973 yd) from Ratlam to Jammu, India, over eight months in 1994. He rolled an average of 10–12 km (6–7 miles) and covered a maximum distance of 21 km (13 miles) per day. The purpose of the rolling journey was to pay homage to the goddess Vaishno Devi to achieve peace and unity for India. During the rolls, he did not eat, and only took sips of water and smoked the occasional cigarette. His body was covered with blisters after completing the journey to the Vaishno Devi temple on the 1,524-m (5,000-ft) mountain in Katra.

LONGEST TAXI RIDE
The longest taxi ride on record covered a distance of 34,908 km (21,691 miles) from London, UK, to Cape Town, South Africa, and back, at a cost of £40,210 ($62,908). It was made by Jeremy Levine, Mark Aylett and Carlos Arrese from 3 June to 17 Oct 1994.

LONGEST JOURNEY IN A 2CV
Between 9 Oct 1958 and 12 Nov 1959, Jacques Seguela and Jean-Claude Baudot (both France) drove 100,000 km (62,139 miles) in a Citroën 2CV (AZ), now housed in the Le Mans Motor Museum, France. They drove through 50 countries and crossed five continents. They spent 2,247 hours at the wheel and used 5,000 litres (1,321 gal) of petrol, achieving an average fuel consumption of 16.27 km/litres (46 mpg).

LONGEST JOURNEY BY AMPHIBIOUS CAR
The longest journey in an amphibious car was undertaken by Ben Carlin (Australia) in the amphibious jeep, *Half-Safe*. He completed the last leg of the Atlantic crossing (the English Channel) on 24 Aug 1951. He arrived back in Montreal, Canada, on 8 May 1958, having completed 62,765 km (39,000 miles) over land and 15,450 km (9,600 miles) by sea and river. He was accompanied on the transatlantic stage of the journey by his ex-wife Elinore.

LONGEST MOPED JOURNEY
Adam Paul rode a record 77,246 km (48,000 miles) from Cape Horn, Chile, to the Cape of Good Hope, South Africa, on a 90cc Honda moped between 10 April 1996 and 15 March 1998.

LONGEST PEDAL-BOAT JOURNEY
Kenichi Horie of Kobe, Japan, set a pedal-boating distance record of 7,500 km (4,660 miles). He left Honolulu, Hawaii, USA, on 30 Oct 1992 and arrived at Naha, Okinawa, Japan, on 17 Feb 1993.

FASTEST TRANSATLANTIC ROW
New Zealanders Phil Stubbs and Robert Hamill rowed across the Atlantic Ocean in a record time of 41 days between 12 Oct and 22 Nov 1997, starting their journey from Tenerife, Canary Islands, and finishing at Port St Charles, Barbados. The previous record for rowing across the Atlantic was 73 days, by Britons Sean Crowley and Mike Nestor in 1986.

LONGEST LAWNMOWER RIDE
In the summer of 1997, 12-year-old Ryan Tripp made a 5,417-km (3,366-mile) journey by lawnmower across the USA, raising $10,400 (£6,500) for a sick baby in his home town. Beginning in Salt Lake City, Utah, Ryan rode the Walker 25-hp mower along secondary roads approved by police, following a lead car driven by friends and family. Ryan's father Todd followed in a pick-up truck with an equipment trailer. The mower was fitted with road tyres and had extra springs and seat padding to make the trip comfortable for Ryan. Nineteen states and 42 days later he arrived at the Capitol in Washington DC, where he was welcomed by Utah senator Orrin Hatch.

FASTEST TRANS-AMERICA CROSSING ON A SKATEBOARD
Jack Smith (USA) skateboarded across the USA in 1976 and 1984. The first trip took 32 days to complete with two companions, and the second trip, which he made with three team members, took just 26 days.

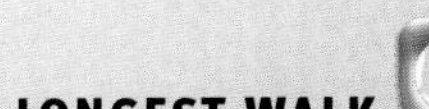

LONGEST WALK
The greatest distance that has ever been walked is 53,350 km (33,151 miles) by Arthur Blessitt of North Fort Myers, Florida, USA. He began his journey on 25 Dec 1969 and has visited 277 nations. He has carried a large wooden cross with him on his entire journey and has been accompanied by his wife Denise to 224 of the countries he has visited.

racing

FASTEST TREE CLIMBER
The record for climbing up and down a 30.5-m (100-ft) fir spar pole is 24.82 seconds, by Guy German of Sitka, Alaska, USA, on 3 July 1988. His climb was part of the World Championship Timber Carnival held in Albany, Oregon, USA.

FASTEST COCONUT TREE CLIMBER
The fastest time in which a 9-m-tall (29-ft 6-in) coconut tree has been climbed barefoot is 4.88 seconds, by Fuatai Solo of Western Samoa (now Samoa) at the Coconut Tree Climbing Competition (held annually at Sukana Park, Fiji), on 22 Aug 1980. After being declared the winner for the third time running, Fuatai climbed the tree again, this time clutching the prize money of $100 (£43) in his mouth.

FASTEST WOOLSACK RACER
Paul Elliot achieved the fastest ever individual time in the World Woolsack Championships held annually at Tetbury, Gloucestershire, UK, with 53.05 seconds in 1994. Competitors have to race up and down a steep hill carrying a 27.21-kg (4-st 4-lb) bag of wool on their shoulders.

FASTEST BOG SNORKELLER
Steve Madeline has won the annual World Bog Snorkelling Championship at Llanwrtyd Wells, Powys, UK, on a record two occasions, in 1989 and 1994. Contestants swim two lengths of a 60-m-long (196-ft 10-in) bog filled with weeds, leeches and newts.

FASTEST BARROW RACERS
The fastest time taken to complete a 1.609-km (1-mile) wheelbarrow race is 4 min 48.51 sec, by Piet Pitzer and Jaco Erasmus at Transvalia High School, Vanderbijlpark, South Africa, on 3 Oct 1987.

FASTEST BED RACERS
The fastest time in the 3.27-km (2-mile 56-yd) Knaresborough Bed Race, Yorkshire, UK, is 12 min 9 sec, by the Vibroplant team in June 1990.

FASTEST BATH TUB RACER
The record time for a 57.9-km (36-mile) bath tub race over water is 1 hr 22 min 27 sec, by Greg Mutton at the Grafton Jacaranda Festival, NSW, Australia, on 8 Nov 1987.

FASTEST PANCAKE RACER
The fastest time in the annual 384-m (420-yd) pancake race held in Melbourne, Australia, is 59.5 seconds, by Jan Stickland on 19 Feb 1985.

FASTEST STILT WALKER
Roy Luiking covered 100 m (328 ft) on 30.5-cm-high (1-ft) stilts in 13.01 seconds at Didam, Netherlands, on 28 May 1992.

FASTEST SPEED MARCHER
Paddy Doyle marched 1.6 km (1 mile) while carrying a rucksack weighing 18.1 kg (2 st 12 lb) on his back in a record time of 5 min 35 sec at Ballycotton, Co. Cork, Republic of Ireland, on 7 March 1993.

BIGGEST PLASTIC DUCK RACE
On 26 May 1997 a record 100,000 yellow plastic ducks raced down a 1-km (1,094-yd) stretch of the River Avon, Bath, UK. Organizers loaded all the ducks into a container and, at a signal from a cannon at precisely 2 pm, tipped them all into the river. It took 2 hr 15 min for duck no. 24,359, owned by Chris Green from Dauntsey, Wilts, UK, to win. With almost half the ducks sponsored at £1 ($1.64) each, the event raised nearly £50,000 ($81,910) for the charity Water Aid.

FASTEST BED MAKER
The shortest time in which one person has made a bed is 28.2 seconds, by Wendy Wall of Hebersham, Sydney, NSW, Australia, on 30 Nov 1978.

FASTEST COAL CARRIER
David Jones carried a 50-kg (7-st 12-lb) bag over the 1.0125-km (3,321-ft) course at Gawthorpe, W Yorkshire, UK, in a record 4 min 6 sec in April 1991.

FASTEST SPEED IN A HUMAN POWERED SUBMARINE
The fastest speed attained by a human powered propeller submarine is 3.445 m/sec (6.696±0.06 knots) by *Substandard*, designed and crewed by William Nicoloff (USA), using a two-blade propeller propulsion system on 30 March 1996. The speed record for a human powered non-propeller submarine is 1.49 m/sec (2.9±0.1 knots) by *Subdude*, designed by the Scripps Institute of Oceanography, University of California, San Diego, USA, using a horizontal oscillating foil propulsion system on 21 Aug 1992. The submarine was crewed by Kimball Millikan and Ed Trevino, with team leader Kevin Hardy.

FASTEST STAMP LICKER

Diane Sheer of London, UK, licked and affixed 225 stamps onto envelopes in a time of five minutes on 3 Aug 1997. According to The Guinness Book of Records *guidelines, one stamp must be gummed securely to the top right-hand corner of each envelope. Stamps are counted if they are placed at an angle but disqualified if they are upside-down.*

FASTEST COAL SHOVELLER
The fastest time in which a 508-kg (1,120-lb) hopper has been filled with coal is 26.59 seconds, by Wayne Miller at Wonthaggi, Victoria, Australia, on 17 April 1995.

FASTEST WIFE CARRIER
Jouni Jussila carried his wife Tiina over the World Wife-Carrying Championship course — a 235-m-long (771-ft) obstacle course that includes chest-high water and two wooden stiles — in a record time of 1 min 5 sec in 1997. It was Jussila's fifth success in the annual contest, which is held in Sonkajärvi, Finland. The winner takes home litres of beer equivalent to the weight of his partner, who need not be his wife but must be over the age of 17 and wear a crash helmet.

FASTEST SACK RACER
Ashrita Furman of Jamaica, New York, USA, completed a 10-km (6-mile 376-yd) sack race in a record time of 1 hr 25 min 10 sec at Mount Rushmore National Park, South Dakota, USA, on 6 Aug 1998.

FASTEST WINDOWCLEANER
On 29 March 1999 Terry Burrows of South Ockenden, Essex, UK, cleaned three standard 114.3-cm² (45-in²) office windows with a 30-cm-long (11¾-in) squeegee and 9 litres (2 gal) of water in 15.59 seconds on the BBC TV programme *Blue Peter*.

FASTEST DRUMMER
Rory Blackwell of Starcross, Devon, UK, played 400 separate drums in a record time of 16.2 seconds on 29 May 1995.

FASTEST INVERTED SPRINTER
On 19 Feb 1994 Mark Kenny of Norwood, Massachusetts, USA, sprinted 50 m (164 ft) on his hands in a time of 16.93 seconds.

FASTEST TYPISTS
Stella Pajunas (now Garnand) typed 216 words in one minute on an IBM machine in Chicago, Illinois, USA.

Gregory Arakelian of Herndon, Virginia, USA, set a speed record of 158 wpm (with two errors) on a PC in the Key Tronic World Invitational Type-Off on 24 Sept 1991.

Michael Shestov set a numerical record by typing spaced numbers from 1 to 801 (without any errors) in five minutes on a PC in New York City, USA, on 2 April 1996.

FASTEST STAIR CLIMBERS
Dennis W. Martz set the record for ascending 100 storeys in June 1978, when he climbed the stairs of the Detroit Plaza Hotel, Michigan, USA, in a time of 11 min 23.8 sec.

The fastest time in which the 1,760 steps of the CN Tower in Toronto, Canada — the world's tallest free-standing structure — have been climbed is 7 min 52 sec, by Brendan Keenoy on 29 Oct 1989.

FASTEST RACING SNAIL
The record-holder at the annual World Snail Racing Championships in Congham, Norfolk, UK, is Archie, trained by Carl Banham. His best time over the 33-cm (13-in) course was 2 min 20 sec.

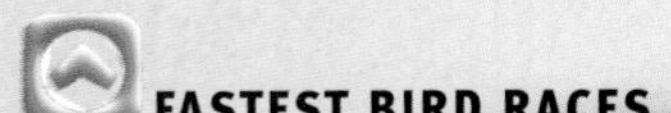

FASTEST BIRD RACES

Ostriches are the fastest birds on land and can run at speeds of up to 72 km/h (45 mph) for 30 minutes without rest. Making the most of the birds' speed and size, the annual Rocky Mountain Ostrich Festival, held in Colorado, USA, features ostrich racing as one of its highlights.

golden oldies

OLDEST PEOPLE
The oldest living person whose date of birth can be authenticated is Sarah Clark Knauss, who was born on 24 Sept 1880. Older than the Eiffel Tower, she was born in Hollywood, Pennsylvania, USA, and now lives in Allentown, Pennsylvania. She was married in 1901 and has a daughter in her nineties, a grandson, three great-granddaughters, five great-great-grandchildren and one great-great-great grandson.

The oldest person for whom there is irrefutable evidence was Jeanne Calment of France. She was born on 21 Feb 1875 and died on 4 Aug 1997, aged 122.

The world's oldest man was Shigechiyo Izumi of Japan, who lived for an authenticated 120 years 237 days. He was born on 29 June 1865 and was recorded as a six-year-old in Japan's first ever census, which took place in 1871. He worked until he was 105, drank *shochu* (liquor distilled from barley) and took up smoking when he was 70. Izumi attributed his long life to 'God, Buddha and the Sun'. He died on 21 Feb 1986 after developing pneumonia.

OLDEST GROOM
Harry Stevens was 103 years old when he married 84-year-old Thelma Lucas at the Caravilla Retirement Home, Wisconsin, USA, on 3 Dec 1984.

OLDEST BRIDE
Minnie Munro became the world's oldest known bride when she married Dudley Reid at the age of 102 in Point Clare, NSW, Australia, on 31 May 1991. The groom was 83.

LONGEST MARRIAGES
Cousins Sir Temulji Bhicaji Nariman and Lady Nariman from India were married when they were both five years old in 1853. Their marriage lasted 86 years, until Sir Temulji's death aged 91 years 11 months in 1940.

Records show that Lazarus Rowe and Molly Webber, who were both born in 1725, married in 1743. Molly died in June 1829 at Limington, Maine, USA, after 86 years of marriage.

LONGEST ENGAGEMENT
Octavio Guillén and Adriana Martínez from Mexico finally married in June 1969 after a 67-year engagement. Both were 82 years old when they wed.

OLDEST DIVORCING COUPLE
The divorcing couple with the highest combined age were Simon and Ida Stern of Milwaukee, Wisconsin, USA. When they ended their marriage in Feb 1984, he was 97 and she was 91.

OLDEST DWARF
Hungarian-born Susanna Bokonyi, alias 'Princess Susanna', of New Jersey, USA, was the world's oldest ever dwarf when she died aged 105 on 24 Aug 1984. She was 1.015 m (3 ft 4 in) tall.

OLDEST CHORUS LINE PERFORMER
Irus Guarino (b. 1909) of Boston, Massachusetts, USA, has been dancing in the chorus line of the Ziegfeld Girls of Florida since 1986. She first performed in a show at the age of 18, and was the centre girl with the Ritz Brothers in New York City, USA.

OLDEST PERSON TO HAVE A NO. 1 HIT
What a Wonderful World gave US jazz trumpeter and singer Louis Armstrong a No. 1 hit in the UK in 1968. It reached No. 1 in several other countries as late as 1970, when he was 69. Armstrong was almost 63 when he had his first US No. 1 hit, *Hello Dolly!*, in 1964. He initially became popular in the 1920s as a result of his recordings with the Hot Five and the Hot Seven.

OLDEST BARMAN
Angelo Cammarata is seen taking a break behind his bar in Pittsburgh, Pennsylvania, USA. The 85-year-old, who is known as 'Camm' to his customers and neighbours, is the world's oldest bartender. He first stepped behind a bar just minutes after the end of Prohibition in 1933, when his father decided to start serving alcohol in the family's grocery store and ice cream parlour. The grocery and ice cream businesses later folded. Today, Camm's bar Cammarata's is run with the help of his two sons, John and Frank.

OLDEST PEOPLE TO FLY

Retired Wing Cdr Kenneth Wallis of Norfolk, UK, is pictured flying the autogyro *Little Nellie*. Wallis is the oldest pilot to set an aviation world record, having made the fastest ever climb to 3,000 m (9,842 ft) in an autogyro on 19 March 1998, at the age of 81 years 336 days. The oldest person ever to qualify as a pilot is Burnet Patten of Victoria, Australia, who obtained his flying licence on 2 May 1997 at the age of 80. Clarence Cornish of Indianapolis, Indiana, USA, piloted aircraft until the age of 97. He died 18 days after his last flight on 4 Dec 1995. The oldest person to fly as a passenger was Charlotte Hughes of Redcar, N Yorkshire, UK, who was given a flight on Concorde from London, UK, to New York, USA, as a 110th birthday present in 1987. She flew again in 1992, aged 115.

OLDEST PERSON TO VISIT BOTH POLES
Major Will Lacy (UK) travelled to the North Pole on 9 April 1990 at the age of 82 and to the South Pole on 20 Dec 1991 at the age of 84. On both trips he arrived and left by light aircraft.

OLDEST DRIVERS
Layne Hall of Silver Creek, New York, USA, was issued with a licence on 15 June 1989 when, according to the licence, he was 109 years old. He died on 20 Nov 1990, but according to his death certificate he was then only 105.

Mrs Maude Tull of Inglewood, California, USA, began driving at the age of 91 after her husband died. She was issued with a replacement licence on 5 Feb 1976, when she was 104.

OLDEST MOTORCYCLIST
Arthur Cook (b. 13 June 1895) of Exeter, Devon, UK, still rides his Suzuki 125 GS Special motorcycle every day.

OLDEST PROFESSIONAL DRAG RACER
Eddie Hill (USA), who is now 63 years old, is still regularly racing at speeds in excess of 485 km/h (300 mph).

OLDEST CRESTA RUN RIDER
Prince Constantin of Liechtenstein rode the Cresta Run toboggan course at the record-breaking age of 86 years 49 days on 10 Feb 1998.

OLDEST BOARDSAILER
Charles Ruijter of the Netherlands took up boardsailing in 1978 at the age of 63. Now 84, he still sails in the lakes around Eindhoven, Netherlands.

OLDEST OLYMPIC MEDALLIST
Oscar Swahn from Sweden was in the winning Running Deer shooting team at the age of 64 in 1912, and was a silver medallist in the same event in 1920, at the age of 72.

OLDEST HOT-AIR BALLOONIST
Florence Laine of New Zealand flew in a balloon at the age of 102 at Cust, New Zealand, on 26 Sept 1996.

OLDEST TIGHTROPE WALKER
William Ivy Baldwin became the world's oldest ever tightrope walker when he crossed South Boulder Canyon, Colorado, USA, on his 82nd birthday on 31 July 1948. The wire he walked across was 97.5 m (320 ft) long and the drop was 38.1 m (125 ft).

OLDEST PARACHUTISTS
Hildegarde Ferrera became the oldest ever parachutist when she made a tandem parachute jump at the age of 99 at Mokuleia, Hawaii, USA, in 1996.

The oldest male parachutist is George Salyer, who made a tandem jump from 3,658 m (12,000 ft) aged 97 years 9 days at Harvey Airfield, Snohomish, Washington, USA, on 27 June 1998.

Sylvia Brett became the oldest female solo parachutist at the age of 80 years 166 days. She jumped at Cranfield, Beds, UK, on 23 Aug 1986.

OLDEST ATHLETE

Baba Joginder Singh throws a discus at the 1998 Indian National Athletics Meet for Veterans, held in Thane, Bombay (Mumbai). Singh, who won the gold medal in the event, is believed to be 105 years old, and was the only competitor aged over 100. As a teenager, he represented India in a 1910 World Championship event held in Berlin, Germany.

eating & drinking

MOST EXPENSIVE MEAL PER HEAD
In Sept 1997 three diners at Le Gavroche, London, UK, spent £13,091.20 ($20,945.92) on one meal. Only £216.20 ($345.92) went on food: cigars and spirits accounted for £845 ($1,352) and the remaining £12,030 ($19,248) went on six bottles of wine. The most expensive bottle, a 1985 Romanée-Conti costing £4,950 ($7,920), proved 'a bit young' so they gave it to the restaurant staff.

MOST EXPENSIVE STEAK
Wagyu cattle, which have been bred around the Japanese city of Kobe for centuries, provide the world's most expensive steak. The herds have a remarkable genetic purity and the cows are treated like royalty, regularly rubbed down with saké and fed huge amounts of beer. Their stress-free life is said to explain the quality of their flesh. On the rare occasions when Kobe beef is available in the West, it costs about $160/lb (£213.80/kg).

MOST EXPENSIVE SPICES
Prices for wild ginseng (the root of *Panax quinquefolium*) from China's Chan Pak mountain area peaked at £310,489/g ($18,678,624/oz) in Hong Kong in Nov 1979. Total annual shipments of the spice — thought by many to be an aphrodisiac — from Jilin province do not exceed 4 kg (8 lb 13 oz).

The most expensive widely-used spice is saffron, made from the dried stigmas of *Crocus sotivus*. It costs £42.50/g ($4/$^1/_{500}$ oz).

HOTTEST SPICE
A single dried gram ($^3/_{100}$ oz) of Red 'Savina' Habanero (1994 special), developed by GNS Spices of Walnut, California, USA, can produce detectable 'heat' in 577 kg (1,272 lb) of bland sauce.

MOST EXPENSIVE CAVIAR
Almas caviar, consisting of the yellow eggs from albino beluga sturgeons, sells for $1,000/1¾ oz (£625/50 g).

MOST EXPENSIVE SHELLFISH
The Percebes barnacle, known as the 'truffle of the seas', costs £241/kg ($176/lb). The barnacles need large amounts of oxygen to survive and so attach themselves to rocks where waves are at their most violent and the water is very aerated. Fishermen risk their lives to catch them in the uninhabited Sisargas Islands off Spain. The molluscs are so highly prized that a festival, the Fiesta de Los Percebes, is held in their honour.

BIGGEST FEAST
A feast held by Atul Dalpatlal Shah to celebrate his inauguration as a monk was attended by a record 150,000 guests. It took place in Ahmadabad, India, on 2 June 1991.

MOST EXPENSIVE CHILLI CON CARNE
The most expensive chilli con carne is served by Chasen's of West Hollywood, USA, and costs $16.75/½ lb (£46.16/kg). Film legend Elizabeth Taylor had some flown to her when she was filming *Cleopatra* (USA, 1963).

BIGGEST FOOD FIGHT
In 1998 about 30,000 people spent one hour throwing around 100 tonnes of tomatoes at each other in the town of Buñol near Valencia, Spain, which holds its annual 'Tomatina' Festival on the last Wednesday of August. The origins of the festival are unclear — some villagers maintain it began by chance when a lorry accidentally discharged its load of tomatoes, others say it started after the Spanish Civil War at a rally opposing General Franco's dictatorship. Today attendants dump the ripe fruit onto the streets from the backs of lorries for people to scoop up and throw.

MOST CREEPY CRAWLIES EATEN
The record for the most creepy crawlies eaten is held by Mark Hogg of Louisville, Kentucky, USA, who consumed 62 nightcrawler worms in 30 seconds on 19 Nov 1998 on the TV show *Guinness® World Records: Primetime.* Mark discovered he had a talent for eating the animals when he was put through army survival training in the jungles of Panama, where he had to survive for six weeks with minimum supplies. He supplemented his rations by eating vegetation, worms and grubs. This need not be as unhealthy as it sounds, since worms contain more protein by weight than chicken and tuna. Mark eats the live worms by tilting his head back and swallowing them whole. He refuses to eat sushi because he thinks eating raw fish is disgusting.

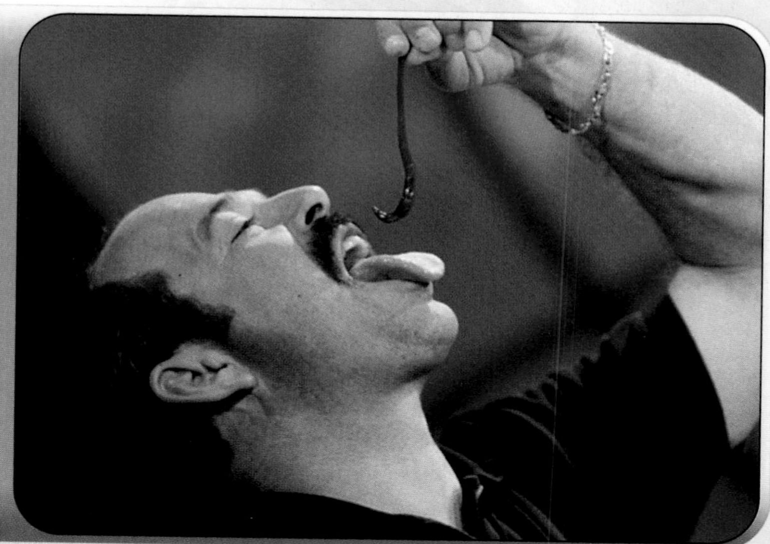

MOST EXPENSIVE FISH

In Jan 1992 a 324-kg (715-lb) bluefin tuna sold for $83,500 (£50,301) — almost $117/lb (£146/kg) — in Tokyo, Japan. The tuna was reduced to 2,400 servings of sushi for wealthy diners at $75 (£45) per serving. The estimated takings from this one fish were $180,000 (£108,000).

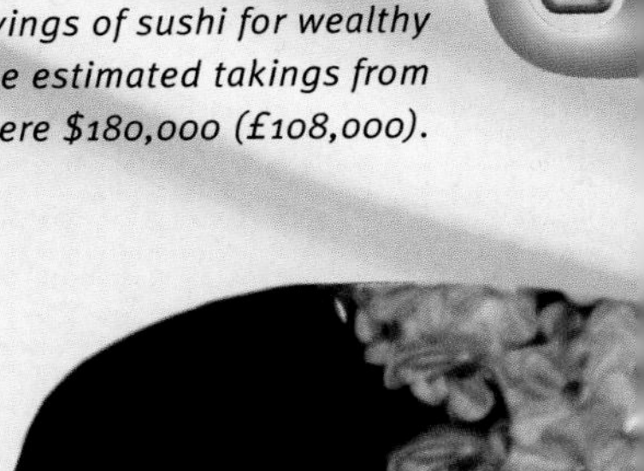

MOST EXPENSIVE FRUIT
In 1977 restaurateur Leslie Cooke paid £530 ($906) for 453 g (1 lb) of strawberries at an auction in Dublin, Republic of Ireland.

MOST EXPENSIVE TRUFFLE
The world's most expensive truffle is *Tuber magmatum pico*, a rare white truffle found in Alba, Italy, which sells for £11,707/kg ($8,820/lb). Scientists have been unable to cultivate the fungus, which is only found by trained pigs or dogs.

MOST EXPENSIVE COFFEE
The Indonesian coffee Kopi Luwak sells for £99.55/250 g ($75/¼ lb), partly because of its rarity but also because of the way it is processed: the beans from which it is made are ingested by a small tree-dwelling animal called the *Paradoxurus* before being extracted from the excreta of the animals and made into Kopi Luwak.

MOST RESTAURANTS VISITED
Fred Magel of Chicago, Illinois, USA, dined out 46,000 times in 60 countries over a period of 50 years as a restaurant grader.

HIGHEST-ALTITUDE DINNER PARTY
The greatest altitude at which a formal meal has been eaten is 6,768 m (22,205 ft), by nine members of the Ansett Social Climbers of Sydney, Australia, who scaled Mt Huascarán, Peru, with a dining table, chairs, wine and a three-course meal on 28 June 1989. At the summit the men dressed up in top hats and thermal black ties and the women in ballgowns.

MOST METAL EATEN
Michel Lotito, also known as Monsieur Mangetout, of Grenoble, France, has been eating metal and glass since 1959. He cuts up objects such as bicycles and supermarket trolleys with an electric power saw to make small pieces which he then swallows like a pill — something that would normally prove fatal and should never be attempted. By Oct 1997 the 47-year-old had eaten nearly eight tonnes of metal in his 22-year career.

STRONGEST ALCOHOL
The Estonian Liquor Monopoly marketed 98% (196° proof) alcohol distilled from potatoes when the country was independent between the two world wars.

Baz's Super Brew, brewed by Barrie Parish at the Parish Brewery, Somerby, Leics, UK, has an alcohol volume of 23%, making it the world's strongest beer.

BIGGEST TOAST
On 26 Feb 1999 a record 197,648 people gathered simultaneously in pubs, restaurants and bars in 74 metropolitan areas of the USA at 11 pm (EST) for 'The Great Guinness Toast'.

BIGGEST WINE TASTING
On 22 Nov 1986 about 4,000 people consumed a total of 9,360 bottles of wine at a tasting sponsored by the TV station KQED in San Francisco, California, USA.

BIGGEST WINE SALE
Andrew Lloyd Webber's 18,000-bottle wine collection sold for £3.69 million ($6 million) at Sotheby's, London, UK, on 21 May 1997. It was described at the time as the greatest single-owner wine collection ever offered at auction. The total price exceeded the estimate of £2–2.7 million ($3.3–4.4 million).

MOST VALUABLE BOTTLE OF WINE
In Dec 1985 £105,000 ($136,248) was paid for a bottle of 1787 Château Lafite at Christie's, London, UK. It was engraved with the initials of Thomas Jefferson, the third US president. In 1986 its cork slipped, spoiling the wine.

MOST EXPENSIVE GLASS OF WINE
A record $1,453 (£982) was paid for the first glass of Beaujolais Nouveau 1993 produced by Maison Jaffelin, Beaune, France. It was bought by Robert Denby at Pickwick's, a British pub in Beaune.

MOST EXPENSIVE SPIRIT
The most expensive spirit on sale is Springbank 1919 Malt Whisky, a bottle of which costs £6,750 ($10,800) at Fortnum & Mason in London, UK.

MOST VALUABLE SPIRIT
The highest price paid for a spirit at auction was $79,552 (£45,200), for a bottle of 50-year-old Glenfiddich whisky. It sold to an anonymous Italian businessman at a charity auction in Milan, Italy, in 1992.

BIGGEST PUB
The Mathäser in Munich, Germany, seats 5,500 people and sells 48,000 litres (84,470 pints) of beer daily.

big food

BIGGEST CURRY
On 17 May 1998 a curry weighing more than 2.65 tonnes was made by a team from the Raj restaurant in Maldon, Essex, UK. The curry, which was made in a specially-designed pot 2.29 m (7 ft 6 in) in diameter and 1.22 m (4 ft) deep, contained 1 tonne of vegetables, 80 kg (176 lb 8 oz) of coconut powder, 20 kg (44 lb 2 oz) of tamarind, 10 kg (22 lb) of tandoori paste, 40 kg (88 lb 3 oz) of food colouring and 3 kg (6 lb 10 oz) of garam masala. It was served in 13,500 portions.

LONGEST SUSHI ROLL
Six hundred members of the Nikopoka Festa committee made a sushi roll (*kappamaki*) 1 km (3,279 ft) long at Yoshii, Japan, on 12 Oct 1997.

BIGGEST CHINESE DUMPLING
The Hong Kong Union of Chinese Food and Culture Ltd and the Southern District Committee made a 480-kg (1,058-lb 3-oz) Chinese dumpling on 5 July 1997 to celebrate the return of Hong Kong to China.

MOST MUSSELS COOKED
On 5 Sept 1998, 12 people cooked 1.5 tonnes of mussels in one pan during a five-hour period at Oostduinkerke-Bad, Flanders, Belgium.

LONGEST SATAY
On 20 June 1998 a satay 83 m (90 yd) in length was made at the Thomson Community Club in Singapore.

BIGGEST BOWL OF SPAGHETTI
On 16 Aug 1998 a bowl of spaghetti weighing 274 kg (605 lb) was cooked by Consolidated Communications in London, UK, on behalf of Walt Disney Home Video to celebrate the re-release of *Lady and the Tramp* (USA, 1955).

BIGGEST RESTAURANT STEAK
A 5.67-kg (12-lb 8-oz) rump steak (pre-cooked weight) is available from the Kestrel Inn, Hatton, Derbyshire, UK. It takes about 40 minutes to cook (to a medium/well-done state) and costs £80 ($128). If a customer finishes the steak, the management will make a donation to charity.

BIGGEST DONER KEBAB
A doner kebab weighing a record 1.03 tonnes and measuring 1.2 m (3 ft 11 in) in width and 1.6 m (5 ft 3 in) in height was created by Kadir Cetinkaya at the Zürich Summer Festival, Switzerland, in July 1998.

BIGGEST HAMBURGER
A 2.5-tonne hamburger was made at the Outagamie County Fairgrounds, Seymour, Wisconsin, USA, on 5 Aug 1989.

BIGGEST SHORTCAKE
A 76.82-m² (827-ft²), 3.687-tonne strawberry shortcake was made by the Greater Plant City Chamber of Commerce in Plant City, Florida, USA, on 19 Feb 1999. It was topped with 617 kg (1,360 lb) of whipping cream and 1.812 tonnes of strawberries.

BIGGEST ONION BHAJI
Chefs at the Jinnah Restaurant, Flaxton, N Yorkshire, UK, created the world's biggest onion bhaji on 10 Nov 1998. It weighed 3.12 kg (6 lb 4 oz) and measured 51 cm (1 ft 8 in) in diameter.

LONGEST STRUDEL
A 1.674-km-long (1-mile 70-yd) apple strudel was made in Karlsruhe, Baden-Württemberg, Germany, on 26 May 1994.

LONGEST BANANA SPLIT
A 7.32-km (4-mile 965-yd) banana split was made by residents of Selinsgrove, Pennsylvania, USA, on 30 April 1988.

BIGGEST ICE CREAM SUNDAE
On 24 July 1988 an ice cream sundae weighing 24.91 tonnes was made by Palm Dairies Ltd of Edmonton, Alberta, Canada. The finished concoction included 20.27 tonnes of ice cream, 4.39 tonnes of syrup and 243.7 kg (537 lb 3 oz) of topping.

BIGGEST ICE CREAM SODA FLOAT
On 3 April 1998 Denny's and Coca-Cola concocted a 9,482-litre (2,505-US gal) ice cream float at North Druid Hill in Atlanta, Georgia, USA. It contained 6,624 litres (1,750 US gal) of Coca-Cola and 340.2 kg (750 lb) of ice cream.

BIGGEST ICE LOLLY
Between 1 and 30 Aug 1997 Iglo-Ola Produktie B.V. of Hellendoorn, Netherlands, manufactured a Rocket Ice weighing 9.081 tonnes. It was 6.5 m (21 ft 4 in) long and 2.26 m (7 ft 5 in) wide and averaged 1.1 m (3 ft 7 in) in thickness.

BIGGEST DOUGHNUT
A jam doughnut weighing 1.7 tonnes and measuring 4.9 m (16 ft) in diameter was made by representatives of Hemstrought's Bakeries, Donato's Bakery and the radio station WKLL-FM at Utica, New York, USA, on 21 Jan 1993.

BIGGEST ONION
Mel Ednie (right) of Anstruther, Fife, UK, grew the world's largest onion, weighing 7.03 kg (15 lb 5 oz), in 1997. Currently, the most successful cultivator of giant vegetables is Bernard Lavery of Rhondda, UK, who holds world records for the heaviest cabbage (56.24 kg or 124 lb), carrot (7.13 kg or 15 lb 11 oz) and courgette (29.25 kg or 64 lb) and for the longest corn cob (92 cm or 3 ft).

BIGGEST SAUSAGES

The longest continuous sausage on record extended a distance of 46.3 km (28 miles 1,354 yd). It was made by M & M Meat Shops and J.M. Schneider Inc at Kitchener, Ontario, Canada, in April 1995. Pictured here are children from Srednja Backa, Yugoslavia, during their attempt to beat the record. The biggest salami weighed 676.9 kg (1,492 lb 5 oz) and was 20.95 m (68 ft 9 in) long. It was made by staff of A/S Svindlands Pølsefabrikk at Flekkefjord, Norway, in July 1992. The biggest ever bratwurst, which measured 3.1 km (1 mile 1,630 yd) in length, was made at Jena, Germany, on 18 Sept 1994.

BIGGEST JELLY
A 35,000-litre (9,246-gal) watermelon-flavoured pink jelly was made by Paul Squires and Geoff Ross at Roma Street Forum, Brisbane, Queensland, Australia, on 5 Feb 1981.

BIGGEST BAR OF CHOCOLATE
A 2.715-m-long (8-ft 11-in), 1.195-m-wide (3-ft 11-in), 30.4-cm-deep (1-ft) Cadbury's Dairy Milk bar weighing 1.1 tonnes was made in Birmingham, UK, on 5 Oct 1998.

TALLEST CHOCOLATE MODEL
In Nov 1997 the Richemont Club built a 14.97-m-long (49-ft 1-in), 4.7-m-wide (15-ft 5-in), 7.47-m-high (24-ft 6-in) chocolate model dinosaur in the Zuid shopping centre, Ghent, Belgium.

BIGGEST CHRISTMAS LOG
On 25 Dec 1997 a 2.3-tonne Christmas log was made, displayed and eaten at the Mercure Hotel in Bangkok, Thailand. The log, which was 8.4 m (27 ft 6 in) long and 60 cm (2 ft) wide, was made by 10 staff and took 360 hours to prepare. The ingredients included 210 kg (462 lb 15 oz) of flour, 300 kg (661 lb 6 oz) of sugar, 120 kg (264 lb 9 oz) of butter, 120 kg (264 lb 9 oz) of evaporated milk and 594 eggs. The log was cut into 19,212 portions.

BIGGEST PINEAPPLE
The world's biggest pineapple was grown by E. Kamuk of Ais Village, Papua New Guinea, in 1994. It weighed 8.06 kg (17 lb 12 oz).

BIGGEST APPLE
The record for the heaviest apple is 1.67 kg (3 lb 11 oz), grown by Alan Smith of Linton, Kent, UK.

BIGGEST BROCCOLI
A head of broccoli weighing 15.87 kg (35 lb) was grown by John and Mary Evans of Palmer, Alaska, USA, in 1993.

BIGGEST GARLIC
The biggest head of garlic, weighing 1.19 kg (2 lb 10 oz), was grown by Robert Kirkpatrick of Eureka, California, USA, in 1985.

BIGGEST MARROW
The biggest marrow ever recorded was grown by John Handbury of Chesterfield, Derbyshire, UK, in 1998. It weighed 61.23 kg (135 lb).

BIGGEST PUMPKIN

Soji Shirai from Ashibetsu City, Japan, stands next to a pumpkin he grew weighing 440 kg (970 lb). An average pumpkin (Cucurbita peto) weighs between 1 and 2 kg (2 lb 2 oz and 4 lb 4 oz). The world's largest ever pumpkin was grown by Gary Burke of Simcoe, Ontario, Canada. It weighed 495 kg (1,092 lb) on 3 Oct 1998.

collectors

BIGGEST JET FIGHTER COLLECTION
Michel Pont, a French winemaker, has a personal collection of 100 jet fighter planes, ranging from British *Vampires* to Russian *MiGs* to a rare French Dassault *Mirage 4*. Pont first started collecting jet fighters in 1986, having collected motorbikes since 1958 and cars since 1970. By Jan 1998 the 66-year-old had accumulated 70 different types of jet fighter, 500 motorcycles and a series of crimson Abarth racing cars.

BIGGEST MODEL AIRCRAFT COLLECTION
Bader Yousif Murad of Bahrain has been collecting model aircraft since his 10th birthday in 1978, when he was given a second-hand model of a KLM B747-200. He now owns 1,105 model aircraft representing more than 440 airlines. Over the last 20 years, his collection, which grows by about 10 models a month, has cost him $30,000 (£18,000).

BIGGEST PASSPORT COLLECTION
Guy Van Keer of Brussels, Belgium, owns 4,260 passports and other travel documents used in lieu of passports. They represent 130 different countries and were issued between 1615 and the present day.

BIGGEST SCRATCH CARD COLLECTION
Darren Haake of Bateau Bay, NSW, Australia, has amassed a total of 277,820 scratch cards since he began collecting in 1993.

BIGGEST BUS TICKET COLLECTION
Yacov Yosipovv of Tel Aviv, Israel, has collected more than 14,000 used bus tickets, each one different in some way.

BIGGEST MARBLE COLLECTION
Over the past 46 years printer Sam McCarthy-Fox from Worthing, W Sussex, UK, has built up a collection of 40,000 marbles. These include antique marbles and fibre-optic examples made from semi-precious stones.

BIGGEST WHISKY COLLECTIONS
Edoardo Giaccone of Brescia, Italy, owned 5,502 unduplicated and unopened full-sized whisky bottles, including bourbons and Irish whiskeys. He died in 1997, leaving his collection to Guiseppe Begnoni of Bologna, Italy.

Claive Vidiz, president of the Brazilian Association of Whisky Collectors, owns 2,571 original — and full — bottles of Scotch whisky. The bottles are kept in a museum that was specially built for the collection in São Paulo, Brazil.

BIGGEST BEER CAN COLLECTION
William Christensen of Madison, New Jersey, USA, has collected more than 75,000 different beer cans from about 125 countries and territories.

BIGGEST COLLECTION OF AEROPLANE SICKBAGS
Nick Vermeulen (Netherlands) has built up a record-breaking collection of 2,112 different aeroplane sickbags. The bags come from a total of 470 different airlines.

LARGEST BALL-POINT PEN COLLECTION
Angelica Unverhau of Dinslaken, Germany, has collected 168,700 ball-point pens. This figure excludes duplicates and includes examples from 137 countries. She began collecting pens nine years ago after becoming fascinated by the many forms and varieties available. The most expensive pen in the collection is one made out of gold and white gold worth over $500 (£334).

BIGGEST GARFIELD COLLECTION
Mike Drysdale and Gayle Brennan of Los Angeles, California, USA, have collected about 3,000 items related to their favourite comic strip character, Garfield. The couple have turned their home into a gigantic shrine to the famous cat. Every corner is crammed with cuddly toys, videos, bedding, crockery, radios, wind-up toys and other Garfield-related items. The collection was started in 1994 when Gayle bought a Garfield bed for the couple's cats.
The characters of the lasagne-loving pet, his canine companion Obie and their long-suffering owner Jon were created by US cartoonist Jim Davis in 1978. The comic strip now has a daily worldwide circulation of 220 million people. Ironically, Davis doesn't own a cat, as his wife is allergic to them.

BIGGEST LAWN MOWER COLLECTION
The Hall and Duck Trust Collection of Vintage Lawn Mowers belonging to Andrew Hall and Michael Duck of Windsor, Berks, UK, contains more than 680 different lawn mowers.

BIGGEST MOVIE CAMERA COLLECTION
Retired postman Dimitrios Pistiola of Athens, Greece, has collected 440 movie cameras dating from 1901 to the present day.

BIGGEST COLOURED VINYL RECORD COLLECTION
Alessandro Benedetti of Monsummano Terme, Italy, has collected 780 records made from coloured vinyl.

BIGGEST BARBIE DOLL COLLECTION
Tony Mattia from Brighton, E Sussex, UK, has 1,125 Barbie dolls in his collection — about half the designs produced since Mattel launched the doll in the USA in 1959. He changes the dolls' costumes once a month and regularly brushes their hair.

BIGGEST PLASTER COLLECTION
Brian Viner from London, UK, has collected about 3,750 unused sticking plasters of many different colours, styles, shapes and sizes.

BIGGEST HANDCUFF COLLECTION
Locksmith Chris Gower from Dorset, UK, has amassed 412 pairs of handcuffs since he began collecting them in 1968. His interest in handcuffs arose from a fascination with escapology.

BIGGEST COLLECTION OF SWATCH WATCHES
Fiorenzo Barindelli from Lombardy, Italy, has amassed 3,524 Swatch watches. He owns an example of every watch documented in every Swatch catalogue since 1983, as well as some prototypes and special-edition pieces, and plans to open a Swatch museum in the year 2000.

BIGGEST COLLECTION OF CHAMBER POTS
Manfred Klauda of Germany has collected 9,400 different chamber pots, some dating back to the 16th century.

BIGGEST PIGGY BANK COLLECTION
Ove Nordström of Spånga, Sweden, has amassed a collection of 4,175 different money holders shaped like pigs.

BIGGEST *STAR WARS* COLLECTION
Jason Joiner of Ealing, London, UK, a special-effects expert who has worked on the Star Wars *prequels, has a collection of more than 20,000* Star Wars *toys. His collection also includes one of the original C3PO robots, an original R2D2 and an original Darth Vader costume, all used in one of the first three* Star Wars *films released.*

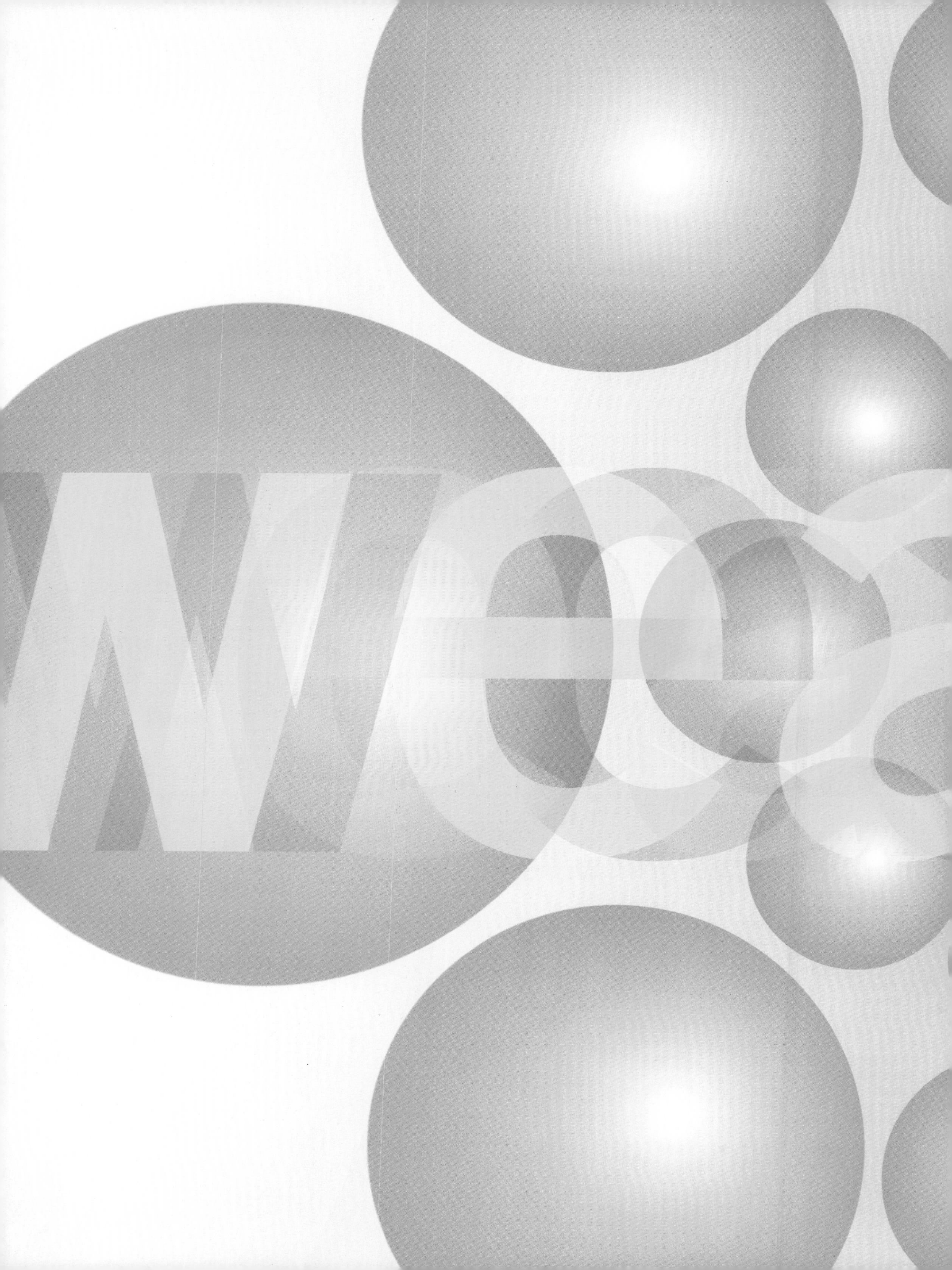

wealth

super rich

RICHEST ROYAL

The world's richest royal is Hassanal Bolkiah, the Sultan of Brunei, with a fortune estimated at $30 billion (£18.1 billion), earned from oil and gas. He is also Asia's richest man, the richest oil tycoon in the world and the owner of the world's biggest residential palace (*see Homes and Hotels*). As well as ruling Brunei, the Sultan is Prime Minister, Defence Minister and Finance Minister, and provides free education and health care for the citizens of his country.

RICHEST WOMEN
The world's richest women are the widow and daughter of Sam Walton, founder of Wal-Mart. *Forbes* estimates that his wife Helen and daughter Alice are each worth $16 billion ($9.65 billion).

Liliane Bettencourt, heiress to the L'Oréal and Nestlé empire, has an estimated fortune of $13.9 billion (£8.4 billion).

RICHEST ROYAL IN EUROPE
The richest royal in Europe is Queen Beatrix of Holland, with a net worth of $5.2 billion (£3.1 billion). She ascended the throne when her mother, Queen Juliana, abdicated on 20 April 1980.

BIGGEST BEQUESTS
In 1991 the US publishing tycoon Walter Annenberg announced his intention to leave his $1-billion (£600-million) collection of art works to the Metropolitan Museum of Art in New York City, USA.

In 1997 the US media tycoon Ted Turner pledged a total of $1 billion (£600 million) to United Nations causes, which include anti-landmine and refugee aid programmes.

MOST EXPENSIVE HOUSES
In 1997 Wong Yuk Kwan, the chairman of Pearl Oriental Holdings, purchased two properties in the Skyhigh development, Hong Kong, China, for $70.2 million (£42.8 million) and $48.9 million (£29.8 million) respectively.

MOST EXPENSIVE ISLANDS
The 16,188-ha (40,000-acre) island of Niihau, Hawaii, is the largest privately owned island in the USA. It has been valued at $100 million (£60 million).

The most expensive island currently on the market is D'Arros in the Seychelles. The atoll, which covers an area of 242.8 ha (600 acres) and has a private lagoon, an airstrip and three homes, can be bought for $21 million (£12.8 million).

MOST LUXURIOUS LINER
The 304-m-long (1000-ft) *The World of ResidenSea*, which is being built by a German shipyard, is expected to cost $529.7 million (£323 million) and will be the most luxurious liner ever built. It will have 500 staff, seven restaurants, a cinema, a casino, a nightclub, bars, a Roman spa, a house of worship, a library, museums, a business service centre, a licensed stock and bond broker, shops, a swimming pool, a retractable marina for water sports, a golf academy, a tennis court and a helipad. Due to be launched in the year 2000, it has 250 ocean-going apartments that are on the market for $1.3–5.8 million (£800,000–3.5 million) each. The most expensive are the 199.92-m² (2,152-ft²) three-bedroom, three-bathroom penthouses.

MOST LUXURIOUS PRIVATE JET
The $35-million (£21.3-million) *Gulfstream V* is able to cruise at 15,850 m (52,000 ft), making it the highest-flying passenger aircraft after Concorde. It is also the fastest long-range executive jet, with a maximum speed of nearly 966 km/h (600 mph) and a range of 12,046 km (7,485 miles) — it can fly to any destination in the world with only one stop for refuelling. If fitted with customized extras, the cost of the *Gulfstream V* rises to $40 million (£24.4 million).

BIGGEST PRIVATE ROLLS-ROYCE FLEET
Sultan Hassanal Bolkiah of Brunei, who was the world's richest man until Microsoft boss Bill Gates (*see Tycoons & High Earners*) exceeded him in wealth, is believed to have the biggest private collection of Rolls-Royce cars. The fleet has been estimated to consist of 150 vehicles. Together with his brother Prince Jefri, the Sultan is reported to own a further 1,998 luxury cars.

GREATEST PHILANTHROPISTS
Doris Bryant (above), the sister of the world's richest investor, Warren Buffett, is known as the 'Sunshine Lady'. She appoints 'sunbeams' who assist her to 'spread a kindly light on the world' and her foundation has awarded $3 million (£1.81 million) to good causes in her home state of North Carolina, USA. The greatest philanthropist of all time was steel and manufacturing magnate Andrew Carnegie, who distributed almost all his fortune to public library construction and the setting up of a number of educational and research institutions. His wealth was estimated at $250 million (£53.46 million) in 1901.

BIGGEST DIVORCE SETTLEMENT

The world's largest ever publicly declared divorce settlement amounted to £500 million ($874 million) plus property. It was secured in 1982 by the lawyers of Soraya Khashoggi (on the left of the picture) from her husband Adnan (right), a Saudi entrepreneur and property owner.

YOUNGEST MULTI-BILLIONAIRE

Athina Onassis Roussel, the granddaughter of shipping magnate Aristotle Onassis, inherited an estimated $5-billion (£3.04-billion) empire and the Greek island of Skorpios in 1988, at the age of three. She will have control of the fortune in 2003, when she is 18.

MOST EXPENSIVE WATCH COLLECTION

Prince Jefri, the younger brother of the Sultan of Brunei, is reported to have paid $5.2 million (£3.12 million), for 10 gem-studded watches.

MOST RAISED BY A PRIVATE ART COLLECTION AT AUCTION

A collection belonging to Victor and Sally Ganz, and including works by Pablo Picasso and Jasper Johns, raised a total of $207.4 million (£129.4 million) at Christie's, New York City, USA, in Nov 1997.

LARGEST STABLE

The Godolphin stable, owned by the ruling Maktoum family of Dubai headed by Sheikh Mohammed al Maktoum, consists of 850 horses in training, 70 brood mares, 18 stallions, 12 studs and 25 trainers. Maintenance costs total $408.98 million (£250 million) a year.

BIGGEST ROCK HEIRESS

Lisa Marie Presley, Elvis' daughter, inherited $130 million (£79.3 million). She received an installment of $38 million (£23.2 million) on her 30th birthday in 1997. When Elvis died his estate faced liquidation, but it has since been turned into one of the world's most successful merchandising enterprises.

tycoons & high earners

RICHEST PERSON OF ALL TIME
John D. Rockefeller's wealth was estimated at about $900 million (£184.88 million) in 1913, equivalent to $189.6 billion (£114.39 billion) in today's terms. Having made a fortune in the oil business, Rockefeller retired in 1897; by 1922 he had given away $1 billion (£248.2 million) to his family and to charity, keeping just $20 million (£4.52 million) for himself.

RICHEST BUSINESSMAN
According to *Forbes* magazine, Bill Gates, the founder, chairman and chief executive officer of Microsoft Corporation, is the richest man in the world today. His fortune is estimated at $90 billion (£54.3 billion).

RICHEST BUSINESSWOMAN
Doris Fisher, half of the husband-and-wife team that opened its first Gap outlet in 1969, is worth an estimated $4.3 billion (£2.6 billion). Often described as the self-made 'king and queen of khaki', Donald and Doris Fisher averaged $9 billion (£5.4 billion) in sales in 1999, with more than 2,500 stores around the world, including GapKids, Old Navy and Banana Republic. Their three sons control shares worth $5.6 billion (£3.38 billion).

RICHEST BUSINESS FAMILY
The Walton family, the children and widow of Wal-Mart founder Sam Walton, are the richest business family in the world, according to *Forbes* magazine, with an estimated combined fortune of $79.8 billion (£48.14 billion). Sam Walton opened his first 'small town discount store' in Arkansas, USA, in 1962. Today, Wal-Mart is the largest retailer in the United States, with sales of $118 billion (£71.9 billion) and 2,399 stores, 451 member-only warehouse clubs and 625 international branches. S. Robson Walton, the current chairman, is estimated to be worth $15.8 billion (£9.5 billion).

RICHEST BUSINESSMAN IN ASIA
Alwaleed Bin Talal Bin Abdulaziz Alsaud is the richest businessman in Asia, with an estimated fortune of $15 billion (£9.05 billion). Building on an inheritance (a small fraction of his present wealth), Alwaleed has made a fortune in the business world by shrewd investment in companies such as Citicorp.

RICHEST BUSINESSMEN IN EUROPE
Theo and Karl Albrecht from Germany and their family have a combined fortune of $13.6 billion (£8.2 billion), which was amassed from their 10% share in Europe's most successful discount food retailer, Aldi. The Aldi Group has 4,000 stores in Europe and 509 stores in the USA.

RICHEST BUSINESSMAN IN LATIN AMERICA
Carlos Slim Helu, the head of the Mexican conglomerate Grupo Carso, is the richest businessman in Latin America. His three sons run Carso and its financial arm Inbursa; their combined family fortune runs to $8 billion (£4.8 billion).

RICHEST BUSINESSMAN IN AFRICA
Nicky Oppenheimer, chairman of the South African diamond and mining empire De Beers, has a family fortune estimated at $2.2 billion (£1.3 billion).

RICHEST MEDIA TYCOON
Kenneth Thomson (Canada), head of publishing and information company Thomson Corp., has a fortune of $11.9 billion (£7.2 billion). Thomson publishes about 70 local and national newspapers in North America, including Toronto's *Globe and Mail*, but the company is now focusing more on electronic information.

RICHEST BUSINESS FAMILY IN EUROPE
Paul Sacher (above) was Europe's richest man, worth an estimated $13.1 billion (£7.9 billion) when he died in May 1999. His family has an inherited fortune of $17 billion (£10.25 billion) from Swiss pharmaceuticals giant Roche, but no longer runs the company. The richest pharmaceuticals tycoon is Novartis chief Pierre Landolt (Switzerland), who has a family fortune of $6.4 billion (£3.9 billion).

GREATEST PERSONAL FINANCIAL RECOVERY

In 1989 Donald Trump, pictured outside his home in Palm Beach, Florida, USA, owned two casinos, an airline, buildings in New York City, and an 85-m (280-ft) yacht, as well as other property worth an estimated $1.7 billion (£1 billion). The onset of the recession, and the slumping property market of the late 1980s, pushed his businesses into $8.8 billion (£5.6 billion) of debt. His assets have now, according to *Forbes* magazine, crept up to $1.5 billion (£937.5 million), although Trump himself claims to be worth $5 billion (£3 billion). In 1998 Trump bought the GM Building in New York City and thanks to the strength of the property market now has few vacancies in his eponymously named buildings.

RICHEST MAN IN RUSSIA

Vladimir Potanin, the richest man in Russia according to Forbes, *is the founder and president of Oneximbank. Worth $1.6 billion (£1 billion) in 1998, which he earned through oil, metals and telecommunications as well as banking, 38-year-old Potanin was also the first ever deputy prime minister of the Russian Federation in 1996.*

RICHEST CONFECTIONERY TYCOONS
The three Mars siblings have a combined fortune of $12 billion (£7.24 billion) from the confectionery giant Mars Inc. and from pet food and prepared-food empires.

RICHEST COSMETICS TYCOONS
Leonard A. and Ronald S. Lauder and their family have a combined fortune of $8.8 billion (£5.3 billion). Leonard runs Estée Lauder, the cosmetics company that was founded by his mother.

RICHEST JEANS TYCOON
Robert D. Haas, the great-great-grandnephew of the founder of jeans manufacturer Levi Strauss Co., has a fortune of $8.2 billion (£5 billion), together with his family.

HIGHEST-EARNING CHIEF EXECUTIVE OFFICER
Michael Eisner, chairman and chief executive officer of Disney, earned $589.1 million (£355.4 million) in the financial year 1998/99 – a figure that includes salary, bonus and stock gains. His total earnings over the five-year period 1995–99 were $631.02 million (£380.7 million).

HIGHEST-EARNING INTERNET CEO
Stephen Case, the founder of America Online, is the highest-paid internet CEO. He earned $159.2 million (£96.05 million) in 1998/99, of which $158.06 million (£95.37 million) was stock gains.

HIGHEST-EARNING CEO IN THE COMPUTER INDUSTRY
Craig Barrett, chief executive officer of Intel, makers of the Pentium processor, earned $116.8 million (£70.47 million) in 1999, including $114.2 million (£68.9 million) in stock gains.

HIGHEST-EARNING CEO IN FINANCIAL SERVICES
In 1998/99 Philip J. Purcell, the CEO of investment bank Morgan Stanley, earned $49 million (£29.6 million), making him the highest-paid financial services CEO. Over the four-year period 1995–99 he earned a total of $108.1 million (£65.2 million).

RICHEST INVESTOR
Warren Buffett, the head of Berkshire Hathaway, is the world's richest investor, estimated to be worth $36 billion (£21.7 billion). His fortune is second only to that of Microsoft chairman and founder Bill Gates.

YOUNGEST 'SUPER-RICH' TYCOON
Jerry Yang, the 30-year-old co-founder of internet search engine Yahoo! Inc., is worth an estimated $4 billion (£2.4 billion) according to *Forbes* magazine. Yahoo!'s recent acquisition of GeoCities extended the company's reach into personal web pages, while its acquisition of broadcast.com has broadened its profile in the web-based audio and video arena. Yang owns about 11% of the company.

RICHEST AUTOMOBILE TYCOON

Ferdinand Piech (below), Volkswagen's chairman, is the richest automobile tycoon. His family, which has a fortune of $5 billion (£3 billion), owns 76% of Porsche AG.

homes & hotels

BIGGEST HOTEL

Workers are pictured putting the finishing touches on the 50-tonne lion which stands at the entrance to the MGM Grand Hotel and Casino in Las Vegas, Nevada, USA. The hotel, which has four 30-storey towers and covers an area of 45.3 ha (112 acres), is the biggest in the world. It has 5,005 rooms (including 751 suites), 10 restaurants, three lounges, four tennis courts, a 15,222-seat arena and a 13.3-ha (32.8-acre) outdoor theme park. Its 170,000-ft² (15,793-m²) casino, which has four separate themed areas, contains thousands of slot machines. When not gambling or spending their money in the hotel's numerous speciality shops, guests can relax in the pool area, which is the biggest in Nevada and features a 40-seater spa tub, two waterfalls and a giant fountain.

BIGGEST NON-PALATIAL RESIDENCE
The largest non-palatial residence in the world is St Emmeram Castle in Regensburg, Germany, which has 517 rooms and a total floor area of 21,460 m² (231,000 ft²). It was owned by Prince Johannes von Thurn und Taxis, whose family used only 95 of the rooms. The castle is valued at more than $202 million (£122 million).

BIGGEST RESIDENTIAL PALACE
Owned by the Sultan of Brunei, Istana Nurul Iman in Bandar Seri Begawan, Brunei, was completed in 1984 at a reported cost of $422 million (£300 million). It has 1,788 rooms, 257 toilets and an underground garage.

BIGGEST HOLLYWOOD HOME
The Manor on Mapleton Drive, Hollywood, California, USA, was built for Aaron Spelling. It occupies 3,390 m² (36,500 ft²) on a 6,040-m² (65,000-ft²) plot of land. The estate includes a doll museum, four bars, three kitchens, a gymnasium, a theatre, eight two-car garages, an Olympic-size swimming pool, a bowling alley, a skating rink, six formal gardens, 12 fountains and a room in which to wrap gifts. Spelling is the producer of a number of TV series, including *Beverly Hills 90210.*

BIGGEST MODERN UNDERGROUND HOUSE
Underhill in Holme, W Yorkshire, UK, has an internal area of 325 m² (3,500 ft²). The home of architect Arthur Quarmby since 1976, it cannot be seen from the surrounding moorland.

MOST 'INTELLIGENT' HOUSE
Bill Gates' house, which was estimated by King County assessors to have cost $55 million (£33 million) to build over seven years, uses state-of-the-art information technology to tailor itself to the preferences of guests. Everyone who enters is given an electronic pin that can be detected by sensors in each room, enabling the house to set the services and entertainments to their requirements. The sensors also control lights and appliances, turning them off automatically when someone leaves a room. Gates' hi-tech home is situated on the eastern shore of Lake Washington, Washington, USA.

MOST ENERGY-EFFICIENT HOUSE
The Autonomous House in Southwell, Notts, UK, produces more energy than it uses. Photovoltaic panels provide electricity, and the 1,450 kWh produced by the house annually is sold back to the UK National Grid.

HIGHEST HOTEL

The Grand Hyatt Shanghai in Pudon, China, is the highest hotel in the world. It occupies the top 35 floors of the 88-storey Jin Mao Tower (pictured above), the tallest building in China and the third tallest in the world. The hotel, which opened for business on 18 March 1999, offers spectacular views over the Bund and the adjacent Huang Pu River.

BIGGEST HOTEL LOBBY
The lobby at the Hyatt Regency, San Francisco, California, USA, is 107 m (350 ft) long and 49 m (160 ft) wide. With its 52-m (170-ft) high ceiling, it is as tall as a 17-storey building.

LONGEST HOTEL ON WHEELS
The longest of the Orient Express luxury trains, which travel between Paris, France, and Istanbul, Turkey, is 501 m (1,644 ft) long. All its carriages are originals from the 1920s and 1930s.

HIGHEST-ALTITUDE HOTEL
The Hotel Everest View above Namche, Nepal – the village closest to Everest base camp – is at a record height of 3,962 m (13,000 ft).

NORTHERNMOST HOTEL
The world's most northerly full-service hotel is the Svalbard Polar Hotel Longyearbyen, Svalbard, Norway. Svalbard consists of several islands from Bjornoya in the south to Rossoya in the north, Europe's northernmost point. About 60% of the archipelago is covered by ice.

MOST EXPENSIVE HOTEL ROOM
The 10-room Bridge Suite at the Royal Towers of Atlantis in the Bahamas can be rented for $25,000 (£15,084) per night. The price includes two entertainment centres, a bar lounge, a baby grand piano and a dining room containing a 22-carat-gold chandelier.

LONGEST HOTEL SWIMMING POOL
The Hyatt Regency Cerromar Beach Resort in Puerto Rico has a 541-m-long (1,755-ft) swimming pool that covers 1.8 ha (4½ acres) and consists of five connected pools with water slides, a subterranean jacuzzi, tropical landscaping and 14 waterfalls. It takes 15 minutes to float from one end of the pool to the other.

MOST FOUNTAINS IN A HOTEL
There are more than 1,000 fountains on the 4.8-ha (12-acre) artificial lake at the Bellagio, Las Vegas, Nevada, USA. The fountains shoot water 74 m (244 ft) into the air, accompanied by surround-sound music and a light display featuring 4,000 programmed lights.

BIGGEST MURAL IN A HOTEL
The biggest hotel mural in the world is *The Great Motherland of China* at the Island Shangri-La hotel in Hong Kong, China. The world's largest Chinese landscape painting, it measures 51 m x 14 m (167 ft x 50 ft) and is 16 storeys high. It can be viewed from a glass elevator between the 41st and the 56th floors.

BIGGEST HOTEL ROLLS-ROYCE FLEET
The Peninsula Group has purchased a total of 50 Rolls-Royces since its first order of seven Brewster Green Silver Shadows in 1970. The most recent order was for nine Silver Spurs. The Peninsula Hong Kong in China has a fleet of 14 Rolls-Royces (13 Silver Spurs and a 1934 Phantom II), while the Palace Hotel Beijing, China, the Peninsula Bangkok, Thailand, and the Peninsula Beverly Hills, California, USA, all have two Rolls-Royce limousines.

HIGHEST DENSITY OF HOTEL ROOMS
Las Vegas, Nevada, USA, which is known for its casino-hotels, has a total of 109,365 hotel rooms. Ten of the largest hotels in the world are in Las Vegas.

HIGHEST CONCENTRATION OF THEME HOTELS
There are more than 16 theme hotels on the Strip in Las Vegas, with themes ranging from Treasure Island to Venetian. The Luxor has a sphinx, a black pyramid and an obelisk, while New York New York features a one-third scale New York skyline and Paris has a half-scale Eiffel Tower.

MOST 'INTELLIGENT' TOWN
Construction workers are pictured posing outside a house in Celebration, Florida, USA. Located south of Orlando, Celebration is a futuristic town designed by Disney. Each of the town's 8,000 homes has a high-speed ISDN link with cable TV, multimedia resources, video on demand and an internet connection. Despite its high-tech amenities, Celebration has been designed to look like an old-fashioned American town, with grid-pattern streets, white picket fences and a traditional downtown area. Cycling and walking paths link every part of the community. Celebration has been under construction since 1996 and has a current population of approximately 1,000, which is expected to reach 20,000 by 2015.

cult objects

MOST EXPENSIVE BARBIE DOLLS SOLD AT AUCTION
The highest price paid for a non-mass-produced Barbie doll was $26,500 (£15,988), at the 95th Harley-Davidson Anniversary Benefit for the Muscular Dystrophy Association in Milwaukee, Wisconsin, USA, on 13 June 1998. The doll was dressed in a genuine leather replica of Harley-Davidson approved clothing and was seated on top of a licensed, replica Harley-Davidson bike, which was actually a telephone.

The most valuable mass-produced Barbie Dolls are #1 Brunettes that have never been removed from their boxes and 1967 Japanese side-part Brunettes with rare pink skin, non-twist waist and bendable legs. Both fetch about $9,500 (£5,731) each.

MOST VALUABLE GI JOE
On 19 August 1994, at an auction at Christie's, New York City, USA, to commemorate the 30th anniversary of GI Joe, a unique GI Joe fighter pilot action figure sold for $5,750 (£3,734).

MOST VALUABLE PAIR OF JEANS
In March 1997 Levi Strauss & Co. paid a vintage denim dealer in New York City, USA, $25,000 (£15,616) for a pair of their Levi's 501 jeans believed to have been made between 1886 and 1902.

MOST VALUABLE SPICE GIRLS COSTUME
The Union Jack costume worn by former Spice Girl Geri Halliwell at the 1997 Brit Awards ceremony sold for £41,320 ($66,112) at an auction at Sotheby's, London, UK, on 16 Sept 1998.

MOST VALUABLE PEZ DISPENSERS
A one-piece shiny Gold Elephant, a Mickey Mouse softhead and a headless dispenser embossed with the words 'PEZ-HAAS', were sold for $6,000 (£3,620) each, a total of $18,000 (£10,860) by David Welch, an author and Pez dealer. The dispensers were made in the late 1940s to early 1950s to dispense Pez sweets, invented in 1927 as an alternative to smoking.

MOST VALUABLE RUBIK'S CUBE
To commemorate the 15th anniversary of Rubik's Cube in 1995, Diamond Cutters International produced the Masterpiece Cube, the only limited edition Rubik's Cube. The actual-size, fully functional replica features 22.5 carats of amethyst, 34 carats of rubies and 34 carats of emeralds, all set in 18-carat gold. It has been valued at about $1.5 million (£905,031). Professor Erno Rubik of Hungary, who invented the original cube, is pictured with an example of his brainchild.

MOST EXPENSIVE PINBALL MACHINE
A one-off pinball machine produced in Feb 1992 is reported to have been sold for $120,000 (£68,000) in Los Angeles, California, USA. It was named *Aaron Spelling* after the American TV producer.

MOST VALUABLE ZIPPO LIGHTER
An original 1933 Zippo lighter was sold for $10,000 (£6,033) by Ira Pilossof on 12 July 1998. The lighter was an early 1933 model without any slash marks on the two corners – all later models had these corner marks. This is the first Zippo model ever produced (formerly referred to as a 1932) and is the most sought after and highly prized among Zippo collectors.

MOST VALUABLE BUBBLE CAR
In March 1997 the British entrepreneur Peter de Savary paid £24,150 ($38,640) for a three-wheeled German-built 1962 Messerschmitt KR 200 'Bubble Top' — a record for any Messerschmitt car. The 191cc two-seater had been expected to sell for £8,000 ($12,800). De Savary also paid record prices for a 1962 Trojan 200 and a 1959 Goggomobil T400, the world's smallest limousine. They were put up for auction at Christie's, London, UK, by Canadian bubble-gum magnate Bruce Weiner.

MOST EXPENSIVE MINI
The Mini Limo, a one-of-a-kind commissioned by Rover Group and built by John Cooper Garages, cost £50,000 ($80,000) when it was delivered in Sept 1997. The two-door Mini boasted an £8,000 ($12,836) Alpine Mini-Disc sound system and seats costing £6,000 ($9,627).

MOST VALUABLE SWISS ARMY KNIFE
An 18-carat gold Swiss army knife produced by Swiss jeweller Luzius Elmer has a current retail price of $4,299 (£2,678).

MOST EXPENSIVE MASS-PRODUCED YOYO

Cold Fusion and Cold Fusion GT yoyos, manufactured by Playmaxx Inc, retail between $150–250 (£90–£150) and are the most expensive mass-produced yoyos in the world. There is also a special version called Gold Fusion, which is plated with 24k gold and sells for between $200 and $300 (£120 and £180). In 1998 Playmaxx Inc. generated approximately $96 million (£57.9 million) in retail sales and was given the 'Craze Of The Year' award by the British Toy Association. Yoyo champion Yo-Hans is pictured publicizing his 1998 single *Walk...(The Dog) Like An Egyptian*.

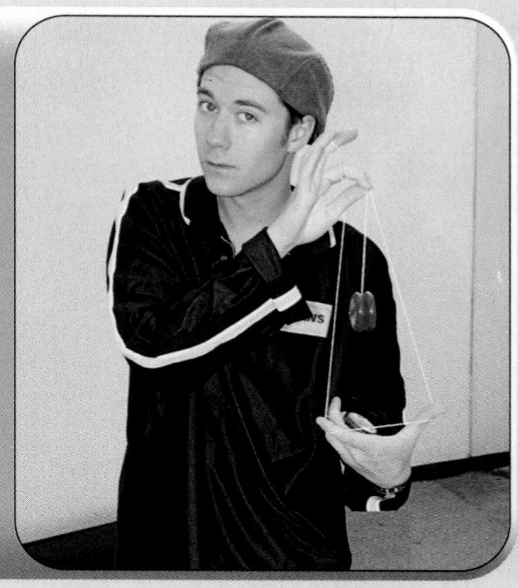

MOST VALUABLE JUKEBOX

The 1933 Wurlitzer Debutante Model (pictured), the world's first jukebox, was sold in Cumming, Georgia, USA, for a record $45,903 (£27,553) on 27 June 1997. The Wurlitzer company was founded in 1856 and also makes electric organs and pianos. The most famous Wurlitzer jukebox is the 1100, designed by Paul Fuller in 1948.

MOST EXPENSIVE MASS-PRODUCED ASTRO LAMP

Lunar by Mathmos, the company which manufactured the original Astro lamp since 1963, retails at £295 ($488). The lamp, which comes in two different colour combinations, is 80 cm (2 ft 7½ in) tall with a polished aluminium base and cap.

MOST VALUABLE SWATCH WATCH
A limited edition Swatch — one of only 120 made — designed in 1985 by French artist Christian Chapiron (known as Kiki Picasso) sold at auction at Sotheby's, Milan, Italy, in 1989 for £34,100 ($45,000). When they were first released the watches were given away free.

LEAST PROFITABLE PHOTOGRAPH
On 5 March 1960 Alberto Diaz Gutiérrez (known as Alberto Korda) took a photograph of the Argentinian revolutionary Ernesto 'Che' Guevara at a memorial ceremony in Havana, Cuba. In 1967, the year Guevara was killed while attempting to foment a revolution in Bolivia, Korda gave the picture to the Italian publisher Feltrinelli, but did not charge him because he considered him 'a friend of the Revolution'. Feltrinelli exploited Guevara's iconic status in the 1960s counter-culture and sold 2 million posters in the next six months. Korda never received a penny in royalties or copyright.

MOST VALUABLE WARHOL PICTURE
Andy Warhol's screen print *Orange Marilyn* sold for $17.3 million (£10.6 million) at Sotheby's, New York, USA, in May 1998. Warhol was one of the leading figures in the Pop Art movement which began in the 1950s and also included Roy Lichtenstein, Claes Oldenburg and Peter Blake. Popular images such as Coca-Cola bottles, Campbell's soup cans and Marilyn Monroe's face were elevated to cult status by Warhol's use of repetition and garish colouring. Warhol, who also made films such as *Flesh* (USA, 1968) and *Andy Warhol's Dracula* (USA, 1974), died in 1987.

valuable stuff 1

MOST VALUABLE BARBIE DOLL

The Mattel toy company celebrated the 40th anniversary of the introduction of its Barbie doll in March 1999 by creating a one-off customized Barbie worth £50,000 ($82,870). Produced in association with the diamond company De Beers, the doll was unveiled at David Morris Jewellers in London, UK, and contains 160 diamonds weighing nearly 20 carats set in 18-carat white gold. The train is secured by a bow created out of diamonds centring around the letter 'B'. The bow itself can be removed and worn as a brooch. A headdress, drop earrings and dress ring, all made of diamonds set in 18-carat white gold, complete the aquamarine silk outfit.

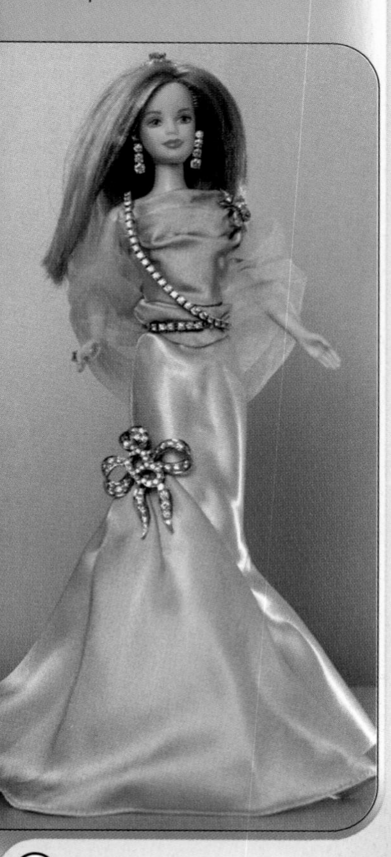

MOST VALUABLE LUGGAGE
A complete set of Louis Vuitton luggage, which includes an armoire trunk, a wardrobe trunk, a steamer trunk, four matching suitcases, a hat box, a cruiser bag and a jewellery case, costs a total of $601,340 (£362,253), making it the most expensive luggage set in the world.

MOST VALUABLE VANITY CASE
A Cartier jewelled vanity case set with a fragment of ancient Egyptian steel was sold at Christie's, New York, USA, for the record sum of $189,000 (£127,651) in Nov 1993.

MOST VALUABLE SHOES
In 1977 Emperor Field Marshall Jean Bédel Bokassa of the Central African Empire (now the Central African Republic) commissioned a pair of pearl-studded shoes from the House of Berluti in Paris, France, for his self-coronation. Costing $85,000 (£48,571), they are the most expensive pair of shoes ever made.

The most expensive shoes on the market cost £18,000 ($28,800) and are made by the design company Gina of London, UK. The UK size 4½ sandals (US size 5) are made out of alligator skin, lined with kid leather and have buckles studded with diamonds. They were designed by Aydin Kurdash.

MOST VALUABLE CUFFLINKS
Gianni Vivé Sulman of Marylebone, London, UK, has produced 73 pairs of cufflinks costing a record £23,983 ($39,750) each. They are made from 18-carat gold set with diamonds.

MOST VALUABLE CIGARS
On 16 Nov 1997 an Asian buyer paid a record £9,890 ($16,560) each for 25 Trinidad cigars made by the Cuban National Factory. The sale took place at Christie's, London, UK.

MOST VALUABLE SLICE OF CAKE
In Feb 1998 a piece of cake left over from the wedding of the Duke of Windsor and Wallis Simpson more than 60 years earlier sold at Sotheby's, New York, USA, for the record sum of $29,900 (£18,231) to Californian entrepreneur Benjamin Yim and his wife Amanda. The cake, which formed part of the Windsor collection auction, had been expected to fetch a maximum of $1,000 (£602) at the sale.

MOST VALUABLE ICE HOCKEY PUCK
The Million Dollar Puck, created by Diamond Cutters International of Houston, Texas, USA, is made of platinum, diamonds and emeralds. The puck, which is actual-size, is covered in 733 stones, including 171 carats in diamonds and four carats in emeralds. It was created for the Houston Aeros Hockey Team in 1996 and is valued at more than $1 million (£602,000).

MOST VALUABLE JIGSAW PUZZLE
Custom-made Stave 'Dollhouse Village' puzzles, which have 2,640 pieces, were created by Steve Richardson of Norwich, Vermont, USA, and cost $14,500 (£8,801) each in June 1999, making them the world's most expensive jigsaw puzzles.

MOST VALUABLE BOARD GAME
The most expensive commercially available board game is the deluxe version of Outrage!, which is produced by Imperial Games of Southport, Merseyside, UK. The game, in which participants have to steal the Crown Jewels from the Tower of London, retails at £3,995 ($6,621).

MOST VALUABLE MONOPOLY SET
An exclusive $2-million (£1.12-million) Monopoly set was created by the jeweller Sidney Mobell of San Francisco, USA, in 1988. The board is made from 23-carat gold and the dice have 42 full cut diamonds for spots.

MOST VALUABLE DINKY TOY
On 14 Oct 1994 a collector paid £12,650 ($20,312) for a 1937 Dinky Bentalls store delivery van at Christie's, London, UK.

MOST VALUABLE WORLD CUP REPLICA
A World Cup 'decoy' trophy sold for the sum of £254,500 ($407,200) — 12 times the estimated price — at Sotheby's, London, UK, in July 1997. The gold painted trophy, a replica of the one that was won by England in 1966, was ordered by the Football Association after the real cup was stolen in 1966. The original was later discovered by a dog named Pickles, but for two years the replica was passed off as the genuine Jules Rimet trophy and was protected by security guards to keep up the pretence for the public.

MOST VALUABLE GEM MODEL CAR
The Gem Prowler, which has been valued at $210,000 (£128,189), was cut from the world's largest amethyst — a rough amethyst from Bolivia that started out at 15,000 carats and finished at 9,600 carats. Its other components include 450 g (1 lb) of white gold and 18 carats of white and canary diamonds. The windshield is carved out of rock crystal. It was created by US firm Diamond Cutters International for Chrysler Plymouth to inaugurate the launch of the latter's new Roadster in 1997.

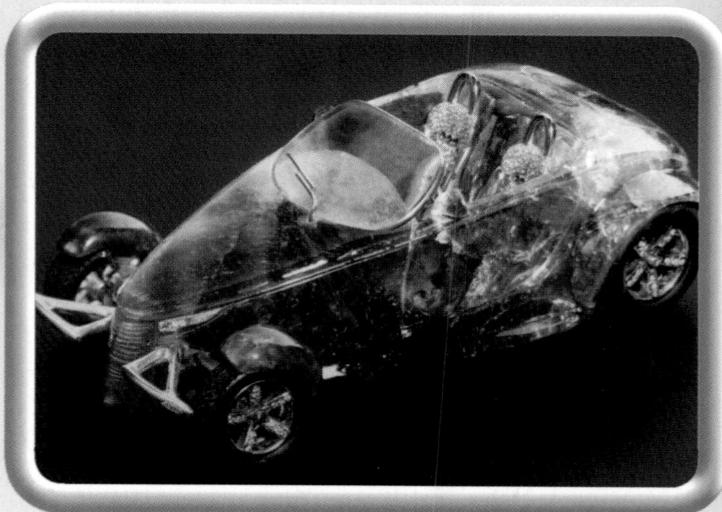

MOST VALUABLE DECKED CHRISTMAS TREE

On 5 Dec 1996 the world's most expensive ever decked Christmas tree was erected in the Place du Rhône, Geneva, Switzerland. It was decorated with baubles donated by Piaget International SA; their total value was $8,885,588 (£5,465,565), excluding tax. Each contained a total of 31 watches and 11 pieces of jewellery.

MOST VALUABLE FRAGMENTS OF OTHER PLANETS

A piece of Martian meteorite fetched $7,333 (£4,583) — more than 1,000 times its weight in gold — at Phillips, New York, USA, in May 1998. The rock, which measures 2 x 2 x 4 mm (7/100 x 7/100 x 3/20 in) and weighs 0.28 g (9/1,000 oz), was found in Brazil in 1958 and was expected to sell for $1,600–3,200 (£1,000–2,000).

Sotheby's, New York, USA, sold 0.33 g (1/100 oz or less than two carats) of rock from the Moon for $442,500 (£283,300) in 1993. A total of 363 kg (800 lb) of lunar rock exists on Earth, compared to 41 kg (90 lb) of Martian rock.

MOST VALUABLE WEDDING DRESS

Sabrina Battaglia (Italy) poses in a wedding dress costing $6 million (£3.75 million), made for her marriage on 7 Dec 1998. The most expensive wedding outfit ever was created by Hélène Gainville, with jewels by Alexander Reza, and was valued at $7.3 million (£4.3 million). The dress was unveiled in Paris, France, on 23 March 1989.

valuable stuff 2

MOST VALUABLE SACRED OBJECT
The 15th-century gold Buddha in Wat Trimitr Temple in Bangkok, Thailand, has the highest intrinsic value of any sacred object — £24 million ($38.3 million) at the June 1999 price of £163/troy oz ($259). It is 3 m (10 ft) tall and weighs an estimated 5½ tonnes. The gold under the plaster exterior was only discovered in 1954.

MOST VALUABLE MISSING ART TREASURE
The Amber Room, presented to Catherine the Great of Russia by Frederick William I of Prussia in 1716, was installed in the Catherine Palace near St Petersburg, Russia. It consisted of intricately carved amber panels and decorated chairs, tables and amber ornaments. In 1941 invading Germans dismantled the room and took it back to Germany, where it was reassembled in the castle at Königsberg, East Prussia (now Kaliningrad, Russia). The Amber Room was crated up and put into storage in 1945 and subsequently disappeared. A single panel resurfaced in Germany in 1997.

MOST VALUABLE DIARY
A dog-eared diary reportedly telling the story of Davy Crockett's last moments at the Alamo but often dismissed as a forgery was sold at auction for $350,000 (£211,000) in Los Angeles, USA, in Nov 1998. The diary, said to have been written by a Mexican officer called José Enrique de la Pena, seems to refute the legend that Crockett met a heroic end in battle, instead stating that he was taken prisoner and executed by the Mexican forces who took the fortress from its Texan defenders in 1836. Sold to an unnamed bidder, the diary consists of two handwritten sheaves bound with ragged ribbons.

MOST VALUABLE ILLUSTRATED MANUSCRIPT
The *Codex Leicester*, an illustrated manuscript in which Leonardo da Vinci predicted the invention of the submarine and the steam engine, sold for $30.8 million (£19,388,141) at Christie's, New York, USA, on 11 Nov 1994. Bought by Microsoft chief Bill Gates, the world's wealthiest man, it is the only Leonardo manuscript in private hands.

MOST VALUABLE LETTERS
The highest price paid for a signed letter is $748,000 (£409,683), for a letter written by Abraham Lincoln on 8 Jan 1863. It was sold to Profiles in History of Beverly Hills, California, USA, at Christie's, New York, on 5 Dec 1991.

The highest price paid for a letter signed by a living person is $12,500 (£6,173), for a letter from President Ronald Reagan praising Frank Sinatra. It was sold at the Hamilton Galleries, USA, on 22 Jan 1981.

MOST VALUABLE MUSIC MANUSCRIPTS
The highest amount paid for a musical manuscript is £2.585 million ($4.136 million), by London dealer James Kirkman at Sotheby's, London, UK, on 22 May 1987, for a 508-page bound volume of nine complete symphonies in the hand of their composer, Wolfgang Amadeus Mozart.

The highest price paid for a single musical manuscript is £1.1 million ($2,008,380), for the autographed copy of the Piano Sonata in E minor, Opus 90 by Ludwig van Beethoven, at Sotheby's, London, UK, on 6 Dec 1991.

MOST VALUABLE BOOK
On 8 July 1998 an original copy of Geoffrey Chaucer's Canterbury Tales *sold at Christie's, London, UK, for a record £4,621,500 ($7,394,400) — more than nine times the expected price. The book was the first major work printed in England by William Caxton, in 1477.*

MOST VALUABLE FLAG
A white Ensign found by the British explorer Captain Robert Falcon Scott on a beach in Antarctica in 1902 sold for £28,750 ($45,868) at Christie's, London, UK, in Oct 1997. It had been expected to fetch £5,000 ($8,151).

MOST VALUABLE BANKNOTES
The highest price achieved at auction for a single lot of banknotes is a record £240,350 ($424,578), paid by Richard Lobel on behalf of a consortium at Phillips, London, UK, on 14 Feb 1991. The lot consisted of a cache of more than 17 million British military notes which were found in a vault in Berlin, Germany.

MOST VALUABLE COIN
An 1804 silver dollar — one of only 15 left, and valued at $500,000 (£306,711) — fetched $1.815 million (£1.1 million) at auction in New York, USA, on 8 April 1997. The coin had been owned by banker Louis Eliasberg, the only person known to have ever owned a complete collection of US coins.

MOST VALUABLE STAMP
A Swedish treskilling was sold for £1.4 million ($2.3 million) in Nov 1996.

MOST VALUABLE SET OF STAMPS
A set of 48 twopenny blue stamps in mint condition were discovered in a rolled-up leather writing case in Dalkeith Palace, Midlothian, UK, by Alexander Martin when he was compiling an inventory of the palace's contents. The set has been valued at £2.75 million ($4.56 million), based on a single mint-condition stamp selling for £5,000 ($8,287). The stamps, which have been owned by three different collectors since their discovery in 1945, are now to be sold on the open market.

MOST VALUABLE CARPET
The Spring carpet of Khusraw, which was made for the audience hall of the

MOST VALUABLE *SS TITANIC* ITEMS

Pictured here is a cast iron name plate and a White Star Line flag retrieved from a lifeboat after the sinking of the *SS Titanic* in April 1912. They were auctioned for $79,500 (£49,687) at Christie's, New York, USA, on 9 June 1998. The demand for items connected to the ill-fated liner has increased massively since the release of the film *Titanic* (USA, 1997).

MOST VALUABLE VIOLIN

The Kreutzer, a violin created by Antonio Stradivari in 1727, was sold for £947,500 ($1,516,000) at Christie's, London, UK, on 1 April 1998.

MOST VALUABLE EGG

Fabergé, the Russian jewellers, created about 56 Imperial Eggs between 1885 and 1917. The most valuable is embellished with more than 3,000 diamonds. In Nov 1994 it sold at Christie's, Geneva, Switzerland, for $5,587,308 (£3,560,539).

Sassanian palace at Ctesiphon, Iraq, was the most valuable carpet ever made. It consisted of about 650 m² (7,000 ft²) of silk and gold thread encrusted with emeralds. The carpet was cut up as booty by looters in 635 AD — had it remained intact it would now be worth approximately £1 million ($1.66 million).

MOST VALUABLE FOUNTAIN PEN
The biggest sum ever paid for a fountain pen was $218,007 (£122,677), for the 'Anémone' fountain pen, made by French company Réden, in Feb 1988. Bought by a Japanese collector, the pen was encrusted with a total of 600 precious stones, including emeralds, amethysts, rubies, sapphires and onyx, and took a team of skilled craftsmen more than a year to complete.

MOST VALUABLE SURGICAL INSTRUMENT
The highest price ever paid for a surgical instrument is $34,848 (£23,368), for a 19th-century German medical chainsaw sold at Christie's, London, UK, on 19 Aug 1993.

MOST VALUABLE PIANO
The highest price ever paid for a piano is £716,500 ($1.2 million), for a Steinway created under the direction of Sir Lawrence Alma-Tadema, which sold at Christie's, London, UK, on 7 Nov 1997. It was acquired by the Sterling and Francine Clark Art Institute, Williamstown, Massachusetts, USA.

MOST VALUABLE MAGIC LANTERN
The highest price ever paid for a magic lantern slide projector is £33,000 ($51,536), for a *c.* 1880 Newton & Co. Triunial lantern sold at Christie's, London, UK, on 17 Jan 1996.

MOST VALUABLE CAMERA
The highest price paid for a camera is £39,600 ($59,459), at Christie's, London, UK, on 25 Nov 1993. The camera had been customized for Sultan Abdel Aziz of Morocco in 1901, when each of its metal components was replaced with gold parts by the manufacturer, at a cost of $9,820 (£2,100) to the sultan.

shopping

BIGGEST CREDIT CARD TRANSACTION

In 1995 Eli Broad of Los Angeles, California, USA, purchased Roy Lichtenstein's painting *I...I'm Sorry* (1965–66) for the sum of $2.5 million (£1.6 million), paying with his American Express card. The highest credit card transaction to date, it earned Broad a total of 2.5 million air miles.

MOST CREDIT CARDS

Walter Cavanagh from Santa Clara, California, USA, has a total of 1,397 different credit cards, which together are worth more than $1.65 million (£1 million) in credit. He keeps his collection in the world's longest wallet, which is 76.2 m (250 ft) in length and weighs 17.49 kg (38 lb 8 oz).

BIGGEST SHOPPING CENTRE

The West Edmonton Mall in Alberta, Canada, was opened in 1981 and completed four years later. The mall is the size of 110 soccer pitches, covers an area of 483,000 m² (5.2 million ft²) on a 49-ha (121-acre) site and houses more than 800 stores and services, as well as 11 major department stores. It serves approximately 20 million customers annually and provides parking for 20,000 vehicles. A water park, golf course, ice rink and chapel can all be found inside.

BIGGEST SHOPPING CENTRE IN EUROPE

Bluewater in Kent, UK, opened in March 1999 and covers an area of 155,669 m² (1.675 million ft²), of which 139,400 m² (1.5 million ft²) is retail space. It currently contains 201 shops, three department stores, three malls and three leisure villages. It has parking for more than 13,000 cars and is surrounded by a landscaped park and a lake.

BIGGEST OPEN-AIR SHOPPING CENTRE

Ala Moana Center in Honolulu, Hawaii, USA, has more than 200 shops over a 20-ha (50-acre) site, making it the world's largest open-air shopping centre. It is visited by more than 56 million shoppers every year.

BIGGEST DEPARTMENT STORE

At 198,500 m² (2.15 million ft²), the world's largest department store by area is Macy's, an 11-storey building occupying an entire block in Herald Square, New York City, USA. The company has a chain of department stores across the USA and was one of the first major retailers to place such stores in shopping centres.

LONGEST MALL

The longest shopping mall in the world is located inside the £40-million ($64-million) shopping centre in Milton Keynes, Bucks, UK. The mall is 720 m (2,360 ft) in length.

BIGGEST UNDERGROUND SHOPPING COMPLEX

The PATH Walkway in Toronto, Canada, has 27 km (16 miles 1,368 yd) of shopping arcades with 371,600 m² (4 million ft²) of retail space.

MOST EXPENSIVE SHOPPING STREET

Shoppers wait outside the jewellery store Tiffany & Co. on Fifth Avenue in New York City, USA. Fifth Avenue is the most expensive street in the world in which to rent shop space, at $580/ft² (£3,767/m²). Other retailers with outlets there include the department store Saks Fifth Avenue and the toyshop FAO Schwarz. It is followed in cost by 57th Street, also in New York City ($500/ft² or £3,251/m²) and Oxford Street, London, UK (£2,594/m² or $400/ft²).

BIGGEST OPEN-AIR MARKET

The San José flea market sits on 48.6 ha (120 acres) of land in the heart of Silicon Valley, California, USA. The market was officially opened in 1960 on an abandoned cattle feed lot and had 20 stallholders and about 100 customers. Today it averages more than 6,000 stallholders and 80,000 visitors each week and has a management staff of 150.

BIGGEST DUTY FREE CENTRE

Heathrow Airport, London, UK, currently has the biggest turnover of any duty free centre in the world, with £247.5 million ($396 million) in 1997. Honolulu Airport, Hawaii, USA, is second, with a turnover of $360 million (£230.5 million), followed by Schiphol Airport, Amsterdam, Netherlands, with $335.3 million (£214.7 million).

MOST MALLS IN ONE COUNTRY

Shoppers are seen streaming through the Forum Shops in Caesar's Palace, a gigantic hotel and casino complex in Las Vegas, Nevada, USA. The Forum Shops, which are set in a replica of an ancient Roman street, attract approximately 20 million visitors per year and feature everything from upmarket fashion boutiques such as Gucci, Versace and Bernini to smaller speciality shops and a number of restaurants. The USA has more shopping malls (defined as enclosed, climate-controlled environments typically anchored by at least one major department store with an area of more than 37,160 m² or 400,000 ft²) than any other country, with a total of 1,897 to date. If they are added to the number of grocery-, drug- or discount-anchored centres (which are generally of open-air design), the total number of shopping centres is 42,048.

MOST SHOPS OWNED BY ONE COMPANY
On 28 Jan 1996 the Woolworth Corporation of New York, USA, had 8,178 retail stores worldwide — the most that any company has ever had. The company's founder, Frank Winfield Woolworth, opened his first shop, The Great Five Cent Store, in Utica, New York, USA, in 1879. Woolworth no longer trades in the USA.

BIGGEST ELECTRONICS RETAILER
Best Buy Co Inc. is the biggest retailer of consumer electronics, home office products, audio-video equipment, entertainment software and domestic appliances, with 1998 sales topping $8.3 billion (£5.01 billion). It is ranked 199th in the *Fortune* 500 list.

MOST ELECTRONICS RETAIL OUTLETS
Radio Shack has more than 6,900 stores and franchises selling electronics and computers across the United States.

BIGGEST TOYSHOP CHAIN
Toys 'R' Us, based in Paramus, New Jersey, USA, has a total of 1,000 stores and 4 million m^2 (43 million ft^2) of retail space worldwide. The largest single Toys 'R' Us store is the branch in Birmingham, W Midlands, UK, at 6,040 m^2 (65,000 ft^2).

GREATEST SALES PER UNIT AREA
The record for the greatest sales figures in relation to area of selling space is held by Richer Sounds plc, a British hi-fi retail chain. Sales at its branch in London Bridge Walk, UK, reached a peak of £195,426/m^2 ($27,830/$ft^2$) for the year ending 31 Dec 1994.

MOST SHOPPERS AT ONE DEPARTMENT STORE
The most visitors to a single department store on one day is an estimated 1.07 million, to the Nextage Shanghai, China, on 20 Dec 1995.

BIGGEST JUMBLE SALES
The record for the greatest amount of money raised at a one-day jumble sale is $214,085.99 (£142,723.93), at the 62nd one-day jumble sale organized by the Winnetka Congregational Church, Illinois, USA, in May 1994.

The White Elephant Sale at the Cleveland Convention Center, Ohio, USA, raised $427,935.21 (£285,785.50) over two days from 18 to 19 Oct 1983.

BIGGEST WHOLESALE MART
The world's biggest wholesale merchandise mart is the Dallas Market Center, Texas, USA, which has a total floor area of approximately 641,000 m^2 (6.9 million ft^2). It houses a total of 2,580 permanent showrooms displaying the merchandise of more than 50,000 manufacturers.

BIGGEST FASHION RETAIL CHAIN

Gap Inc. has over 2,500 shops selling its casual clothing in Canada, France, Germany, Japan, the UK and the USA. The company, which was founded in San Francisco, California, USA, in 1969, had sales of $6,507.8 million (£3,926.5 million) in 1998. It is currently rated No. 174 in the Fortune *500 list. Its profile has risen in recent years thanks to its innovative advertising, featuring stars such as Kylie Minogue and Iggy Pop.*

gambling

BIGGEST CASINO
Foxwoods Resort in Connecticut, USA, houses the biggest casino in the world, with a gaming area of 17,900 m² (192,670 ft²). Its facilities include a total of 3,854 slot machines, 234 gaming tables and seats for 3,500 bingo players.

BIGGEST LOTTERY
In the 1997/98 financial year the UK National Lottery, currently operated by Camelot plc, was ranked as the single largest lottery in sales terms by an independent survey in *La Fleur's Lottery World* magazine. Its total ticket sales for the year came to £5,513.7 million ($9,256.5 million).

MOST MILLIONAIRES CREATED BY A SINGLE LOTTERY DRAW
Millions 2000, which culminates on 1 Jan 2000, aims to award a top prize of $48 million (£28.96 million) and make 2,000 other people millionaires. Tickets costing $9.60 (£5.79) give entry to monthly draws. The lottery pays out a monthly jackpot of $96,000 (£57,900) in cash, as well as awarding prizes such as cars and holidays. Four billion tickets will have to be sold to meet the anticipated jackpots. It has been set up by the International Lottery In Liechtenstein Foundation in order to raise more than $1.5 billion (£905 million) for various humanitarian causes around the world.

BIGGEST POKER PRIZE
Huck Seed (below right) of Las Vegas, Nevada, USA, won a pot of $2.3 million (£1.4 million) from Dr Bruce Van Horn (below left) of Ada, Oklahoma, USA, en route to winning the 27th annual World Series poker championship on 16 May 1996. Seed's first-place finish in the $10,000 (£6,400) Buy-in No-limit Texas Holdem competition also earned him a prize of $1 million (£640,328). Van Horn won a $585,000 (£374,500) runner-up prize. An engineering student, Seed took a leave of absence from university in 1989, began making money as a professional poker player, and never returned to his studies.

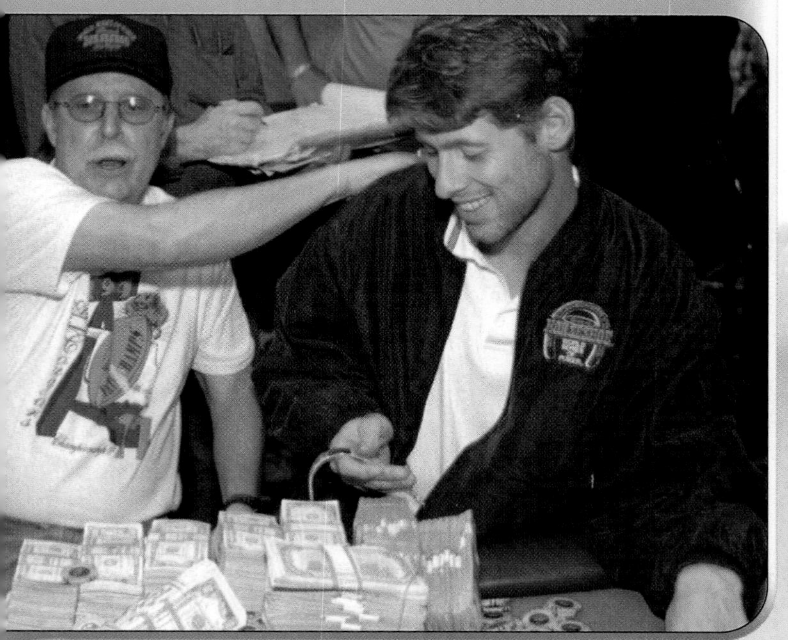

MOST EFFICIENT LOTTERY
The UK National Lottery returns more money to good causes and the government, both in terms of money and as a percentage of sales revenue, than any other lottery, according to an independent survey in *La Fleur's Lottery World* magazine. Camelot, the lottery organizer, returned £2,448 million ($4,105.1 million) — 44.3% of its total sales — in 1997/98.

HIGHEST SPENDING PER CAPITA IN A LOTTERY
The Massachusetts Lottery in the USA is the top lottery in the world in terms of ticket sales per person — $525 (£328.13) per capita was spent on tickets (over three times more than the level in the UK National Lottery) in 1998.

FASTEST-SELLING LOTTERY TICKETS
Powerball lottery tickets in Wisconsin, USA, were selling at a rate of 380,000 an hour when the jackpot reached a lump-sum payment of $137 million (£82.66 million), or the sum of $10 million (£6.03 million) every year for the next 25 years.

BIGGEST SLOT MACHINE JACKPOT
The biggest ever slot machine jackpot was $27,582,539 (£16,642,053), won by an anonymous Las Vegas woman on a Megabucks machine at the Palace Station Hotel and Casino, Las Vegas, Nevada, USA, on 15 Nov 1998. The winner, a former flight attendant in her mid-60s, had won over $680,000 (£410,281) on another slot machine (the Wheel Of Fortune MegaJackpot) less than a month before.

BIGGEST VIDEO POKER JACKPOT
In April 1998 a grandmother from San Antonio, Texas, USA, hit a jackpot of $839,306.92 (£508,670) — the world's biggest ever video poker jackpot — on the Five Duck Frenzy™ machine at the Las Vegas Club, Las Vegas, Nevada, USA.

BIGGEST HOUSE IN BINGO
The record for the largest ever house in a bingo session was 15,756 people, at the Canadian National Exhibition, Toronto, on 19 Aug 1983. The competition, which was staged by the Variety Club of Ontario, Canada, offered total prize money of $202,872 (£132,710) and a record one-game payout of $81,084 (£53,149).

EARLIEST FULL HOUSE
'Full House' calls were made on the 15th number by Norman A. Wilson at Guide Post Working Men's Club, Bedlington, Northumberland, UK, on 22 June 1978; Anne Wintle of Bryncethin, Mid Glamorgan, UK, in Bath, Avon, on 17 Aug 1982; and Shirley Lord at Kahibah Bowling Club, NSW, Australia, on 24 Oct 1983.

LATEST FULL HOUSE
'House' was not called until the 86th number at the Hillsborough Working Men's Club, Sheffield, S Yorks, UK, on 11 Jan 1982. There were 32 winners.

MOST BINGO NUMBERS CALLED IN ONE HOUR
The greatest number of numbers called in one hour by an individual is 2,668, by Paul Scott at The Riva Bingo Club, Brighton, E Sussex, UK, on 16 Feb 1997.

BIGGEST BOOKMAKER
Ladbrokes had a peak turnover of £2,855.5 million ($4,570 million) from gambling in 1998 and is the world's largest chain of betting shops, with more than 2,000 outlets in the United Kingdom and the Republic of Ireland at the end of that year, and other branches throughout the world.

BIGGEST HORSE RACING PAYOUT
The largest payout for a bet on a horse race was $1,627,084 (£988,211) after tax, paid to Britons Anthony Speelman and Nicholas Cowan on their $64 (£39.25) nine-horse accumulator at Santa Anita racecourse, California, USA, in 1987.

LARGEST RACECOURSE JACKPOT IN RELATION TO STAKE
On 15 June 1997 the race day Triple Trio (predicting the first, second and third horses in the second, third and fifth races on the card) jackpot at Happy Valley Racecourse, run under the auspices of the Hong Kong Jockey Club, stood at $25.9 million (£15.8 million) for a stake of $1.39 (£0.85).

BIGGEST NON-PROFIT RACING CLUB
All money made by the Hong Kong Jockey Club, after payment of prizes, operating costs, betting tax and investments to improve racing and betting facilities, is donated to community projects, both social and educational. In 1998 the club donated more than $131.9 million

(£79.6 million), making it the biggest non-profit racing club in the world.

HIGHEST ANNUAL BETTING TURNOVER FOR A RACING CLUB
The total betting turnover of the Hong Kong Jockey Club for the 1997/98 season was $12.1 billion (£7.3 billion). Approximately one third of Hong Kong's adult population bets on horse racing during the season. Bets can be placed on the racecourse, or at 120 sanctioned betting stations throughout Hong Kong.

MOST ACCURATE TIPSTERS
The only recorded instance of a horse racing correspondent forecasting 10 out of 10 winners on a single race card was at Delaware Park, Wilmington, Delaware, USA, on 28 July 1974, by Charles Lamb of the *Baltimore News American*.

In greyhound racing the best performance is 12 out of 12, by Mark Sullivan of *The Sporting Life* newspaper for a meeting at Wimbledon, London, UK, on 21 Dec 1990.

HIGHEST EVER ODDS SECURED FOR AN ACCUMULATOR
The highest odds for an accumulator bet were 3,072,887 to 1, by an unnamed woman from Nottingham, UK, on 2 May 1995. She placed a £0.05 ($0.08) accumulator at Ladbrokes on five horses that won at odds of 66-1, 20-1, 20-1, 12-1 and 7-1, and won £153,644.40 ($242,496.95) for the accumulator and £208,098.79 ($328,442.32) in total.

Edward Hodson of Wolverhampton, W Midlands, UK, won a 3,956,748 to 1 bet with a £0.55 ($0.73) stake on 11 Feb 1984, but his bookmaker had a £3,000 ($4,008) payout limit.

BIGGEST TOTE WIN
The biggest recorded Totalizator win was one of £341 2s 6d ($1,659) from a stake of 2s ($0.49), representing odds of 3,410 to 1, by Catharine Unsworth of Liverpool, UK, at Haydock Park on a race won by Coole on 30 Nov 1929.

BIGGEST WIN ON FOOTBALL POOLS
The world record individual payout is £2,924,622.60 ($4,483,153.90), paid by Littlewoods Pools to a syndicate at the Yew Tree Inn, Worsley, Greater Manchester, UK, for matches played on 19 Nov 1994.

BIGGEST INDIVIDUAL LOTTERY WIN
Maria Grasso, a childminder from Boston, Massachusetts, USA, won the $197-million (£122-million) Big Game Jackpot in the Massachusetts Lottery in April 1999 — the largest ever win by an individual.

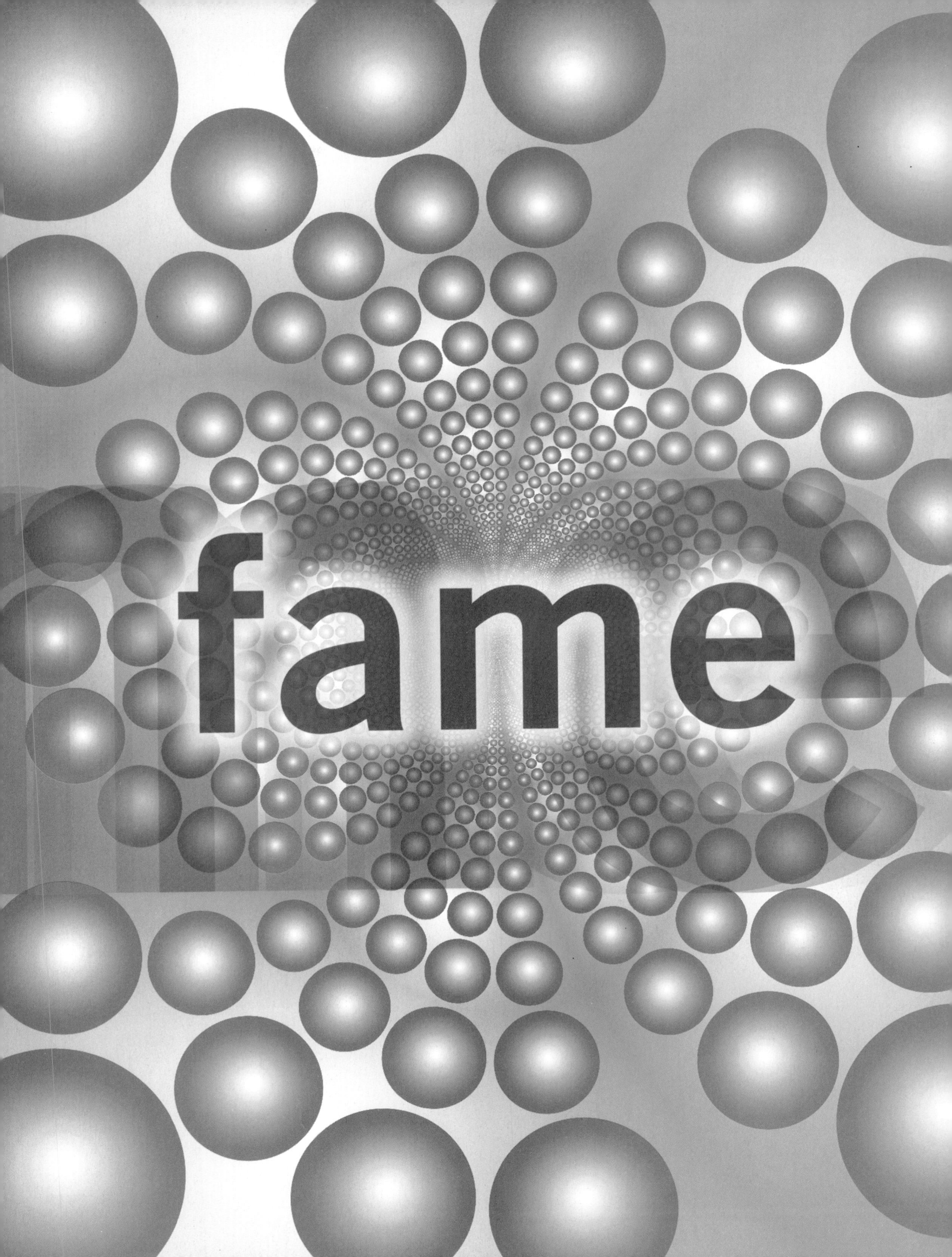
fame

movie stars

MOST LEADING ROLES
John Wayne acted in 153 films in the course of his career, starting with *The Drop Kick* (USA, 1927) and ending with *The Shootist* (USA, 1976). He played the lead in all but 11 of them.

LONGEST SCREEN CAREER
Curt Bois made his debut in *Der Fidele Bauer* (Germany, 1908) at the age of eight. His final film appearance was 80 years later in Wim Wenders' *Wings of Desire* (Germany, 1988).

LONGEST SCREEN PARTNERSHIPS
The Indian stars of Malayalam cinema Prem Nazir and Sheela played opposite each other in a total of 130 movies until she retired in 1975.

The longest Hollywood partnership (excluding performers billed together solely in 'series' films) was 15 films, by Charles Bronson and Jill Ireland from 1968 to 1986.

LONGEST COMEDY PARTNERSHIPS
Americans Stan Laurel and Oliver Hardy acted together in more than 50 comedy films between 1927 and 1940. They first appeared together in *Lucky Dog* (US, 1917) but did not act together again until 1926. *The Music Box* (USA, 1932) received an Oscar for best short film.

Myrna Loy and William Powell acted together in 13 films between 1934 and 1947, including the MGM *Thin Man* series, in which they starred as Nick and Nora Charles, a husband-and-wife detective team.

MOST FILMS BY A DANCING PARTNERSHIP
Fred Astaire and Ginger Rogers appeared as a dancing partnership in nine films, starting with *Flying Down to Rio* (USA, 1933) in which they had a brief dance number called the Carioca. Their subsequent films included *The Gay Divorcee* (USA, 1934) and *Shall We Dance?* (USA, 1937).

YOUNGEST NO. 1 BOX-OFFICE STAR
Shirley Temple was seven years old when she became the No. 1 star at the US box office in 1935.

HIGHEST-PAID CHILD PERFORMER
Macaulay Culkin was paid $1 million (£565,000) for *My Girl* (USA, 1991) when he was 11 years old. He subsequently earned $5 million (£2.8 million) plus 5% gross for *Home Alone II: Lost in New York* (USA, 1992) and a reputed $8 million (£5.2 million) for *Richie Rich* (USA, 1994).

MOST DEVOTED METHOD ACTORS
Daniel Day Lewis is reputed to have spent many nights without sleep in a mock jail cell in order to prepare for his role in *In the Name of the Father* (Ireland/GB/USA, 1993), while for *Last of the Mohicans* (USA, 1992) he went to a survival camp to learn to track and kill animals and make canoes from trees.

Nicolas Cage had two teeth removed without painkillers for his part in *Vampire's Kiss* (USA, 1988). He also ate six live cockroaches to make the scene "really shock".

HIGHEST-EARNING MOVIE STAR
The world's top-earning movie actor is Harrison Ford (above), who earned $58 million (£35 million) in 1998. Ford has appeared in nine of the 45 highest-grossing films of all time. His signature roles include Indiana Jones in the trilogy beginning with Raiders of the Lost Ark *(US, 1981) and Han Solo in the original* Star Wars *trilogy.*

GREATEST AGE RANGE PORTRAYED BY AN ACTOR IN ONE FILM
Dustin Hoffman was 33 when he played the role of Jack Crabb in *Little Big Man* (USA, 1970). In the course of the film his character ages from 17 to 121.

MOST CHARACTERS PLAYED BY AN ACTOR IN ONE FILM
Alec Guinness played eight members of the ill-fated d'Ascoyne family in *Kind Hearts and Coronets* (UK, 1949).

FEWEST ACTORS IN A NARRATIVE FILM
Yaadein (Reminiscences, India, 1964) was written, directed and produced by Sunil Dutt, who was also its only actor. The two-hour film was shot entirely in one location and featured cartoon characters and balloons representing other people. The movie's only other living presence is the actress Nargis (Dutt's wife), who is shown in silhouette.

MOST APPEARANCES AS JAMES BOND
Sean Connery and Roger Moore have both starred as British secret agent 007 seven times. Connery appeared in the first Bond movie, *Dr No*, in 1962 and apparently bowed out after *Diamonds Are Forever* (1971) but made a comeback in *Never Say Never Again* in 1983. Roger Moore made his debut in *Live and Let Die* in 1973 and last played 007 in *A View to a Kill* in 1985.

MOST WEIGHT LOST AND GAINED FOR FILM APPEARANCES

Many stars go to extremes in their efforts to change size for a role. For example, Jennifer Jason Leigh (pictured) went down to a weight of 39 kg (6 st 2 lb) for her role as an anorexic teenager in *The Best Little Girl in the World* (USA, 1981). Gary Oldman lost 13.6 kg (2 st 2 lb) to play punk star Sid Vicious in *Sid and Nancy* (UK, 1986) and ended up in hospital suffering from malnutrition. However, the record-holder is Robert De Niro, who gained 27.2 kg (4 st 4 lb) for his role as Jake La Motta in Martin Scorsese's *Raging Bull* (USA, 1980), portraying the middleweight boxer's decline from world-class athlete to bloated has-been.

TALLEST MALE STAR
Christopher Lee, veteran of horror films such as *Dracula* (GB, 1958), is the tallest major movie star, at 1.95 m (6 ft 5 in) in height.

SHORTEST ADULT FEMALE STAR
Linda Hunt, who won an Oscar for her role as a Eurasian cameraman in *The Year of Living Dangerously* (Australia, 1982), is 1.44 m (4 ft 9 in) tall.

HIGHEST MOVIE INSURANCE QUOTE
The troubled actor Robert Downey Jr was reputedly working uninsured on *The Gingerbread Man* (USA, 1998). The premium for insuring him would have cost a record $1.4 million (£845,000) on a film with a budget of less than $42 million (£25 million).

TALLEST FEMALE STARS AND SHORTEST ADULT MALE STAR

US actress Sigourney Weaver (pictured left) is 1.83 m (6 ft) tall, the same height as two other leading ladies, Brigitte Nielsen and Geena Davis. Danny DeVito (on the right) who starred opposite Arnold Schwarzenegger in Twins *(USA, 1988), is 1.54 m (5 ft) in height.*

TOP-GROSSING FEMALE STAR

The US gross from the 20 films in which Julia Roberts has appeared up to 20 June 1999 is $1.202 billion (£725 million). They include Steel Magnolias *(USA, 1989),* Pretty Woman *(USA, 1990),* My Best Friend's Wedding *(USA, 1997) and* Notting Hill *(UK, 1999).*

pop stars

HIGHEST-EARNING POP STAR
Celine Dion ranked 12th on *Forbes* magazine's list of the 40 richest entertainers, with an income of $55.5 million (£33.5 million), making her the world's highest-earning pop star of 1998. She has had many No. 1 hits around the world and her success has been boosted by movie tie-ins such as *My Heart Will Go On*, the love theme from the movie *Titanic* (1997).

HIGHEST-EARNING GIRL BAND
The Spice Girls ranked 20th on *Forbes* magazine's list of the 40 richest entertainers of 1998, with an income of $49 million (£29.6 million).

MOST VALUABLE POP STAR ON THE STOCK MARKET
David Bowie commands an estimated fortune of £150 million ($250 million). In 1997 Bowie raised £33 million ($55 million) through the issue of bonds, which he sold to Prudential Insurance. Other stars thought to be following suit include members of the Rolling Stones.

MOST FAN CLUBS
There are more than 480 active Elvis Presley fan clubs worldwide — more than for any other musical star. This is particularly astonishing in view of the fact that Presley, who died in Aug 1977, did not record in other languages, except for a few soundtrack songs, and only once performed in concert beyond the borders of the USA, in Canada in 1957.

MOST APPEARANCES ON THE COVER OF *ROLLING STONE* MAGAZINE
Mick Jagger, the singer with the Rolling Stones, has appeared on the cover of *Rolling Stone* magazine a total of 16 times.

MOST GRAMMYS WON IN A YEAR
The most Grammy awards won in a single year is eight, by Michael Jackson in 1984. Jackson began his career as a child star in his brothers' band, the Jackson Five. He launched his solo career in 1972 with the song *Got To Be There*, and 10 years later released the album *Thriller*, which sold more than 48 million copies worldwide.

MOST BRIT AWARDS
Annie Lennox, formerly of the Eurythmics, has won seven Brit awards — more than any other artist or act. Her most recent award was Best British Female Artist in 1996.

British band Blur hold the record for the most wins in a year, with four in 1995.

PIANO PLAYED BY THE MOST POP STARS
A Bechstein grand piano was used by a number of influential pop stars during the 1960s and 1970s, including the Beatles on *The White Album*, David Bowie on *The Rise And Fall Of Ziggy Stardust And The Spiders From Mars* and *Hunky Dory*, and Elton John on *Goodbye Yellow Brick Road* and *A Single Man*. The instrument, which is now valued at £15,000–18,000 ($24,861–29,833), was hired from the Samuels music shop in London, UK, and became the resident piano at Trident Studios, London, UK.

BIGGEST RECORD CONTRACT LAWSUIT
George Michael fought a nine-month court battle during 1993 and 1994 in an attempt to end his contract with Sony Music. He eventually lost the case, which cost him an estimated £3 million ($1.96 million), and his contract was eventually bought out by US company Dreamworks.

MOST VALUABLE LYRICS
In Feb 1998 the autographed lyrics to *Candle In The Wind 1997* sold for $442,500 (£240,963) in Los Angeles, California, USA. The lyrics were rewritten by Bernie Taupin and the song was performed by Elton John at the funeral of Diana, Princess of Wales in Sept 1997. The three-page manuscript, signed by John and Taupin, was bought by the Lund Foundation For Children which funds programmes for disadvantaged children.

MOST CHARITIES SUPPORTED BY A POP STAR
Michael Jackson has supported 39 charity organisations either with monetary donations through sponsorships of their projects or through participating in their silent auctions. The charities involved include AIDS Project L.A., American Cancer Society, BMI Foundation, Inc., Childhelp USA., United Negro College Fund (UNCF), YMCA — 28th Street/Crenshaw, The Sickle Cell Research Foundation and Volunteers of America.

HIGHEST-EARNING POP GROUP
The Rolling Stones are the world's wealthiest pop group, with earnings of £57 million ($94.5 million) in 1998 alone. The band was formed in April 1962 in London, UK, and has been fronted ever since by Mick Jagger pictured here with Keith Richards and Ron Wood. By 1964 they were the only serious rivals to the Beatles and the next few years saw a string of classic singles such as *(I Can't Get No) Satisfaction*. In 1970 Austrian financial adviser Prince Rupert Loewenstein took over their affairs, translating their 'bad boy' image and live reputation as 'The Greatest Rock 'n' Roll Band in the World' into unprecedented earnings.

MOST EXPENSIVE PROMOTIONS FOR AN ALBUM BY A POP STAR
Promotions for Michael Jackson's album *HIStory* (1995) included a 9.1-m-high (30-ft) inflated statue of the star on top of Tower Records in Hollywood, California, USA, a huge sign in Times Square, New York City, USA, and another statue floated on a barge down the River Thames in London, UK. Jackson's record company Sony spent a total of $40 million (£24.25 million) on the launch of the album in the USA, the United Kingdom, Italy, Australia, Japan, South Africa and the Netherlands.

MOST PRODUCT ENDORSEMENTS BY A POP GROUP IN A YEAR
The Spice Girls hold the record for the greatest number of promotions by a group in any one year, with 10 different advertisers in 1997, including Sony PlayStation and Mercedes. A $1-million (£625,000) deal with Pepsi involved 40,000 Pepsi drinkers being flown to Istanbul, Turkey, for a Spice Girls concert and after-show party.

MOST PAID TO A POP STAR FOR ADVERTISING RIGHTS
The software company Microsoft acquired the rights for the Rolling Stones' hit single *Start Me Up* for $8 million (£4.85 million) and featured it in its *Windows '95* campaign.

BIGGEST ADVERTISING DEAL TO BE TURNED DOWN
The record for the largest sum of money ever rejected by a pop star for an advertising deal is $12 million (£7.32 million) by Bruce Springsteen in 1987. The sum had been offered by US car manufacturer Chrysler for the use of Springsteen's 1984 hit *Born in the USA* in a car commercial.

HIGHEST-EARNING MUSIC PRODUCER
Master P, chief executive officer of No Limit Records, based in New Orleans, Louisiana, USA, is estimated to have a net worth of $56.5 million (£34.1 million) . Born Percy Miller, Master P has stayed out of the East Coast-West Coast rappers' feud and is currently the world's most successful rap star.

MOST PSEUDONYMS USED BY A POP STAR
Prince Rogers Nelson made his first album, For You, *as Prince in 1978. He has since used the names Tora Tora, Coco, Alexander Nevermind, Victor, Camille, Christopher, Jamie, [symbol], The Artist Formerly Known As Prince and The Artist for his work as performer, producer and songwriter.*

tv stars

MOST WATCHED TV STAR IN LATIN AMERICA

Brazil's Maria da Graça Meneghel, known as Xuxa, is the most watched Latin American TV star. A Spanish-language version of the four-and-a-half-hour-long *Xuxa Show* (originally in Portuguese) is shown in 16 countries. The 36-year-old blue-eyed blonde began her TV career as a children's presenter in Dec 1982 and is renowned for her love of children: in Oct 1989 she established the Xuxa Meneghel Foundation, which provides food, shelter and education for Brazilian young people. She has also spearheaded campaigns against AIDS, drug abuse and polio.

HIGHEST-PAID TV COMEDY ACTOR
Jerry Seinfeld, former star of *Seinfeld*, tops the 1999 *Forbes* Celebrities 100 List, with estimated earnings of $267 million (£161 million).

Tim Allen was the highest-paid star of a show broadcast during the 1998/99 season. He drew a salary of $1.25 million (£754,193) per show for the 1999 series of *Home Improvement*.

HIGHEST-PAID TV DRAMA ACTOR
Anthony Edwards, who plays Dr Mark Greene in *ER*, earns $400,000 (£241,342) per episode, as a result of the $35 million (£21.12 million) deal which keeps him on the show until the 2001/02 season.

HIGHEST-PAID CHAT SHOW HOST
Oprah Winfrey placed fourth in the 1999 *Forbes* Celebrities 100 List, with an income for the year of $125 million (£75.42 million). She has also appeared in films such as *Beloved* (USA, 1999).

HIGHEST-PAID NEWS BROADCASTER
Barbara Walters (USA) reputedly earns in excess of $13 million (£7.84 million) a year as news correspondent and co-anchor of *ABC News Magazine*, *20/20*, *The Barbara Walters Specials* and *The View*. She has interviewed every US president since Richard Nixon and made journalistic history by arranging the first joint interview of President Anwar Sadat of Egypt and Prime Minister Menachem Begin of Israel in Nov 1977.

HIGHEST-PAID MAGICIAN TO APPEAR ON TV
The highest-paid magician to appear on TV is David Copperfield, who earned $50 million (£30.2 million) in 1999 according to the *Forbes* Celebrities 100 List. Copperfield's stunts include making the Statue of Liberty disappear.

HIGHEST-PAID TV WRITER
Larry David (USA), co-writer of the hit comedy *Seinfeld*, was second only to the show's star on the 1999 *Forbes* Celebrities 100 List, despite leaving the show in 1996. He returned to pen the finale in 1998. His earnings for 1999 are estimated at $242 million (£146 million).

Chris Carter (USA), creator of *The X-Files* and *Millennium*, is the wealthiest active TV writer, earning $52 million (£31.37 million) in 1999.

LONGEST TIME IN THE SAME ROLE
William Roache has been playing the character Ken Barlow without a break since the first episode of the British soap opera Coronation Street *in 1960. The character was first seen as a student, and since then he has had three wives and 23 girlfriends, been a newspaper editor and a teacher, and survived a suicide attempt.*

HIGHEST-PAID TV PRODUCER
Mike Judge (USA), creator of animated series such as *Beavis and Butt-head* and *King of the Hill*, was the leading TV producer in the *Forbes* 1999 rich-list, with earnings of $53 million (£32 million).

MOST WATCHED TV STAR
David Hasselhoff is the star and producer of *Baywatch*, which has an estimated weekly audience of 1.1 billion in 142 different countries. Hasselhoff, the only actor to have been with the show through its entire run, also starred in the TV show *Knight Rider* (1982–85) and is a major pop star in Germany. He has been named as one of TV's 10 most powerful stars by *TV Guide* magazine. Female *Baywatch* stars have included Pamela Anderson, Gena Lee Nolin and Yasmine Bleeth.

MOST WATCHED TV STAR IN JAPAN
Akashiya Sanma (real name Sugimoto Takafumi) polled 56.8 points in Video Research (Japan) Ltd's twice-yearly survey of television popularity. Japanese television stars flit from show to show as featured or special guests, so in any given week a star could be on several different programmes across four different networks.

MOST WATCHED TV STAR IN FRANCE
News presenter Patrick Poivre d'Arvor is watched by more viewers than any other French television personality. On 2 Dec 1997 his news show *TF1 20 hrs* had a record 15.02 million viewers across the country. The star receives extensive press attention and in April 1996 was the victim of *l'entarteur* — the Belgian anarchist Noel Godin, who pelts his targets with custard pies.

MOST WATCHED TV STAR IN GERMANY
Thomas Gottschalk currently hosts Germany's top-rating show *Wetten Daß* (*I Bet That...*), in which guest celebrities are asked to bet on whether contestants will succeed in record attempts. The programme receives 23% of the total audience share. Gottschalk,

Germany's most popular TV personality, has appeared in many other TV shows as well as a great number of national advertising campaigns.

MOST WATCHED TV STAR IN RUSSIA

Valdis Pelsh, the star of the music show *Uguday Melodiyu* (*Guess the Melody*), is Russia's most popular television personality. The show, which is shown six times a week (three original broadcasts and three morning repeats), receives up to 56% of the total audience share in Russia.

MOST WATCHED MALE PRESENTER IN THE UNITED KINGDOM

Chris Tarrant hosts the quiz show *Who Wants To Be A Millionaire?*, in which contestants have the chance to win £1 million ($1.66 million). The show on 7 March 1999 resulted in BARB ratings of 19.21 million and an audience share of 67.8%. Tarrant, who first came to national prominence fronting the children's show *TISWAS*, is also a successful radio disc jockey.

MOST WATCHED FEMALE PRESENTER IN THE UNITED KINGDOM

Cilla Black, who hosts the popular British dating show *Blind Date*, is currently the most watched TV presenter in the UK. The show, which has been running since 1984, had an average of 9.1 million viewers per episode in the 1997/98 season. In 1997 Cilla was made an OBE (Officer of the Order of the British Empire) by Queen Elizabeth II for her services to British entertainment.

LONGEST CAREER AS A TV PRESENTER

The astronomy programme *The Sky at Night*, which airs monthly on British television, has been presented by Patrick Moore without a break or a missed show since 24 April 1957. By Jan 1999 a total of 541 episodes had been broadcast.

RICHEST ACTRESS ON TV

Helen Hunt, the star of Mad About You, *is the world's wealthiest TV actress, with a net worth of $31 million (£18.7 million). Her TV debut was on* The Mary Tyler Moore Show *and she won an Oscar for* As Good As It Gets *(USA, 1997).*

sports stars

HIGHEST EARNINGS IN A YEAR
The greatest earnings by a sports star in a year, excluding monies from sponsorship and endorsements, is $75 million (£46 billion) by US boxer Mike Tyson. In 1986 Tyson had become the youngest boxing heavyweight world champion of all time when he beat Trevor Berbick (USA) to win the WBC version at the age of 20 years 144 days.

HIGHEST CAREER EARNINGS BY A SPORTSMAN
Retired basketball legend Michael Jordan earned more money during his 13-year basketball career than any other sportsman in history, including endorsement deals. Now aged 36, Jordan earned $33 million (£19.91 million) in salary with the Chicago Bulls for his last season (1998) plus a further $47 million ($29 million) in endorsements, making him *Forbes* magazine's highest-paid sportsman for the fifth time in six years. By 1998 his career earnings had exceeded $300 million (£187.5 million).

HIGHEST-EARNING TENNIS PLAYERS
By May 1999 US tennis player Pete Sampras' career earnings from prize money alone totalled $36.1 million (£22.5 million). In 1997 he was paid a total of $8 million (£5 million) for his biggest endorsement deals, with Nike and Wilson. Sampras also holds the men's record for earnings in a season, at $6.5 million (£4.06 million) in 1997.

Andre Agassi (USA) made a total of $15.8 million (£9.87 million) during 1998 – the most made by a tennis player in one year. This includes his prize money plus endorsement deals with companies such as Nike, Canon and Head.

HIGHEST-EARNING SOCCER PLAYER
Brazilian footballer Ronaldo Luis Nazario de Lima, known simply as Ronaldo, is the world's highest-earning soccer player. In 1998 the Inter Milan striker earned a total of $8.9 million (£5.5 million). This figure included a monthly wage of $324,000 (£200,000), $162,000 (£100,000) in bonuses and $4.8 million (£3.01 million) in advertising and other sponsorship deals.

The earnings of Manchester United midfielder David Beckham reached £2.9 million ($4.7 million) in 1998, making him the highest-earning soccer player in the United Kingdom and the second highest in the world.

HIGHEST-EARNING GOLFERS
The highest all-time career earnings on the US PGA circuit is $12.29 million (£7.41 million), by Australia's Greg Norman between 1976 and May 1999. Norman has had more than 70 victories worldwide.

The season's record on the US PGA Tour is $2.96 million (£1.79 million), by US player David Duvall to June 1999.

Hale Irwin (USA) won a record-breaking $2.86 million (£1.43 million) on the US Seniors PGA Tour in 1997.

The record career earnings for a woman golfer is $6.28 million (£3.78 million), by Betsy King (USA) from 1977 to 1998.

The record season's earnings by a woman golfer is $1.24 million (£772,993), by Annika Sorenstam of Sweden in 1997.

Colin Montgomerie (GB) won a season's record of £993,077 ($1.64 million) in European Order of Merit tournaments in 1998.

FASTEST $1 MILLION EARNED BY A GOLFER FROM TURNING PRO
In 1996 US golfer Tiger Woods broke South African Ernie Els' record for the fewest events played since turning professional to earn $1 million (£625,000). Woods needed only nine pro starts. By the end of his debut season he had won five tournaments and earned more than $2 million (£1.25 million). He was the highest-earning golfer of 1997 and the second highest-paid endorser in sport, collecting $2.1 million (£1.3 million) in salary and winnings and $24 million (£15 million) in endorsements. In Sept 1996 he signed a $40-million (£25.3-million) contract with Nike, which brought out a new Woods apparel line in June 1997.

OLDEST HIGH-EARNING SPORTSMAN
In 1997 the 68-year-old US golfer Arnold Palmer earned a total of $16.1 million (£10 million) from salary, winnings and endorsements, making him the 12th highest-earner in sport. Palmer, who was the first golfer to win more than $1 million (£625,000) on the PGA Tour, still plays on the PGA Senior Tour.

HIGHEST EARNINGS BY A SPORTSWOMAN

Steffi Graf (Germany) had earned a total of $21,512,490 (£12,437,638) in prize money by 21 June 1999, beating the record set by her fellow tennis star Martina Navrátilová (USA, formerly Czechoslovakia). However, Navrátilová still holds the record if endorsements and sponsorship deals are included in the figure.

BIGGEST SPORTS CONTRACTS

Kevin Garnett signed a $126-million (£77-million) 6-year contract extension with the Minnesota Timberwolves on 3 Oct 1997, the biggest contract in the NBA. In 1997 Alonzo Mourning of the Miami Heat (pictured), Shaquille O'Neal (LA Lakers) and Juwon Howard (Washington Wizards) also signed nine-figure deals.

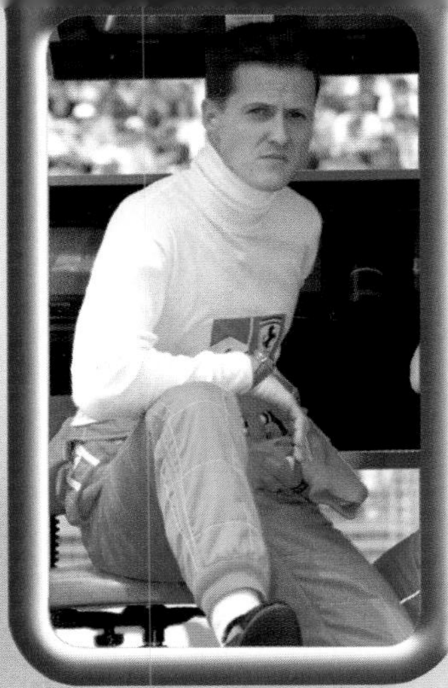

HIGHEST-EARNING FORMULA ONE DRIVER

In 1996 German Formula One driver Michael Schumacher was paid a record $25 million (£15.6 million) to drive for Ferrari's Formula One team – the highest salary in the history of Formula One. Schumacher's total earnings in 1997 have been estimated at $35 million (£22 million), including salary and winnings as well as sponsorships and endorsements.

MOST SUCCESSFUL MUSICAL CAREER BY A SPORTSMAN

Shaquille O'Neal, hoopster for the Los Angeles Lakers, also has a highly successful music career. He released his debut album, *Shaq Diesel* (1993), when he was 21, and in 1997 his record label TWIsM (The World Is Mine) formed a joint venture with A&M Records to produce a fourth album.

HIGHEST-EARNING CRICKETER

Indian cricketer Sachin Tendulkar earns around $4 million (£2.5 million) per year. The vast majority of this figure comes from sponsorship deals for companies such as Pepsi, Visa, Cadbury's and Colgate. He appears in almost a quarter of all Indian TV commercials and is one of the most well-known faces on the Indian subcontinent.

HIGHEST-EARNING ICE HOCKEY PLAYER

The highest-earning ice hockey player is Sergei Federov, who plays for the Detroit Red Wings. Federov earned a record $29.8 million (£18.6 million) from wages and endorsements in 1998.

HIGHEST-EARNING AMERICAN FOOTBALL PLAYER

Green Bay NFL player Brett Favre made a record total of $13.1 million (£8.03 million) in 1998.

HIGHEST-EARNING SNOOKER PLAYER

The most successful snooker player in terms of tournament earnings is Stephen Hendry (GB). He has won a record total of £6.2 million ($9.92 million), when he won the World Championship for the seventh time in 1999 – itself a record for the modern era – Hendry won £230,000 ($368,000), taking his earnings from World Championship competitions alone to over £1.5 million ($2.4 million).

MOST PRIZE MONEY WON IN A SEASON

Marion Jones (USA) notched up one of the greatest seasons by any athlete, male or female, in 1998, when she won all but one of the 36 events she contested and remained undefeated at both 100 m and 200 m. Jones took the overall Grand Prix title as well as individual titles at 100 m and long jump, which meant she received one third of the Golden League Jackpot – giving her $633,333 (£395,833) from the Grand Prix final alone.

supermodels

TALLEST SUPERMODEL
Australian-born Elle MacPherson is 1.85 m (6 ft 1 in) tall and is known as 'The Body' because her dimensions — 91-61-89 cm (36-24-35 in) — are regarded as perfect.

SHORTEST SUPERMODEL
British supermodel Kate Moss was discovered by Storm Agency's Sarah Doukas at JFK Airport, New York City, USA, in 1990. At just over 1.69 m (5 ft 6 in) in height, she seemed an unlikely choice but went on to revolutionize modelling, making way for a new type of model and a new trend called 'grunge'. The first big designer to use her was Calvin Klein, with whom she signed a $2-million (£1.1-million) contract in 1991.

LONGEST-LEGGED SUPERMODEL
Of all the supermodels, German model Nadja Auermann has the longest legs, at 1.14 m (45 in). She shot to fame in 1993, when the fashion world rejected grunge in favour of glamour. By 1994 she had appeared on the covers of both *Harper's Bazaar* and *Vogue*.

RICHEST SUPERMODEL
Elle MacPherson is said to be worth $38.12 million (£23 million), making her the richest supermodel in the world. Although she no longer appears regularly on the catwalk, she still commands huge fees and has various business interests. These include a share in the Fashion Café chain and her own line of lingerie, Elle MacPherson Intimates. Elle has also appeared in several films, including *Sirens*, *Jane Eyre* and *Batman & Robin*.

Cindy Crawford is the world's second-richest supermodel, with an estimated wealth of $34.8 million (£21 million).

BIGGEST SUPERMODEL JOINT VENTURE
Claudia Schiffer, Elle MacPherson and Naomi Campbell all own shares in the Fashion Café theme restaurants. The chain, which aims to reflect the glamour and excitement of the fashion world, has seven branches in major cities worldwide, including Barcelona, Spain, and New York City, USA. Two more restaurants are under construction in Dubai and Singapore, and the chain has secured 27 other locations around the world.

LONGEST CONTRACT
Christy Turlington (USA) has represented Calvin Klein for over 10 years — an industry record. She gave up catwalk modelling in 1995 and graduated from New York University, USA, in May 1999 with a liberal arts degree.

BIGGEST COSMETICS CONTRACT
In 1993 Claudia Schiffer signed the biggest ever cosmetics contract when she was offered the sum of $6 million (£4 million) to become the face of Revlon. Claudia has done campaigns for all the big fashion houses and was a particular favourite of Karl Lagerfeld. She has also made her own fitness video, and made her movie debut in 1998 with *The Blackout*.

TOP-PAYING CATWALK SHOWS
One of the main forces behind the supermodel phenomenon was the late Italian designer Gianni Versace. Versace is reported to have paid top models as much as $50,000 (£30,000) per half-hour show in the late 1980s on the proviso that they would only appear in his show that season. This is said to have created the elite group of girls — Christy Turlington, Naomi Campbell and Linda Evangelista — who dominated fashion magazines in the early 1990s.

LARGEST INTERNATIONAL MODELLING AGENCY
Elite Model Management is currently based in 22 countries round the world, with 11 offices in Europe and five in the USA. The company has bases as far apart as São Paulo, Brazil, and Hong Kong, China.

MOST MAGAZINE COVERS
Claudia Schiffer was spotted in a disco in Germany when she was 17, and has not stopped working since. She has appeared on approximately 550 magazine covers, more than any other supermodel.

LONGEST SUPERMODEL CAREER

Christy Turlington has been modelling for a longer period of time than any other supermodel since being discovered at the age of 13. She began modelling full-time in 1987, when she was 17. By 1988 she was the face of the perfume Eternity and had secured a deal with Maybelline worth $800,000 (£440,000) for 12 days' work.

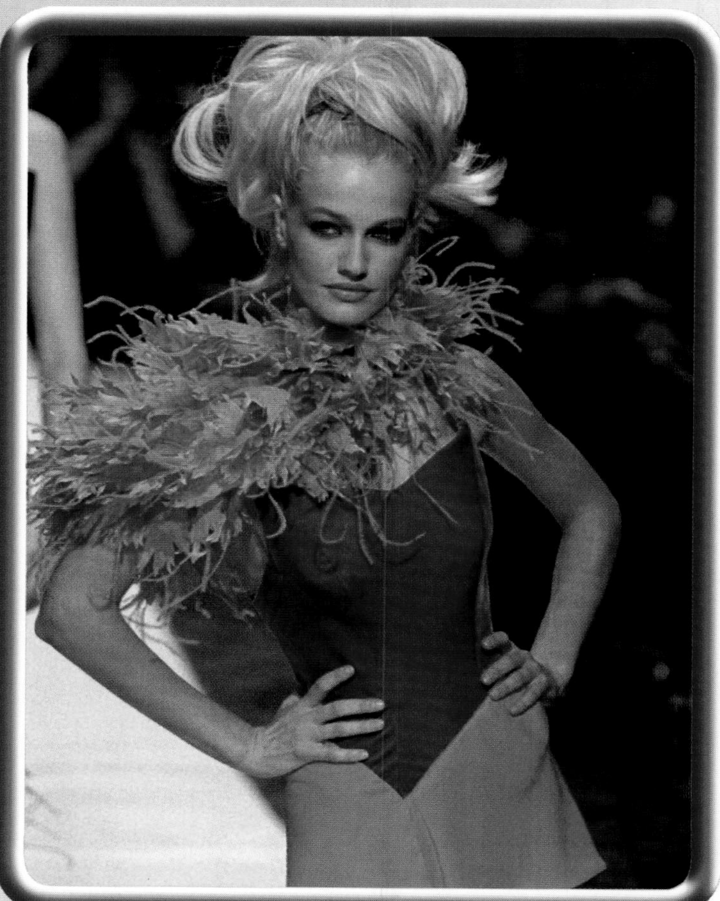

MOST SUCCESSFUL MODELLING AGENCY

The agency Elite has a record 35 supermodels on its books, including Karen Mulder (pictured), Claudia Schiffer, Cindy Crawford and Amber Valletta. It currently bills more than $100 million (£60 million) in modelling fees every year. Set up by John Casablanca (USA) in Paris, France, in 1971, Elite only represents female models, and has approximately 500 women on its books worldwide.

YOUNGEST SUPERMODEL TO WIN A MAJOR COSMETICS CONTRACT

Niki Taylor was just 13 when she won $500,000 (£295,000) in a 'Fresh Faces' contest run by a New York model agency in 1989. This is the largest sum that any girl who has gone on to become a supermodel has won in a contest of this kind. She went on to sign a deal with L'Oréal for Cover Girl, the youngest model ever to win a major cosmetics contract.

MOST VOGUE COVERS
Christy Turlington has appeared on the cover of British *Vogue* a record 21 times. Her first appearance was in July 1986 and her most recent appearance was in Jan 1996.

LONGEST CATWALK CAREER
Carmen Dell'Orefici was born in 1931 and has been modelling for the Ford Agency since the 1940s. At the age of 68 she is still in demand for contracts and international shows.

Daphne Self is 70 years old but has had an on/off modelling career. She is signed to Models 1 in London, UK, has been photographed for *Vogue* and *Marie Claire* and features in the 1999 Laura Ashley campaign.

HIGHEST-PAID SUPERMODEL

According to Forbes *magazine Claudia Schiffer earns $10.5 million (£6.3 million) a year — more than any other supermodel. Her wealth is currently estimated at $34 million (£20.5 million), making her the richest European supermodel.*

oscars & awards

MOST VERSATILE AWARD-WINNER
Actress/singer/director Barbra Streisand has won two Oscars, five Emmys, seven Grammys, seven Golden Globes and a special Tony in 1970 as Broadway Actress of the Decade.

MOST BEST DIRECTOR OSCARS
John Ford won four Oscars as Best Director, for *The Informer* (USA, 1935), *The Grapes of Wrath* (USA, 1940), *How Green Was My Valley* (USA, 1941) and *The Quiet Man* (USA, 1952).

MOST BEST DIRECTOR NOMINATIONS
William Wyler was Oscar-nominated a record 12 times between 1936 and 1965 and won the award three times, for *Mrs Miniver* (USA, 1942), *The Best Years of Our Lives* (USA, 1946) and *Ben-Hur* (USA, 1959).

MOST BEST ACTRESS OSCARS
Katharine Hepburn won four Oscars, for *Morning Glory* (USA, 1933), *Guess Who's Coming to Dinner* (USA, 1967), *The Lion in Winter* (UK, 1968 — award shared) and *On Golden Pond* (USA, 1981). She also had the longest award-winning career, spanning 48 years.

MOST BEST ACTOR OSCARS
Seven people have won the Best Actor Academy Award twice: Spencer Tracy for *Captains Courageous* (USA, 1937) and *Boys Town* (USA, 1938); Fredric March for *Dr Jekyll and Mr Hyde* (USA, 1932) and *The Best Years of Our Lives* (USA, 1946); Gary Cooper for *Sergeant York* (USA, 1941) and *High Noon* (USA, 1952); Marlon Brando for *On the Waterfront* (USA, 1954) and *The Godfather* (USA, 1972 — award declined); Jack Nicholson for *One Flew Over the Cuckoo's Nest* (USA, 1975) and *As Good As It Gets* (USA, 1997); Dustin Hoffman for *Kramer vs. Kramer* (USA, 1979) and *Rain Man* (USA, 1988); and Tom Hanks for *Philadelphia* (USA, 1993) and *Forrest Gump* (USA, 1994).

MOST BEST SUPPORTING ACTOR OSCARS
Walter Brennan won Oscars for Best Supporting Actor in *Come and Get It* (USA, 1936), *Kentucky* (USA, 1938) and *The Westerner* (USA, 1940).

MOST BEST SUPPORTING ACTRESS OSCARS
The record is two: Shelley Winters won Oscars for her roles in *The Diary of Anne Frank* (USA, 1959) and *A Patch of Blue* (USA, 1965); and Dianne Wiest won for *Hannah And Her Sisters* (USA, 1986) and *Bullets Over Broadway* (USA, 1994). Both of Wiest's roles were in films directed by Woody Allen.

MOST AWARDS FOR ONE ROLE
Marlon Brando won (but declined) the Best Actor award for his role as Vito Corleone in *The Godfather* (USA, 1972) and Robert De Niro won a Best Supporting Actor award for his performance as the younger Corleone in *The Godfather Part II* (USA, 1974).

Barry Fitzgerald was nominated for both Best Actor and Best Supporting Actor for *Going My Way* (USA, 1944), winning the latter. This is the only time that one actor has been nominated in two acting categories for the same film.

YOUNGEST OSCAR-WINNERS
Tatum O'Neal was 10 years old when she was voted Best Supporting Actress for *Paper Moon* (USA, 1973).

Shirley Temple was awarded an honorary Oscar at the age of five in 1934.

OLDEST OSCAR-WINNER
Jessica Tandy won the Best Actress award for *Driving Miss Daisy* (USA, 1990) at the age of 80.

MOST CONSECUTIVE EMMY AWARDS
The US comedy series Frasier *has won five consecutive Emmy awards as Best Comedy Series. Kelsey Grammer (third from right) has also won three Emmys for Best Actor for his role as psychiatrist Dr Frasier Crane, and David Hyde Pierce (right of picture), who plays Frasier's brother Niles, has won two Best Supporting Actor awards.*

MOST GOLDEN RASPBERRIES

The Spice Girls (right) made history at the 1999 Golden Raspberries when all five were given the Worst Actress Award for their collective performance in *Spiceworld: The Movie* (UK, 1997); they were the most people ever to share the prize. The Golden Raspberries (or 'Razzies') were instituted by author John Wilson in 1980 to complement the Academy Awards by highlighting the worst the film industry had to offer. Other 'winners' have included Bruce Willis, Demi Moore, Leonardo DiCaprio, Pamela Anderson, Kevin Costner and Madonna. The 20th ceremony, in 2000, will name the 100 Worst Films of the 20th Century. Votes are being taken on the Golden Raspberry website www.razzies.com.

MOST FAMILY MEMBERS TO HAVE WON OSCARS

Walter Huston was named Best Supporting Actor for The Treasure of the Sierra Madre *(USA, 1948), his son John won Best Director for the same film and John's daughter Anjelica won Best Supporting Actress for* Prizzi's Honour *(USA, 1985). Francis Ford Coppola took the Best Director award for* The Godfather Part II *(USA, 1974), his father Carmine won the Best Original Score award for the same film and Nicolas Cage (Francis' nephew, left) was named Best Actor for* Leaving Las Vegas *(USA, 1995).*

MOST CESAR AWARDS

French star Isabelle Adjani is the only person to have won four Césars, awarded by the French Académie des Arts. Her first was in 1982 for her role in Andrzej Zulawski's Possession. *She went on to win further awards for her work in* L'Eté Meurtrier *in 1984,* Camille Claudel *in 1989 and* La Reine Margot *in 1995.*

MOST OSCAR NOMINATIONS WITHOUT AN AWARD

Both Richard Burton and Peter O'Toole have been nominated for the Best Actor Award seven times, but neither have won. Burton was nominated for *My Cousin Rachel* (USA, 1952), *The Robe* (USA, 1953), *Beckett* (UK, 1964), *The Spy Who Came in from the Cold* (UK, 1965), *Who's Afraid of Virginia Woolf?* (USA, 1966), *Anne of the Thousand Days* (UK, 1970) and *Equus* (UK, 1977). O'Toole's nominations were for *Lawrence of Arabia* (UK, 1962), *Beckett* (UK, 1964), *The Lion In Winter* (UK, 1968), *Goodbye Mr Chips* (UK, 1969), *The Ruling Class* (UK, 1969), *The Stunt Man* (USA, 1980) and *My Favourite Year* (USA, 1982).

MOST OSCARS FOR BEST FOREIGN LANGUAGE FILM BY ONE COUNTRY

Italy has won 13 Oscars for Best Foreign Language Film, the most recent being *Life Is Beautiful* in 1999.

MOST APPEARANCES AS HOST AT THE OSCARS

Bob Hope hosted the Academy Awards a record 13 times: in 1940 (the second half of the show), 1945, 1946, 1953, 1955, 1958, 1959, 1960, 1966, 1967, 1968, 1975 and 1978.

YOUNGEST PEOPLE TO WIN TONYS

Daisy Eagan was 11 years old when she won the Tony Award for Best Actress in a Featured Role in a Musical (equivalent to a Best Supporting Actress award) for her part in *The Secret Garden* in 1991.

Liza Minnelli, at the age of 19, was the youngest person to win a lead role Tony. She won for her performance in *Flora, The Red Menace* in 1965.

MOST CONSECUTIVE BAFTA WINS

Robbie Coltrane won three consecutive Best Television Actor awards for his role as forensic psychiatrist Fitz in Granada Television's series *Cracker*, from 1994 to 1996.

MOST GRAMMYS

The individual who won the most Grammys was the Hungarian-born British composer Sir Georg Solti, who had 31 by the time of his death in 1997.

world leaders

YOUNGEST PRESIDENT
The youngest head of state of a republic is Yaya Jammeh, who became president of the provisional council and head of state of the Gambia at the age of 29 on 26 July 1994 and was elected president at the age of 31 on 27 Sept 1996.

OLDEST PRIME MINISTER
Sirimavo Bandaranaike became prime minister of Sri Lanka at the record age of 78 in 1994. She had become the first female prime minister anywhere in the world when she first took office, in 1960.

SHORTEST PRESIDENCY
Pedro Lascurain was president of Mexico for one hour on 18 Feb 1913. The legal successor to President Madero, who was murdered on 13 Feb 1913, Lascurain was sworn in, appointed General Victoriano Huerta as his successor and resigned.

MOST RE-ELECTED PRIME MINISTERS
Cambodia, Iraq and Lebanon have all had prime ministers who were re-elected to office eight times. Prince Norodom Sihanouk was first elected prime minister of Cambodia in March 1945 and last served from 1961 to 1962. Iraq's Nuri as-Said first served as prime minister in 1930 and then served intermittently until his last re-election in 1958. Rashid Karami was elected prime minister of the Lebanon for the first time in 1955 and his last term ran between 1984 and 1987.

OLDEST PRESIDENT AND YOUNGEST PREMIER
The oldest republican head of state is 82-year-old Kiro Gligorov, president of the Former Yugoslav Republic of Macedonia (right). The country also has the youngest prime minister, Ljupco Georgievski of the Internal Macedonian Revolutionary Organization–Democratic Party of Macedonian National Unity (VMRO-DPMNE), who was born on 17 Jan 1966 (left). He took office on 30 Nov 1998 when he was 32 years old.

President Suharto won six consecutive elections from 1967, holding the reins of power in Indonesia for 31 years until he was forced out of power in 1998 following violent rioting by university students.

HIGHEST PERSONAL MAJORITIES
Boris Yeltsin, the president of the Russian Federation, had a personal majority of 4.73 million votes in elections in the Soviet Union in March 1989. He received 5.12 million votes out of the 5.72 million cast in his Moscow constituency.

Benazir Bhutto achieved 98.48% of the poll in the Larkana-III constituency in the 1990 general election in Pakistan, with 94,462 votes. The next highest candidate obtained 718 votes.

MOST WOMEN LEADERS SERVING SIMULTANEOUSLY
Fourteen women served as prime minister, president or co-captain regent between 1 Jan and 31 Dec 1993, in Dominica, Norway, Pakistan, Bangladesh, Poland, Canada, Turkey, Burundi, Rwanda, Iceland, Nicaragua, Ireland and San Marino.

BIGGEST PRESIDENTIAL STAFF
The republican head of state with the biggest staff is the US president Bill Clinton. There are more than 1,000 employees at the White House, including domestic staff, caterers, groundspeople, security personnel and interns. Some of this number also work for Hillary Rodham Clinton, the First Lady.

MOST EXPENSIVE PRESIDENTIAL INAUGURATION
The inauguration of the US president in Washington DC, which takes place every fourth year, is the most expensive in the world. The most expensive ever US presidential inauguration was that of George Bush in 1989, which cost a total of $30 million (£18.9 million).

PRESIDENT WITH MOST FAMILY MEMBERS IN POWER
Until 1995 Barzan Ibrahim, a half-brother of Iraqi president Saddam Hussein, was ambassador to the UN

LONGEST TIME IN POWER
Fidel Castro became prime minister of Cuba in July 1959 and has been president and head of government since 3 Dec 1976. He came to power after his third attempt to overthrow the country's dictator Fulgencio Batista. He nationalized all US-owned businesses in Cuba in 1960, which led to numerous CIA-backed actions against him, ranging from the unsuccessful Bay of Pigs invasion of 1961 to an attempt to kill him with an exploding cigar. The continuing US economic blockade, combined with the Soviet Union's cancellation of economic support in 1991, has caused increasing hardship in the country, although Cuba still maintains one of the highest literacy rates in the world.

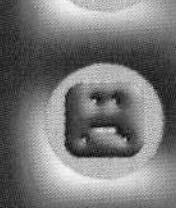

MOST-MARRIED PRIME MINISTER

Currently the most-married prime minister in a monogamous society is Gerhard Schroeder, who has been married four times. The German Chancellor is pictured here on the far right, with (right to left) his fourth wife, Doris, French prime minister Lionel Jospin and Jospin's wife Sylviane.

and controlled much of the family fortune. Another of Saddam's half-brothers, Watban Ibrahim, was minister of the interior, and a third half-brother, Sabaoni Ibrahim, was chief of general security. Saddam's son-in-law Saddam Kamal Hussein was commander of the presidential guard until he fled to Jordan in 1995, and his sons, Udday and Qusay, hold various state and other offices. The latter was head of security services but was replaced by one of Saddam's in-laws.

MOST DESCENDANTS TO BECOME PRIME MINISTER

Pandit Jawaharlal Nehru became India's first prime minister when the country attained independence on 15 Aug 1947 and remained in power until his death in 1964. His daughter Indira Gandhi served as prime minister from 1966 to 1977 and from 1980 until she was assassinated by her own bodyguards in 1984. Rajiv Gandhi, Indira's eldest son, became prime minister following his mother's death and won the 1984 elections by a landslide. He served until 1989 and was assassinated while campaigning for the premiership in 1991.

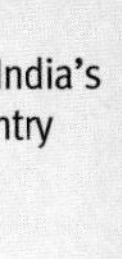

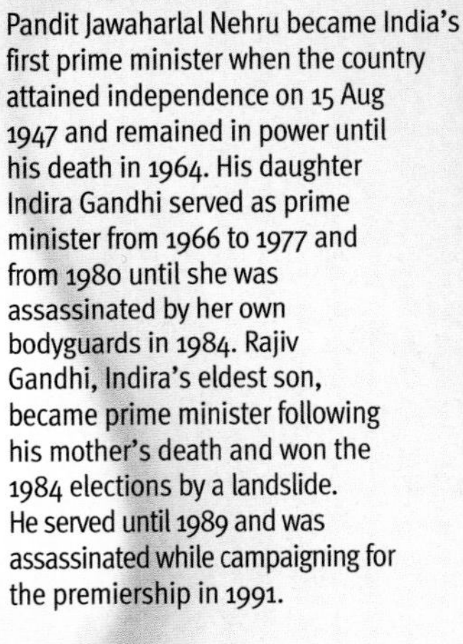

LONGEST 20TH-CENTURY HOUSE ARREST

Nobel Peace Prize winner Aung San Suu Kyi, leader of the National League for Democracy, was placed under house arrest on 20 July 1989 by Burma's military government and held until 10 July 1995. The daughter of assassinated Burmese leader General Aung San, she was held under martial law that allows detention for up to three years without charge or trial. It was extended to six years in 1994.

PRESIDENT TO HAVE SPENT THE LEAST TIME IN HIS COUNTRY

Valdus Adamkus, who became president of Lithuania in 1998, returned to the republic in 1997 after living in Chicago, Illinois, USA, for more than 50 years.

MOST ACCESSIBLE PRIME MINISTER

With the exception of the leaders of some 'micro-states', the most accessible head of government is the Danish premier Poul Nyrup Rasmussen, whose home phone number is in the public domain. Rasmussen often personally answers telephone queries from Danish citizens. Openness in government in Denmark extends to the sovereign — any citizen may request an audience with Queen Margrethe II.

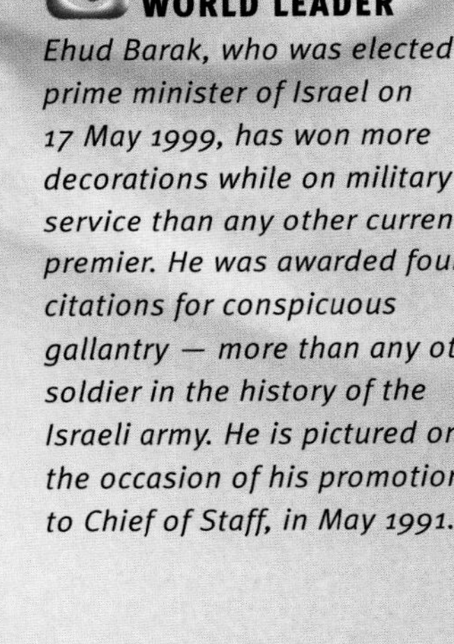

MOST DECORATED WORLD LEADER

Ehud Barak, who was elected prime minister of Israel on 17 May 1999, has won more decorations while on military service than any other current premier. He was awarded four citations for conspicuous gallantry — more than any other soldier in the history of the Israeli army. He is pictured on the occasion of his promotion to Chief of Staff, in May 1991.

MOST HOSPITALIZED PRESIDENT

Boris Yeltsin has had 13 known hospital stays between his election as president of the Russian Federation in 1991 and May 1999. He has still managed to surpass the average age attained by Russian males — 58 — by more than nine years.

LONGEST SERIES OF SPEECHES BY A POLITICIAN

Chief Mangosuthu Buthelezi, the leader of the Inkatha Freedom Party and South African home affairs minister, spoke for an average of 2½ hours on 11 of the 18 days of the KwaZulu legislative assembly in 1993.

campaigns & charities

BIGGEST TELETHONS

The Jerry Lewis 'Stars Across America' Muscular Dystrophy Association Labor Day Telethon has raised $954 million (£596 million) since it was first broadcast in 1966. The debut show was the first televised fundraising event of its kind to raise more than $1 million (£358,000). In 1998 it raised a total of $51.58 million (£31.12 million) in pledges and contributions.

The Comic Relief programme broadcast on BBC television on 12 March 1999, raised £32 million ($53.04 million). Comic Relief was launched in the UK in 1985 and has since raised over £171 million ($283.4 million), all of which goes to help some of the poorest and most vulnerable people in the UK and Africa. Apart from comedians such as French & Saunders and Rowan Atkinson, film stars such as Johnny Depp and Hugh Grant have performed in the programmes, which are broadcast every two years.

BIGGEST ENVIRONMENTAL FUNDRAISING EVENT

The Rainforest Foundation International, established by the musician Sting and his wife Trudi Styler in 1989, has raised more than $9 million (£5.4 million) net to support indigenous people and the rainforest. A celebrity benefit concert held in Carnegie Hall, New York City, USA, in April 1998 raised a record $2 million (£1.2 million) gross. It included singers such as Madonna, Elton John and Billy Joel. The street sign outside Carnegie Hall was renamed 'Rainforest Way' during Rainforest Awareness Week, and the Empire State Building was lit up in green.

MOST MONEY RAISED FOR CHARITY BY A SINGLE SPORTING EVENT

The London Marathon, run through the streets of London, UK, since 1981, raises more money for charity than any other single sporting event in the world. In the 1998 race a record £15.7 million ($26 million) was raised.

LONGEST-RUNNING CHARITY FOOTBALL MATCH

The Football Association Charity Shield was inaugurated in 1908 and has been played annually at Wembley Stadium, London, UK, since 1924. Money raised from ticket sales is distributed to an average of 90 establishments and causes, including sports charities, hospitals, drug rehabilitation centres and inner city development programmes. The 1998 charity match between Arsenal and Manchester United raised almost £500,000 ($828,700).

BIGGEST ROCK BENEFIT

Live Aid, the first ever simultaneous rock concert with satellite links between two countries, took place at Wembley Stadium, London, UK, and JFK Stadium, Philadelphia, Pennsylvania, USA, on 13 July 1985. The 17-hour concert was attended by 150,000 people (80,000 in Philadelphia and 70,000 in London) and more than 1.6 billion people around the world

MOST MONEY RAISED BY AN INDIVIDUAL IN A MARATHON

Retired advertising executive John Spurling (pictured above) raised £1.13 million ($1.87 million) for charity by running the London Marathon on 18 April 1999. This more than doubled the previous record of £440,000 ($769,560) set by Sir Roger Gibbs in the 1982 race. The money Spurling raised was divided between the Lord's Taverners — a group of ex-Test cricketers and celebrities who take part in regular charity cricket matches — and the Animal Health Trust.

BIGGEST SINGLE DONATION TO AIDS RESEARCH

In May 1999, the world's richest man, Bill Gates, and his wife, Melinda, donated a record $25 million (£15.08 million) to research into AIDS and HIV. Other recent donations by the couple have included $1.5 million (£905,000) for Kosovo refugees and a $5-billion (£3.1-billion) grant on 2 June 1999 to the William H. Gates Foundation, believed to be the largest donation made by a living person to charity. The Foundation supports initiatives in education, global health and community giving in the Pacific Northwest.

watched it on television. The concert, which included Queen, Madonna, Tina Turner and Paul McCartney on the bill, raised £51.36 million ($80 million) for the Ethiopian Famine Relief Fund, and the charity has raised more than £37.5 million ($60 million) since then.

BIGGEST MUSICAL BENEFIT FOR AIDS
A concert held in memory of rock star Freddie Mercury, who died of AIDS in Nov 1991, was held at Wembley Stadium, London, UK, on 20 April 1992. It was attended by about 75,000 people and is estimated to have been seen by almost 1 billion people in more than 70 countries. The concert raised £20 million ($35 million) for AIDS charities, and featured artists such as U2, David Bowie and Liza Minnelli.

MOST MONEY RAISED BY A WAR RELIEF BENEFIT
Opera star Luciano Pavarotti's War Child charity concert *Pavarotti and Friends* staged on 1 June 1999 raised a record $3.4 million (£2.1 million). Held annually in Modena, Italy, since 1995, the concerts have included performances by artists such as Eric Clapton, Mariah Carey, Gloria Estefan and Sheryl Crow. Bono of U2 wrote the hit song *Miss Sarajevo* for the 1995 event.

MOST MONEY RAISED IN A SECOND-HAND CLOTHES SALE
Elton John's wardrobe has had to be cleared many times due to its size. The star's last two sales made a total of £530,000 ($875,000) for the Elton John AIDS Foundation. The Stage Costume and Memorabilia section of his 1988 sale at Sotheby's, London, UK, which included personal possessions as well as clothes, raised £421,185 ($758,133).

BEST-SELLING MAGAZINE FOR THE HOMELESS
The Big Issue was established in London, UK, by John Bird with the assistance of Gordon Roddick in Sept 1991. Between 8,000 and 10,000 homeless and vulnerably housed people sell over 1.1 million copies a month in Los Angeles, California, USA; Cape Town, South Africa; Melbourne, Sydney and Brisbane, Australia; and throughout the UK.

MOST OSCAR DRESSES SOLD AT A CHARITY AUCTION
On 18 March 1999 a record 56 dresses and evening gowns that had been worn to the Oscars by actresses such as Julia Roberts, Sharon Stone and Uma Thurman were auctioned at 'Unforgettable: Fashion of the Oscars' at Christie's, New York City, USA. A total of $786,120 (£474,309) was donated to the American Foundation for AIDS Research (AmFAR). The most valuable lot was the blue and violet faille crepe dress worn by Elizabeth Taylor to the 1969 Academy Awards. It sold for $167,50 (£101,062).

memorabilia

MOST VALUABLE DRESS
A blue silk and velvet gown worn by Diana, Princess of Wales, when she danced with John Travolta at a White House dinner in 1985, sold for $200,000 (£134,000) at Christie's, New York, USA, on 26 June 1997.

MOST VALUABLE FILM COSTUME
The costume for the Cowardly Lion (played by Bert Lahr) in *The Wizard of Oz* (USA, 1939) fetched $250,000 (£167,500) at auction in Beverly Hills, California, USA, on 12 Dec 1998.

MOST VALUABLE FILM SHOES
The red slippers worn by Judy Garland in *The Wizard of Oz* (USA, 1939) fetched $165,000 (£90,000) at Christie's, New York, USA, on 2 June 1988.

MOST VALUABLE FILM PROP
The eponymous statuette from *The Maltese Falcon* (USA, 1941) sold for $398,500 (£265,666) at Christie's, New York, USA, in 1994.

MOST VALUABLE CARTOON POSTER
A poster for Disney's *Alice's Day at Sea* (USA, 1924) sold for £23,100 ($34,273) at Christie's, London, UK, in April 1994.

MOST VALUABLE PIECE OF JAMES BOND CLOTHING
On 17 Sept 1998 the steel-rimmed bowler hat used as a weapon by Oddjob in *Goldfinger* (UK, 1964) sold for £61,750 ($98,800) at an auction at Christie's, London, UK.

MOST VALUABLE GUITAR
A Fender Stratocaster that once belonged to Jimi Hendrix was sold by his former drummer 'Mitch' Mitchell for £198,000 ($353,628) at Sotheby's, London, UK, on 25 April 1990.

MOST VALUABLE JAZZ INSTRUMENT
A saxophone once owned by American jazz legend Charlie Parker sold for £93,500 ($146,328) at Christie's, London, UK, in Sept 1994.

MOST VALUABLE ROCK ITEM
John Lennon's 1965 Rolls-Royce Phantom V touring limousine sold for $2.229 million (£1.768 million) at Sotheby's, New York, USA, on 29 June 1985. It was bought by Jim Pattison, Chairman of the Expo '86 World Fair in Vancouver, British Columbia, Canada, and at the time was the greatest price paid for a used car.

BIGGEST ROCK COLLECTION
The Hard Rock Café in Philadelphia, Pennsylvania, USA, has 45,000 pieces of rock memorabilia on display, including Madonna's black bustier and vinyl trousers that belonged to Sid Vicious, bass guitarist for the Sex Pistols.

MOST VALUABLE PIECES OF ROCK STAR CLOTHING
In 1997 an Afghan coat worn by John Lennon on the cover of the Beatles' *Magical Mystery Tour* album (1967) was bought for £34,999 ($57,750) on behalf of his son Julian.

MOST VALUABLE STAR DOLL
Elizabeth Taylor and Jamie Lee Curtis are seen here with a one-off Elizabeth Taylor doll featuring 27 diamonds set in platinum. It sold for $25,000 (£15,625) at an auction held on 24 Oct 1998 to raise money for the Children Affected By AIDS Foundation.

A complete stage costume worn by (The Artist Formerly Known as Prince) sold for £12,100 ($20,570) at Christie's, London, UK, in Dec 1991.

A white rhinestone glove owned by Michael Jackson sold for £16,500 ($28,050) in Dec 1991.

MOST VALUABLE ROCK STAR GLASSES
A pair of glasses worn by Buddy Holly sold for $45,000 (£30,000) at auction in New York, USA, in 1990.

MOST VALUABLE TOP HAT SOLD AT AUCTION
On 15 July 1998 a top hat worn on formal occasions by former British prime minister Sir Winston Churchill sold for a record £25,300 ($40,480) at Sotheby's, London, UK. The hat was sold to an anonymous buyer after a fierce bidding battle.

MOST VALUABLE TOOTH
In 1816 a tooth belonging to British scientist Sir Isaac Newton sold for £730 ($3,785) – equivalent to £23,250 ($38,535) today – in London, UK.

MOST VALUABLE HAIR
In 1988 a lock of hair from the British naval hero Horatio Nelson, who died at the Battle of Trafalgar in 1805, sold for £5,575 ($9,475) to a bookseller from Cirencester, Glos, UK.

MOST VALUABLE SKULL
The skull of Emmanuel Swedenborg, the Swedish philosopher and author of *Divine Love And Wisdom*, was bought by the Royal Swedish Academy of Sciences for £5,500 ($10,560) in London, UK, on 6 March 1978.

MOST VALUABLE BIRTH CERTIFICATE
Sir Paul McCartney's original birth certificate sold for £52,591 ($84,146) at Bonhams, London, UK, in March 1997. The pre-sale estimate was £8,125 ($13,000). The certificate was put on the market by an American collector and the purchaser remained anonymous.

MOST VALUABLE FORMULA ONE MEMORABILIA
A pair of overalls worn by Brazilian driver Ayrton Senna, who was killed in a high-speed crash at the 1994 San Marino Grand Prix, was bought by an

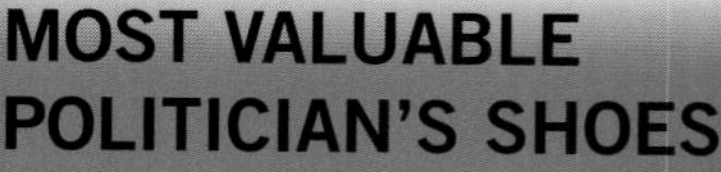

MOST VALUABLE POLITICIAN'S SHOES

A young boy is seen here wearing the ostrich-skin shoes that Nelson Mandela wore in 1990 when he walked free after 27 years in a South African prison. They were sold at Christie's, London, UK, in May 1995 for £4,500 ($7,100) to Sterling and Hunt, the company that originally made them. Half the proceeds went to help needy children in South Africa, the other half to fund research into premature births in the United Kingdom. The company made a replica of the shoes and presented them to Mandela.

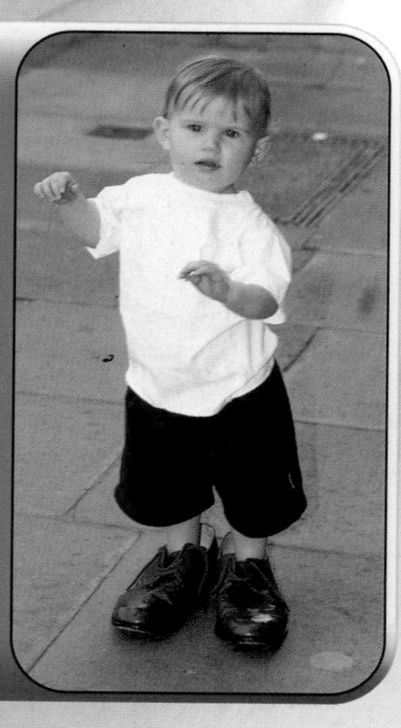

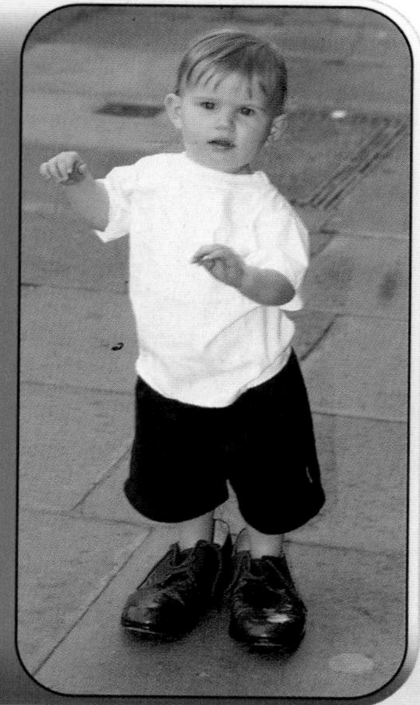

anonymous bidder at Sotheby's, London, UK, in Dec 1996 for £25,300 ($42,140). Senna had worn the overalls in his first Formula One race for the Toleman team in Monaco in 1984. A pair of gloves worn by Senna during the 1987 season went for £2,530 ($4,048) to an anonymous bidder and a race helmet he wore in 1982 fetched £28,750 ($46,000). It was bought by British racing fan Peter Radcliffe.

MOST VALUABLE PIECE OF BOXING MEMORABILIA

A calf-length white robe that once belonged to boxing legend Muhammad Ali sold for $140,000 (£85,000) at Christie's, Los Angeles, USA, in Oct 1997. The buyer chose to remain anonymous. Ali had worn the robe when he defeated George Foreman to regain the world heavyweight championship in the legendary 'Rumble in the Jungle' match in Zaïre (now Congo) in 1974.

MOST VALUABLE PIECE OF MADONNA CLOTHING

A model is pictured wearing one of Madonna's distinctive studded bras, which sold for £4,000 ($6,400) at Christie's, London, UK, in 1997. The biggest sum ever paid for an item of clothing belonging to Madonna is £12,100 ($19,360), for a corset designed by Jean-Paul Gaultier and sold at Christie's, London, UK, in May 1994.

MOST VALUABLE BASEBALL

The highest price paid for a baseball is $3.054 million (£1.909 million), including sales commission, at auction in New York City, USA, on 12 Jan 1999. The ball, which was bought by Todd McFarlane, had been hit by Mark McGwire in Sept 1998 for a major league record of 70 home runs in a season. It was retrieved at the game by a fan.

fans & followers

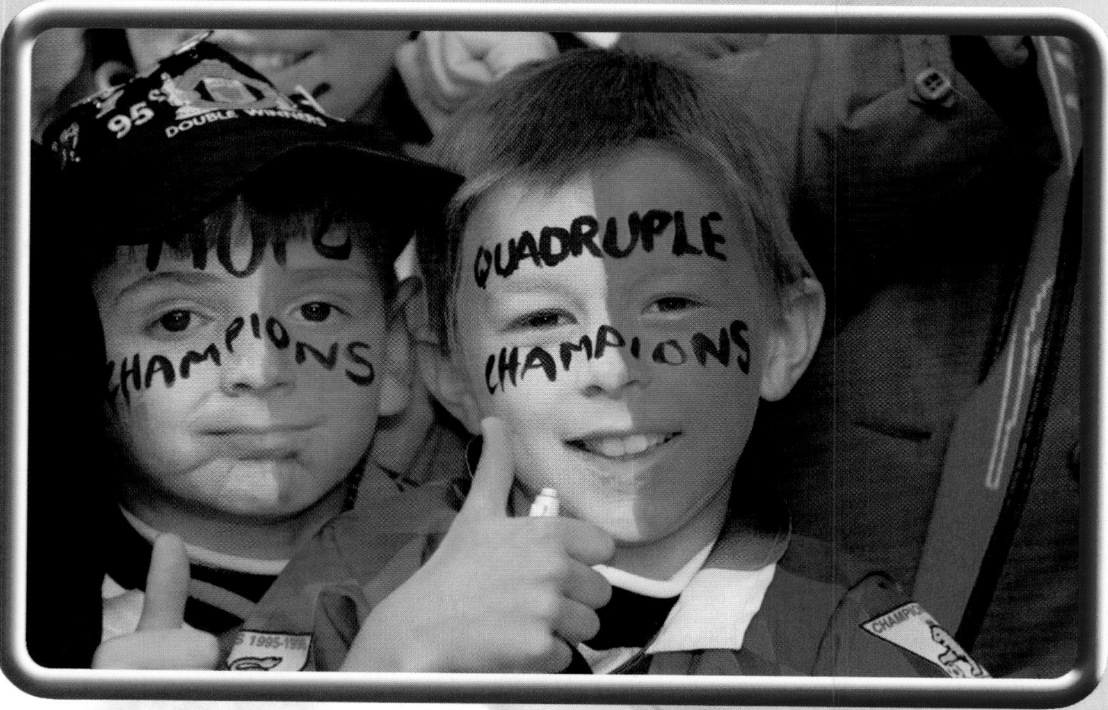

MOST-VISITED GRAVE SITE
Graceland, the former home and final resting place of Elvis Presley, receives more than 700,000 visitors annually from all over the world — more than any other grave site. The record for the greatest number of visitors to Graceland in one year is 753,962, in 1995. On 17 Aug 1977, the day after his death, Elvis sold in excess of 20 million albums — more than any other artist in a single day.

BIGGEST FLORAL TRIBUTE
Between 1 and 8 Sept 1997 an estimated 10,000–15,000 tonnes of flowers were laid in memory of Diana, Princess of Wales, at Kensington Palace, St James's Palace and Buckingham Palace, London, UK. This figure was given by the authorities who removed the flowers at the end of the mourning period; newspapers estimated that there were a total of 5 million bouquets.

MOST IMPERSONATED ICON
There are estimated to be more than 48,000 Elvis Presley impersonators around the world, including 'the Chinese Elvis' (Paul Chan) and 'the Sikh Elvis' (Elvis Singh). One recent addition was James Brown from Belfast, Northern Ireland, who performs as 'The King'. He specializes in performing songs that were written after Presley's death; favourites include Nirvana's *Come As You Are*, The Sex Pistols' *Anarchy in the UK* and *Whole Lotta Rosie* by AC/DC.

MOST WIDELY-SUPPORTED FOOTBALL CLUB
The Supporters Club of Manchester United FC (English Premier Division) has approximately 138,000 members. There is a total of 276 branches in the British Isles and a further 24 branches in countries as diverse as Malaysia and Iceland. The Scandinavian branch is the largest overseas group, with around 30,000 members. Accurate figures for unaffiliated supporters are impossible to calculate, but it has been estimated that there are about 20 million Manchester United fans in China alone – enough to fill the club's Old Trafford ground more than 350 times.

BIGGEST TOTAL AUDIENCE FOR A ROCK TOUR
U2 played to 3,940,010 people during their Pop Mart tour, which began in Las Vegas, Nevada, USA, in April 1997 and ended in Johannesburg, South Africa, in March 1998, after 93 concerts.

BIGGEST TV AUDIENCE
More people watched the funeral of Diana, Princess of Wales, on 6 Sept 1998 than any other TV broadcast in history. The global audience was estimated at 2.5 billion people.

MOST ARDENT FILM WATCHER
Gwilym Hughes of Gwynedd, UK, has seen and had logged 22,990 films since he saw his first film while in hospital in 1953. He keeps a diary that contains details of all the films he has seen. He now watches most of them on video.

MOST ARDENT THEATRE-GOERS
Dr H. Howard Hughes, Professor Emeritus of Texas Wesleyan College, Fort Worth, USA, attended a record 6,136 shows from 1956 to 1987.

Edward Sutro saw a record 3,000 first-night theatrical productions in the United Kingdom from 1916 to 1956 and possibly more than 5,000 shows in his 60 years of theatre-going.

Nigel Tantrum of East Kilbride, S Lanarkshire, UK, attended a record

MOST POPULAR CULT FILM

Sal Piro, the president of the US *Rocky Horror Show* fan club, has seen *The Rocky Horror Picture Show* (UK, 1975) about 1,000 times. *The Rocky Horror Show*, the stage show on which the film is based, was written by Richard O'Brien and opened at the Royal Court Theatre, London, UK, in 1973. It rapidly crossed from cult status to the mainstream, and today it has played in all major European countries as well as Australia and the Far East. The film, featuring Tim Curry, Susan Sarandon and Meat Loaf, is still showing in more than 100 cinemas in the USA, and many more across the world, to the delight of fans who dress as their favourite characters (such as Frank N. Furter and Magenta, right), throw rice, water and toast at appropriate moments and chant responses along to the film's soundtrack.

169 separate performances at the 1994 Edinburgh Festival between 13 Aug and 4 Sept.

MOST PUBS VISITED
Bruce Masters of Flitwick, Beds, UK, has visited a total of 31,241 pubs and 1,568 other drinking establishments since 1960, drinking locally-brewed beer wherever it is available.

MOST SEASON TICKETS HELD
Spanish team Barcelona FC sells around 98,000 season tickets (the stadium's capacity) to games at its home ground Camp Nou, making it the football stadium with the greatest number of season-ticket holders.

YOUNGEST FAN TO TOUR EVERY FOOTBALL LEAGUE GROUND
Oliver Newton, from Wakefield, W Yorkshire, UK, had visited every one of the 92 Premiership and Football League grounds in England and Wales by the age of five months, in 1998. He first visited Nottingham Forest's City Ground when he was just four weeks old, and ended his tour at the home of Lincoln City, Sincil Bank. He was accompanied on his travels by his football-mad parents, who have photographed their son next to all of the pitches.

MOST ARDENT TRAINSPOTTER
Bill Curtis from Clacton-on-Sea, Essex, UK, is the official world champion trainspotter, or 'gricer' (a nickname coined in honour of Richard Grice, the first ever champion, who held the title from 1896 to 1931). Curtis' recorded sightings include approximately 60,000 locomotives, 11,200 electric units and 8,300 diesel units over 40 years in a number of different countries.

MOST ARDENT BIRDSPOTTERS
Phoebe Snetsinger from Webster Groves, Missouri, USA, has spotted 8,040 (82.9%) of the 9,700 known bird species since 1965. She has now seen members of all of the families on the official list and more than 90% of the genera.

The record for the greatest number of bird species to have been spotted in a 24-hour period is 342, by Terry Stevenson, John Fanshawe and Andy Roberts (all from Kenya) on 30 Nov 1986, the second day of Birdwatch Kenya '86.

BIGGEST SCI-FI FOLLOWING

The TV series Star Trek *was first shown in 1966 and there are now more than 350* Star Trek *web sites and 500 fan publications. After more than 400,000 requests from fans (known as 'Trekkers'), NASA named one of its space shuttles* Enterprise, *after the ship in the series.*

pet superstars

HIGHEST-EARNING ANIMAL ARTIST
Ruby the elephant started painting when her keepers at Phoenix Zoo, Arizona, USA, saw her making patterns in the dirt with a stick clutched in her trunk and gave her paints, brushes and an easel to work with. Ruby's canvases sell for up to $3,500 (£2,187).

BIGGEST DOGS

The tallest breeds of dog are the Irish Wolfhound (below) and the Great Dane. The tallest dog was Shangret Damzas, a Great Dane owned by Wendy and Keith Comley of Milton Keynes, Bucks, UK. He was 1.054 m (3 ft 5 1/2 in) tall at the shoulder and weighed up to 108 kg (17 st). The heaviest dog on record was Aicama Zorba of La Susa, an Old English mastiff owned by Chris Eraclides of London, UK. He weighed in at 155.58 kg (24 st 7 lb) at his heaviest, in Nov 1989.

HIGHEST-EARNING LITERARY DOG
In 1991 springer spaniel Mildred Kerr, known as Millie, brought in a salary more than four times that of her master, the then US president George Bush, when her 'autobiography' sold 400,000 copies. 'Dictated' to First Lady Barbara Bush, *Millie's Book* was described as 'an under-the-table look at life in the Bush family'. It made a total of $900,000 (£510,000).

MOST TRICKS PERFORMED BY A DOG
Chanda-Leah, a champagne-coloured toy poodle from Hamilton, Ontario, Canada, performs more than 500 tricks. Chanda-Leah's owner Sharon Robinson has taught the six-year-old to play the piano, count and spell. The dog has appeared on numerous US television shows, including *Regis and Kathie Lee* and *The Maury Povich Show*, and now has her own publicist.

MOST SKILLED TALKING PARROT
Alex, an African Grey parrot, has learned words for more than 35 objects and seven colours and can make a distinction between three-, four-, five- and six-sided shapes. His accuracy averages 80%.

MOST PATSYS WON BY AN ANIMAL
Francis the mule was the first animal to be awarded first place at the PATSY awards, which were held annually from 1951 to 1987 to honour the Picture/Performing Animal Top Stars of the Year and promote the health and safety of showbiz animals. The star of *Francis the Talking Mule* (USA, 1949) received his award from actor James Stewart. He went on to win a further six PATSYs — more than any other animal.

MOST SUCCESSFUL DRUG-SNIFFER
Iowa, a black Labrador retriever used by the Port of Miami, Florida, USA, made 155 drug seizures worth a record $2.4 billion (£1.45 billion). Iowa was trained by Armando Johnson and handled by Chuck Meanders, Chief of Canine Operations for the Port of Miami.

The greatest number of seizures by dogs is 969 in one year (worth $182 million or £103.4 million) by Rocky and Barco, a pair of malinoises patrolling the Rio Grande Valley along the US/Mexico border. The pair were so proficient that Mexican smugglers put a $30,000 (£17,000) price on their heads.

MOST EXTREME SPORTS PARTICIPATED IN BY A DOG
Part-Ex belongs to John-Paul Eatock, the manager of Tyf No Limits Adventure Centre, south Wales, UK. The three-year-old Jack Russell terrier joins his owner in a wide range of extreme sports activities including kayaking, abseiling, surfing, windsurfing and climbing.

MOST SUCCESSFUL MOUSER
Towser, a tortoiseshell cat owned by Glenturret Distillery Ltd near Crieff, Perth and Kinross, UK, caught 28,899 mice (an average of three a day) before her death in 1987.

MOST PEOPLE AT A PET'S FUNERAL
In 1920 the funeral of Jimmy the canary from New Jersey, USA, was attended by 10,000 mourners. Jimmy's owner, cobbler Edidio Rusomanno, had the bird's body placed in a white casket. The funeral cortege was followed by two coaches and a 15-piece band.

RICHEST CAT
Blackie, the last in a household of 15 cats, was left $24 million (£15 million) in the will of his owner, Ben Rea.

RICHEST DOGS
The biggest legacy ever left to a dog was $15 million (£3 million), bequeathed by Ella Wendel of New York, USA, to her standard poodle Toby in 1931. All of Wendel's dogs were served prime lamb chops by personal butlers and slept in their own bedrooms in hand-carved miniature four-poster beds with silk sheets.

Bathroom fixture magnate Sidney Altman of Beverly Hills, California, USA, left $6 million (£3.6 million) to his pure-bred cocker spaniel Samantha when he died aged 60 in 1996. His widow Marie Dana Altman, who was given a $60,000 (£36,486) annual stipend providing she took care of Samantha, is currently sueing the dog for a greater share of her late husband's fortune.

SMALLEST DOGS
The smallest dog ever was a matchbox-sized Yorkshire terrier owned by Arthur Marples of Blackburn, Lancs, UK, a former editor of *Our Dogs* magazine. He was 6.3 cm (2 1/2 in) tall and 9.5 cm (3 3/4 in) long, and weighed 113 g (4 oz). He died in 1945, aged nearly two.

The smallest living dog is Big Boss, a Yorkshire terrier owned by Dr Chai Khanachanakom of Bangkok, Thailand.

BIGGEST AND SMALLEST RABBITS

The largest breed of rabbit is the Flemish Giant (left of picture), which weighs an average of 10 kg (1 st 8 lb), and the smallest are the Netherland Dwarf and the Polish — a hybrid of which weighed 397 g (14 oz) in 1975. The biggest rabbit of all time was a French lop weighing 12 kg (1 st 12 lb 7 oz), exhibited in Spain in April 1980.

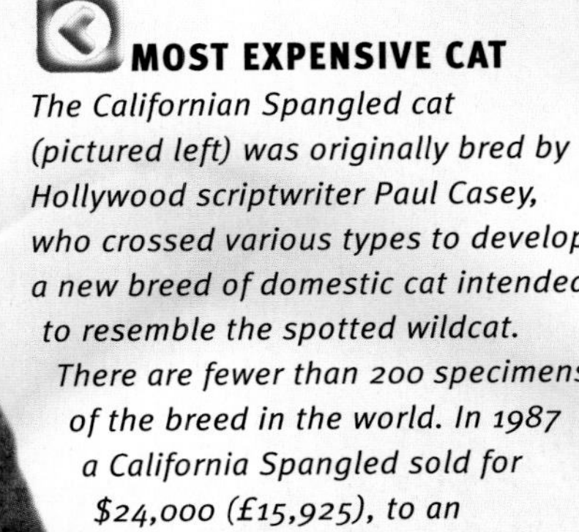

MOST EXPENSIVE CAT

The Californian Spangled cat (pictured left) was originally bred by Hollywood scriptwriter Paul Casey, who crossed various types to develop a new breed of domestic cat intended to resemble the spotted wildcat. There are fewer than 200 specimens of the breed in the world. In 1987 a California Spangled sold for $24,000 (£15,925), to an anonymous film star.

On 7 Dec 1995 he was 11.94 cm (4⁷/₁₀ in) tall and 12.95 cm (5¹/₁₀ in) long, and weighed 481 g (1 lb 1 oz).

SMALLEST CAT
Tinker Toy, a male blue point Himalayan-Persian cat owned by Katrina and Scott Forbes of Taylorville, Illinois, USA, is 7 cm (2¾ in) tall and 19 cm (7½ in) long.

BIGGEST CATS
The heaviest ever cat was Himmy, a tabby owned by Thomas Vyse of Cairns, Queensland, Australia. Himmy weighed 21.3 kg (3 st 4 lb 15¼ oz) when he died in 1986. He was so fat he had to be transported in a wheelbarrow.

Orange Thing of Minnetonka, Minnesota, USA, is believed to be the heaviest living cat. The tabby, owned by John Posthumus, weighed 18.5 kg (40 lb 13 oz) on 30 Oct 1998.

The longest domestic cat is four-year-old Snowbie, who measured 1.03 m (3 ft 4½ in) from his nose to the tip of his tail on 21 Nov 1997. He weighs 9½ kg (1 st 7 lb), is 33 cm (13 in) tall and has a 31-cm-long (12-in) tail. Owned by Lorna Sutherland of Ellon, Aberdeenshire, UK, he thrives on a diet of turkey, tuna, rice pudding and coffee.

BIGGEST SINGLE-SEX DOG LITTERS
Llana, a four-year-old greyhound/saluki owned by Nigel Wood of Bolsover, Derbyshire, UK, gave birth to 16 female puppies (three stillborn) on 27 June 1998.

Alpenblick's Great Lady (Cleo) gave birth by Caesarian section to 14 male puppies, the largest ever single-sex male litter on 19 Feb 1998 in Ladysmith, British Columbia, Canada.

MOST-TRAVELLED CAT
Hamlet the cat escaped from his cage during a flight from Toronto, Canada, and travelled more than 965,600 km (600,000 miles) in just over seven weeks. He was caught in Feb 1984.

SLOWEST-TRAVELLED PET
Chester the tortoise, who was painted with a white streak for identification, escaped from his home in Lyde, Herts, UK, in 1960 and was found by a neighbour in 1995. He had travelled 686 m (2,250 yd) in 35 years.

MOST-STROKED DOG
Josh the Wonder Dog, owned by Richard Stack of Glen Burnie, Maryland, USA, was stroked by 478,802 people between 1989 and his death on 23 July 1997.

UGLIEST DOG
Chi Chi, a rare African sand dog, has won the World Championship Ugly Dog Contest at Petaluma, California, USA, five times and took first place in the contest's 'Ring of Champions', which pitted the winners from the previous 25 years against one another. Chi Chi has made several TV appearances and is the star of a comic strip called *The Ugliest Dog*.

BIGGEST DOG WALK
On 20 Feb 1999, 2,114 dogs (accompanied by their walkers) participated in the Mighty Texas Dog Walk in Austin, Texas, USA. The 4.8-km (3-mile) walk was in aid of Texas Hearing & Service Dogs, an organization that adopts dogs from animal shelters and trains them as working partners for disabled people.

religions, rites & cults

MOST-VISITED SIKH TEMPLE

The Golden Temple in Amritsar, India, is the largest and most important Sikh shrine, attracting up to 20,000 visitors per day. This figure rises to 200,000 on special occasions such as Guru Purab (the birthday of one of the 10 Sikh gurus) and Baisakhi (the festival marking the day Sikhism was established). The second storey of the temple is covered by an estimated 400 kg (881 lb) of gold leaf and hundreds of precious stones. The temple's architecture is influenced by both Hindu and Muslim styles. Its sanctuary contains the *Adi Grantha*, the sacred scripture of the Sikhs.

BIGGEST RELIGION
Christianity is the world's predominant religion, with some 1.94 billion adherents in 1998, or 32.8% of the world's population. However, religious statistics are necessarily only tentative, because the test of adherence to religion varies widely in rigour, while many individuals, particularly in the East, belong to two or more religions.

BIGGEST CHRISTIAN DENOMINATION
The largest Christian denomination in the world is the Roman Catholic Church, which in 1998 had 1.03 billion members, or 17.3% of the total world population.

BIGGEST NON-CHRISTIAN RELIGION
The world's largest non-Christian religion is Islam, which has over 1.16 billion followers.

LARGEST RELIGION WITHOUT RITES
The Baha'i faith, which is practised worldwide by about 6 million people, has no ceremonies, no sacraments and no clergy. Baha'ism emphasizes the importance of all religion and the spiritual unity of humanity. It emerged through the teaching of two 19th-century Iranian visionaries and is now adhered to in over 70 countries.

FASTEST-GROWING MODERN CHURCH
The Kimbanguist Church was founded in Congo (now Democratic Republic of Congo) in 1959 by Simon Kimbangui, a Baptist student. By 1996 the Church, which is a member of the World Council of Churches, had over 6.5 million members.

BIGGEST RELIGIOUS CROWD
The greatest number of human beings known to have assembled with a common purpose is the estimated 20 million Hindu pilgrims who gathered at a 'half' Kumbh Mela held in Prayag (Allahabad), Uttar Pradesh, India, on 30 Jan 1995. An estimated 200,000 people entered Prayag every hour on the day before the festival. By 10 am an estimated 15 million people had been in the water and another 5 million were waiting their turn.

BIGGEST TEMPLE
The largest religious structure is Angkor Wat, Cambodia, which covers 162.6 ha (402 acres). It was built to the Hindu god Vishnu by Suryavarman II between 1113 and 1150 AD.

BIGGEST RADIO AUDIENCE FOR A REGULAR RELIGIOUS BROADCAST

Decision Hour, *a religious radio show that has been broadcast regularly since 1957 by the US Baptist evangelist Billy Graham (pictured above), attracts an average audience of 20 million people.*

BIGGEST CATHEDRAL
The largest cathedral in the world is St John the Divine, cathedral church of the Diocese of New York, USA, with a floor area of 11,240 m² (121,000 ft²). The cornerstone was laid on 27 Dec 1892, but work on the building was stopped in 1941 and only restarted in earnest in July 1979. The cathedral nave is the longest in the world, at 183.2 m (601 ft) in length, and has a vaulted ceiling 37.8 m (124 ft) high.

BIGGEST MOSQUE
The Shah Faisal Mosque, Islamabad, Pakistan, can accommodate 100,000 worshippers in the prayer hall and the courtyard and a further 200,000 people in the adjacent grounds, giving a total capacity of 300,000. The complex area is 18.97 ha (46.87 acres) and the covered area of the prayer hall takes up 0.48 ha (1.19 acres).

BIGGEST BUDDHIST TEMPLE
Borobudar, near Jogjakarta, Indonesia, built in the 8th century, is 31.4 m (103 ft) tall and has an area of 123 m² (403 ft²).

BIGGEST SYNAGOGUE
Temple Emanu-El on Fifth Avenue at 65th Street, New York City, USA, has an area of 3,523.47 m² (37,928 ft²). When the adjoining Beth-El Chapel and the Temple's other three sanctuaries are in use, a total of 5,500 people can be seated in the synagogue.

MOST-VISITED HINDU TEMPLE
Tirupati Temple in Andhra Pradesh, India, attracts 30,000–40,000 visitors per day and an estimated 75,000 on New Year's Day. The temple is also the richest Hindu temple in the world, with an annual budget of $57.02 million (£35.2 million). Collection boxes alone raise more than $22.67 million (£14 million) every year, and a similar sum is raised through the auction of hair donated by devotees visiting the temple. It also earns rent from cottages housing devotees and from special services. The temple has 13,000 full-time employees and an additional 2,000 contract staff.

LONGEST RELIGIOUS CIRCUIT
The longest circuit around a religious site as part of a pilgrimage is 85 km (52 miles 1,440 yd), walked by Hindu worshippers around Lake Mansarovar, Tibet.

BIGGEST FUNERALS
In Feb 1969 the funeral of C.N. Annadurai, the charismatic chief minister of Madras, India, was attended by 15 million people, according to a police estimate.

The queue at the grave of the 42-year-old singer and folk hero Vladimir Visotsky at the Vagankovsyoye Cemetery, Moscow, USSR (now Russia), after his death in 1980 was 10 km (6 miles) long.

SMALLEST CHRISTIAN SECT

The Sabbathday Lake community of Shakers in Maine, USA, currently has seven members, making it the smallest surviving Christian sect. Sister Frances Carr and Brother Arnold Hadd are pictured rehearsing songs for their 1995 album Simple Songs, *the first recording ever made by Shakers of their own music.*

BIGGEST PERCENTAGE OF A POPULATION TO ATTEND A FUNERAL

About 10.2 million people — 16.6% of the population of Iran — lined the 32-km (20-mile) route to Tehran's Behesht-e Zahra cemetery for the funeral of Ayatollah Khomeini, the creator of the Islamic State, on 11 June 1989, according to official Iranian estimates. It is believed that 2 million people paid their respects as the body lay in state. In the crush eight people were killed and 500 injured. At the funeral people shredded the white shroud, partly exposing the body of the Ayatollah in his casket.

MOST HUMAN SACRIFICES IN A RELIGIOUS CEREMONY

The most human sacrifices made at a single ceremony is believed to have been the 20,000 people killed by Aztec priests at the dedication ceremony for the Great Temple (Teocalli) at Tenochtitlán (now Mexico City) to the war-god Huitzilpochtli in 1486.

MOST FEMALE-DOMINATED RELIGIOUS SECT

Dianic Wicca, a neo-pagan movement, worships a goddess and has female-only covens. The feminist witchcraft sect was founded in California, USA, in the 1920s.

MOST MALE-DOMINATED SOCIETY

Mount Athos, a 336-km^2 (129-mile^2) autonomous monastic republic within Greece, bars all females, including domestic animals and birds, and women are not even allowed to approach its shores by boat. The republic has a population of 1,400 men occupying its 20 Orthodox monasteries and their dependencies.

MOST PROLIFIC CRYING STATUE

A 40-cm-high (15-in) statue of the Virgin Mary brought from Medjurorje, Bosnia, by a curate from Civitavecchia, Italy, in 1994 appeared to cry tears of blood on 14 days between 2 Feb and 17 March 1995. One manifestation was witnessed by the diocesan bishop.

LONGEST PERIOD OF STIGMATA

Padre Pio (Francesco Forguione), a devout Italian Capuchin friar, bore the stigmata (the wounds received by Christ on the Cross) from 1918 until his death in 1968. They were seen by thousands of pilgrims. He was beatified by Pope John Paul II in May 1999.

MOST SAINTS CREATED BY A POPE

Pope John Paul II has created more saints than any other pope. By Jan 1999 he had canonized 283 people and beatified 805 (given them the title 'Blessed' on behalf of the Roman Catholic Church) — 10 times as many as all his 20th-century predecessors put together and more than any other pontiff. Born in Wadowice, Poland, on 18 May 1920 as Karol Wojtyla, he ascended the papal throne in 1978, becoming the first non-Italian to be elected pope in 456 years and the youngest pope this century.

criminals

MOST PROLIFIC MURDERERS
Behram, a member of the Thuggee cult, strangled at least 931 victims with his *ruhmal* (yellow and white cloth strip) in Oudh, India, between 1790 and 1840.

The most prolific murderer in the western world, and the most prolific ever female murderer, was Elizabeth Bathori of Transylvania (now in Romania). She is alleged to have killed more than 600 girls and young women in order to drink and bathe in their blood, ostensibly to preserve her youth. When the crimes were discovered, the countess was walled up in her home from 1610 until her death in 1614.

The most prolific murderer of the 20th century was the bandit leader Teófilo 'Sparks' Rojas, who is said to have killed between 592 and 3,500 people from 1945 until his death in an ambush in Colombia on 22 Jan 1963.

The world's biggest ever mass killing carried out by one person took place in April 1982, when policeman Wou Bom-kon went on a drunken eight-hour rampage in the Kyong Sang-namdo province of South Korea. He killed 57 people and wounded 35 with 176 rounds of rifle ammunition and hand grenades, before blowing himself up.

The most prolific known serial killer of recent times was Pedro Lopez, who killed 300 young girls in Colombia, Peru and Ecuador. Known as the 'Monster of the Andes', Lopez was sentenced to life imprisonment in Ecuador in 1980.

The Mexican sisters Delfina and María de Jesús González, who abducted girls to work in brothels, formed the world's most prolific ever murder partnership. Known to have murdered at least 90 of their victims but suspected to have killed many more, Delfina and Maria were sentenced to 40 years' imprisonment in 1964.

The world's most prolific murderer by poison was nurse Jane Toppan of Massachusetts, USA, who killed between 30 and 100 patients with morphine or atropine over 20 years. In 1902 Toppan confessed to 30 murders but claimed that they had been acts of mercy. She was subsequently committed to a mental institution.

BIGGEST CRIMINAL ORGANIZATION
The Six Great Triads of China form the largest organized crime association in the world today, with an estimated 100,000-plus members worldwide.

BIGGEST DRUGS HAUL
On 28 Sept 1989 a record 20 tonnes of cocaine with an estimated street value of \$6–7 billion (£3.7–4.4 billion) was seized in a raid on a warehouse in Los Angeles, California, USA.

BIGGEST ROBBERIES
The plundering of the Reichsbank following the collapse of Germany during April and May 1945 was the world's biggest bank robbery. The book *Nazi Gold* estimated that the total haul would have been worth \$3.34 billion (£2.5 billion) at 1984 values.

During the civil disorder that took place in Beirut, Lebanon, in 1976, a guerrilla force blasted its way into the vaults of the British Bank of the Middle East in Bab Idriss and cleared out safe-deposit boxes with contents valued by the former finance minister Lucien Dahdah at \$50 million (£22 million) and by another source at an "absolute minimum" of \$20 million (£9 million).

The biggest ever jewel robbery on record took place in Aug 1994, when gems with an estimated value of \$46 million (£30 million) were stolen from the jewellery shop at the Carlton Hotel in Cannes, France, by a three-man gang.

BIGGEST BANK FRAUD
In 1989 the Banca Nazionale del Lavoro, Italy, admitted that it had been defrauded of a huge amount of money when its branch in Atlanta, Georgia, USA, made unauthorized loan commitments to Iraq. The loss was subsequently estimated to be about \$5 billion (£3 billion).

MOST DANGEROUS CAR SECURITY DEVICE
The Blaster was invented by Charl Fourie (South Africa) to deter carjackers. A switch controls the flow of gas from a canister in the boot. The gas exits over a spark via nozzles beneath the doors and 2-m (6-ft 6-in) fireballs shoot out from both sides of the car.

BIGGEST RANSOM
Two Hong Kong businessmen, Walter Kwok and Victor Li, paid gangster Cheung Tze-keung, also known as 'Big Spender', a record total of \$127 million (£77.5 million) for their freedom after he kidnapped them in 1996 and 1997 respectively. The case created further notoriety when the businessmen reported the abductions to the authorities in mainland China (where the death penalty is in force) rather than to those in Hong Kong (which, because of its status, does not have the death penalty). Cheung, who was also involved in smuggling and armed robbery, was arrested and charged in Canton, on the Chinese mainland, and executed by firing squad in Nov 1998. Four of his accomplices were also shot, and 31 of his gang members received long jail sentences.

BIGGEST WHITE-COLLAR CRIME
In Feb 1997 Japanese copper trader Yasuo Hamanaka pleaded guilty to fraud and forgery in connection with illicit trading that had cost his employer Sumitomo, Japan's largest trading company, an estimated $2.6 billion (£1.58 billion) over 10 years of unauthorized transactions.

MOST PRISONERS ON DEATH ROW
In 1998 there were more than 3,549 prisoners on death row in the 38 US states in which the death penalty is still exercised.

LONGEST TIME ON DEATH ROW
Sadamichi Hirasawa of Japan was convicted of poisoning bank employees with potassium cyanide in order to steal $370 (£100) in 1948. He died in Sendai Prison, Japan, aged 94, after 39 years on death row.

LONGEST SENTENCES
Chamoy Thipyaso and seven of her associates were each jailed for 141,078 years by the Bangkok Criminal Court, Thailand, on 27 July 1989. They had been found guilty of swindling the public.

The longest sentence ever imposed on a mass murderer was 21 consecutive life sentences and 12 death sentences, on John Wayne Gacy, who killed 33 boys and young men between 1972 and 1978. He was sentenced by a jury in Chicago, Illinois, USA, in March 1980 and executed in May 1994.

LONGEST TIME SERVED
Paul Geidel was convicted of second-degree murder at the age of 17 in Sept 1911 and released from the Fishkill Correctional Facility, Beacon, New York, USA, at the age of 85, in 1980. Geidel, who was refused parole in 1974, served 68 years 245 days.

MOST MAFIA CONVICTIONS

Salvatore 'Toto' Riina (right), the head of the Sicilian Mafia and the most wanted man in Italy, was tried with 38 other alleged mob bosses at Caltanissetta, Italy. Riina was given a life sentence along with 23 others, six were given more lenient terms and nine were acquitted on 26 Sept 1997.

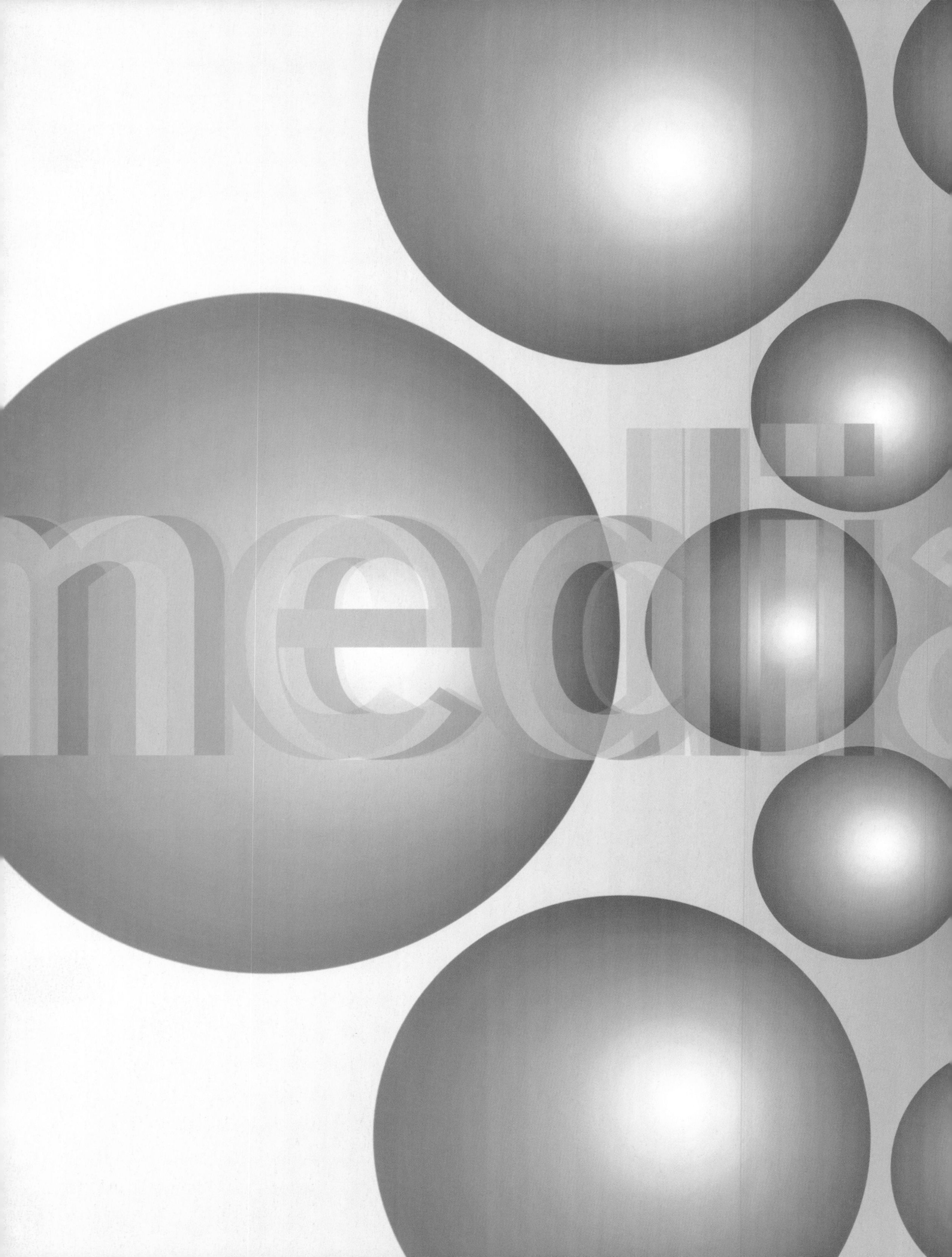

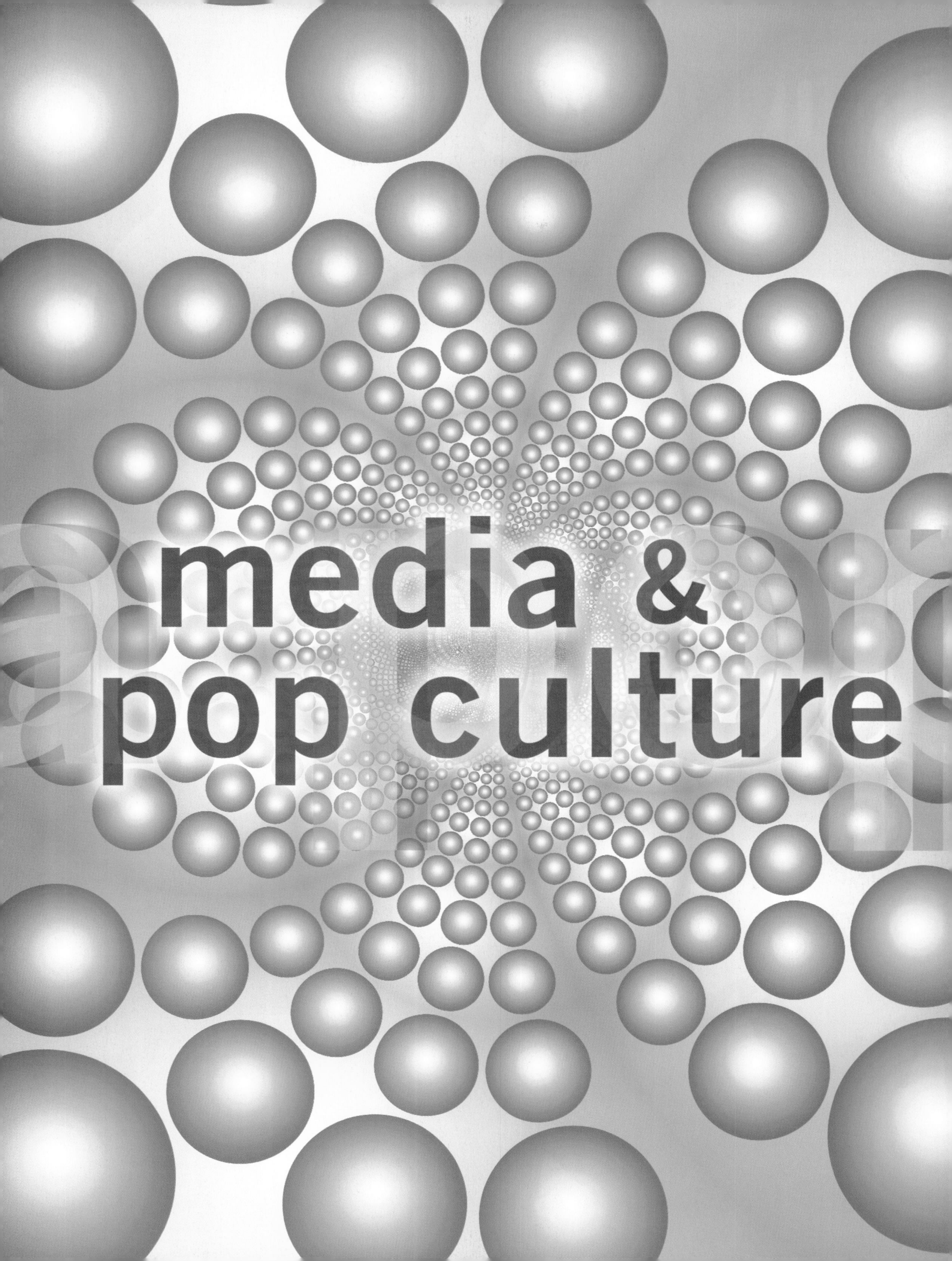
media &
pop culture

hollywood

MOST EXPENSIVE FILMS
Paramount's *Titanic* (USA, 1997), starring Leonardo DiCaprio and Kate Winslet and directed by James Cameron, was due to be released in July 1997 but was delayed until Dec 1997 due to post-production problems. This delay added at least $20 million (£12.5 million) to the budget, making *Titanic* the most expensive movie ever made at almost $250 million (£158.7 million).

The most expensive film ever made in terms of real costs adjusted for inflation was Joseph L. Mankiewicz's *Cleopatra* (USA, 1963), which starred Elizabeth Taylor and Richard Burton. The $44-million (£15.7-million) budget would equal more than $260 million (£156.9 million) in 1999.

MOST EXPENSIVE SCI-FI FILM
Waterworld (USA, 1995), starring Kevin Costner, suffered a series of setbacks when the set broke free from its moorings in the Pacific Ocean on several occasions. This problem and additional technical failures made it the most expensive sci-fi movie ever made, at an estimated $160 million (£102 million).

HIGHEST-GROSSING FILMS
Titanic (USA, 1997) was released on 19 Dec 1997 and had grossed $1.835 billion (£1.107 billion) worldwide by May 1999.

MOST PROFITABLE FILM SERIES
Pierce Brosnan is pictured above as British secret agent James Bond in a scene from The World Is Not Enough *(USA, 1999). The 20 Bond movies, based on the novels by Ian Fleming and largely produced by Cubby Broccoli, have grossed more than $1 billion (£603 million) worldwide — more than any other film series. It is estimated that over 50% of the world's population have seen at least one Bond film.*

HIGHEST-GROSSING HORROR FILMS

Miramax's *Scream* (USA, 1996), directed by Wes Craven and starring Drew Barrymore and Neve Campbell, cost about $15 million (£9.6 million) to make and had grossed $161.6 million (£98.6 million) by July 1997. *Scream 2* (USA, 1997), which starred David Arquette and Courteney Cox (pictured below), grossed $33 million (£20.1 million) on its opening weekend and took $160.5 million (£96.8 million) from Dec 1997 to Aug 1998. A second sequel, *Scream 3*, is due for release in 1999. If inflation and the increased price of cinema tickets are taken into account, *The Exorcist* (USA, 1973), directed by William Friedkin, is the highest-grossing horror movie ever made. The film has grossed more than $381 million (£230 million) in today's terms.

MGM's *Gone With The Wind* (USA, 1939) took $193.6 million (£43.2 million) from 197.55 million admissions in North America alone. Taking into account inflation and the increased price of cinema tickets, this is equivalent to $885.3 million (£534.2 million) today. In an inflation-adjusted list of the highest-grossing movies in the US, *Gone With The Wind* would be first, while *Titanic* would be fifth with a figure of $600.8 million (£362.5 million).

HIGHEST-GROSSING SCI-FI FILMS
The original and remastered versions of George Lucas' *Star Wars* (USA, 1977 and 1997) have grossed a record total of $1.19 billion (£717 million), taking into account inflation and the rise in the price of cinema tickets.

Fox's *Independence Day* (USA, 1996) has grossed $811 million (£506 million) worldwide — the highest box office gross of any science-fiction film on its first release.

HIGHEST-GROSSING COMEDY
Austin Powers: The Spy Who Shagged Me (USA, 1999) grossed a record $54.92 million (£33.14 million) during its first weekend of release (11–13 June 1999). In two days it earned more than the entire run of its predecessor, *Austin Powers: International Man Of Mystery* (USA, 1997).

BIGGEST LOSS
MGM's *Cutthroat Island* (USA, 1995), starring Geena Davis and directed by her then husband Renny Harlin, cost more than $100 million (£63.4 million) to produce, promote and distribute. By May 1996 it had reportedly earned back just $11 million (£7 million).

MOST EXPENSIVE FILM RIGHTS
The highest price ever paid for film rights was $9.5 million (£4.9 million), for the Broadway musical *Annie*. The deal was announced by Columbia in 1978 and the film was released in 1982. It was directed by John Huston and starred Albert Finney.

MOST FILMED AUTHOR
A total of 350 films based on plays by William Shakespeare have been made to date. Of these, 309 are straight or relatively straight versions of the original text, while 41 are modern versions such as *10 Things I Hate About You* (USA, 1999), based on *The*

FASTEST BOX OFFICE GROSS

Star Wars: The Phantom Menace opened in the USA on 19 May 1999 and took $28.54 million (£17.72 million) in its first 24 hours; $100 million (£60.33 million) in five days; $200 million (£120.67 million) in 13 days; and $300 million (£181 million) in four weeks. The Phantom Menace, which stars Ewan McGregor (pictured), Liam Neeson and Natalie Portman, is the prequel to the original Star Wars trilogy, released between 1977 and 1983.

Taming Of The Shrew. There have also been innumerable parodies. *Hamlet* is the most popular choice of play for filmmakers, with 75 versions made, followed by *Romeo And Juliet* with 51. The most recent of these was *William Shakespeare's Romeo And Juliet* (USA, 1996), which starred Leonardo DiCaprio and Claire Danes.

MOST FILMED HORROR AUTHOR
More than 20 of horror writer Stephen King's novels and short stories have been made into movies, including *Carrie* (USA, 1976), *The Shining* (UK, 1980) and *Misery* (USA, 1990).

MOST FILMED STORY
There have been a record 95 films based on the classic fairy tale *Cinderella*, including cartoon, modern ballet, operatic, all-male and parody versions. The first ever version was *Fairy Godmother* (UK, 1898), while the most recent was *Ever After* (USA, 1998).

MOST FREQUENTLY PORTRAYED CHARACTERS
The French emperor Napoleon Bonaparte has been the subject of more than 175 films since 1897 — a record for any historical figure.

The fictional character most frequently portrayed on the big screen is Sherlock Holmes, the detective created by Sir Arthur Conan Doyle. He has been portrayed by 75 actors in more than 211 films since 1900.

LONGEST FILM
The 85-hour *Cure For Insomnia* (USA, 1987), which was directed by John Henry Timmis IV, premiered in its entirety at the School of Art Institute of Chicago, USA, from 31 Jan to 3 Feb 1987. Much of the film consists of L. D. Groban reading his own 4,080-page poem, interspersed with scenes of a rock band and some X-rated footage.

MOST COSTUMES IN ONE FILM
A record 32,000 costumes were worn in *Quo Vadis* (USA, 1951).

MOST COSTUME CHANGES IN ONE FILM
Madonna changed costume a record 85 times in *Evita* (USA, 1996) and wore a total of 39 hats, 45 pairs of shoes and 56 pairs of earrings. The costumes were based on Eva Perón's own clothes, many of which are kept in an Argentinian bank vault.

OLDEST HOLLYWOOD DIRECTOR
Hollywood's oldest director was George Cukor (1899–1983), who made his 50th and final film, MGM's *Rich And Famous*, in 1981 at the age of 81.

YOUNGEST HOLLYWOOD PRODUCER
Steven Paul was 20 years old when he produced and directed *Falling In Love Again* (USA, 1980), which starred Elliott Gould and Susannah York.

LARGEST FILM STUDIO COMPLEX
Universal City in Los Angeles, California, USA, covers 170 ha (420 acres) and has 561 buildings and 34 sound stages.

bollywood

MOST GENERATIONS OF ACTRESSES IN ONE FAMILY

Kajol, who has starred in a string of recent box office successes, is one of three generations of Bollywood actresses. Her mother Tanuja and aunt Nutan were both leading actresses in the 1960s, while her grandmother Shobhana Samarth starred in numerous 1940s hits.

BIGGEST FILM OUTPUT
In 1990 a record 948 films in 21 languages (including Hindi, Tamil, Telegu, Bengali and Gujarati) were produced in India.

HIGHEST-GROSSING BOLLYWOOD FILM
Hum Aapke Hain Kaun (1994), starring Madhuri Dixit and Salman Khan, is the highest-grossing Bollywood film of all time. It earned more than $63.8 million (£40.4 million) in its first year, breaking the record set by the 'curry western' *Sholay* in 1975.

LONGEST BOLLYWOOD CAREERS
P. Jairaj, who made his debut in 1929, has had an acting career spanning 70 years. Although he has acted in more than 300 films, he is better known for character roles than as a lead.

Since making his debut in *Jeevan Naiya* in 1936, Ashok Kumar, affectionately known as Dadamoni, has been acting continuously for 63 years. A three-time winner of the *Filmfare* Best Actor award, his most famous role was in *Kismet* (1943), which in real terms is the highest-grossing Indian film of all time. Although no longer a lead actor, Ashok continues to play character roles and to make appearances on TV.

The Bollywood actress with the longest film career was Lalita Pawar, who acted continuously for 70 years. She made her debut at the age of 12 and appeared in more than 700 films. Her best-known role was as the scheming mother in *Ramshastri* (1944). Lalita's last film, *Bhai*, was completed two months before her death in 1998.

MOST APPEARANCES IN INTERNATIONAL FILMS
Saeed Jaffrey has appeared in 18 international films, including *Gandhi* (UK, 1982), *A Passage To India* (UK, 1984), *Masala* (Canada, 1991) and *My Beautiful Launderette* (UK, 1985). He made his film debut in the 1977 Indian film *The Chess Players* (*Shatranj Ke Khiladi*) and has appeared in almost 100 Hindi films and one Punjabi film. In 1998 Jaffrey opted out of Indian commercial cinema in favour of acting in international films and on British television. He recently became part of the first Asian family to feature regularly in the United Kingdom's longest-running soap opera, *Coronation Street*.

Shabana Azmi has acted in nine international films — more than any other Indian actress. These include *Madame Souzatska* (USA, 1988), *City Of Joy* (UK/Fra, 1992) and *Fire* (Canada, 1995). She has won four National Awards and three *Filmfare* awards.

MOST INTERNATIONAL FILM AWARDS
Satyajit Ray, nicknamed 'God' in Bombay film circles, was India's most celebrated movie director. Prior to his death in 1992 he received a total of 34 international film awards, including an Oscar for Lifetime Achievement. He was also awarded the *Bharat Ratna* and the *Padmashree*, India's highest civilian and arts awards.

MOST BEST ACTOR AWARDS
Dilip Kumar has won eight *Filmfare* awards for Best Actor and one award for Lifetime Achievement in a career spanning more than 50 years.

MOST BEST ACTRESS AWARDS
Nutan (1936–91) won five *Filmfare* awards for Best Actress and one for Best Supporting Actress during a career which spanned 47 years. Widely considered the most versatile actress of her generation, she came from a family of top Hindi performers.

MOST BEST SINGER AWARDS
Kishore Kumar, who died in 1987, won eight *Filmfare* awards for Best Male Playback Singer. He appeared in several comedies in the 1940s before becoming a full-time singer. Although best known for his yodelling and

HIGHEST-EARNING MALE STAR

The highest-earning male star in Bollywood is Shah Rukh Khan (pictured right), who is reported to earn $599,460 (£361,687) per film. It is said he plans to increase this to $717,986 (£433,200) in the year 2000. Khan, whose most successful movies include *Dilwale Dulhaniya Le Jayenge* (1995), *Dil to Pagal Hai* (1997) and *Kuch Kuch Hota Hai* (1998), made his debut in 1991 and has since won a total of seven Filmfare awards. He is well known for playing unconventional or controversial roles, and portrayed psychopaths in both *Baazigar* (1993) and *Darr* (1994). Amitabh Bachchan, the star of most of Bollywood's hits in the 70s and 80s, is currently said to command $717,986 (£433,200) per film. However, a string of recent box offices failures seems likely to push his future earnings down.

BIGGEST BOLLYWOOD SCREEN FAMILY

Twenty-four members of the Kapoor extended family have acted in films since Prithviraj Kapoor first took to the screen in 1929. He was followed into acting by his three sons, Raj, Shammi and Shashi. Other famous relatives through marriage include top star Amitabh Bachchan, directors Ramesh Sippy and Manmohan Desai, and Shashi's sister-in-law, British actress Felicity Kendall. One of Bollywood's current leading ladies, Karishma Kapoor (left), is Prithviraj's great granddaughter.

jazz-scat rhythms with nonsense lyrics, it was his melancholic songs which won him the most awards.

MOST PROLIFIC BOLLYWOOD RECORDING ARTIST

Since 1948 Lata Mangeshkar is reported to have recorded more than 5,000 songs in Hindi and thousands in 14 other Indian languages. Lata is the older sister of singer Asha Bhosle, celebrated by UK band Cornershop in their hit single *Brimful of Asha*.

MOST ROLES PLAYED IN ONE FILM

Sivaji Ganesan played all nine roles in the Tamil film *Navarathri* (1964), which was directed by A. P. Nagarajan. It was remade in Hindi in 1974 as *Naya Din Nayi Raat*, with Sanjeev Kumar taking all the parts.

MOST PROLIFIC BOLLYWOOD STUNTWOMAN

Mary Evans, known as Fearless Nadia, starred in many action movies from 1934 until her retirement in 1961. Her most famous films include *Hunterwali* (1935), *Jungle Princess* (1942) *Stunt Queen* (1947) and *Tigress* (1948). Born in 1909 to an English father and a Greek mother, Mary first came to Bombay at the age of five. She returned in the mid-1920s to work in a touring theatre company and got her first big break in Indian films in 1934, in *Desh Deepak* and *Noor-e-Yaman*. She changed her name to Nadia on the advice of a fortune-teller, and later married the film-maker Homi Wadia.

LONGEST PRODUCTION OF A BOLLYWOOD FILM

Love and God (*Qais aur Laila*) (1986) took more than 20 years to make after running into a series of difficulties, including the deaths of lead actor Guru Dutt in 1964 and director K. Asif in 1971. The incomplete film was finally released in 1986, with Sanjeev Kumar taking over the lead role. K. Asif was also the director of *Mughal-e-Azam* (1960), which took more than 14 years to complete following the death of the lead actor Chandramohan. He was replaced by Dilip Kumar.

LONGEST INTERVAL BETWEEN SCREEN KISSES

The earliest kiss in Indian cinema took place in 1929, in *Prapancha Pash*. Kissing was subsequently prohibited in Indian films, and was not seen again until 1983, in *Betaab*.

HIGHEST-GROSSING BOLLYWOOD FILMS AT THE UK BOX OFFICE

In 1998 *Dil Se* and *Kuch Kuch Hota Hai* became the first two Indian films to reach the UK box office Top 10. *Kuch Kuch Hota Hai* earned £171,418 ($284,108) in its first three days of release in the UK alone.

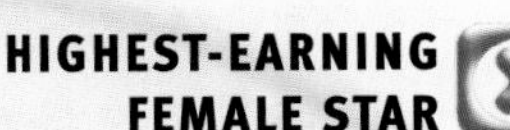

HIGHEST-EARNING FEMALE STAR

Bollywood's highest-earning actress is Madhuri Dixit (right), who reportedly has an asking price of $599,460 (£361,687) per film. The star of India's highest-grossing movie ever, Hum Aapke Hain Kaun *(1994), she made her debut in* Abodh *in 1984 and went on to act in over 60 hit films throughout the late 1980s and the 1990s.*

tv & video

MOST PROLIFIC TV PRODUCER

Aaron Spelling (USA) has produced more than 3,842 episodes of TV shows since 1956. If they were all shown end-to-end they would take 128 days to screen. His output has included *Charlie's Angels*, starring Farrah Fawcett-Majors, Kate Jackson and Jaclyn Smith (pictured below), *Starsky And Hutch*, *Dynasty* and *Beverly Hills 90210*, which featured his daughter Tori. Spelling's awards include two Golden Globes — for *Burke's Law* in 1964 and *Dynasty* in 1983 — two Emmys, the Writers Guild of America Award and the NAACP Image Award a record six times.

BIGGEST TV CONTRACT
On 24 Sept 1998 it was announced that King World Productions Inc. would pay Harpo Productions Inc., Oprah Winfrey's company, a $75 million (£45.25 million) advance against minimum payments for both the 2000/01 and 2001/02 seasons of Winfrey's top-rated chat show, which she hosts and produces.

MOST EXPENSIVE TV DEAL
In Jan 1998 the National Football League (NFL) signed contracts with CBS, ABC, Fox and ESPN totalling $17.6 billion (£10.6 billion). The contracts give each network rights to NFL games for eight years starting with the 1998/99 season. ESPN will pay the NFL $600 million (£360.5 million) per year, ABC and Fox will each pay an annual fee of $550 million (£330.5 million), and CBS will pay $500 million (£300.4 million) per year.

MOST EXPENSIVE TV SHOW
In Jan 1998 NBC agreed to pay $13 million (£8.2 million) for each hourly episode of the medical drama *ER*. It had previously paid $1.6 million (£1 million) per episode. The programme is the top US primetime show, with a weekly audience of 32 million people. The three-year deal with *ER* creators Warner Bros. will work out at $873.68 million (£536 million) for 66 episodes.

MOST WATCHED TV STATION
The state-owned station China Central Television (CCTV) is transmitted to 84% of all Chinese viewers in China; it is estimated that more than 900 million people tune in. The total broadcasting time of its nine channels each day is 162 hours, in Mandarin, Cantonese, English and French. The single most-watched show is the daily *Xin Wen Lian Bo* (*News Hookup*), which attracts 315 million viewers.

BIGGEST GLOBAL TV NETWORK
CNN International can be seen in over 149 million households in 212 countries and territories through a network of 23 satellites.

BIGGEST TV AUDIENCES
The American life guard drama *Baywatch*, whose stars have included David Hasselhoff and Pamela Anderson, is the world's most widely viewed TV series, with an estimated weekly audience of more than 1.1 billion people in 142 countries.

MOST SUCCESSFUL SOAP OPERA

Dallas, *starring Larry Hagman (left of picture) and Patrick Duffy (right of picture), began in 1978 and by 1980 had an estimated 83 million US viewers every week (a record 76% share of the TV audience). It ran for 356 episodes, from April 1978 to May 1991, and has been aired in 130 countries.*

'Goodbye, Farewell and Amen', the final episode of the Korean War black comedy *M*A*S*H*, was transmitted to 77% of all US viewers on 28 Feb 1983. It was estimated that about 125 million people tuned in.

MOST VIEWED TRIAL
From Jan to Oct 1995 a daily average of 5.5 million US viewers watched the trial of O.J. Simpson, the American footballer and actor charged with the murder of his ex-wife Nicole and her friend Ronald Goldman.

BIGGEST SOAP OPERA PRODUCER
The Brazilian network Rede Globo is the largest and most profitable producer of *telenovelas* (soap operas) in Latin America, which run on average for more than 100 episodes. It shows soaps from 6 pm each night.

In the 1960s the *telenovela Simply Mary* was sold to every Spanish-speaking country and once attracted more viewers than the World Cup.

Escrava Isaura (*Isaura The Slave*) has been dubbed and exported to all Spanish-speaking countries, dubbed into Mandarin and shown in Asia.

LONGEST-RUNNING SOAP OPERA
The British soap opera *Coronation Street*, about the inhabitants of the fictional district of Weatherfield, Manchester, UK, was first shown on 9 Dec 1960 and at least two episodes per week have been broadcast ever since. The show was devised by Tony Warren and is made by Granada TV.

LONGEST-RUNNING RELIGIOUS SOAP OPERA
Mahabharat, the most popular soap opera in India, was shown every Sunday morning for two years from 1994 to 1996.

MOST EXPENSIVE SOAP OPERA
The Brazilian soap opera *Torre De Babel* (*Tower Of Babel*) cost $17 million (£10.25 million) to make, with each individual episode costing $100,000 (£60,335). The story was written by Silvio de Abreu.

MOST EXPENSIVE CHINESE SOAP OPERA
The Romance Of Three Kingdoms cost £8.3 million ($12.96 million) to make. There were 300,000 people involved in the 44-episode production, which was made in 1996.

BEST-SELLING VIDEO

Walt Disney's The Lion King *(USA, 1994) had sold 55.7 million copies worldwide by May 1999. The 32nd Disney animated feature, it was the first without human characters and the first based on an original story. It featured the voices of Whoopi Goldberg, Jeremy Irons and Rowan Atkinson.*

MOST EXPENSIVE STRAIGHT-TO-TV FILM

Dominique Swain (right) played the lead in Adrian Lyne's adaptation of Lolita *(USA, 1997). With a budget of $58 million (£35.4 million), it was the most expensive film to debut on US cable television. US rights were bought by cable company Showtime Networks after the film controversially failed to gain an initial US theatrical release. It was first shown on US TV on 2 Aug 1998 and was released in US cinemas a month later.*

MOST ACTORS IN A SOAP OPERA
Torre de Babel set the record for the soap opera with the most actors — 300 were under permanent contract, although the show could not use more than 180 at one time.

MOST EXPENSIVE GAME SHOW
Production costs for NTV's *Trans-America Ultra Quiz* (Japan) rose to over $657,030 (£391,432) per episode in 1990, more than three times that of conventional quiz shows. The show featured ever-changing foreign stopovers, including Hawaii, Europe and South America.

MOST GAME SHOW CONTESTANTS
A record 28,523 contestants entered the Japanese quiz show *Trans-America Ultra Quiz*. It featured a total of 213,430 contestants throughout its 16-year run from 1977 to 1993, only 31 of whom ever made it to the final stage at the foot of the Statue of Liberty, New York, USA.

MOST PROLIFIC GAME SHOW PRODUCER
The most prolific game show producer is Mark Goodson (USA). He has produced more than 39,000 episodes of game shows, taking up a total of 21,240 hours of airtime.

HIGHEST PRICE PAID FOR TV RIGHTS TO A FILM
The Fox network paid $82 million (£50 million) for the TV rights to Steven Spielberg's *Jurassic Park: The Lost World* in June 1997, before its international release.

HIGHEST PRICE PAID FOR TV RIGHTS TO A MINI SERIES
In 1991 a group of US and European investors, led by CBS, paid $8 million (£4.5 million) for the TV rights to Alexandra Ripley's *Scarlett*, the sequel to Margaret Mitchell's 1936 novel *Gone With The Wind*.

MOST RENTED VIDEO
George Lucas' *Star Wars* (USA, 1977) has made $270.9 million (£166.2 million) through video rentals in North America alone. Revenues include the proceeds from the original video release and the 1997 digitally remastered version. The rental revenue of the first *Star Wars* trilogy (original and remastered) as a whole, including *The Empire Strikes Back* (USA, 1980) and *Return Of The Jedi* (USA, 1983) has reached a total of $636.4 million (£383.9 million).

FASTEST VIDEO PRODUCTION
Tapes of the royal wedding of Prince Andrew and Sarah Ferguson on 23 July 1986 were produced by Thames Video Collection. Live filming ended at 4:42 pm and the first VHS tapes were purchased in London, UK, at 10:23 pm, 5 hr 41 min later.

MOST SPENT ON TV AND VIDEO PRODUCTS
The leading consumer market for video and TV products is Japan, with an average expenditure of $43.66 (£26.23) per person a year.

COUNTRY WITH MOST TV SETS
There are a record 227.5 million households with TV sets in China.

COUNTRY WITH MOST VCRS
A record 81% of US households (78.125 million) own at least one video recorder.

CITY WITH MOST VIDEO LIBRARIES
Bombay (Mumbai), India, has a total of 15,000 video libraries and 500 video parlours — more than any other city in the world.

music video

MOST EXPENSIVE VIDEO
The video for Michael and Janet Jackson's hit single *Scream* (1995) cost a record $7 million (£4.4 million) to make and was directed by Mark Romanek (USA). Shot on seven different sound stages, it features flying electric guitars and complex morphing effects. *Scream* won the MTV Music Video Award for Dance in 1995 and the Grammy for Music Video, Short Form, in 1996.

LONGEST VIDEOS
Michael Jackson's part feature film, part music video *Ghosts* (1996) is 35 minutes long and was based on an original concept by cult horror writer Stephen King. Jackson plays five different roles in the video, which was directed by Stan Winston.

Michael Jackson's legendary *Thriller* (1983) video and Snoop Doggy Dogg's *Murder Was The Case* (1994) both run for 18 minutes. Snoop's video was directed by fellow rap artist Dr Dre and the star-studded line-up also included Dr Dre, Ice Cube, Jewell and Jodeci.

SHORTEST VIDEOS
German TV station VIVA-TV made a video to accompany UK grindcore band Napalm Death's single *The Kill* (1992), which is 10 seconds long.

The shortest video made by a record company is German artist Klaus Beyer's *Die Glatze*, a super-8 movie transferred to videotape, which has a total running time of 1 min 23 sec.

MOST VIDEOS MADE FOR ONE SONG
There are five different videos for the track *Timber* (1998) by UK dance act Coldcut: the original mix, the EBN remix (New York), the LPC remix (Sweden), the Clifford Gilberto remix (Germany) and the Gnomadic remix (UK). Coldcut offered the *Timber* track to video-makers to encourage them to remix videos in the same way that DJs and producers remix records. Coldcut have been regarded as pioneers of the remixing concept since their radical reworking of US rappers Eric B and Rakim's *Paid In Full* (1987) turned the track into a worldwide hit.

Swedish group the Cardigans produced three different videos for *Lovefool* (1996): one European version and two US versions, one of which featured scenes from the film *William Shakespeare's Romeo And Juliet* (USA, 1996).

MOST-PLAYED SONG ON MTV EUROPE
US grunge band Nirvana's *Smells Like Teen Spirit* (1991) is the most-played music video on MTV Europe. It ranked first in the Top 10 Singles of the 1990s poll held by the music station in 1996.

BIGGEST MUSIC TV STATION
MTV is beamed into 281.7 million households in 79 countries around the globe, which means it can be seen by one in four of the world's total TV audience. MTV began broadcasting in 1981 and added three new channels to its existing range in July 1999, thus doubling its output. The three new channels are MTV Base (featuring R&B, rap and dance), MTV Extra (featuring items from MTV UK and Ireland to complement the main MTV channel) and VH1 Classic (focusing on classic hits by artists such as Abba and Eric Clapton).

COSTLIEST SPECIAL EFFECTS IN A VIDEO
The video for What's It Gonna Be? *(1999) by Busta Rhymes and Janet Jackson, directed by Hype Williams, cost $2.4 million (£1.44 million) to produce. Computer-morphing effects accounted for much of this expenditure. The track was taken from Rhymes' millennium-themed album* E.L.E. — The Final World Front.

MOST-PLAYED MUSIC VIDEOS ON THE BOX
The Box is a music-video channel available worldwide. Viewers phone a video 'jukebox' line to request the video and artist they want to see. Between its release in Jan 1998 and July 1999, the love theme from the movie *Titanic* (USA, 1997), Celine Dion's *My Heart Will Go On* (1997), received an unprecedented 60,474 requests.

The Box's most popular video by a dead artist is by rapper Tupac Shakur (USA), who was killed in Sept 1996. His single *Changes*, which features a sample from Bruce Hornsby and the Range's *The Way It Is* (1986), received 21,380 requests in the 18 weeks following its first showing on The Box in Feb 1999.

MOST STARS FROM DIFFERENT MUSIC GENRES ON ONE VIDEO
A charity recording of the Lou Reed song *Perfect Day*, commissioned to show the diversity of music played on BBC Television and Radio, features 27 artists from 18 genres, including jazz (Courtney Pine), reggae (Burning Spear), country (Tammy Wynette and

MOST MTV VIDEO AWARDS WON BY A FEMALE ARTIST
Madonna won a record six MTV Music Video awards in 1998, after being nominated in nine categories — eight for *Ray Of Light* and one for *Frozen*. The *Ray Of Light* video, directed by Jonas Okerlund, won for Video of the Year, Best Direction, Best Female Video, Best Editing and Best Choreography. *Frozen*, directed by Chris Cunningham, picked up the Best Special Effects award. Both tracks were taken from her album *Ray Of Light*, which went triple-platinum in the USA. Madonna performed *Ray Of Light* at the ceremony, in which her new video for *Power Of Goodbye* received its world premiere. Madonna is shown here performing *Nothing Really Matters* at the 41st Grammy Awards on 24 Feb 1999.

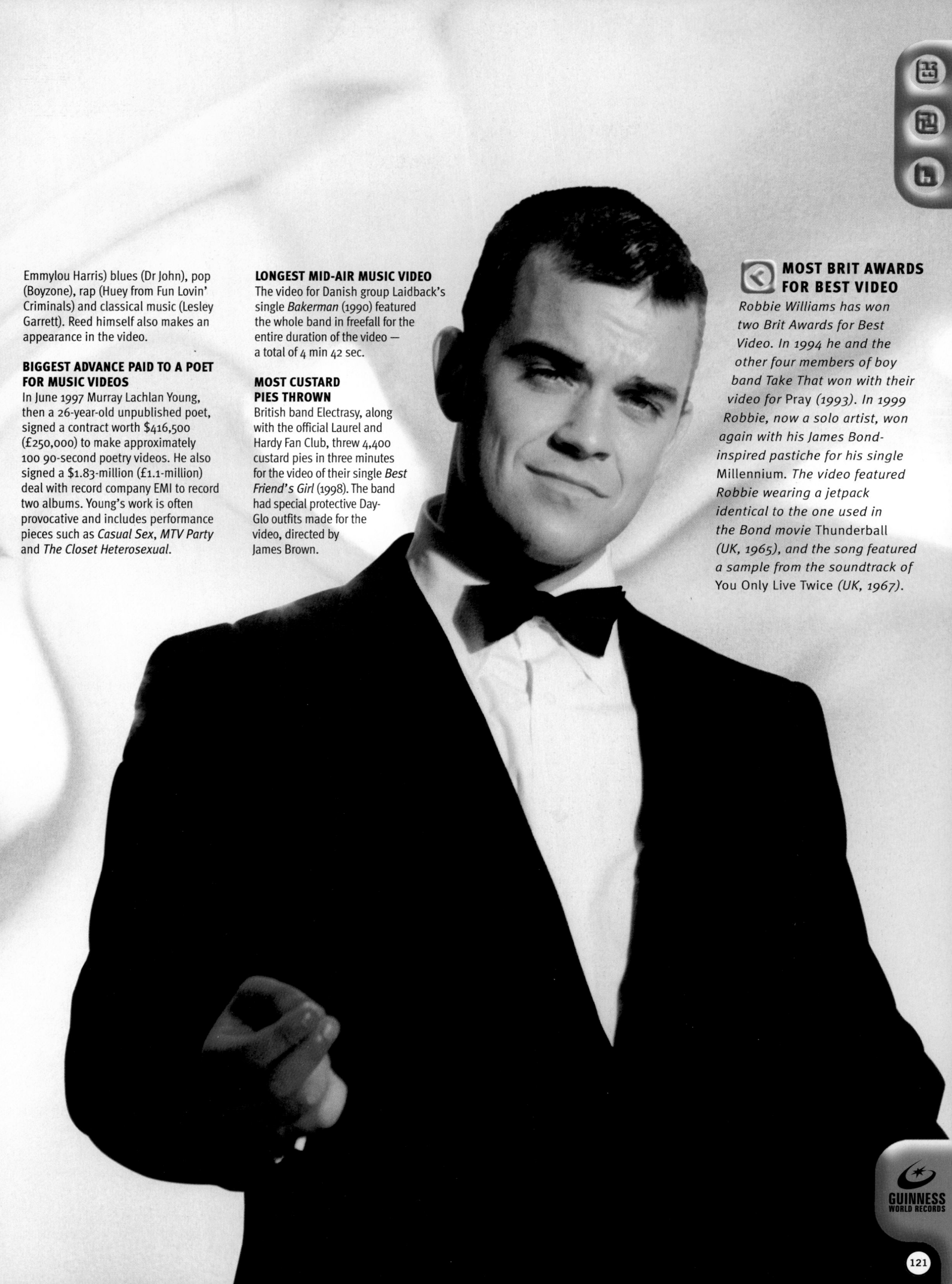

Emmylou Harris) blues (Dr John), pop (Boyzone), rap (Huey from Fun Lovin' Criminals) and classical music (Lesley Garrett). Reed himself also makes an appearance in the video.

BIGGEST ADVANCE PAID TO A POET FOR MUSIC VIDEOS

In June 1997 Murray Lachlan Young, then a 26-year-old unpublished poet, signed a contract worth $416,500 (£250,000) to make approximately 100 90-second poetry videos. He also signed a $1.83-million (£1.1-million) deal with record company EMI to record two albums. Young's work is often provocative and includes performance pieces such as *Casual Sex*, *MTV Party* and *The Closet Heterosexual*.

LONGEST MID-AIR MUSIC VIDEO

The video for Danish group Laidback's single *Bakerman* (1990) featured the whole band in freefall for the entire duration of the video — a total of 4 min 42 sec.

MOST CUSTARD PIES THROWN

British band Electrasy, along with the official Laurel and Hardy Fan Club, threw 4,400 custard pies in three minutes for the video of their single *Best Friend's Girl* (1998). The band had special protective Day-Glo outfits made for the video, directed by James Brown.

MOST BRIT AWARDS FOR BEST VIDEO

Robbie Williams has won two Brit Awards for Best Video. In 1994 he and the other four members of boy band Take That won with their video for Pray *(1993). In 1999 Robbie, now a solo artist, won again with his James Bond-inspired pastiche for his single* Millennium. *The video featured Robbie wearing a jetpack identical to the one used in the Bond movie* Thunderball *(UK, 1965), and the song featured a sample from the soundtrack of* You Only Live Twice *(UK, 1967).*

pop

MUSIC RECORDS
Because of the localized nature of the music industry, the records on the music pages are a mixture of US, British and world records.

MOST SUCCESSFUL ARTIST
Elvis Presley was the world's most successful solo artist of the rock era, with 18 No. 1 singles and nine No. 1 albums in the USA and 17 No. 1 singles and six No. 1 albums in the UK. He had 94 chart entries in the USA and 98 in the UK.

MOST SUCCESSFUL GROUP
The Beatles have sold around 1 billion records and had a record 20 No. 1 singles and 18 No. 1 albums in the USA and 17 No. 1 singles and 14 No. 1 albums in the UK.

MOST SUCCESSFUL FEMALE ARTIST
No female artist has sold more records around the world than Madonna, with total sales of more than 100 million. She is the most successful female artist in both the USA and the UK, with a US total of 32 Top 10 singles and 11 Top 10 albums and a UK total of 44 separate Top 10 singles and 13 Top 10 albums (including six that reached No. 1 — a UK record for any female artist).

MOST SUCCESSFUL FAMILY GROUP
Between 1968 and 1999 the Bee Gees had 24 Top 20 singles in the USA and the UK. They have also had 13 Top 20 albums in the USA and 12 in the UK.

MOST SUCCESSFUL PRODUCER
The producer with the most No. 1 singles in the UK and the USA during the rock era is George Martin, who saw 28 of his productions head the British chart and 23 reach No. 1 in the USA. He also holds the record for longest span of UK- and US-produced hits. In the UK, there was an interval of 36 years 4 months between *You're Driving Me Crazy* by the Temperance Seven in April 1961 and *Candle in the Wind 97* by Elton John in Sept 1997. In the USA, the gap between *I Want to Hold Your Hand* by the Beatles and *Candle in the Wind 97/Something About the Way You Look Tonight* by Elton John is 33 years 8 months.

FIRST FEMALE GROUP DEBUT AT NO. 1
*On 6 Jun 1998 Irish pop group B*Witched became the first female group to enter the UK chart at No. 1, with their debut single* C'est La Vie. *The group followed through with two more No. 1 hits —* Rollercoaster *on 3 Oct 1998 and* To You I Belong *on 19 Dec 1998, becoming one of only two acts to have entered at No. 1 with their first three singles. The other act to achieve this feat was duo Robson Green and Jerome Flynn.*

OLDEST FEMALE VOCALIST TO REACH NO. 1
The lead singer of Blondie, Deborah Harry, became the oldest female vocalist to top the UK chart when she went to No. 1 with *Maria* on 13 Feb 1999 at the age of 53 years 8 months. She broke the record previously held by Cher, who reached No. 1 in Oct 1998 with *Believe* at the age of 52 years 6 months. Blondie are also the only US act to have had UK hits in the 1970s, the 1980s and the 1990s (excluding collaborations) and are the act with the longest gap between newly recorded UK No. 1 hits, stretching from *The Tide Is High* in Nov 1980 to *Maria* in Feb 1999. Furthermore, Blondie are the only US act to have had three successive UK No. 1s in the 1980s — *Atomic*, *Call Me* and *The Tide Is High*.

BIGGEST-SELLING ALBUMS
Michael Jackson's *Thriller* (1982) has sold more than 45 million copies globally. Of these, 25 million were in the USA – a total unsurpassed in that country.

The biggest-selling album in the UK is *Sgt Pepper's Lonely Hearts Club Band* by the Beatles, with reported sales of 4.5 million since its release in 1967.

BIGGEST-SELLING SINGLE
In the UK *Candle in the Wind 97/ Something About the Way You Look Tonight* by Elton John sold 658,000 copies on its first day, 1.5 million in week one, 2 million in eight days, 3 million in 15 days and had passed 5.4 million sales by the sixth week. In the USA there were advance orders of 8.7 million and a first week ship-out of 3.4 million. In total, 11 million sales were certified in the USA alone. Elton John performed the song at the funeral of Diana, Princess of Wales, and proceeds went to her charitable trust. The single also spent 45 weeks at the top of the Canadian chart. It went in at No. 1 on 22 Sept 1997 and had earned 19 Canadian platinum discs by Christmas. It remained in the Top 3 until March 1999, 18 months later.

MOST PLAYED SONGS
Only two songs have received more than 7 million plays on US radio — *Yesterday*, written by John Lennon and Paul McCartney, and *You've Lost That Lovin' Feelin'*, written by Phil Spector, Barry Mann and Cynthia Weill.

MOST HIT SINGLES
Elvis Presley holds the record for the most hit singles in the USA, with 151 entries on the *Billboard* Top 100 chart since 1956.

Cliff Richard has had a record 120 UK chart entries since Sept 1958.

MOST CONSECUTIVE NO. 1 SINGLES
The record for most consecutive No. 1 singles in the UK is 11, set by the Beatles between 1963 and 1966. The run started with *From Me to You* and ended with *Yellow Submarine*.

Elvis Presley holds the US record for most consecutive No. 1 singles, with 10.

MOST NO. 1 ENTRIES ON UK CHARTS

The act with the most entries at No. 1 in the UK is Take That with eight. The female act with the most No. 1 entries is the Spice Girls, with seven, and the solo male act with the most is George Michael, with four. Robbie Williams (pictured), former member of Take That, holds the record for most Brit Award nominations, receiving six in 1999.

The run started with *Heartbreak Hotel* in 1956 and ended with *Don't* in 1958.

MOST SUCCESSFUL UK DEBUT

Irish boy band Boyzone's first 15 UK singles all reached the Top 5, beating a record held by Kylie Minogue (Australia). The group is also the only Irish act to have six UK No. 1 singles, up to May 1999.

YOUNGEST CHART-TOPPERS

The youngest solo artist to have topped the UK charts was Little Jimmy Osmond, who was at No. 1 for five weeks in 1972 with *Long Haired Lover From Liverpool*, when he was 9 years 8 months old. In second place is fellow American Frankie Lymon who was 13 years 9 months old when he reached No. 1 with *Why Do Fools Fall In Love?* in 1956, followed by Jimmy's older brother Donny, who was 14 years 6 months when *Puppy Love* reached the No. 1 spot in 1972.

FINEST FEMALE YEAR

In 1998 female artists, or female fronted acts, headed the UK singles chart for a record 26 weeks of the year and in the last week of the year they were featured on nine of the Top 10 singles on the chart. On 19 Dec 1998, for the first time, the Top 5 artists on the UK chart were all female: B*Witched, Cher, Billie, Mariah Carey and Whitney Houston, and The Honeyz.

MOST SUCCESSFUL UK SOLO ARTIST

Elton John, who was knighted in 1998, is the most successful UK solo artist in both the USA and the UK, with total sales of more than 150 million records around the world. In the USA he had at least one Top 40 entry every year between 1970 and 1999, making a record run of 30 consecutive years. Elton John also holds the records for the biggest-selling album by a British male soloist in both the USA and UK. In the USA, *Elton John's Greatest Hits* (1974) has sold 15 million, while in the UK *The Very Best of Elton John* (1990) has certified sales of 2.7 million.

LONGEST SPAN OF US/UK TOP 20 ALBUMS

Frank Sinatra holds the record for the longest span of Top 20 albums in the USA and the UK. His first US chart entry in the rock era was *In The Wee Small Hours*, which entered on 28 May 1955, and his most recent was *Duets II*, which exited the Top 20 on 31 Dec 1994, 39 years 7 months later. In the UK he first entered on 8 Nov 1958 with *Come Fly With Me* and his most recent Top 20 album, *My Way — The Best of Frank Sinatra*, exited 39 years 7 months later in June 1998, two months after his death. He also had several top-selling albums before the UK album chart started in 1958.

BEST-SELLING LATIN ARTIST

Spanish vocalist Julio Iglesias is the most successful Latin music artist in the world, with reported global sales of more than 200 million albums. Iglesias' album *Julio* (1994) is also the only foreign-language album to have gone double platinum (2 million copies) in the USA.

MOST SUCCESSFUL LATIN RECORD

Macarena by Spanish duo Los Del Rio is the most successful Latin recording, selling more than 10 million around the world. It topped the US chart for 14 weeks in 1996 and spent 60 weeks on the Top 100.

MOST SUCCESSFUL RECORD LABEL

Since the US Top 100 was launched in Aug 1958, the record label with the most No. 1 hits is Columbia, with 83 up to May 1999. They have almost twice as many chart-toppers as their closest rivals, Capitol Records, with 46, and RCA Records, with 42.

MOST SUCCESSIVE NO. 1s BY A NEW ACT

The record for the most successive UK No. 1 singles by a new act is held by the Spice Girls (the lead singer of which, Mel G, is pictured), who reached No. 1 with their first six singles in the UK. They also topped the chart with two of their next three hits.

rock

LONGEST UK NO. 1 TITLE

The longest title (without brackets) of a UK No. 1 single is *If You Tolerate This Your Children Will Be Next* by the Manic Street Preachers, which reached No. 1 in Sept 1998. The band, comprising Nicky Wire (pictured), Richey Edwards, James Dean Bradfield and Sean Moore, released their first single in 1989. They attracted critical acclaim and a devoted cult following, but when Edwards disappeared in Feb 1995 a split looked inevitable. However, they returned in 1996 to achieve a new level of commercial success. In 1999 they won Brit awards for Best British Band and Best Album (*This Is My Truth, Tell Me Yours*). Richey Edwards' whereabouts remain a mystery.

BIGGEST-SELLING ALBUM
The Eagles' *Greatest Hits 1971–75* is the biggest-selling rock album in the USA, with sales of 25 million.

BIGGEST-SELLING HEAVY ROCK ALBUM
Led Zeppelin IV (Four Symbols) by British band Led Zeppelin has sold over 21 million copies in the USA since 1971.

BIGGEST-SELLING SOLO ROCK ALBUM
Bruce Springsteen's *Born In The USA* (1984) is the top-selling album by a US solo rock act in the USA, with sales of over 15 million.

BIGGEST-SELLING ROCK CONCEPT ALBUM
The Wall by British band Pink Floyd has sold 23 million copies in the USA.

MOST WEEKS ON THE US ALBUM CHART
Dark Side Of The Moon by Pink Floyd entered the US chart on 17 March 1973 and is still there. It had spent 741 weeks in the Top 200 and 411 weeks on the Pop Catalogue chart by May 1999, topping the latter in its 1,154th chart week.

MOST US PLATINUM ALBUMS
Led Zeppelin holds the record for the most US platinum albums by a rock act, having amassed 94 by June 1999.

FASTEST-SELLING ALBUM IN THE UK
Be Here Now (1997) by Oasis sold a record 345,000 copies in the UK on the day it was released. By its third day it had sold 700,000 copies and within 17 days sales had passed the 1 million mark. Like Oasis' first two albums, *Be Here Now* entered the chart at No. 1, giving the band the record for the most consecutive releases to enter in this position. It also entered the charts at No. 1 in nine other countries.

BIGGEST-SELLING ROCK ALBUM IN JAPAN
Japan's top-selling rock album is *Review* by the Japanese band Glay, which has sold more than 4.7 million copies in its native country alone.

MOST SUCCESSFUL POSTHUMOUS ALBUMS IN THE USA
Nirvana topped the US chart with *MTV Unplugged In New York* in Nov 1994 and *From The Muddy Banks Of The Wishkah* in Oct 1996. The band's lead singer, Kurt Cobain, committed suicide in April 1994.

BIGGEST-SELLING HEAVY ROCK ALBUM IN THE UK
Bat Out Of Hell *by Meat Loaf has sold more than 2.1 million copies in the UK since 1978. The first collaboration between Meat Loaf (real name Marvin Lee Aday) and writer/producer Jim Steinman, it had spent 472 weeks on the UK album chart by April 1999. Later successes included* Dead Ringer *(1981) and* Bat Out Of Hell II: Back Into Hell *(1993), which spawned the single* I'd Do Anything For Love (But I Won't Do That)*, the best-selling single in the UK that year.*

LONGEST TIME BETWEEN A HIT ALBUM AND SINGLE
The first UK hit single by Led Zeppelin, *Whole Lotta Love*, entered the chart on 13 Sept 1997. This was a record-breaking 28 years 5 months after the group's debut album, *Led Zeppelin,* had first charted.

MOST SUCCESSFUL ROCK SINGLE
In 1991 *Everything I Do (I Do It For You)* by Bryan Adams spent a record 16 consecutive weeks at No. 1 in the UK and seven weeks at No. 1 in the USA. It also reached No. 1 in 16 other countries, including France, Germany, Australia, Canada and Belgium.

BIGGEST SCREEN AT A CONCERT
The set for U2's 1997 PopMart tour featured the world's largest LED (light-emitting diodes) screen. Measuring 16.7 x 51.8 m (54.8 x 170 ft), the screen showed animation and pop art masterpieces. U2 (whose singer Bono is pictured) were originally identified with guitar-based anthems but by the 1990s were experimenting with samplers, dance rhythms and visual effects.

MOST MODERN ROCK NO. 1 SINGLES IN THE USA
The act to have had the most No. 1 singles on the *Billboard* Modern Rock chart is US group R.E.M., with six.

The British acts to have had the highest number are the Cure and Depeche Mode, with four each.

MOST MAINSTREAM ROCK NO. 1 SINGLES IN THE USA
The act to have had the most No. 1 singles on the *Billboard* Mainstream Rock Tracks chart is Van Halen, with 11.

The solo artist to have had the highest number is John Mellencamp, with eight.

LONGEST US HIT SINGLE
November Rain by Guns 'N' Roses is the longest single to have reached the US Top 20, with a playing time of 8 min 40 sec. It reached No. 3 in Aug 1992.

MOST SIMULTANEOUS UK INDIE HITS
The Smiths held the top three places on the UK indie chart on 28 Jan 1984.

On 1 July 1995 Oasis had six singles in the top seven of the UK indie chart.

MOST VALUABLE US ROCK RECORD
There are only two known copies of *The Freewheelin' Bob Dylan* (Columbia CS-8796, in stereo) as the album was later re-pressed with four songs removed. Copies in near-mint condition would be worth between $20,000 and $30,000 (£12,000 and £18,000) today.

MOST CONTINENTS PLAYED IN A DAY
On 24 Oct 1995 UK heavy metal band Def Leppard staged shows on three different continents. They appeared in Tangiers, Morocco, London, UK and Vancouver, Canada.

MOST DEATHS AT A ROCK CONCERT
Eleven fans were trampled to death at a gig by the Who in Cincinnati, Ohio, USA, in 1979.

HIGHEST US CHART ENTRY BY A ROCK ACT
Aerosmith (whose singer Steven Tyler is pictured) are the only rock group to have entered the US singles chart at No. 1. They achieved this with I Don't Want To Miss A Thing *in Sept 1998.*

dance, r&b & hip hop

BIGGEST-SELLING DANCE ALBUM IN THE UK
Bizarre Fruit (1994) by the British group M People has sold more than 1.5 million copies in the United Kingdom — more than any other dance album. The album features the hits *Sight for Sore Eyes*, *Open Your Heart* and *Search for the Hero*.

BIGGEST-SELLING DANCE ALBUM IN THE USA
The soundtrack to *Purple Rain* by Prince (now [symbol]) and the Revolution topped the US chart for a record 24 weeks and has sold more than 13 million copies there since its release in 1985. The film, which starred Prince, was an apparently autobiographical story set on the club scene of Minneapolis, Minnesota, USA. The album yielded the hits *When Doves Cry* and *Let's Go Crazy*.

MOST SIMULTANEOUS HITS BY A DANCE ACT
On 20 April 1996 all of Prodigy's 10 hit singles were in the UK Top 100. The group's previous nine singles, all of which had originally made the UK Top 15, had been reissued after *Firestarter*, released in March 1996, gave them their first ever No. 1 single.

FASTEST-SELLING DANCE ALBUM IN THE UK
The Fat Of The Land (1997) by Prodigy sold a record 317,000 copies in its first week. In the USA it sold more than 200,000 copies in its first week. The album entered the chart at No. 1 in a total of 20 countries.

MOST SUCCESSFUL CHART DEBUTS
The only act to have entered the US pop chart at No. 1 with its first three albums is rapper Snoop Dogg (aka Snoop Doggy Dogg), with *Doggy Style* (1993), *Tha Dogfather* (1996) and *Da Game Is To Be Sold, Not To Be Told* (1998).

The only act to have entered at No. 1 with its first two albums within a year is rapper DMX, with *It's Dark And Hell Is Hot* (June 1998) and *Flesh of My Flesh Blood Of My Blood* (Jan 1999).

MOST CONSECUTIVE US NO. 1 SINGLES
The record for the most consecutive No. 1 pop singles by an artist is seven, by R&B vocalist Whitney Houston between 1985 and 1988. These included *Saving All My Love For You* (1985), *I Wanna Dance With Somebody (Who Loves Me)* and *So Emotional* (both 1987).

SHORTEST US TOP 10 TITLE
The shortest-titled record to reach the US pop Top 10 is *7*, by Prince (now [symbol]) in 1992.

MOST US TOP 40 HITS WITHOUT REACHING NO. 1
The artist to have had the most US Top 40 pop hits without hitting No. 1 is James Brown, with 44. The next four acts are also R&B artists: Brook Benton (24), Sam Cooke (24), Jackie Wilson (23) and Fats Domino (22).

LONGEST US CHART SPAN
The act with the longest chart span on the US pop Top 100 is R&B group the Isley Brothers. They first entered the chart with their much-covered composition *Shout* in Sept 1959 and last charted 37 years 4 months later, with *Tears* in Jan 1997.

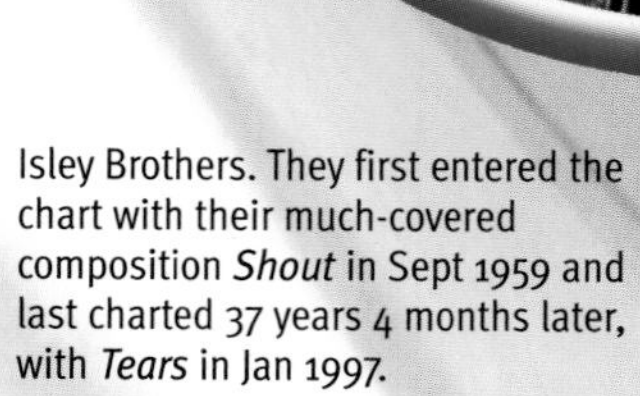

LONGEST US SPAN OF NO. 1 HITS
The R&B artist with the longest span of US No. 1 pop hits is Michael Jackson. His first solo No. 1 was *Ben* in Oct 1972 and he last topped that chart 22 years 11 months later with *You Are Not Alone* in Sept 1995. The latter was also the first ever single to enter the US chart at No. 1. Jackson had also topped the US chart as lead singer of the Jackson 5 on four occasions before his first solo No. 1.

MOST NO. 1 US RAP SINGLES
The artist who has had the greatest number of No. 1 singles on the Billboard *Rap Chart is L L Cool J, with a total of eight. These included* I'm That Type Of Guy, Around The Way Girl, Loungin' *and* Father. *L L Cool J is on the Def Jam label, which holds the record for the greatest number of US No. 1 rap singles, with 15. Other artists on the label include Public Enemy, MC Serch and Boss.*

MOST SUCCESSFUL RAP PRODUCER IN THE USA

Sean 'Puff Daddy' Coombs is the most successful US rap producer, having been responsible for four singles that consecutively headed the US rap chart for a total of 36 weeks in 1997. These included *Hypnotize* and *Mo Money, Mo Problems* by The Notorious B.I.G. Puff Daddy's tribute to The Notorious B.I.G. (aka Christopher Wallace) — *I'll Be Missing You*, made with Faith Evans and featuring 112 — headed the US chart for 11 weeks and was No. 1 on the UK chart for six weeks in 1997, making it the most successful ever R&B tribute song in the USA and UK. Puff Daddy recorded the single after B.I.G. was gunned down as he left a party in Los Angeles, California, USA, on 4 March 1997.

MOST SUCCESSFUL BENELUX SINGLE IN THE UK
No Limits by Belgian dance music duo 2 Unlimited is the most successful ever single from the Benelux countries on the UK chart. It was No. 1 for five weeks in 1993.

MOST SUCCESSFUL NON ENGLISH-LANGUAGE RAP RECORDS
In 1993 *Dur Dur d' Etre Bébé (It's Tough To Be A Baby)* by the then four-year-old French rapper Jordy (Lemoine) sold more than 1 million copies in France and was also a minor hit on the *Billboard* chart in the USA. In Feb 1994 France's main TV channel, TF1, banned Jordy, saying his parents were exploiting him.

Da Ya Ne by the Japanese rap trio East End X Yuri sold 1 million copies in Japan in 1995.

MOST SUCCESSFUL FEMALE RAP ALBUM IN THE USA
Chyna Doll by New York rapper Foxy Brown is the only all-rap album by a female artist to have topped the US chart. It reached No. 1 in Feb 1999.

MOST CHARTED FEMALE SINGER
No female singer has had more US Top 100 pop chart entries than R&B star Aretha Franklin, who had 76 chart entries between 1961 and 1998.

MOST SUCCESSFUL HIT BY A FEMALE DUO
The most successful single by a female duo on the US pop chart is *The Boy Is Mine* by Brandy & Monica, which was No. 1 for 13 weeks from June 1998.

LONGEST-RUNNING GROUP
The Four Tops were the longest-running successful group with the same members from the start. Levi Stubbs, Renaldo 'Obie' Benson, Abdul Fakir and Lawrence Payton formed the group in 1953 and sang together until Payton's death in 1997.

LONGEST-RUNNING US R&B NO. 1
The longest-running R&B No. 1 hit is *Nobody's Supposed To Be Here* by Canadian vocalist Deborah Cox, which headed the chart for 14 weeks from 24 Oct 1998 to 6 Feb 1999.

MOST SUCCESSFUL REGGAE SINGLE IN THE UK
The double-sided hit *Rivers Of Babylon/Brown Girl In The Ring* by Germany-based band Boney M is the most successful ever reggae recording in the United Kingdom. It headed the chart for five weeks in 1978 and sold more than 2 million copies.

BIGGEST-SELLING HIP HOP/RAP ALBUM IN THE USA
Please Hammer Don't Hurt 'Em (1990) by M.C. Hammer and *Crazysexycool* (1994) by TLC share the record for the biggest-selling hip hop/rap album in the USA, with certified sales of 10 million.

MOST GRAMMY NOMINATIONS
In 1999 Lauryn Hill received 10 Grammy nominations — a record for a female recording artist. Most were for her chart-topping album The Miseducation Of Lauryn Hill. *She won five awards (another female record): Album of the Year, Best New Artist, Best R&B Album, Best Female R&B Vocal Performance and Best R&B Song.*

country music

MOST SUCCESSFUL COUNTRY ARTISTS IN THE USA

Garth Brooks is the most successful country recording artist of all time, with album sales expected to equal the Beatles' record-breaking total of 100 million by the end of 1999. Despite his enormous success on the US album chart, Brooks did not have a US Top 100 single until Dec 1998, with *It's Your Song*.

Reba McEntire is the biggest-selling female country vocalist in the USA, with 13 platinum and six gold albums to her name by Jan 1999. These include *Sweet Sixteen* (1989), *Read My Mind* (1994) and *If You See Him* (1998).

MOST SUCCESSFUL COUNTRY DUO

Kix Brooks and Ronnie Dunn are the most successful country duo of all time. Six of their albums have sold over 1 million copies and 12 of their singles have reached No. 1, including *Boot Scootin' Boogie* (1992), *Little Miss Honky Tonk* (1995) and *Husbands & Wives* (1998).

MOST SUCCESSFUL COUNTRY GROUP

Alabama hold the records for the most No. 1 singles, albums and total sales by a country group. They have had 32 No. 1 singles and 10 No. 1 albums and have sold over 57 million records.

MOST PLAYED COUNTRY SONGS IN THE USA

Dolly Parton's composition *I Will Always Love You*, Jim Webb's song *By The Time I Get To Phoenix* and *Gentle On My Mind* by John Hartford have each been played on air a certified 4 million times in the USA. This figure includes versions by non-country performers.

MOST POPULAR US JUKEBOX TRACK

The most played record of all time on American jukeboxes is Patsy Cline's recording of *Crazy* (1961). The song was one of the first hits to be composed by Willie Nelson.

BIGGEST-SELLING COUNTRY ALBUMS IN THE USA

Garth Brooks' 1990 album *No Fences* sold a record total of more than 16 million copies.

The biggest-selling country album ever by a group in the USA is *Greatest Hits* (1986) by Alabama, which has sold more than 5 million copies.

MOST WEEKS AT NO. 1 BY A US ALBUM

No record has topped any US album chart for longer than *12 Greatest Hits* (1967) by Patsy Cline, which headed the country catalogue chart in *Billboard* for 251 weeks.

MOST SIMULTANEOUS ALBUM HITS IN THE USA

On 10 Oct 1992 four of the Top 5 albums on the US country chart were by Garth Brooks. The albums — *The Chase*, *Beyond Season*, *No Fences* and *Ropin' The Wind* — all featured on the US Top 20 pop album chart too.

HIGHEST-PAID COUNTRY ARTIST

In 1998 Garth Brooks earned $35 million (£21 million) — more than any other country music star. On 6 Dec 1997 Brooks had a record 12 separate tracks on the Billboard *Top 75 country chart. The highest-paid female artist of 1998 was Canadian Shania Twain, who grossed over $33.5 million (£20.2 million) that year.*

MOST NO. 1 COUNTRY ALBUMS IN THE USA

'Outlaw' stars Willie Nelson and Merle Haggard have both had a record 15 US No. 1 country albums.

Loretta Lynn has had 10 No. 1 country albums in the USA — more than any other female artist.

The most US No. 1 country albums by a group is 10, by Alabama.

MOST ENTRIES AT NO. 1 IN THE USA

The country artist who has had the most albums entering the US pop chart at No. 1 is Garth Brooks, with six.

MOST SIMULTANEOUS ALBUM HITS IN THE UK

On 24 Sept 1964 the late Jim Reeves had a record-breaking eight entries in the UK Top 20 pop album chart.

Irish singer Daniel O'Donnell occupied a record six of the top seven places on the UK country album chart on 16 Nov 1991.

BEST-SELLING DOUBLE LP

The US sales record for a double album was broken by Garth Brooks' *Double Live* in Dec 1998. The album, which narrowly missed selling 1 million copies on its first day, had initial orders of a record 7 million copies. It sold 1,085,373 copies in its first week, 1.7 million copies in two weeks and 2.158 million copies in three. *Double*

MOST DUETS RECORDED

Willie Nelson (right) has recorded duets with around 100 recording artists, including Bob Dylan, Julio Iglesias, Frank Sinatra, Ray Charles, Sinead O'Connor, Neil Young, Joni Mitchell, Bonnie Raitt and fellow country music legends such as Merle Haggard, Jim Reeves, Johnny Cash, Brenda Lee and Dolly Parton. Nelson's first break in country music came when he financed and recorded *No Place For Me* in 1957. Shortly afterwards he sold his first song, *Family Bible,* for $50 (£18). Nelson went on to write hits for many top country artists in the 1960s, including *Crazy* for Patsy Cline. However, it was his first album for Columbia records, *Red Headed Stranger,* that established him as one of country music's most popular artists.

Live was Brooks' third No. 1 pop album that year — a total only equalled in record history by Elvis Presley, the Beatles and the Monkees.

MOST COUNTRY RADIO STATIONS
In the USA there are over 2,350 specialist radio stations that play predominantly country music — this far exceeds the number playing other musical formats. Sales of country music records in the USA in 1998 went up to 62.1 million from 59 million the previous year.

BIGGEST BOXED SET TO TOP THE US CHARTS
The six-CD set *The Limited Series* by Garth Brooks is the biggest boxed set to have topped the US pop chart. It reached No. 1 in May 1998.

BIGGEST-SELLING COUNTRY SINGLE IN THE USA
The only country single with sales of 3 million in the USA is *How Do I Live* by LeAnn Rimes, which reached No. 2 on the pop chart in 1998.

MOST NO. 1 COUNTRY SINGLES IN THE USA
The most No. 1 hits on the *Billboard* country chart by one act is 40, by Conway Twitty between 1968 and 1986.

MOST CONSECUTIVE NO. 1 US COUNTRY SINGLES
The group Alabama notched up a record-breaking 21 consecutive country No. 1 singles between 1980 and 1987.

MOST NO. 1 SINGLES BY A WOMAN
The record for the most No. 1 hits on the *Billboard* country charts by a female artist is 24, by Dolly Parton, from *Joshua* (1970) to *The Rockin' Years* (1991), a duet with Ricky Van Shelton. Parton has also had 56 Top 10 singles and 41 weeks in total at No. 1. In 1986 her company, Parton Enterprises, opened Dollywood, a 35-ha (87-acre) theme park near her birthplace in Sevier County, Tennessee, USA.

MOST WEEKS ON SINGLES CHART IN THE USA
How Do I Live by LeAnn Rimes spent a record 69 weeks on the US Top 100 from 21 June 1997 to 10 Oct 1998. It also broke the record for the most weeks in the Top 40, with 61, and the record (set 55 years earlier) for the most weeks in the Top 10, with 32.

TOP-SELLING FEMALE COUNTRY ALBUM
The top-selling country album by a female artist in the USA is The Woman In Me *(1996) by Shania Twain, which has sold 11 million copies. It is also the third biggest-selling album of all time by any female artist. Her 9-million-selling album* Come On Over *is the second biggest-selling country album by a female artist.*

classical music, opera & jazz

BEST-SELLING CLASSICAL ALBUM
The Three Tenors In Concert, recorded by José Carreras, Placido Domingo (both Spain) and Luciano Pavarotti (Italy) for the 1990 football World Cup Finals, has sold an estimated 13 million copies.

BIGGEST CLASSICAL AUDIENCE
An estimated 800,000 people attended a free open-air concert by the New York Philharmonic Orchestra on the Great Lawn of Central Park, New York City, USA, on 5 July 1986.

BIGGEST ORCHESTRA
On 23 Nov 1998, Music For Youth organized the world's largest orchestra, consisting of 3,503 musicians at the National Indoor Arena, Birmingham, UK. Conducted by Sir Simon Rattle, they played Malcolm Arnold's *Little Suite No. 2*, lasting 7 min 40 sec.

MOST PROLIFIC CONDUCTOR
Herbert von Karajan (Austria), who died in 1989, made more than 800 classical recordings. He conducted the London Philharmonic Orchestra, the Vienna State Opera, La Scala Opera of Milan and the Berlin Philharmonic Orchestra, and founded the Salzburg Festival in 1967.

LONGEST SYMPHONY
Victory at Sea, written by the American composer Richard Rodgers for the documentary film of the same name and arranged by Robert Russell Bennett for NBC TV in 1952, lasts 13 hours.

LONGEST OPERAS
The Life and Times of Joseph Stalin by Robert Wilson, performed from 14 to 15 Dec 1973 at the Brooklyn Academy of Music, New York City, USA, lasted almost 13 hr 25 min.

The longest frequently performed opera in the world is Wagner's *Die Meistersinger von Nürnberg* (1868). An uncut version performed by the Sadler's Wells company in London, UK, in 1968 lasted a total of 5 hr 15 min.

SHORTEST OPERA
The shortest published opera is *The Sands of Time* by Simon Rees and Peter Reynolds, which lasted 4 min 9 sec when first performed by Rhian Owen and Dominic Burns at The Hayes, Cardiff, UK, in March 1993. A 3-min 34-sec version was performed under the direction of Peter Reynolds in London, UK, in Sept 1993.

LOWEST NOTE
The lowest vocal note in the classical repertoire is in Osmin's aria in *Die Entführung aus dem Serail* by Wolfgang Amadeus Mozart. It calls for a low D (73.4 Hz).

HIGHEST NOTE
The highest vocal note in the classical repertoire is G^3, which occurs in Mozart's *Papolo di Tessaglia*.

LONGEST OPERATIC APPLAUSE
Placido Domingo (Spain) was applauded for a record 1 hr 20 min through a total of 101 curtain calls after a performance of *Otello* at the Vienna State Opera House, Austria, in July 1991.

BEST-SELLING JAZZ ARTIST
US saxophonist Kenny G has sold an estimated 50 million albums, including the best-selling jazz album of all time, Breathless *(of which an estimated 13 million copies have been sold). Kenny, born Kenneth Gorelick in 1959, has worked with Whitney Houston, Aretha Franklin, Smokey Robinson and Barry White, and is President Clinton's favourite saxophonist.*

LONGEST OPERATIC CAREER
Danshi Toyotake of Hyogo, Japan, sang *Musume Gidayu* (a traditional Japanese narrative) for 91 years from the age of seven, from 1898 to 1989.

BIGGEST OPERA HOUSE
The Metropolitan Opera House at the Lincoln Center, New York City, USA, was completed in Sept 1966 at a cost of $45.7 million (£16.3 million). It has a capacity of 4,065 people; the auditorium alone seats 3,800.

OLDEST OPERA HOUSE
In 1737 King Carlo VI commissioned Giovanni Medrano to build the Teatro S. Carlo in Naples, Italy. It was rebuilt under the direction of architect A. Niccolini after a fire in 1816 and has remained essentially the same building ever since. Containing 184 boxes in six tiers, the theatre can seat 1,500 people.

OLDEST CLASSICAL MUSIC
The earliest classical music in written records is Classical Chinese music, a musical theory that can be traced back 3,000 years when the philosopher Confucius advocated the practice of music.

BEST-SELLING OPERA SINGER
Italian tenor Luciano Pavarotti made his professional debut in 1961 and has sold about 60 million albums worldwide. His entire stage repertoire has reached disc and every recording is a best-seller. He also holds the record for the most curtain calls in an opera, receiving 165 after singing the part of Nemorino in Donizetti's *L' Elisir d' Amore* at the Deutsche Oper, Berlin, Germany, on 24 Feb 1988. The applause lasted 1 hr 7 min. Pavarotti reached a huge worldwide audience in the early 1990s when he began performing with Placido Domingo and José Carreras as 'The Three Tenors', under the baton of Zubin Mehta. The partnership was originally formed to celebrate the 1990 World Cup Finals, held in Italy.

LONGEST RECORDING CONTRACT

In 1931 the violinist and conductor Yehudi Menuhin signed a recording contract with EMI that remained in force until his death in March 1999. As well as the classical recordings for which Menuhin was renowned, he made a number of recordings with the jazz violinist Stéphane Grappelli and the Indian sitar-player Ravi Shankar.

OLDEST MUSICAL INSTRUMENT
An ancient bone flute, estimated to be about 43,000–82,000 years old, was found by Dr Ivan Turk, a palaeontologist at the Slovenian Academy of Science at a Neanderthal campsite in Ljubljana, Slovenia, in 1998. The oldest known musical instrument, it is made of an old cave-bear femur segment with four holes (two complete and two partial).

EARLIEST JAZZ RECORD
The first jazz record made was *Indiana/ The Dark Town Strutters Ball*, recorded for the Columbia label in New York City, USA, on or around 30 Jan 1917 by the Original Dixieland Jazz Band. It was released on 31 May 1917.

BIGGEST JAZZ FESTIVAL
The Festival International de Jazz de Montreal in Québec, Canada, is the world's largest jazz festival. Lasting 11 days, it attracts 1.5 million people to watch 400 concerts by 2,000 musicians from 20 countries.

LONGEST JAZZ CAREER
Saxophonist and pianist Benny Waters (b. 1902) from Maryland, USA, has been performing since his mid-teens and is still recording at the age of 97.

OLDEST JAZZ CLUB
The Village Vanguard cellar jazz club opened in New York City, USA, in the 1930s and has hosted mainstream jazz ever since.

MOST SUCCESSFUL PRE-TEEN CLASSICAL FEMALE PERFORMER

Charlotte Church was just 12 years old when she earned a double platinum album, for the 300,000 sales of her 1998 album Voice Of An Angel. *The record also earned the young Welsh soprano gold discs in Australia and New Zealand. Signed to Sony Music UK, she has played high-profile concerts at the London Palladium and the Royal Albert Hall.*

cartoons

HIGHEST-GROSSING FIRST RUN
Walt Disney's *The Lion King* (USA, 1994) grossed a record $766.9 million (£500.2 million) on its first run, when it was screened in over 60 countries. The film took 600 animators three years to make. In 1995 its hit theme tune, *Can You Feel The Love Tonight*, was awarded an Oscar for Best Original Song.

HIGHEST-GROSSING ANIMATED FILM
Walt Disney's *The Jungle Book* (USA, 1967) is the highest-grossing animated film ever made, with $205.8 million (£124.2 million).

Disney's *Snow White* (USA, 1937), which has taken $175.3 million (£105.7 million), would almost certainly top the list if inflation were taken into account.

HIGHEST-GROSSING JAPANESE ANIMATED FILM
Princess Mononoke (Japan, 1997) is Japan's highest-grossing animated film, making $156.6 million (£94.5 million) in Japan alone. When the film was shown on the Nippon Television Network (NTV) on 22 Jan 1999, it attracted the biggest audience for a movie in 15 years.

LONGEST-RUNNING ANIMATED FILM SERIES
Harry 'Bud' Fisher's series *Mutt and Jeff* began as a supplement to the *Pathé's Weekly* cinema newsreel on 10 Feb 1913 and continued as separate weekly reels from 1 April 1916 to 1 Dec 1926. At least 323 *Mutt and Jeff* films are known to have been made.

LONGEST-SERVING ACTOR IN AN ANIMATED SERIES
Actor Jack Mercer (USA) provided the voice of Popeye in the *Popeye The Sailor Man* series for a record-breaking 45 years. The series was produced for the cinema between 1933 and 1957 and was then made for television during the 1970s.

MOST CELEBRITIES FEATURED IN AN ANIMATED SERIES
The Simpsons has featured the voices of 228 celebrities, including Magic Johnson, Elizabeth Taylor and Paul and Linda McCartney.

MOST VALUABLE CARTOON CELLS
A black-and-white drawing from Walt Disney's *Orphan's Benefit* (1934) raised a record £171,250 ($280,000) when it was sold at Christie's, London, UK, in 1989.

One of the 150,000 colour cells from Walt Disney's animated film *Snow White* (USA, 1937) was sold in 1991 for $203,000 (£115,000).

MOST FITS CAUSED BY A TV SHOW
In Dec 1997 more than 700 children in Japan were rushed to hospital when an episode of an animated series based on the Nintendo game *Pocket Monsters* caused them to have convulsions. A total of 208 children aged three and above were detained in hospital after the broadcast. According to experts, the fits were caused by a sequence in which red lights flashed from the eyes of the character Pikachu.

MOST EXPENSIVE ANIMATED FILM
DreamWorks' The Prince Of Egypt *(USA, 1998) cost $60 million (£36.2 million) to make. It was in production for four years and was worked on by 350 artists and animators. The four-minute Red Sea sequence alone took 350,000 working hours to complete.*

BIGGEST CARTOON MUSEUM
The International Museum of Cartoon Art in Boca Raton, Florida, USA, has a collection of over 160,000 original animated drawings from 50 different countries. The collection also includes 10,000 books on animation and 1,000 hours of cartoons, interviews and documentaries on film and tape.

LONGEST-RUNNING COMIC
The Dandy, which was first published by D.C. Thomson on 4 Dec 1937, brought out its 3,007th edition on

MOST CONSECUTIVE OSCAR NOMINATIONS

Between 1991 and 1997 Aardman Animation of Bristol, UK, received six consecutive Oscar nominations for Best Short Animated Film — a record for any Oscar category. Three of the nominations, *Creature Comforts*, *The Wrong Trousers* and *A Close Shave*, all directed by Aardman's founder Nick Park, went on to win Oscars. The last two of these featured the cheese-loving inventor Wallace and his long-suffering canine companion Gromit (pictured). The animation technique for Park's films requires thousands of minute adjustments to modelling-clay figures, so each scene can take weeks to complete.

10 July 1999. Featuring Desperate Dan, the creation of cartoonist Dudley Watkins, the comic currently has a fan club of over 350,000 members.

MOST SYNDICATED COMIC STRIP

Peanuts by Charles Schulz was first published in Oct 1950 in the USA. The comic strip, which features the characters Charlie Brown and Snoopy, currently appears in 2,620 different newspapers in 75 countries.

LONGEST-RUNNING NEWSPAPER COMIC STRIP

The world's longest-running newspaper comic strip is *The Katzenjammer Kids*, which was first published in the *New York Journal* in Dec 1897 and is still running. Created by Rudolph Dirks, *The Katzenjammer Kids* is now drawn by cartoonist Hy Eisman and is syndicated to 50 newspapers by King Features Syndicate.

MOST VALUABLE COMIC

The most valuable comic book is a first-issue copy of *Action Comics* from June 1938, in which Superman made his first appearance. It was sold for $100,000 (£68,771) in 1997 and, according to the *Overstreet Comic Book Price Guide*, it is now valued at $185,000 (£115,625).

MOST PROLIFIC COMICS WRITER

Paul S. Newman (USA) had more than 4,000 stories published in 360 different comic books, including *Superman*, *Mighty Mouse*, *Prince Valiant*, *Fat Albert*, *Tweety & Sylvester* and *The Lone Ranger*.

MOST FILMED COMIC CHARACTER

Zorro has been portrayed in 69 films to date. Invented by Johnston McCulley, he was also the first comic strip character to be the subject of a major feature film, *The Mark of Zorro* (USA, 1920) starring Douglas Fairbanks. The movie appeared just one year after the comic strip was printed, giving Zorro the record for the fastest transition from comic strip to silver screen. The most recent version was *The Mask Of Zorro* (USA, 1998), in which the identity of the masked avenger was passed from Anthony Hopkins to Antonio Banderas.

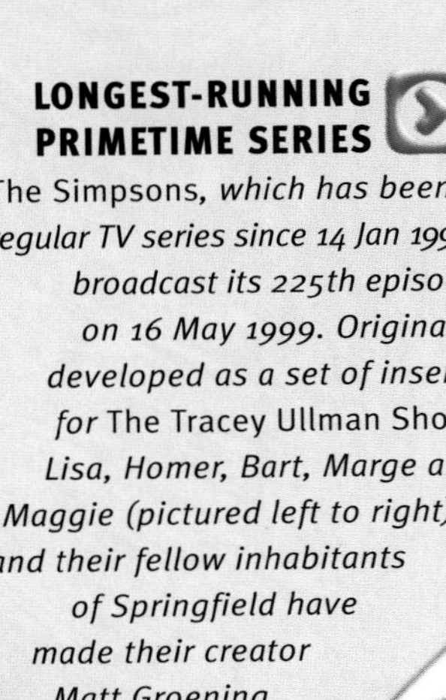

LONGEST-RUNNING PRIMETIME SERIES

The Simpsons, which has been a regular TV series since 14 Jan 1990, broadcast its 225th episode on 16 May 1999. Originally developed as a set of inserts for The Tracey Ullman Show, Lisa, Homer, Bart, Marge and Maggie (pictured left to right) and their fellow inhabitants of Springfield have made their creator Matt Groening (USA) a multi-millionaire.

theme parks & rides

MOST EXPENSIVE THEME PARK
Disney is reported to have spent about $1 billion (£625 million) on the design, development and realization of its Animal Kingdom in Florida, USA.

BIGGEST THEME PARK
Disney World near Orlando, Florida, USA, covers 12,140 ha (30,000 acres), making it the largest theme park in the world today. Opened on 1 Oct 1971, it cost approximately $400 million (£163.5 million) to develop.

MOST-VISITED THEME PARK
In 1997 Tokyo Disneyland in Japan attracted a total of 17.83 million visitors. Opened on 15 April 1983, the 46.25-ha (114.2-acre) park includes areas dedicated to the Wild West, tropical exploration, fairy tales, space travel and the future, and can accommodate up to 85,000 visitors at once.

MOST RIDES AT A THEME PARK
Cedar Point in Ohio, USA, has a total of 67 different rides — the most of any theme park in the world today. They include classic wooden roller coasters such as *Blue Streak*, which was built in 1964, hair-raising state-of-the-art rides such as *Mantis* (1996), and children's rides such as *Jr. Gemini* (1978).

MOST ROLLER COASTERS AT A THEME PARK
A record-breaking 13 roller coasters dominate the skyline at Cedar Point, Ohio, USA, which has been nicknamed 'America's Roller Coast' as a result. At its opening in 1892, the theme park had just one roller coaster, which shuttled riders around at a sedate 16 km/h (10 mph). Today it has some of the tallest, fastest and most technically advanced coasters in the world.

FASTEST ROLLER COASTER
Superman The Escape, at Six Flags Magic Mountain, California, USA, is the fastest coaster in the world. Riders are shot from 0 to 160 km/h (100 mph) in seven seconds and taken up to a height of 126 m (415 ft) in 15-seater gondolas before reaching the record-breaking speed once more on the backwards descent.

TALLEST GRAVITY-BASED COASTER
Fujiyama at Fujikyu Highland Park, Japan, reaches a height of 79 m (259 ft), with a first drop of 70 m (239 ft). The ride was built with a design speed of 130 km/h (81 mph), though it does not actually reach it during the ride.

TALLEST FREEFALL COASTER
The Drop Zone at King's Island Theme Park, Ohio, USA, has an 80-m (262-ft) drop from its 96.6-m (317-ft) vertical lift-tower, in an 88-second ride. Up to 40 riders freefall 43 m (141 ft) at zero G, reaching a speed of 108 km/h (67 mph).

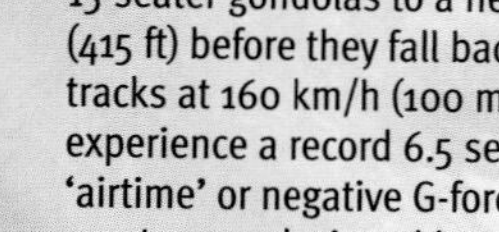

TALLEST THRILL RIDE
The Giant Drop at Dreamworld in Australia is the tallest freefall ride in the world, at 119 m (390 ft) or 39 storeys. Passengers on the open-air gondolas are winched skyward with their legs hanging freely. The ride, which lasts 1 min 46 sec, reaches speeds of up to 160 km/h (100 mph) before freefalling from 0 to 135 km/h (84 mph) within five seconds.

BIGGEST LOOPING ROLLER COASTER
The Viper coaster at Six Flags Magic Mountain, California, USA, has a 57.3-m (188-ft) drop. The ride turns upside-down seven times at a speed of 133 km/h (70 mph). It has three loops and a 12-m (40-ft) corkscrew.

FASTEST LAUNCHED COASTER
Superman the Escape, a steel coaster installed at Six Flags Magic Mountain, Valencia, California, USA, launches its 15-seater gondolas to a height of 126 m (415 ft) before they fall back along the tracks at 160 km/h (100 mph). Riders experience a record 6.5 seconds of 'airtime' or negative G-force. The coaster was designed by Intamin AG of Switzerland.

BIGGEST BIG WHEEL
The British Airways London Eye, designed by London architects David Marks and Julia Barfield, is scheduled to be unveiled at Jubilee Gardens, London, UK, in Jan 2000. When it is completed, it will be 136.1 m (446 ft 7 in) tall with a diameter of 135 m (443 ft). Each of the 32 capsules will be able to carry up to 25 passengers, giving views over a 48.28-km (30-mile) radius. The wheel will be the fourth biggest structure in London.

LARGEST ALL-WEATHER INDOOR WATER PARK

The Ocean Dome is part of a leisure resort at Miyazaki on the island of Kyushu, Japan. The park is 300 m (984 ft 1 in) long, 100 m (328 ft 1 in) wide and 38 m (124 ft 8 in) tall, and has a 140-m-long (459-ft 3-in) beach made up of polished crushed marble from China. The Ocean Dome is a popular destination for honeymoon couples and can accommodate a maximum of 10,000 people at one time, with a constant air temperature within the complex of 30°C (86°F) and a water temperature of 28°C (82.4°F). It also contains the world's largest wave-making machine, capable of producing waves up to 2.5 m (8 ft 2 in) high.

LONGEST ROLLER COASTER
The Ultimate roller coaster at Lightwater Valley, N Yorkshire, UK, is 2.298 km (1 mile 753 yd) long and the ride lasts 5 min 50 sec. Built in 1991, *The Ultimate* has steel tracks supported in places by a wooden superstructure.

ROLLER COASTERS WITH MOST INVERSIONS
The twisting steel coaster *Dragon Khan* takes riders upside-down eight times. The sit-down ride is the main attraction at Port Aventura, Salou, Spain. Built in 1995, the year the park opened, the track is 1.27 km (4,166 ft 1 in) long.

The *Monte Makaya* at Terra Encantada, Rio de Janeiro, Brazil, also turns riders upside-down eight times during each complete circuit of its 851.36-m (2,793-ft 4-in) steel track. Track elements include one Vertical Loop, two Cobra Rolls, a Double Corkscrew and three Zero-G-Heart Rolls.

BIGGEST PORTABLE THRILL RIDE
Taz's Texas Tornado has been in service at Six Flags Astroworld, Texas, USA, since 14 March 1998, but was originally assembled in Germany in 1986. The twisting steel coaster is 34.1 m (112 ft) in total height and has a maximum speed of 97 km/h (60 mph). Its steepest turn is at an angle of 80°.

OLDEST CONTINUALLY OPERATING ROLLER COASTER
Tivoli Gardens, Copenhagen, Denmark, was founded in 1843, and is one of the oldest amusement parks in the world. It is home to *Rutschebanen* (Scenic Railway) *Mk II*, which was built in 1913 and is the world's oldest operational roller coaster.

BIGGEST THEME PARK WEDDING
On 2 May 1997, at the opening of *Giant Drop* — a 69-m-high (227-ft) freefall tower at the Six Flags Great America theme park, USA — a record 144 couples were married seconds before a three-second plummet towards the ground at a speed of 100 km/h (62 mph). Most of the wedding ceremony took place in the park's 3,200-seat stunt show arena. The couples then ascended to the 22-storey Giant Drop, where the Reverend Herring completed the ceremony. The couples, who came from all over the USA, had been selected by radio stations to participate in the mass wedding.

FASTEST STAND-UP ROLLER COASTER
The Riddler's Revenge, *a steel stand-up coaster at Six Flags Magic Mountain, California, USA, is 47.5 m (156 ft) tall and has a top speed of 104.6 km/h (65 mph) — the highest of any roller coaster in which the riders stand up. It has six inversions (where the rider turns upside-down), including a 360° vertical loop with a record height of 37.8 m (124 ft).*

advertising

BIGGEST ADVERTISING AGENCY
Japanese advertising agency Dentsu Inc. had sales of $11.8 billion (£7.02 billion) by the end of March 1998 and 5,683 employees worldwide.

MOST EXPENSIVE TV ADVERT
A commercial for Apple Computers Inc cost a total of $600,000 (£360,000) to produce and $1 million (£600,000) to show. Directed by Ridley Scott, who also made *Blade Runner* (USA, 1982) and aired only once (in 1984), the ad registered such high viewer recall that it is believed to be one of the most cost-effective commercials ever made.

BIGGEST REVENUE BY A TV NETWORK IN ONE DAY
Fox TV is reputed to have earned a record $150 million (£90.5 million) on Super Bowl Sunday (31 Jan 1999), making it the most successful day in terms of advertising revenue for any network in TV history. About $45 million (£24.13 million) was made from pre-game advertising revenue.

MOST EXPENSIVE COMMERCIAL BREAK
The US TV network Fox earned $2 million (£1.25 million) for a 30-second spot during the transmission peak of the 1999 Super Bowl. The average cost of a 30-second spot during the day was $1.6 million (£970,000).

BIGGEST SINGLE TERRITORY AD CAMPAIGN
The 1996 US campaign for AT&T telephone services cost parent company AT&T Corporation a record $474 million (£296.25 million).

MOST ADVERTS FOR A PRODUCT IN ONE EVENING
All 17 versions of a Castlemaine XXXX commercial were shown on Granada Sky Broadcasting, UK, on 1 Oct 1996.

MOST AWARDS WON BY AN INTERNATIONAL COMMERCIAL
The Levi 501 jeans *Drugstore* TV advert won 33 awards in 1995.

FASTEST PRODUCTION OF AN ADVERT
A television ad for Reebok's InstaPUMP shoes was created, filmed and aired during Super Bowl XXVII at the Atlanta Georgia Dome, USA, on 31 Jan 1993. Filming took place up to the beginning of the fourth quarter of play, editing began in the middle of the third quarter and the ad was aired during the break at the two-minute warning of the fourth quarter. The commercial lasted for 30 seconds.

MOST ADVERTISING PAGES
The most pages of advertisements sold in a single issue of a periodical is 938.79 out of a total of 1,162 pages, in the Feb/March 1998 American edition of *Brides Magazine*.

SHORTEST ADVERT
An advert lasting four frames (equivalent to 0.133 seconds) was aired on KING-TV's *Evening Magazine* on 29 Nov 1993. The ad, for Bon Marché's Frango sweets, cost $3,780 (£2,500).

MOST POPULAR FILM TRAILER
When a 2-min 10-sec trailer for Star Wars: The Phantom Menace *(USA, 1999) was first shown in cinemas in 1998, many* Star Wars *fans all over the world paid the full price for a cinema ticket to watch the trailer and then walked out before the feature presentation. Many came back to see the trailer time after time. When LucasFilms, the film's production company, made the trailer available to download on its official website, it is reported to have received 3.5 million visits in five days.*

MOST CONTROVERSIAL CAMPAIGN
The Italian fashion company Benetton is unusual in that it creates all its advertising in-house, rather than using an outside agency. Over the years its campaigns have consistently caused outrage among many people: typical images have included a picture of a person with AIDS at the point of death, and a child with hair shaped into devil's horns. The advertisement featuring a newborn baby, pictured here, prompted more than 800 complaints to the British Advertising Standards Authority during 1991, when it ran as part of a press and billboard hoarding campaign. Benetton's images have won many awards, however, including Best Campaign of 1991 by the European Art Directors Club and the Infinity Award of the International Center of Photography in Houston, Texas, USA.

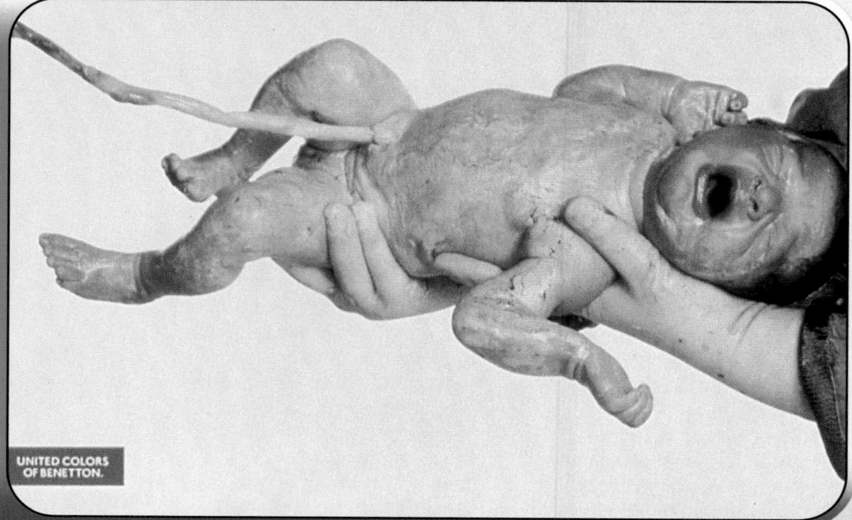

MOST CHART HITS PRODUCED BY AN AD CAMPAIGN

Levi Strauss' ads have resulted in chart success for more of the records they have featured than any other ad campaign. Eight songs from the company's ads have reached the No. 1 position in the United Kingdom, including two that went straight to No. 1 — Spaceman *by Babylon Zoo on 6 Jan 1996 and* Flat Beat *by Mr Oizo (pictured) on 3 April 1999.*

BIGGEST CAST IN AN ADVERT

Saatchi and Saatchi's ad *Face*, for British Airways, was filmed in Utah, USA, in Oct 1989 and starred 6,300 people wearing coloured tracksuits. Shot from the air, the ad showed the cast assembled in different configurations to create images of an ear, an eye, a pair of lips and, finally, a whole face and a globe.

BIGGEST CAST OF BABIES IN AN ADVERT

As of Right, a British television commercial made for the Vauxhall Astra car by Tony Kaye in 1996, featured 2,000 babies and no adults. The most babies on set at any one time was 984.

BIGGEST BILLBOARD

On 2 Feb 1999 a 16.88-m-high (55-ft 5-in), 126.48-m-long (414-ft 11-in) billboard was installed on the facade of the Ukraina Department Store in Kiev, Ukraine. Advertising Organics shampoo, the billboard remained in place for three months.

LONGEST FIXED BILLBOARD

The Bassat Ogilvy promotional hoarding for Ford España is 145 m (475 ft 9 in) in length and 15 m (49 ft 3 in) in height. It is sited at Plaza de Toros Monumental de Barcelona in Barcelona, Spain, and was installed on 27 April 1989.

BIGGEST MOVING BILLBOARD

A 268.25-m-long (880-ft 1-in) billboard covering an area of 1072.19 m² (11,541 ft²) was placed on a train travelling through Gauteng province, South Africa, on 11 May 1998.

BIGGEST NEON ADVERTISING SIGN

The largest neon advertising sign in the world is 91 m (298 ft 6 in) wide and 46 m (150 ft 11 in) high and covers 4,186 m² (45,041 ft²) on a wall at Tai Sing Container and Godown Centre, Hong Kong, China. Depicting eight horses, it was constructed in Dec 1997 and contains more than 5,000 light bulbs.

LONGEST ADVERTISING POSTER

A poster produced by Saatchi & Saatchi for the Rome Opera House and set up at the Piazza del Popolo in Rome, Italy, on 27 July 1998, was 274 m (898 ft 11 in) long and 2 m (6 ft 6 in) high.

MOST MARKETABLE SPORTSMAN

Fortune *magazine has estimated Michael Jordan's worth at over $10 billion (£6.033 billion), including revenue created through endorsements, television, ticket sales and merchandising, including Nike goods. When Jerry Reinsdorf bought 56% of the Chicago Bulls the year after Jordan arrived, his investment grew more than 1,000%. When Jordan announced his retirement in 1999, shares in Nike are reported to have fallen by 5.4%.*

publishing

BEST-SELLING AUTHOR
The top-selling fiction writer of all time is Agatha Christie, creator of Hercule Poirot and Miss Marple. Her 78 crime novels have sold an estimated 2 billion copies in 44 different languages.

BEST-SELLING BOOKS
The world's best-selling and most widely distributed book is the Bible, with an estimated 3.88 billion copies sold between 1815 and 1999.

Excluding non-copyright works, the all-time best-selling book is *The Guinness Book of Records*, first published by Guinness Superlatives in Oct 1955. Global sales in 37 languages had surpassed 85 million by July 1999.

BEST-SELLING CHILDREN'S BOOK SERIES
The 110 titles in the *Goosebumps* series by R.L. Stine have sold 220 million copies worldwide since the first book, *Welcome To Dead House* was published by Scholastic, Inc. in 1992.

BEST-SELLING NOVELS
Three novels have been credited with sales of over 30 million, all of them by American female authors. They are *Gone With The Wind* (1936) by Margaret Mitchell; *To Kill A Mockingbird* (1960) by Harper Lee; and *Valley Of The Dolls* (1966) by Jacqueline Susann, which sold 6.8 million copies in the six months following its publication.

Scottish author Alistair Maclean wrote a total of 30 novels, 28 of which have sold more than 1 million copies in the United Kingdom alone. It has been estimated that a novel by Maclean is purchased somewhere in the world every 18 seconds.

BEST-SELLING DIARY
The Diary of Anne Frank, the young author's account of events that took place when her family and their friends were hiding from the Nazis in Amsterdam, Netherlands, during the Second World War, has been translated into 55 languages and has sold more than 25 million copies.

LONGEST STAY ON A BEST-SELLER LIST
The Road Less Traveled by M. Scott Peck spent a record-breaking 694 weeks on the *New York Times* paperback best-seller list before dropping out on 6 April 1997. The book has sold more than 5 million copies.

MOST PROLIFIC NOVELIST
The Brazilian novelist José Carlos Ryoki de Alpoim Inoue had a total of 1,046 sci-fi novels, westerns and thrillers published between June 1986 and Aug 1996 — more than any other writer.

OLDEST AUTHORS
US sisters Sarah and Elizabeth Delany published *The Delany Sisters' Book Of Everyday Wisdom* in Oct 1994, when they were 105 and 103 years old respectively. In 1997 Sarah wrote the sequel *On My Own At 107*.

LONGEST BIOGRAPHY
The longest biography in publishing history is the life story of British wartime leader Sir Winston Churchill. Co-authored by his son Randolph and Martin Gilbert, who has been the sole author since Randolph's death in 1968, the book currently comprises a record 22 volumes, though writing and research is still on-going.

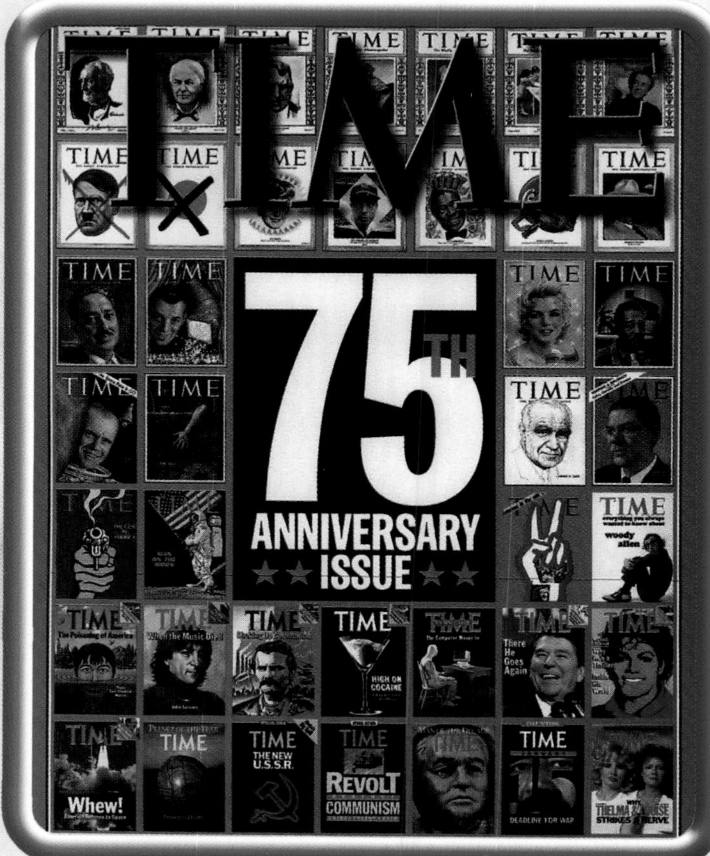

TOP-SELLING NEWS MAGAZINE
Time, which was launched in 1923, had a circulation of 4.06 million, for the six months ending Dec 1998 in the US alone. Time Inc has built up a large newsgathering organization and owns other best-selling magazines, including Fortune, Life *and* People.

BIGGEST BOOKSHOP
The biggest bookshop in the world is the Barnes and Noble Bookstore in New York City, USA. It covers an area of 14,330 m² (154,250 ft²) and has 20.71 km (12 miles 4,594 ft) of shelving.

OLDEST SEX MANUAL
Vatsyayana's *Kama Sutra* is believed to be the oldest sex manual in existence. Generally considered the standard work on love in Sanskrit literature, the book is thought to have been written between the 1st and 6th centuries AD. Today the *Kama Sutra* is widely available and has been translated into a number of languages.

TOP-SELLING NEWSPAPERS
The newspaper with the highest circulation in the world is Tokyo's *Yomiuri Shimbun*, established in 1874. By March 1999 its circulation was 14.42 million — 10.18 million for the morning edition and 4.24 million for the evening edition.

Komsomolskaya Pravda, the youth paper of the former Soviet Communist Party, reached a peak daily circulation of 21.9 million copies in May 1990.

More newspapers are sold in the United Kingdom than in any other country in the European Union. News International's *The Sun* has the highest circulation of any British daily newspaper, with 3.7 million copies sold, while *The Sun's* sister paper, the *News of the World*, has a record Sunday circulation of 4.2 million.

HIGHEST-EARNING HORROR AUTHOR

US novelist Stephen King (pictured playing in the celebrity band The Rock Bottom Remainders with writer Amy Tan) is the highest-earning horror author in the world, making $40 million (£24.1 million) in 1998 alone. His novels include Carrie *(1974),* The Shining *(1978),* Pet Sematary *(1983) and* Misery *(1987), all of which have been made into successful films.*

BEST-SELLING LIVING AUTHOR

The top-selling living author is British romantic novelist Dame Barbara Cartland. Her 635 titles have sold more than 650 million copies worldwide.

MOST NEWSPAPERS PUBLISHED IN ONE COUNTRY
In 1995 India had more than 4,235 different newspapers, most of them regional and published in different languages, including Hindi, Urdu, Punjabi, Gujarati and English.

HEAVIEST NEWSPAPER
The heaviest single issue of a newspaper was the 14 Sept 1987 edition of the Sunday *New York Times*, which weighed more than 5.4 kg (12 lb) and contained 1,612 pages.

TOP-SELLING MAGAZINES
Reader's Digest, which was established in Feb 1922, has a monthly circulation of more than 27 million copies in 18 different languages. Its US edition alone sells more than 15 million copies each month, while its UK edition has a monthly readership of around 1.63 million copies.

In 1974 the US *TV Guide* became the first weekly periodical to sell a billion copies in a single year. It currently has a weekly circulation of 11 million copies.

TOP-SELLING SOCIETY MAGAZINE
Spain's *¡Hola!* sells 627,514 copies a week — 116,962 more copies than its British sister publication, *Hello!*.

TOP-SELLING GAY MAGAZINE
Los Angeles-based *Advocate* magazine sells more than 2 million copies a year in the USA.

performance

LONGEST CONTINUOUS THEATRICAL RUN
The Mousetrap, a thriller written by Agatha Christie, opened at the Ambassadors Theatre, London, UK, on 25 Nov 1952. On 25 March 1974, after a total of 8,862 performances, it moved to St Martin's Theatre next door. On 14 April 1999 the 19,301st performance took place. The box office has grossed £20 million ($33.3 million) from more than 9 million theatre-goers.

LONGEST-RUNNING MUSICALS
The off-Broadway musical *The Fantasticks* by Tom Jones and Harvey Schmidt opened on 3 May 1960. By 8 March 1999 the show had been performed a record 16,127 times at the Sullivan Street Playhouse, Greenwich Village, New York, USA.

Cats is the longest-running musical in the history of the West End and Broadway, with the 7,675th and 6,896th show performed respectively on 14 April 1999. It opened on 11 May 1981 at the New London Theatre, UK, and has since been seen by an estimated 48 million people in approximately 250 cities around the world. Based on the poems in *Old Possum's Book Of Practical Cats* by T.S. Eliot, with music by Andrew Lloyd Webber, it has grossed more than £1.25 billion ($2 billion) worldwide.

LONGEST-RUNNING COMEDY
No Sex Please, We're British which was written by Anthony Marriott and Alistair Foot and presented by John Gale, opened at the Strand Theatre, London, UK, on 3 June 1971, transferred to the Duchess Theatre, London, on 2 Aug 1986 and finally ended on 5 Sept 1987 after 16 years 3 months – a total of 6,761 performances. The play was directed by Allan Davis throughout its run.

HIGHEST ADVANCE SALES
The musical *Miss Saigon*, written by Alain Boublil and Claude-Michel Schönberg, produced by Cameron Mackintosh and starring Jonathan Pryce and Lea Salonga, opened on Broadway in April 1991 after generating record advance sales of $36 million (£21.98 million).

HIGHEST-INSURED SHOW
The producers of *Barnum*, which opened at the London Palladium, UK, on 11 June 1981, insured the musical for the record sum of £5 million ($10 million). The individual insurance for its star Michael Crawford, who had to walk a high wire and slide down a rope from the highest box to the stage, accounted for £3 million ($6 million) of the total.

GREATEST THEATRICAL LOSS
The largest ever loss sustained by a theatrical show was borne by the American producers of the Royal Shakespeare Company's musical *Carrie*, which was based on the novel by Stephen King. The production closed after five performances on Broadway on 17 May 1988 at a cost of $7 million (£3.93 million).

HIGHEST-PAID DANCER
Michael Flatley (USA), the star of Lord Of The Dance, *earned $1.6 million (£1 million) a week for his Irish-style dancing at the peak of the show's success. This included profits from ticket, video and merchandise sales. The Chicago-born star first found international fame when he performed at the 1994 Eurovision Song Contest in Dublin, Republic of Ireland. He is seen here with members of the* Lord Of The Dance *troupe at the 1997 Academy Awards ceremony.*

LARGEST AUDIENCE FOR A COMEDIAN

On 24 Aug 1996 Danish-born US satirist Victor Borge performed before a paying audience of 12,989 people at The Hollywood Bowl, Los Angeles, California, USA, a record for a comedian. Borge is renowned for his send-ups of classical music and his 'audible punctuation' routine. The UK record is 11,230, by Eddie Izzard (pictured) on 24 Feb 1999 at Wembley Arena, London, UK, during his *Dressed To Kill* world tour. The event raised £150,000 ($240,675) for the Prince's Trust, a charity that provides young people with training and support for new businesses. Izzard, whose surreal routines range in subject matter from accountants on *Star Trek* to cats armed with pneumatic drills, has been known to perform in a mini-skirt and full make-up. His movie appearances have included *Velvet Goldmine* (UK/USA, 1998) and *The Avengers* (USA, 1998).

MOST PERFORMANCES IN ONE PRODUCTION
Steven Wayne (UK), the longest-serving cast member of a musical, has been with the West End production of *Cats* since rehearsals began for the opening on 11 May 1981. During that time he has played and understudied most of the male roles in the show.

LONGEST PLAY
The longest known play is *The Non-Stop Connolly Show* by John Arden (UK), which took 26 hr 30 min to perform in Dublin, Republic of Ireland, in 1975.

SHORTEST PLAY
The world's shortest ever play is the 30-second *Breath*, written by the Irish-born playwright and novelist Samuel Beckett in 1969. The play consists of the sound of a single human breath. Beckett, who won the Nobel Prize for Literature in 1969 and died in 1992, was a pivotal figure in the Theatre of the Absurd.

BIGGEST DANCE FESTIVAL
The Festival de Dança de Joinville in Santa Catarina, Brazil, is the largest dance festival in the world, both in terms of the number of dancers and the number of performance categories. About 3,000 dancers from all over the world gather to participate.

MOST CURTAIN CALLS FOR A BALLET
The record for the greatest number of curtain calls received at any ballet is 89, by Dame Margot Fonteyn (UK) and Rudolf Nureyev (USSR) after their performance of Tchaikovsky's *Swan Lake* at the Vienna Staatsoper, Austria, in Oct 1964.

LONGEST CHORUS LINES
The longest chorus lines in performing history contained up to 120 dancers, as part of some of the early *Ziegfeld's Follies*, which were created in 1907 by Florenz Ziegfeld, the greatest exponent of the American revue. Over the years the Ziegfeld Girls included future Hollywood stars such as Barbara Stanwyck, Paulette Goddard and Irene Dunne.

When the show *A Chorus Line* by Nicholas Dante and Marvin Hamlisch broke the then record as the longest-running Broadway show on 29 Sept 1983, the finale featured a one-off total of 332 top-hatted 'strutters'.

FASTEST TAP DANCER
The fastest rate ever measured for tap dancing is 38 taps per second, achieved by James Devine in Sydney, NSW, Australia, on 25 May 1998.

FASTEST FLAMENCO DANCER
Solero de Jérez attained a rate of 16 heel taps per second in a routine in Brisbane, Queensland, Australia, in Sept 1967.

BIGGEST ARTS FESTIVAL
The annual Edinburgh Fringe Festival, UK, began in 1947 and saw its busiest year in 1993, when 582 groups gave a total of 14,108 performances of 1,643 shows between 15 Aug and 4 Sept. Although all kinds of performance art are represented on the programme, the Fringe has become particularly popular in recent years for its comedy and cabaret acts, such as the Kamikaze Freak Show (above). The Fringe runs alongside the 'official' Festival, which concentrates on international theatre and classical music.

art & installations

HIGHEST INSURANCE PREMIUM QUOTED FOR A PAINTING

The *Mona Lisa* (*La Gioconda*) by Leonardo Da Vinci was valued at $100 million (£35 million) by insurers for a move from the Louvre, Paris, France, to the USA for an exhibition in 1962. The painting was not insured, as the premiums would have cost more than the tightest security precautions.

MOST VALUABLE 20TH-CENTURY PAINTING

Les Noces de Pierette by Pablo Picasso (Spain) sold for a record $80.44 million (£51.89 million) in Paris, France, in 1986.

MOST VALUABLE PAINTING BY A FEMALE ARTIST

In the Box by the US Impressionist artist Mary Cassatt, who died in 1926, sold at Christie's, New York City, USA, for $3.67 million (£2.45 million) on 23 May 1996. Seven of the 10 highest prices paid for works by female artists have been for paintings by Cassatt.

MOST VALUABLE PAINTING BY AN ANONYMOUS ARTIST

Departure of the Argonauts (1487) sold at Sotheby's, London, UK, for £4.2 million ($6.7 million) on 9 Dec 1989.

MOST VALUABLE PHOTOGRAPH

Hand With Thimble (1920), Alfred Stieglitz's photograph of one of the hands of his wife, artist Georgia O'Keeffe, raised $398,500 (£260,458) at an auction at Christie's, New York City, USA, on 8 Oct 1993.

MOST VALUABLE POSTER

A poster by the Scottish designer, architect and painter Charles Rennie Mackintosh, advertising an 1895 art show at the Glasgow Institute of Fine Arts, UK, sold for £68,200 ($105,028) at Christie's, London, UK, in Feb 1993.

MOST AUCTION SALES BY AN ARTIST

By May 1999, works by Pablo Picasso, the Spanish pioneer of Cubism, had been sold at auction 3,595 times. The total value of these sales is $1.23 billion (£765.3 million).

MOST EXPENSIVE PAINTING

Portrait of Dr Gachet by Vincent Van Gogh was bought by the Japanese businessman and collector Ryoei Saito at Christie's, New York City, USA, for $82.5 million (£46.1 million) in May 1990. It depicts the doctor into whose care the disturbed artist was placed, and was completed only weeks before Van Gogh's suicide in 1890. Ironically in view of the huge sums his works command today, he sold only one painting in his lifetime.

BIGGEST FLOWER SCULPTURE

In 1992 US artist Jeff Koons created Puppy, *a 12.3-m x 5.5-m x 6 m (40-ft x 18-ft x 19-ft 6-in) sculpture made out of flowers at the Documenta exhibition in Kassel, Germany. The plants chosen vary according to the climate in which the piece is exhibited. The work has an internal sprinkling system and 1.5-m (5-ft) steel rods attached to a frame to create the coat. Koons is renowned for controversial pieces in media including sculpture, ceramics and photography.*

MOST VALUABLE SCULPTURE

The Three Graces by Antonio Canova was jointly purchased by the Victoria & Albert Museum, London, UK, and the National Gallery of Scotland, Edinburgh, UK, for £7.5 million ($11.5 million) in 1994. The statue, which is scheduled to make the 644-km (400-mile) journey between London and Edinburgh every seven years, has been permanently disfigured by a hairline fracture sustained during its travels.

BIGGEST SCULPTURE

The figures of Jefferson Davis, Robert Edward Lee and Thomas 'Stonewall' Jackson are 27.4 m (90 ft) high and cover 0.5 ha (1.33 acres) on Stone Mountain, Atlanta, Georgia, USA. Sculptor Walker Kirtland Hancock worked with Roy Faulkner and other helpers to create it from 12 Sept 1963 to 3 March 1972.

BIGGEST OUTDOOR INSTALLATION

Desert Breath covers 10 ha (25 acres) and is made up of 178 cones, 89 sand cones and 89 conical depressions cut into the floor of the desert near the town of Hurghada in Egypt. It took a team of three Greek artists nine months to create, and will have been eroded within a few years.

BIGGEST LAND PORTRAIT

US crop artist Stan Herd uses his tractor to carve enormous pictures into the landscape. His largest work to date is a 65-ha (160-acre) portrait of the 1930s Hollywood star Will Rogers on the plains of south-west Kansas, USA.

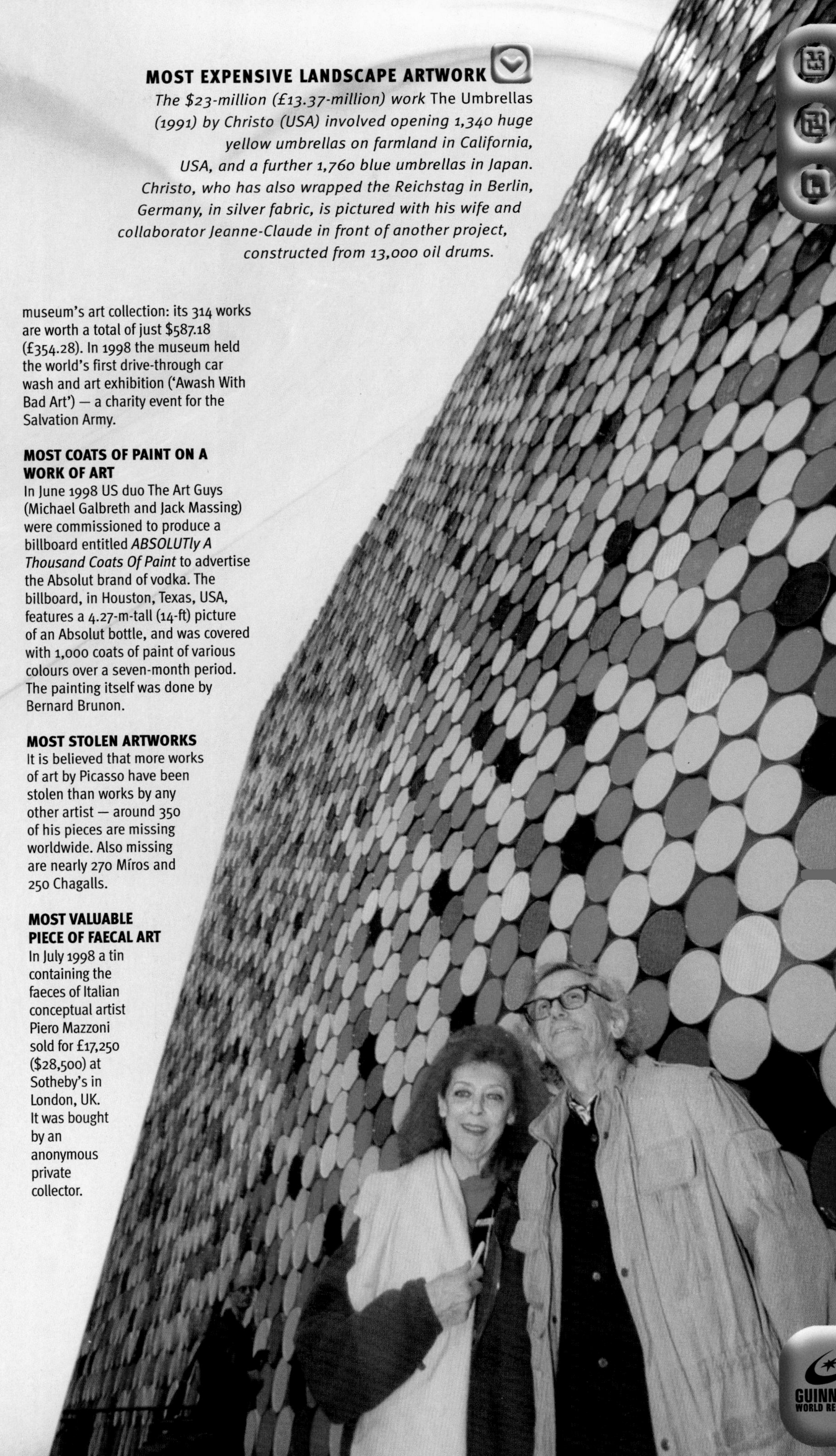

MOST EXPENSIVE LANDSCAPE ARTWORK

The $23-million (£13.37-million) work The Umbrellas *(1991) by Christo (USA) involved opening 1,340 huge yellow umbrellas on farmland in California, USA, and a further 1,760 blue umbrellas in Japan. Christo, who has also wrapped the Reichstag in Berlin, Germany, in silver fabric, is pictured with his wife and collaborator Jeanne-Claude in front of another project, constructed from 13,000 oil drums.*

BIGGEST ARCHITECTURAL INSTALLATION

Tight Roaring Circle, a 12-m-tall (39-ft), 19-m-wide (62-ft) bouncy castle made of 2,725 m² (29,333 ft²) of white PVC-coated polyester, was designed by Dana Caspersen and William Forsythe. It was constructed inside the Roundhouse, a converted railway turntable shed in London, UK, in 1997. Visitors were invited to interact with the structure, spurred on by low lighting, an ambient soundtrack by Joel Ryan and text by the Japanese writer Yukio Mishima printed on the courtyard walls.

LONGEST SKETCH PROJECT

Alan Whitworth (UK) has been sketching Hadrian's Wall, the second-century Roman fortification marking England's northern boundary with Scotland, for more than 13 years. His sketch will be 117 km (73 miles) long when it is finished in 2007.

BIGGEST GALLERY ENDOWMENT

The J. Paul Getty Trust was set up in Jan 1974 with $1.64 billion (£700 million) and has an annual budget of more than $100 million (£60 million). It runs the Getty Center in Los Angeles, California, USA, which opened on 15 Dec 1997, as well as the smaller J. Paul Getty Museum, Malibu, California, USA.

MOST VISITORS TO AN ART GALLERY IN ONE YEAR

In 1995 the Centre Pompidou in Paris, France, had a record 6.3 million visitors.

BIGGEST ROUND-THE-CLOCK ART EXHIBITION

Buenos Aires No Duerme ('Buenos Aires Doesn't Sleep') is a multidisciplinary art exhibition that runs for 10 days and 10 nights non-stop every year. A total of 1.2 million people visited the exhibition, held at the Centro Municipal de Exposiciones, Buenos Aires, Argentina, in 1998.

LEAST VALUABLE ART COLLECTION IN A PUBLIC MUSEUM

The MOBA (Museum Of Bad Art) in Garden Grove, California, USA, is the only museum in the world dedicated to the worst excesses of creative endeavour. The maximum sum paid for an artwork is $6.50 (£3.92) and the average is $1.80 (£1.08). Most works are either pulled from rubbish dumps or donated. MOBA's collection has the lowest value of any public museum's art collection: its 314 works are worth a total of just $587.18 (£354.28). In 1998 the museum held the world's first drive-through car wash and art exhibition ('Awash With Bad Art') — a charity event for the Salvation Army.

MOST COATS OF PAINT ON A WORK OF ART

In June 1998 US duo The Art Guys (Michael Galbreth and Jack Massing) were commissioned to produce a billboard entitled *ABSOLUTly A Thousand Coats Of Paint* to advertise the Absolut brand of vodka. The billboard, in Houston, Texas, USA, features a 4.27-m-tall (14-ft) picture of an Absolut bottle, and was covered with 1,000 coats of paint of various colours over a seven-month period. The painting itself was done by Bernard Brunon.

MOST STOLEN ARTWORKS

It is believed that more works of art by Picasso have been stolen than works by any other artist — around 350 of his pieces are missing worldwide. Also missing are nearly 270 Míros and 250 Chagalls.

MOST VALUABLE PIECE OF FAECAL ART

In July 1998 a tin containing the faeces of Italian conceptual artist Piero Mazzoni sold for £17,250 ($28,500) at Sotheby's in London, UK. It was bought by an anonymous private collector.

high fashion

OLDEST DESIGNER LABEL

Charles Edward Worth, who died in 1895, was the first designer to sign his work with a label and to show garments on live models. Born in Lincolnshire, UK, Worth moved to Paris, France, in 1845, where his talent for design was soon discovered by the ladies of the court of Napoleon III. He then started his own business and by 1871 had 1,200 people in his employment, making £14,981 (then $80,000) a year. His business was inherited by his son after his death and continues today through the perfumes of the House of Worth, such as Worth Pour Homme and Je Reviens.

BIGGEST-SELLING DESIGNER CLOTHING LABEL

The biggest-selling designer clothing brand in the world is Ralph Lauren, which had annual global sales of $1.5 billion (£905 million) in 1998. Boasting labels such as Polo Ralph Lauren, Polo Sport and the Ralph Lauren Collection, the company has nearly 200 Polo STORES and outlet stores worldwide, and also sells its designs through approximately 1,600 department stores and speciality shops.

RICHEST LUXURY GOODS MAKER

Bernard Arnault (France), who heads the luxury goods empire LVMH (Moet Hennessy Louis Vuitton), is worth an estimated $6 million (£3.6 billion). The company sells Christian Lacroix, Givenchy and Kenzo Mode fashions, Louis Vuitton bags and Christian Dior, Guerlain and Givenchy perfumes, as well as top drinks brands such as Dom Perignon and Hennessy. In 1998 the company had sales of $7.5 billion (£4.52 billion), 57% of which came from their fragrance, cosmetics, fashion and leather goods lines.

BIGGEST-SELLING DESIGNER PERFUME

The world's biggest-selling designer perfume is Chanel No. 5, which sells more than 10 million bottles a year. Developed in 1925, Chanel No. 5 has more than 80 ingredients. Its creator, Coco Chanel, was the first ever couturier to attach her name to a perfume.

BIGGEST STOCKIST OF DESIGNER CLOTHING

The US department store Saks Fifth Avenue currently stocks a total of 1,252 designer brands — more than any other store in the world. Saks, which was founded in 1924, has a total of 59 stores throughout the USA and employs approximately 1,200 people.

OLDEST DESIGNER

British designer Sir Hardy Amies, who was born in 1909, is still actively involved in the fashion industry. Sir Hardy joined the fashion house Lachasse in Farm Street, London, UK, in 1934 and founded his own dressmaking business in nearby Savile Row in 1946. He is currently dressmaker by appointment to Queen Elizabeth II.

FASTEST RISE TO HEAD OF A DESIGN HOUSE

Stella McCartney, the daughter of Paul and Linda McCartney, was appointed as the new designer at Parisian fashion house Chloé in April 1997, just 18 months after graduating from Central Saint Martins College of Art and Design in London, UK. McCartney, who replaced Karl Lagerfeld, currently commands a six-figure salary. She famously dedicated her 1999 spring collection to the memory of her mother.

MOST EXPENSIVE DESIGNER HAT

In 1977 UK designer David Shilling created a straw-coloured hat valued at £19,950 ($34,833). The hat was decorated with a selection of diamond-encrusted jewellery, all of which could be worn separately. A chain of diamonds covering the crown of the hat could be worn as a necklace, a rose decoration as a brooch and a dewdrop design as a pair of earrings. The hat would be worth £66,234 ($109,776) in today's terms.

MOST EXPENSIVE TIARAS

The world's most expensive tiara was designed by Gianni Versace and had an estimated retail value of $5 million (£3.2 million) in 1996. Set in yellow gold and decorated with 100-carat diamonds, the tiara weighed approximately 300 g (10½ oz).

An 18-carat gold crown set with cut diamonds and surmounted by a 6.9-carat yellow diamond retailed for £250,000 ($414,000) at Harrods, London, UK, in 1998. The tiara was designed by Slim Barrett, whose headwear is worn by celebrities such as Madonna and Sinead O'Connor.

MOST EXPENSIVE JACKET

In 1998 Naomi Campbell modelled the world's most expensive jacket as part of Gai Mattioli's 1998 collection. Worth $1 million (£600,000), it has 100-carat Burmese rubies — the biggest on the market — and 250-year-old, 36-carat emeralds as buttons.

MOST EXPENSIVE METALLIC SHOES

Manolo Blahnik made six pairs of gold shoes with heels covered in 18-carat gold and 18-carat gold front bands for Antonio Berardi's 1999 spring/summer catwalk show. The shoes were priced from £6,000 ($9,944), depending on their size. During the show the shoes were protected by bodyguards.

MOST EXPENSIVE BRA

The Dream Angels Bra was designed by Janis Savitt for M+J Savitt. Costing $5 million (£3.02 million), it is embellished with 77 carats of rubies and has straps studded with 330 carats of diamonds set in platinum. It was available exclusively through Victoria's Secret Christmas Dreams and Fantasy Catalogue 1998.

YOUNGEST INTERNATIONALLY ESTABLISHED DESIGNER

British designer Julien MacDonald (pictured), who was born in 1973, was spotted by Karl Lagerfeld during his graduation show at the Royal College Of Art in London, UK, when he was 24, and was asked to design a knitwear range for Chanel. After success in Paris, France, MacDonald went on to present his own collection, 'Mermaids', in 1997. The youngest established designer of all time is Frenchman Yves Saint-Laurent (b.1936), who became Christian Dior's assistant at the age of 17 and was named head of the House of Dior in 1957.

MOST EXPENSIVE JEANS

Gucci 'genius jeans' — original Guccis decorated with African beading, tribal feather trims and silver metal buttons and rivets — went on sale in Gucci shops worldwide after being launched in Milan, Italy, in Oct 1998. Although they cost $3,050 (£1,840) a pair, they were quickly snapped up by buyers, many of whom had put their names down on a waiting list after seeing the jeans on the catwalk. 'Genius jeans' spend two weeks at a distressing plant after being manufactured, where they are faded and ripped before having their decorations sewn on by hand.

MOST EXPENSIVE CANCELLED CATWALK SHOW

Giorgio Armani's Emporio show during Paris fashion week in March 1998 was cancelled by French police concerned about safety at the venue. By that time Armani had spent $300,000 (£187,500) on the show and a further $1 million (£625,000) on the after-show party, making it the most expensive fashion show never to have happened.

MOST SPENT ON A DESIGNER STORE

Helena Christiansen is seen modelling an outfit by Gianni Versace. Versace's shop in Bond Street, London, UK, opened in 1992 and is said to have cost more to set up than any other designer store, at £12 million ($21.2 million). Versace is one of the most commercially successful fashion houses in the world, grossing $50.8 million (£26.5 million) in 1978 and $533.8 million (£325.8 million) in 1997.

RICHEST DESIGNER

Ralph Lauren, pictured below with US president Bill Clinton, has a personal fortune estimated at $1.7 billion (£1.03 billion) — the highest of any designer. Described by New York *magazine as 'the first image-maker', Lauren was born Ralph Lipschitz in New York, USA, in 1939. He began his career as a sales assistant and changed his name before opening his first shop — which sold ties — in the 1960s. The Ralph Lauren empire is currently valued at around $3 billion (£1.8 billion).*

GUINNESS WORLD RECORDS

street fashion

FASTEST-GROWING DESIGNER LABEL

Tommy Hilfiger clothes are sold in more than 2,000 department and speciality stores and in about 55 specialized retail outlets all over the world. In 1998 the company had sales of $847.1 million (£511.1 million) — an increase of 28% on the previous year. In 1995 Hilfiger won the 'From Catwalk to Sidewalk' award, which honours the designer whose clothing is most easily worn unaltered by the man or woman on the street. The company is also the official clothing supplier to the Ferrari Formula 1 motor racing team.

BIGGEST SPORTSWEAR COMPANY
The sportswear giant Nike was founded in Oregon, USA, by Bill Bowerman, one of the country's top athletics coaches and his former student Phil Knight. The company had revenues of $9.55 billion (£5.76 billion) in 1998, making it the 166th largest company on the *Fortune* 500 list. Nike controls more than 40% of the US sportswear market.

BEST-SELLING BRAND OF CLOTHING
Levi Strauss is the world's biggest brand-named clothing manufacturer. Their clothes, sold under the Levis, Dockers and Slates brands, are sold in more than 30,000 retail outlets in 60 countries. In 1998 the company's sales totalled $6 billion (£3.62 billion).

Dockers, a brand of casual wear created by Levi Strauss and Co, was launched in the USA in 1986 and by the early 1990s had become the fastest-growing sub-brand in US history, with the highest level of brand awareness of any casual trousers. After a $10-million (£6.82-million) promotion campaign, Dockers were the best-selling brand in the casual wear market.

BIGGEST FASHION STORE
On 3 Oct 1998 the high street fashion chain Top Shop unveiled its new three-level store at Oxford Circus, London, UK, covering an area of 7,897 m² (85,000 ft²) — 25% bigger than the previous Oxford Circus store. The menswear shop Top Man is located in the same building and covers 1,022 m² (11,000 ft²) of floor space. In total, the building, which already attracted 7 million customers per year, now has six sections on its upper floors and three sections below ground. The 18-month refurbishment included checks on 98 columns, 3,300 girders, 12 million rivets and repairs to 4.89 km (3 miles) of concrete beams. A total of 9,000 m³ (96,875.1 ft³) of rubble and rubbish was removed.

BIGGEST FASHION FRANCHISE
The Benetton Group dresses customers in more than 120 countries through its 7,000 franchised stores and company-owned megastores. The Italian company's clothing consists primarily of knitwear and sportswear, and it is the world's largest consumer of wool in the garment sector. Today it has nine factories in different parts of the world. Its sales totalled $2.3 billion (£1.4 billion) in 1998.

BIGGEST SURFWEAR MANUFACTURER
Quiksilver had a revenue in the fiscal year 1998 of approximately $316 million (£190.66 million), making it the largest manufacturer of surfwear in the world to date. The company sells to more than 130 countries and sponsors hundreds of athletes, including surf champions Robbie Naish, Kelly Slater and Lisa Andersen.

BIGGEST CHARITY SHOP CHAIN
Oxfam opened its first charity shop in 1948 and now has 836 shops in the United Kingdom and Ireland, making it the biggest charity shop chain in the world. In 1998 the company — which fights hunger, disease, exploitation and poverty worldwide regardless of race or religion — had an income of £16.2 million ($26.52 million) from its shops. This is almost one third of its annual income from voluntary work.

BIGGEST SECONDHAND CLOTHES SHOP
Domsey's Warehouse and Annex in Brooklyn, New York, USA, is the largest secondhand clothes shop, with an area of 23,225 m² (250,000 ft²), of which 3,720 m² (40,000 ft²) is the sales floor. The family business has been handed down through three generations and has been based in Brooklyn for 18 years. It stocks about 350,000 garments at any one time.

BIGGEST FOOTWEAR RETAILER AND MANUFACTURER
The Bata Shoe Organization was founded in Zlin, Bohemia (now Czech Republic), in 1894, and now has 4,458 company-run stores worldwide as well as more than 100,000 independent retailers and franchisees. It has more than 62 manufacturing units, which together produce about 170 million pairs of shoes. Bata sells its shoes through companies in more than 60 countries.

BIGGEST-SELLING SKATE SHOES
Vans is the ninth largest footwear manufacturer in the USA and according to *Sporting Goods Intelligence* leads the market in alternative footwear. The company, which is known mainly for its skateboarding shoes, had sales of $187 million (£112.8 million) in 1998, $143 million (£86.3 million) of which were in the USA.

OLDEST ATHLETIC SHOE ENDORSEMENT
Converse's basketball shoes, cross-training casual shoes and children's shoes are sold under the Chuck Taylor Converse All-Star brand, named after Chuck Taylor, who became the very first athletic shoe endorser in 1923. Taylor's name was added to the ankle patch to honour his contribution to basketball.

BIGGEST-SELLING BRAND OF DESIGNER UNDERWEAR
The world's most popular designer underwear brand is Calvin Klein (USA). In the 1980s Klein identified the trend among women of buying men's underwear for themselves and launched boxers for women. In 1998 the company sold 30 million pairs of briefs and knickers, with a total retail value of $425 million (£256 million).

BEST-SELLING BRA
Sara Lee controls 32% of the US bra market. The company, which had total sales of $20 billion (£12 billion) in 1998, owns the Wonderbra and the best-selling Playtex brand, which includes the 18-hour, Cross-Your-Heart and Playtex Secrets lines.

BIGGEST TIGHTS MANUFACTURER
One in every five pairs of tights in the world is made by Sara Lee, making it the largest tights manufacturer, with 51% of the US market in 1998. Its hosiery brands include L'Eggs, Hanes and Pretty Polly.

BIGGEST DESIGNER HAT COMPANY
Kangol was founded in northern England in 1938. The company's hats have been long worn by golfers and members of the British armed forces (who wore Kangol berets) but have recently been adopted by young people because of the hats' connection with hip-hop stars. Sales are reported to have increased by 50% in the wake of Quentin Tarantino's film *Jackie Brown* (USA, 1998), in which Samuel L. Jackson wore a Kangol hat.

FASTEST-SELLING WATCH
The Swatch watch, which was invented by the Swiss watchmaker Dr. Ernest Thomke and Nicholas Hayek in 1981, had sold more than 100 million units within 10 years, making it the fastest-selling brand of watch in history. In 1989 the company asked Italian artist Mimmo Paladino to design a Swatch, which was produced in a limited edition of 120. Two years later a Paladino Swatch sold at an auction in Europe for $24,000 (£13,946).

MOST POPULAR SUNGLASSES
Ray-Ban sunglasses sold 10 million units worldwide in 1998. Ray-Ban's best known model, the Wayfarer, has been available since 1953 and is reported to be the best-selling style in history.

BIGGEST CLOTHING INDUSTRIES
The largest clothing industry in the world in terms of the value of the goods produced is that of the USA, which manufactured approximately $39.5 billion (£24.7 billion) worth of clothing, excluding footwear, in 1996. It had about 800,000 employees in 1997.

The biggest clothing industry in terms of the number of employees is China's. Its total clothing production (excluding footwear) was worth $17.9 billion (£11.2 billion) in 1996.

BIGGEST-SELLING UNDERWEAR
Marks & Spencer sells 50 million pairs (counting multi-packs as a pair) of its own brand women's knickers globally each year — nearly 137,000 pairs a day. The company operates almost 700 stores in some 30 countries and sells mid-price clothing, food and household items under its popular St Michael brand. It also owns more than 190 Brooks Brothers clothing stores in the USA and Asia.

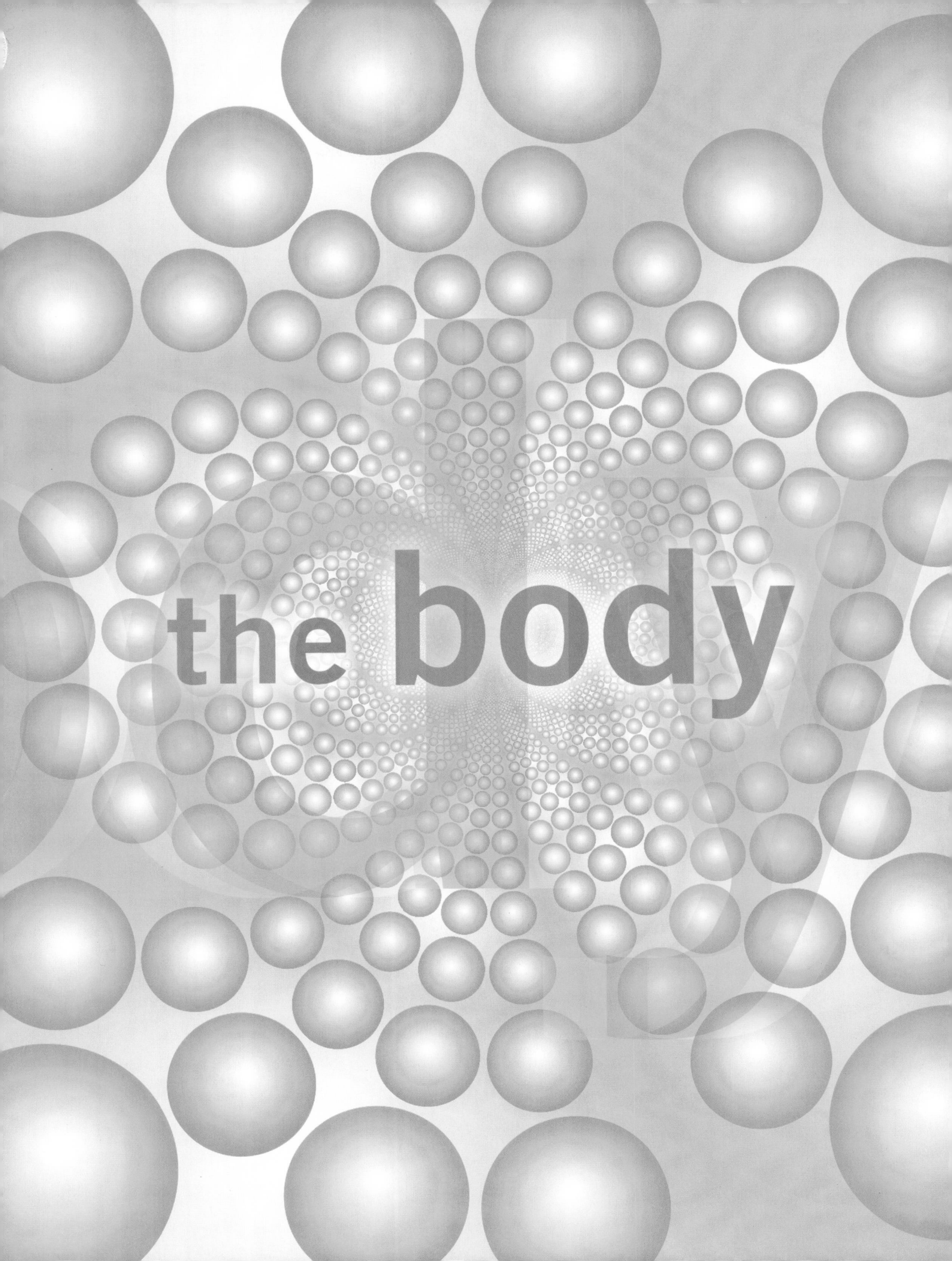
the body

body transformation

MOST ARTISTS TATTOOING SIMULTANEOUSLY

Enigma, an American circus star, was tattooed by 22 artists simultaneously during the Amsterdam Tattoo Convention, Netherlands, on 9 May 1996. A star of Jim Rose's Circus, Enigma has had his body covered in jigsaw-puzzle tattoos. He also has horns, a tail and porcupine quills, which were implanted into his body using coral. Bone is growing around the implants and the horns on his head grow at a rate of 3.8 cm (1½ in) a year.

LONGEST TATTOO SESSION

The longest tattoo session lasted 25 hours, when Chris Masterson had his legs and arms tattooed for charity by Ian Barfoot in Reading, Berks, UK, in 1992.

GREATEST COVERAGE BY TATTOOS

Tom Leppard, a retired soldier who lives on the Isle of Skye, UK, has had 99.9% of his body tattooed with a leopard-skin design. His body is now covered with dark spots and the skin between them is tattooed saffron yellow. The only parts of his body that remain free of tattoos are the insides of his ears and the skin between his toes.

The record for tattoo coverage of a woman is 95%, held by Julia Gnuse of Foothill Ranch, California, USA, who appeared on the TV show *Guinness® World Records: Primetime* on 6 Oct 1998, and 'Krystyne Kolorful' from Alberta, Canada.

MOST INDIVIDUAL TATTOOS

Bernie Moeller of Pennsylvania, USA, had had his body covered by a total of 14,006 individual tattoos by 3 April 1997. His tattoos have made him a popular guest at various outdoor events and he has made several television appearances.

BIGGEST TATTOO ARCHIVE

The Tattoo Archive is run by the Paul Rodgers Foundation in Berkeley, California, USA, and has tens of thousands of items relating to the history of tattooing and to modern tattoos. It is the world's first ever tattoo research resource centre. Lyle Tuttle of the Tattoo Archive has a private collection of American tattoo memorabilia including tens of thousands of business cards and machines.

BIGGEST TATTOO MUSEUM

The Tattoo Museum, opened in 1995 in Amsterdam, Netherlands, is the world's largest collection of tattoos on view to the public. It puts on demonstrations and has a library and a permanent exhibition of memorabilia and ethnographic tattoo history. It attracts up to 23,000 visitors a year.

OLDEST TATTOOS

Ötzi, the world's oldest preserved human body, has 15 tattoos. Found in a glacier near the Ötz Valley, on the Italy–Austria border, in 1991, Ötzi is believed to be 5,300 years old and to have died at the age of 40. He has a series of blue parallel lines covering his lower spine, as well as stripes across his right ankle and a tattoo of a cross behind his right knee.

Two Egyptian mummies dating back to 2160–1994 BC have abstract patterns of dots and dashes on their bodies. The tattoos were probably believed to offer protection from evil spirits.

MOST PIERCED MAN

Alex Lambrecht of Belgium has acquired a total of 137 piercings with a combined weight of approximately 500 g (1 lb 1 oz) over a period of 40 years, making him the most pierced man in the world. At an average of $83 (£50) a time, Lambrecht's piercings would have cost him $11,400 (£6,850) had he not done them himself. Most of them are on his face but he also has more than 50 on his genitals.

MOST COMMON FORM OF COSMETIC SURGERY

Liposuction is the most common form of cosmetic surgery in the USA. The American Society of Plastic and Reconstructive Surgeons estimates that 149,042 liposuction procedures were performed in 1997, the latest year for which figures are available.

MOST EXPENSIVE FORM OF COSMETIC SURGERY

Facelifts are the most expensive form of cosmetic surgery: the minimum cost is $6,000 (£3,620) to tighten and pull the skin behind the ears. The removal of eye bags and laser resurfacing of the skin starts at $10,000 (£6,030), while a full facelift costs from $20,000 (£12,060).

MOST PLASTIC SURGERY UNDERGONE BY A CRIMINAL

Drugs baron Richie Ramos of Philadelphia, USA, had an extra 16 months of freedom from the FBI after plastic surgery. He had five bullet scars removed and the skin on his fingertips changed, in addition to work on his 'bull-like chest, flabby waist and fleshy face'. The operations cost $74,900 (£45,000).

THICKEST MAKE-UP

The thickest three-dimensional make-up is 'Chutti', unique to the South Indian Kathakali dance-theatre tradition. The make-up takes hours to apply and the colours used, together with the styles of the costumes, denote the different nature of each of the characters. Green, for example, represents a heroic, divine character, while a white beard represents piousness. The villainous Redbeard characters have mask-like attachments, built up using rice paste and paper, that extend 15 cm (6 in) from the face.

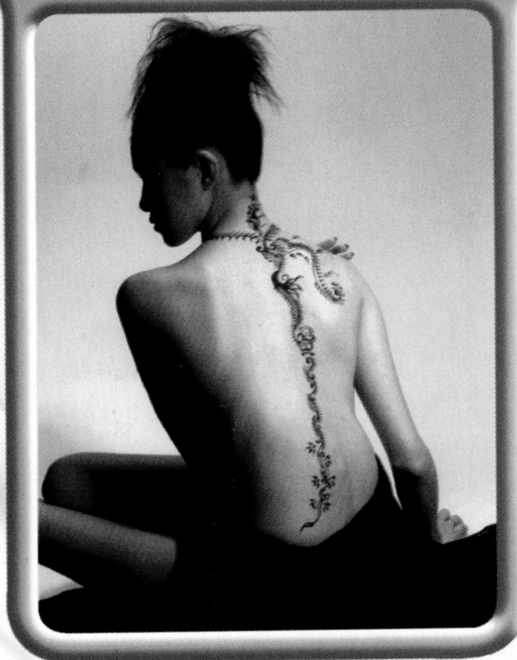

FASTEST HENNA ARTIST

Jyoti Taglani completed 64 henna armband tattoos in one hour (each measuring a minimum of 10.16 cm x 2.54 cm (4 in x 1 in) as per Guinness® Book of Records *guidelines) at the* Cosmopolitan *Show, held at Earl's Court, London, UK, on 30 April 1999. One of her designs is pictured.*

MOST PLASTIC SURGERY

Cindy Jackson has spent $99,600 (£60,000) on 27 operations over a period of nine years. Born on a pig farm in Ohio, USA, 43-year-old Jackson has had three full facelifts, two nose operations, knee, abdomen and jawline surgery, thigh liposuction, breast reduction and augmentation, and semi-permanent make-up. Her look is based on Leonardo Da Vinci's theory of a classically proportioned face. Dubbed the 'human Barbie doll', Cindy is now the director of the London-based Cosmetic Surgery Network.

MOST DOUBLES CREATED BY PLASTIC SURGERY

The dictator Stalin, who controlled the USSR between 1924 and 1953, was reportedly so paranoid that he employed several doubles to lessen the likelihood of being assassinated. The lookalikes, who had plastic surgery to make them resemble him, are said to have attended most state funerals, and even Stalin's own guards often failed to tell the difference.

MOST PLASTIC SURGERY FOR ART

Since May 1990 Orlan, a French performance artist whose most recent work has been herself, has undergone a series of plastic surgical operations to transform herself into a new being, *The Reincarnation of Saint Orlan*, modelled on Venus, Diana, Europa, Psyche and Mona Lisa. Orlan has been exhibited worldwide and is supported by the French Ministry of Culture. Her video *New York Omnipresence* shows implants being sewn into her temples.

MOST SEX CHANGES

It is estimated that there are around 12,000 surgeons in the USA who carry out sex change operations, making it the sex change center of the world. (It has been suggested that Thailand leads the field, and there is great demand for operations in Asia, but no figures are available.)

OLDEST SEX CHANGE

The greatest age at which a person is known to have had sex change surgery is 74. According to the US Educational Gender Information Service, retirement age is a common time for individuals to change their gender roles.

MOST WEIGHT GAINED

Doris James from San Francisco, California, USA, is alleged to have gained 147 kg (23 st 3 lb) in the 12 months before her death at the age of 38 in Aug 1965, when she weighed 306 kg (48 st 3 lb). She was 1.57 m (5 ft 2 in) tall.

big & small

HEAVIEST PEOPLE
The heaviest person in medical history was Jon Minnoch from Bainbridge Island, Washington State, USA, who was 1.85 m (6 ft 1 in) in height and weighed more than 635 kg (100 st) when he was rushed to hospital suffering from heart and respiratory failure in 1978, although much of that was due to fluid retention. It took 12 firemen and an improvised stretcher to move him from his house to the ferry that was needed to take him to the hospital, where he was put into two beds lashed together. After two years on a 1,200-calorie-per-day diet, he had reduced to 216 kg (34 st), but when he died, on 10 Sept 1983, his weight had gone back up to 362 kg (57 st).

HEAVIEST MODEL

US model Teighlor reached a peak weight of 326.14 kg (51 st 5 lb) in the early 1990s and has forged a successful modelling career, appearing in films and on greetings cards and advertising posters. She has now lost 81.65 kg (12 st 12 lb) after her weight started to affect her health.

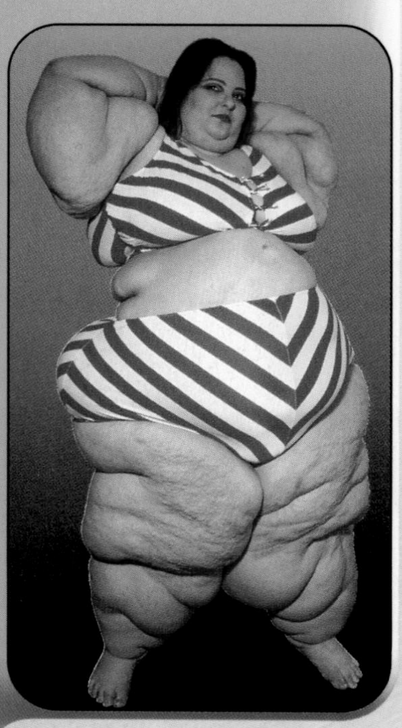

The heaviest ever woman is Rosalie Bradford (USA), who registered a peak weight of 544 kg (85 st 10 lb) in Jan 1987, before she developed heart failure and began a rigorous diet in order to save her life. By Feb 1994 her weight had reduced to 128.3 kg (20 st 3 lb). She appeared on the TV show *Guinness® World Records* on 4 Aug 1998.

HEAVIEST SINGLE BIRTH
Anna Bates (Canada) gave birth to a 10.8-kg (1-st 10-lb) boy in Seville, Ohio, USA, in 1879.

HEAVIEST TWINS
The world's heaviest twins were Billy and Benny McCrary of Hendersonville, North Carolina, USA. Normal in size until they were six years old, Billy and Benny weighed in at 337 kg (53 st 1 lb) and 328 kg (51 st 9 lb) respectively in Nov 1978, when each had a waist measurement of 2.13 m (7 ft). They were billed at weights of up to 349 kg (55 st) when they took part in wrestling bouts.

LARGEST WAIST
Walter Hudson (USA) had a waist measurement of 3.02 m (9 ft 11 in) in 1987, when he weighed 543 kg (85 st 7 lb).

LIGHTEST PERSON
Lucia Xarate, a 67-cm-tall (26½-in) dwarf from San Carlos, Mexico, weighed just 2.13 kg (4 lb 11 oz) at the age of 17. She had increased to 5.9 kg (13 lb) by her 20th birthday.

LIGHTEST SINGLE BIRTHS
A premature baby girl weighing 280 g (9$\frac{9}{10}$ oz) is reported to have been born at the Loyola University Medical Center, Illinois, USA, on 27 June 1989.

The lowest definite birthweight recorded for a surviving infant is 283 g (10 oz), for Marian Taggart (née Chapman), who was born six weeks premature in Tyne & Wear, UK, in 1938. The 30-cm-long (12-in) child was nursed by Dr D. A. Shearer, who fed her hourly for the first 30 hours with brandy, glucose and water through a fountain-pen filler.

SMALLEST WAISTS
The smallest waist of a person of normal height was 33 cm (1 ft 1 in), for Ethel Granger of Peterborough, Cambs, UK. She reduced from a natural 56 cm (1 ft 10 in) between 1929 and 1939.

SMALLEST LIVING WOMAN

Madge Bester (third from left) of Johannesburg, South Africa, is the shortest woman alive, measuring just 65 cm (2 ft 1½ in) in height, with a weight of 30 kg (4 st 10 lb). She suffers from Osteogenesis imperfecta, *a hereditary condition that results in brittle bones and other deformities of the skeleton. She is pictured at a news conference in Taipei, Taiwan, with the country's shortest man and shortest women.*

The 19th-century French actress Mlle Polaire (Emile Marie Bouchand) also claimed to have a waist measurement of 33 cm (1 ft 1 in).

TALLEST PEOPLE
The tallest ever person for whom there is irrefutable evidence was Robert Wadlow (USA), who was 2.72 m (8 ft 11$\frac{1}{10}$ in) tall in 1940, shortly before his death. He would probably have exceeded 2.74 m (9 ft) in height had he survived for another year.

The world's tallest 'true' (non-pathological) giant was Angus McCaskill, who stood 2.36 m (7 ft 9 in) when he died in Canada in 1863.

The tallest living man in the USA is Manute Bol, who is 2.31 m (7 ft 6¾ in) tall. He was born in 1962 in Sudan and is now a US citizen. He has played for the Philadelphia 76ers and other basketball teams.

The tallest living man in the UK is Christopher Greener, who is 2.29 m (7 ft 6¼ in) tall.

The tallest woman ever was Zeng Jinlian of Yujiang village in the Bright Moon Commune, Hunan Province, China. She was 2.48 m (8 ft 1¾ in) when she died in 1982 (taking into account her severe curvature of the spine).

Sandy Allen (USA) is the tallest living woman, at 2.317 m (7 ft 7¼ in). By the age of 10 she stood 1.905 m (6 ft 3 in) tall. She weighs 209.5 kg (33 st).

The tallest married couple were Anna Hanen Swan of Nova Scotia, Canada, and Martin van Buren Bates of Kentucky, USA, who stood 2.27 m (7 ft 5½ in) and 2.20 m (7 ft 2½ in) tall respectively when they married in 1871.

TALLEST TWINS
The tallest living twins are Michael and James Lanier of Troy, Michigan, USA, who were born in 1969 and are both 2.235 m (7 ft 4 in) tall.

The tallest female twins are Heather and Heidi Burge from Palos Verdes, California, USA. Born in 1971, they are both 1.95 m (6 ft 4¾ in) tall.

TALLEST PERSON

The tallest living person is Radhouane Charbib of Tunisia. When he was measured under controlled conditions on 22–23 April 1999 in Tunisia he was 2.359 m (7 ft 8 9/10 in) tall.

TALLEST TRIBE

The tallest major tribe in the world is the Tutsi (also known as the Watussi) of Rwanda and Burundi, central Africa, whose young adult males average 1.83 m (6 ft).

SHORTEST PEOPLE

The shortest ever mature human of whom there is independent evidence was Gul Mohammed of New Delhi, India. In 1990 he was 57 cm (1 ft 10½ in) in height and weighed 17 kg (2 st 9½ lb). He died aged 36 in 1997, of a heart attack after a long struggle with asthma and bronchitis.

The shortest female was Pauline Musters, who measured 30 cm (1 ft) at birth in Ossendrecht, Netherlands, in 1876 and at the age of nine was 55 cm (1 ft 9¾ in) tall. An examination after her death from pneumonia with meningitis at the age of 19 in New York City, USA, showed her to be exactly 61 cm (2 ft) in height (there was some evidence of elongation of the body after death).

The shortest twins ever were Matyus and Béla Matina of Budapest, Hungary (later the USA), who were both 76 cm (2 ft 6 in) tall.

SMALLEST TRIBE

The Mbutsi pygmies of Congo (formerly Zaïre) have an average height of 1.37 m (4 ft 6 in) for men and 1.35 m (4 ft 5 in) for women. Pygmy children are not significantly shorter than other children but they do not grow in adolescence because they produce too little IGF (insulin-like growth factor).

MOST VARIABLE STATURE

Adam Rainer (Austria) was only 1.18 m (3 ft 10½ in) tall at the age of 21 but then started growing at a rapid rate and by the age of 32 was 2.18 m (7 ft 1¾ in) tall. He became so weak as a result of this unprecedented growth spurt that he remained bedridden for the rest of his life. At the time of his death aged 51 in 1950, he had grown another 16 cm (6¼ in), reaching a height of 2.34 m (7 ft 8 in).

MOST DISSIMILAR COUPLE

When 94-cm-tall (3-ft 1-in) Natalie Lucius married 1.885-m (6-ft 2-in) Fabien Pretou at Seyssinet-Pariset, France, in 1990 there was a record height difference of 94 cm (3 ft 1 in) between bride and groom.

SMALLEST TWINS

John and Greg Rice of West Palm Beach, Florida, USA, are both 86.3 cm (2 ft 10 in) tall, making them the world's smallest living twins. Their size has not prevented them from becoming highly successful businessmen. Having made their fortunes as real-estate speculators in the 1970s, they now own and run a multi-million dollar motivational speaking company called Think Big, which organizes seminars on creative problem-solving.

bodily phenomena

MOST FINGERS AND TOES
A baby boy was found to have 14 fingers and 15 toes at an inquest held in London, UK, in Sept 1921.

FEWEST TOES
Some members of the Wadomo tribe of Zimbabwe and the Kalanga of Botswana have only two toes on each foot.

MOST ARMS AND LEGS ON ONE PERSON
Rudy Santos of Bacolad City, Philippines, has four arms and three legs. The extra limbs belong to a dead twin lodged in his abdomen.

LONGEST TIME A TWIN HAS REMAINED UNDISCOVERED
In July 1997 a foetus was discovered in the abdomen of 16-year-old Hisham Ragab of Egypt, who had been complaining of stomach pains. A swollen sac found pressing against his kidneys turned out to be his 18-cm-long (7-in), 2-kg (4-lb 6-oz) identical twin. The foetus, which had been growing inside him, had lived until 32 or 33 weeks after conception.

LONGEST-LIVING CONJOINED TWINS
Chang and Eng Bunker, the conjoined twins from Siam (now Thailand), were born on 11 May 1811, married sisters Sarah and Adelaide Yates of Wilkes County, North Carolina, USA, and fathered 22 children between them. They died within three hours of each other at the age of 63 on 17 Jan 1874. The pair, who were never separated as it was thought that to do so would endanger both their lives, earned their living in the USA as a circus attraction in the Barnum & Bailey Circus.

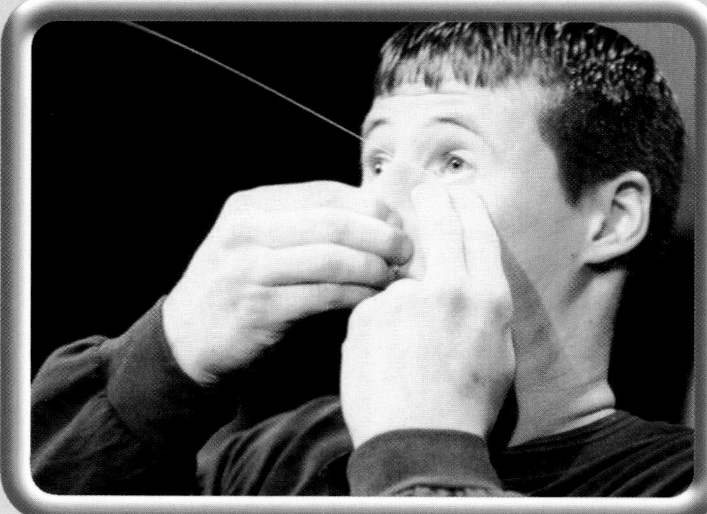

GREATEST DISTANCE MILK SHOT FROM EYE
Jim Chichon from Milford, Pennsylvania, USA, squirted milk from his eye a distance of 2.02 m (6 ft 7½ in) on Guinness® World Records: Primetime *on 20 Nov 1998, beating the old record of 1.52 m (5 ft) set by Mike Moraal (Canada). Chichon can squirt liquid from his eye because his tear ducts work in two directions rather than one. He realized he had this ability when, as a child, he held his nose underwater and bubbles emerged from his eyes.*

MOST SUCCESSFUL CONJOINED TWIN OF MODERN TIMES
Andy Garcia, the US actor who has starred in films such as *The Godfather Part 3* (USA, 1990) and *Things To Do In Denver When You're Dead* (USA, 1995), was born with a twin attached to his shoulder in Cuba in 1956. The twin was no bigger than a tennis ball and was removed by surgeons soon after birth.

LONGEST-LIVING TWO-HEADED PERSON
The Two-Headed Boy of Bengal was born in 1783 and died from a cobra bite at the age of four. His two heads, each of which had its own brain, were the same size and were covered with black hair at their junction. When the boy cried or smiled the features of the upper head were not always affected and their movements were thought to be reflex.

LONGEST HUMAN TAIL
In 1889 the magazine *Scientific American* described a 12-year-old boy from Thailand who had a soft tail almost 30 cm (1 ft) in length. In ancient literature there are many reports of adult men and women with 15–17-cm-long (6–7-in) tails. Today human tails are usually removed at birth.

OLDEST BABY TOOTH
A maxillary right cuspid (baby tooth) was extracted from the mouth of Mary H. Norman of N Carolina, USA, on 15 Dec 1998. She was born on 16 Dec 1915, so the tooth was 82 years 364 days old.

LONGEST BEARDS
Hans Langseth had a record-breaking 5.33-m-long (17½-ft) beard at the time of his death in Kensett, Iowa, USA, in 1927. The beard was presented to the Smithsonian Institute in Washington DC in 1967.

Janice Deveree from Bracken County, Kentucky, USA, had a 36-cm (14-in) beard in 1884 — the longest of any 'bearded lady'.

GREATEST EYEBALL PROTRUSION

Kimberley Goodman, a former medical courier from Chicago, Illinois, USA, can protrude her eyeballs a distance of 1.1 cm (2/5 in). Using an exometer, she was measured on *Guinness® World Records: Primetime* on 17 June 1998 by Dr Martin Greenspoon, an optical special-effects designer. Kimberely gained the ability to 'pop' her eyes after being hit on the head with a hockey mask, but medical experts do not know how she and a few others in the world are able to perform this feat. She is pictured here alongside Keith Smith from Columbus, Ohio, USA, who was one of two others participating in the 'pop-off' challenge.

MOST STRAWS STUFFED IN MOUTH

Jim 'The Mouth' Purol of Whitter, California, USA, stuffed 151 regular drinking straws in his mouth on Guinness® World Records: Primetime *on 11 Aug 1998.*

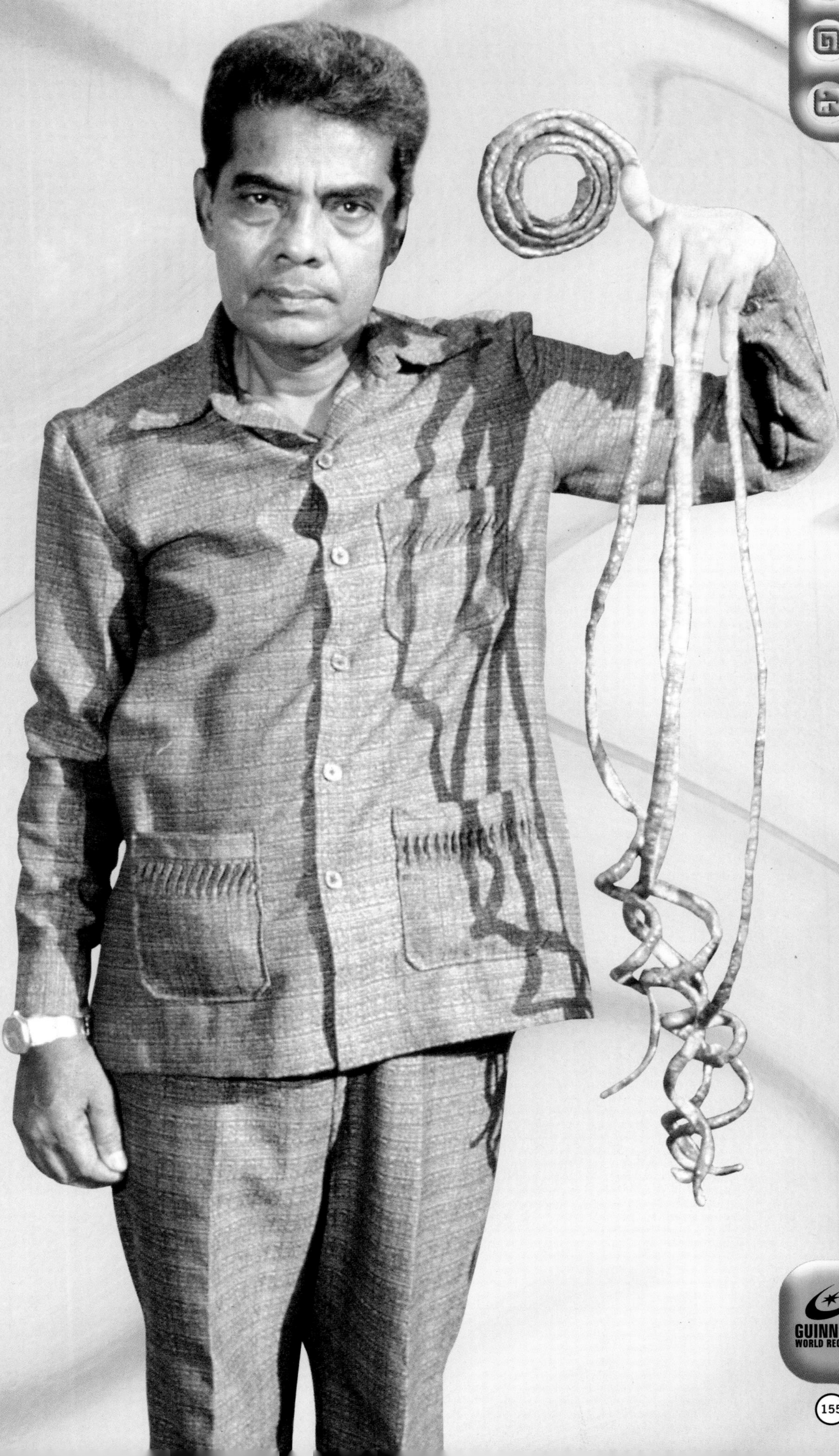

LONGEST MOUSTACHE
Kalyan Ramji Sain of India began growing a moustache in 1976. In July 1993 it had a total span of 3.39 m (11 ft 11 in).

BIGGEST FEET
If cases of elephantiasis are excluded, the biggest feet of a living person are those of Matthew McGrory of Los Angeles, California, USA, who wears UK size 29 (US size 29½) shoes.

LONGEST NOSE
Thomas Wedders (UK) had a record 19.05-cm-long (7½-in) nose. He was exhibited as a freak in a circus.

LONGEST FINGERNAILS

The world's longest fingernails are those of Shridhar Chillal (pictured right) of Pune, India; nails on his left hand were measured on Guinness® World Records: Primetime *on 10 July 1998 as having a total length of 6.15 m (20 ft 2¼ in). The nail on his thumb is 1.42 m (4 ft 8 in) long, on his index finger 1.09 m (3 ft 7 in), on his middle finger 1.17 m (3 ft 10¼ in), on his ring finger 1.26 m (4 ft 1½ in) and on his little finger 1.21 m (3 ft 11½ in).*

medical extremes

HEAVIEST BRAIN
The heaviest brain ever recorded was that of a 30-year-old male, and weighed 2.3 kg (5 lb 1 oz). It was reported by Dr T. Mandybur of the Department of Pathology and Laboratory Medicine at the University of Cincinnati, Ohio, USA, in Dec 1992.

LIGHTEST BRAIN
The lightest 'normal' or non-atrophied brain on record weighed 680 g (1 lb 8 oz). It belonged to Daniel Lyon, who died aged 46 in New York, USA, in 1907. He was just over 1.5 m (5 ft) in height and weighed 66 kg (10 st 5 lb).

LARGEST GALL BLADDER
On 15 March 1989, at the National Naval Medical Center in Bethesda, Maryland, USA, Professor Bimal C. Ghosh removed a gall bladder weighing 10.4 kg (23 lb) from a 69-year-old woman. The patient had been complaining of increasing swelling around the abdomen. After the gall bladder — which was more than three times the weight of an average newborn baby — was removed, the patient made a full recovery.

BIGGEST TUMOUR
In 1905 Dr Arthur Spohn reported operating on an ovarian cyst estimated to weigh 148.7 kg (328 lb) in Texas, USA. It was drained during the week prior to surgical removal of the shell and the patient made a full recovery.

BIGGEST TUMOUR TO HAVE BEEN REMOVED INTACT
The largest tumour ever removed intact by a surgeon was a multicystic mass of the right ovary weighing 137.6 kg (303 lb). The operation, which took more than six hours, was performed by Professor Katherine O'Hanlan of Stanford University Medical Center, California, USA. The growth had a diameter of 91 cm (3 ft) and was removed in its entirety from the abdomen of an unnamed 34-year-old woman in Oct 1991. The patient, who weighed 95 kg (15 st) after the operation and made a full recovery, left the operating theatre on a stretcher. The cyst left on another.

MOST PILLS TAKEN
The record for the greatest number of pills known to have been taken by one patient is 565,939, by C.H.A. Kilner of Bindura, Zimbabwe, between 9 June 1967 and 19 June 1988. This works out at an average of 73 tablets per day. It is estimated that if all the pills he took were laid out end to end they would form an unbroken line 3.39 km (2 miles 186 yd) long.

LONGEST COMA
Elaine Esposito from Tarpon Springs, Florida, USA, fell into a coma at the age of six, after undergoing an appendectomy on 6 Aug 1941. She died at the age of 43 years 357 days on 25 Nov 1978, having remained unconscious for a record period of 37 years 111 days.

LOWEST BODY TEMPERATURE
The lowest authenticated body temperature was 14.2°C (57.5°F), by two-year-old Karlee Kosolofski (Canada) on 23 Feb 1994. She had been locked outside for six hours in a temperature of –22°C (–8°F), and had to have her frostbitten left leg amputated, but otherwise made a full recovery. Pictured above is a thermograph, showing relative temperatures inside a human head. The red areas are the hottest.

MOST INJECTIONS RECEIVED
Samuel Davidson from Glasgow, UK, has had at least 78,900 insulin injections since 1923 when he was 11.

LONGEST TIME SPENT IN AN IRON LUNG
James Farwell from Chichester, W Sussex, UK, has been using a negative pressure respirator since May 1946.

John Prestwich from Kings Langley, Herts, UK, has been dependent on a respirator since 24 Nov 1955.

LONGEST-LASTING TRACHEOSTOMY
Winifred Campbell from Wanstead, London, UK, breathed through a silver tube in her throat for a record-breaking 86 years. She died in 1992.

OLDEST MOTHER
Arceli Keh (USA) is said to have been 63 years old when she gave birth at the University of Southern California, USA, in 1996. Menopause occurs in the majority of women between 45 and 55 years but recent hormonal techniques have led to post-menopausal women becoming fertile. It is now theoretically feasible for women of any age to become pregnant.

MOST ORGANS TRANSPLANTED
Daniel Canal, aged 13, of Miami, Florida, USA, received his third set of four new organs in June 1998. Daniel was given a new stomach, liver, pancreas and small intestine at Jackson Children's Hospital, Miami, USA, three times in a little over a month, having waited five years for his first transplant. His first multi-organ transplant was in early May, but his body rejected it. The second, on 2 June, was unsuccessful when the liver failed. After the third he remained critical. However he went on to make a full recovery. All three procedures were performed by Dr Andreas Tzakis, who gave Daniel a total of 12 organs.

LARGEST MULTIPLE BIRTHS
In 1971 Dr Gennaro Montanino from Rome, Italy, claimed to have removed 15 foetuses from the uterus of a 35-year-old woman after four months of pregnancy. A fertility drug was responsible for this unique instance of quindecaplets.

The record for surviving births is seven (septuplets), born to Bobbie McCaughey in Iowa, USA, on 19 Nov 1997, and to Hasna Mohammed Humair in Aseer, Saudi Arabia, on 14 Jan 1998. Geraldine Broderick gave birth to nine babies in Sydney, NSW, Australia, on 13 June 1971, but two were stillborn. Nkem Chukwu gave birth to octuplets (eight babies) at the Texas Children's Hospital, Houston, Texas, USA, — one born naturally on 8 Dec 1998, the others delivered by caesarean section on 20 Dec 1998. Seven babies survived.

LONGEST GESTATION INTERVAL OF A POST-MORTEM BIRTH
On 5 July 1983 a baby girl was delivered from a woman who had been classified as brain-dead for 84 days in Roanoke, Virginia, USA.

LONGEST CARDIAC ARREST
On 7 Dec 1987 fisherman Jan Egil Refsdahl suffered a cardiac arrest lasting a record four hours after falling overboard in the freezing waters off Bergen, Norway. He was rushed to hospital when his body temperature fell to 24°C (75°F) and his heart stopped beating, but he went on to make a complete recovery after being hooked up to a heart-lung machine.

BIGGEST BLOOD TRANSFUSION
Warren Jyrich, a 50-year-old haemophiliac, required a record 2,400 donor units of blood — the equivalent of 1,080 litres (237 gal) — during open-heart surgery at the Michael Reese Hospital, Chicago, Illinois, USA, in Dec 1970.

HIGHEST BODY TEMPERATURE
On 10 July 1980 — a day when the temperature reached 32.2°C (90°F) — 52-year-old Willie Jones was admitted to Grady Memorial Hospital in Atlanta, Georgia, USA, with heatstroke and found to have a body temperature of 46.5°C (115.7°F) — the highest on record. He was discharged after 24 days.

LOUDEST SNORER
Snores by Kåre Walkert of Kumla, Sweden, who suffers from the breathing disorder apnea, were recorded at 93 dBA at the Örebro regional hospital on 24 May 1993.

LONGEST DREAM
The longest recorded period of REM sleep (the rapid eye movements that characterize dreaming) lasted 3 hr 8 min. It was recorded in David Powell at the Puget Sound Sleep Disorder Center, Seattle, Washington, USA, on 29 April 1994.

LONGEST HICCOUGHING FIT
Charles Osborne from Anthon, Iowa, USA, began hiccoughing in 1922 and continued until Feb 1990. He was unable to find a cure but led a normal life, marrying twice and fathering eight children.

OLDEST PERSON TO HAVE AN OPERATION
The oldest person ever to have undergone an operation was James Henry Brett Jr, whose hip was operated on in Houston, Texas, USA, on 7 Nov 1960 when he was 111 years 105 days old.

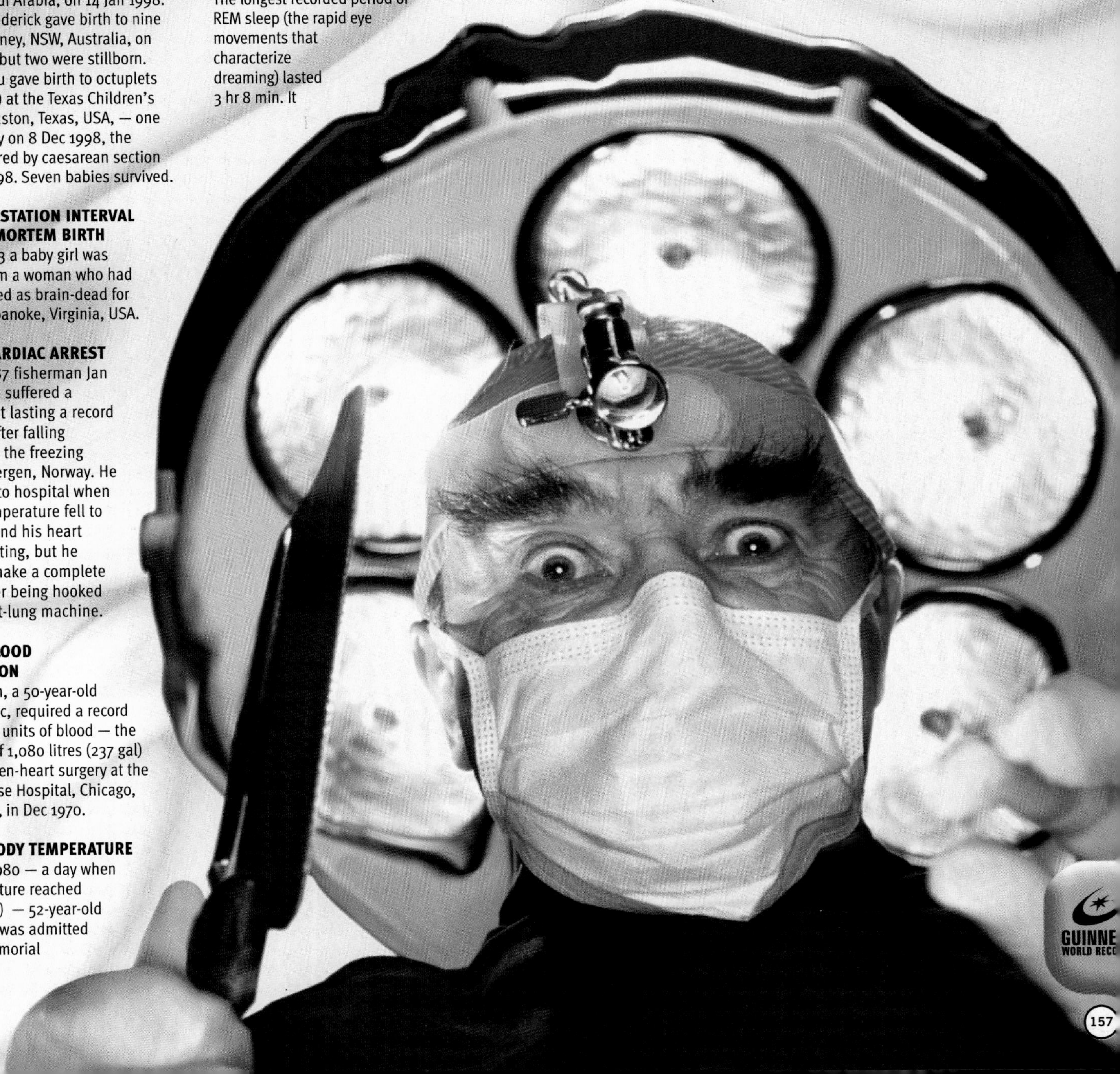

body building

GREATEST STRONGMEN
Magnus Ver Magnusson (Iceland) won the World's Strongest Man contest four times, in 1991, 1994, 1995 and 1996, becoming only the second man (after Bill Kazmaier of the USA) to win three years in a row. He began powerlifting in 1984 and won senior titles in Europe in 1989 and 1990. He also won the World Muscle Power Championship in 1995. Born in 1963, he is 1.87 m (6 ft 2 in) tall, weighs 130.18 kg (20 st 7 lb) and has a chest measurement of 1.3 m (4 ft 3 in). He now owns Magnus' Gym in Reykjavik, Iceland.

Jon Pall Sigmarsson (Iceland) also won the World's Strongest Man contest four times, in 1984, 1986, 1988 and 1990. Sigmarsson, who weighed 133 kg (21 st) and had a 1.44-m (4-ft 9-in) chest, dominated the WSM competition in the mid and late 1980s and won five World Muscle Power titles. He died of a heart attack while weightlifting in 1993.

BIGGEST BICEPS
The biceps of Denis Sester of Bloomington, Minnesota, USA, each measure 77.8 cm (2 ft 6⅝ in) when cold. He began building his biceps as a teenager when he wrestled pigs on his parents' farm.

BIGGEST MUSCULAR CHEST MEASUREMENT
Isaac 'Dr Size' Nesser of Greensburg, Pennsylvania, USA, has a record muscular chest measurement of 1.905 m (6 ft 3 in). Now 37 years old, he has been lifting weights since he was eight years old.

LONGEST-RUNNING BODY BUILDING TV SHOW

Jack LaLanne, who is now 84, opened the first health club in the USA in 1936, as well as hosting the longest-running exercise TV show, in which he encouraged housewives to use broomsticks and chairs to get fit. *The Jack LaLanne Show* was first transmitted in San Francisco in 1951, went coast-to-coast in 1959 and ran until 1984.

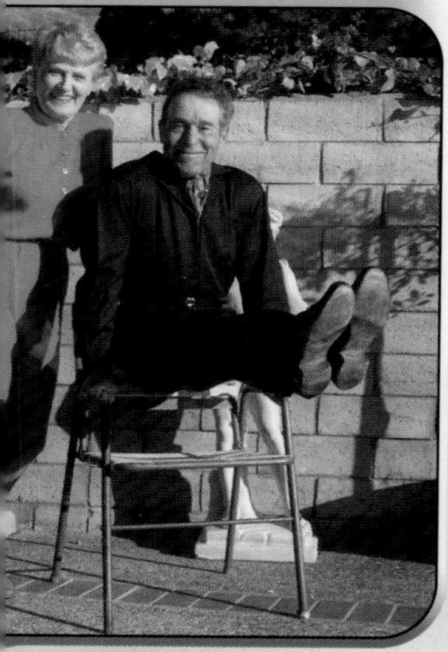

MOST PRIZE MONEY
The 1998 Mr Olympia pageant, held by the International Federation of Body Builders (IFBB), had a total prize pot of $310,000 (£187,040), with $110,000 (£66,370) going to the champion.

BIGGEST ATTENDANCE AT A BODY BUILDING SHOW
Although Mr Olympia is more prestigious, the Arnold Schwarzenegger Classic weekend show ('Arnold Classic') draws about 50,000 people every year.

MOST ARNOLD CLASSICS TITLES
Ken 'Flex' Wheeler, nicknamed the 'Sultan of Symmetry', won the 'triple crown' (the Ironman, the Arnold Classic and the San Jose Classic) in 1997 and the Arnold Classic in 1993, 1997 and 1998. He has been training since the age of 15.

MOST MR OLYMPIA CONTESTANTS
In 1989, at the Mr Olympia event held in Rimini, Italy, a record 26 contestants vied for the title, which was won by Lee Haney (USA). He equalled Arnold Schwarzenegger's then record of six consecutive titles.

FEWEST MR OLYMPIA CONTESTANTS
In 1968 Sergio Oliva (USA), known as 'The Myth', defended his Mr Olympia title unopposed at the Brooklyn Academy of Music, New York City, USA. In Paris, France, Arnold Schwarzenegger (Austria) was also unopposed in 1971. Oliva and Schwarzenegger had a series of epic battles for the title between 1969 and 1972. Oliva won three times, from 1967 to 1969, but the 1969 title was a close run. Schwarzenegger won the 1970 and 1972 titles, edging Oliva into second place both times.

MOST FILMS MADE BY A BODY BUILDER
Arnold Schwarzenegger has appeared in 25 feature films, including The Terminator *(USA, 1984),* Terminator 2: Judgment Day *(USA, 1991),* Total Recall *(USA, 1990),* True Lies *(USA, 1994) and* Batman And Robin *(USA, 1997). He has won 13 world titles (seven Mr Olympia titles, five Mr Universe titles and one Mr World title) and has been producing body building contests for 20 years.*

HEAVIEST MR OLYMPIA CHAMPION
In 1993 Dorian Yates (UK) weighed 116.57 kg (18 st 5 lb) when he was crowned Mr Olympia for the second year in succession in Atlanta, Georgia, USA. Yates went on to win the Mr Olympia title six times in a row, from 1992 to 1997.

TALLEST MR OLYMPIA CONTESTANT
Lou Ferrigno (USA) was 6 ft 5 in (1.95 m) tall when he competed in the 1974 Mr Olympia contest held at the Felt Forum, Madison Square Garden, New York City, USA.

SHORTEST MR OLYMPIA CONTESTANT
Flavio Baccanini from San Francisco, California, USA, competed in the 1993 Mr Olympia contest held in Atlanta, Georgia, USA. Baccanini, originally from Italy, was 1.47 m (4 ft 10 in) tall and weighed 72.57 kg (11 st 6 lb). He failed to win a medal.

BIGGEST TIME GAP BETWEEN MR OLYMPIA WINS
Arnold Schwarzenegger won the contest for the sixth time in 1975 and announced his retirement immediately afterwards. In 1980 he was seen training but it was assumed that he was preparing for a new film. When he boarded a flight to Australia (where Mr Olympia was held that year) with the other competitors, they thought he was making a TV documentary. That year he won the Mr Olympia title for the seventh time.

MOST CONSECUTIVE MR UNIVERSE TITLES
Lou Ferrigno of California, USA, is the only man in history to have won the Mr Universe title two years in succession, in 1973 and 1974. He starred in the TV show *The Incredible Hulk* and has appeared in a succession of films, including *Hercules* (USA, 1983) and *The Adventures Of Hercules* (USA, 1985). He is 1.95 m (6 ft 5 in) tall and weighs 136 kg (21 st 6 lb).

MOST IFBB PRO WINS
Vince Taylor of Pembroke Pines, Florida, USA, has had a record 19 wins from competitions all over the world recognized by the International Federation of Body Builders (IFBB). He won the Masters Olympia for those aged 40 and over in 1996 and 1997.

BIGGEST MS OLYMPIA CONTEST
In 1990 a total of 30 women competed in the Ms Olympia contest, which has been held annually since 1980.

SMALLEST MS OLYMPIA CONTEST
In 1996 just 12 competitors participated in the contest.

HEAVIEST MS OLYMPIA CONTESTANT
Nicole Bass (USA) weighed 92.53 kg (14 st 8 lb) when she participated in 1997. She was also the tallest ever contestant, at 1.88 m (6 ft 2 in)

SHORTEST MS OLYMPIA CONTESTANT
Michele Ralabate (USA), who competed in 1995, is 1.5 m (4 ft 11 in) tall.

LIGHTEST MS OLYMPIA CONTESTANT
Erika Mes from the Netherlands weighed 45.36 kg (7 st 2 lb) when she competed in 1984.

YOUNGEST MS OLYMPIA CONTESTANT
Lorie Johnson from the USA was 17 years old when she took part in the first Ms Olympia competition in 1980.

OLDEST MS OLYMPIA CONTESTANT
Christa Bauch (Germany) was 47 years old when she competed in the 1994 competition.

MOST CONSECUTIVE MS UNIVERSE CONTESTS ENTERED
Laura Creavalle, a Guyanan national resident in the USA, participated in 10 contests from 1988 to 1997.

BIGGEST CHAIN OF GYMS
Gold's Gym opened in Venice, California, USA, in 1965 and became internationally famous when it featured in *Pumping Iron* (USA, 1975), which featured up-and-coming stars Arnold Schwarzenegger and Lou Ferrigno. It is now the world's biggest international gym chain, with more than 500 centres. Its many star clients include Janet Jackson, Charlie Sheen, Jodie Foster and Hollywood Hogan, and it boasts its own motion picture and TV divisions.

MOST SUCCESSFUL TRAINERS
Jake Steinfeld has trained film director Steven Spielberg and actors Harrison Ford and Priscilla Presley and heads a multi-million-dollar fitness empire that includes a cable television network, FiT TV — the world's only 24-hour fitness channel — a national magazine, home videos and branded equipment and merchandise. In three years, his Body By Jake Enterprises sold more than $250 million (£156 million) in licensed products through 'infomercials'.

Radu Teodorescu, known as the 'Grand Master' of exercise, has been a personal trainer for more than 20 years. Voted 'Toughest Trainer In Town' by *New York* magazine, Radu has been featured in more than 400 magazine articles and created Cindy Crawford's multi-million-selling fitness video *Shape Your Body Workout*.

MOST MR OLYMPIA TITLES
Lee Haney of South Carolina, USA, won the Mr Olympia contest eight times from 1984 to 1991. After winning his final title in Orlando, Florida, USA, Haney announced his retirement from the sport. Haney, who has been body building for 28 years, holds seminars at correctional institutions, motivating inmates to maximize their physical and spiritual potential.

techn

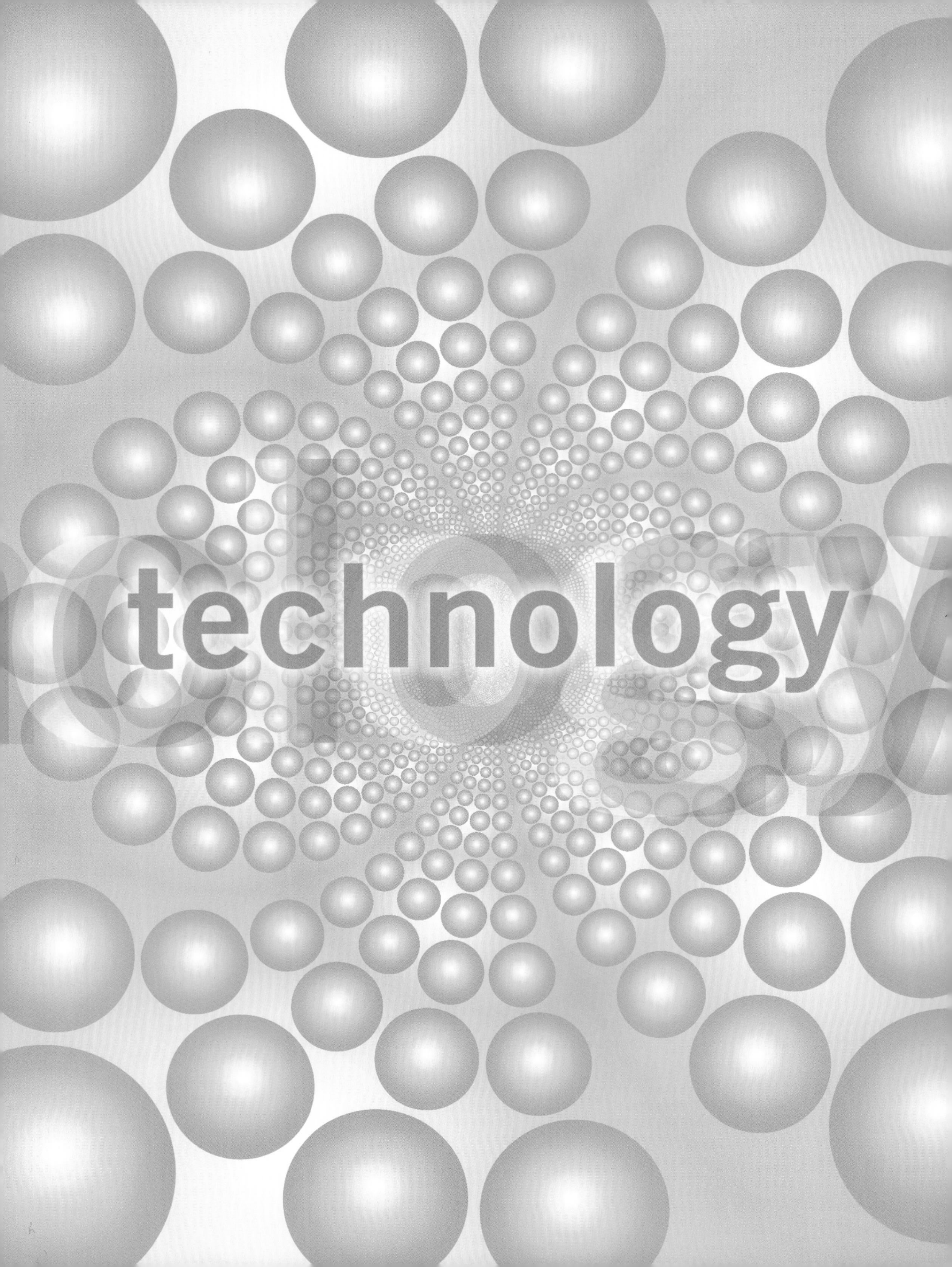
technology

the internet 1

MOST INTERNET USERS
At the end of 1998 there were about 150 million internet users — an increase of 246% over two years. The global figure is expected to increase to 327 million by the end of 2000. There may be more computers hidden behind corporate 'firewalls' designed to exclude electronic visitors, including hackers.

MOST WIRED COUNTRY
The USA had over 76 million internet users in Dec 1998 — nearly 51% of the worldwide total. Japan is second, with 9.75 million users, and the UK is third, with 8.1 million.

MOST INTERNET USERS PER CAPITA
Of every 1,000 people in Finland, 244.5 are internet users, according to the 1998 *Computer Industry Almanac*.

BIGGEST INTERNET DOMAIN OWNERSHIP
According to NetNames Ltd, the USA has a total of 1.35 million domains, which represents 50.9% of the overall domain ownership in the world. The United Kingdom is the second largest, with 160,004, or 6%.

BIGGEST FREE E-MAIL PROVIDER
Hotmail is the world's largest free web-based e-mail service provider, with more than 35 million subscribers.

GREATEST NUMBER OF ACTIVE ON-LINE NET ACCOUNTS
Charles Schwab & Co., the US stockbroker, has more than 900,000 on-line accounts holding in excess of $66.6 billion (£40.02 billion) in assets and accounting more than one-third of their 99,000 daily trading operations.

BIGGEST INTERNET CRASH
At 11:30 am Eastern Standard Time on 25 April 1997 the global computer network ran into major problems and much of the system became unusable. Human error and equipment failure had led a network in Florida, USA, to claim 'ownership' of 30,000 of the internet's 45,000 routes. Data packets were routed incorrectly and connections across the internet failed. Some providers took action within 15 minutes, but the problem persisted until 7 pm.

SMALLEST WEB SERVER
The web page of the Wearables Laboratory at Stanford University, Palo Alto, California, USA, is supported by Jumptec's DIMM-PC, a single-board AMD 486-SX computer with a 66MHz CPU, 16 MB RAM, and 16 MB flash ROM. The set-up is big enough to hold a useful amount of RedHat 5.2 Linux including the HTTP daemon that runs the web server. At relatively low usage levels it consumes 800 milliwatts from a 5V power supply, rising to 2 watts at 100% CPU usage. By Jan 1999 it was averaging 40 hits a minute. The 'matchbox' server is only slightly higher and wider than a box of matches but is one third the thickness, measuring 6.86 x 4.32 x 0.64 cm ($2\frac{7}{10}$ x $1\frac{7}{10}$ x $\frac{1}{4}$ in). It has a volume of about 16.39 cm^3 (1 in^3) — less than a tenth the size of the previous record-holder.

MOST QUESTIONS RECEIVED ON AN INTERNET SITE IN 30 MINUTES
On 17 May 1997 former Beatle Sir Paul McCartney received more than 3 million questions from fans in 30 minutes during a web event to promote his album Flaming Pie. *On 19 Nov 1997 McCartney also set a record for the first ever debut performance of a classical work live on the internet, when he performed his new work, the 75-minute symphonic poem* Standing Stones, *live from Carnegie Hall, New York, USA.*

MOST POPULAR INTERNET NEWS SERVICE

The seven sites of the international news service CNN, based in Atlanta, Georgia, USA, have a combined average of 55 million page views per week. The sites also receive more than 3,000 user comments per day via the CNN message boards. The sites currently contain more than 210,000 pages but grow by 90–150 pages daily. The 24-hour television news channel, which began broadcasting on 1 June 1980, is part of Turner Broadcasting, owned by Time Warner Inc. A total of 1 billion people worldwide have access to a CNN service.

BIGGEST MULTILINGUAL WEB BROADCAST
The opening and closing ceremonies of the Third Conference of the Parties of the United Nations Framework Convention on Climate Change in Kyoto, Japan, in Dec 1997 were broadcast simultaneously via the internet in seven languages — Arabic, Chinese, English, French, Japanese, Russian and Spanish.

BIGGEST FINE AS A RESULT OF INTERNET CRIME
US anti-abortion activists who operated a site called *The Nuremberg Files* that contained 'Wanted' posters listing the names and addresses of doctors who perform abortions were ordered to pay more than $107.7 million (£65 million) in damages on 3 Feb 1999. Four doctors

BIGGEST SEARCH ENGINE

The biggest search engine is AltaVista, with 150 million indexed pages. Its closest rival is Northern Light, which has 125 million pages. AltaVista is also the most popular search engine, with more than 21 million users and in excess of 1 billion page views every month worldwide.

and two clinic workers who had been killed by activists since 1993 had their names crossed off on the site, and the wounded were highlighted in grey. The defendants were 12 individuals and organizations known collectively as the American Coalition of Life Activists and Advocates for Life Ministries. The case is currently under appeal.

BIGGEST SAVING OF PAPER THROUGH USING THE INTERNET

The delivery firm Federal Express has announced that it saves approximately 2 billion sheets of paper a year in the USA by tracking packages online.

BIGGEST VOLUNTARY INTERNET SAFETY ORGANIZATION

Formed in June 1995 by Colin Gabriel Hatcher (USA), the Cyber Angels (the cyber-branch of the Guardian Angels) has dealt with more than 200 cases of cyber-stalking. The Cyber Angels have recently been commissioned by the United Nations Educational Scientific and Cultural Organization (UNESCO) to monitor the internet.

MOST DOWNLOADED WOMAN

Images of Cindy Margolis (USA) have been downloaded an estimated 7 million times. In 1995 Margolis was filmed by a television crew modelling a swimsuit. A picture of her was then posted on the internet, and 70,000 people downloaded her image in the first 24 hours. She subsequently featured in a TV programme, which resulted in her image being downloaded once every 10 seconds for 48 hours. In 1998 a poll in the magazine Internet Life *recognized Margolis as the most downloaded women of the year for the third year running. She has also appeared in several advertising campaigns, in a number of TV shows, including* Baywatch *and* Married... With Children *and in the movie* Austin Powers: International Man Of Mystery *(USA, 1997), in which she played one of the deadly, seductive Fembots.*

the internet 2

BIGGEST CYBERSTAR MERCHANDISE SALES
During 1998 Dancing Baby T-shirt sales in the USA totalled more than $2.8 million (£1.7 million) wholesale. Music CD sales exceeded $425,000 (£256,000) wholesale, while international and US sales of the electronic Dancing Baby doll topped $550,000 (£331,845) wholesale. Other merchandise across the USA, Australia and Europe grossed over $900,000 (£543,019).

MOST COMMERCE CONDUCTED ON THE INTERNET
Businesses in the USA will exchange an estimated $17 billion (£10.26 billion) in goods and services in 1999 — more than any other country.

BIGGEST INTERNET SHOPPING MALL
The Internet Mall has a record 27,000 on-screen virtual shops and more than 1 million subscribers in the UK alone. It uses 65,000 shops around the globe to create the service, which is available in more than 150 countries. Products ranging from popcorn to car insurance are delivered within 48 hours.

BIGGEST NETWORKED ROLE-PLAYING GAME

With each of its 10 servers able to hold 2,500 players at the same time, Origin's *Ultima Online* is the largest multiplayer networked role-playing game in the world. At present, up to 14,000 players take part each day, many of them staying on-line for up to four hours at a time. In its first three months on the market, it sold 100,000 copies. With 32,000 interacting 'inhabitants', 15 major cities, nine sites of religious significance and at least seven dungeons, Britannia (the setting for *Ultima Online*) is the largest parallel universe on the internet. With more inhabitants joining daily, and with enormous regions of this parallel universe left to explore, Britannia seems likely to grow ever larger.

MOST DOWNLOADED CYBERPET

More than 10 million people worldwide have downloaded MOPy, a lifelike pet fish screensaver, since its release on the web in Oct 1997. MOPy was designed for Hewlett Packard by Global Beach, a digital communications agency. It will respond to care and attention from its owner and thrive on regular feeding but will grow sulky, ill and may even 'die' if neglected. In addition to MOPy, Global Beach has designed three more pets: two cyber-tarantulas and a cyber-scorpion.

BIGGEST CYBERSTORE
Amazon.com was founded in 1994 by Jeff Bezos (USA) and has now sold products to more than 5 million people in more than 160 countries. Its catalogue of 4.7 million books, CDs and audiobooks makes it the largest on-line shop in the world.

BIGGEST INTERNET AUCTION
In Oct 1996 Nick Nuttall displayed 1,400 items of oriental art in the biggest collection of items for auction shown on the internet at the same time. The items ranged from Japanese wooden carvings to bronzes and antique furniture. Prospective buyers could e-mail questions about the lots, order the catalogue and e-mail bids.

BIGGEST INTERNET MUSIC DATABASE
ProMusicFind.Com, a site for buying and selling new and used musical instruments and audio and electronic music equipment, as well as new, used and rare records, CDs, videos and books, has more than 1 million items on its database.

BIGGEST INTERNET ALBUM RELEASE
In March 1998 British band Massive Attack launched the whole of its third album *Mezzanine* on-line, together with a preview of the video for the first single from the album, three weeks before it was available in the shops. The site received 1,313,644 hits, and the songs were downloaded a total of 101,673 times before the album went on sale on 20 April. A further 1,602,658 hits were recorded a month after the shop release. Despite its availability on

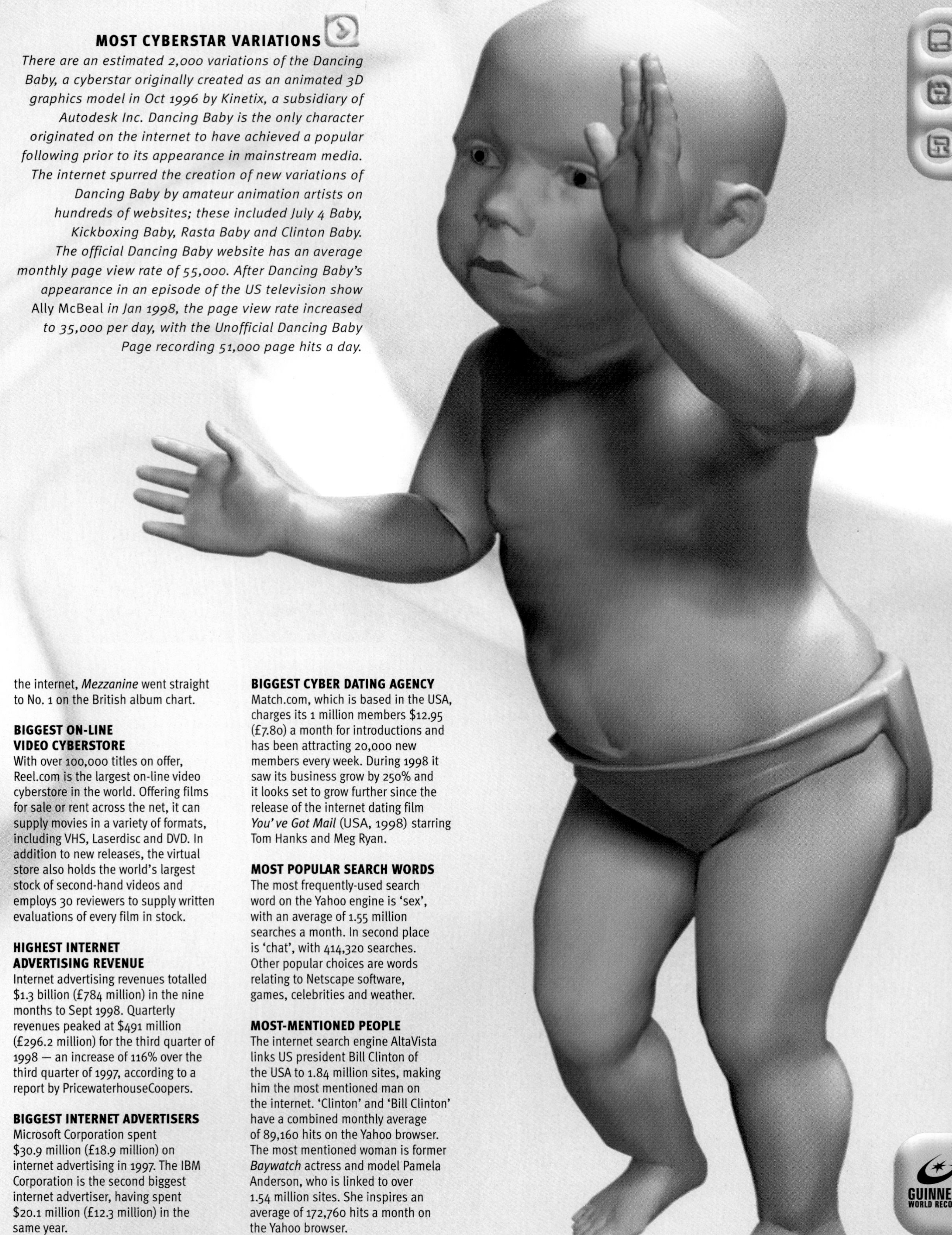

MOST CYBERSTAR VARIATIONS

There are an estimated 2,000 variations of the Dancing Baby, a cyberstar originally created as an animated 3D graphics model in Oct 1996 by Kinetix, a subsidiary of Autodesk Inc. Dancing Baby is the only character originated on the internet to have achieved a popular following prior to its appearance in mainstream media. The internet spurred the creation of new variations of Dancing Baby by amateur animation artists on hundreds of websites; these included July 4 Baby, Kickboxing Baby, Rasta Baby and Clinton Baby. The official Dancing Baby website has an average monthly page view rate of 55,000. After Dancing Baby's appearance in an episode of the US television show Ally McBeal *in Jan 1998, the page view rate increased to 35,000 per day, with the Unofficial Dancing Baby Page recording 51,000 page hits a day.*

the internet, *Mezzanine* went straight to No. 1 on the British album chart.

BIGGEST ON-LINE VIDEO CYBERSTORE

With over 100,000 titles on offer, Reel.com is the largest on-line video cyberstore in the world. Offering films for sale or rent across the net, it can supply movies in a variety of formats, including VHS, Laserdisc and DVD. In addition to new releases, the virtual store also holds the world's largest stock of second-hand videos and employs 30 reviewers to supply written evaluations of every film in stock.

HIGHEST INTERNET ADVERTISING REVENUE

Internet advertising revenues totalled $1.3 billion (£784 million) in the nine months to Sept 1998. Quarterly revenues peaked at $491 million (£296.2 million) for the third quarter of 1998 — an increase of 116% over the third quarter of 1997, according to a report by PricewaterhouseCoopers.

BIGGEST INTERNET ADVERTISERS

Microsoft Corporation spent $30.9 million (£18.9 million) on internet advertising in 1997. The IBM Corporation is the second biggest internet advertiser, having spent $20.1 million (£12.3 million) in the same year.

BIGGEST CYBER DATING AGENCY

Match.com, which is based in the USA, charges its 1 million members $12.95 (£7.80) a month for introductions and has been attracting 20,000 new members every week. During 1998 it saw its business grow by 250% and it looks set to grow further since the release of the internet dating film *You' ve Got Mail* (USA, 1998) starring Tom Hanks and Meg Ryan.

MOST POPULAR SEARCH WORDS

The most frequently-used search word on the Yahoo engine is 'sex', with an average of 1.55 million searches a month. In second place is 'chat', with 414,320 searches. Other popular choices are words relating to Netscape software, games, celebrities and weather.

MOST-MENTIONED PEOPLE

The internet search engine AltaVista links US president Bill Clinton of the USA to 1.84 million sites, making him the most mentioned man on the internet. 'Clinton' and 'Bill Clinton' have a combined monthly average of 89,160 hits on the Yahoo browser. The most mentioned woman is former *Baywatch* actress and model Pamela Anderson, who is linked to over 1.54 million sites. She inspires an average of 172,760 hits a month on the Yahoo browser.

computers

HIGHEST MARKET VALUATION OF A COMPUTER COMPANY
The Microsoft Corporation was valued at $418.6 billion (£252.56 billion) at the end of the 1998 fiscal year. Its annual revenue was $14.5 billion (£8.75 billion). The corporation develops, sells and licenses software and online services to computer users around the world. Its chairman Bill Gates, who currently owns about 30% of Microsoft, founded the company with Paul Allen in 1975, and it has made him the richest man in the world.

BIGGEST PC MANUFACTURER
Compaq — the name is derived from 'compatibility' and 'quality' — was founded in Houston, Texas, USA, by Rod Canion, Jim Harris and Bill Murto. Since 1995 the company has held the largest slice of the worldwide PC market. In 1998 Compaq sold a total of 13,275,204 PCs — equivalent to one every 2.38 seconds. It provides the systems for 75% of the world's cashpoint transactions and 60% of lotteries.

BIGGEST DIRECT MARKETING COMPUTER SALES COMPANY
The Dell Computer Corporation, founded by Michael Dell in 1984, employs 17,800 people worldwide. Dell's revenue figures for the year ending 29 Jan 1999 were $18.2 billion (£11 billion) — an increase of 48% on the previous year. For the fourth quarter Dell averaged customer sales of $14 million (£8.4 million) a day via its website.

BEST-SELLING SOFTWARE
Since its release on 24 Aug 1995, approximately 193 million copies of the Microsoft operating system *Windows '95* have been sold. The update *Windows '98* is now bundled with 90% of the desktop computers that are sold around the world and 22.3 million copies have been sold since it became available in June 1998. Only sales of MS-DOS, the basic operating system that is pre-installed on almost all desktop PCs, have outstripped sales of this software.

FASTEST COMPUTERS
The fastest general-purpose vector-parallel computer is the Cray Y-MP C90 supercomputer, which has two gigabytes of central memory and 16 CPUs (central processing units), giving a combined peak performance of 16 gigaflops.

The fastest supercomputer was installed by Intel at Sandia National Laboratories, Texas, USA, in 1996. Using 9,072 Intel Pentium Pro processors, each running at about 200 MHz, and 608 gigabytes of memory, it has a peak performance of about 1.8 tetraflops (1.8 trillion conversions per second).

'Massively parallel' computers have a theoretical aggregate performance exceeding that of a C-90. Performances on real-life applications are often less impressive, perhaps because it is harder to harness the power of many small processors than a few large ones.

DENSEST HARD DRIVE
The IBM micro-disk can fit 2.5 gigabytes of data into 6.45 cm² (1 in²) of disk space. The disk was unveiled in March 1999 by a team at IBM's Storage System's Division in San José, California, USA. High density drives that are light in weight consume less energy, which is particularly important for designers of portable computers.

In Sept 1997 the US Defense Projects Research Agency (DARPA) commissioned researcher John McDonald to build the world's first PetOps supercomputer — a machine that can perform 1,000 trillion operations per second. DARPA gave $1 million (£625,000) to finance this three-year project, which will result in the fastest computer ever to have been

SHORTEST INSTRUCTION MANUAL FOR A HOME COMPUTER
The Apple iMac personal computer was released in the USA in Aug 1997 and in the UK the following month. The distinctive one-piece machine with translucent casing comes with an instruction manual that consists of just six pictures and 36 words, allowing the computer to live up to the sales pitch stating that a user can just take it out of the box and plug it in. Worldwide iMac sales were approaching 2 million units by April 1999 and the success of the iMac has helped boost Apple's profits, which had been flagging for a number of years. After having lost nearly $2 billion (£1.2 billion) between 1995 and 1997, the company has turned in six consecutive quarters in profit.

commissioned. They want to use the system to simulate battles and natural disasters for training purposes.

The World Supercomputing Speed Record was set in Dec 1994 by a team of scientists from Sandia National Laboratories and Intel Corporation, who linked together two of the largest Intel Paragon parallel-processing machines. The system achieved a performance of 281 gigaflops on the Linpack benchmark. The massively parallel supercomputer also achieved 328 gigaflops running a program used for radar signature calculations. The two-Paragon system used 6,768 processors working in parallel.

FASTEST-SPREADING COMPUTER VIRUS

Melissa, a macro virus operating in the Microsoft *Outlook* package through Microsoft *Word* documents, was discovered on 26 March 1999. The virus mails itself to the first 50 addresses in the affected computer's mailbox. One large organization reported that up to 500,000 e-mail messages were generated by the virus in less than three hours — enough to swamp a company's communications system and shut it down. Experts calculate that within five generations *Melissa* has the capacity to infect more than 312 million PCs.

MOST PHYSICALLY DAMAGING VIRUS

The *CIH* virus has affected 1 million PCs since it was first triggered on 26 April 1998, the 12th anniversary of the nuclear reactor disaster in Chernobyl, USSR (now Ukraine). *CIH* irreversibly alters a computer's BIOS chip, which is soldered onto the motherboard. The damage can make a computer totally useless.

BIGGEST NUMBER CRUNCHED

In April 1997 it was announced that computer scientists at Purdue University, Indiana, USA, had co-ordinated researchers around the world to find the two largest numbers that, multiplied together, equal a known 167-digit number, $(3^{349}-1)\div2$. The breakthrough came after about 100,000 hours of computing time. The two factors had 80 digits and 87 digits. The previous factorization record was 162 digits.

BIGGEST PRIME NUMBER FOUND USING A COMPUTER

On 27 Jan 1998, 19-year-old student Roland Clarkson discovered the prime number $23{,}021^{377}-1$. This number, which is 909,526 digits long when written out in full, was traced using software written by George Woltman and Scott Kurowski. It is the 37th known 'Mersenne prime'. Clarkson, one of several thousand volunteers contributing to the Great Internet Mersenne Prime Search (GIMPS), found the number on his ordinary 200 MHz Pentium desktop computer.

'MOST HUMAN' COMPUTER SYSTEM

A computer running the program *Albert* was awarded the 1999 Loebner Prize for the 'most human' computer system, winning $2,000 (£1,250) for its author, Robby Garner from Georgia, USA. *Albert* is a program that a user can communicate with using human speech. The 11 judges of the annual Loebner Prize put systems through a restricted version of the Turing Test, the classic test of machine intelligence. *Albert One* won the 1997 Loebner Prize and Mr Garner won the 1998 award with another program called *Sid*.

SMALLEST COMPUTER WITH 'FULL SCREEN' CAPABILITY

The main unit of the Wearable PC, developed by IBM in Japan, is roughly the same size as a personal stereo. The 'screen' is a 1.5-cm² (¼-in²) viewer worn 3 cm (1⅕ in) from the eye. The screen gives the illusion of a full-size display without impairing depth perception or lateral vision. Technicians who need to refer to complex manuals as they work can look at the documentation without taking their attention away from the job at hand.

computer games

MOST ADVANCED GAMES CONSOLE

Bernard Stolar, the president and chief operating officer of the US arm of SEGA, is pictured displaying SEGA's new Dreamcast video game console. The SEGA Dreamcast, which was released in Tokyo, Japan, on 20 Nov 1998, is a 128-bit 200MHz games console with a 33.6-Kbps on-board modem. Its graphic engine is capable of drawing more than 3 million polygons a second, and its maximum simultaneous colour capacity is 16.77 million colours.

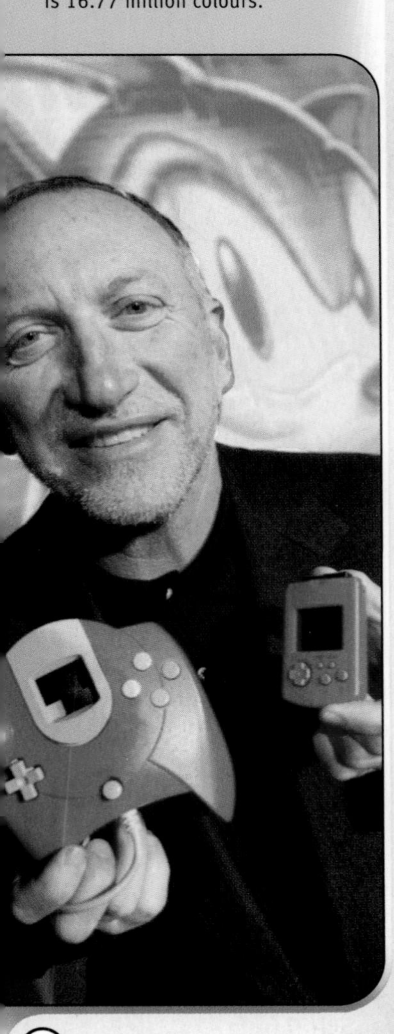

MOST GAMES SALES
In 1998 worldwide retail sales of video games were worth $15 billion (£9.05 billion). The games industry has grown dramatically since the 1970s, when the majority of consoles were produced by Atari. Today, the leading players in the market are Nintendo, SEGA and Sony.

MOST POPULAR HAND-HELD GAME SYSTEM
The world's most popular video game system is the Nintendo Game Boy, which sold more than 80 million units between 1989 and 1999. The company currently occupies more than 99% of the US hand-held games market through its Game Boy, Game Boy Pocket and Game Boy Colour units. Game Boy Colour features an eight-bit processor and a high-quality LCD screen with the ability to display up to 56 different colours simultaneously from a palette of 32,000. More than 1,000 Game Boy titles are available worldwide.

BEST-SELLING GAMES CONSOLE
The Sony PlayStation console had sold approximately 54.42 million units worldwide by March 1999, making it the best-selling computer games console in the world. Sony Computer Entertainment Inc. has spent more than $300 million (£181 million) developing the PlayStation, which runs hit games such as *Tomb Raider* and *Final Fantasy VII*, and about 430 million units of PlayStation software have been produced.

BIGGEST CHAIN OF VIDEO GAME ARCADES
SEGA Gameworks, a partnership between the games company SEGA, movie studio DreamWorks and music/entertainment company MCA, has 11 video entertainment super-centres in the USA and Guam. The largest of the centres, in Las Vegas, Nevada, USA, has a floor area of 4,180 m² (45,000 ft²) and 300 game units.

MOST SUCCESSFUL GAMES MANUFACTURER
In the year ending March 1999, Electronic Arts of California, USA, reported sales of $1.22 billion (£736 million) and profits of $73 million (£44 million). The company develops, publishes and distributes software for PCs and entertainment systems including Sony PlayStation and Nintendo 64.

BEST-SELLING FLIGHT SIMULATOR

MS Flight Simulator *was released by Microsoft in April 1992 and had sold a total of 21 million units by June 1999. Aircraft featured in* Flight Simulator 2000 *include Concorde, the Boeing 737-400 and 777-300, the Learjet 45, the Bell 206B JetRanger helicopter and the Sopwith Camel.*

BEST-SELLING GAMES
The Nintendo game *Super Mario Brothers* has sold a total of 40.23 million copies worldwide.

The 26 games featuring Mario, the character who first appeared in the arcade game *Donkey Kong* in 1982, have sold more than 152 million copies in total since 1983.

MOST ADVANCE ORDERS FOR A GAME
More than 325,000 US consumers put down deposits for copies of *The Legend of Zelda: Ocarina of Time*, a Nintendo 64 game, to ensure that they received their copy as soon as it went on sale on 23 Nov 1998.

FASTEST-SELLING GAMES
Resident Evil 2 by Capcom Entertainment of Sunnyvale, California, USA, was released on 21 Jan 1998 and sold more than 380,000 units in its first weekend, making more than $19 million (£11.5 million). The game, developed for the Sony PlayStation platform, broke records set by some of the industry's most popular video games, including *Final Fantasy VII* and *Super Mario 64*. It was supported by a $5-million (£3-million) advertising campaign. Over 5 million units had been sold by June 1999.

FASTEST-SELLING PC GAME
Myst, which was developed by Cyan and released by Broderbrund in 1993, sold 500,000 copies in its first year. Sales of the game have now topped 4 million and it has made total profits of over $100 million (£60 million). *Myst* was the first CD-ROM entertainment to sell more than 2 million copies. *Riven*, the sequel to *Myst*, was developed by Cyan and released by Broderbrund in Dec 1997. By May 1998 it had sold over 1 million units and made $43.7 million (£26.4 million). *Riven* comprises five CD-ROMS and has three times more animation than *Myst*.

MOST COMPLEX GAME
Jane's Combat Simulations' game *688(I) Hunter/Killer* is reportedly the most realistic submarine simulation developed for PCs. The game was developed by defence contractors who design submarine simulators for the US Navy, and a knowledge of flight dynamics is an advantage for players, who have to master sonar and weapons systems, develop real target solutions and outfit a boat with the latest weaponry.

BEST-SELLING FITNESS GAME
Released in March 1998, *Pocket Pikachu* by Nintendo sold 1.5 million

BEST-SELLING FOOTBALL GAME

The FIFA *series of games, developed by EA Sports, has sold more than 16 million units.* FIFA 99 *provides more teams and more methods of play than any other game currently on the market. Launched on PC format on 27 Nov 1998, the game features a full pop soundtrack including* Rockafeller Skank *by Fatboy Slim.*

units in its first three months. Pikachu is a yellow squirrel-like character based on the popular Japanese cartoon *Pocket Monsters*. The aim of the game is to keep Pikachu's cheeks rosy by taking it for regular walks. Pikachu is kept in its owner's pocket and 'complains' when it is not being exercised enough.

BEST-SELLING STRATEGY WAR GAMES

The *Command & Conquer* line of war games, developed by Westwood Studios (USA), sold more than 10 million units between its release in 1995 and Dec 1998. The line includes the original *Command & Conquer* for MS-DOS, Windows, Macintosh, Sony PlayStation and *Sega Saturn; The Covert Operations*; and *Command & Conquer Red Alert*, the prequel to *Command & Conquer*.

MOST POPULAR DJ SIMULATION ARCADE GAME

By May 1999 Japanese company Konami had released 6,700 copies of the arcade game *Beatmania* (known as *Hiphopmania* outside Japan), a DJ simulation game in which the player has to handle two record decks and an 'effects' button. They are then rated on their competence at mixing effectively and timing the additional sound effects.

MOST RIGOROUS SOFTWARE REGULATIONS

Germany has regulations stipulating that blood shown on computer games be green, and that 'victims' that are likely to end up getting killed are portrayed as 'zombies', or as far from human as possible.

MOST POPULAR GAME CHARACTERS

Lara Croft, the heroine of the Tomb Raider *series, was created by Core Design and the games featuring her have sold a total of 15 million copies. She has also featured in advertisements for SEAT cars and Lucozade and in Nov 1998 she was appointed the UK's Ambassador for Scientific Excellence by the British Department of Trade and Industry. The most popular male character is Mario the plumber, the star of Nintendo's* Super Mario Brothers *(see 'Best-Selling Computer Games'). Mario, with his brother Luigi, has also featured in three cartoon series and the film* Super Mario Brothers *(USA, 1993), in which he was played by Bob Hoskins.*

robots & artificial intelligence

BIGGEST ROBOT
In 1993 US company Amblin Entertainment, which is owned by Steven Spielberg, created a 5.5-m-tall (18-ft), 14-m-long (46-ft), 4,082-kg (9,000-lb) robotic *Tyrannosaurus rex* for the film *Jurassic Park*. Made of latex, foam rubber and urethane, it was the same size as the original dinosaur and the biggest robot ever made for a motion picture.

SMALLEST ROBOT
The light-sensitive Monsieur microbot, developed by the Seiko Epson Corporation, Japan, in 1992, measures less than 1 cm³ (3/50 in³) and weighs 1.5 g (1/20 oz). Made from 97 separate watch parts, it can move at a speed of 1.13 cm/sec (2/5 in/sec) for about five minutes when charged.

TOUGHEST ROBOT
A robot named Commander Manipulator has been developed by British Nuclear Fuels Ltd to help with the clean-up of contamination at Windscale Pile 1 (now called Sellafield), Cumbria, UK — the scene of one of the world's worst nuclear accidents, in 1957. The technology available at the time of the accident was unable to cope with the extreme conditions in the plant's defective reactor, so the 15 tonnes of uranium fuel contained inside it were simply buried under several metres of concrete. The robot is largely resistant to the effects of radiation and its hydraulically-powered five-jointed arm can shift weights of up to 127 kg (280 lb).

CHEAPEST ROBOT
Walkman, a 12.7-cm-tall (5-in) robot, was built from the remains of a Sony Walkman for $1.75 (£1.12) at the Los Alamos National Laboratory, New Mexico, USA, in 1996. In tests it struggled to get free when its legs were held, without being programmed to do so and without making the same movement twice.

MOST-USED INDUSTRIAL ROBOT
Puma (Programmable Universal Machine for Assembly), designed by Vic Schienman in the 1970s and manufactured by Swiss company Staubli Unimation, is the most commonly used robot on assembly lines and in university laboratories.

FASTEST INDUSTRIAL ROBOT
In July 1997 Japanese company Fanuc developed the LR Mate 100I high-speed conveyance robot, the axis speed of which is estimated to be 79% faster than previous models. The robot can carry objects for up to 3 km (1 mile 1,513 yd), and can move up and down 2.5 cm (1 in) and back and forth 30 cm (12 in) in a time of 0.58 seconds — 60% faster than previous models and an industry record.

MOST HUMANOID ROBOT
In 1997 Japanese company Honda launched the 1.6-m-tall (5-ft 3-in) P3 robot. The robot, which has three-dimensional sight, can turn its head, step over obstacles, change direction and correct its balance if pushed. Developed by 150 engineers over 11 years at a total cost of $80 million (£48.8 million), it is intended for use in nursing and for tasks that are too dangerous or strenuous for humans.

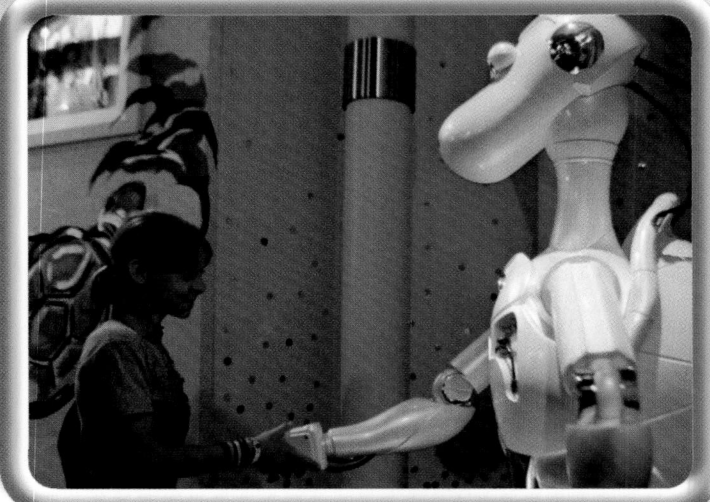

BIGGEST VIRTUAL-REALITY MARINE SIMULATION
A girl shakes hands with a turtle-shaped robot at Expo 98, held in Lisbon, Portugal. The exhibition was the setting for the world's biggest ever virtual-reality marine simulation. Visiting 'divers' could explore the Atlantic, Pacific, Indian and Antarctic oceans by means of a VR headset and an Onyx 2 supercomputer.

MOST ADVANCED ROBOT TOY
In Jan 1998 the Danish toy company Lego unveiled MindStorms, 'intelligent' plastic building blocks that can be made into 'thinking' robots and brought to life through a home computer. Developed over more than 10 years by Professor Papert of Massachusetts Institute of Technology (MIT), Cambridge, Massachusetts, USA, the bricks contain a microchip and sensors.

FASTEST-SELLING ROBOT PET
Aibo (Japanese for 'partner') is Sony's robot dog, which retails for $2,066 (£1,260). When Aibo made its first appearance on Sony's website on 31 May 1999, 3,000 were sold within 20 minutes. The 27.9-cm (11-in) tall Aibo can recognize its surroundings with a built-in sensor. It can play independently, or be programmed to do tricks. When another 2,000 Aibos went on sale on the internet in the USA on 1 June 1999 the initial rush to buy the pet caused web servers to crash.

MOST ADVANCED ROBOTIC ARM
In 1997 the US company Barret Technology developed a $250,000 (£153,000) robotic arm that has cables that act like tendons and that can hold weights of 5 kg (11 lb) in any position. The arm has a total of seven gearless joints, driven by brushless motors.

MOST SOPHISTICATED SURGICAL APPLICATION

Dr Robert Lazzara of Seattle, Washington, USA, is seen practising a coronary artery bypass on a model thorax using Computer Motion Inc.'s Zeus robot. Zeus, which was released in Feb 1998, allows surgeons to perform heart bypasses through three incisions the width of pencils, using thin instruments that fit inside tubes in the patient's body. Computer Motion Inc. is currently planning to produce a new version of the robot that allows surgeons to operate over a high-speed telephone line.

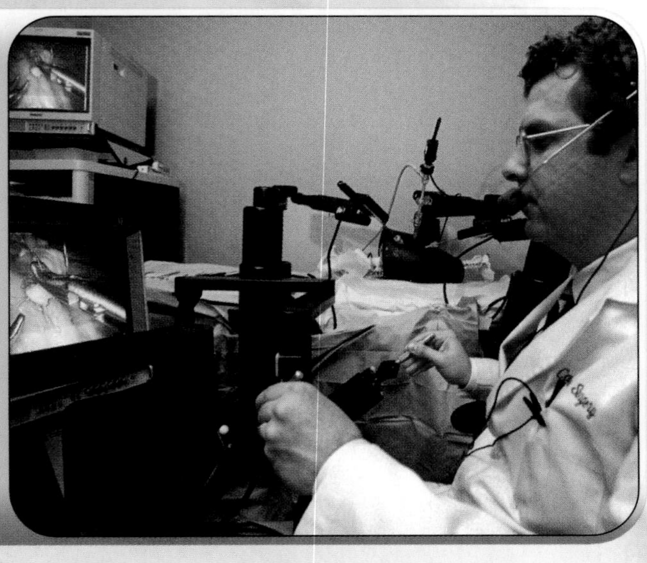

It can throw a ball, and could also be developed for cleaning, assisting people in and out of the bath, opening doors and preparing meals.

MOST ADVANCED FORM OF ARTIFICIAL INTELLIGENCE
Deep Blue, IBM's RS/6000 SP chess-playing parallel supercomputer, beat world chess champion Garry Kasparov by 3½ games to 2½ in 1997. Equipped with chess specific co-processors, *Deep Blue* can examine 200 million moves a second, which translates as 50 billion possible moves in three minutes (the time normally allowed for a single move in chess competitions). This astonishing amount of processing power allows *Deep Blue* to be, in Kasparov's words, 'brilliantly subtle'.

BIGGEST ROBOTIC TELESCOPE
The world's largest robotic telescope, situated at La Palma in the Canary Islands, has been built as a joint project between the Royal Observatory in Greenwich, London, and the astrophysics department at Liverpool John Moores University, both in the UK. Remotely controlled from an office at the university's astronomy department, the telescope has a 2-m (6-ft 7-in) aperture that will allow researchers to study black holes, red giants and distant galaxies.

BIGGEST PRODUCER OF COMMERCIAL ROBOTS
Formed in 1982, Japanese robot manufacturer Fanuc is the largest producer of commercial robots. Fanuc Robotics in the USA has more than 1,100 employees and 21,000 robots in service.

COUNTRY WITH THE MOST INDUSTRIAL ROBOTS
Since 1991 approximately 325,000 robots have been installed in Japan — more than half of the 580,000 installed worldwide. For every 10,000 people that are employed in the Japanese manufacturing industry, there are now 265 robots in use.

MOST AUTOMATED FACILITY
In March 1997 the Fanuc assembly plant in Yamanashi, Japan, became the most automated facility in the world when a number of two-armed intelligent robots began to assemble mini-robots, resulting in a completely automated manufacturing system.

LONGEST JOURNEY BY A ROBOT
On 4 July 1997 NASA's Sojourner robot rover completed its 129-million-km (80-million-mile) journey to Mars, landing on its surface within sight of the earlier Pathfinder lander. Weighing just 17.55 kg (38 lb 10 oz), the robot was remote controlled from Earth and roamed the surface of Mars conducting scientific experiments. Because it was so far away from its Earth-based controller, manoeuvring instructions took almost 20 minutes to reach it.

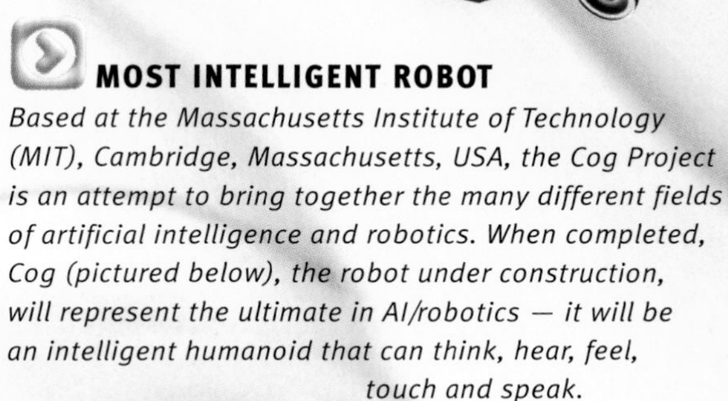

MOST INTELLIGENT ROBOT
Based at the Massachusetts Institute of Technology (MIT), Cambridge, Massachusetts, USA, the Cog Project is an attempt to bring together the many different fields of artificial intelligence and robotics. When completed, Cog (pictured below), the robot under construction, will represent the ultimate in AI/robotics — it will be an intelligent humanoid that can think, hear, feel, touch and speak.

satellites & communications

WIDEST MOBILE PHONE COVERAGE

In May 1998 the Iridium mobile phone network launched its final five communications satellites, bringing the size of its fleet up to 66 spacecraft — the largest number of networked communications satellites in existence. The system, which is to be operated and maintained on behalf of Iridium by Motorola, provides the world's widest mobile phone coverage. The phones are a little larger than normal mobiles and the Iridium network allows users to make calls from anywhere on the surface of the planet. Pictured is a refugee from Kosovo at a camp in Macedonia using an Iridium satellite phone to contact relatives.

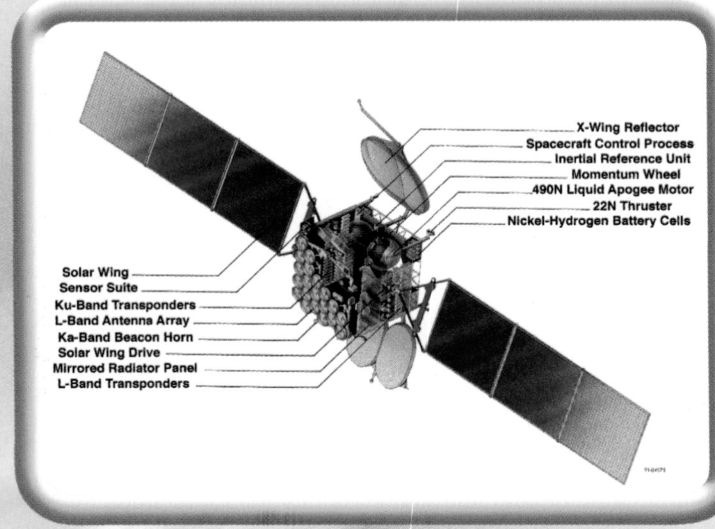

MOST POPULAR COMMUNICATIONS SATELLITE MODEL

The best-selling model of commercial communications satellite in the world, with 73 orders placed by the end of 1998, is the Hughes Space and Communications HS601. The list of customers using HS601s includes the US Navy and NASA. ICO Global Communication, of London, UK, has a fleet of 12 satellites, making the company the largest single user of HS601s.

BRIGHTEST ARTIFICIAL SATELLITE VISIBLE FROM EARTH

The *Mir* space station is the brightest artificial object that can be seen from Earth. In astronomers' terms it is about zeroth magnitude, which sets it at a similar brightness in the night sky to the nearest star to Earth, Alpha Centauri.

MOST DISTANT ARTIFICIAL OBJECT VISIBLE FROM EARTH

In 1998 NASA's *Near Earth Asteroid Rendezvous* (*NEAR*) spacecraft made a slingshot around the Earth to propel itself out to the giant asteroid Eros. It swung by closest to Earth in January — making it the first interplanetary craft to be visible to the naked eye — but on 1 April it was photographed by astronomer Gordon Garradd of Loomberah, NSW, Australia. At 33.65 million km (20.90 million miles) from Earth — 100 times the distance to the Moon — it became the most distant artificial object ever to be seen from Earth.

CLOSEST APPROACH TO THE MOON BY A COMMERCIAL ORBITER

The communications satellite *HGS-1* was left in an unusable elliptical orbit when its rocket malfunctioned shortly after launch in 1998. To correct the spacecraft's orbit, mission controllers slingshotted the satellite around the Moon. During the manoeuvre, it passed within 6,212 km (3,858 miles) of the lunar surface — the closest any commercial communications satellite has ever got to the Moon.

MOST POWERFUL COMMUNICATIONS SATELLITE

The Hughes Space and Communications' *HS702* satellite is capable of emitting a 15kW signal, making it the most powerful commercial communications satellite in the world. To achieve such a high output, the satellite draws upon twin high-efficiency solar cells.

OLDEST MAN-MADE SATELLITE STILL ORBITING

On 17 March 1958 a US satellite called *Vanguard 1* was boosted into orbit around the Earth. It is now the world's oldest orbiting satellite.

HEAVIEST SATELLITE LAUNCHED BY A SPACE SHUTTLE

The heaviest spacecraft ever carried into orbit and deployed by a US space shuttle is the Compton Gamma Ray Observatory (CGRO), which weighs 17.27 tonnes. CGRO is an astronomy satellite that has spent its eight-year orbital lifetime studying high-energy cosmic rays.

MOST PROLIFIC SATELLITE LAUNCHER

Russia and the other former states of the USSR have launched a total of 1,337 satellites into orbit, making it the world's most prolific satellite launching nation.

MOST PROLIFIC COMMUNICATIONS SATELLITE MANUFACTURER

Hughes Space and Communications Company, based in Los Angeles, California, USA, has supplied 137 communications satellites to the commercial sector — nearly 40% of those currently in operation.

BIGGEST COMMERCIAL SATELLITE FACTORY

With 56,000 m² (602,799 ft²) of floor space dedicated to satellite manufacture, the Hughes Integrated Satellite Factory in El Segundo, California, USA, is the world's largest commercial communications satellite factory. The factory is now the central location for the construction of Hughes Space and Communications' satellites.

MOST EXPENSIVE SATELLITE FAILURE

The world's most costly satellite accident happened on 12 Aug 1998, when a US Air Force *Titan 4* rocket exploded 41 seconds after lift-off from Cape Canaveral, Florida, USA, destroying the $1.035-billion (£625-million) spy satellite it was carrying. The rocket's guidance system is believed to have been responsible for the failure.

BIGGEST TELECOMMUNICATIONS FAILURE

The most disruptive failure of a telecommunications system happened in May 1998, when *Galaxy 4*, a $265-million (£160-million) Hughes Space and Communications satellite, operated by PanAmSat, developed a fault. An estimated 41 million people in the USA temporarily lost the use of their pagers as a result of the failure.

BIGGEST ORBITAL LITTERBUG
Space debris, which includes rocket stages left behind in orbit by space missions, is an ongoing problem for mission planners. Having left a total of 3,173 pieces of space debris in orbit around the Earth, the USA scoops the title of biggest orbital litterbug.

BIGGEST STRUCTURE IN SPACE

The International Space Station is the largest structure in Space. When completed in 2004, it will be 79.9 m (290 ft) long, have a wingspan of 108.6 m (356 ft 4½ in) and weigh 456 tonnes. It will take 44 launches to complete and is the largest international space project ever undertaken, involving teams from the USA, Russia, Canada, Japan, Brazil and 11 European countries.

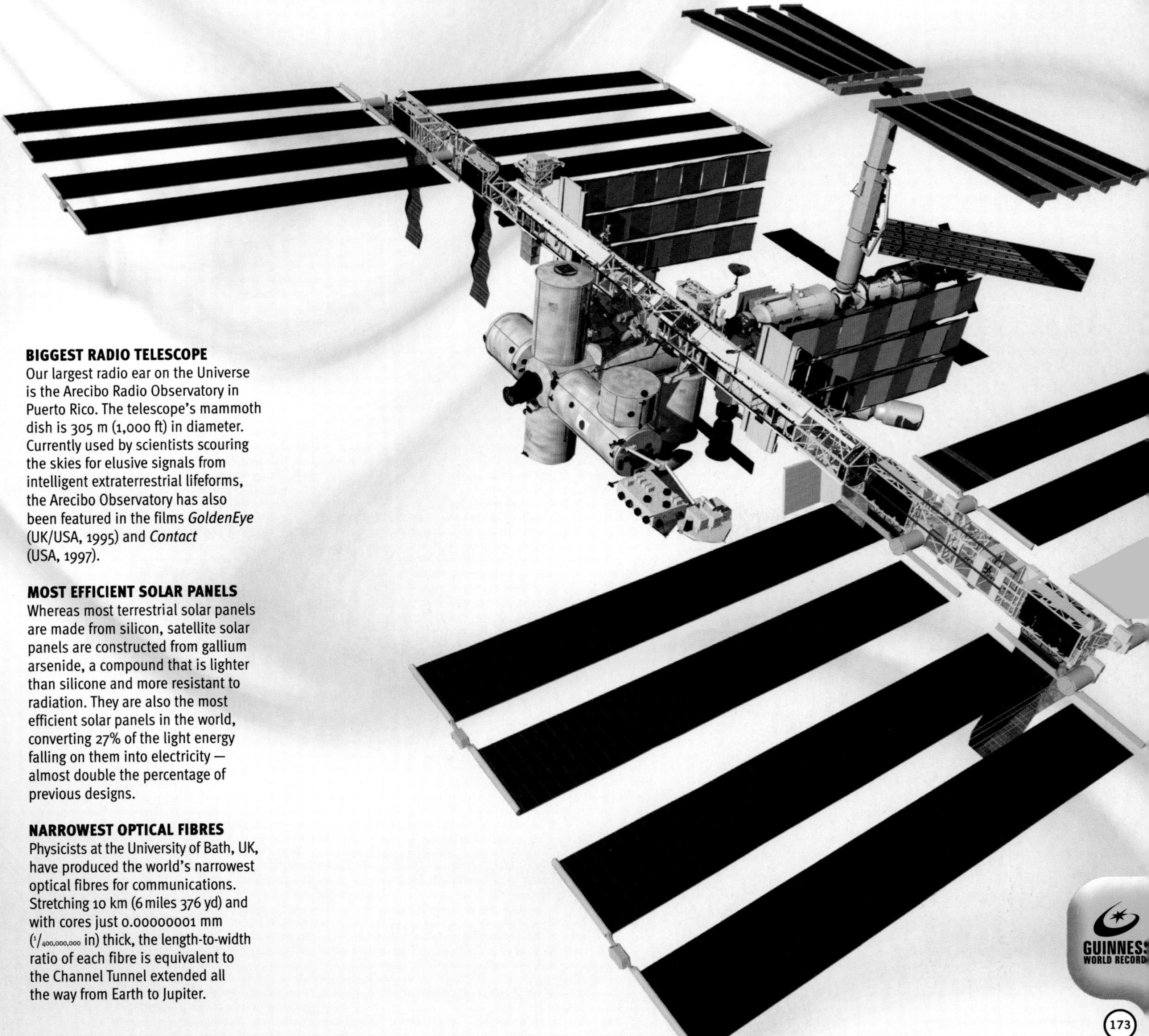

BIGGEST RADIO TELESCOPE
Our largest radio ear on the Universe is the Arecibo Radio Observatory in Puerto Rico. The telescope's mammoth dish is 305 m (1,000 ft) in diameter. Currently used by scientists scouring the skies for elusive signals from intelligent extraterrestrial lifeforms, the Arecibo Observatory has also been featured in the films *GoldenEye* (UK/USA, 1995) and *Contact* (USA, 1997).

MOST EFFICIENT SOLAR PANELS
Whereas most terrestrial solar panels are made from silicon, satellite solar panels are constructed from gallium arsenide, a compound that is lighter than silicone and more resistant to radiation. They are also the most efficient solar panels in the world, converting 27% of the light energy falling on them into electricity — almost double the percentage of previous designs.

NARROWEST OPTICAL FIBRES
Physicists at the University of Bath, UK, have produced the world's narrowest optical fibres for communications. Stretching 10 km (6 miles 376 yd) and with cores just 0.00000001 mm (1/400,000,000 in) thick, the length-to-width ratio of each fibre is equivalent to the Channel Tunnel extended all the way from Earth to Jupiter.

gadgets

SMALLEST CELLULAR PHONE
The PHS (Personal Handyphone System), made by the Nippon Telegraph and Telephone Corp., is a wristwatch-style phone that dispenses with the conventional keypad. Numbers are selected by voice recognition circuitry. The unit weighs 70 g ($2\frac{2}{5}$ oz) and measures 5.5 x 4 x 1.6 cm (2 x $1\frac{1}{2}$ x $\frac{3}{5}$ in).

SMALLEST SOLID-STATE STORAGE DEVICE
The SanDisk Multimedia Card, which was developed by SanDisk and Siemens for use in portable equipment such as mobile phones and digital voice recorders, is 3.2 x 2.4 x 0.14 cm ($1\frac{1}{4}$ x $\frac{9}{10}$ x $\frac{1}{20}$ in) thick and can store up to 10 megabytes of data.

SMALLEST VIDEO RECORDER
Sony's EVO 220 Micro 8 mm weighs 680 g (1 lb 8 oz) and measures 6 x 21.7 x 14.6 cm ($2\frac{3}{10}$ x $8\frac{1}{2}$ x $5\frac{7}{10}$ in). It can record up to five hours of video onto 8-mm ($\frac{3}{10}$-in) tape.

SMALLEST VIDEO TRANSMITTER
The VID1 from AE Inc. allows the wireless transmission of a picture to a base station 609 m (2,000 ft) away. Measuring 1.5 x 2.28 x 0.76 mm ($\frac{3}{5}$ x $\frac{9}{10}$ x $\frac{3}{10}$ in), it transmits either PAL or NTSC encoded video at 900 MHz, reducing the need for powerful output and allowing use for up to 11 hours.

SMALLEST VIDEO-CD PLAYER
The smallest video-CD player with its own screen is Panasonic's SL-DP70, which measures 13 x 3.6 x 14.4 cm (5 x $1\frac{2}{5}$ x $5\frac{3}{5}$ in). It can function for up to two hours with six AA batteries and costs about $528 (£330).

SMALLEST DVD PLAYER-MONITOR
The Panasonic PalmTheatre has an area of 40.7 cm² ($6\frac{1}{3}$ in²), is 4.2 cm ($1\frac{3}{5}$ in) thick and weighs 911 g (2 lb) without the battery. Its 14.73-cm ($5\frac{4}{5}$-in) LCD screen has 280,000 pixels and can handle 16:9 and 4:3 aspect ratio films. The unit also boasts stereo speakers and virtual surround sound.

MOST SHOCK-PROOF CD PLAYER
The PCD-7900, manufactured by Sanyo-Fisher, is the first personal CD player to incorporate a 40-second anti-shock memory, which compensates for errors in the disk tracking caused by external shock. The shock-guard capability is so extensive that the user can listen to music from the original disk while changing disks.

MOST EXPENSIVE POWER AMPLIFIER
The AudioNote Ongaku costs $93,200 (£56,000), making it the world's most expensive power amplifier. The Ongaku is a valve amplifier with a Class A output configuration, giving purity of sound at the expense of electrical efficiency. The main reason for its high cost is the solid silver windings for the output transformers.

MOST EXPENSIVE PRODUCTION 35-MM SLR CAMERA
The Canon Eos 1N-RS costs $3,840 (£2,400), making it the most expensive production 35-mm SLR camera in the world to date. The 1N-RS has a shutter speed from $\frac{1}{8,000}$ th of a second up to 30 seconds, accepts film speeds from 25 to 5,000 ASA and can shoot up to three frames every second. Its Pentaprism viewfinder offers 100% of the view that is relayed to the film and the main body can accept any Canon EF mount lenses.

MOST SOPHISTICATED TOILET
The Washlet Zoë, first sold in May 1997 by Toto of Japan, has a seat and lid that lift automatically and a flush 'simulator' — a sound effect that serves to cover any embarrassing noises. The seat is heated and the toilet can wash and dry the user. The entire unit can be remote controlled and it automatically freshens the air after every use. The Zoë retails for $699 (£422). Toto is also developing a toilet that can analyse your urine and take your blood pressure, then transmit these statistics to a doctor via a built-in modem.

SMALLEST COMPUTER
The smallest handheld computer is the Psion Series 5, which weighs 345 g (12 oz) including batteries. It has a touch-type keyboard and touch-sensitive screen.

SMALLEST CALCULATOR
Scientists at IBM's Research Laboratory in Zürich, Switzerland, have designed a calculating device with a diameter of less than 0.000001 mm ($\frac{39}{100,000,000}$ in).

MOST 'INTELLIGENT' PEN
The SmartQuill, developed by British Telecom, can function as a diary, calendar, contacts database, alarm, note taker, calculator, pager, e-mail receiver and pen. It can store the equivalent of 10 A4 pages before information is downloaded to the 'inkwell'. Silicon strips measure the gravity against the fingers, so no matter how bad your handwriting is the pen will recognize it. The SmartQuill is expected to be in the shops by 2001, priced around £200 ($330).

SMALLEST SHEET-FEED SCANNER
The CanoScan 300S, which uses Canon's LED InDirect Exposure (LIDE) technology, weighs just 1.5 kg (3 lb 4 oz).

SMALLEST CAMCORDER
The Sony CCD-CR1 Ruvi measures 12.5 x 6.7 x 4.4 cm (5 x $2\frac{1}{2}$ x $1\frac{3}{4}$ in) and can store 30 minutes of moving images. The camera has a 6.35-cm ($2\frac{1}{2}$-in) LCD screen and an optical zoom and the tape is enclosed in a plastic cartridge along with the record and playback heads, which plug in and out with every new cartridge inserted.

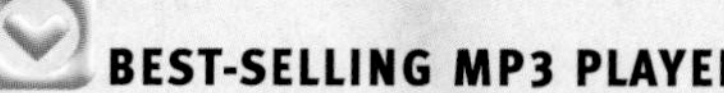

BEST-SELLING MP3 PLAYER

The Diamond Rio PMP300 MP3 player sold 400,000 units between its release in Nov 1998 and May 1999. The MP3 format, available on the internet, is a digital method of storing and retrieving audio files. The PMP300, measuring 9 x 6.5 x 1.5 cm ($3\frac{1}{2}$ x $2\frac{1}{2}$ x $\frac{3}{5}$ in), stores up to 60 minutes of digital-quality sound. MP3 players are smaller than an audio cassette and have no moving parts, so they never skip.

THINNEST MINIDISC RECORDER

Sony's MZ-R55 is 1.89 cm ($\frac{3}{4}$ in) thick and weighs 190 g (6 oz) with its lithium ion battery and alkaline AA cells. It can play for up to 16 hours.

SMALLEST DOCUMENT SHREDDER
Piranha's PRO26 measures 17 x 6 x 4 cm ($6\frac{1}{2}$ x $2\frac{1}{3}$ x $1\frac{1}{2}$ in) and deals with any kind of document by nibbling off slices and shredding them into slivers.

SMALLEST FAX MACHINE
Philips' smart phone add-on connects to the Philips PCS 1900 Digital Phone to send faxes and e-mails, access the internet and provide other communication services. It makes the PCS 1900, at 17 cm ($6\frac{7}{10}$ in) in length and 159 g ($5\frac{3}{5}$ oz) in weight, the smallest and lightest mobile fax.

SMALLEST BINOCULARS
The U-C 8x18 series binoculars, with 8x magnification and optics that allow focusing down to 2 m (6 ft 7 in), weighs 145 g (5 oz) and measures 8.5 x 7 x 1.8 cm (3 x $2\frac{7}{10}$ x $\frac{7}{10}$ in).

CHEAPEST GPS RECEIVER
The cheapest portable Global Positioning by Satellite receiver in the world today is the GPS Pioneer, which is manufactured by Magellan Systems Corporation in the USA. The Pioneer is the first GPS receiver to cost less than $100 (£62) and allows users to find their location on the planet through its ability to decode information from the NavStar network of 24 orbiting geostationary satellites.

BEST-SELLING MATCHMAKER

The Lovegety, manufactured by Erfolg in Japan, has sold more than 1.3 million units since its release in Feb 1998. The palm-sized beeper, which retails for $22 (£13), recognizes signals sent from a Lovegety held by someone of the opposite sex within a range of 4.6 m (15 ft). It was invented by Takeya Takafuji, who wanted to create "a machine that can recognize the other's mind".

cars

FASTEST ROAD CAR
The highest speed ever reached by a standard production car is 386.7 km/h (240.1 mph), by a McLaren F1 driven by Andy Wallace at the Volkswagen Proving Ground, Wolfsburg, Germany on 31 March 1998.

FASTEST DIESEL-ENGINED CAR
The prototype 3-litre Mercedes C 111/3 attained 327.3 km/h (203.3 mph) in tests on the Nardo Circuit, southern Italy, on 5–15 Oct 1978. In April 1978 the car maintained an average speed of 314.5 km/h (195.4 mph) over a period of 12 hours, covering a record distance of 3773.5 km (2344 miles 1,232 yd).

FASTEST ELECTRIC CAR
The highest speed achieved by an electric vehicle is 295.832 km/h (183.822 mph) over a two-way flying kilometre (1,094 yd), by General Motor's Impact, driven by Clive Roberts (UK) at Fort Stockton Test Center, Texas, USA, on 11 March 1994

FASTEST ACCELERATION
The fastest road-tested acceleration on record is 0–96 km/h (0–60 mph) in 3.07 seconds, by a Ford RS200 Evolution driven by Graham Hathaway at Millbrook Proving Ground, Beds, UK, in May 1994.

MOST POWERFUL CAR
The most powerful production car currently on the market is the McLaren F1 6.1, which develops in excess of 627 bhp. The vehicle can accelerate to 96 km/h (60 mph) in 3.2 seconds.

LOWEST PETROL CONSUMPTIONS
In 1989 Stuart Bladon drove a Citroën AX 14DTR 180.26 km (112 miles 18 yd) on one gallon of fuel on the M11 motorway, UK.

A vehicle designed by Team 1200 from Honda in Suzuka City, Japan, achieved 3,336 km/litre (9,426 mpg) in the Pisaralla Pisimmälle mileage marathon at Nokia, Finland, on 1 Sept 1996.

LONGEST FUEL RANGE
The greatest distance ever travelled by a vehicle on the contents of a standard fuel tank (80.1 litres or 17½ gallons) is 2,153.4 km (1,338 miles 18 yds), by an Audi 100 TDI diesel car. The car was driven by Stuart Bladon from John O'Groats, Highland, to Land's End, Cornwall, UK, and back again between 26 and 28 July 1992.

GREATEST DISTANCE COVERED ON A SINGLE CHARGE BY A PRODUCTION VEHICLE
A Solectria force NiMH electric sedan established a new distance record by completing 400.72 km (249 miles) on a single charge in the 1997 North East Sustainable Energy Association (NESEA) American Tour de Sol, using state of the art nickel metal hydride batteries produced by the Ovonic Battery

LONGEST CAR
A 30.5-m-long (100-ft), 26-wheeled limo (pictured below) designed by Jay Ohrberg of Burbank, California, USA, includes a swimming pool with a diving board and a king-sized waterbed among its many features. It can be driven as a rigid vehicle or altered to bend in the middle. Designers of these super-stretched cars try to outdo each other not just with the length of their creations but with the add-ons – for example, the 22-wheel, 20.73-m (68-ft) Cadillac *Hollywood Dream* has six telephones, a satellite dish, a putting green and a helicopter landing pad.

SMALLEST CAR IN PRODUCTION

The Smart car made by Daimler-Benz is the smallest car currently in production; with an exterior length of just under 2.5 m (8 ft 4 in) it beats its nearest rival, the Rover Mini, by 55 cm (1 ft 8 in). The two-seater car has removable body panels made out of thermoplastic, allowing owners to change the colour of their vehicles.

Company. Solectria broke their existing record of 392.67 km (244 miles) set at the 1996 Tour de Sol.

HIGHEST CAR MILEAGE
The highest recorded mileage for a car is 2,719,800 km (1,690,000 miles), by a 1966 Volvo P-1800S owned by Irvine Gordon of East Patchogue, New York, USA, up to Feb 1999.

BIGGEST CAR
The biggest car ever to have been produced for private use was the Bugatti 'Royale' type 41, assembled at Molsheim, France, by the Italian designer Ettore Bugatti. First built in 1927, the car has an eight-cylinder engine with a capacity of 12.7 litres (2¾ gal) and is more than 6.7 m (22 ft) long. The bonnet alone is 2.13 m (7 ft) in length.

WIDEST CARS
The Koenig Competition:2417, built in 1989, and the Koenig Competition Evolution:2418, built in 1990, both in Germany, are both 2.195 m (7 ft 2⅖ in) in width.

SMALLEST CAR
The Peel P50, which was constructed by Peel Engineering Company on the Isle of Man in 1962, was 1.34 m (4 ft 5 in) in length, 99 cm (3 ft 3 in) in width and 1.34 m (4 ft 5 in) in height. It weighed 59 kg (132 lb).

LIGHTEST CAR
The world's lightest ever car was built and driven by Louis Borsi of London, UK, and weighs 9.5 kg (21 lb). It has a 2.5cc engine and can reach a maximum speed of 25 km/h (15 mph).

HEAVIEST CAR
The heaviest car in recent production is the Soviet-built Zil–41047 limousine, which has a 3.88-m (12-ft 9-in) wheel-base weighing 3.335 tonnes. A 'stretched' Zil, of which only two or three were made annually, was used by former Soviet president Mikhail Gorbachev until Dec 1991. It weighed 6 tonnes and used 75-mm (3-in) armour-plated steel for protection in key areas. The eight-cylinder, 7-litre engine guzzled fuel at the rate of 2.1 km/litre (6 mpg).

CHEAPEST CAR
The 1922 Red Bug Buckboard, built by the Briggs & Stratton Company, Milwaukee, Wisconsin, USA, was on the market for $125–150 (£28–34). This would be equivalent to $1,130–1,870 (£680–826) in 1999 terms. It had a 1.57-m (62-in) wheelbase and weighed 111 kg (245 lb). Early models of the King Midget cars, which were made in the USA in kit form for self-assembly, sold for as little as $100 (£25) in 1948, the equivalent of $842 (£507) in 1999 terms.

LONGEST PRODUCTION RUN
The Morgan 4/4, built by the Morgan Motor Car Company of Malvern, Worcs, UK, celebrated its 63rd birthday in Dec 1998. There is currently a waiting list of between six and eight years for the car.

BEST-SELLING SPORTS CAR
Mazda manufactured 492,645 MX5 sports cars between 1989 and 1998. The car, which is called a Miata in the USA and a Roadster in Japan, became so successful that the market was subsequently flooded with two-seater sports cars.

MOST CARS PRODUCED IN A YEAR
In 1997 a record 57.84 million vehicles were constructed worldwide. Of this total, more than 41 million were cars, making 1997 a record-breaking year for car production.

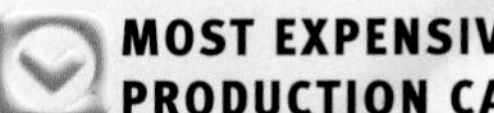

MOST EXPENSIVE PRODUCTION CAR

The world's most expensive production car is the Mercedes Benz CLK/LM, which costs $1,547,620 (£957,093.33). It has a top speed of 320 km/h (200 mph) and can travel from 0 to 100km/h (62 mph) in 3.8 seconds.

bikes

BIGGEST BICYCLE
The largest bicycle in the world, as measured by wheel diameter, is *Frankencycle*, which was built by Dave Moore of Rosemead, California, USA, and first ridden by Steve Gordon of Moorpark, California, on 4 June 1989. The wheel diameter is 3.05 m (10 ft) and the bicycle itself is 3.4 m (11 ft 2 in) tall.

LONGEST BICYCLE
The longest true bicycle (defined as a two-wheeled cycle without a third stabilizing wheel) was designed and built by Terry Thessman of Pahiatua, New Zealand. It measures 22.24 m (72.96 ft) in length and weighs 340 kg (750 lb). It was ridden a distance of 246 m (807 ft) by a team of four people on 27 Feb 1988. It performs well when ridden in a straight line but cornering remains a problem.

SMALLEST BICYCLE
The world's smallest wheeled rideable bicycle has wheels of 1.9 cm (3/4 in) in diameter. It was ridden by its constructor Neville Patten of Gladstone, Queensland, Australia, for a distance of 4.1 m (13 ft 5 in) on 25 March 1988.

TALLEST UNICYCLE
Steve McPeak (USA) rode a 31.01-m-tall (101-ft 9-in) unicycle, with a safety wire suspended from an overhead crane, a distance of 114.6 m (376 ft) in Las Vegas, Nevada, USA, in Oct 1980.

BIGGEST TRICYCLE
The world's biggest tricycle was designed and constructed by 16 students at Bay de Noc Community College, Escabana, Michigan, USA, in July 1998. It has a front wheel diameter of 4.67 m (15 ft 3 in), the back wheels have a diameter of 2.23 m (7 ft 3 in) and the overall height of the tricycle is 7.13 m (23 ft 4 3/4 in).

MOST EXPENSIVE MOTORCYCLE
The world's most expensive production motorbike is the Morbidelli 850 V8, which retails for $102,872 (£62,983).

SMALLEST UNICYCLE

The smallest ridden unicycle is 20 cm (8 in) high with a wheel diameter of 1.8 cm (7/10 in), and it has no attachments or extensions fitted. It was made by Signar Berglund of Sweden. It has been ridden on a number of occasions by Peter Rosendahl (Sweden), the greatest distance being 8.5 m (27 ft 10 in) on the TV show *Laß Dich Überrachen (Let Me Surprise You)* at the ZDF Studios, Unterföhring, Germany, on 29 March 1998.

SMALLEST TANDEM
Jacques Puyoou of Pau, Pyrénées-Atlantiques, France, has built a tandem that is 36 cm (14 in) in length. It has been ridden by himself and his wife.

MOST EXPENSIVE MOUNTAIN BIKE
'The Flipper', the most expensive retail mountain bike in the world, costs £7,244 ($12,025). Made by Stif (UK), it weighs just 9.07 kg (20 lb) and is designed for off-road racing circuits. It includes some of the world's most expensive bicycle components — the brakes, gears and pedals are made in Japan, the frame is from the USA, the forks and handlebars are British and the saddle is Italian.

BIGGEST PRODUCER OF FOLDING BICYCLES
Dahon California, Inc. (USA) is the world's largest producer of folding bicycles. Since 1982 Dahon has produced over 1.2 million bicycles, their best-selling model being the Classic, with over 400,000 units sold worldwide.

LONGEST MOTORCYCLE
Douglas and Roger Bell of Perth, Western Australia, designed and built a 7.6-m-long (24-ft 11-in) motorbike weighing nearly 2 tonnes.

SMALLEST MOTORCYCLE
Simon Timperley and Clive Williams of Progressive Engineering Ltd, Ashton-under-Lyne, Greater Manchester, UK, designed and constructed a motorcycle with a wheel-base of 10.8 cm (4 1/4 in), a seat height of 9.5 cm (3 3/4 in) and a wheel diameter of 1.9 cm (3/4 in) at the front and 2.4 cm (9/10 in) at the back. The bike was ridden a distance of 1 m (3 ft 3 in).

BIGGEST MOTORCYCLE MANUFACTURER
The Honda Motor Company of Japan is the largest manufacturer of motorcycles in the world. The company has 95 production facilities in 34 countries for motorcycles and automobiles. In 1998 Honda sold a total of 5.1 million units to retailers worldwide.

EARLIEST MOTORCYCLE
The first internal combustion engine motorized bicycle was *Einspur*, a wooden-framed machine built by

LIGHTEST FOLDABLE BICYCLE

The Triancle 6500 B-PEHT23, developed in Japan by the National Bicycle Industrial Co., Matsushita Electric Industrial Co. and the East Japan Railway Co., weighs 6.5 kg (14 lb 5 oz). The frame and front fork are made of titanium. The bicycle is small enough to be carried easily onto a train or to fit into a locker at a station.

Gottlieb Daimler in Bad Cannstatt, Germany, in 1885 and first ridden by Wilhelm Maybach. It had a top speed of 19 km/h (12 mph) and developed ½ hp from its single-cylinder 264 cc four-stroke engine at 700 rpm.

LARGEST-CAPACITY SCOOTER
The Suzuki Bergman 400 cc has the largest capacity of any scooter that is currently in production. It has a power output of 31.5 bhp @ 8,000 rpm, together with a torque output of 14.46 lb ft² @ 6,000 rpm.

MOST EXPENSIVE PRODUCTION SCOOTER
The Suzuki AN 400 is the most expensive scooter currently in production, costing $6,628 (£3,999), with an on-road charge of $456 (£275).

LONGEST-RUNNING SCOOTER MANUFACTURER
Vespa of Italy is the oldest company manufacturing scooters. The prototype of the first Vespa scooter was tested and approved in Dec 1945, with production beginning in April 1946. In 1949 the company was awarded a royal warrant to supply the Duke of Edinburgh with scooters.

FASTEST PRODUCTION BIKE

The Suzuki Hayabusa Gsx1300R is reported to reach speeds of 312 km/h (194 mph), making it the fastest production bike in the world. The motorcycle is a 1298 cc DOHC with four valves per cylinder, a narrow 14° valve angle and electronic fuel injection with ram-air. The result is a powerful bike with 173 bhp at 9800 rpm but an overall weight of 215 kg (474 lb). 'Hayabusa' is Japanese for peregrine falcon.

planes & boats

FASTEST SAILING VESSEL

On 26 Oct 1993 the trifoiler *Yellow Pages Endeavour* (pictured below) reached a speed of 46.52 knots (86.21 km/h or 53.57 mph) while on a timed run of 500 m (547 yd) at Sandy Point near Melbourne, Victoria, Australia. This is the highest speed ever reached by any craft under sail on water. The trifoiler, which has a 12-m-high (40-ft) sail and three short planing hulls, was designed by Lindsay Cunningham (Australia), who also designed Australia's Little America's Cup catamarans. It was piloted on its record-breaking run by Simon McKeon and Tim Daddo, both of Australia.

FASTEST AIRLINERS

The Tupolev Tu-144, first flown in 1968, was reported to have achieved Mach 2.4 (2,575 km/h or 1,600 mph), although its normal cruising speed was Mach 2.2. In May 1970 it became the first commercial transport to exceed Mach 2.

The BAC/Aérospatiale Concorde was first flown in 1969. It cruises at speeds of up to Mach 2.2 (2,333 km/h or 1,450 mph) and is the fastest supersonic airliner.

FASTEST AIRCRAFT

The USAF Lockheed SR-71, a reconnaissance aircraft, was the fastest ever jet, reaching a speed of 3,529.56 km/h (2,193.22 mph). First flown in its definitive form in 1964, the Lockheed was reportedly capable of attaining an altitude of 30,000 m (98,000 ft). It was 32.73 m (107 ft 5 in) long, had a wingspan of 16.94 m (55 ft 7 in) and weighed 77.1 tonnes at take-off. Its reported range at Mach 3 was 4,800 km (3,000 miles) at 24,000 m (79,000 ft).

The fastest propeller-driven aircraft was the Soviet Tu-95/142, which had four 11,033-kW (14,795-hp) engines driving eight-blade contrarotating propellers and a maximum level speed of Mach 0.82 or 925 km/h (575 mph).

The highest speed achieved by a piston-engined aircraft is 850.24 km/h (528.33 mph) over a 3-km (1-mile 1584-yd) course, by *Rare Bear*, a modified Grumman F8F Bearcat piloted by Lyle Shelton, in Las Vegas, Nevada, USA, in Aug 1989.

The fastest biplane was the one-off Italian Fiat CR42B, which had a 753-kW (1,010-hp) Daimler-Benz DB601A engine. It reached a speed of 520 km/h (323 mph) in 1941.

FASTEST FLYING BOAT

The Martin XP6M-1 SeaMaster, a four-jet-engined US Navy minelayer flown from 1955 to 1959, had a top speed of 1,040 km/h (646 mph).

BIGGEST AIRCRAFT

The jet airliner with the highest capacity is the Boeing 747-400, which first entered service in 1989. It has a wingspan of 64.9 m (213 ft) and a range of 13,340 km (8,290 miles) and can carry up to 566 passengers.

SMALLEST BIPLANE

The smallest biplane ever flown was Bumble Bee Two *(pictured above), which was designed and constructed by Robert Starr of Tempe, Arizona, USA. Capable of carrying just one person,* Bumble Bee Two *was 2.69 m (8 ft 10 in) in overall length and had a wingspan of 1.68 m (5 ft 6 in). It weighed 179.6 kg (396 lb) when empty. In 1988 it crashed and was totally destroyed after attaining an altitude of 120 m (394 ft).*

The airliner that holds the record for the greatest volume is the Airbus Super Transporter A300-600 ST Beluga, which has a 1,400-m³ (49,440-ft³) main cargo compartment, a maximum take-off weight of 150 tonnes, a 44.84-m (147-ft 1-in) wingspan and an overall length of 56.16 m (184 ft 2 in). The usable length of its cargo compartment is 37.7 m (123 ft 8 in).

BIGGEST WINGSPANS

The $40-million (£24-million) Hughes H4 Hercules flying boat, also known as the *Spruce Goose*, had the biggest ever wingspan of any aircraft, at 97.51 m (320 ft). The 193-tonne, 66.65-m-long (218-ft 8-in), eight-engined aircraft reached a height of 21.3 m (70 ft) in a 914-m (1,000-yd) test run piloted by US tycoon Howard Hughes off Long Beach Harbor, California, USA, in 1947 but never flew again.

The biggest wingspan of a current aircraft is 73.3 m (240 ft 6 in), on the Ukrainian Antonov An-124 Ruslan.

SMALLEST MONOPLANE

The smallest monoplane ever flown is *Baby Bird*, which was designed and built by Donald Stits. It is 3.35 m (11 ft) long, has a wingspan of 1.91 m (6 ft 4 in) and weighs just 114.3 kg (252 lb) when empty. First flown in 1984, the plane has a maximum speed of 177 km/h (110 mph).

SMALLEST TWIN-ENGINED AIRCRAFT

The world's smallest ever twin-engined aircraft is believed to be the Colombian MGI5 Cricri, which was first flown in 1973. The Cricri has a wingspan of 4.9 m (16 ft) and an overall length of 3.91 m (12 ft 10 in). It is powered by two 11.25-kW (15-hp) JPX PUL engines.

BIGGEST SAILING VESSEL

The biggest sailing vessel currently in service is the 109-m-long (358-ft) *Sedov*, built in 1921 in Kiel, Germany, and now used by the Russian Navy. It has a beam of 14.6 m (48 ft), a displacement of 6,300 tonnes and a sail area of 4,192 m² (45,124 ft²). *Sedov* can reach speeds of up to 17 knots (31 km/h or 19 mph) and has a crew of 65 cadets and 120 officer trainees.

LONGEST SAILING VESSEL

The longest sailing vessel in the world is the 187-m (614-ft) French-built *Club Med 1*, which has five aluminium masts and 2,800 m² (30,100 ft²) of

BIGGEST PRODUCTION AIRCRAFT

The production airliner with the greatest volume is the Ukrainian Antonov An-124 Ruslan (pictured left), the cargo hold of which has a usable volume of 1,014 m^3 (35,800 ft^3) and a maximum take-off weight of 405 tonnes. The heavy-lift version of the An-124, the An-225 Mriya, has a stretched fuselage providing as much as 1,190 m^3 (42,000 ft^3) of usable volume. Its cargo compartment includes an unobstructed 43-m-long (141-ft) hold and has a maximum width and height of 6.4 m (21 ft) and 4.4 m (14 ft 5 in) respectively.

computer-controlled polyester sails. It operates as a Caribbean cruise ship for the Club Med holiday company and can carry 425 passengers.

BIGGEST AIRCRAFT CARRIERS
The Nimitz class US Navy aircraft carriers *USS Nimitz*, *Dwight D. Eisenhower*, *Carl Vinson*, *Theodore Roosevelt*, *Abraham Lincoln*, *George Washington* and *John C. Stennis* (the last three of which displace 103,637 tonnes) have the biggest full-load displacement of any warships. They are 332.9 m (1,092 ft) in length with 1.82 ha (4½ acres) of flight deck. Driven by four nuclear-powered 260,000-shp geared steam turbines, they can reach speeds of more than 30 knots (56 km/h or 35 mph). The *Nimitz* has four C-13 Mod 1 catapults or 'cats' that propel aircraft off the flight deck. These can accelerate even the heaviest carrier-based aircraft to speeds of 273 km/h (170 mph) from a standing start.

BIGGEST CARGO VESSEL
The oil tanker *Jahre Viking* (formerly known as *Happy Giant* and *Seawise Giant*) is 458.45 m (1,504 ft) long and weighs 564,763 dwt. It has a beam of 68.8 m (226 ft) and a draught of 24.61 m (80 ft 8 in). The tanker was almost totally destroyed during the Iran–Iraq war but underwent a $60-million (£34-million) renovation in Singapore and the United Arab Emirates. It was relaunched under its new name in Nov 1991.

BIGGEST CONTAINER SHIP
The biggest container vessel currently in service is *Regina Maersk*, which was built in Odense, Denmark, in 1996. It has a gross tonnage of 81,488 and a capacity of 6,000 TEU.

BIGGEST HYDROFOIL
The 64.6-m-long (212-ft) *Plainview* naval hydrofoil, which weighs 314 tonnes with a full load, was launched by the Lockheed Shipbuilding and Construction Co. at Seattle, Washington, USA, on 28 June 1965. It has a service speed of 92 km/h (57.2 mph).

BIGGEST YACHTS
The Saudi Arabian royal yacht *Abdul Aziz*, which was built in Denmark and completed at Vospers Yard, Southampton, Hants, UK, in June 1984, is 147 m (482 ft) long.

The biggest non-royal yacht in the world is the 124-m-long (407-ft) *Savarona*, which was built for Turkish president Mustafa Kemal Atatürk in 1931.

BIGGEST JUNK
The sea-going *Zheng He* had a displacement of 3,150 tonnes and an estimated length of 164 m (538 ft). The flagship of Admiral Zheng He's 62 treasure ships *c.* 1420, it is believed to have had nine masts.

FASTEST HOVERCRAFT
On 25 Jan 1980 a 24-m-long (79-ft), 110-tonne US Navy test hovercraft reached a speed of 105.8 km/h (65.7 mph) in the Chesapeake Bay Test Range, Virginia, USA.

OLDEST COMMISSIONED WARSHIP
Ordered in 1758, *HMS Victory* took a total of six years to build. It has 43.5 km (27 miles) of rigging and 1.6 ha (4 acres) of sails. Now being restored to its original condition, the ship is the only remaining specimen of its kind anywhere in the world. It is currently docked at Portsmouth, Hants, UK.

OLDEST IRON STEAMSHIP
The *SS Great Britain* was launched in Bristol, UK, in 1843 and was the first propeller-driven iron vessel to cross the Atlantic. It was also used on the UK–Australia route and from 1855 to 1856 carried troops to the Crimean War. After running into trouble off Cape Horn in 1884, the ship sailed to Port Stanley in the Falkland Islands for shelter, where it was subsequently used as a storage vessel. It was salvaged from the Falklands in 1970 and brought back to Bristol, where it was restored to its original appearance.

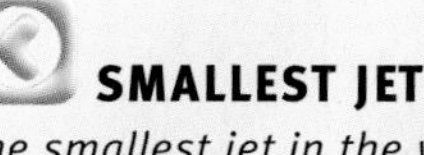

SMALLEST JET

The smallest jet in the world is the Silver Bullet, *which was built by Bob and Mary Ellen Bishop of Aguila, Arizona, USA, in 1976. It is 3.7 m (12 ft) long, has a wingspan of 5.2 m (17 ft) and weighs approximately 198 kg (437 lb). The* Silver Bullet *can fly straight and level at a speed of 483 km/h (300 mph).*

rockets

MOST SATELLITES DESTROYED AT A LAUNCH

This artist's impression shows the *Ariane 5* launcher lifting off from the launch pad at Kourou, French Guiana. The launcher, an upgrade of the *Ariane 4* rocket, is capable of delivering an 18-tonne satellite into a low-earth orbit and a 5.9-tonne payload into geostationary orbit. On 6 June 1996 *Ariane 5*'s first flight ended in disaster when its on-board computer malfunctioned 40 seconds after launch, causing it to veer wildly off-course. An automatic self-destruct mechanism then blew it into pieces. The rocket was carrying four identical Cluster satellites. *Ariane 5* has since made two successful launches, in Oct 1997 and Oct 1998.

BIGGEST ROCKET
The US craft *Saturn V* was the biggest ever rocket, at a record 110.6 m (363 ft) in height with the *Apollo* spacecraft on top. It weighed 2,903 tonnes on the launch pad.

SMALLEST ROCKET
The smallest satellite launch vehicle in the world was *Pegasus*, a 15-m-long (49-ft 3-in) three-stage booster. The original *Pegasus*, which has since been succeeded by an operational *Pegasus XL* version, was air-launched from an aircraft in 1990.

MOST EXPENSIVE ROCKETS
The *Saturn V* rocket was constructed for the *Apollo* moon landing programme, which had cost approximately $25 billion (£10.5 billion) by the time of the first flight to the Moon in July 1969.

Commercial customers have been charged more than $120 million (£72.4 million) in total for launches to orbit communications satellites aboard the US commercial rocket *Titan*, which is no longer on the market.

CHEAPEST SATELLITE LAUNCHER
The least expensive US satellite launcher was *Pegasus*, which was developed with a budget of $45 million (£27 million) and cost approximately $10 million (£6 million) per launch.

MOST INTELLIGENT ROCKETS
The launch and flight of the space shuttles are computer-controlled and guided from nine minutes before lift-off to the crafts' arrival in orbit eight minutes after launch.

MOST ADVANCED ROCKET ENGINE
The revolutionary Aerospike engine, which will be used to power the next generation of shuttle craft, has no nozzle, unlike conventional rocket engines. Instead, exhaust gas flows over a centrally positioned ramp that changes position in flight, to give better efficiency and more power. Prototypes of the Aerospike are already flying on converted SR-71 spy planes.

MOST POWERFUL ROCKET ENGINE
Built in the former USSR by the Scientific Industrial Corporation of Power Engineering in 1980, the RD-170 has a thrust of 806 tonnes in open space and 704 tonnes at the Earth's surface. It also has a turbopump rated at 190MW, and burns liquid oxygen and kerosene. The RD-170 powered the four strap-on boosters of the *Energiya* booster, launched in 1987 but now grounded by budget cuts.

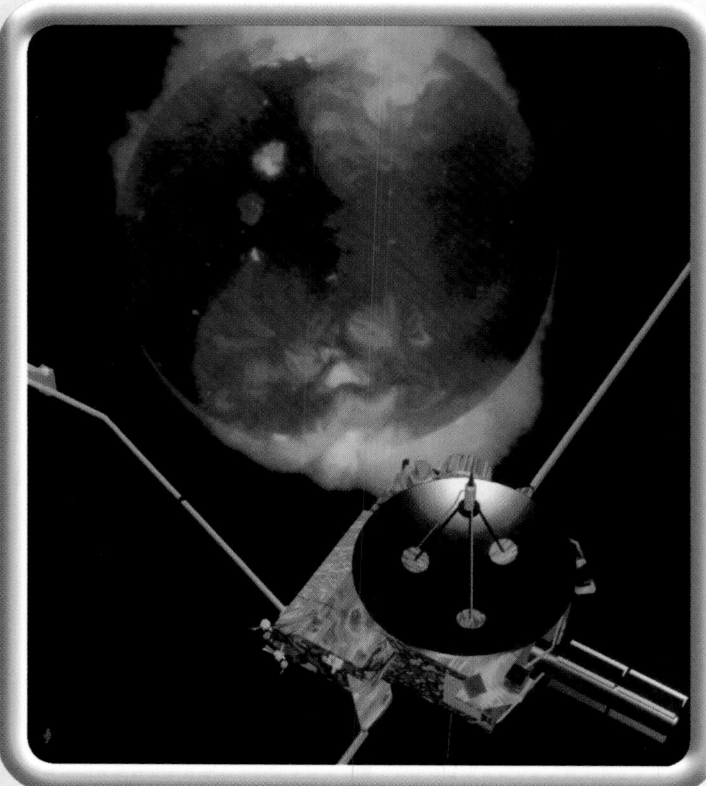

FASTEST ESCAPE VELOCITY FROM EARTH

The ESA Ulysses *spacecraft is seen passing over one of the Sun's poles. The craft, which is powered by an IUS-PAM upper stage, achieved a record escape velocity of 54,614 km/h (33,936 mph) from the Earth after deployment from the space shuttle* Discovery *on 7 Oct 1990. The information it is relaying back to Earth has allowed scientists to build up a new three-dimensional picture of the Sun.*

MOST COMPLEX HEAT SHIELD
The heat shield fitted to the space shuttle on its early missions, to protect it from the heat of re-entry, consisted of 32,000 silica tiles that had to be individually glued into position and tested for strength — a difficult, expensive and time-consuming job. Improvements to the shuttle's heat protection system have slightly reduced the number of tiles needed today. The shuttle's replacement, the Reusable Launch Vehicle, will not use tiles — its body will be made from advanced graphite compounds instead.

MOST SPECTACULAR LAUNCH FAILURE
Designed as a key part of the Soviet programme to land a human on the Moon, the giant *N1* rocket was abandoned after its third failure to launch on 3 July 1969, less than two weeks before the start of the USA's successful *Apollo 11* mission. The last failure of *N1* resulted in a huge explosion that killed many people at the launch site.

LEAST RELIABLE LAUNCH SYSTEM
The Russian–Ukrainian *Zenit* launcher has had 21 successful and seven failed missions since 1985 — a success rate of 72%.

LONGEST-SERVING LAUNCH VEHICLE
The *A2* rocket, now used to launch *Soyuz* ferry craft to the *Mir* space

MOST RELIABLE LAUNCH SYSTEMS

Mission STS-78 of the US space shuttle Columbia *is seen lifting off from Cape Canaveral, Florida, USA, on 20 June 1996. Between April 1981 and Jan 1998 the US space shuttle completed a total of 89 launches with only one failure — a 98% success rate. The Russian* Soyuz U *series has flown a total of 781 times with 766 successes since 1973, twice recording 100 consecutive successful launches.*

station, is a more advanced version of the one used to launch *Sputnik* in 1957. Beginning life in the mid-1950s as the *SS-6*, it was the first Soviet Inter-Continental Ballistic Missile (ICBM). Over the years it has achieved many important milestones — including launching the first animal and the first human into Space in 1961. In its sixth decade it will play an important part in the servicing of the new International Space Station.

SMALLEST MANNED SPACECRAFT

The Manned Manoeuvring Unit (MMU), used by astronauts working outside the space shuttle, is 1.24 m (4 ft) tall, 0.83 m (2 ft 8 in) wide and 1.12 m (3 ft 8 in) deep and weighs just 109 kg (240 lb). Powered by nitrogen thrusters, it was first used on shuttle mission STS-41-B when astronaut Bruce McCandless manoeuvred up to 100 m (328 ft) away from *Challenger*.

CLOSEST APPROACH TO THE SUN BY A ROCKET

On 16 April 1976 the research spacecraft *Helios B* approached within 43.5 million km (27 million miles) of the Sun, carrying both US and West German instrumentation.

MOST SUCCESSFUL AMATEUR ROCKETS

The *Halo* rocket, built by a US group called HAL5, reached an altitude of 57.92 km (36 miles) on 11 May 1998. *Halo* was carried to a height of 18.3 km (11 miles 654 yd) by a helium-filled balloon before being launched. The height it achieved is just 22.5 km (14 miles) short of NASA's official definition of the beginning of Space.

The highest altitude reached by a ground-launched amateur-built rocket is 36 km (22 miles 634 yd). The *Hyperion I* rocket, built by Korey Kline, was launched from NASA's Wallops Island facility, Virginia, USA, on 7 Jan 1997. The 48-kg (106-lb) rocket accelerated to three times the speed of sound using a mixture of solid and liquid fuel.

LOUDEST LAUNCH

The noise created by the launch of the unmanned Apollo 4 *(pictured right) on 9 Nov 1967 was so great that the resulting air-pressure wave was detected at the Lamont-Doherty Geological Observatory 1,770 km (1,100 miles) away. The reverberations from the launch also caused the roof to be torn from the press site 4.8 km (3 miles) away. Subsequent* Saturn V *launches were muffled in order to reduce noise levels.*

lethal weapons

BIGGEST SUBMARINE

The Russian Akula submarine (pictured below), which has the NATO codename 'Typhoon', is believed to have an overall length of 171.5 m (562 ft 8 in) and a displacement of 26,500 tonnes. The launch of the first 'Typhoon' is reported by NATO to have taken place at the secret covered shipyard at Severodvinsk on the White Sea on 23 Sept 1980. At present, six Akula submarines are said to be in service, each of them armed with 20 multiple warhead SS-N-20 missiles with a range of 8,300 km (5,158 miles).

MOST PEOPLE KILLED BY A BOMB
The atomic bomb dropped on Hiroshima, Japan, by the USA on 6 Aug 1945 killed more than 100,000 people instantly. A further 55,000 people died from radiation sickness within a year.

MOST POWERFUL NUCLEAR WEAPON
The most powerful ICBM (Intercontinental Ballistic Missile) is the former USSR's SS-18 (Model 5), which is thought to be armed with 10,750-kilotonne MIRVs (Multiple Independently Targetable Re-entry Vehicles). All SS-18 ICBMs had been returned to Russia by the end of April 1995, where 150 are still operational. If the START 2 (Strategic Arms Reduction Talks 2) agreement is fully implemented, the remaining SS-18s and all other ICBMs with more than one warhead will be destroyed.

MOST POWERFUL THERMONUCLEAR DEVICE
A thermonuclear device with power equivalent to around 57 megatonnes of TNT was detonated by the former USSR in the Novaya Zemlya area in Oct 1961. The shock wave circled the Earth three times, with the first circuit taking 36 hr 27 min. Estimates put the power of the device at between 62 and 90 megatonnes.

LONGEST-RANGE ATTACKS
In Jan 1991 seven B-52G bombers took off from Barksdale Air Force Base, Louisiana, USA, to deliver cruise missiles against Iraq just after the start of the Gulf War. Each flew 22,526 km (14,000 miles), refuelling four times in the 35-hour round trip.

In Sept 1996 B-52s flew non-stop from Guam in the western Pacific to launch cruise missiles around Baghdad, Iraq — a distance of 20,284 km (12,604 miles).

LONGEST-RANGE MISSILES
The US Atlas missile entered service in 1959 and had a range of 16,669 km (10,360 miles) — about 4,828 km (3,000 miles) more than was necessary to hit any point in Soviet territory from launch sites in the West.

The longest-range Russian missile is the SS-18, codenamed 'Satan', which entered service in the early 1980s and has a range of 12,070 km (7,500 miles).

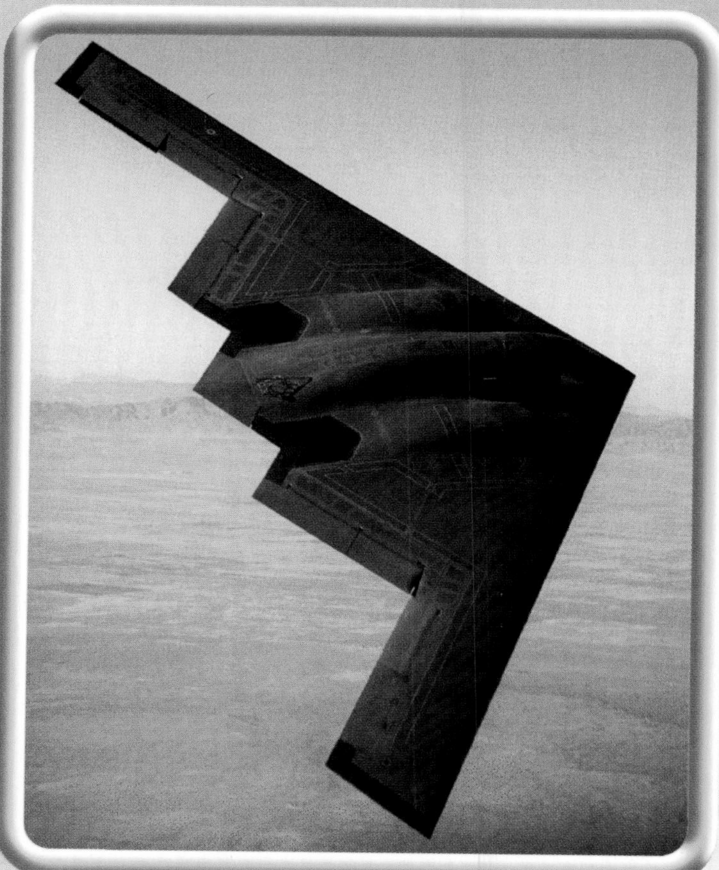

MOST EXPENSIVE MILITARY AIRCRAFT

The world's most expensive military aircraft is the US B2 Spirit (pictured above), which is priced at $1.3 billion (£780 million). A long-range multi-role bomber, it is capable of delivering both conventional and nuclear munitions, and has a number of stealth characteristics that enable it to penetrate an enemy's defences without being observed: these include its special coatings and flying-wing design. The B2 has an unfuelled range of 9,600 km (5,965 miles), and can carry a payload of 18.144 tonnes. It made its first flight on 17 July 1989.

MOST ADVANCED FIGHTER PLANE
The US F22 Raptor was developed by Lockheed Martin Aeronautical Systems, Lockheed Martin Fort Worth and Boeing in the late 1990s. It cost around $13.3 billion (£8 billion) — twice as much as its European counterpart, the Eurofighter. The F22 is capable of carrying a number of different air-to-air weapons in its internal bays: these include radar-guided AIM-120C medium-range air-to-air missiles (AMRAAMS), longer-finned AIM-120A AMRAAMS and heat-seeking short-range AIM-9M sidewinders. It will also carry an internal M61A2 20-mm cannon, an advanced version of the M61 Gatling-type gun. The F22 is 18.9 m (62 ft) long with a wingspan of 13.4 m (43 ft 11 in).

FASTEST COMBAT JET
The world's fastest combat jet is the Mikoyan MiG-25 fighter — the NATO codename for which is 'Foxbat' — developed by the former USSR. The single-seat 'Foxbat-A' has a wingspan of 13.95 m (45 ft 9 in), is 23.82 m (78 ft 2 in) long and has an estimated maximum take-off weight of

MOST ACCURATE PORTABLE ANTI-AIRCRAFT MISSILE

US Marines are seen with a Stinger missile launcher during exercises. The Stinger missile, which was introduced in the early 1980s, is 1.52 m (5 ft) long, weighs 10 kg (22 lb) and has a range of about 4.83 km (3 miles) and a speed of about 2,092 km/h (1,300 mph). The Stinger's cryogenically-cooled infra-red seeker distinguishes between an aircraft's infra-red signature and counter-measures such as flares. In the early 1990s the US Army took delivery of the Stinger POST (Passive Optical Seeker Technology), which is flown to target by a programmable microprocessor. The missile can 'think', and once it is locked on, there is little the pilot of the target aircraft can do other than outfly the missile or eject.

37.4 tonnes. The reconnaissance 'Foxbat-B' has been tracked by radar at speeds of about Mach 3.2.

FASTEST BOMBERS
The US variable-geometry or 'swing-wing' General Dynamics FB-111A has a maximum speed of Mach 2.5.

The Russian 'swing-wing' Tupolev Tu-22M, which is known to NATO as 'Backfire', has an estimated over-target speed of Mach 2 but could be as fast as Mach 2.5.

FASTEST DESTROYER
The highest speed ever attained by a destroyer is 45.25 knots (83.4 km/h or 52 mph), by the 3,251-tonne French ship *Le Terrible* in 1935. Built in Blainville, France, and powered by four Yarrow small tube boilers and two Rateau geared turbines, giving 100,000 shaft horsepower, the destroyer was decommissioned at the end of 1957.

FASTEST MILITARY HOVERCRAFT
On 25 Jan 1980 the 23.7-m-long (78-ft), 100-tonne test vehicle SES-100B, a US Navy hovercraft, achieved a record-breaking speed of 91.9 knots (170 km/h or 106 mph).

MOST ADVANCED COMBAT SHIP
In July 1998 the UK Defence Evaluation Research Agency (DERA) commissioned Vosper Thornycroft of Southampton, UK, to build the world's biggest steel ocean-going trimaran, which could shape the future of naval ship development in the next century. The diesel-electric driven vessel, *Triton*, will be 97 m (318 ft) long, displace 1,100 tonnes and have a maximum speed of 20 knots (37 km/h or 23 mph). Its advanced design offers 20% less drag than a conventional monohull and the stability to mount detection systems higher up on the ship. The *Triton*'s launch date is April 2000; this will be followed by 18 months of sea trials.

BIGGEST UNMANNED AIR VEHICLE
The biggest unmanned air vehicle in development is the Global Hawk, which was unveiled at Teledyne Ryan Aeronautical in San Diego, California, USA, on 20 Feb 1997. Its first flight was at Edwards Air Force Base, California, USA, on 28 Feb 1998. The aircraft, which has a 35.4-m (116-ft) wingspan and a 22,526-km (14,000-mile) range, will be used by the USAF for aerial reconnaissance.

MOST POWERFUL TORPEDO
The Russian Type 65, a 66-cm (26-in) torpedo, carries a warhead of nearly one tonne of conventional explosive or a 15-kilotonne nuclear warhead — giving it slightly less explosive power than the bombs that destroyed Hiroshima and Nagasaki in 1945. It can home in acoustically on the turbulence left in the wake of a ship more than 80.5 km (50 miles) away and can close at more than 43½ knots (80.5 km/h or 50 mph) — far in excess of the speed of the fastest surface ships.

MOST ADVANCED HELICOPTER
The Russian Ka-52 Alligator is the world's most advanced helicopter. A two-seat derivative of the Ka-50 Black Shark, it is intended primarily as a gunship and is equipped with a wide range of weapons as well as devices that allow it to fly missions in extreme weather conditions.

FASTEST-FIRING MACHINE GUN

Designed for use in helicopters and armoured vehicles in the late 1960s, the 7.62-mm (3/10-in) M 134 Minigun (pictured above, mounted in the nose turret of a Cobra gunship) is the world's fastest-firing machine gun. Based on the multiple-barrelled Gatling design, it has six barrels that are revolved by an electric motor and fed by a 4,000-round link belt. This allows for a rate of fire of 6,000 rounds per minute — about 10 times that of an ordinary machine gun.

danger

danger &
disaster

danger zones

HIGHEST MURDER RATE

The country with the highest murder rate in proportion to its population varies from year to year, but the rate for Colombia was consistently high throughout the 1990s, with an average of 77.5 murders per 100,000 people. This is nine times higher than the US rate. More than 27,000 murders a year currently take place in Colombia.

The city with the highest murder rate in proportion to its population is Bogota, Colombia's capital. More than 8.600 murders take place there every year (an average of nearly one an hour), and violence is the leading cause of death for males aged 11 to 59.

HIGHEST RAPE RATE

The country with the highest rape rate in the world is South Africa. Official figures released by the South African Police Service, based on estimates calculated from the 1996 census results, indicate a rape rate of 116 per 100,000 people in 1998.

MOST ROAD FATALITIES

India's roads are rated as the most dangerous in the world. The country contains only 1% of the world's road vehicles but accounts for 6% of its road accidents. Of 9.34 million deaths in India in 1998, 217,000 — or 1 in 43 — were as a result of road traffic accidents.

Portugal had a rate of 28.9 deaths per 100,000 people in 1996, giving it the worst record in Europe. Greece has the second highest number of road deaths in Europe, with an average of 22.5 deaths for every 100,000 people.

MOST AIR CRASHES

The number of people killed in air crashes on scheduled flights has decreased sharply since 1988, when there were an average 175 fatalities per million departures. By 1998 the figure had fallen to 75 fatalities per million departures.

The chances of being killed in an air accident are highest in the skies over Africa, where there were an average 190 fatalities per million departures in 1998. The second most dangerous continent is Asia, with 160 fatalities per million departures.

MOST FATAL SHOOTINGS

There are currently more than 200 million guns in the USA, where one in four adults owns a firearm and about 40,000 fatalities are caused by guns each year. In the last 10 years gun-related homicides in the country have risen by 18%.

HIGHEST INCIDENCE OF PIRACY

In the last 10 years about 1,500 acts of piracy have been reported in southeast Asia. Most pirates operating in the region are armed with sub-machine guns and use small speedboats to 'jump' targeted vessels. Financial losses from piracy in the Pacific area alone are estimated to exceed approximately $100 million (£60 million) a year.

MOST CONTAMINATED AGRICULTURAL LAND

Members of a delegation to the Chernobyl nuclear power plant view the 'sarcophagus' built over the destroyed fourth reactor after it exploded in April 1986. The former Soviet republic of Belarus suffered more damage than anywhere else in the region from the disaster — almost 99% of the land there has been contaminated to degrees above internationally accepted levels. Despite the fact that a third of the total fallout fell on land used for agriculture, food produced in the country continues to be consumed. An estimated 1.5 million people have suffered adverse physical effects as a result of the disaster.

LARGEST CITY TO BE THREATENED BY AN EARTHQUAKE

Children at a Tokyo primary school are seen taking part in an earthquake drill. Since being struck by an earthquake with a magnitude of 8.4 on the Richter scale in Dec 1854, the Tokyo region has been subjected to thousands of small tremors every year. The area is now an urban sprawl housing almost 30 million people, with skyscrapers, overhead expressways and millions of tonnes of fuel oil and poisonous chemicals stored in tanks around Tokyo Bay. Scientists predict that at some point in the future, another earthquake will occur in the Tokai region, and that it will be much larger than the quake which wrecked the western Japanese city of Kobe in 1995.

WORST PLACE FOR KIDNAPPINGS

Families of kidnapping victims and supporters from various non-governmental organizations parade through the streets of Medellin, Colombia, to call for an end to kidnappings. Of the 8,000 kidnap cases reported worldwide in 1996, 6,500 took place in Latin America and more than 4,000 occurred in Colombia, where an average of 10 people are kidnapped every day. The crime is alleged to be worth $200 million (£120 million) a year in the country. Only 3% of Colombia's kidnappers are convicted, compared to 95% in the USA.

WORST PLACE IN WHICH TO BE A JOURNALIST

The most dangerous place in the world in which to be a journalist is Algeria, where over 70 journalists were murdered between 23 May 1993 and 1998. On arriving in the country, journalists are now met by a government protection team.

A total of 190 journalists and media workers were killed worldwide between 1995 and 1998: 46 in Europe and the republics of the former Soviet Union, 44 in the Americas, 62 in Africa and 38 in Asia. Between 1990 and 1994, 370 journalists were murdered worldwide.

LARGEST CITY TO BE THREATENED BY A VOLCANIC ERUPTION

Mt Vesuvius near Naples, Italy, is regarded as one of the most dangerous volcanoes in the world. More than 700,000 people live within a 10-km (6-mile 376-yd) radius of its summit crater, and the outskirts of Naples are within 15 km (9 miles 564 yd) of the vent. If enough warning of an eruption can be given, the Italian government envisages an evacuation of at least 600,000 people. This would take a week, during which time Naples' outer suburbs could suffer the same fate as Pompeii.

MOST 'UNINTENTIONAL' DEATHS

The World Health Organization defines 'unintentional' deaths as road traffic accidents, poisonings, falls, fires, drownings and other accidental injuries (not counting homicide, violence and war). Of a total of 9.34 million deaths in India in 1998, 723,000 — or 1 in 13 — were defined as 'unintentional'. They included 32,000 poisonings, 50,000 falls, 135,000 fires and 92,000 drownings.

MOST LIKELY PLACE IN WHICH TO BE KILLED BY A SNAKE

Humans are most likely to die from a snakebite in Sri Lanka, where an average of 800 people a year are killed by snakes.

WORST PLACE FOR LANDMINES

The United Nations estimates that more than 110 million active landmines are currently buried in 70 countries, with an equal number stockpiled in readiness for use. However, the International Campaign To Ban Landmines puts the stockpile figure at 250 million.

The country with the most landmines is Egypt, with approximately 13 million, left after the Battles of El Alamein in 1942 and the Arab/Israeli conflicts between 1948 and 1973. Pictured right is Mohammed Saber, an Afghani boy who lost both his legs when he stepped on a landmine while out collecting firewood.

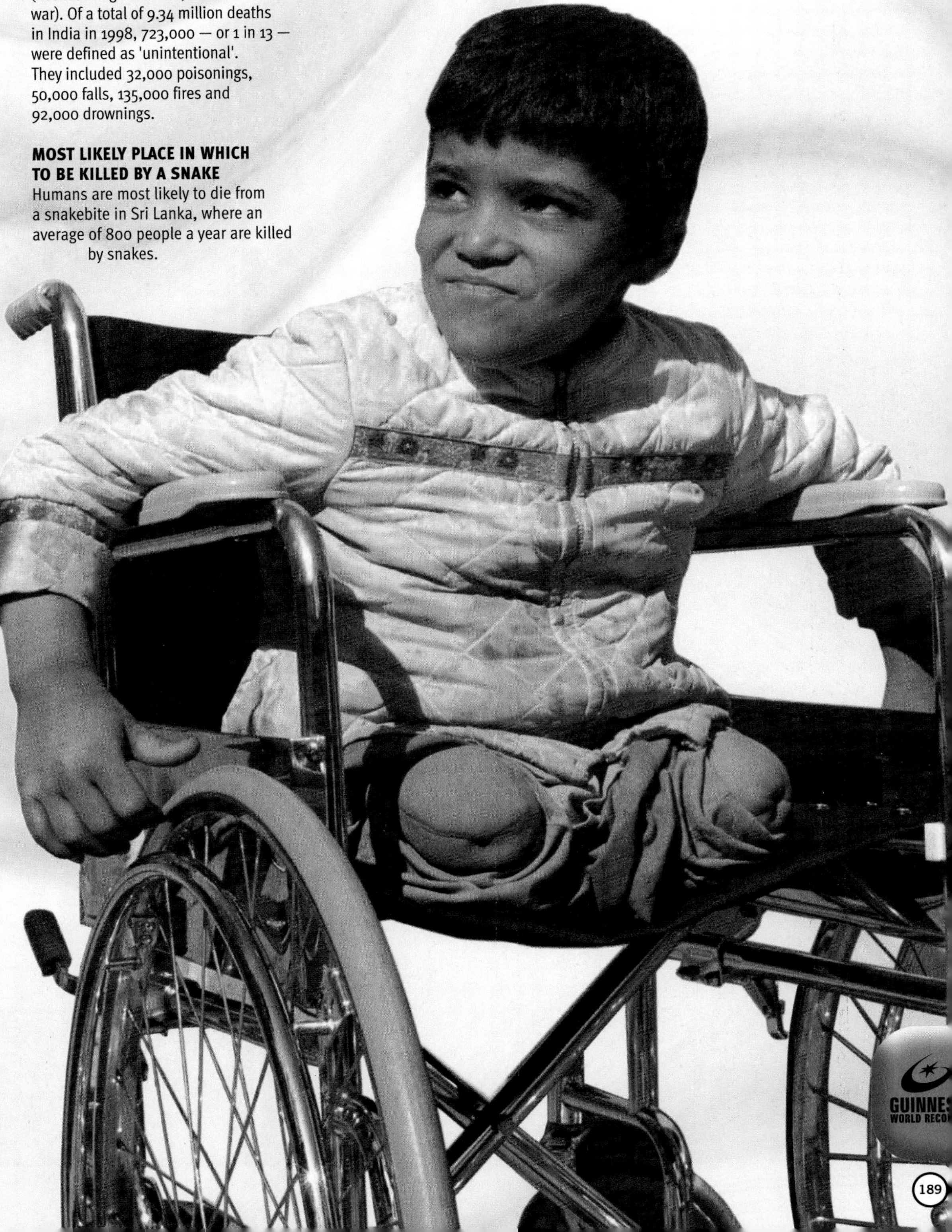

war & terrorism

BIGGEST WARTIME ASSAULT ON THE ENVIRONMENT

In Jan 1991 Iraqi president Saddam Hussein gave the order for an estimated 816,000 tonnes of crude Gulf oil to be pumped from Kuwait's Sea Island terminal and from seven large oil tankers. During the same campaign, Iraqi forces set fire to 600 oil wells, creating clouds of black smoke up to 2.13 km (1 mile 569 yd) high, enveloping warships 80 km (50 miles) offshore and depositing soot as far away as the Himalayas. The last blazing well was extinguished on 6 Nov 1991.

MOST EXPENSIVE WAR

The material cost of the Second World War (1939–45) has been estimated at $1.5 trillion (£940 billion) — more than the cost of all other wars put together.

MOST TELEVISED WARS

In terms of transmission hours, the Vietnam War is likely to remain the most televised war in history for many decades to come. In 1965 the US network NBC screened *Actions of a Vietnamese Marine Battalion*, showing shocking action sequences, and as its ratings rocketed CBS, ABC and foreign broadcasters rushed to put camera teams into Vietnam as well. It is estimated that the three major US networks and their subsidiaries devoted about 10,000 hours of prime viewing time to coverage of the war between 1965 and 1975.

The collapse of the former Yugoslavia and associated conflicts between 1991 and 1996 eclipsed Vietnam in density of TV coverage because by then it was much easier for freelance journalists to travel with their own equipment and satellite dishes. During the five years of conflict journalists shot and recorded millions of hours of footage, of which only a tiny percentage was broadcast.

BLOODIEST WARS

The costliest war in terms of human life was the Second World War, in which the total number of military and civilian fatalities was an estimated 56.4 million. In Poland 6.028 million people were killed — 17.2% of the pre-war population.

In Paraguay's war against Brazil, Argentina and Uruguay from 1864 to 1870, Paraguay's population was reduced from 525,000 to 221,000. Fewer than 28,000 survivors were adult males.

HIGHEST BATTLEFIELD

Since 1984 the Indian and Pakistani armies have faced each other on the Siachen Glacier, Kashmir, at a height of up to 6,705.6 m (22,000 ft), in temperatures as low as −60°C (−76°F). Reports suggest that Pakistan spends as much as $588,000 (£354,773) a month and India about $1 million (£603,355) a month maintaining troops on the glacier.

MOST DEATHS CAUSED BY CHEMICAL WEAPONS IN ONE WAR

Exact figures for those wounded and killed by chemical weapons between Jan 1915 and Nov 1918, during the First World War, are unreliable, but at least 100,000 people died and 900,000 were injured. The Russian army, which was equipped with inadequate respirators, sustained some 56,000 fatalities and 475,000 casualties.

BIGGEST SINGLE CHEMICAL WARFARE ATTACK

The greatest number of people killed in a single chemical warfare attack is an estimated 4,000, at Halabja, Iraq, in March 1988. President Saddam Hussein used chemical weapons against his country's Kurdish minority for the support it had given to Iran in the Iran–Iraq war.

BLOODIEST UN PEACEKEEPING OPERATION

The ongoing conflict in the Balkans has led to more fatalities than any other UN peacekeeping mission. The total number of fatalities for all missions in the region is 268, including 210 fatalities in UNPROFOR (United Nations Protection Force) alone.

LONGEST-RUNNING UN PEACEKEEPING OPERATION

The longest-running UN peacekeeping mission is UNTSO (United Nations Truce Supervision Organization), which has been in place since June 1948. UNTSO's headquarters are in Jerusalem, but it maintains military observation posts throughout the Middle East.

MOST TIME ELAPSED BETWEEN WAR CRIMES AND TRIAL

In 1997 Maurice Papon was indicted for 'crimes against humanity' committed 56 years earlier during the Second World War. In 1942 Papon was responsible for the deportation of Jews from unoccupied Vichy France to the German Occupied Zone in the north of the country, from where they were taken to Auschwitz concentration camp. He was sentenced to 10 years' imprisonment in 1998.

BIGGEST REWARD FOR COUNTER-TERRORISM

The US State Department offers a maximum reward of $5 million (£3 million) for information that leads to the prevention of terrorist acts or the capture of international terrorists. The most recent maximum reward was offered at the time of the bombing of the US embassies in Kenya and Tanzania in Aug 1998. A total of 243 people were killed in the attack in Nairobi, Kenya (pictured) — the highest death toll from terrorist action against an embassy. The US State Department appealed for information on Osama bin Laden, believed to have been behind the bombing. Since the counter-terrorism reward was established, a total of $7 million (£4.2 million) has been awarded for information.

MOST EXPENSIVE PEACEKEEPING OPERATION

The most expensive United Nations peacekeeping mission to date was UNPROFOR (United Nations Protection Force), which cost $4.6 billion (£2.9 billion) from 12 Jan 1992 to 31 March 1996 and included all the missions deployed in the former Yugoslavia during this period.

MOST PEOPLE KILLED IN A TERRORIST ATTACK

The highest ever death toll from any single terrorist attack was 329 people, when a bomb exploded aboard the Air India Boeing 747 'Kanishka' above the Atlantic Ocean in June 1985.

LONGEST EMBASSY SIEGE

In response to the exiled Shah of Iran's admission to the USA for medical treatment in Sept 1979, a crowd of about 500 people seized the US embassy in Tehran, Iran. Of the approximately 90 people inside the embassy, 52 remained in captivity until the end of the crisis, 444 days later on 20 Jan 1981. This was the day of President Reagan's inauguration, when the US released almost $8 billion (£3.95 billion) in Iranian assets.

MOST HOSTAGES HELD

The greatest number of hostages to have been held by a terrorist organization was over 500 people captured by Tupac Amaru terrorists at the Japanese embassy in Lima, Peru, on 17 Dec 1996. The group gradually released the majority of the hostages, and the final 72 were rescued when Peruvian commandos stormed the embassy on 22 April 1997, killing all 14 rebels, including the group's leader Nestor Cerpa.

During the Palestinian Liberation Front's hijacking of the Italian cruise liner *Achille Lauro* in Oct 1985, 413 people were held hostage for two days until the terrorists surrendered to the Egyptian authorities. The US passengers are considered to have been at the greatest risk, because they were separated from the other passengers as key targets by the hijackers. One US passenger, 69-year-old Leon Klinghoffer, was shot as he sat in his wheelchair, then thrown overboard.

MOST FATALITIES FROM AN ATTACK IN AN UNDERGROUND TRAIN

Members of the Aum Shinrikyo cult released poisonous sarin gas on rail lines on the Tokyo underground, Japan, during the morning rush hour on 20 March 1995. Twelve commuters died as a result of the attack and over 5,000 required treatment due to inhalation of noxious fumes.

LONGEST TIME HELD HOSTAGE

Terry Anderson (USA) was held in Beirut, Lebanon, for 2,454 days (6 years 264 days) by Hezbollah terrorists. After his release on 4 Dec 1991 he saw his six-year-old daughter for the first time — she was born shortly after he was kidnapped.

GUINNESS WORLD RECORDS

disasters: air, land & sea

WORST AIR ACCIDENTS
The world's worst ever air disaster took place on 27 March 1977, when two Boeing 747s, operated by Pan Am and KLM, collided on the runway at Los Rodeos Airport, Tenerife, Canary Islands, killing 583 people. Amazingly, 63 people on the Pan Am flight survived the disaster.

The worst air accident involving a single aircraft occurred on 12 Aug 1985, when a JAL Boeing 747, flight 123, crashed between Tokyo and Osaka, Japan, killing 520 passengers and crew on board.

WORST MID-AIR COLLISION
On 12 Nov 1996 a total of 351 passengers and crew were killed in a collision between a Saudi Boeing 747 scheduled flight and a Kazakh Illushin 76 charter flight 80 km (50 miles) south-west of New Delhi, India. Only the tail section of the Saudi aircraft remained intact after the planes plunged to the ground.

WORST BALLOONING DISASTER
The greatest loss of life to have resulted from a hot-air balloon accident occurred on 13 Aug 1989, when two passenger balloons that were launched a few minutes apart for a sightseeing flight over Alice Springs, Northern Territory, Australia, collided at a height of 610 m (2,000 ft). The basket of one of the balloons tore a hole in the fabric of the other, which then collapsed, sending the pilot and 12 passengers to their deaths.

WORST DISASTER IN SPACE
The worst ever disaster during actual spaceflight took place on 29 June 1971, when astronauts Georgi Dobrovolsky, Viktor Patsayev and Vladislav Volkov (all USSR), who were not wearing spacesuits, died when their *Soyuz 11* spacecraft depressurized during re-entry.

The worst space disaster on the ground took place when a rocket exploded during fuelling at the Baikonur Cosmodrome, USSR (now Kazakhstan), on 24 Oct 1960, killing 91 people.

WORST MARITIME COLLISION
On 15 Dec 1977 the tanker *Venoil* (330,954 deadweight tonnes) struck her sister ship *Venpet* (330,869 dwt) off the coast of southern Africa, causing the worst ever collision at sea.

WORST SHIPWRECK
The 321,186-deadweight-tonne VLCC (very large crude carrier) *Energy Determination* blew up and broke in two in the Strait of Hormuz, Persian Gulf, on 12 Dec 1979, causing the world's biggest ever shipwreck.

WORST FERRY DISASTER
In the early hours of 21 Dec 1987 the ferry *Dona Paz* collided with the tanker *Victor* while it was sailing from Tacloban to Manila, Philippines. After being engulfed by flames, both vessels sank within minutes. The *Dona Paz* officially had 1,550 passengers but overcrowding is common in the region and it may actually have held 4,000.

WORST UNDERGROUND TRAIN DISASTER
On 28 Oct 1995 approximately 300 people were killed in a fire that broke out in an underground train at Baku, Azerbaijan. Apart from those who were burned to death, many people died from smoke inhalation, being crushed or electrocution on the live rails. The Azerbaijan Interior Ministry blamed the disaster on a technical fault. The picture above shows the funeral of one of the victims.

WORST SKI-LIFT DISASTER

The world's worst ever ski-lift accident occurred at the resort of Cavalese, Italy, on 9 March 1976, when a ruptured cable caused the death of 42 people. Italy was also the scene of the recent disaster when an EA-6B Prowler Jet piloted by Capt. Richard Ashby of the US Marine Corps severed the cables of a car on Mt Cermis (pictured right) on 3 Feb 1998. Twenty passengers plunged to their deaths. Ashby was acquitted of manslaughter but found guilty of obstructing justice by destroying a video of the incident. The US government paid compensation of $51,172 (£30,875) to the family of each victim, plus $20 million (£12 million) to the village to replace the lift.

WORST AIR SHOW DISASTER

At Ramstein Air Base, Germany, on 28 Aug 1988, three Italian jets collided in mid-air during an air show. One of the jets exploded and ploughed into the crowd below, killing 70 people and injuring more than 400.

WORST SUBMARINE DISASTER DURING PEACETIME

On 10 April 1963 the 3,759-tonne US nuclear submarine *Thresher* failed to surface while carrying out deep-diving tests in the Atlantic, off Cape Cod, Massachusetts, USA. It had 112 officers and 17 civilian technicians on board. The following year, the US Navy announced that large sections of the vessel's hull had been discovered at a depth of 2,560 m (6,400 ft) by the bathyscape *Trieste II*, but the cause of the tragedy has never been properly explained.

WORST TRAIN DISASTER

On 6 June 1981 more than 800 passengers died when their train plunged off a bridge into the River Bagmati in Bihar, India.

WORST TRAIN TUNNEL DISASTER

On 2 March 1944, 521 passengers and crew suffocated when their train stalled in a tunnel near Salerno, Italy.

WORST LIFT ACCIDENT

A lift operating at the Vaal Reefs gold mine, South Africa, fell 490 m (1,600 ft) on 11 May 1995, killing 105 workers.

WORST MASS PANIC

In 1991, 1,426 Muslim pilgrims were trampled to death in a stampede along a tunnel between Mecca and Medina, Saudi Arabia.

WORST FOOTBALL RIOTS

In May 1964, 318 fans were killed and 500 injured in a riot at an Olympic qualifying match between Argentina and Peru in Lima, Peru. The riot was sparked when a last-minute Peruvian goal was disallowed by the referee. Had the goal stood, it would have sent Peru to the Olympics that year.

On 21 Oct 1982 a large number of supporters of Spartak Moscow were crushed to death in an icy corridor at the end of a UEFA Cup game against Haarlem (Netherlands) at the Luzhniki stadium, Moscow, USSR. Following the relaxation of reporting restrictions under *glasnost*, estimates of up to 340 fatalities were given to the world's media.

WORST BULLFIGHT DISASTER

On 20 Jan 1980 in Sincelejo, Colombia, a stand at a bullring collapsed, leaving 222 people dead.

WORST SPACE MISSION DISASTER

The greatest number of people to have perished in a manned spaceflight is seven (five men and two women) — the crew of Challenger 51L, *which exploded 73 seconds after lift-off from the Kennedy Space Center, Florida, USA, on 28 Jan 1986.*

natural disasters

COSTLIEST YEAR FOR NATURAL DISASTERS
The year ending 31 Dec 1995 was the costliest ever in terms of natural disasters, with a total bill amounting to $180 billion (£114.05 billion), much of which was accounted for by the Kobe earthquake in Japan. The figures are collated every year by Munich Re, the world's largest re-insurers.

BIGGEST POWER FAILURE CAUSED BY A NATURAL DISASTER
During Hurricane George in Sept 1998 winds of 177 km/h (110 mph) hit the Dominican Republic, leaving 100,000 people homeless and almost the entire population (8 million) without power.

MOST PEOPLE KILLED BY EARTHQUAKES
In July 1201 approximately 1.1 million people are believed to have been killed by an earthquake in the eastern Mediterranean. Most of the casualties were in Egypt and Syria.

The earthquake that struck the Shaanxi, Shanxi and Henan provinces of China on 2 Feb 1556 is believed to have been responsible for the death of 830,000 people.

The highest death toll in modern times was caused by the quake in Tangshan, eastern China, on 28 July 1976. According to the first official figure, 655,237 people were killed. This was subsequently adjusted to 750,000 and then to 242,000.

MOST PEOPLE MADE HOMELESS BY AN EARTHQUAKE
More than 1 million Guatemalans in a 1,310-km² (3,400-mile²) area were made homeless on 4 Feb 1976, when an earthquake ripped along the Montagua Fault between the Caribbean and North American plates. The material damage was estimated at $1.4 billion (£780 million) and the quake is widely cited as the worst natural disaster in Central American history. It was almost matched by the 1972 Nicaraguan earthquake, which devastated Managua and caused $1.3 billion (£720 million) worth of material damage.

An earthquake on Japan's Kanto plain on 1 Sept 1923 destroyed 575,000 homes in Tokyo and Yokohama. The official figure for the number of people killed and missing in the quake and its resultant fires is 142,807.

MOST PEOPLE TRAPPED BY AVALANCHES
A total of 240 people died and more than 45,000 were trapped when a series of avalanches thundered through the Swiss, Austrian and Italian Alps on 20 Jan 1951. The avalanches were caused by a combination of hurricane force winds and wet snow overlaying powder snow.

MOST DEVASTATING ICE STORM
In Jan 1998 an ice storm wreaked havoc across eastern Canada and parts of the north-eastern USA, shutting down airports and train stations, blocking roads and cutting off power to 3 million people. After two weeks, 1 million people were still without power, and some areas remained without power for three weeks. The total cost of the damage was estimated at $650 million (£406 million).

MOST PEOPLE KILLED BY LANDSLIDES
On 31 May 1970 about 18,000 people were killed by a landslide on the slopes of Huascaran in the Yungay region of Peru, making it the most devastating single landslide in history. Ten villages and most of the town of Yungay were buried by the landslide, which was caused by an earthquake. It was one of the worst disasters of the 20th century in terms of the number of fatalities.

On 16 Dec 1920 a series of landslides triggered by a single earthquake that hit Gansu province, China, killed about 180,000 people.

MOST PEOPLE KILLED BY AN AVALANCHE
During the First World War between 40,000 and 80,000 men are believed to have been killed by avalanches triggered by the sound of gunfire in part of the south Tyrolean Alps, Austria (now in Italy). The Tyrol was also the scene of a disaster (right) on 23 Feb 1999, when 31 people in Galtuer in the Paznaun Valley, Austria, were killed in one of a series of avalanches that swept through villages and ski resorts in the area. Seven more people died in avalanches in the Tyrol that month, bringing the death toll to 38.

MOST MADE HOMELESS BY A HURRICANE

Hurricane Mitch, which struck Central America in late 1998, caused 9,745 deaths and destroyed 93,690 dwellings. Approximately 2.5 million people were left dependent on international aid efforts.

MOST PEOPLE KILLED BY A VOLCANIC ERUPTION
When the Tambora volcano in Sumbawa, Indonesia (then the Dutch East Indies), erupted in April 1815, 92,000 people were killed, either directly or as a result of the subsequent famine.

MOST PEOPLE KILLED BY A FLOOD
In Oct 1887 the Huang He (Yellow River) in Huayan Kou, China, flooded its banks, killing about 900,000 people. Despite causing devastating seasonal floods, the Huang He suffers from water shortages and is the biggest river to dry up. The river's dry periods are getting longer, jeopardizing 7 million ha (17.3 million acres) of crops and the livelihoods of 52 million people.

MOST DEVASTATING MONSOONS
Monsoons in Thailand in 1983 killed around 10,000 people and caused more than $396 million (£264 million) worth of damage. Up to 100,000 people are estimated to have contracted diseases and around 15,000 people had to be evacuated.

MOST DEVASTATING CYCLONE
Between 300,000 and 500,000 people are estimated to have died in the worst known cyclone, which hit East Pakistan (now Bangladesh) on 12 Nov 1970. Winds of up to 240 km/h (150 mph) and a 15-m-high (50-ft) tidal wave lashed the coast, the Ganges Delta and the offshore islands of Bhola, Hatia, Kukri Mukri, Manpura and Rangabali.

MOST PEOPLE KILLED BY A TORNADO
On 26 April 1989 approximately 1,300 people lost their lives and as many as 50,000 people were made homeless when a tornado hit the town of Shaturia in Bangladesh.

MOST PEOPLE KILLED BY A TYPHOON
Approximately 10,000 people died when a violent typhoon with winds of up to 161 km/h (100 mph) struck Hong Kong on 18 Sept 1906.

MOST PEOPLE KILLED BY A DROUGHT
A drought in China between 1876 and 1879 led to the death of between 9 million and 13 million people.

MOST PEOPLE KILLED BY A GEYSER
In Aug 1903 four people were killed when Waimangu geyser in New Zealand erupted. The victims had been standing 27 m (90 ft) away from it but their bodies were found up to 800 m (875 yd) away. One was jammed between rocks and another was suspended from a tree.

MOST PEOPLE KILLED BY A LIGHTNING STRIKE
On 8 Dec 1963 a Boeing 707 jet airliner was struck by lightning near Elkton, Maryland, USA, causing it to crash. A total of 81 passengers were killed.

COSTLIEST NATURAL DISASTER

The Kobe earthquake of Jan 1995 resulted in overall losses of $100 billion (£63.04 billion), making it the costliest natural disaster to befall any one country. Japan, with its large fiscal resources and modern construction techniques, is relatively well prepared for the inevitable tremors that occur there due to its geographic location on the Pacific 'Rim of Fire'.

environmental disasters

MOST ENDANGERED ECOSYSTEM
Western Asia's coastal zone is the most fragile ecosystem in the world, due to the decline of its coral reefs and forests. The region lost 11% of its natural forest in the 1980s, and many countries suffer from water scarcity. In addition, about 191 million litres (42 million gal) of oil are spilled into the Persian Gulf annually.

MOST CONTAMINATED SPOT
Chelabinsk, Russia, is the most radioactive point on the planet and has probably been so since 1940, when the Mayak weapons complex was built. Since then there have been three nuclear disasters in the area, affecting up to 500,000 people with levels of radiation similar to those in Chernobyl. Scientists designated it the most contaminated spot on Earth in 1992.

BIGGEST TOXIC DUMP
In Feb 1990, 3,000 tonnes of waste were found dumped near the seaport of Sihanoukville, Cambodia. The waste, which came from Taiwanese company Formosa Plastics Corp, contains unsafe levels of mercury. Several villagers who rummaged through the waste have complained of nausea, exhaustion and stomach pains.

BIGGEST TOXIC CLOUD
In Sept 1990 a fire at a factory handling beryllium in Ust Kamenogorsk, USSR (now Kazakhstan), released a toxic cloud that extended at least as far as the Chinese border, more than 300 km (190 miles) away.

WORST NUCLEAR ACCIDENTS
The worst ever nuclear reactor disaster took place at Chernobyl No. 4 in the USSR (now Ukraine), in 1986. Contamination was experienced over 28,200 km² (10,900 miles²) and about 1.7 million people were exposed to varying amounts of radiation. A total of 850,000 people are still living in contaminated areas.

The worst nuclear waste accident occurred at Kyshtym, USSR (now Russia), in 1957, when an overheated waste container exploded, releasing radioactive compounds that dispersed over 23,000 km² (8,900 miles²). Within three years more than 30 small communities within a 1,200-km² (460-mile²) radius were eliminated from maps of the USSR and about 17,000 people were evacuated, but 8,015 people died over 32 years of observation as a direct result of the accident.

GREATEST OZONE DEPLETION
The largest 'hole' in the ozone layer is above the Antarctic region. Each austral spring, a 23-km-high (14-mile) area of ozone $1^1/_4$ times the size of the USA disappears. Above this height the ozone is unaffected, so the gap is perhaps better described as a 'thinning' rather than a 'hole'.

BIGGEST EMISSIONS OF 'GREENHOUSE GASES'
The USA is home to 4% of the world's population but produces 25% of the world's annual emissions of carbon dioxide and other greenhouse gases.

MOST POLLUTED MAJOR CITY
Levels of sulphur dioxide, carbon monoxide and suspended atmospheric particulate matter in Mexico City, the capital of Mexico, are more than double those deemed acceptable by the World Health Organization (WHO).

The biggest emitter of carbon dioxide in relation to its population is Luxembourg, which produces 18% more per head than the USA.

MOST ACIDIC ACID RAIN
A pH reading of 2.83 was recorded over the Great Lakes in the USA and Canada in 1982.

MOST DESTRUCTIVE FIRES
The worst year in recorded history for the destruction of the natural environment was 1997, mainly because of fires that were deliberately lit to clear forest areas but also because of fires resulting from the droughts caused by the El Niño effect in the Pacific. The largest and most numerous fires occurred in Brazil, where they raged on a 1,600-km (1,000-mile) front. People from the Xingu Reservation, Mato Grosso, Brazil, are pictured surveying the damage caused by fires that burned over 1,500 km² (579 miles²) of the state. About 30,000 km² (11,600 miles²) of Brazilian rainforest is also deliberately felled and burned by subsistence farmers and big business every year.

MOST CHEMICALLY POLLUTED TOWN

The Russian town of Dzerzhinsk, which has a population of 287,000, is home to dozens of factories producing chlorine and pesticides. The Kaprolaktam plant in particular emits 600 tonnes of vinyl chlorine, a carcinogenic gas, every year. Greenpeace has named Dzerzhinsk the site of the worst chemical pollution in Russia and its lake — the source of the fish pictured here — the most poisonous in the world. Average life expectancy in the town is only 42 years for men and 47 for women.

GREATEST SULPHUR DIOXIDE POLLUTION
The Maritsa power complex in Bulgaria releases a record 350,000 tonnes of the acidic gas sulphur dioxide into the River Maritsa every year. Sulphur dioxide is a major cause of acid rain.

MOST DEVASTATING AIR POLLUTION
More than 6,300 people have died from the effects of a poisonous cloud of methyl isocyanate that escaped from Union Carbide's pesticide plant near Bhopal, India, on 3 Dec 1984. The company made a settlement of $380.1 million (£293 million) to compensate victims and their relatives.

BIGGEST THREAT TO ANCIENT FORESTS
About 80% of the world's large areas of ancient forest have been destroyed, mainly by big logging companies. The ancient forests contain 90% of the world's land-based species, and millions of flora and fauna species have been rendered extinct by their loss. In total, 76 countries have lost all of their ancient forest areas.

WORST LAND POLLUTION
From Feb to Oct 1994 thousands of tonnes of crude oil flowed across the Arctic tundra of the Komi Republic, Russia. An estimated 100,000 tonnes of oil were lost in a slick up to 18 km (11 miles 325 yd) long.

MOST OIL SPILT IN A YEAR
The largest quantity of oil spilt into the sea in one year is 608,000 tonnes, in 1979. The *Atlantic Empress* produced the biggest offshore oil spill that year when it collided with the *Aegean Captain* off the coast of Tobago, in the Caribbean. It was responsible for 287,000 tonnes of the spillage.

WORST COASTAL OIL DAMAGE
The *Exxon Valdez* oil tanker ran aground in Prince William Sound, Alaska, USA, in March 1989, spilling more than 30,000 tonnes of oil and polluting a 2,400-km-long (1,500-mile) stretch of coast. The ship's owner, Exxon, was fined $5 billion (£3.2 billion) and was ordered to pay a clean-up bill of $3 billion (£1.9 billion).

WORST RIVER POLLUTION
In Nov 1986 firefighters attending a blaze at the Sandoz chemical works in Basel, Switzerland, flushed 30 tonnes of agricultural chemicals into the Rhine, killing around 500,000 fish.

WORST MARINE POLLUTION
Between 1953 and 1967 a plastics factory in Minimata Bay, Kyushu, Japan, deposited mercury waste into the sea. Up to 20,000 people were affected and 4,500 were seriously harmed. Between 43 and 800 people died.

disease, plagues & epidemics

DEADLIEST DISEASES
The deadliest disease is rabies encephalitis. The only known survivor of rabies was Matthew Winkler (USA), who was bitten by a rabid animal in 1970.

The most widespread fatal disease of our era is Acquired Immune Deficiency Syndrome (AIDS), believed to result from the Human Immunodeficiency Virus (HIV). The virus has now caused more cases in heterosexuals than homosexuals. Recent research shows that some African victims apparently remain healthy after seemingly repeated exposure to the virus, offering hope that the epidemic may be conquered.

Yellow fever is a mosquito-borne infection prevalent in the Caribbean and Brazil and on the west coast of Africa. Some reports suggest it kills as many as 90% of those infected.

OLDEST DISEASES
Cases of leprosy were described in ancient Egypt as early as 1350 BC.

Tuberculosis schistosomiasi, an infectious disease of the liver and kidneys, has been discovered in Egyptian mummies from the 20th dynasty (1250 to 1000 BC).

NEWEST GERM
The most recently discovered disease that infects humans is the prion, a malformed nerve protein that spreads through the brain cells. It produces a human spongiform encephalopathy known as new variant Creutzfeldt Jacob Disease (*nv*CJD). In 1999 there were 40 cases, all of which were fatal.

MOST URGENT HEALTH PROBLEM
The World Health Organization (WHO) estimates that by 2020 tobacco-related illness will be the leading killer, responsible for more deaths than AIDS, tuberculosis, road accidents, murder and suicide put together. Populations in developing countries face the greatest risk as 85% of all smokers will come from the world's poorer countries by the mid-2020s. The WHO estimates that tobacco-related illness will be killing 7 million people per year in these countries by 2030.

BIGGEST KILLER OF WOMEN
Tuberculosis (TB) has now become the single biggest killer of women globally. It has been estimated that one third of all women in Asia are infected with it. Some recently discovered strains are resistant to all conventional antibiotics.

MOST SUCCESSFUL IMMUNIZATION CAMPAIGN
The WHO declared the world free of smallpox on 1 Jan 1980. Formerly one of the world's deadliest plagues (it caused an estimated 2 million deaths per year in the mid-1960s), smallpox was eradicated by one type of vaccine that was effective against all forms of the disease. The last known death from smallpox was in Aug 1978, when a medical photographer at Birmingham University, UK, was infected with a sample kept for research purposes.

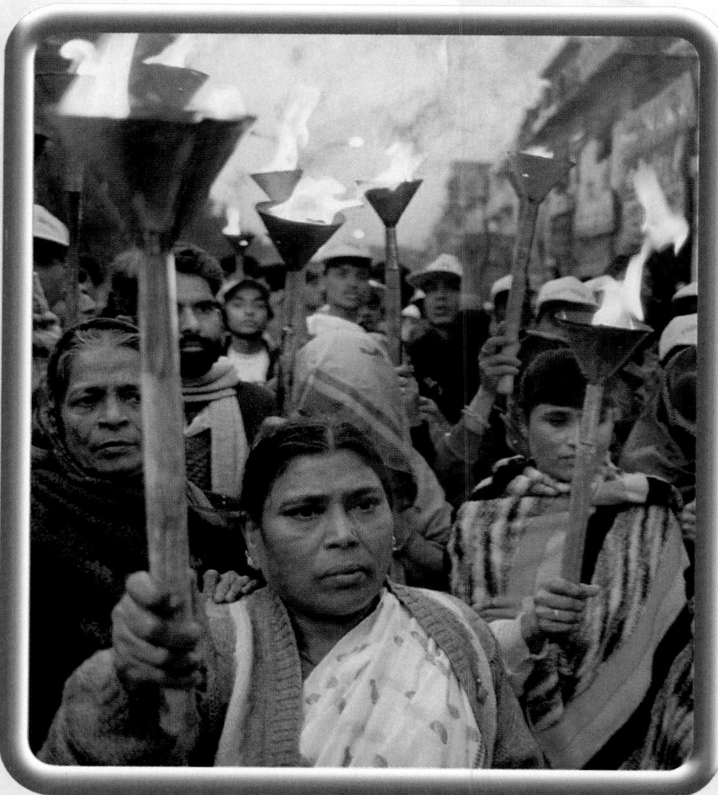

FASTEST-GROWING DISEASE
According to the UN AIDS report of Dec 1998, 5.8 million people were infected with HIV in that year. The number of people living with the virus had risen by 10% since 1997 to 33.4 million worldwide. India has the largest infected population – an estimated 4 million people. In the picture above, protesters march through the Indian capital, New Delhi, demanding jobs and medical facilities for HIV and AIDS sufferers.

DEADLIEST MALARIAL INFECTION

The deadliest strain of malaria is *Plasmodium falciparum*, which causes malignant tertian malaria. It can affect the brain, causing fits, coma or even sudden death. The women shown here, in Kisii, Kenya, were among thousands hospitalized in a malaria outbreak after four months of unseasonal rain — possibly due to the El Niño weather phenomenon — caused extensive flooding in the north-east and west of the country. Over 14,000 Kenyans were diagnosed as having contracted the infection and, according to United Nations and Oxfam reports, 1,500 people died of the disease between Dec 1997 and Feb 1998. The problem was exacerbated by the fact that Kenya has more drug-resistant mosquitoes than any other country on the African continent.

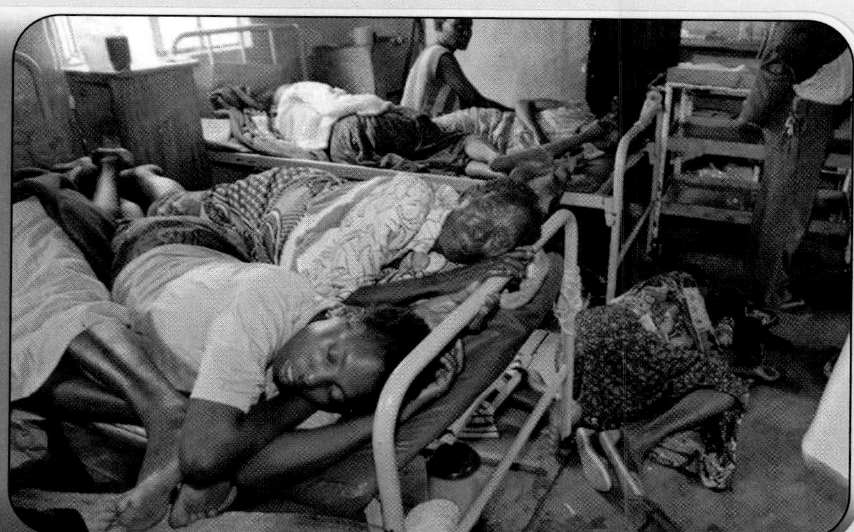

MOST RESURGENT DISEASE
The deterioration in health services following the collapse of the Soviet Union in 1991 has been a major factor in the spread of diphtheria in the area. The International Red Cross estimates that there were between 150,000 and 200,000 cases in the countries of the former USSR in 1997. This compares with 2,000 cases in the Soviet Union in 1991. Cases of tuberculosis and cholera are also increasing rapidly there.

DEADLIEST FLU OUTBREAK
A record 21.64 million people died of influenza in 1918 and 1919.

DEADLIEST AVIAN FLU OUTBREAK
Avian flu, a strain of influenza previously only known to affect birds, was found to have infected 16 people in Hong Kong, China, in 1997. Four people died from the virus, which is the first to have been passed directly from birds to humans.

DEADLIEST *E. COLI* OUTBREAK
Twenty people died and 500 became ill after consuming contaminated meat from a butcher's shop in Wishaw, UK, in 1998. It was infected with *Escherichia coli* O157-H7, a dangerous strain of a normally harmless bacterium, which is believed to be transmitted by food.

More than 9,500 cases of *E. coli* food poisoning were reported in Japan during an outbreak in summer 1996, and 11 people died as a result of being infected by O157-H7.

DEADLIEST EBOLA OUTBREAK
The highest known toll in an Ebola fever outbreak is 232 fatalities out of 296 possible cases, in the Democratic Republic of Congo (formerly Zaïre) in 1995. The disease causes massive bleeding and throws the body into shock.

GREATEST INCIDENCE OF LEPROSY
The country with the most cases of leprosy is Brazil, with 160,000 cases per annum; that is 10.2 people per 100,000 of the population. Leprosy causes damage to the skin and nerves.

MOST PEOPLE KILLED BY INFECTION
The West African island-republic of Sao Tome and Principe has a record 241 deaths per annum through infectious diseases for every 100,000 people.

LEADING CAUSE OF DEATH
Diseases of the heart and blood account for more than 50% of all deaths in industrialized nations. The most prevalent direct causes of death are heart attacks and strokes.

DEADLIEST PANDEMIC

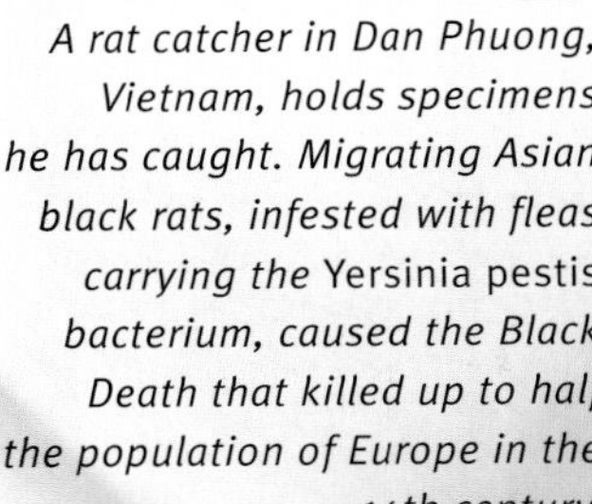

A rat catcher in Dan Phuong, Vietnam, holds specimens he has caught. Migrating Asian black rats, infested with fleas carrying the Yersinia pestis *bacterium, caused the Black Death that killed up to half the population of Europe in the 14th century.*

animal attack

MOST DANGEROUS ANIMAL
Malarial parasites of the genus *Plasmodium* carried by mosquitoes of the genus *Anopheles* have probably been responsible for half of all human deaths since the Stone Age, excluding those caused by wars and accidents. According to 1997 World Health Organisation estimates, malaria is still causing 1.5 million deaths every year.

MOST POISONOUS ANIMAL
Poison arrow frogs (*Dendrobates* and *Phyllobates*) from South and Central America secrete some of the deadliest biological toxins in the world. The skin secretion of the golden poison arrow frog (*Phyllobates terribilis*) is the most poisonous of all. Scientists have to wear thick gloves when handling specimens.

MOST VENOMOUS SNAKE
The most venomous snake in the world is Belcher's sea snake (*Hydrophis belcheri*) from the region around Ashmore Reef off northwestern Australia. Its myotoxic venom is many times more potent than the venom of any land snake.

The most venomous land snake is the 1.7-m-long (5-ft 7-in) small-scaled snake (*Oxyuranus microlepidotus*) of western Australia, which is closely related to the taipan. One specimen can yield enough venom to kill 250,000 mice.

MOST VENOMOUS SPIDER
The Brazilian huntsman (*Phoneutria fera*) has the most active neurotoxic venom of any spider. Large and aggressive, huntsmen hide in clothing or shoes and bite furiously several times if disturbed. Hundreds of accidents involving the Brazilian huntsman are reported annually, but an antivenin is now available. Most of the deaths that do occur are of children under the age of seven.

BIGGEST PREDATORY FISH
*The largest predatory fish is the rare Great White shark (*Carcharodon carcharias*). Adult specimens average 4.5 m (14 ft 9 in) in length and generally weigh around 650 kg (102 stone 5 lb). There is evidence to suggest that some Great Whites grow to more than 6 m (20 ft) in length.*

MOST DANGEROUS CROCODILIAN

The saltwater crocodile (*Crocodylus porosus*) kills an estimated 2,000 people every year, although most of these deaths go unrecorded. The largest reputed death toll in a crocodile attack occurred towards the end of World War II, on the night of 19–20 Feb 1945. Allied troops invaded Ramree Island off the coast of Burma (now Myanmar), trapping between 800 and 1,000 Japanese infantrymen in a coastal mangrove swamp. By the following morning only 20 of the Japanese soldiers were still alive: most of the rest are believed to have been eaten alive by crocodiles.

MOST POISONOUS FISH
The death puffer fish or maki-maki (*Arothron hispidus*) of the Red Sea and Indo-Pacific region contains a deadly toxin called tetrodotoxin, one of the most powerful non-proteinous poisons. Less than 0.1 g (0.004 oz) of this poison — which is contained in the fish's ovaries, eggs, blood, liver, intestines and skin — is enough to kill an adult human in as little as 20 minutes.

The stonefish (*Synanceia horrida*), found in the tropical waters of the Indo-Pacific, has the largest venom glands of any known fish. Contact with the spines of its fins, which contain neurotoxic poison, can be fatal for humans.

MOST FEROCIOUS FISH
Razor-toothed piranhas of the genera *Serrasalmus* and *Pygocentrus* will attack any creature that is injured or makes a commotion in the water, regardless of its size. In 1981 more than 300 people are reported to have been eaten by piranhas when an overloaded boat capsized and sank while docking at Obidos, Brazil.

MOST SHOCKING FISH
The electric eel or paroque (*Electrophorus electricus*) lives in fresh water in Brazil and the Guianas. Live from head to tail, it has two pairs of longitudinal organs that can release an electric shock of up to 650 volts. This force is strong enough to light an electric bulb or incapacitate an adult human.

MOST VENOMOUS JELLYFISH
The cardiotoxic venom of the Flecker's sea wasp or box jellyfish (*Chironex fleckeri*) has killed at least 70 people off the coast of Australia in the last hundred years. If medical aid is unavailable, some victims have been known to die within four minutes. One effective defence is women's hosiery — the jellyfish's stinging cells cannot penetrate the material.

MOST DANGEROUS SEA URCHIN
Toxin from the spines and pedicellaria (small pincer-like organs) of the flower sea urchin (*Toxopneustes pileolus*) causes severe pain, respiratory problems and paralysis in humans.

MOST DANGEROUS BEE
The venom of the hybrid Africanized honey bee (*Apis mellifera scutellata*) is no more potent than that of other bees but the number of stings that the species inflicts when in swarms is sometimes sufficient to kill humans.

MOST VENOMOUS CENTIPEDE
In the Solomon Islands there is a peculiarly dangerous form of centipede called *Scolopendra subspinipes*. So potent is its venom, injected into its victim by a modified pair of front limbs rather than by its jaws, that human victims have been known to plunge their bitten hands into boiling water in order to mask the pain.

MOST DANGEROUS ANT
Native to South America, the fire ant (*Solenopsis invicta*) first reached the USA in the 1930s in ships carrying earth. In May 1998 an estimated 23,000 rainbow trout were killed after ingesting fire ants in a 24-km (15-mile) stretch of the Guadaloupe River in central Texas. The fire ant is attracted to electrical sources and often bites through insulation, causing electricity blackouts and fires.

MOST VENOMOUS LIZARDS
Unusually for lizards, both the Gila monster (*Heloderma suspectum*) of Mexico and the south-western USA and its close relative the Mexican beaded lizard (*H. horridum*) from western coastal Mexico have a venomous bite. The venom contained in their glands is powerful enough to kill two adult humans.

MOST DANGEROUS SMALL MAMMALS
The small mammals that pose the most danger to humans are rats. More than 20 pathogens are carried by them, including the bacterium that causes the bubonic plague or 'Black Death'. They also carry leptospirosis (Weil's disease), Lassa fever, rat-bite fever, and murine typhus, all of which can be fatal.

MOST DANGEROUS BEAR
The only species of bear that actively preys on humans is the polar bear (*Ursus maritimus*). Most attacks occur during the night and are made by hungry adolescent males that are probably inexperienced hunters and are likely to have been driven from their usual prey by larger bears.

MOST DANGEROUS BIG CAT
Tigers attack humans more frequently than other cats do, probably because humans fall within the natural size range of a tiger's prey and are fairly easy to catch, even for old or injured tigers.

STRONGEST ANIMAL BITE
Experiments carried out with a 'Snodgrass gnathodynamometer' (shark-bite meter) at the Lerner Marine Laboratory in Bimini, Bahamas, revealed that a dusky shark (*Carcharhinus obscurus*) 2 m (6 ft 6 in) long could exert a force of 60 kg (132 lb) between its jaws. This is equivalent to a pressure of 3 tonnes/cm² (19.6 tons/in²) at the tips of the teeth. The bites of larger sharks, such as the Great White (*Carcharodon carcharias*), must be considerably stronger but have never been measured.

LONGEST DEADLY SNAKE
*The reticulated python (*Python reticulatus*), a specimen of which is seen here with a handler from London Zoo, UK, regularly exceeds 6.25 m (20 ft 6 in) in length. The length of pythons and their relatives, anacondas and boas, helps them to kill prey by constriction.*

parasites

LONGEST TAPEWORM
The broad or fish tapeworm, *Diphyllobothrium latum*, which lives in the small intestine of fish and sometimes humans, can reach 12 m (40 ft) in length. Over 10 years it would shed bodily segments 8 km (5 miles) long and release about 2 billion eggs.

Taeniarhynchus saginatus, the beef tapeworm, usually grows to around 5 m (16 ft) but the largest known specimen was over 23 m (75 ft) long — three times longer than a human intestine.

BIGGEST TICK
Ticks are parasitic arachnids that prey on mammals and birds. They swell up as they suck blood through the skin. The largest belong to the sub-order Ixodida and can measure 3.6 cm (1 2/5 in) in length when fully bloated.

BIGGEST FLUKE
A didymozoid digenean species *Nematobibothriodes histoidii* found in the body wall tissues of the sunfish *Mola mola* can grow to 12 m (40 ft) long.

BIGGEST ROUNDWORM
The world's largest parasitic species of nematode or roundworm is *Placentonema gigantissimus*, which can reach a length of 7.5 m (25 ft). It inhabits the placenta of sperm whales.

BIGGEST FLEA
The giant flea *Hystrichopsylla schefferi*, dubbed 'super flea', can measure 1 cm (1/2 in) in length. Its only known host is the North American mountain beaver *Aplodontia rufa*.

BIGGEST LEECH
Haementeria ghilianii, an Amazonian leech, grows up to 30 cm (1 ft) in length.

BIGGEST PARASITIC PROTOZOANS IN HUMANS
Balantidium coli, which sometimes lives in the large intestine of humans, is only 0.08 mm x 0.06 mm (4/125 in x 3/125 in).

LONGEST THORNY-HEADED WORM
Acanthocephalan (or thorny-headed) worms are usually no more than 2.5 cm (1 in) long but at over 90 cm (3 ft) in length, female specimens of *Nephridiacanthus longissimus* are the world's longest acanthocephalan worms. Each species of thorny-headed worm inhabits different species – *Nephridiacanthus longissimus* inhabits the intestines of aardvarks.

MOST BLOODTHIRSTY PARASITES
The indistinguishable eggs of the hookworms *Ancylostoma duodenale* and *Necator americanus* are found in the faeces of 1.3 billion people worldwide. In cases of heavy infestation, the lining of the gut is so thickly covered with worms that they look like the pile of a carpet. The bleeding that results from their feeding adds up to a total of 10 million litres of blood worldwide every day.

LONGEST-LIVING PARASITE
A lifespan of 27 years has been reliably recorded for the medicinal leech *Hirudo medicinalis*.

MOST USEFUL PARASITE
The medicinal leech *Hirudo medicinalis*, traditionally used by doctors for blood-letting, has made a comeback. In 1991 a team of Canadian surgeons led by Dr Dean Vistnes took advantage of the anti-coagulants in leeches' saliva to drain away blood and prevent it from clotting during an operation to reattach a patient's scalp. The animals used in these procedures have been specially cultured in sterile conditions.

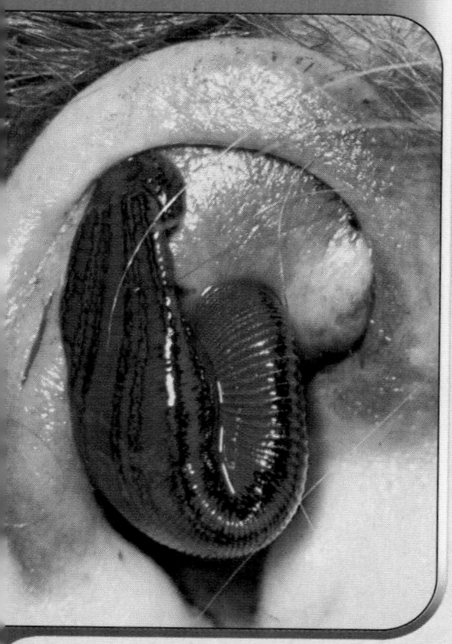

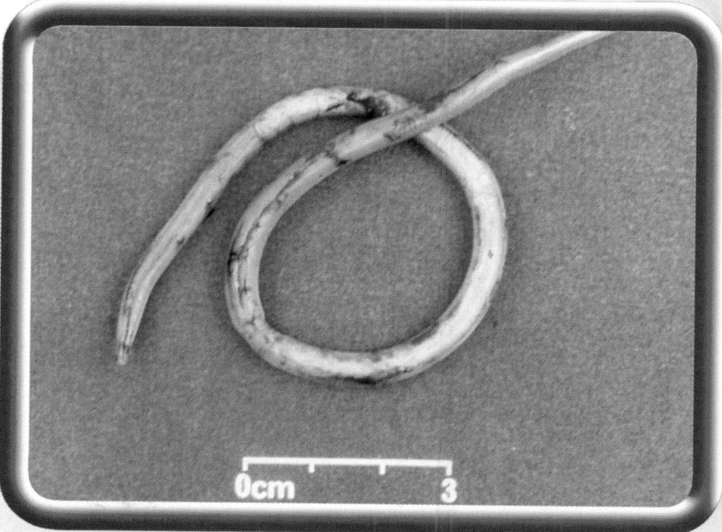

MOST FERTILE PARASITES
One female Ascaris lumbricoides *roundworm (above) can produce up to 200,000 eggs every day of her adult life, and has a total reproductive capacity of 26 million eggs. The body of the beef tapeworm* Taeniarhynchus saginatus, *meanwhile can consist of more than 1,000 segments, each of which contains approximately 80,000 eggs. A human host infected with a single specimen (which can live for up to 25 years) is liable to excrete about nine of the constantly-renewed segments, and therefore approximately 720,000 eggs, each day.*

LONGEST PARASITIC FASTS
The common bedbug *Cimex lectularius*, which feeds upon human blood is famously able to survive without feeding for more than a year. However the soft tick *Ornithodoros turicata* (which spreads the spirochaete that causes relapsing fever) can survive for periods of up to five years without food.

MOST PARASITIZED HOST SPECIES
Stagnicola emarginata, a type of freshwater snail from the Great Lakes of the USA and Canada, transmits parasites that cause 'swimmer's itch'. This snail is a host for the larvae of at least 35 species of parasitic fluke.

MOST ADAPTABLE FLUKE
Most flukes infect very few different organisms, but the liver fluke *Fasciola hepatica* has been found as an adult in the liver, gall bladder and associated ducts in a range of mammalian species, including sheep, cattle, goats, pigs, horses, rabbits, squirrels, dogs and humans.

MOST SIGNIFICANT NEW PARASITE
Many new species of new parasite are discovered every year but none are more zoologically significant than a microscopic ectoparasite known as *Symbion pandora*. Discovered living on the lips of the scampi lobster *Nephrops norvegicus*, it is fundamentally distinct from all other groups of animals – so much so that in Dec 1995 an entirely new phylum, the Cycliophora, was created in order to accommodate it.

MOST SUCCESSFUL PARASITIC WORM IN HUMANS
Parasitizing the small intestine and measuring up to 45 cm (1 ft 6 in) in length, the large roundworm *Ascaris lumbricoides* infects approximately 25% of the world's human population. Victims are usually infected with an average of 10–20 specimens, though much higher numbers have been recorded. The simultaneous migration of large quantities of *Ascaris* larvae through the lungs can cause severe haemorrhagic pneumonia.

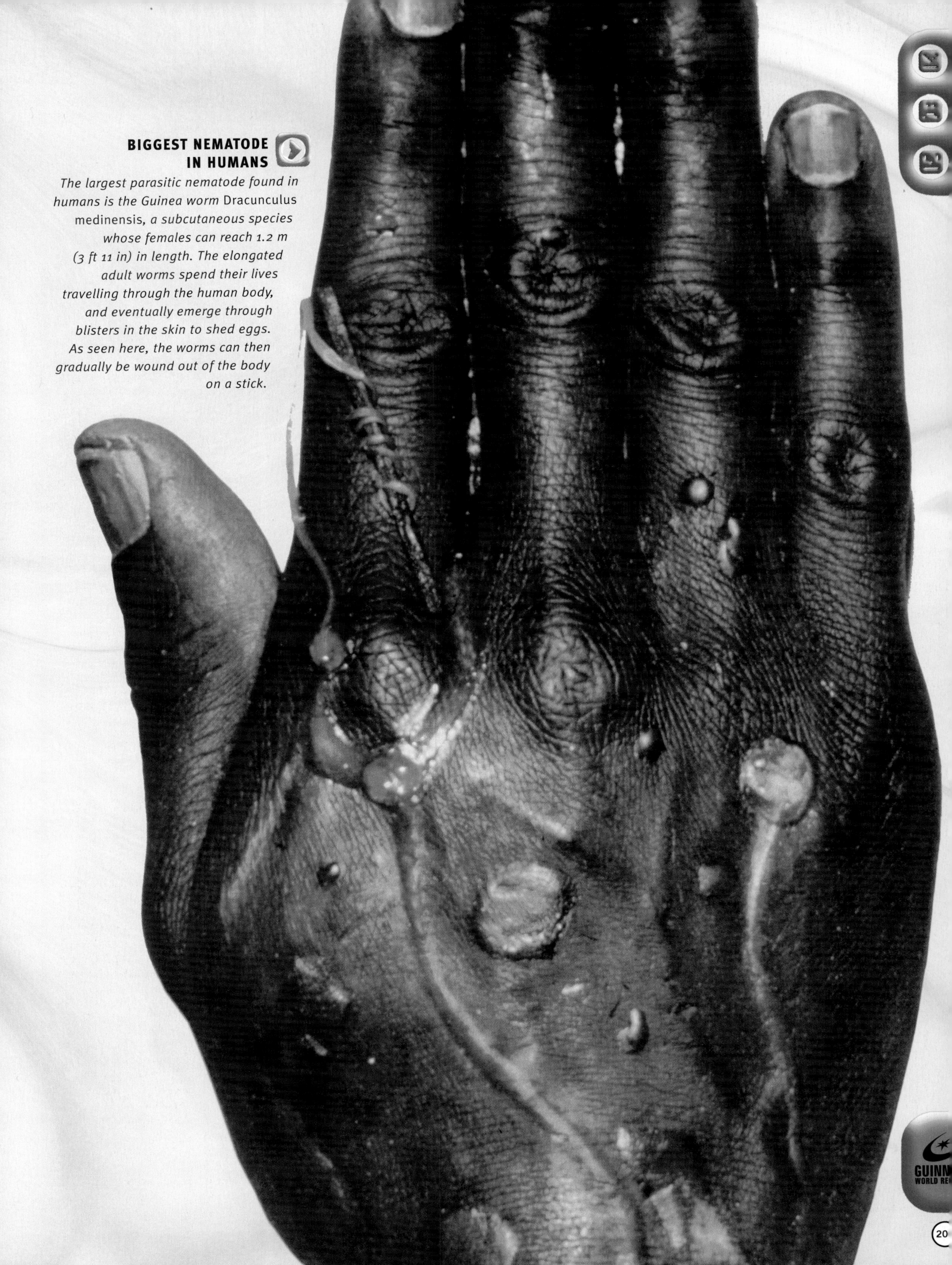

BIGGEST NEMATODE IN HUMANS

The largest parasitic nematode found in humans is the Guinea worm Dracunculus medinensis, *a subcutaneous species whose females can reach 1.2 m (3 ft 11 in) in length. The elongated adult worms spend their lives travelling through the human body, and eventually emerge through blisters in the skin to shed eggs. As seen here, the worms can then gradually be wound out of the body on a stick.*

dangerous & strange plants

BIGGEST CACTUS

The largest cactus is the saguaro (*Cereus giganteus* or *Carnegiea gigantea*) found in the south-western USA. The green fluted column is surmounted by candelabra-like branches rising to a height of 17.67 m (57 ft 11 in) in a specimen discovered in the Maricopa Mountains, near Gila Bend, Arizona, USA, on 17 Jan 1988. The characteristic spines that protect many species of cactus from animal attack are actually reduced leaves.

MOST POISONOUS PLANT
The castor oil plant (*Ricinus communis*), which is cultivated worldwide to make castor oil, contains ricin, the most lethal plant poison. A single seed weighing 0.25 g ($^{9}/_{1,000}$ oz) is enough to kill a human being. If the poison is injected, 1 microgram per kg ($^{1}/_{10,000,000}$ oz per stone) of body weight is fatal.

MOST DANGEROUS TREES
The manchineel tree (*Hippomane mancinella*) of the Caribbean coast and the Florida Everglades has had an evil reputation since Spanish explorers learnt to fear it in the 16th century. The whole tree exudes a highly poisonous and caustic sap, once used as an arrow poison. One drop in the eye can blind a person and one bite of the fruit causes blistering and severe pain. The slightest contact causes the skin to erupt in blisters.

For sheer numbers of victims, nothing rivals *Toxicodendron*, the genus that includes poison oak and poison ivy. Both produce the poison urushiol, which causes severe skin reactions in millions of Americans every year and is a major cause of disability in people who work outdoors.

MOST POISONOUS FLOWER
All parts of the attractive oleander *(Nerium oleander)*, a plant that is common throughout the world, are extremely dangerous. Bees that gather too much nectar from its flowers make poisonous honey and people have died after eating meat cooked on skewers made from oleander wood.

MOST CARCINOGENIC PLANT
The microscopic fungus *Aspergillus flavus* produces aflatoxin B1, one of the most powerful carcinogens known. As little as 10 micrograms ($^{1}/_{3,333,333}$ oz) triggers liver cancer in rats. *A. flavus* contaminates certain foodstuffs, most notoriously peanuts.

MOST FATAL FUNGI
The toadstool *Galerina sulcipes* is the world's most lethal fungus, with a fatality rate of 72% in humans who eat it.

The yellowish-olive death cap (*Amanita phalloides*), which can be found worldwide, is responsible for 90% of fatal poisonings caused by fungi. Its total toxin content is 7–9 mg (0.105–0.135 grains) dry weight. The estimated lethal amount of amatoxins for humans, depending on bodyweight, is 5–7 mg (0.075–0.105 grains), which is equivalent to less than 50 g ($1\frac{3}{4}$ oz) of a fresh fungus. The death cap belongs to a group that contains both edible and poisonous fungi. The effects of eating it are vomiting, delirium, collapse and death after 6–15 hours.

NASTIEST STINGERS
New Zealand's tree nettle (*Urtica ferox*) can kill a horse. Its stinging hairs inject a mixture of potent poisons; in 1961 a man in New Zealand's hill country stumbled into the plant and by the time he reached hospital was blind, paralysed and had severe breathing problems. He died within five hours.

Australia's stinging trees, armed with large hollow hairs on their leaves and twigs, are as feared as New Zealand's tree nettle. The worst, the gympie bush (*Dendrocnide moroides*), causes intense stabbing pains that can recur months later.

NASTIEST UNDERWATER STINGER
Toxins produced by *Lyngbya majuscula*, a fine, hairlike cyanobacterium found worldwide, cause a burn-like rash known as seabather's dermatitis. In severe cases, the skin blisters and peels and the victim suffers irritation of the eyes, nose and throat, skin sores, headache and tiredness. Sores can last two weeks. However its toxins are now being investigated as a cure for cancer.

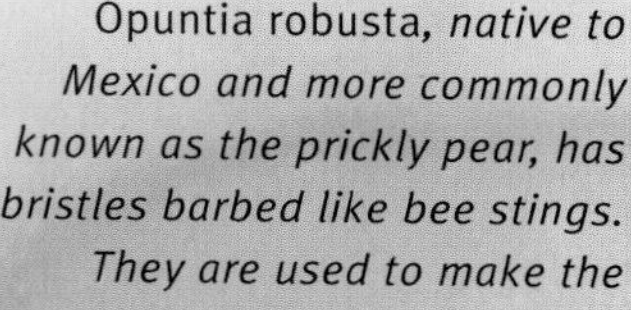

ITCHIEST CACTUS

Opuntia robusta, *native to Mexico and more commonly known as the prickly pear, has bristles barbed like bee stings. They are used to make the world's itchiest itching powder.*

MOST DAMAGING WEED
The weed that attacks the largest number of crops in the most countries is the purple nutgrass or nutsedge (*Cyperus rotundus*). The land weed is native to India but attacks 52 crops in 92 countries.

EARLIEST BOTANICAL WEAPON
The Christmas rose (*Helleborus niger*) is said to have played a part in breaking the siege of Kirra in central Greece in 600 BC. The attackers added poisonous hellebore roots to the town's water supply, triggering an outbreak of severe diarrhoea in the defending troops, who gave up the fight.

FASTEST-ACTING PLANT TRAP
The *Utricularia* genus of plants has the fastest-acting trap of any plant. The underwater plant acts by sucking its prey into its bladders in 0.03 seconds.

SMALLEST PLANT PREY
The underground leaves of *Genlisea* have recently been discovered to capture and digest soil-dwelling protozoa. Attracted by a chemical lure, thousands of micro-organisms a day squeeze through microscopic slits to the interior of the leaf, where the plant produces digestive juices. This is the only known example of a plant feeding on microscopic animals.

BEST ANIMAL MIMIC
Some orchids famously imitate the bees and wasps that pollinate them. The best mimic is *Drakaea glyptodon*, a hammer orchid from western Australia, which has flowers that look like wingless female thynnid wasps and produce an identical pheromone to the insect. When a male wasp finds a mate he grabs her round the waist and carries her off. If he grabs a dragon orchid by mistake, the hinged lip of the flower hurls him against the pollen-bearing sex organs so that sacs of pollen stick to him. If the wasp then approaches another orchid, he delivers the sacs and pollinates the flower.

MOST UNUSUAL POLLINATION
Flowers of *Microloma sagittatum*, a South African milkweed, clip parcels of pollen to the tip of a sunbird's tongue with a snap-lock device. The bird carries this pollen to the next flower inside its beak. All other identical milkweeds are pollinated by insects.

HARDIEST PLANT
Buellia frigida, a lichen that lives in the Antarctic, can survive the temperature of liquid nitrogen (-196°C or -321°F). Along with the world's most southerly plant, *Lecidea cancriformis* (found at latitude 86°S), it endures natural temperatures as low as -70°C (-94°F) in winter and 30°C (86°F) in summer – a range of 100°C (180°F). These hardy lichens can carry out photosynthesis between -20°C (-4°F) and 20°C (68°F).

BIGGEST CARNIVOROUS PLANTS
Plants of the *Nepenthes* genus have vines that reach a length of up to 10 m (33 ft), making them the largest species of carnivorous plant. They capture some of the biggest prey of any plants, including creatures as large as frogs.

MOST DEVIOUS PLANT

Sarracenia leucophylla *uses a series of lures to trap and digest insects. Around the mouth of each tube is an array of glands producing sweet-smelling nectar, surrounding patterns of glistening tissue that attract flies. The tube is lined with downward-pointing hairs so that once the flies have alighted they find it impossible to escape. Their struggle weakens them to the point of exhaustion, and they drop into a pool of powerful enzymes that digests them alive.*

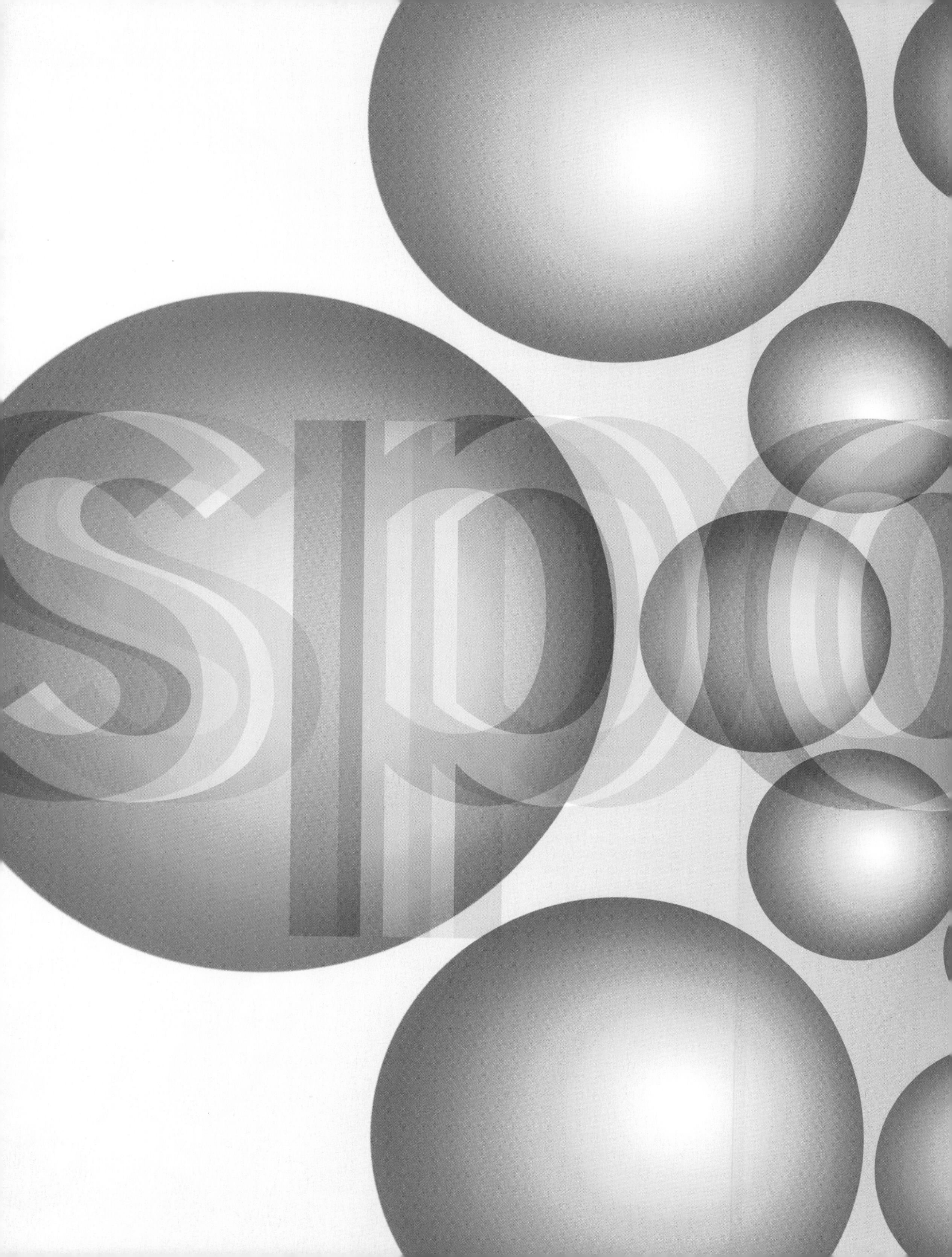

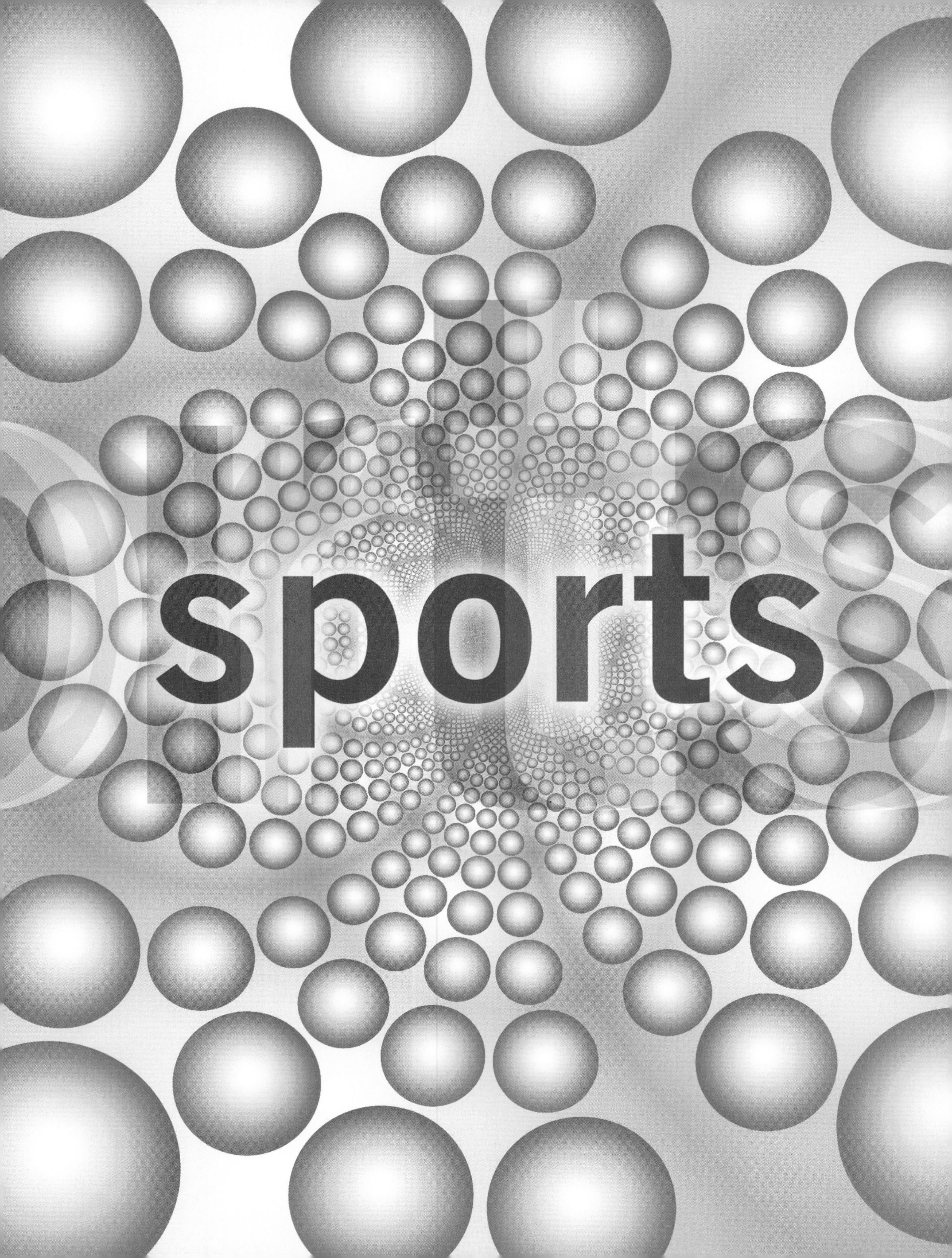
sports

extreme sports: air

BIGGEST BUNGEE JUMP
On 19 Sept 1997 Jochen Schweizer (Germany) made a bungee jump from a height of 2.5 km (1 mile 974 yd) above the town of Reichelsheim, near Frankfurt, Germany. Making the jump from an SA 365 Dauphine helicopter, Schweizer used a 284-m-long (931-ft 9-in) bungee cord. The first freefall phase, using the cord, covered 380 m (1,246 ft 8 in) — the cord had a natural expansion length of more than 95 m (311 ft 6 in) and the total distance jumped was 1.012 km (3,320 ft 3 in). From the jump out of the helicopter to the lower turning point took 17 seconds. Schweizer detached at 1.7 km (1 mile) and then freefell for 16 seconds, opening his parachute at an altitude of 900 m (2,952 ft).

BIGGEST MASS BUNGEE JUMP

On 6 Sept 1998, 25 people jumped from a 52-m-high (170-ft) platform suspended in front of the twin towers of the Deutsche Bank headquarters in Frankfurt, Germany. The event, organized by Frankfurt City Council, was part of a 'skyscraper festival' held to draw public attention to the city's modern architecture and burgeoning business district. The people involved in the jump were volunteers who had been attending the festival.

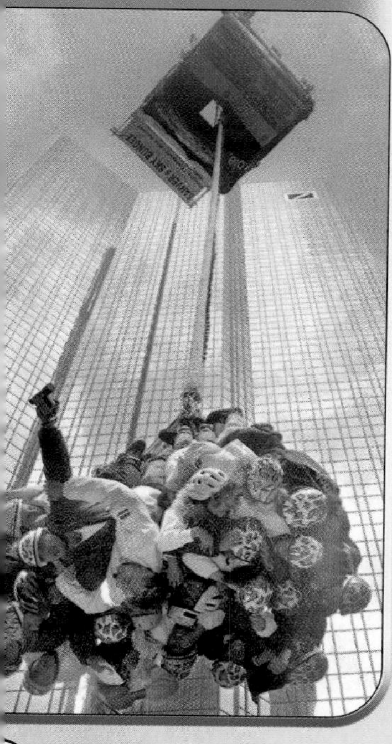

HIGHEST LAND-BASED BUNGEE JUMP
David Kirke, a member of the Oxford University Dangerous Sports Club, UK, leapt from the Royal Gorge Bridge, Colorado, USA, in 1980. The distance from the jump-point to the ground was 315 m (1,050 ft). Kirke used 126 m (420 ft) of unstretched bungee rope in the attempt.

HIGHEST TOY BALLOON FLIGHT
In Sept 1987 Ian Ashpole (UK) set a world altitude record for toy balloon flight when he reached a height of 3.05 km (1 mile 1,575 yd) over Ross-on-Wye, Herefordshire, UK. Ashpole was lifted to the target altitude by the hot-air balloon *Mercier*. When he reached the desired height he cut himself free from the balloon, then one by one from the 400 helium-filled toy balloons that suspended him in mid-air. Once freed from all the balloons, he freefell at a speed of approximately 144 km/h (90 mph) before parachuting to the ground.

HIGHEST BALLOON SKYWALK
Mike Howard (UK) walked on an aluminium bar between two hot-air balloons at a height of 5.73 km (3 miles 986 yd) over Marshall, Michigan, USA, on 4 May 1998. He used only a pole for balance and no safety ropes. The feat was later shown on the TV show *Guinness® World Records*.

LONGEST FORMATION SKYDIVING SEQUENCE (FOUR-WAY)
Thierry Boiteux, Marin Ferre, Marial Ferre and David Moy (France) arranged themselves into 36 different formations while freefalling over Pujaut, France, on 27 June 1997.

MOST JUMPS BY A SKYSURFER
Eric Fradet from Le Tignet, France, has logged 17,200 jumps, including 4,700 skysurfing jumps and 500 team jumps since 1976.

MOST PARACHUTING DESCENTS
Cheryl Stearns (USA) holds the record for the most descents undertaken by a woman, with 12,800, mainly over the USA, up to the end of 1998.

BIGGEST MASS FREEFALL FORMATION

On 26 July 1998 a record 246 skydivers came together for 7.3 seconds in the sky above Ottawa, Illinois, USA, to set a new world record for the world's largest freefall formation.

LONGEST DELAYED DROPS BY PARACHUTE
Joseph Kittinger fell a record 25.82 km (16 miles) from a balloon at an altitude of 31.33 km (19 miles 872 yd) over Tularosa, New Mexico, USA, on 16 Aug 1960.

Elvira Fomitcheva (USSR) made the longest ever delayed parachute drop by a woman, falling 14.8 km (9 miles 352 yd) in the skies over Odessa, USSR (now Ukraine), on 26 Oct 1977.

LONGEST PARACHUTE FALL
William Rankin fell for a record 40 minutes over North Carolina, USA, on 26 July 1956. The great length of the fall was due to thermals.

HIGHEST PARACHUTE BASE JUMP
Glenn Singleman and Nicholas Feteris jumped from a 5.88-km (3-mile 1,102-yd) ledge on the Great Trango Tower, Kashmir, on 26 Aug 1992.

BIGGEST PARACHUTE CANOPY STACK
The world's largest ever canopy stack involved a total of 53 people from a number of countries over Kassel, Germany in Sept 1996. They held the stack for six seconds.

LONGEST UPSIDE-DOWN FLIGHT
The longest period spent flying in an inverted position was 4 hr 38 min 10 sec. The record was set by Joann Osterud, who flew between Vancouver and Vanderhoof, British Columbia, Canada, in July 1991.

HIGHEST BUNGEE JUMP FROM A BUILDING

In Oct 1998 A.J. Hackett made a 180.1-m (590-ft 11-in) jump from the Sky Tower, the highest building in Auckland, New Zealand. He attached himself to two steel cables to avoid hitting the tower. Hackett was also the first man to bungee jump from the Eiffel Tower, and from a helicopter.

MOST INSIDE LOOPS DURING FLIGHT
David Childs (USA) achieved a record 2,368 inside loops in a Bellanca Decathalon. He performed the feat over Alaska, USA, on 9 Aug 1986.

MOST OUTSIDE LOOPS
Joann Osterud made a total of 208 outside loops in a 'Supernova' Hyperbipe over North Bend, Oregon, USA, on 13 July 1989.

The greatest height gained by a woman is 4.325 km (2 miles 1,209 yd), by Kat Thurston (UK) at Kuruman, South Africa, on 1 Jan 1996.

The record for the greatest height gained with a tandem paraglider is 4.38 km (2 miles 1,271 yd), set by Richard and Guy Westgate (UK) at Kuruman, South Africa, on 1 Jan 1996.

LONGEST MICROLIGHT DISTANCE
The greatest distance ever covered in a straight line by a microlight was 1,627.78 km (1,011 miles 845 yd). The record was set by Wilhelm Lischak (Austria), flying from Volsau, Austria, to Brest, France, on 8 June 1988.

GREATEST MICROLIGHT ALTITUDE
The record for the greatest altitude ever reached in a microlight is 9.72 km (6 miles 70 yd), by Serge Zin (France). He achieved this over Saint Auban, France, in 1994.

LONGEST PARAGLIDING FLIGHTS
The men's paragliding distance record is 289.63 km (179 miles 1,703 yd), set by Will Gadd (USA) on 30 May 1998.

The greatest distance flown by a female paraglider is 285 km (177 miles 169 yd), by Kat Thurston (UK) at Kuruman, South Africa, on 25 Dec 1995.

The greatest distance flown on a tandem paraglider is 200 km (124 miles 493 yd), by Richard and Guy Westgate (UK) at Kuruman, South Africa, on 23 Dec 1995.

GREATEST PARAGLIDER HEIGHT GAINS
The height gain record is 4.526 km (2 miles 1,429 yd), by British paraglider Robby Whittal at Brandvlei, South Africa, on 6 Jan 1993.

LONGEST HANG GLIDES
The record for the greatest ever straight line distance is 495 km (307 miles 1,165 yd), by Larry Tudor (USA) from Rock Springs, Wyoming, USA, on 1 July 1994.

The greatest distance by a woman is 353.1 km (219 miles 715 yd), by Tiki Mashy (USA) on 19 June 1998.

GREATEST HEIGHT BY A HANG GLIDER
Larry Tudor (USA) gained 4.343 km (2 miles 1,232 yd) over Owens Valley, California, USA, in 1985.

MOST PARACHUTE DESCENTS
Don Kellner (USA) holds the record for the most sport parachuting descents. By 1998 he had completed 26,000. It is estimated that the human body reaches 99% of its low level terminal velocity after falling 573 m (1880 ft).

extreme sports: land

FASTEST STREET LUGER

On 29 May 1998 Tom Mason (below) from Van Nuys, California, USA, set an official world record for street luge when he achieved a speed of 130.8 km/h (81.28 mph) at Mount Whitney, California, USA. Mason, who took up street luge in 1995, set the record on a 10-kg (23-lb) board and was timed by Bob Pererya from the street luge sanctioning body RAIL (Road Racing Association for International Luge). RAIL was formed in 1990 and is based in Los Angeles, California, USA. The association currently has over 100 members, both racing and non-racing.

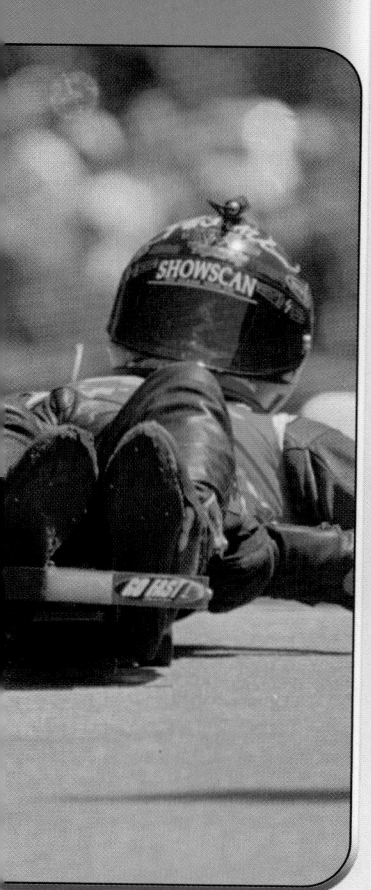

LONGEST SKATEBOARD JUMP

Tony Alva set a long-jump record of 5.18 m (17 ft), clearing 17 barrels at the World Professional Skateboard Championships held at Long Beach, California, USA, on 25 Sept 1977.

FASTEST SKATEBOARDERS
Gary Hardwick from Carlsbad, California, USA, set a skateboard record (standing position) of 100.66 km/h (62.55 mph) at Fountain Hills, Arizona, USA, on 26 Sept 1998. The event was sanctioned by Alternative International Sports, based in Phoenix, Arizona, USA.

Eleftherios Argiropoulos covered 436.6 km (271 miles 510 yd) in 36 hr 33 min 17 sec at Ekali, Greece, from 4 to 5 Nov 1993.

HIGHEST SKATEBOARD JUMP
The skateboarding high-jump record is 1.67 m (5 ft 5¾ in), by Trevor Baxter (UK) at Grenoble, France, on 14 Sept 1982.

BIGGEST MOUNTAINBOARD SPIN
While doing a 360° aerial spin during competition in Big Bear, California, USA, Mike Reinoehl (USA) reached a height of about 2.135 m (7 ft) and covered a distance of about 6.1 m (20 ft).

FASTEST BUTT BOARDER
Darren Lott (USA) achieved a record speed of 105 km/h (65.24 mph) on a butt board in Fountain Hills, Arizona, USA, on 26 Sept 1998.

HIGHEST JUMP ON IN-LINE SKATES
The record for the highest ever jump on in-line skates is 2.7 m (8 ft 11 in), by Randolph Sandoz (Switzerland) at Amsterdam, Netherlands, on 15 Dec 1996.

FASTEST BACKWARDS ROLLER SKATER
Jay Edington (USA) achieved a record speed of 75.14 km/h (46.69 mph) while roller-skating backwards in Fountain Hills, Arizona, USA, on 26 Sept 1998.

FASTEST IN-LINE SKATING ROAD TIMES
Eddy Matzger (USA) skated 34.82 km (21 miles 1,126 yd) in one hour at Long Beach, California, USA, in Feb 1991.

Jonathan Seutter (USA) holds the 12-hour road record, having covered a distance of 285.86 km (177 miles 1,109 yd) at Long Beach, California, USA, on 2 Feb 1991.

MOST MOUNTAIN-BOARDING TITLES

Jason T. Lee (USA) won the overall titles at Dirt Duel '97 and Dirt Duel '98, the mountainboarding World Championship. Lee had the fastest qualifying times at both events and has had the fastest times at all but one event in the past four years of local and national races.

Kimberly Ames (USA) set the 24-hour road record when she skated 455.5 km (283 miles 123 yd) in Portland, Oregon, USA, on 2 Oct 1994.

HIGHEST IN-LINE SKATING SPEED
Graham Wilkie and Jeff Hamilton (both USA) both achieved a speed of 103.03 km/h (64.02 mph) in Arizona, USA, on 26 Sept 1998, in an official attempt sanctioned by Alternative International Sports.

FASTEST STREET SKIER
The highest speed achieved downhill on a public road on an in-line wheeled frame not exceeding 1.07 m (42 in) in length and attached to the feet by ski bindings and boots is 101 km/h (63 mph), by Douglas Lucht (USA) in Arizona, USA, on 7 March 1998.

FASTEST ROLLER-SKIING RELAY
The greatest distance achieved by a team of four roller-skiers in 24 hours is 488.736 km (303 miles 1,223 yd), by a team of four at RAF Alconbury, Cambs, UK, from 23 to 24 May 1998.

FASTEST SANDBOARDERS
Nancy Sutton (USA) was clocked at 71.94 km/h (44.7 mph) in Nevada, USA, on 19 Sept 1998.

Marco Malaga (Peru) attained a speed of 71.13 km/h (44.2 mph) — the highest speed by a man — at Dumont Dunes, California, USA, on 26 Nov 1998.

MOST SANDBOARDING WORLD CHAMPIONSHIPS
Marco Malaga (Peru) holds the record for the most sandboarding World Championships won by a man, with three wins (1996, 1997 and 1998) in championships sanctioned by Dune Riders International, the world governing body for sandboarders.

Julie Pilcic (USA) is the female record-holder, having won three World Championships (1996, 1997 and 1998).

FASTEST SAND YACHTERS
The official top speed reached in a sand yacht is 107 km/h (66.48 mph), by Christian-Yves Nau (France) in *Mobil* at Le Touquet, France, on 22 March 1981.

MOST MOUNTAIN-BIKING WORLD CHAMPIONSHIPS
The most downhill World Championship wins by a man is seven, by Nicolas Vouilloz (France) — three in the junior championships from 1992 to 1994 and four in the senior class from 1995 to 1998.

The most downhill wins by a woman is five, by Anne-Caroline Chausson (France) — two in the junior championship in 1994 and 1995 and three in the senior class from 1996 to 1998.

The most cross-country wins is three, by Henrik Djernis (Denmark) from 1992 to 1994 and by Alison Sydor (Canada) from 1994 to 1996.

MOST MOUNTAIN-BIKE WORLD CUP WINS
The most mountain-biking cross-country World Cup wins by a woman is 28, by Juli Furtado (USA) from 1991 to 1996.

The most downhill World Cup wins by a woman is 13, by Anne-Caroline Chausson (France) from 1993 to 1998.

The most downhill World Cup wins by a man is seven, by Nicolas Vouilloz (France) from 1992 to 1998.

HIGHEST BUNNY HOP
The highest bunny hop achieved on a mountain bike was 1.125 m (45 in), by Steve Geall (UK) on 18 April 1998.

MOST DIRT JUMPING TITLES
Ryan Nyquist from Los Gatos, California, USA, has won the National Bicycle League's Dirt Circuit, the Pioneer King of Dirt and the K2 Pro Dirt Jump Series and has been crowned the ABA King of Dirt.

MOUNTAIN-BIKING WORLD CUP WINS

The most cross-country World Cup wins by a man is 15, by Thomas Frischknecht (Switzerland, right) from 1991 to 1998.

extreme sports: water

BIGGEST SURFING COMPETITION

The G-Shock US Open of Surfing, which takes place at Huntington Beach, California, USA, is generally regarded as the biggest surfing competition in the world today. The competition, which forms part of the world qualifying series, has attracted an average of 200,000 spectators every year since it started in 1994, and has about 700 competitors. The total prize money is $155,000 (£97,000). Of this, $100,000 (£62,500) goes to the winner of the men's surfing contest and $15,000 (£9,375) goes to the winner of the women's contest.

MOST WORLD PROFESSIONAL SERIES SURFING TITLES

The men's title has been won six times by Kelly Slater (USA), in 1992 and from 1994 to 1998.

The women's professional title has been won a record four times by: Frieda Zamba (USA), 1984–86 and 1988; Wendy Botha (Australia, formerly South Africa), 1987, 1989, 1991 and 1992; and Lisa Anderson (Australia), 1993–96.

MOST WORLD AMATEUR CHAMPIONSHIP SURFING TITLES

The most titles is three, by Michael Novakov (Australia) in the Kneeboard event in 1982, 1984 and 1986.

The most titles won by a woman is two, by Joyce Hoffman (USA) in 1965 and 1966 and Sharon Weber (USA) in 1970 and 1972.

MOST SUCCESSFUL WAKEBOARDERS

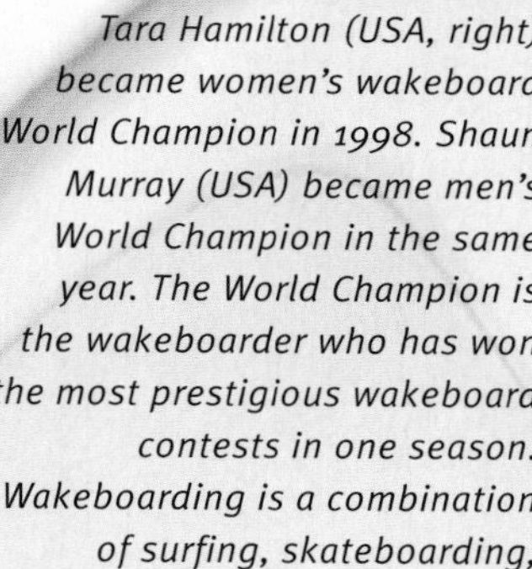

Tara Hamilton (USA, right) became women's wakeboard World Champion in 1998. Shaun Murray (USA) became men's World Champion in the same year. The World Champion is the wakeboarder who has won the most prestigious wakeboard contests in one season. Wakeboarding is a combination of surfing, skateboarding, snowboarding and waterskiing. The board resembles a fat snowboard with a pair of bindings attached to it.

MOST BODYBOARDING CHAMPIONSHIPS

Mike Stewart has won nine World Championships, eight national tour titles and 11 pipeline championships. He has won every bodyboarding competition he has entered in the last seven years as well as every *BodyBoarding Magazine* Readers' Poll.

LONGEST SWELL RIDDEN BY A BODYBOARDER

Mike Stewart (USA) surfed a swell in Tahiti on 19 July 1996, then flew to Hawaii, USA, to meet it again. He surfed it a third time in California, and finally in Alaska on 27 July.

HIGHEST WAVE RIDDEN BY A BODYBOARDER

In Jan 1996 Mike Stewart (USA) rode an 18.3-m (60-ft) wave off the coast of Jaws, Maui, Hawaii, USA. He was towed in by a Wave Runner. He also holds the record for the highest wave ever paddled into — 15.25 m (50 ft).

MOST KNEEBOARDING WORLD CHAMPIONSHIPS

Mario Fossa (Venezuela), known to his fans as the 'King Of Dizzy', won five consecutive Pro Tour Titles from 1987 to 1991. Kneeboarders perform their tricks while kneeling on a short, squat board.

TOP BOARDSAILING SPEED

The fastest overall speed by a boardsailer is 45.34 knots (84.02 km/h or 52.21 mph), by Thierry Bielak (France) at Camargue, France, in 1993.

The women's record is 40.36 knots (74.74 km/h or 46.44 mph), by Elisabeth Coquelle of France at Tarifa, Spain, on 7 July 1995.

MOST WATERSKIING TITLES

The record for the greatest number of individual discipline titles won is eight, by Liz Allan-Shetter (USA). She is also the only person to have won all four titles — slalom, jumping, tricks

BAREFOOT WATERSKIING

The greatest number of men's World Barefoot Championship Overall titles is three, by Brett Wing (Australia, right) in 1978, 1980 and 1982, and Ron Scarpa (USA) in 1992, 1996 and 1998. The most World Barefoot Championship Overall titles is four, by Kim Lampard (Australia) in 1980, 1982, 1985 and 1986, and Jennifer Calleri (USA) in 1990, 1992, 1994 and 1996. The World Barefoot Championship team title has been won by the USA a record six times between 1988 and 1998. Barefoot skiers perform without waterskis, boards or shoes.

MOST SUCCESSFUL AQUABIKER

Since 1997 the Union Internationale Motonautique, based in Monaco, has staged World Championships in three aquabike disciplines. Marco Sickerling of Germany, competing in the freestyle discipline, was crowned UIM European and World Champion in 1997 and European Champion in 1998.

and overall — in one year, at Copenhagen, Denmark, in 1969.

The USA won the team championship on 17 successive occasions from 1957 to 1989.

The World Overall Championships have been won five times by Patrice Martin (France), in 1989, 1991, 1993, 1995 and 1997.

The record for the most women's titles in the World Overall Championships is three, by Willa McGuire (USA) in 1949, 1950 and 1955, and Liz Allan-Shetter (USA) in 1965, 1969 and 1975.

HIGHEST WATERSKIING SPEED
The highest speed known to have been attained by any waterskier is 230.26 km/h (143.08 mph), by Christopher Massey (Australia) on the Hawkesbury River, Windsor, NSW, Australia, on 6 March 1983.

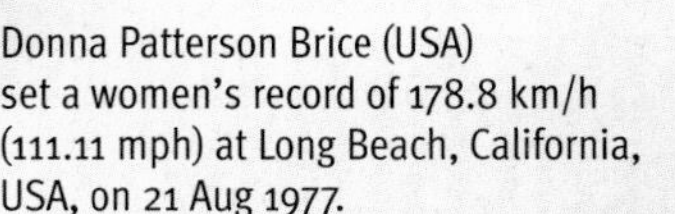

Donna Patterson Brice (USA) set a women's record of 178.8 km/h (111.11 mph) at Long Beach, California, USA, on 21 Aug 1977.

MOST WATERSKIERS TOWED BY ONE BOAT
On 18 Oct 1986 a record-breaking 100 skiers were towed on double skis over a nautical mile (1.8 km) by the cruiser *Reef Cat* at Cairns, Queensland, Australia. The tow was organized by the Cairns and District Powerboating and Ski Club.

MOST WORLD AND OLYMPIC CANOEING TITLES
A record 34 world titles (including Olympic titles) were won by Birgit Schmidt from 1979 to 1998.

The men's record is 13, jointly held by Gert Fredriksson from 1948 to 1960, Rüdiger Helm (GDR, now Germany) from 1976 to 1983, and Ivan Patzaichin (Romania) from 1968 to 1984.

HIGHEST CANOEING SPEEDS
At the 1995 World Canoeing Championships, the Hungarian four-man team won the 200-m title in 31.155 seconds, at an average speed of 23.11 km/h (14.36 mph).

On 3 Aug 1996 at the Olympic Games in Atlanta, Georgia, USA, the four-man kayak team from Germany covered 1,000 m in 2 min 51.52 sec — an average speed of 20.98 km/h (13.04 mph).

FASTEST CROSS-CHANNEL PADDLEBOARDERS
In July 1996 seven members of the Southern California Paddleboard Club – Derek and Mark Levy, Crag Wellay, Tim Ritter, Michael Lee, Charlie Didinger and John Matesich – completed a crossing of the English Channel from Dover, UK, to Cap Gris-Nez, France, in 6 hr 52 min.

MOST SUCCESSFUL NATION IN WHITE WATER FREESTYLE KAYAKING
The most successful nation to date in white water freestyle kayaking is Germany. They won the inaugural World Championships in St David's, Dyfed, UK, in 1991, and then in front of their home crowd at Augsburg in 1995.

HIGHEST-EARNING SURFERS

Kelly Slater (USA), pictured right, had earned a record $708,230 (£427,314) by April 1999. In 1991 he was the subject of a bidding war between the major surfwear companies, eventually won by Quiksilver. The women's career record is $270,275 (£168,922), by Pam Burridge (Australia) up to April 1999.

extreme sports: snow

MOST X GAMES SNOWBOARDING MEDALS

The most X Games snowboarding medals won by a woman is six, by Barrett Christy (USA). Christy took the gold medal in the Big Air event and the silver medal in the Slopestyle discipline at the 1999 Winter X Games. She also won both events in the inaugural X Games, and silver for both in 1998. The Winter X Games were launched by ESPN in 1977 and feature ice-climbing, snow mountain biking, free-skiing, skiboarding, snowboarding and snowcross.

SNOWBOARDING CHAMPIONS

The record for the most World Cup titles is 11, by Karine Ruby (France; pictured below). She won the overall from 1996 to 1998, the slalom from 1996 to 1998, the giant slalom from 1995 to 1998 and the snowboard cross in 1997. Mike Jacoby (USA) has won a record three men's World Cup titles: the overall in 1996 and the giant slalom in 1995 and 1996.

MOST WORLD CHAMPIONSHIP SNOWBOARDING TITLES

Karine Ruby (France) holds the record for the most World Championship titles (including Olympics titles), with three. She won the giant slalom in 1996 and 1998 and the snowboard cross in 1997. No man has ever won more than one World Championship title.

FASTEST SNOWBOARDER

The highest officially recorded speed attained by a snowboarder is 201.907 km/h (125.463 mph), by Daren Powell (Australia) at Les Arcs, France, on 1 May 1999.

MOST 'VERTICAL METRES' SNOWBOARDED IN A DAY

Over 15 hours on 20 April 1998 Tammy McMinn snowboarded down a slope in Sloko Range, Canada, 101 times, making a total vertical descent of 93.124 km (57 miles 1,524 yd). She was lifted back to the top each time by helicopter. She performed her feat alongside skier Jennifer Hughes (see below).

MOST 'VERTICAL METRES' SKIED IN A DAY

Edi Podivinsky, Luke Sauder, Chris Kent (all Canada) and Dominique Perret (Switzerland) hold the record for the most 'vertical metres' skied in a day. On 29 April 1998 they skied a total of 107.777 km (66 miles 1,709 yd) in 14 hr 30 min on a slope at Blue River, British Columbia, Canada, 73 times and were lifted back to the summit each time by helicopter.

The women's record is 93.124 km (57 miles 1,524 yd), set by Jennifer Hughes (USA) at Sloko Ridge, Canada, on 20 April 1998 alongside snowboarder Tammy McMinn (see above).

MOST SKIBOARDING MEDALS

Mike Nick (USA) won a gold medal in the 1998 ESPN Winter X Games Skiboarding Slopestyle and silver in the Triple Air discipline at the 1999 Games. The 1998 Winter X Games gave skiboarders their first opportunity to take part in a full international skiboarding competition.

MOST SNOW MOUNTAIN BIKING MEDALS

The most medals won for snow mountain biking is three, by Cheri Elliott (USA) — the 1997 gold speed medal, the 1998 silver speed medal and the silver difficulty medal.

MOST X GAMES MEDALS WON BY A MALE SNOWBOARDER

Shaun Palmer (USA; above left) battles for position with Norway's Tor Bruserud during the 1999 ISF Boardercross World Championships at Passo del Tonale, Italy. Palmer has claimed a record three gold medals at the Winter ESPN X Games for the Boarder X discipline, winning every year since the inaugural X Games in 1997. This is in addition to a 1997 X Games gold in the Snow Mountain Biking Dual Downhill event.

MOST TWO-SEATER LUGEING TITLES

Stefan Krauße and Jan Behrendt (both GDR, now Germany) have won a record six two-seater titles (1989, 1991–93, 1995 and 1998).

FASTEST LUGER

The highest photo-timed speed was 137.4 km/h (85.1 mph), by Asle Strand (Norway) at Tandådalens Linbana, Sälen, Sweden, on 1 May 1982.

CLOSEST OLYMPIC LUGE RACE

The final of the women's luge event at the 1998 Winter Olympic Games in Nagano, Japan, on 11 Feb 1998 was decided by a margin of 0.002 seconds. Germany's Silke Kraushaar edged out team-mate Barbara Niedernhueber to take the gold with a combined time of 3 min 23.779 sec over four runs on the championship course.

MOST WORLD SKI-BOB TITLES

The most World Championship titles won by a man is three, by Walter Kronseil (Austria) from 1988 to 1990.

The record for the most individual World Championship combined titles is four, by Petra Tschach-Wlezcek (Austria) from 1988 to 1991.

FASTEST SKI-BOBBER

The record for the highest speed reached in a ski-bob is 173 km/h (105 mph), by Romuald Bonvin (Switzerland) at Les Arcs, France, on 1 May 1999.

HIGHEST ICE-YACHTING SPEED

The highest officially recorded speed ever reached by an ice-yacht is 230 km/h (143 mph), by John Buckstaff (USA) on Lake Winnebago, Wisconsin, USA, in 1938.

MOST SINGLE-SEATER LUGE TITLES

The record for the most World Championship luge titles won (including Olympic titles) is six, by Georg Hackl (GDR, now Germany), who won the single-seater in 1989, 1990, 1992, 1994, 1997 and 1998. Steffi Walter (GDR) won a record two Olympic single-seater titles, at the women's event in 1984 and 1988. Margit Schumann (GDR) won the most women's titles overall, with five between 1973 and 1977.

MOST ICE-CLIMBING MEDALS

The record for the most ice-climbing medals ever won at the X Games is three, by Will Gadd (USA). He took the gold speed and difficulty medals in 1998, and the gold difficulty medal in 1999.

FASTEST OLYMPIC SPEED-SKIERS

The highest speed reached in an Olympic event is 229 km/h (142.47 mph), by Michel Pruefer (France) at the 1992 Winter Olympic Games in Albertville, France, when the sport was introduced as a demonstration event.

The youngest speed-skier to reach 161 km/h (100 mph) is Tatiana Fields (USA). She achieved this record aged 12, at the 1999 Red Bull US Speed-Skiing Championships in Snowmass, Colorado, USA.

MOST WORLD SKI-ORIENTEERING TITLES

The most individual titles is four, by Ragnhild Bratberg (Norway). She won the classic in 1986 and 1990 and the sprint in 1988 and 1990.

The men's record is three, by Anssi Juutilainen of Finland (classic 1984 and 1988, sprint 1992) and Nicolo Corradini of Italy (classic 1994 and 1996, sprint 1994).

FASTEST MONOSKIER

David Arnaud (France) reached a speed of 196.507 km/h (122.107 mph) at Les Arcs, France, on 1 May 1999.

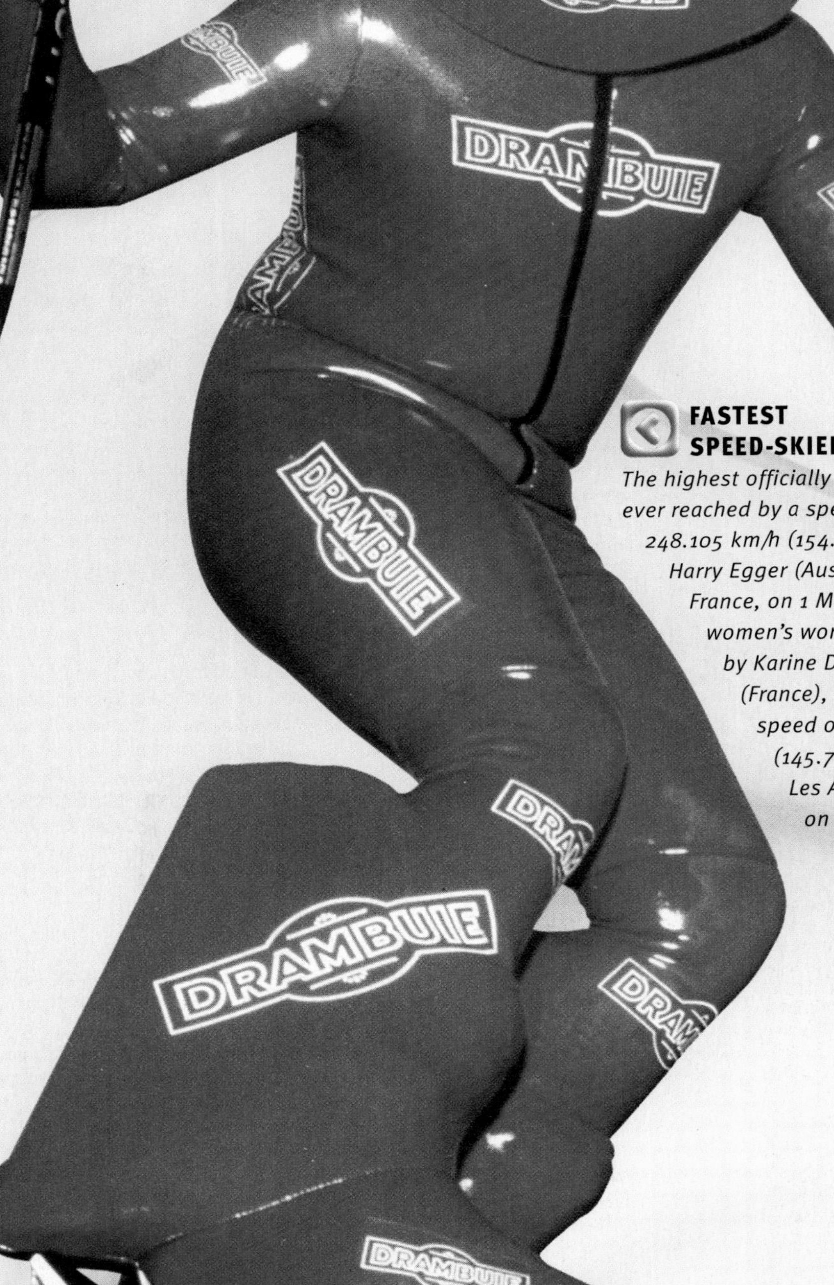

FASTEST SPEED-SKIERS

The highest officially recorded speed ever reached by a speed-skier is 248.105 km/h (154.17 mph), by Harry Egger (Austria) at Les Arcs, France, on 1 May 1999. The women's world record is held by Karine Dubouchet (France), who reached a speed of 234.528 km/h (145.733 mph) at Les Arcs, France, on 1 May 1999.

skiing

MOST WORLD TITLES

The most titles won by a skier (including Olympic titles) is 18, by Bjørn Dæhlie (Norway, pictured below), who won 12 individual and six relay titles in the Nordic discipline from 1991 to 1998. Dæhlie won a record 29 medals between 1991 and 1999. The most titles won by a woman is 17, by Yelena Välbe (Russia), with 10 individual and seven relay titles from 1989 to 1998. The most titles by a jumper is five, by Birger Ruud (Norway) in 1931 and 1932 and from 1935 to 1937. Ruud is the only person to have won Olympic events in both the Alpine and Nordic disciplines: the ski-jumping and the Alpine downhill in 1936.

MOST WORLD ALPINE CHAMPIONSHIP TITLES

The record for the most titles in the World Alpine Championships is 12, by Christl Cranz (Germany), who won seven individual (four slalom, 1934 and 1937–39, and three downhill, 1935, 1937 and 1939) and five combined (1934–35 and 1937–39). Cranz also won the gold medal for the combined in the 1936 Olympics.

The most titles won by a man is seven, by Toni Sailer (Austria), who won all four Alpine events (giant slalom, slalom, downhill and the non-Olympic Alpine combination) in 1956 and the downhill, giant slalom and combined in 1958.

MOST WORLD NORDIC CHAMPIONSHIP MEDALS

The most medals won by a woman in the World Nordic Championships is 23, by Raisa Petrovna Smetanina (USSR, later CIS), including a total of seven golds (1974–92).

MOST ALPINE WORLD CUP WINS

The record for the greatest number of individual event wins in the Alpine discipline is 86 (46 giant slalom and 40 slalom) from a total of 287 races, by Ingemar Stenmark (Sweden) from 1974 to 1989. This included a men's record of 13 wins in one season (1978/79). Of these, 10 were part of a record 14 successive giant slalom wins from March 1978 to Jan 1980.

Franz Klammer (Austria) won 25 downhill races from 1974 to 1984.

Annemarie Moser (Austria) won a women's record of 62 individual events from 1970 to 1979. She also had a record 11 consecutive downhill wins from 1972 to 1974.

MOST NORDIC WORLD CUP WINS

Bjørn Dæhlie of Norway holds the record for the most World Cup titles won in the cross-country discipline, with six (1992–93, 1995–97 and 1999).

Yelena Välbe (USSR, now Russia) has won a women's record of four cross-country titles (1989, 1991–92, 1995).

MOST SKI-JUMPING WORLD CUP WINS

The most titles won by a ski-jumper in the World Cup is four, by Matti Nykänen of Finland (1983, 1985–86, 1988).

MOST OLYMPIC TITLES

Katja Seizinger of Germany (pictured above) is one of two women to have won a record three Olympic Alpine titles and five Olympic Alpine medals. The other is Vreni Schneider of Switzerland. Seizinger won the downhill in 1994 and 1998 and the combined in 1998, and took bronze in the super giant slalom in 1992 and 1998. She has also won a record five super giant slalom World Cup titles (1993–96, 1998).

MOST FREESTYLE TITLES

Edgar Grospiron (France) has won a record three World Championship titles (moguls in 1989 and 1991 and aerials in 1995). He also won an Olympic title in 1992.

The record for the most men's overall titles in the World Cup is five, by Eric Laboureix (France) from 1986 to 1988 and in 1990 and 1991.

The most women's overall titles in the World Cup is 10, by Connie Kissling (Switzerland) from 1983 to 1992.

HIGHEST SPEEDS

The highest speed reached in a World Cup downhill is 112.4 km/h (69.84 mph), by Armin Assinger (Austria) at Sierra Nevada, Spain, on 15 March 1993.

The highest average speed reached in an Olympic downhill is 107.24 km/h (66.64 mph), by Jean-Luc Cretier (France) at Nagano, Japan, on 13 Feb 1998.

The record time for a 50-km (31-mile) race in a major championship is 1 hr 54 min 46 sec, by Aleksey Prokurorov (Russia) at Thunder Bay, Canada, in 1994. His average speed was 26.14 km/h (16.24 mph).

The highest speed ever attained by a person skiing on one leg is 185.567 km/h (115.309 mph), by Patrick Knaff (France) in 1988.

The highest speed reached by a grass-skier is 92.07 km/h (57.21 mph), by Klaus Spinka (Austria) in Waldsassen, Germany, on 24 Sept 1989.

LONGEST RACES

The longest Nordic ski race is the 89-km (55-mile 528-yd) annual Vasaloppet in Sweden. There were a record 10,934 starters in 1977.

The longest downhill race is the 15.8-km (9-mile 1,439-yd) Inferno from the top of the Schilthorn to Lauterbrunnen, Switzerland. The record time for the race is 13 min 53.4 sec, set by Urs von Allmen of Switzerland in 1991.

LONGEST ALL-DOWNHILL SKI RUN

The Weissfluhjoch-Küblis Parsenn skiing course near Davos, Switzerland, is a record 12.23 km (7 miles 1,038 yd) in length.

BIGGEST RACE

The Finlandia Ski Race is 75 km (46 miles 1.056 yd) long and runs from Hämeenlinna to Lahti, Finland.

MOST WORLD CUP WINS IN ONE SEASON

Vreni Schneider (Switzerland) is pictured taking part in the women's giant slalom event at the 1988 Winter Olympics. Schneider holds the record for the most World Cup wins in a single season: in 1988/89 she won a record total of 13 individual events and one combined event, including all seven slalom events.

In Feb 1984 it had a record 13,226 starters and 12,909 finishers.

GREATEST DISTANCE COVERED
Seppo-Juhani Savolainen (Finland) covered 415.5 km (258 miles 352 yd) in 24 hours at Saariselkä, Finland, from 8 to 9 April 1988.

The women's 24-hour record is 330 km (205 miles), by Sisko Kainulaisen (Finland) at Jyväskylä, Finland, from 23 to 24 March 1985.

MOST WORLD GRASS-SKIING CHAMPIONSHIP TITLES
The World Grass-skiing Championships have been held biennially since 1979. The most titles won is 14, by Ingrid Hirschhofer (Austria) between 1979 and 1993.

The most titles won by a man is seven, by Erwin Gansner of Switzerland (1981–87) and Rainer Grossman of Germany (1985–93).

Only two people have ever won all four titles (Super-G, giant slalom, slalom and combined) in one year: Rainer Grossman (Germany) in 1991 and Ingrid Hirschhofer (Austria) in 1993.

LONGEST SKI-JUMPS

The longest ski-jump ever officially recorded in the finals stage of a World Cup event is 214.5 m (704 ft), by Martin Schmitt (Germany; pictured right) at Planica, Slovenia, on 19 March 1999. This distance was achieved in the second of his two jumps in the competition. His first jump had been measured at 219 m (718 ft) but he fell, so the distance was not officially recorded. On the following day Tommy Ingebrigsten (Norway) completed a jump of 219.5 m (720 ft) in the qualifying round.

ice sports

MOST WOMEN'S SPEED-SKATING TITLES

Gunda Neimann-Stirnemann (Germany) holds the record for most world titles won in women's speed-skating events. In total she took seven titles from 1991 to 1993 and 1995 to 1998. After a disastrous fall in the 1994 Olympics, she returned to form in the 1998 Olympics in Calgary, Canada, when she set a new record (4:01.67) in the women's 3,000-m. She is seen here setting a new world record in the women's 5,000-m event during the World All-Round Speed-Skating Championships in Hamar, Norway, on 7 Feb 1999. She recorded a time of 6:57.24, scoring an all-time low of 161.479 points overall.

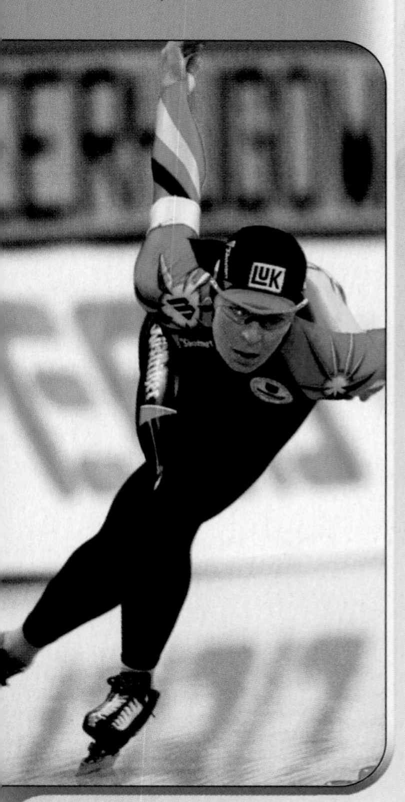

FASTEST SKATERS
Jeremy Wotherspoon (Canada) set a new 500-m speed-skating record with a time of 34.76 seconds in Calgary, Canada, on 20 Feb 1999.

The women's 500-m record is 37.55 seconds, set by Catriona Le May Doan (Canada) in Calgary, Canada, on 29 Dec 1997.

Jan Bos (Netherlands) skated 1,000 m in 1 min 8.55 sec in Calgary, Canada, on 21 Feb 1999 — a men's record.

The women's 1,000-m record is held by Monique Garbrecht (Germany), who skated the distance in 1 min 15.61 sec at Calgary, Canada, on 21 Feb 1999.

MOST MEN'S WORLD SPEED-SKATING TITLES
The greatest number of world overall titles won by a male skater is five, by Oscar Mathisen (Norway), 1908–09 and 1912–14, and by Clas Thunberg (Finland), 1923, 1925, 1928–29 and 1931.

MOST OLYMPIC SPEED-SKATING TITLES
The most Olympic gold medals won is six, by Lidiya Pavlovna Skoblikova (USSR) in 1960 (two) and 1964 (four).

The most Olympic gold medals won by a man is five, by Clas Thunberg (Finland) in 1924 and 1928, and Eric Arthur Heiden (USA) at one Games at Lake Placid, New York, USA, in 1980.

MOST WORLD FIGURE-SKATING TITLES
The greatest number of men's individual world figure-skating titles is 10, by Ulrich Salchow (Sweden) in 1901–05 and 1907–11.

The women's individual record is also 10, by Sonja Henie between 1927 and 1936.

The most world pair titles is 10, by Irina Rodnina — four with Aleksey Nikolayevich Ulanov from 1969 to 1972 and six with her husband Aleksandr Gennadyevich Zaitsev from 1973 to 1978.

HIGHEST FIGURE-SKATING MARKS
The highest tally of maximum six marks awarded in an international championship is 29, to Jayne Torvill and Christopher Dean (GB) at the World Ice Dance Championships in Ottawa, Canada, in March 1984. It comprised seven in the compulsory dances, a perfect set of nine for presentation in the set pattern dance and 13 in the free dance.

The most sixes by a soloist is seven: by Donald Jackson (Canada) in the World Men's Championships at Prague, Czechoslovakia (now Czech Republic), in 1962; and by Midori Ito (Japan) in the World Women's Championships in Paris, France, in 1989.

MOST FIGURE-SKATING GRAND SLAMS

Katarina Witt (GDR, now Germany) achieved a rare double 'Grand Slam' when she won the World, Olympic and European titles in both 1984 and 1988. The only other figure-skaters to have matched this feat were Austria's Karl Schäfer and Norway's Sonja Henie, both in 1932 and 1936.

FASTEST CRESTA RUN TIMES
The Cresta Run course at St Moritz, Switzerland, is 1,212 m (3,977 ft) long with a drop of 157 m (514 ft). The fastest time recorded there is 50.09 seconds, by James Sunley (GB) on 13 Feb 1999. His average speed was 87.11 km/h (54.13 mph).

MOST CRESTA RUN WINS
The most wins in the Cresta Run Grand National is eight, by the 1948 Olympic champion Nino Bibbia (Italy) from 1960 to 1964 and in 1966, 1968 and 1973,

and by Franco Gansser (Switzerland) in 1981, from 1983 to 1986, from 1988 to 1989, and in 1991.

MOST WORLD TWO-MAN BOBSLEIGH TITLES
Switzerland has won the two-man world title a record 17 times (1935, 1947–50, 1953, 1955, 1977–80, 1982–83, 1987, 1990, 1992 and 1994). This total includes a record four Olympic successes (in 1948, 1980, 1992 and 1994).

Eugenio Monti (Italy) won 11 titles — eight two-man from 1957 to 1961 (a record five consecutive titles) and in 1963, 1966, 1968, and three four-man (1960, 1961, 1968).

MOST INDIVIDUAL FOUR-MAN BOBSLEIGH TITLES
Bernhard Germeshausen (GDR, later Germany) won four titles (1976, 1977, 1980, 1981), as did Wolfgang Hoppe (GDR, later Germany, 1984, 1991, 1995, 1997).

MOST OLYMPIC BOBSLEIGH MEDALS
The most Olympic gold medals won by an individual is three, by Meinhard Nehmer and Bernhard Germeshausen (both GDR, later Germany) in the 1976 two-man and the 1976 and 1980 four-man events.

The most medals won is seven (one gold, five silver, one bronze), by Bogdan Musiol (GDR, later Germany) from 1980 to 1992.

OLDEST OLYMPIC BOBSLEIGH CHAMPION
Jay O'Brien (USA) was 48 years 357 days old when he was a member of the four-man bobsleigh team that won a gold medal at the Winter Olympics in Lake Placid, New York, USA, in 1932.

YOUNGEST OLYMPIC BOBSLEIGH CHAMPION
William Guy Fiske was in the US team that won the five-man bobsleigh event at the Winter Olympics in St Moritz, Switzerland, in 1928, when he was 16 years 260 days old.

MOST WORLD CURLING CHAMPIONSHIP TITLES
The most men's World Championship titles are held by Canada, which has won 25 times (1959–64, 1966, 1968–72, 1980, 1982–83, 1985–87, 1989–90, 1993–96, 1998).

The most women's titles held is 10, by Canada (1980, 1984–87, 1989, 1993–94, 1996–97).

LONGEST CURLING THROW
A curling stone was thrown a record distance of 175.66 m (576 ft 4 in) by Eddie Kulbacki (Canada) at Park Lake, Manitoba, Canada, on 29 Jan 1989. The attempt took place on a specially prepared sheet of curling ice.

FASTEST CURLING GAME
Eight curlers from the Burlington Golf and Country Club curled an eight-end game in a record time of 47 min 24 sec, with time penalties of 5 min 30 sec, at Burlington, Ontario, Canada, on 4 April 1986.

MOST WORLD FOUR-MAN BOBSLEIGH TITLES
Switzerland has won the four-man bobsleigh world title a record 20 times (1924, 1936, 1939, 1947, 1954–57, 1971–73, 1975, 1982–83, 1986–90 and 1993). This total includes a record five Olympic victories (1924, 1936, 1956, 1972 and 1988). The Swiss team — Marcel Rohner (driver), Silvio Schaufelberger, Markus Nuessli and Beat Hefti of Swiss 1 — is seen here on the way to second place in the World Championships in Cortina d'Ampezzo, Italy, in Feb 1999.

ice hockey

MOST GAMES PLAYED
Gordie Howe (Canada) played in a record 1,767 regular season games (and 157 play-off games) over a record 26 seasons in the National Hockey League (NHL), from 1946 to 1971 (for the Detroit Red Wings) and then in the 1979/80 season (for the Hartford Whalers). He also played 419 regular season games (and 78 games in the play-offs) for the Houston Aeros and for the New England Whalers in the World Hockey Association (WHA) between 1973 and 1979, giving him a career total of 2,421 major league games.

MOST GOALS SCORED
The most goals scored in professional hockey is 1,072 by Wayne Gretzky (Edmonton Oilers, Los Angeles Kings, St Louis Blues and New York Rangers). In the NHL he scored 894 goals in the regular season and 122 in Stanley Cup games between 1979 and 1999. He also scored 56 goals in the WHA in 1978/79. He broke Gordie Howe's record of 1,071 goals on 29 March 1999 for the New York Rangers against the New York Islanders. By the time he had played his last professional game, against the Pittsburgh Penguins on 18 April 1999, Gretzky had amassed 61 NHL records.

MOST GOALS AND POINTS IN A SEASON
Wayne Gretzky holds the record for the most goals scored in one season — 92 for the Edmonton Oilers, in 1981/82. He also scored a record 215 points, including a record 163 assists in 1985/86. In all his games in 1984/85, including Stanley Cup play-offs, he scored a record 255 points (90 goals, 165 assists).

MOST GOALS IN A GAME
The most goals in a game is seven, by Joe Malone for the Québec Bulldogs against Toronto St Patricks in Québec City on 31 Jan 1920.

MOST ASSISTS IN A GAME
The record for the most assists in a game is seven, achieved once by Billy Taylor for Detroit against Chicago on 16 March 1947 and three times by Wayne Gretzky for Edmonton against Washington on 15 Feb 1980, against Chicago on 11 Dec 1985 and against Québec on 14 Feb 1986.

MOST POINTS IN A GAME
The most points scored by one player in a North American major league game is 10, by Jim Harrison (three goals, seven assists) for Alberta, later Edmonton Oilers, in a WHA match at Edmonton on 30 Jan 1973, and by Darryl Sittler (six goals, four assists) for Toronto Maple Leafs against Boston Bruins in an NHL match at Toronto on 7 Feb 1976.

MOST TEAM GOALS
The most goals by a team in a World Championship match is 58, a record set by Australia against New Zealand (who failed to score) at Perth, Australia, on 15 March 1987.

The most team goals scored in an NHL season is 446, by the Edmonton Oilers in the 1983/84 season, when they also achieved a record 1,182 scoring points.

MOST TEAM POINTS
The Montréal Canadiens scored a record 132 team points (60 wins, 12 ties) from 80 games played in 1976/77. Their tally of eight losses was also the lowest ever in a season of 70 or more games.

MOST SUCCESSFUL TEAMS
The Detroit Red Wings won a record 62 games in 1995/96.

The highest percentage of wins in a season was .875% by the Boston Bruins, with 38 wins in 44 games in the 1929/30 season.

LONGEST UNDEFEATED RUN
The longest unbeaten run in a season is 35 games (25 wins, 10 ties), by the Philadelphia Flyers from 14 Oct 1979 to 6 Jan 1980.

FASTEST GOAL
The shortest time taken to score from the opening whistle is five seconds, by Doug Smail for the Winnipeg Jets on 20 Dec 1981, by Bryan Trottier for the New York Islanders on 22 March 1984 and by Alexander Mogilny for the Buffalo Sabres on 21 Dec 1991.

MOST STANLEY CUP POINTS
Wayne Gretzky scored 382 points, 122 goals and 260 assists (all records) in Stanley Cup games.

The most points scored in a single game is eight, by Mario Lemieux, with five goals and three assists for Pittsburgh against Philadelphia on 25 April 1989 and by Patrik Sundström, with three goals and five assists for New Jersey against Washington on 22 April 1988.

MOST STANLEY CUP GOALS
The most goals in a game is five, by Newsy Lalonde for Montréal against Ottawa on 1 March 1919, Maurice Richard for Montréal against Toronto on 23 March 1944, Darryl Sittler for Toronto against Philadelphia on 22 April 1976, Reggie Leach for Philadelphia against Boston on 6 May 1976, and Mario Lemieux for Pittsburgh against Philadelphia on 25 April 1989.

The record for the most goals in a season is 19, set by Reggie Leach for Philadelphia in 1976 and by Jari Kurri for Edmonton in 1985.

MOST STANLEY CUP ASSISTS
The most assists in a game is six, by Mikko Leinonen for New York against Philadelphia on 8 April 1982 and by Wayne Gretzky for Edmonton against Los Angeles on 9 April 1987.

MOST OLYMPIC GOLD MEDALS
The most Olympic gold medals is three, by Vitaliy Davydov, Anatoliy Firsov, Viktor Kuzkin and Aleksandr Ragulin (USSR, 1964, 1968, 1972), Vladislav Tretyak (USSR, 1972, 1976, 1984) and Andrey Khomutov (USSR, 1984, 1988; CIS, 1992).

MOST WORLD AND OLYMPIC TITLES

The USSR won 22 world titles (including the Olympic titles in 1956, 1964 and 1968) from 1954 to 1990 as well as one title playing as Russia in 1993. They won a further five Olympic titles in 1972, 1976, 1984, 1988 and 1992 (as the CIS, with an all-Russian team) for an Olympic record of eight. The USSR also hold the record of a 47-game unbeaten sequence in the World Championships. Canada have secured 21 world titles and hold the record for the most medals (gold, silver and bronze) won in both the World Championships and the Olympics, with 42 and 12 respectively. The US women's ice hockey team won the first Olympic title at Nagano in 1998, beating arch rivals Canada 3–1.

MOST STANLEY CUP WINS

The Montréal Canadiens have had a record 24 wins (1916, 1924, 1930–31, 1944, 1946, 1953, 1956–60, 1965–66, 1968–69, 1971, 1973, 1976–79, 1986 and 1993) from a record 32 finals. Henri Richard of the Canadiens played on a record 11 cup-winning teams from 1956 to 1973. Stephane Quintal of the Canadiens is shown here up-ending Trevor Linden of the New York Islanders.

MOST NCAA WINS
Michigan has won the NCAA Championships a record nine times, in 1948, 1951–53, 1955–56, 1964, 1996 and 1998.

MOST WOMEN'S WORLD CHAMPIONSHIPS
Canada won the first five women's World Championships (1990, 1992, 1994, 1997 and 1999) without losing a single game.

MOST SUCCESSFUL GOALTENDERS

Three-time Stanley Cup winner Patrick Roy (pictured) of the Colorado Avalanche has won 110 playoff games, more than any other goaltender. Terry Sawchuk played a record 971 NHL regular season games as goaltender for five teams from 1949 to 1970. He had a record 447 wins and a record 103 shutouts. Jacques Plante holds the record for the most regular season wins by a goalie in a professional career, with 449 victories (434 in the NHL and 15 in the WHA).

GUINNESS WORLD RECORDS

athletics

MOST OLYMPIC TITLES

The most gold medals won is 10 (an absolute Olympic record), by Raymond Ewry (USA): standing high, long and triple jumps in 1900, 1904, 1906 and 1908.

The most gold medals won by a woman is four, by Fanny Blankers-Koen (Netherlands) in the 100 m, 200 m, 80-m hurdles and 4 x 100-m relay, 1948; Betty Cuthbert (Australia) in the 100 m, 200 m and 4 x 100-m relay, 1956, and the 400 m, 1964; Bärbel Wöckel (GDR) in the 200 m and 4 x 100-m relay, 1976 and 1980; and Evelyn Ashford (USA) in the 100 m, 1984, and 4 x 100-m relay, 1984, 1988 and 1992.

MOST OLYMPIC MEDALS

The most medals is 12 (nine gold, three silver), by distance runner Paavo Nurmi (Finland) in 1920, 1924 and 1928.

The most medals by a female athlete is seven, by Shirley de la Hunty (Australia), with three gold, one silver and three bronze in 1948, 1952 and 1956. A re-read of the photo-finish indicated that she was third, not fourth, in the 1948 200-m event, which unofficially makes her medal count eight. Irena Szewinska (Poland), the only female athlete to win a medal in four successive Games, also won seven medals (three gold, two silver and two bronze in 1964, 1968, 1972 and 1976), as did Merlene Ottey (Jamaica), with two silver and five bronze in 1980, 1984, 1992 and 1996.

MOST WORLD CHAMPIONSHIP MEDALS

Merlene Ottey (Jamaica) has won a record 14 medals in the World Athletics Championships, with three gold, four silver and seven bronze from 1983 to 1997. The most medals won by a man is 10, by Carl Lewis (USA): a record eight gold (100 m, long jump and 4 x 100-m relay, 1983; 100 m, long jump and 4 x 100-m relay, 1987; and 100 m and 4 x 100-m relay, 1991), a silver at long jump in 1991 and a bronze at 200 m in 1993.

MOST WINS AT ONE GAMES

The most gold medals at one Games is five, by Paavo Nurmi (Finland) in 1924 (1,500 m, 5,000 m, 10,000-m cross-country, 3,000-m team and cross-country team).

The most medals at individual events is four, by Alvin Kraenzlein (USA) in 1900 (60 m, 110-m hurdles, 200-m hurdles and long jump).

OLDEST OLYMPIC CHAMPIONS

The oldest winner of an Olympic event was Patrick 'Babe' McDonald (USA), who was 42 years 26 days old when he won the 25.4-kg (56-lb) weight throw in Belgium in Aug 1920.

The oldest female champion was Lia Manoliu (Romania), who was 36 years 176 days old when she won the gold medal for the discus in Mexico in 1968.

YOUNGEST OLYMPIC CHAMPIONS

The youngest gold medallist was Barbara Jones (USA), who was a member of the winning 4 x 100-m relay team at Helsinki, Finland, when she was 15 years 123 days in July 1952.

The youngest male champion was Bob Mathias (USA), who won the decathlon aged 17 years 263 days in London, UK, in 1948.

MOST WORLD CHAMPIONSHIP GOLD MEDALS

Sergey Bubka (Ukraine, formerly USSR) won the pole vault at a record six consecutive championships from 1983 to 1997.

The most gold medals won by a woman is four, by Jackie Joyner-Kersee (USA) in the long jump in 1987 and 1991 and the heptathlon in 1987 and 1993.

OLDEST AND YOUNGEST RECORD-BREAKERS

Marina Styepanova (USSR) set a 400-m hurdle record (52.94 seconds) at Tashkent, USSR (now Uzbekistan), in 1986 at the age of 36 years 139 days.

Wang Yan (China) set an individual women's 5,000-m walk record of 21 min 33.8 sec aged 14 years 334 days in China on 9 March 1986.

The youngest man to break an individual record was Thomas Ray (GB), who pole-vaulted 3.42 m (11 ft 21/4 in) aged 17 years 198 days on 19 Sept 1879.

MOST RECORDS SET IN A DAY

Jesse Owens (USA) set six world records in 45 minutes at Ann Arbor, Michigan, USA, on 25 May 1935. He ran 100 yd in 9.4 seconds at 3:15 pm, made an 8.13-m (26-ft 81/4-in) long jump at 3:25 pm, ran 220 yd (and 200 m) in 20.3 seconds at 3:45 pm and covered the 220-yd (and 200-m) low hurdles in 22.6 seconds at 4 pm. The following year Owens won four gold medals at the Olympics in Berlin, Germany.

FASTEST 100 M

Maurice Greene (USA) is pictured setting a new world record of 9.79 seconds in the men's 100 m on 16 June 1999 in Athens, Greece. Greene took 0.05 seconds off the previous record, set by Canada's Donovan Bailey at the 1996 Olympics in Atlanta, Georgia, USA. This was the biggest margin taken off the 100-m record since electronic timing was introduced in the 1960s. Greene also equalled the time set by Ben Johnson (Canada) in 1988. Johnson's time was subsequently invalidated after a positive drugs test.

FASTEST 1,500 M

Hicham el-Guerrouj (Morocco) broke the 1,500-m world record in Rome, Italy, on 14 July 1998. His time of 3:26.00 bettered the previous record set by Noureddine Morceli (Algeria) by more than a second.

LONGEST WINNING SEQUENCES
The record winning sequence at a track event is 122, by Ed Moses (USA) at the 400-m hurdles between Aug 1977 and June 1987.

Iolanda Balas (Romania) won a record 150 consecutive high-jump competitions between 1956 and 1967.

HIGHEST JUMP ABOVE OWN HEAD
The greatest height cleared by an athlete above his own head was 59 cm (1 ft 11¼ in), by 1.73-m-tall (5-ft 8-in) Franklin Jacobs (USA), who jumped 2.32 m (7 ft 7¼ in) in New York City, USA, on 27 Jan 1978.

The greatest height cleared by a female athlete above her own head was 32 cm (1 ft ¾ in), by 1.68-m-tall (5-ft 6-in) Yolanda Henry (USA), who jumped 2.00 m (6 ft 6¾ in) in Seville, Spain, on 30 May 1990.

BEST STANDING JUMPS
The best high jump from a standing position was 1.9 m (6 ft 2¾ in), by Rune Almen (Sweden) at Karlstad, Sweden, on 3 May 1980.

The women's best is 1.52 m (4 ft 11¾ in), by Grete Bjørdalsbakka (Norway) in 1984.

FASTEST MASS RELAYS
The fastest 100 x 100-m was 19 min 14.19 sec, by a team from Antwerp in Belgium on 23 Sept 1989.

The fastest time over 160.9 km (100 miles) by 100 runners was 7 hr 35 min 55.4 sec, by the Canadian Milers Athletic Club at York University, Toronto, Canada, on 20 Dec 1998.

The greatest distance covered by 10 runners in 24 hours is 487.343 km (302 miles 494 yd), by Puma Tyneside Running Club in Jarrow, Tyne and Wear, UK, in Sept 1994.

FASTEST FEMALE SPRINTER

Florence Griffith Joyner, known to her fans as Flo-Jo, caused a sensation when she smashed two world records – the women's 100 m and 200 m – at the US Olympic trials in July 1988. Her 100-m time of 10.49 seconds still stands, but she went on to break her 200-m record twice at the Olympic Games in Seoul, South Korea, setting a time of 21.56 in the semi-final, and then achieving 21.34 seconds in the final on 29 Sept 1988. Flo-Jo died on 21 Sept 1998.

golf

BEST SCORES IN THE OPEN

The best score in a round is 63, by Mark Hayes (USA) at Turnberry, UK, in 1977; Isao Aoki (Japan) at Muirfield, UK, in 1980; Greg Norman (Australia) at Turnberry in 1986; Paul Broadhurst (GB) at St Andrews, UK, in 1990; Jodie Mudd (USA) at Royal Birkdale, UK, in 1991; Nick Faldo (GB) at Royal St George's, UK, in 1993; and Payne Stewart (USA) in 1993, also at Royal St George's.

Nick Faldo completed the first 36 holes at Muirfield, UK, in a record 130 strokes (66, 64) from 16 to 17 July 1992.

BEST US OPEN SCORES

The best score in a round in the US Open is 63, by Johnny Miller (USA) on the 6,328-m (6,920-yd), par-71 Oakmont Country Club course, Pennsylvania, in June 1973 and by Jack Nicklaus and Tom Weiskopf (both USA) at Baltusrol Country Club (6,414 m or 7,014 yd) in Springfield, New Jersey, on 12 June 1980.

The best score over two rounds is 134, by Jack Nicklaus of the USA (63, 71) at Baltusrol in 1980; Chen Tze-chung of Taiwan (65, 69) at Oakland Hills, Michigan, in 1985 and Lee Janzen of the USA (67, 67) at Baltusrol in June 1993.

The best score over four rounds is 272, by Jack Nicklaus (63, 71, 70, 68) at Baltusrol Country Club, Springfield, New Jersey, in June 1980, and his fellow US player Lee Janzen (67, 67, 69, 69) at Baltusrol in June 1993.

OLDEST US OPEN CHAMPION

US golfer Hale Irwin won the US Open at the age of 45 years 15 days on 18 June 1990. Irwin won the tournament in 1974 and 1979, but had not been a contender for several years, and was only eligible via a special exemption given to him by the USGA. Although he has never been the top player in the world, he has been in the US top 10 money winners eight times, from 1973 to 1978, in 1981 and in 1990.

BEST US MASTERS SCORES

The top score in a round is 63, by Nick Price (Zimbabwe) in 1986 and Greg Norman (Australia) in 1996.

The best score over two rounds is 131 (65, 66) by Raymond Floyd (USA) in 1976.

BEST US PGA SCORES

The best ever score in any round in the US PGA is 63, by Bruce Crampton (Australia) at Firestone, Akron, Ohio, in 1975; Raymond Floyd (USA) at Southern Hills, Tulsa, Oklahoma, in 1982; Gary Player (South Africa) at Shoal Creek, Birmingham, Alabama, in 1984; Vijay Singh (Fiji) at Inverness Club, Toledo, Ohio, in 1993 and Michael Bradley and Brad Faxon (both USA) at the Riviera Golf Club, Pacific Palisades, California, in 1995.

The record aggregate is 267, by Steve Elkington (Australia), with 68, 67, 68, 64, and Colin Montgomerie (GB), with 68, 67, 67, 65, both at Riviera Golf Club, Pacific Palisades, California, in 1995.

MOST WORLD CUP WINS

US golfers Arnold Palmer (left of picture) and Jack Nicklaus (right of picture), seen here with Tom Watson, have been on a record six winning teams in the World Cup: Palmer in 1960, 1962–64 and 1966–67; and Nicklaus in 1963–64, 1966–67, 1971 and 1973. Nicklaus has also taken the most individual titles, winning three times (1963–64 and 1971).

MOST TOURNAMENT WINS

In 1945 Byron Nelson (USA) won a record 18 tournaments and an unofficial tournament; his 11 consecutive wins was also a record.

US golfer Sam Snead turned professional in 1934 and by 1965 had won 81 official US PGA tour events.

The womens' record in the USLPGA is 88, by Kathy Whitworth (USA) between 1959 and 1991.

The most career victories in European Order of Merit tournaments is 55, by Spaniard Severiano Ballesteros from 1974 to 1995.

BIGGEST WINNING MARGIN

The record for the greatest margin of victory in a professional tournament is 21 strokes, by Jerry Pate (USA), who won the 1981 Colombian Open with a score of 262.

YOUNGEST AND OLDEST NATIONAL CHAMPIONS

Thuashni Selvaratnam won the Sri Lankan Ladies' Amateur Open Golf Championship when she was aged 12 years 324 days in 1989.

Pamela Fernando was a record 54 years 282 days old when she won the Sri Lankan Women's Championship on 17 July 1981.

BEST FOUR ROUNDS IN THE US MASTERS

Eldrick 'Tiger' Woods holds the record for the best four rounds in the US Masters, with 270 (70, 66, 65, 69) in 1997. At the same time, he broke the record for shots below par in the championship, with -18, and became the youngest person ever to win the tournament, at 21 years 104 days. He also equalled Raymond Floyd's 54-hole record of 201, set in 1976. Born on 30 Dec 1975, Woods became the youngest ever golfer to reach number one in the Official World Golf Ranking at the age of 21 years 167 days on 15 June 1997, getting to the top after only his 42nd week as a professional.

BEST FOUR ROUNDS IN THE OPEN

Greg Norman (Australia) holds the record for the best score in four rounds at the Open, with 267 (66, 68, 69, 64). He set the record at Royal St George's, Sandwich, Kent, UK, from 15 to 18 July 1993.

MOST HOLES PLAYED
Eric Freeman (USA) played 467 holes, using a cart, at the Glen Head Country Club, New York, USA, in 12 hours in 1997. The nine-hole course is 2,992 m (3,272 yd) long.

Ian Colston played a record 401 PGA holes on foot in 24 hours at Bendigo Golf Club, Victoria, Australia (par 73, 5,542 m or 6,061 yd), in 1971.

Using a motorized buggy, Joe Crowley (USA) completed 1,702 holes at Green Valley Country Club, Clermont, Florida, USA, from 23 to 29 June 1996.

LONGEST PUTT
The longest holed putt in a major tournament was 100.6 m (110 ft), achieved by Jack Nicklaus in the 1964 Tournament of Champions and Nick Price in the 1992 United States PGA.

MOST BALLS HIT IN ONE HOUR
The most balls driven in one hour, over 91.5 m (100 yd) and into a target area, is 2,146, by Sean Murphy of Canada at Swifts Practice Range, Carlisle, Cumbria, UK, on 30 June 1995.

LONGEST STRAIGHT HOLE IN ONE SHOT
The longest ever straight hole achieved in one shot was the 10th (408 m or 446 yd) at the Miracle Hills Golf Club, Nebraska, USA, by Robert Mitera on 7 Oct 1965. Mitera was a two-handicap player who normally drove 224 m (245 yd). An 80-km/h (50-mph) gust of wind carried his shot over a 265-m (290-yd) drop-off.

The women's record is 359 m (393 yd), by Marie Robie on the first hole of the Furnace Brook Golf Club, Wollaston, Massachusetts, USA, on 4 Sept 1949.

LONGEST 'DOG-LEG' HOLE
The longest 'dog-leg' hole achieved in one stroke is 453 m (496 yd) 17th, by Shaun Lynch at Teign Valley Golf Club, Christow, Devon, UK, on 24 July 1995.

MOST CONSECUTIVE ACES
There are at least 20 cases of holes-in-one being achieved at two consecutive holes. Perhaps the greatest was Norman Manley's unique 'double albatross' on the par-4 301-m (330-yd) seventh and par-4 265-m (290-yd) eighth holes on the Del Valle Country Club course, Saugus, California, USA, on 2 Sept 1964.

BEST WORLD CUP SCORE

Fred Couples holds the record for the lowest ever individual score in the World Cup. He achieved a score of 265 from 10 to 13 Nov 1994, when he and Davis Love III represented the USA at the championships in Dorado, Puerto Rico. Couples and Love also broke the record for the lowest aggregate score for 144 holes, with 536. The USA has won the World Cup a record 21 times.

tennis

YOUNGEST TENNIS MILLIONAIRE

In 1997, at 16 years of age, Martina Hingis (Switzerland) became the youngest sportswoman to earn $1 million (£610,426). When she won her quarter final at the 1998 Italian Open, she became the youngest tennis player to earn $6 million (£3.74 million), at the age of 17 years, seven months and eight days.

MOST GRAND SLAM WINS
The most singles championships won in grand slam tournaments is 24, by Margaret Court (Australia): 11 Australian, five US, five French and three Wimbledon, 1960–73.

The record for the most men's singles championships is 12, won by Roy Emerson (Australia): six Australian and two each French, US and Wimbledon, from 1961 to 1967.

The most grand slam tournament wins by a doubles partnership is 20, by Althea Brough and Margaret Du Pont (USA): 12 US, five Wimbledon and three French from 1942 to 1957; and Martina Navrátilová and Pam Shriver (USA): seven Australian, five Wimbledon, four French and four US, 1981–89.

MOST WIMBLEDON WINS
Billie-Jean King (USA) won a record 20 women's titles between 1961 and 1979: six singles, 10 women's doubles and four mixed doubles.

Martina Navrátilová (USA) won nine women's singles titles: 1978–79, 1982–87 and 1990.

Elizabeth Ryan (USA) won 19 women's doubles titles (12 women's, seven mixed) from 1914 to 1934.

The most titles won in the men's championships is 13, by Hugh Doherty (GB), with five singles titles (1902–06) and a record eight men's doubles (1897–1901 and 1903–05). He was partnered by his brother Reginald in all tournaments.

The most men's singles wins since the abolition of the Challenge Round in 1922 is five, a record jointly held by Björn Borg (Sweden), 1976–80, and Pete Sampras (USA), 1993–95 and 1997–98. Sampras is still competing at top level.

YOUNGEST AND OLDEST WIMBLEDON CHAMPIONS
Lottie Dod (GB) was 15 years 285 days old when she won the women's singles title in 1887.

Margaret Du Pont (USA) was 44 years 125 days old when she won the mixed doubles in 1962.

MOST US OPEN WINS
Margaret Du Pont (USA) won 25 titles from 1941 to 1960: a record 13 women's doubles (12 with Althea Brough, USA), nine mixed doubles and three singles.

The most women's singles titles is eight, by Molla Mallory (USA), 1915–18, 1920–22 and 1926.

The record for the most men's US Open titles is 16, by Bill Tilden (USA); this includes a total of seven singles (1920–25, 1929). Seven singles titles were also won by Richard Sears (USA), 1881–87, and William Larned (USA), 1901–02, 1907–11.

YOUNGEST AND OLDEST US OPEN WINNERS
Vincent Richards (USA) was 15 years 139 days old when he won the men's doubles in 1918.

The oldest champion was Margaret Du Pont (USA), who won the mixed doubles at the age of 42 years 166 days in 1960.

MOST WINS IN THE AUSTRALIAN OPEN
Margaret Court (Australia) won a record total of 21 titles: 11 women's singles (1960–66, 1969–71 and 1973), eight women's doubles and two mixed doubles.

Roy Emerson (Australia) won a record six men's singles (1961, 1963–67).

Adrian Quist (Australia) won 10 men's doubles and three men's singles titles between 1936 and 1950.

MOST FRENCH OPEN WINS
Margaret Court (Australia) won a record 13 titles from 1962 to 1973: five singles, four women's doubles and four mixed doubles.

BIGGEST ATP TOUR EARNERS

Stefan Edberg (Sweden) is one of only three players to have won more than $20 million (£12.5 million) on the ATP (Association of Tennis Professionals) Tour, the others being Boris Becker (Germany) and Pete Sampras (USA). The ATP Tour was launched in 1990 as a partnership of players and tournaments and replaced the Men's Tennis Council as the governing body for the men's professional tennis circuit. Edberg first captured the imagination of the tennis world in 1983 when he won the junior singles titles at all four Grand Slam tournaments in one year. He went on to win full singles titles at all the Grand Slam tournaments with the exception of the French Open.

FASTEST SERVES

The record for the fastest timed women's service was set by Venus Williams (USA) during the European Indoor Championships at Zürich, Switzerland, on 16 Oct 1998, and stands at 205 km/h (127.4 mph). The record for the fastest service timed with modern equipment is 239.8 km/h (149 mph), achieved by Greg Rusedski (GB) during the ATP Champions' Cup at Indian Wells, California, USA, on 14 March 1998.

The men's record is nine, by Henri Cochet (France), with four singles, three men's doubles and two mixed doubles from 1926 to 1930.

The singles record is seven, by Chris Evert (USA): 1974–75, 1979–80, 1983 and 1985–86.

Björn Borg (Sweden) won six men's singles titles: 1974–75 and 1978–81.

MOST DAVIS CUP WINS

The USA has won the Davis Cup 31 times since 1900.

MOST WINS IN THE ATP TOUR CHAMPIONSHIP

Ivan Lendl (USA, formerly Czechoslovakia) won a total of five titles: 1982, 1983, 1986 (two) and 1987.

Seven doubles titles were won by the legendary pairing of John McEnroe and Peter Fleming (both USA) from 1978 to 1984.

LONGEST GRAND SLAM MATCH

A 5-hr 31-min match between Alex Corretja (Spain) and Hernan Gumy (Argentina) took place in the third round of the French Open on 31 May 1998. Corretja eventually won 6–1, 5–7, 6–7, 7–5, 9–7.

YOUNGEST WINNER IN THE FEDERATION CUP

Anna Kournikova (Russia) came to attention in 1996 when she became the youngest player to compete and win in the Federation Cup competition, at the age of 14, helping Russia to defeat Sweden 3-0. She turned professional in 1995, reached the singles semi-finals at Wimbledon in 1997 and won the Princess Cup doubles in 1998, with Monica Seles.

soccer 1

MOST EXPENSIVE PLAYER
The highest ever transfer fee for a footballer is $46.4 million (£28 million), paid by Internazionale to Lazio (both of Italy) for Christian Vieri. It was the Italian striker's ninth transfer in 10 seasons and took his salary from $3.31 million (£2 million) to $5.14 million (£3.1 million).

MOST EXPENSIVE DEFENDER
In May 1998 Dutch defender Jaap Stam struck a deal to go to Manchester United for a record transfer fee of £10.75 million ($18 million). The 26-year-old PSV Eindhoven star accepted a seven-year deal that is worth £11 million ($18.3 million) including bonuses. He began his professional career at 19 and made his international debut in 1996 for the Netherlands.

MOST APPEARANCES
British goalkeeper Peter Shilton made a record 1,390 senior appearances, including a record 1,005 national league matches: 286 for Leicester City (1966–74), 110 for Stoke City (1974–77), 202 for Nottingham Forest (1977–82), 188 for Southampton (1982–87), 175 for Derby County (1987–92), 34 for Plymouth Argyle (1992–94), one for Bolton Wanderers in 1995, nine for Leyton Orient (1996–97); one League play-off, 86 FA Cup matches, 102 League Cup matches, 125 internationals for England, 13 Under-23 matches, four Football League XI matches and 53 European and other club competitions.

MOST CAREER GOALS
The greatest number of goals scored by a player in a specified period is 1,281, by Pelé (Edson Arantes do Nascimento) for Santos, the New York Cosmos and Brazil between 7 Sept 1956 and 1 Oct 1977.

Artur Friedenreich of Brazil scored an undocumented 1,329 goals in a 26-year first-class career from 1909 to 1935.

Franz 'Bimbo' Binder scored 1,006 goals in 756 games in Austria and Germany between 1930 and 1950.

MOST GOALS IN A MATCH
The most goals scored by one player in a first-class match is 16, by Stephan Stanis for Racing Club de Lens v. Aubry-Asturies in a wartime French Cup game in Lens, France, on 13 Dec 1942.

MOST CONSECUTIVE HAT-TRICKS
The record for the most consecutive league games in a top division in which one player has scored a hat-trick is four: Masahi Nakayama of Jubilo Iwata scored five, four, four and three goals in successive matches in the Japanese League in April 1998.

FASTEST GOALS
In first-class football the record for the fastest goal is six seconds, by Albert Mundy for Aldershot v. Hartlepool United in a British Fourth Division match at Victoria Ground, Hartlepool, Co. Durham, UK, in Oct 1958; by Barrie Jones for Notts County v. Torquay United in a British Third Division match in March 1962, and by Keith Smith for Crystal Palace v. Derby County in a British Second Division match at the Baseball Ground, Derby, UK, on 12 Dec 1964.

MOST EUROPEAN CUP WINS
The European Cup, contested since 1956 by the champion teams of the various national leagues in Europe, has been won a record seven times by Real Madrid of Spain (1956–60, 1966 and 1998). Clarence Seedorf (left of picture) is seen fending off Edgar Davids of Juventus (Italy) in the 1998 final, which Real won 1–0.

FASTEST HAT-TRICK
The fastest confirmed time in which three goals have been scored is 2 min 13 sec, by Jimmy O'Connor for Shelbourne against Bohemians at Dallymount Park, Dublin, Republic of Ireland, on 19 Nov 1967.

Maglioni is said to have scored a hat-trick in 1 min 50 sec when playing for Independiente against Gimnasia y Escrima de la Plata in Argentina on 18 March 1973.

HIGHEST SCORE
The highest score recorded in a first-class match was 36, in the Scottish Cup match between Arbroath and Bon Accord on 5 Sept 1885. Arbroath won 36–0 at their home ground.

BIGGEST VICTORY MARGINS IN NATIONAL CUP FINALS
In 1935 Lausanne-Sports beat Nordstern Basel 10–0 in the Swiss Cup Final. Lausanne were defeated by the same scoreline by Grasshopper Club (Zürich) in the 1937 Swiss Cup Final.

MOST NATIONAL LEAGUE CHAMPIONSHIPS
CSKA Sofia of Bulgaria hold a European post-war record of 27 league titles, including two under the name CFKA Sredets (renamed CSKA).

Dynamo Berlin (German Democratic Republic) won 10 successive national championships from 1979 to 1988.

MOST CUP-WINNERS CUP WINS
The Cup-Winners Cup, contested between 1960 and 1999 by the winners of the major national cup competitions in Europe, was won a record four times by the Spanish club Barcelona (1979, 1982, 1989 and 1997). The club has been home to many international greats, including Johan Cruyff (Netherlands), Gary Lineker (England) and Brazilian stars Rivaldo (back row, second from right) and Ronaldo.

LONGEST-HELD NATIONAL SOCCER LEAGUE TITLE
The Cairo club Al Ahly maintained the Egyptian national soccer title from the 1948/49 season until the 1959/60 season. However, the 1952 championship was abandoned because of the Egyptian revolution and the 1955 league programme was not completed.

MOST COPA LIBERTADORES WINS
Independiente (Argentina) have won the Copa Libertadores, contested since 1960 by the champions of the South American leagues, a record seven times (1964–65, 1972–75 and 1984).

MOST WORLD CLUB CHAMPIONSHIPS
The record for wins in the World Club Championship, contested since 1960 between the winners of the European Cup and the Copa Libertadores, is three, held by: Peñarol of Uruguay (1961, 1966 and 1982); Nacional of Uruguay (1971, 1980 and 1988); and AC Milan of Italy (1969, 1989 and 1990).

MOST CUP OF CHAMPION CLUBS WINS
The Cup of Champion Clubs, contested since 1964 by the winners of the African national leagues, has been won a record four times by Zamalek of Egypt (1984, 1986, 1993 and 1996).

MOST AFRICAN CUP-WINNERS CUP WINS
Al Ahly (Egypt) have won the African Cup-Winners Cup a record four times (1984–86 and 1993).

MOST SUCCESSFUL GOALKEEPER
The longest period that a goalkeeper has prevented goals being scored past him in top-class competition is 1,275 minutes, by Abel Resino of Athletico Madrid, Spain, in 1991.

BIGGEST CROWD
The record attendance at a European Cup match is 136,505, at the semi-final between Celtic and Leeds United at Hampden Park, Glasgow, UK, on 15 April 1970.

FURTHEST DISTANCE TRAVELLED FOR A LEAGUE GAME
The furthest distance travelled between two clubs in the top division of a national soccer league is 4,766 km (2,979 miles), between the grounds of LA Galaxy, California, and New England Revolution, Massachusetts, in the US Major League.

MOST UNDISCIPLINED MATCH
On 1 June 1993 it was reported that referee William Weiler sent off 20 players in a league match between Sportivo Ameliano and General Caballero in Paraguay. Trouble flared after two Sportivo players were sent off. A 10-minute fight ensued, and Weiler dismissed a further 18 players, including the rest of the Sportivo team. The match was then abandoned.

MOST GOALS SCORED BY A GOALKEEPER

José Luis Chilavert, who plays for Paraguay and for Vélez Sarsfeld of Argentina, scored 44 official league and international goals between July 1992 and May 1999. A penalty and free-kick specialist, he is also the only goalkeeper to have scored in a World Cup qualifying match and the only 'keeper to have scored twice in one game.

soccer 2

BIGGEST FOOTBALL STADIUM
The Maracaña Stadium in Rio de Janeiro, Brazil, has a normal capacity of 205,000, with seats for 155,000.

BIGGEST CROWD
The largest ever crowd at a football match consisted of 199,854 people, for the World Cup deciding match between Brazil and Uruguay at the Maracaña Stadium, Rio de Janeiro, Brazil, on 16 July 1950.

The record for the greatest number of spectators at a tournament is 3,587,538, for the 52 matches in the 1994 World Cup in the USA.

MOST INTERNATIONAL APPEARANCES
The record for the greatest number of matches played for a national team is 147, by Majed Abdullah Mohammed of Saudi Arabia from 1978 to 1994.

MOST INTERNATIONAL GOALS
The most goals by a player in an international match is 10, by Sofus Nielsen for Denmark v. France (17–1) in the 1908 Olympics and by Gottfried Fuchs for Germany v. Russia (16–0) in the 1912 Olympic tournament (consolation event) in Sweden.

MOST SUCCESSFUL INTERNATIONAL GOALKEEPER
The longest period that a goalkeeper has prevented goals in international matches is 1,142 minutes, by Dino Zoff (Italy) from Sept 1972 to June 1974.

HIGHEST INTERNATIONAL MARGIN
The highest winning margin in an international is 17, by England in their 17–0 victory over Australia at Sydney, Australia, on 30 June 1951 (not listed by England as a full international) and by Iran in their 17–0 win over the Maldives at Damascus, Syria, in June 1997.

FASTEST INTERNATIONAL HAT-TRICK
The fastest time in which three goals have been scored in an international is 3½ minutes, by George Hall of Tottenham Hotspur for England against Ireland at Old Trafford. Manchester, UK, on 16 Nov 1938.

MOST INDIVIDUAL WORLD CUP WINS
Pelé (Brazil) is the only player to have been a member of three World Cup-winning teams, in 1958, 1962 and 1970.

MOST WORLD CUP GOALS
Gerd Müller (West Germany) scored a record 14 goals in the World Cup; 10 in 1970 and four in 1974.

Just Fontaine (France) has scored the most goals in one tournament, with a total of 13 in six games in 1958.

Alcides Ghiggia (Uruguay, 1950) and Jairzinho (Brazil, 1970) are the only players to have scored in every match in every round of a final series.

Brazil hold the team record, having scored 173 goals in a total of 80 matches since 1930.

MOST EUROPEAN CHAMPIONSHIPS WINS
Germany has won the European Championships a record three times, in 1972 and 1980 (as West Germany) and in 1996. Jürgen Klinsmann is pictured (centre) after the 1996 final at Wembley, London, UK. Germany beat the Czech Republic 2–1 in the first final of any senior championship to be decided by a 'golden goal'.

MOST GOALS IN A WORLD CUP GAME
The record for the most goals in a game in the finals stage of the World Cup is 11. This has been achieved three times: when Brazil beat Poland 6–5 in Italy on 5 June 1938; in Hungary's 8–3 victory over Germany in Switzerland on 20 June 1954; and when Hungary beat El Salvador 10–1 in Spain on 15 June 1982.

Oleg Salenko scored five goals in Russia's 6–1 win over Cameroon on 28 June 1994 — a record for a player in one game.

MOST GOALS IN A WORLD CUP FINAL
The record for the most goals in a World Cup final is seven, when Brazil beat Sweden 5–2 in Stockholm, Sweden, on 29 June 1958.

Geoff Hurst scored three goals — the only hat-trick in a final — when England beat West Germany 4–2 at Wembley Stadium, London, UK, on 30 June 1966.

FASTEST WORLD CUP GOALS
Bryan Robson (England) scored 27 seconds into a match against France at Bilbao, Spain, on 16 June 1982.

Based on timing from film, Vaclav Masek of Czechoslovakia scored against Mexico in 15 seconds at Viña del Mar, Chile, in 1962.

MOST WORLD CUP APPEARANCES
The record number of World Cup tournaments participated in by a player is five, by Antonio Carbajal of Mexico (1950, 1954, 1958, 1962 and 1966); and Lothar Matthäus of (West) Germany (1982, 1986, 1990, 1994 and 1998). Matthäus also holds the record for matches played, with 25.

MOST WORLD CUP HAT-TRICKS
Four players have scored two hat-tricks in World Cup tournaments: Sandor Kocsis (Hungary) at the 1954 tournament in Switzerland; Just Fontaine (France) in Sweden in 1958; Gerd Müller (West Germany) at the 1970 tournament in Mexico; and Gabriele Batistuta (Argentina, pictured) in his World Cup debut against Greece in the USA in 1994 and against Jamaica in France in 1998.

YOUNGEST WORLD CUP PLAYER
Norman Whiteside was 17 years 41 days old when he played for Northern Ireland against Yugoslavia in June 1982.

OLDEST WORLD CUP PLAYER
Roger Milla was 42 years 39 days old when he played for Cameroon against Russia on 28 June 1994.

MOST OLYMPIC WINS
The Olympic football championship has been won three times by Great Britain (1900, 1908 and 1912) and Hungary (1952, 1964 and 1968).

MOST COPA AMERICA WINS
The record for wins in the Copa America (the South American Championships until 1974) is 14, by Uruguay (1916–17, 1920, 1923–24, 1926, 1935, 1942, 1956, 1959, 1967, 1983, 1987 and 1995); and Argentina (1921, 1925, 1927, 1929, 1937, 1941, 1945–47, 1955, 1957, 1959, 1991 and 1993).

MOST CONCACAF GOLD CUP WINS
The CONCACAF Gold Cup (the CONCACAF Championships until 1990) has been won 10 times by Costa Rica (1941, 1946, 1948, 1953, 1955, 1960, 1961, 1963, 1969 and 1989).

MOST ASIAN CUP WINS
The Asian Cup, held every four years since 1956, has been won three times by Iran (1968, 1972 and 1976) and Saudi Arabia (1984, 1988 and 1996).

MOST AFRICAN CUP OF NATIONS WINS
The African Cup Of Nations was first contested in 1957. Two countries have each won four times: Ghana in 1963, 1965, 1978 and 1982, and Egypt in 1957, 1959, 1986 and 1998.

MOST WOMEN'S WORLD CUP WINS
The women's cup was initiated in 1991 and is held every four years. It was won by the USA in 1991 and by Norway in 1995.

HIGHEST SCORE IN A WOMEN'S INTERNATIONAL
The record score in a women's international game is 21–0, by China against the Philippines at the 1995 Asian Women's Championship in Malaysia; by Canada against Puerto Rico at Centennial Park, Toronto, Canada, on 28 Aug 1998; by Australia against American Samoa at Mt Smart Stadium, Auckland, New Zealand, on 9 Oct 1998; and by New Zealand against Samoa on the same date and at the same place.

The highest ever score during the women's World Cup Finals, 8–0, was by Sweden against Japan in Foshan, China, on 19 Nov 1991 and by Norway against Nigeria on 6 June 1995 in Karlstad, Sweden.

MOST WORLD CUP WINS

Brazil have won the World Cup a record four times (1958, 1962, 1970 and 1994); Romario is pictured holding the trophy after their most recent win. Brazil are the only team to have taken part in all 16 finals tournaments and have won a record 53 matches out of 80 in the finals stage.

american football

MOST SUPER BOWL WINS
The greatest number of team wins is five, by the San Francisco 49ers (1982, 1985, 1989–90 and 1995) and by the Dallas Cowboys (1972, 1978, 1993–94 and 1996).

The individual player to have been on the most winning teams is Charles Hayley, who won five Super Bowls, two for the San Francisco 49ers (1989–90) and three for the Dallas Cowboys (1993–94 and 1996).

Chuck Noll holds the record for the most wins by a coach. He led the Pittsburgh Steelers to four Super Bowl titles between 1975 and 1980: IX, X, XIII and XIV.

HIGHEST SUPER BOWL SCORES
The highest team score was set by the San Francisco 49ers when they beat the Denver Broncos 55–10 at New Orleans, Louisiana, USA, on 28 Jan 1990. As well as being the highest victory margin, San Francisco's eight touchdowns is also a Super Bowl record.

In 1995 the San Francisco 49ers also set the record for the highest aggregate score when they beat the San Diego Chargers 49–26.

HIGHEST NFL ATTENDANCE
The record for the greatest number of spectators at a regular season game is 102,368, on 10 Nov 1957. The game was between the LA Rams and the San Francisco 49ers, and was played at the Los Angeles Coliseum, California, USA.

MOST YARDS GAINED RUSHING
On 26 Nov 1998 Barry Sanders of the Detroit Lions became only the second back to rush for more than 15,000 yards, with a career total at the end of the 1998 season of 15,269 yards. The record is held by Walter Payton of the Chicago Bears, who rushed for 16,726 yards between 1975 and 1987.

MOST NFL TITLES
The Green Bay Packers have won a record 13 NFL/NFC titles: 1929–31, 1936, 1939, 1944, 1961–62, 1965–67, 1996 and 1997.

MOST AFL TITLES
The record for the most AFL/AFC titles is held by the Buffalo Bills, who won six titles, in 1964 and 1965 and from 1990 to 1993. The last four titles led to Super Bowl finals, but the Bills lost on each occasion — another record.

MOST CONSECUTIVE NFL WINS
The Chicago Bears hold the record for the most consecutive NFL regular season victories, winning 17 games in succession in 1933 and 1934.

The Miami Dolphins set a record for the most consecutive games won in a single season, with 14 in 1972.

LONGEST UNBEATEN NFL RUN
The most consecutive games played without defeat in the NFL is 25, by the Canton Bulldogs, with a total of 22 wins and three ties between 1921 and 1923.

MOST NFL WINS IN A SEASON
The record for the most wins in a season is 15, by the San Francisco 49ers in 1984, the Chicago Bears in 1985 and the Minnesota Vikings in 1998.

The Miami Dolphins won all their games in the 1972 season (14 regular season matches and three play-off games, including the Super Bowl).

HIGHEST NFL SCORES
The highest individual team score in a regular season game is 72, by the Washington Redskins against the New York Giants (who scored 41) on 27 Nov 1966. This game also holds the record for the highest aggregate score for an NFL game.

The Chicago Bears beat the Washington Redskins 73–0 in the NFL Championship game on 8 Dec 1940.

MOST NFL GAMES PLAYED
George Blanda played in 340 games in a record 26 seasons in the NFL (Chicago Bears 1949–58, Baltimore Colts 1950, Houston Oilers 1960–66 and Oakland Raiders 1967–75).

MOST SUCCESSFUL NFL COACH
The record for the greatest number of games won as coach is 347, by Don Shula for the Baltimore Colts (1963–69) and the Miami Dolphins (1970–95).

MOST NFL GAMES LOST
The Tampa Bay Buccaneers lost a record 26 consecutive games in 1976 and 1977.

LONGEST NFL PASS COMPLETION
A pass completion of 99 yards has been achieved on eight occasions and has always resulted in a touchdown. The most recent 99-yard pass was from Brett Favre to Robert Brooks of the Green Bay Packers against the Chicago Bears on 11 Sept 1995.

LONGEST FIELD GOAL
The longest field goal kicked is 63 yards, by Tom Dempsey of the New Orleans Saints and Jason Elam (pictured) of the Denver Broncos. Dempsey's record was set on 8 Nov 1970 while playing against the Detroit Lions — with two seconds remaining, and with the Saints trailing 17–16, Dempsey stepped up and made his historic kick. The record was equalled on 25 Oct 1998 when Elam's kick for the Broncos at the end of the first half against the Jacksonville Jaguars sailed between the posts. Dempsey was watching the game on TV and said he cheered when the record was equalled. Elam also holds the record for being the most accurate point-after-touchdown maker in NFL history, having converted 259 out of 260 during his six-year career with the Broncos.

LONGEST NFL PUNT
Steve O'Neal kicked a punt of 98 yards for the New York Jets against the Denver Broncos on 21 Sept 1969.

LONGEST NFL PUNT RETURN
The longest return is 103 yards, by Robert Bailey for the Los Angeles Rams against the New Orleans Saints on 23 Oct 1994.

LONGEST INTERCEPTION RETURNS IN AN NFL GAME
The longest recorded return for a touchdown is 104 yards. It was achieved by James Willis and Troy Vincent for the Philadelphia Eagles in a game against the Dallas Cowboys on 3 Nov 1996. Willis returned the ball 14 yards and lateralled it to Vincent, who returned it for the remaining 90 yards.

The longest interception return for a touchdown by an individual player is 103 yards. The record was set by Vencie Glenn for the San Diego Chargers in a game against the Denver Broncos on 29 Nov 1987. This was equalled by Louis Oliver for the Miami Dolphins against the Buffalo Bills on 4 Oct 1992.

LONGEST NFL KICKOFF RETURN
The record for the longest ever NFL kickoff return for a touchdown is 106 yards, by three players: Al Carmichael for the Green Bay Packers against the Chicago Bears on 7 Oct 1956; Noland Smith for the Kansas City Chiefs against the Denver Broncos on 17 Dec 1967; and Roy Green for the St Louis Cardinals against the Dallas Cowboys on 21 Oct 1979.

MOST NFL KICKOFF RETURNS
The New York Giants hold the record for the most kickoff returns in one game, making 12 against Washington on 27 Nov 1966. Washington themselves had seven returns, so there was a record number of kickoff returns in one game.

LONGEST RUNS FROM SCRIMMAGE (NCAA)
The record for the longest run from scrimmage is 99 yards, by: Gale Sayers (Kansas *v.* Nebraska), 1963; Max Anderson (Arizona State v. Wyoming), 1967; Ralph Thompson (West Texas State *v.* Wichita State), 1970; and Kelsey Finch (Tennessee *v.* Florida), 1977.

LARGEST CROWD (NCAA BOWL GAMES)
A record 106,869 people were at the 1973 Rose Bowl when Southern Cal. beat Ohio State 42–17.

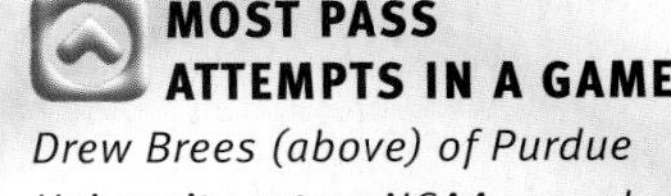

MOST PASS ATTEMPTS IN A GAME

Drew Brees (above) of Purdue University set an NCAA record of 83 pass attempts against Wisconsin in Oct 1998. He also made 55 pass completions, equalling the record set by Rusty LaRue of Wake Forest. The NFL record for pass attempts is 70 (45 completions) by Drew Bledsoe for the New England Patriots against the Minnesota Vikings on 13 Nov 1994.

MOST PASSES COMPLETED

Dan Marino of the Miami Dolphins has completed more passes than any other NFL footballer, with 4,763 between 1983 and 1998. Marino also holds records for the most passing attempts (7,989); the most yards gained passing in a career (58,913) and in a season (5,084 in 1984); and the most touchdown passes in a career (408) and in a season (48 in 1984).

cricket

HIGHEST TEAM INNINGS
Victoria scored 1,107 runs in 10 hr 30 min v. New South Wales in an Australian Sheffield Shield match at Melbourne in Dec 1926.

The Test record is 952 for six, by Sri Lanka v. India at Colombo, Sri Lanka, from 4 to 6 Aug 1997.

LOWEST TEAM INNINGS
The traditional first-class record is 12, shared by two teams: Oxford University (a man short) v. Marylebone Cricket Club at Cowley Marsh, Oxford, UK, in 1877, and Northamptonshire v. Gloucestershire at Gloucester, UK, in June 1907.

A team called 'The Bs' scored six in their second innings against England at Lord's, London, UK, in 1810.

The Test match record is 26, by New Zealand v. England at Auckland, New Zealand, in 1955.

MOST SIXES IN AN INNINGS
Andrew Symonds hit 16 sixes in an innings of 254 not out for Gloucestershire v. Glamorgan in a County Championship match at Abergavenny, UK, in Aug 1995. He added four in his second innings of 76, for a record match total of 20.

Chris Cairns hit a record 14 sixes in a limited-overs international, in his 157 (from 89 deliveries) for New Zealand against Kenya at Nairobi, Kenya, on 7 Sept 1997.

MOST SIXES IN A TEST INNINGS
Wasim Akram hit a record 12 sixes in his 257 not out for Pakistan against Zimbabwe at Sheikhupura, Pakistan, from 18 to 20 Oct 1996. Akram also holds the record for the greatest number of wickets taken in a one-day international career, with a total of 371 in 265 matches — an average of 23.49 — between 1985 and 1999.

MOST WICKETS IN A MATCH
Jim Laker took 19 wickets for 90 runs (9–37 and 10–53) for England v. Australia at Old Trafford, UK, in July 1956.

MOST WICKETS IN AN INNINGS
Alfred Freeman of Kent, UK, took all 10 wickets in an innings on a record three occasions, against Lancashire in 1929 and 1931 and against Essex in 1930.

The fewest runs to have been scored off a bowler taking all 10 wickets is 10, off Hedley Verity for Yorkshire v. Nottinghamshire at Leeds, UK, in 1932 (the full analyses for earlier performances of the feat are unknown).

MOST CATCHES (FIELDER)
The greatest number of catches in an innings is seven, by Michael Stewart for Surrey against Northamptonshire at Northampton, UK, on 7 June 1957, and by Anthony Brown for Gloucestershire against Nottinghamshire at Trent Bridge, Nottingham, UK, on 26 July 1966.

MOST CATCHES IN A MATCH (FIELDER)
Walter Hammond held a total of 10 catches for Gloucestershire in a game against Surrey at Cheltenham, UK, from 16 to 17 Aug 1928.

MOST CATCHES IN A TEST MATCH (FIELDER)
Seven catches were made by Greg Chappell for Australia v. England at Perth, Australia, in 1974, Yajurvindra Singh for India v. England at Bangalore, India, in 1977, and Hashan Prasantha Tillekeratne for Sri Lanka v. New Zealand at Colombo, Sri Lanka, in 1992.

MOST DISMISSALS (WICKET KEEPER)
The record for the most ever dismissals in an innings is nine, by Tahir Rashid (eight catches and a stumping) for Habib Bank against Pakistan Automobile Corporation at Gujranwala, Pakistan, in Nov 1992, and by Wayne James (seven catches and two stumpings) for Matabeleland against Mashonaland Country Districts at Bulawayo, Zimbabwe, on 19 April 1996.

The most stumpings in an innings is six, by Hugo Yarnold for Worcestershire against Scotland at Broughty Ferry, Dundee, UK, on 2 July 1951.

The most dismissals in a match is 13, by Wayne James (11 catches, two stumpings) for Matabeleland v. Mashonaland Country Districts at Bulawayo, Zimbabwe, from 19 to 21 April 1996.

The most stumpings in a match is nine, by Frederick Huish for Kent v. Surrey at The Oval, London, UK, in 1911.

MOST DISMISSALS IN TESTS (WICKET KEEPER)
The record dismissals in an innings is seven (all caught), by Wasim Bari for Pakistan v. New Zealand at Auckland, New Zealand, in Feb 1979, Bob Taylor for England v. India at Bombay, India, in Feb 1980, and Ian Smith for New Zealand v. Sri Lanka at Hamilton, New Zealand, in Feb 1991.

The record in a match is 11, all caught, by Jack Russell for England v. South Africa at Johannesburg, South Africa, from 30 Nov to 3 Dec 1995.

MOST TEST APPEARANCES
Allan Border of Australia played 156 Test matches between 1979 and 1994.

MOST ONE-DAY CENTURIES IN CAREER
In Sept 1998 Sachin Ramesh Tendulkar scored his 18th one-day international century playing for India against Zimbabwe in Bulawayo, Zimbabwe. In doing so he broke the record held by Desmond Haynes of the West Indies. Tendulkar has since scored three further one-day centuries and also holds the record for the highest number of runs in a calendar year in limited-overs international cricket.

FASTEST BOWLERS
Allan Donald of South Africa is one of the fastest bowlers playing today, with deliveries that are regularly recorded at speeds of up to 150 km/h (93 mph). Nicknamed 'White Lightning', Donald gives the batsman only about 4/10 of a second to react from the moment a ball leaves his hand to the moment it arrives at the wicket. This devastating speed contributed to his 107 international wickets in Test matches and one-day internationals in 1998, which made him the world's leading wicket-taker. The highest electronically measured speed for a bowled ball is 160.45 km/h (99.7 mph), bowled by Jeff Thomson of Australia against the West Indies in Dec 1975.

MOST CAREER MATCHES PLAYED IN ONE-DAY INTERNATIONALS
Mohammad Azharuddin of India played 315 international games from the start of his career in 1985 to 1999. He has also made a record 148 career catches by a fielder.

MOST CAREER RUNS SCORED IN ONE-DAY INTERNATIONALS
Desmond Haynes of the West Indies scored a total of 8,648 runs in 238 matches (an average of 41.37 a match) from 1977 to 1994.

MOST CAREER DISMISSALS IN ONE-DAY INTERNATIONALS
Ian Healy of Australia made 234 (195 caught, 39 stumped) in 168 matches from 1988 to 1997.

MOST WICKETS IN A TEST INNINGS

India's Anil Kumble took all 10 wickets in his country's defeat of Pakistan at Delhi, India, in Feb 1999, which squared the two-match Test series. He equalled the record held by Jim Laker, who also took 10 wickets for England against Australia at Old Trafford, UK, in July 1956. While Laker conceded fewer runs than Kumble — 53 compared to 74 — Kumble took less deliveries, completing his feat in 26.3 overs to Laker's 51.2 overs.

HIGHEST INDIVIDUAL INNINGS

Brian Lara scored 501 not out in 7 hr 54 min for Warwickshire against Durham at Edgbaston, UK, in June 1994. His innings included the most runs in a day (390) and the most runs from strokes worth four or more (308: 62 fours and 10 sixes). Lara also holds the Test record, with a score of 375 in 12 hr 48 min for the West Indies against England at Recreation Ground, St John's, Antigua, in April 1994.

rugby

MOST WORLD CUP MATCH WINS

Since the Rugby Union World Cup was first contested in 1987, the competition has been won by New Zealand (1987), Australia (1991) and South Africa (1995). New Zealand hold the record for the most matches won in the championships, with 16 (six in 1987, five in 1991 and five in 1995). The All Blacks, as they are known to their fans, also set the World Cup record for the highest score when they beat Japan 145–17 at Bloemfontein, South Africa, on 4 June 1995. During the match New Zealand scored 21 tries — another World Cup record. Wing three-quarter Jonah Lomu (below) shared the tournament record for the most tries (seven) with team-mate Marc Ellis.

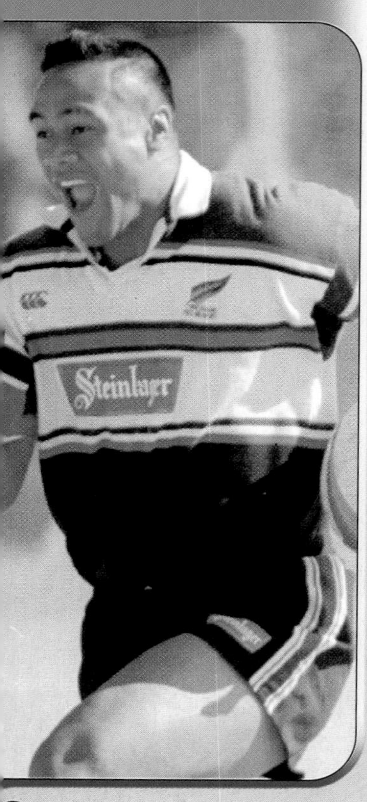

RUGBY UNION

MOST WORLD CUP POINTS

The leading scorer in World Cup matches is Gavin Hastings (Scotland), with 227 points. Hastings holds the overall record for penalties (36) and conversions (39).

The most points scored in a World Cup match by one player is 45, by Simon Culhane for New Zealand against Japan in 1995. This total included a record 20 conversions.

MOST WORLD CUP TRIES

The leading try scorer in World Cup matches is Rory Underwood (England), with a total of 11.

The most tries scored in a match by an individual is six, by Marc Ellis of New Zealand against Japan in 1995.

MOST WORLD CUP APPEARANCES

The most individual appearances is 17, by Sean Fitzpatrick of New Zealand.

MOST POINTS SCORED IN AN INTERNATIONAL

The record for the highest score in any full international was set when Hong Kong beat Singapore 164–13 in a World Cup qualifying match at Kuala Lumpur, Malaysia, on 27 Oct 1994.

The highest aggregate score between two of the eight major nations under the modern points system is 109. This occurred when South Africa beat Wales 96–13 at Pretoria, South Africa, on 27 June 1998.

The most points scored by one player in an international match is 50 points (10 tries), by Hong Kong's Ashley Billington in the World Cup qualifying match between Hong Kong and Singapore at Kuala Lumpur, Malaysia, on 27 Oct 1994.

The highest individual points score in any match between the major nations is 27, by Rob Andrew (one try, two conversions, five penalty goals and a drop goal) for England against South Africa at Pretoria, South Africa, on 4 June 1994.

The record number of tries scored by one participant in a match between the major nations is five, by George Lindsay for Scotland against Wales on 26 Feb 1887, and by Douglas 'Daniel' Lambert for England against France on 5 Jan 1907.

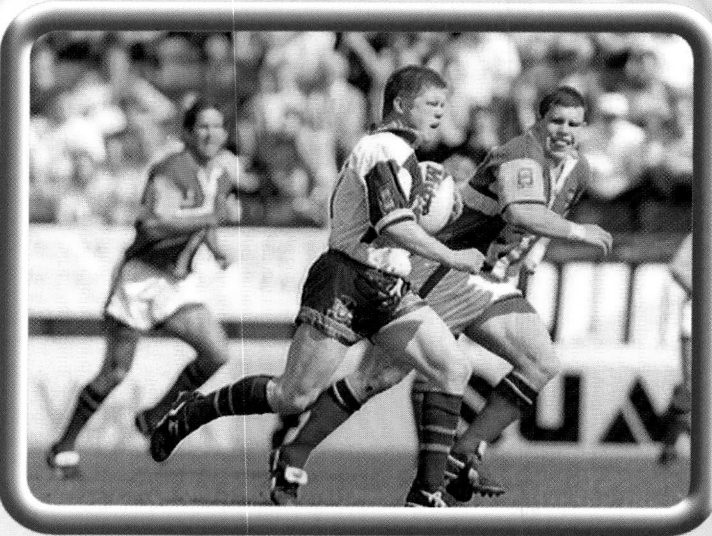

MOST POINTS IN A RUGBY LEAGUE MATCH

Dean Marwood (centre of picture) scored 42 points in two separate games, when Workington beat Highfield 78–0 on 1 Nov 1992 and when they beat Leigh 94–4 on 26 Feb 1995. This is a record for a League match. The most points scored in any game was 53, by George 'Tich' West for Hull Kingston Rovers in their 73–5 defeat of Brookland Rovers in the Challenge Cup on 4 March 1905.

MOST GOALS KICKED IN AN INTERNATIONAL

The most penalty goals kicked in a match is eight, by: Mark Wyatt (Canada) against Scotland at St John, New Brunswick, Canada, on 25 May 1991; Neil Jenkins (Wales) against Canada at Cardiff, S Glamorgan, UK, on 10 Nov 1993; Santiago Meson (Argentina) against Canada at Buenos Aires, Argentina, on 12 March 1995; Gavin Hastings (Scotland) against Tonga at Pretoria, South Africa, on 30 May 1995; Thierry Lacroix (France) against Ireland at Durban, South Africa, on 10 June 1995; and Paul Burke (Ireland) against Italy at Dublin, Republic of Ireland, on 4 Jan 1997.

FASTEST TRIES

The fastest try in an international game occurred when Herbert 'Bart' Price scored less than 10 seconds after kick-off for England against Wales at Twickenham, UK, on 20 Jan 1923.

The fastest known try in any game was scored eight seconds after kick-off, by Andrew Brown for Widden Old Boys against Old Ashtonians at Gloucester, UK, on 22 Nov 1990.

MOST POINTS SCORED IN INTERNATIONAL CAREERS

Michael Lynagh scored a record 911 points in 72 international matches for Australia between 1984 and 1995.

The most tries is 64, by David Campese in 101 internationals for Australia between 1982 and 1996.

MOST INTERNATIONAL APPEARANCES

Philippe Sella (France) played 111 times for France between 1982 and 1995.

The most consecutive appearances is 63, by Sean Fitzpatrick (New Zealand) between 1986 and 1995.

MOST HONG KONG SEVENS WINS

Fiji have won the Hong Kong Sevens nine times (1977–78, 1980, 1984, 1990–92 and 1998–99). The 1997 event was replaced by the World Cup Sevens, which was also won by Fiji.

BIGGEST CROWD

The biggest ever paying attendance was 104,000 people, for Scotland's 12–10 win over Wales at Murrayfield, Edinburgh, UK, on 1 March 1975.

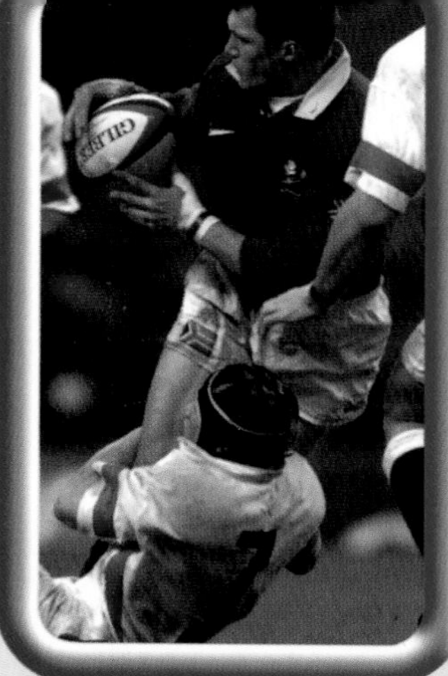

MOST CONSECUTIVE UNION WINS

The record for consecutive international wins is 17, shared by South Africa and New Zealand. England's Neil Back is pictured tackling South Africa's Andre Snyman when the teams met at Twickenham, UK, on 5 Dec 1998. England won 13–7, preventing the Springboks from taking the record outright.

RUGBY LEAGUE

MOST WORLD CUP WINS

Australia have won the World Cup seven times, in 1957, 1968, 1970, 1977, 1988, 1992 and 1995. They also won the International Championship of 1975.

HIGHEST SCORE IN AN INTERNATIONAL

Australia defeated South Africa 86–6 at Gateshead, Tyne & Wear, UK, on 10 Oct 1995.

MOST CAREER POINTS

Neil Fox scored 6,220 points (2,575 goals, including four drop goals, and 358 tries) in a senior Rugby League career that lasted from 10 April 1956 to 19 Aug 1979. Of those, 4,488 were for Wakefield Trinity, 1,089 were for five other clubs, 228 were for Great Britain and 147 were for Yorkshire; the remaining 268 were scored in other representative games.

MOST CAREER TRIES

Brian Bevan (Australia) scored a total of 796 tries in 18 seasons from 1945 to 1964. He scored 740 tries for Warrington, 17 for Blackpool and 39 in representative matches.

MOST CAREER GOALS

Jim Sullivan (Wigan) kicked 2,867 goals in his club and representative career from 1921 to 1946.

MOST INTERNATIONAL MATCHES

Jim Sullivan played 60 internationals for Wales and Great Britain from 1921 to 1939, kicked the most goals (160) and scored the most points (329).

MOST INTERNATIONAL TRIES

Michael Sullivan (Huddersfield, Wigan, St Helens, York and Dewsbury) scored a record 45 tries in 51 matches for England and Great Britain from 1954 to 1963.

MOST POINTS SCORED IN A RUGBY LEAGUE INTERNATIONAL

A record 32 points were scored by Bobby Goulding (right; three tries, 10 goals) for England v. Fiji at Nadi, Fiji, on 5 Oct 1996 and by Andrew Johns (two tries, 12 goals) for Australia v. Fiji at Newcastle, NSW, Australia, on 12 July 1996.

BIGGEST CROWD

The highest attendance was 104,583 people, for a double header (Newcastle Knights v. Manly Sea Eagles and Parramatta Eels v. St George Illawarra Dragons) in Sydney, NSW, Australia, on 7 March 1999.

basketball

HIGHEST AVERAGE POINTS (NBA)

Michael Jordan, who retired from the game on 13 Jan 1999, set 21 NBA records while playing for the Chicago Bulls, including the highest average number of points per game (31.5), the most seasons as the league's leading scorer (10), the most seasons as the league's leading scorer of field goals (10) and the most seasons as the league player with the highest number of field goal attempts (10). On 20 April 1986 he scored 63 points in a play-off game against the Boston Celtics — a record number of points by an individual player in an NBA play-off game. He also played in the gold-medal-winning US Olympic teams of 1984 and 1992. Off the court Jordan owns a restaurant, has presented the TV show *Saturday Night Live* and starred in *Space Jam*, a film in which he plays basketball with cartoon characters. He has earnt more from endorsement deals than any other player.

MOST WORLD TITLES

The record for the most men's World Championship (instituted in 1950) titles is four, by Yugoslavia (1970, 1978, 1990 and 1998).

The record for the most women's World Championship titles is six, jointly held by the USA and the USSR.

HIGHEST INTERNATIONAL SCORE

In a senior international match Iraq beat Yemen by 251 to 33, at the Asian Games in New Delhi, India, in Nov 1982.

MOST NBA TITLES

The Boston Celtics have won 16 National Basketball Association titles: in 1957, from 1959 to 1966, and in 1968, 1969, 1974, 1976, 1981, 1984 and 1986.

HIGHEST NBA SCORES

The highest aggregate score in a match was 370, when the Detroit Pistons beat the Denver Nuggets 186–184 at Denver, Colorado, USA, on 13 Dec 1983. Three overtimes were played after a 145–145 tie in regulation time.

The highest ever aggregate score in regulation time was 320, when the Golden State Warriors beat the Denver Nuggets 162–158 at Denver, Colorado, USA, on 2 Nov 1990.

The highest-scoring individual in an NBA game was Wilt Chamberlain, who scored a record 100 points for the Philadelphia Warriors against the New York Knicks at Hershey, Pennsylvania, USA, on 2 March 1962. This included a record 36 field goals and 28 free throws from 32 attempts, as well as a record 59 points in one half.

Chamberlain's free throws record was equalled by Adrian Dantley for Utah against Houston at Las Vegas, Nevada, USA, in Jan 1984.

GREATEST NBA WINNING MARGIN

The Cleveland Cavaliers beat the Miami Heat 148–80 on 17 Dec 1991 — a record margin of 68 points.

MOST NBA SEASON WINS

The Chicago Bulls had 72 NBA wins in the 1995/96 season — a record number within a single season.

LONGEST NBA WINNING STREAK

The Los Angeles Lakers won a record 33 games in succession from 5 Nov 1971 to 7 Jan 1972.

MOST NBA DEFENSIVE PLAYER AWARDS

Dikembe Mutombo (number 55, bottom left of picture) of the Atlanta Hawks secured a record-breaking third NBA Defensive Player of the Year award in May 1998. He first won the title in the 1994/95 season with the Denver Nuggets, then again in the 1996/97 season with Atlanta. Here he is seen preparing to rebound in a game against the LA Lakers.

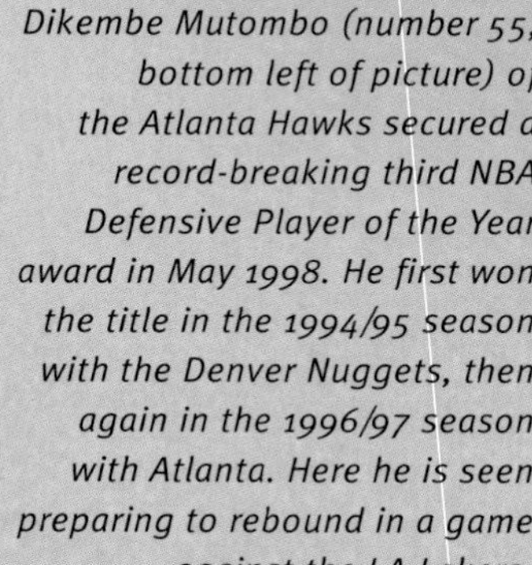

MOST NBA GAMES

Robert Parish played 1,611 regular season games over 21 seasons for the Golden State Warriors (1976–80), the Boston Celtics (1980–94), the Charlotte Hornets (1994–96) and the Chicago Bulls (1996–97).

The record for the greatest number of complete games played in a single season is 79, by Wilt Chamberlain for Philadelphia in 1961/62. During this period he was on court for a record total of 3,882 minutes.

The record for most consecutive games is 1,028, by A.C. Green for the LA Lakers, Phoenix Suns and Dallas Mavericks from 19 Nov 1986 to 4 May 1999.

MOST NBA POINTS

Kareem Abdul-Jabbar scored a record 38,387 points during his NBA career — an average of 24.6 points per game. This included a record 15,837 field goals in regular season games and 5,762 points and a record 2,356 field goals in NBA play-off games.

MOST POINTS IN NBA SEASON

In 1961/62 Wilt Chamberlain set season records for Philadelphia for points and scoring average, with 4,029 at 50.4 per game, and for field goals (1,597).

YOUNGEST NBA PLAYER

Jermaine O'Neal was 18 years 53 days old when he made his debut for the Portland Trail Blazers against the Denver Nuggets on 5 Dec 1996.

OLDEST REGULAR NBA PLAYER

Robert Parish of the Chicago Bulls was still playing at the age of 43 years 231 days on 19 April 1997.

BIGGEST NBA CROWD

Atlanta Hawks forward Tyrone Corbin (right of picture) drives past Chicago Bulls guard Ron Harper in Atlanta, Georgia, USA, on 27 March 1998. The Bulls defeated the Hawks 89–74 before an NBA record crowd of 62,046 people.

HIGHEST MATCH ATTENDANCE
The biggest ever crowd at a basketball match was 80,000 people, for the final of the European Cup Winners' Cup between AEK Athens and Slavia Prague at the Olympic Stadium, Athens, Greece, on 4 April 1968.

HIGHEST VERTICAL DUNK
Sean Williams and Michael Wilson, both of the Harlem Globetrotters, dunked a basketball at a rim height of 3.58 m (11 ft 8 in) at Disney-MGM Studios, Orlando, Florida, USA, on 16 Sept 1996.

LONGEST FIELD GOAL IN A GAME
Christopher Eddy scored a 27.49-m (90-ft 2¼-in) field goal for Fairview High School against Iroquois High School at Erie, Pennsylvania, USA, on 25 Feb 1989. The record-breaking shot was made in overtime and won the game 51–50 for Fairview.

TOP SHOOTING SPEEDS
John Connolly scored 280 out of 326 attempts in 10 minutes using one basketball and one rebounder at St. Peter's School, Pacifica, California, USA, on 12 Oct 1998.

Jeff Liles scored 53 points in one minute, shooting from seven positions as stated by Guinness World Records rules, at the YMCA in Carthage, Missouri, USA, on 8 May 1997.

In 24 hours on 29 and 30 Sept 1990 Fred Newman scored 20,371 free throws from a total of 22,049 taken (a success rate of 92.39%) at Caltech, Pasadena, California, USA.

Ted St. Martin scored a record 5,221 consecutive free throws at Jacksonville, Florida, USA, on 28 April 1996.

MOST BALLS SPUN
On 26 May 1999 Michael Kettman (USA) spun 28 basketballs across his chest on the *Guinness® World Records* show.

MOST BALLS DRIBBLED
Joseph Odhiambo of Arizona, USA, has demonstrated the unique ability to dribble five basketballs — two with each hand, the fifth between his feet.

LONGEST DRIBBLE
Jamie Borges (USA) dribbled a ball 155.9 km (96.89 miles) in 24 hours without 'travelling' at Barrington High School, Rhode Island, USA, in May 1998.

MOST OLYMPIC TITLES
The USA has won 11 men's Olympic titles, winning 100 matches and losing just two since 1936. When the rules on amateurism were relaxed, star NBA players such as Shaquille O'Neal (pictured with actress Meagan Good), Michael Jordan, Magic Johnson and Charles Barkley made the 'Dream Teams' of 1992 and 1996 even stronger. The women's title has been won a record three times by the USSR in 1976, 1980 and 1992 (the last as the Unified team from the ex-USSR) and by the USA in 1984, 1988 and 1996.

baseball & softball

BIGGEST CONTRACT
The biggest baseball contract is an average of $15 million (£9.1 million) per year for seven years. It was signed by Kevin Brown of the LA Dodgers on 12 Dec 1998. On completion, Brown's contract will be worth a total of $105 million (£63.7 million).

MOST SPECTATORS
An estimated 114,000 spectators watched a demonstration game between Australia and an American Services team during the Olympic Games in Melbourne, Australia, on 1 Dec 1956.

The record attendance for a single game in the USA is 92,706, for a game between the Los Angeles Dodgers and the Chicago White Sox on 6 Oct 1959.

The record for the highest ever season's attendance in all major league baseball games is 70,372,221, in 1998.

MOST VALUABLE WORLD SERIES PLAYER
Three players have won the Most Valuable Player award twice: Sandy Koufax (Los Angeles NL, 1963 and 1965); Bob Gibson (St Louis NL, 1964 and 1967); and Reggie Jackson (Oakland AL, 1973, New York AL, 1977).

OLDEST PLAYER
Leroy 'Satchel' Paige pitched for the Kansas City As (AL) at the age of 59 years 80 days on 25 Sept 1965.

YOUNGEST PLAYER
Joseph Nuxhall played one game for Cincinnati in June 1944, aged 15 years 314 days, and did not play again in the National League until 1952.

MOST CONSECUTIVE HITS
Pinky Higgins had 12 consecutive hits for Boston (AL) from 19 to 21 June 1938. This record was equalled by Moose Droppo for Detroit (AL) from 14 to 15 July 1952.

Joe DiMaggio hit in 56 consecutive games for the New York Yankees in 1941, earning him the nickname 'Joltin' Joe'. In 223 times at bat, he had 91 hits – 56 singles, 16 doubles, four triples and 15 home runs.

MOST WORLD SERIES WINS
The New York Yankees (AL) hold the record for the most World Series wins, achieving their 24th in 1998, the year they set an American League record for the most wins in a regular season, with 114, and a total season record of 125. Here Scott Brosius, the Series' Most Valuable Player, celebrates the Yankees' triumph.

MOST HOME RUNS
Hank Aaron scored 755 career home runs: 733 for the Milwaukee Braves (NL, 1954–65) and the Atlanta Braves (NL, 1966–74), and 22 for the Milwaukee Brewers (AL) from 1975 to 1976.

The record for the most home runs in a major league game is four. This was first achieved by Bobby Lowe for Boston against Cincinnati on 30 May 1894 and has been repeated 11 times since.

The most consecutive games hitting home runs is eight, achieved by Dale Long for Pittsburgh (NL) in May 1956, Don Mattingly for New York (AL) in July 1987 and Ken Griffey Jr for Seattle (AL) in July 1993.

LONGEST HOME RUN
The record for the longest measured home run in a major league game is 193 m (634 ft), by Mickey Mantle for the New York Yankees against the Detroit Tigers at Briggs Stadium, Detroit, USA, in Sept 1960.

LONGEST GAME
The Brooklyn Dodgers (NL) and the Boston Braves played to a 1–1 tie after 26 innings on 1 May 1920. The Chicago White Sox (AL) played the longest game in elapsed time – 8 hr 6 min – before beating the Milwaukee Brewers 7–6 in the 25th inning on 9 May 1984.

MOST GAMES PLAYED
Pete Rose played in 3,562 games and was at bat a record 14,053 times for Cincinnati (NL, 1963–78, 1984–86), Philadelphia (NL, 1979–83) and Montreal (NL, 1984).

Cal Ripken played a total of 2,632 consecutive games for the Baltimore Orioles between 30 May 1982 and 19 Sept 1998.

MOST GAMES PITCHED
The record for the most games pitched in a single career is 1,071, by Dennis Eckersly. He played for five different teams between 1975 and 1998.

MOST STRIKEOUTS

Kerry Wood (below) of the Chicago Cubs (NL) threw 20 strikeouts in a nine-inning game on 6 May 1998, equalling the major league record. Here he's shown pitching in the fifth inning of the game, against the Houston Astros in Chicago. Wood matched the record of five-time Cy Young award-winner Roger Clemens, who struck out 20 batters on two occasions when playing for the Boston Red Sox (AL).

HIGHEST-PAID CATCHER
Mike Piazza (right) of the NY Mets has the most lucrative contract ever signed by a catcher. Over seven years he stands to earn a total of $91 million (£56.2 million). He also gets the use of a luxury box for family and friends at all home games, and a hotel suite when the club is on the road.

MOST GAMES WON BY A PITCHER
The most games won by a pitcher is 511, by Cy Young, who also played a record 749 complete games in his career for Cleveland (NL, 1890 to 1898), St Louis (NL, 1899 to 1900), Boston (AL, 1901 to 1908), Cleveland (AL, 1909 to 1911) and Boston (NL, 1911). Young also pitched a record total of 7,356 innings.

MOST CONSECUTIVE SCORELESS INNINGS
Orel Hershiser IV of the LA Dodgers pitched a record 59 consecutive scoreless innings from 30 Aug to 28 Sept 1988.

MOST CY YOUNG AWARDS
Five Cy Young awards have been won by Roger Clemens (Boston AL, in 1986, 1987 and 1991, and Toronto AL, in 1997 and 1998).

The most Cy Young awards won by a National League pitcher is four, by Steve Carlton (Philadelphia, 1972, 1977, 1980 and 1982) and Greg Maddux (Chicago, 1992 and Atlanta, from 1993 to 1995).

FASTEST PITCHER
The greatest reliably recorded speed at which a baseball has been pitched is 162.3 km/h (100.9 mph), by Lynn Nolan Ryan at Anaheim Stadium, California, USA, on 20 Aug 1974.

LONGEST THROW
Glen Gorbous (Canada) threw a baseball 135.88 m (445 ft 10 in) on 1 Aug 1957.

LONGEST THROW BY A WOMAN
Mildred 'Babe' Didrikson threw a baseball 90.2 m (296 ft) on 25 July 1931.

FASTEST BASE RUNNER
The record for the fastest time for circling bases is 13.3 seconds, set by Ernest Swanson at Columbus, Ohio, USA, in 1931. His average speed around the bases was 29.7 km/h (18.45 mph).

MOST WORLD SOFTBALL TITLES
The men's fast-pitch World Championship has been won four times by the USA, in 1966, 1968, 1976 (shared) and 1980, and by Canada, in 1972, 1976 (shared), 1988 and 1992.

The women's fast-pitch World Championship has been won a record six times by the USA, in 1974, 1978, 1986, 1990, 1994 and 1998.

Dot Richardson (USA) has won a record eight individual world titles.

MOST RUNS IN SOFTBALL
The most runs scored by an individual in a World Championship tournament is 19, by Marty Kernaghan (Canada) in 1988.

The most runs scored by a woman in a World Championship tournament is 13, by Kathy Elliott (USA) in 1974.

MOST STRIKEOUTS IN SOFTBALL
The most strikeouts by a pitcher in a World Championship tournament is 99, by Kevin Herlihy (New Zealand) in 1972.

The record for the most strikeouts by a woman in a World Championship tournament is 76, by Joan Joyce (USA) in 1974.

BIGGEST REPLICA BAT
The world's biggest ever replica baseball bat is 36.6 m (120 ft) high and weighs 30.85 tonnes. Modelled on the 'R43' bat made for Babe Ruth, who is credited with inventing the modern baseball bat, the replica stands in front of bat maker Hillerich & Bradsby's headquarters in Louisville, Kentucky, USA.

MOST HOME RUNS

Mark McGwire hit 70 home runs in 162 games for the St Louis Cardinals (NL) in the 1998 season. He broke Roger Maris's record of 61 home runs in 162 games for the New York Yankees (AL), which had stood since 1961. McGwire was chased most of the way to the record by Sammy Sosa of the Chicago Cubs (NL), who finished the season with 66 home runs.

auto sports

MOST SUCCESSFUL GRAND PRIX DRIVERS

The World Drivers' Championship was won five times by Juan-Manuel Fangio (Argentina), in 1951 and from 1954 to 1957. When Fangio retired in 1958 he had won 24 Grand Prix races (two shared) from a total of 51 starts.

Alain Prost (France) had 51 wins from a total of 199 races between 1980 and 1993. During his career he gained a record 798.5 Grand Prix points.

The most pole positions is 65, by the late Ayrton Senna (Brazil) from 161 races (41 wins) between 1985 and 1994.

The most Grand Prix starts is 256, by Ricardo Patrese (Italy) from 1977 to 1993.

The most Grand Prix wins in a year is nine, by Nigel Mansell (GB) in 1992 and by Michael Schumacher (Germany) in 1995.

MOST SUCCESSFUL GRAND PRIX MANUFACTURERS

The greatest number of Grand Prix race victories by a manufacturer is 119, a record held by Ferrari at the end of the 1998 Grand Prix season. Excluding the Indianapolis 500 race, included at that time in the World Drivers' Championship, Ferrari won all seven races in 1952 and the first eight (of nine) in 1953.

Williams have won a record nine Grand Prix championships (1980–81, 1986–87, 1992–94 and 1996–97).

The McLaren team won 15 of the 16 Grand Prix races in the 1988 season: Ayrton Senna had eight wins and Alain Prost had seven.

CLOSEST GRAND PRIX FINISH

Peter Gethin (GB) beat Ronnie Peterson (Sweden) by 0.01 seconds in the 1971 Italian Grand Prix.

FASTEST GRAND PRIX RACE

Peter Gethin (GB) drove at an average speed of 242.615 km/h (150.759 mph) in a BRM during the 1971 Italian Grand Prix at Monza.

FASTEST QUALIFYING LAP IN A GRAND PRIX

Keke Rosberg (Finland) set a record lap time of 1 min 5.59 sec in a Williams-Honda at the 1985 British Grand Prix at the Silverstone track. His average speed for the circuit was 258.802 km/h (160.817 mph).

OLDEST AND YOUNGEST GRAND PRIX DRIVERS

The oldest Grand Prix driver was Louis Alexandre Chiron (Monaco), who finished sixth in the Monaco Grand Prix on 22 May 1955, aged 55 years 292 days.

The youngest driver was Michael Thackwell (NZ), who drove in the Canadian Grand Prix on 28 Sept 1980 aged 19 years 182 days.

The oldest winner of a Grand Prix race was Tazio Nuvolari (Italy) at Albi, France, on 14 July 1946, aged 53 years 240 days.

The youngest winner was Bruce McLaren (NZ), who won the US Grand Prix at Sebring, Florida, aged 22 years 104 days.

Troy Ruttman (US) was just 22 years 80 days old when he won the Indianapolis 500 on 30 May 1952. It was part of the World Drivers' Championship at the time.

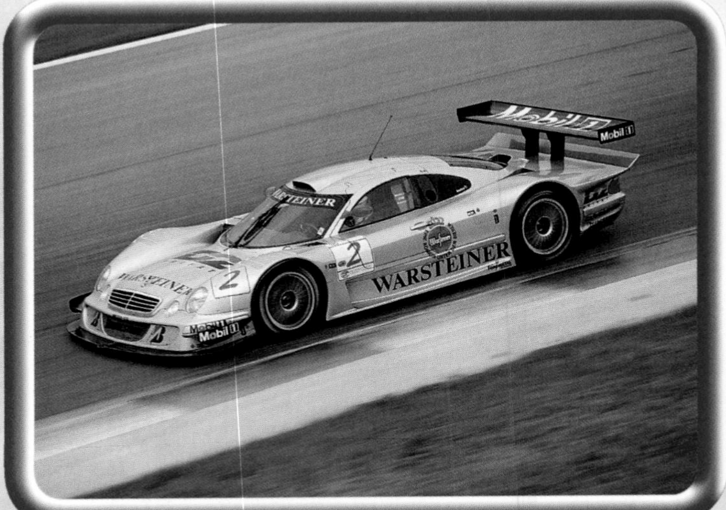

MOST SUCCESSFUL FIA GT CHAMPIONSHIP CAR

The Mercedes-Benz CLK-LM won all 10 races (winning the first two meets as the CLK-GT) of the 1998 FIA GT Championships. The two competing CLK-LM cars took double pole (places one and two on the grid) in all 10 races that make up the Championship season.

MOST SUCCESSFUL INDIANAPOLIS 500 DRIVERS

Three drivers have each won the Indianapolis 500 race four times: A.J. Foyt Jr (USA) in 1961, 1964, 1967 and 1977; Al Unser Sr (USA) in 1970, 1971, 1978 and 1987; and Rick Mears (USA) in 1979, 1984, 1988 and 1991.

BEST INDIANAPOLIS 500 STARTING STATISTICS

A.J. Foyt Jr started a record 35 consecutive Indianapolis 500 races from 1958 to 1992.

Rick Mears has started the race in pole position a record six times (1979, 1982, 1986, 1988, 1989 and 1991).

FASTEST INDIANAPOLIS 500 RACE

Arie Luyendyk (Netherlands) won in 2 hr 41 min 18.404 sec on 27 May 1990. His average speed was 299.307 km/h (185.986 mph).

FASTEST QUALIFYING LAPS IN THE INDIANAPOLIS 500

The highest average speed over the four qualifying laps is 381.392 km/h (236.992 mph), by Arie Luyendyk (Netherlands) in a Reynard-Ford Cosworth on 12 May 1996. This time included a record speed for a single lap of 382.216 km/h (237.498 mph). On 10 May 1996 Luyendyk had also set the unofficial track record of 385.041 km/h (239.26 mph).

MOST CONSECUTIVE WORLD RALLY TITLES

Tommi Makinen and his co-driver Risto Mannisenmaki (Finland) won a record third consecutive World Rally Championship title in Nov 1998. They are seen (right) in the first leg of the 18th Argentine Rally on 21 May 1998, in Cordoba, and (far right) celebrating their win in the 67th Monte Carlo Rally on 20 Jan 1999, which improves their chances of taking a fourth title. They are posing on the bonnet of the Mitsubishi Lancer that took them to their record.

BIGGEST INDIANAPOLIS 500 PRIZES
The record for the largest ever prize fund is $9,047,150 (£5.65 million), in 1999.

The biggest individual prize awarded was $1,568,150 (£957,240), won by Arie Luyendyk (Netherlands) in 1997.

MOST LE MANS WINS
The most wins by one driver is six, by Jacky Ickx (Belgium): 1969, 1975–77 and 1981–82.

The record for the most Le Mans wins by a manufacturer is 16, by Porsche (1970–71, 1976–77, 1979, 1981–87, 1993, 1996–98).

FASTEST LAPS AT LE MANS
The fastest ever lap in the Le Mans 24-hour race is 3 min 21.27 sec, by Alain Ferté (France) in a Jaguar XJR-9 on 10 June 1989. His average speed over the 13.536-km (8-mile 728-yd) lap was 242.093 km/h (150.429 mph).

Hans Stück (West Germany) set the fastest practice lap speed on 14 June 1985, attaining a speed of 251.664 km/h (156.381 mph).

GREATEST DISTANCE COVERED IN A LE MANS RACE
Dr Helmut Marko (Austria) and Gijs van Lennep (Netherlands) covered a distance of 5,335.302 km (3,315 miles 363 yd) in their 4,907 cc Flat-12 Porsche 917K Group 5 sports car from 12 to 13 June 1971.

The greatest distance covered on the current Le Mans circuit is 5,331.998 km (3,313 miles 264 yd), by Jan Lammers (Netherlands), Johnny Dumfries and Andy Wallace (both GB) in a Jaguar XJR-9 from 11 to 12 June 1988. Their average speed was 222.166 km/h (138.047 mph).

LONGEST RALLY
The Singapore Airlines London–Sydney Rally covered 31,107 km (19,330 miles) from Covent Garden, London, UK, to Sydney Opera House, Australia, in 1977. It was won by Andrew Cowan, Colin Malkin and Michael Broad (GB) in a Mercedes 280E.

MOST MONTE CARLO RALLY WINS
The Monte Carlo Rally has been won four times by Sandro Munari (Italy), in 1972 and from 1975 to 1977, and by Walter Röhrl (West Germany), with co-driver Christian Geistdorfer, in 1980 and from 1982 to 1984.

MOST WORLD RALLY CHAMPIONSHIP WINS
Juha Kankkunen (Finland) won four times, in 1986, 1987, 1991 and 1993.

Carlos Sainz (Spain) has won a record 22 World Championship races.

MOST RAC RALLY WINS
Hannu Mikkola (Finland), with co-driver Arne Hertz (Sweden), has had four wins, in a Ford Escort in 1978 and 1979 and in an Audi Quattro in 1981 and 1982.

FASTEST RACE
The Busch Clash race over a distance of 80.5 km (50 miles) on a 4.02-km-long (2-mile 880-yd), 31° banked track at Daytona, Florida, USA, is the world's fastest race. In 1987 Bill Elliott (USA) averaged a record speed of 318.331 km/h (197.802 mph) in a Ford Thunderbird during the race.

MOST SUCCESSFUL GRAND PRIX FAMILY
Graham Hill (GB) was World Drivers' Champion in 1962 and 1968 and runner-up three times. His son Damon (right) became World Drivers' Champion on 13 Oct 1996.

bike sports

MOST WORLD CHAMPIONSHIP CYCLING TITLES
Koichi Nakano of Japan won 10 professional sprint titles in a row, from 1977 to 1986.

The most wins at a men's amateur event is seven, by Daniel Morelon (France) in the sprint (1966, 1967, 1969–71, 1973 and 1975) and Leon Meredith (GB) in the 100-km motor paced (1904–05, 1907–09, 1911 and 1913).

MOST OLYMPIC CYCLING TITLES
The record for the most gold medals won in cycling events at the Olympic Games is three, by Paul Masson (France) in 1896, Francisco Verri (Italy) in 1906, Robert Charpentier (France) in 1936 and Daniel Morelon (France) in 1968 (two) and 1972. Morelon also won a silver medal at the 1976 Olympic Games and a bronze medal at the 1964 Games.

MOST TOUR DE FRANCE WINS
The greatest ever number of wins in the annual Tour de France race is five, by Jacques Anquetil (France) in 1957 and from 1961 to 1964; Eddy Merckx (Belgium) from 1969 to 1972 and in 1974; Bernard Hinault (France) in 1978, 1979, 1981, 1982 and 1985; and Miguel Induráin (Spain) from 1991 to 1995.

FASTEST TOUR DE FRANCE SPEED
The fastest average speed in the Tour de France was 39.504 km/h (24.547 mph), by Miguel Induráin (Spain) in 1992. Induráin won five consecutive Tour de France races, and won both the Giro d'Italia and the Tour de France in 1992 and 1993. He retired at the end of 1996, having never won the Vuelta a España, the major tour of his native country.

LONGEST ONE-DAY CYCLING RACE
The longest single-day 'massed start' road race is the 551 to 620-km (342 to 385-mile) event from Bordeaux to Paris, France. The highest average speed was 47.186 km/h (29.32 mph), by Herman van Springel (Belgium) in 1981. He covered 584.5 km (363 miles 176 yd) in 13 hr 35 min 18 sec.

MOST SUCCESSFUL MOTORCYCLIST
The most World Championship titles won is 15, by Giacomo Agostini (Italy): seven at 350 cc from 1968 to 1974 and eight at 500 cc from 1966 to 1972 and in 1975. Agostini is also the only man to have won two World Championships in five consecutive years (350 cc and 500 cc titles from 1968 to 1972). He won 122 races (68 at 500 cc and 54 at 350 cc) in the World Championship series between 24 April 1965 and 25 Sept 1977, including 19 in 1970. That season's total equalled the record set by Mike Hailwood (GB) in 1966.

MOST SUPERCROSS WINS
The record for the most Supercross wins is six, by Jeremy McGrath (USA), who won the AMA (American Motorcycle Association) Supercross Champion 250 cc title from 1993 to 1996 and in 1998 and 1999. McGrath also won the World Supercross title in 1994 and 1995.

MOST TOURIST TROPHY WINS
The record for the greatest number of victories in the Isle of Man TT races is 23, by Joey Dunlop (Ireland) between 1977 and 1998.

The most events won in the Isle of Man TT races in one year is four (Formula One, Junior, Senior and Production), by Phillip McCallen (Ireland) in 1996.

HIGHEST TOURIST TROPHY SPEEDS
The Isle of Man TT circuit record is 198.92 km/h (123.61 mph), set by Carl Fogarty on 12 June 1992.

On 12 June 1992 Steve Hislop set the race speed record of 1 hr 51 min 59.6 sec — an average speed of 195.17 km/h (121.28 mph) — when he won the Senior TT on a Norton.

The record for the fastest average speed around the 'Mountain' circuit by a woman is 181.29 km/h (112.65 mph), by Sandra Barnett (GB) in the Junior TT on 4 June 1997.

MOST TRIALS WINS
Jordi Tarrès (Spain) won seven World Trials Championships: in 1987, from 1989 to 1991 and from 1993 to 1995. He secured his first World Championship at the age of 20 and has also been runner-up twice.

YOUNGEST WORLD CUP WINNER
The youngest rider to win an event at the World Cup is Marco Melandri (Italy), who won the Dutch TT Grand Prix at Assen in June 1997 aged 15 years 10 months, riding for the Benetton team on a 125 cc Matteoni.

PURSUIT RECORDS
Since its introduction at the 1974 Commonwealth Games, the 4,000-m team pursuit has been won by the Australian team a record five times. They also hold the Games record of 4 min 3.84 sec, set in Victoria, British Columbia, Canada, in 1994. The world record is currently held by Italy, who recorded a time of 4 min 00.94 sec at the Manchester Velodrome, UK, in 1996.

BIGGEST BEACH RACE
More than 250,000 spectators turned out for Le Touquet Beach Race, France, on 22 Feb 1998. This annual event features 800 riders pitting themselves against Le Touquet beachfront. In the 1997 race only 100 riders completed the course. Beach racing is an offshoot of motocross, which is a popular off-road motorcycle sport. The most prestigious international motocross competition in the world is the Motocross des Nations, where the world's best riders represent their countries in a two-day contest. This annual 'World Cup' is held in a different country each year and regularly includes riders representing more than 30 countries. Each country enters three riders, one in each class — a 125 cc, a 250 cc and an open class racer.

MOST WINS IN ONE SEASON

Australian Michael Doohan's 12 wins in the 500 cc class during 1997 gave him the record for the most wins in a single class in one season. Doohan's victory on 4 Oct 1998 at the Australian Grand Prix gave him a fifth consecutive World 500 cc Motorcycle Championship, the most achieved by a currently competitive motorcyclist.

LONGEST MOTORCYCLE CIRCUIT
The 59.8-km (37-mile 284-yd) 'Mountain' circuit on the Isle of Man has hosted the principal TT races since 1911 (with minor amendments in 1920). It has 264 curves and corners and is the longest circuit used for any motorcycle race.

FASTEST MOTORCYCLE CIRCUIT
The highest average lap speed attained on any closed circuit on a motorcycle is 257.958 km/h (160.288 mph), by Yvon du Hamel (Canada) on a modified 903 cc four-cylinder Kawasaki Z1 at the 31° banked 4-km (2 $^{1}/_{2}$-mile) Daytona International Speedway, Florida, USA, in March 1973. His lap time was 56.149 seconds.

MOST WOMEN'S ROAD CHAMPIONSHIPS

The record for the most women's World Cycling Championship titles is 11, by Jeannie Longo-Ciprelli (France). She won titles for pursuit (1986 and 1988–89), road (1985–87, 1989 and 1995), points (1989) and time-trial (1995 and 1996). She also holds the world one-hour record, covering 48.159 km (29 miles 1,629 yd) in Mexico City, Mexico, on 26 Oct 1996 — the same year in which she won an Olympic gold medal.

swimming & diving

MOST OLYMPIC MEDALS
The most individual Olympic gold medals is five, by Krisztina Egerszegi (Hungary) – the 100-m backstroke in 1992, the 200-m backstroke in 1988, 1992 and 1996 and the 400-m medley in 1992.

The most individual gold medals won by a man is four by: Charles Daniels (USA) in the 220-yd freestyle in 1904, the 440-yd freestyle in 1904 and the 100-m freestyle in 1906 and 1908; Roland Matthes (GDR) in the 100-m and 200-m backstroke in 1968 and 1972; Tamás Daryni (Hungary) in the 200-m and 400-m medley in 1988 and 1992; Aleksandr Popov (Russia) in the 50-m and 100-m freestyle in 1992 and 1996; and Mark Spitz (see below).

The most golds won by a swimmer is nine, by Mark Spitz (USA) in the 4 x 100-m and 4 x 200-m freestyle in 1968, the 100-m and 200-m freestyle, the 4 x 100-m and 4 x 200-m freestyle, the 100-m and 200-m butterfly and the 4 x 100-m medley in 1972. He set a world record time in all but one (the 1968 4 x 200-m freestyle).

The most golds won by a woman is six, by Kristin Otto (GDR) in 1988: the 100-m freestyle, backstroke and butterfly, the 50-m freestyle, the 4 x 100-m freestyle and the 4 x 100-m medley.

Mark Spitz has won most medals, 11: a silver (100-m butterfly) and a bronze (100-m freestyle) in 1968 as well as his nine golds. This record was equalled by Matt Biondi (USA), with a gold in 1984, five golds, one silver and one bronze in 1988, and two golds and a silver in 1992. Spitz's record of seven medals at a single Games (1972) was also equalled by Biondi in 1988.

The most medals won by a woman is eight, by Dawn Fraser (Australia) with four gold and four silver from 1956 to 1964, Kornelia Ender (GDR) with four gold and four silver from 1972 to 1976 and Shirley Babashoff (USA) with two gold and six silver from 1972 to 1976.

MOST WINS IN ONE EVENT
Two swimmers have won the same event at three Olympic Games: Dawn Fraser (Australia) in the 100-m freestyle (1956, 1960, 1964) and Krisztina Egerszegi (Hungary) in the 200-m backstroke (1988, 1992, 1996).

MOST MEDALS IN THE WORLD CHAMPIONSHIPS
Michael Gross (West Germany) won 13 World Championship medals (five gold, five silver and three bronze) from 1982 to 1990.

The most medals won by a woman is 10, by Kornelia Ender (GDR) — eight gold and two silver in 1973 and 1975.

The most golds won by a man is six (two individual and four relay) by James Montgomery (USA) in 1973 and 1975.

The most medals at a single championship is seven, by Matt Biondi (USA) with three gold, one silver and three bronze in 1986.

DEEPEST CONSTANT-BALLAST DIVE
On 30 Nov 1998 Tanya Streeter (Cayman Islands) broke the world record for constant-ballast free-diving in fresh water, reaching a depth of 56.39 m (185 ft) at a sinkhole in Florida, USA. In a constant-ballast dive weights are worn for the ascent as well as the descent. Streeter also holds the record for the assisted free-dive using a balloon, attaining a depth of 112.77 m (370 ft) on 9 May 1998. She made this free-dive with a single breath and used a weighted sled. The Caymans have produced some of the world's best divers because of their excellent diving infrastructure and superb water conditions.

FASTEST BUTTERFLY SWIMMER
James Hickman (GB) currently holds two world records for the butterfly stroke — he took the world short-course record for 200 m in Paris, France, on 28 March 1998, in a time of 1 min 51.76 sec and then on 13 Dec of the same year went on to beat Michael Klim's world 100-m short-course record with a time of 51.02 seconds, shaving 0.02 seconds off the previous time. Hickman was in top form at the European short-course championships in Sheffield, UK, winning both the 200-m butterfly and the 200-m individual medley, as well as gaining a bronze in the 100-m individual medley. The butterfly stroke developed from a loophole in the rules governing breaststroke, and was officially recognized as a distinct stroke in 1952.

MOST WORLD RECORDS
The most world records set by a man is 32, by Arne Borg (Sweden) between 1921 and 1929.

The most world records set by a woman is 42, by Ragnhild Hveger (Denmark) from 1936 to 1942.

The most world records set by a man in currently recognized events (metric distances in 50-m pools) is 26, by Mark Spitz (USA) from 1967 to 1972.

The most world records set by a woman in currently recognized events is 23, by Kornelia Ender (GDR, now Germany) from 1973 to 1976.

The most world records set in one pool is 86, in the North Sydney pool, NSW, Australia, between 1955 and 1978. This includes 48 imperial distance records.

LONGEST SWIMS
The greatest distance known to have been swum in the ocean is 207.3 km (128 miles 1,432 yd), by Walter Poenisch Snr (USA) from Havana, Cuba, to Little Duck Key, Florida, USA, in 34 hr 15 min from 11 to 13 July 1978.

Fred Newton swam 2,938 km (1,826 miles) down the Mississippi River, USA, between Ford Dam and Carrollton Ave, New Orleans, Louisiana, from 6 July to 29 Dec 1930. He was in the water for a total of 742 hours.

The greatest distance swum in 24 hours is 101.9 km (63 miles 559 yd), by Anders Forvass (Sweden) at the 25-m Linköping public swimming pool, Sweden, from 28 to 29 Oct 1989.

The greatest distance swum by a woman in 24 hours is 95.657 km (59 miles 771 yd), by Kelly Driffield at the Mingara Leisure Centre Pool, Tumbi Umbi, NSW, Australia, in June 1997.

The greatest distance ever swum underwater is 78.92 km (49 miles 68 yd) in 24 hours, by Paul Cryne (GB) and Samir Sawan al Awami (Qatar) from Doha to Umm Said, Qatar, and back again in 1985.

The greatest distance ever to have been swum underwater by a relay team is 151.987 km (94 miles 774 yd), by six people in a swimming pool in Czechoslovakia (now Czech Republic) from 17 to 18 Oct 1987.

LONGEST RELAYS
The 20-strong New Zealand national relay team swam a record 182.807 km (113 miles 1,040 yd) in Lower Hutt, New Zealand, in a time of 24 hours from 9 to 10 Dec 1983.

BIGGEST RELAYS
The most participants in a one-day swim relay was 2,454, each of whom swam one length at the Karosa swimming club, Vysoké Myto, Czech Republic, on 1 April 1998.

MOST OLYMPIC DIVING MEDALS
The greatest number of Olympic medals ever won by a diver is five, by Klaus Dibiasi (Italy), with three gold and two silver from 1964 to 1976, and by Greg Louganis (USA), with four gold and one silver in 1976, 1984 and 1988. Dibiasi is also the only diver to have ever won the same event (highboard) at three successive Olympic Games (1968, 1972 and 1976).

MOST WORLD DIVING TITLES
Greg Louganis has won a record five world titles — highboard in 1978 and both highboard and springboard in 1982 and 1986, as well as four Olympic gold medals in 1984 and 1988.

The record for the greatest number of gold medals ever to have been won in a single event since the inaugural World Championship in 1973 is three, by Philip Boggs (USA) in the springboard in 1973, 1975 and 1978 and Greg Louganis (see above). Boggs also won the 1976 Olympic springboard title.

YOUNGEST DIVING CHAMPIONS
Canadian Alexandre Despatie (seen here left of picture with British diver Tony Ali) won gold in the 1998 Commonwealth Games platform diving final in Kuala Lumpur, Malaysia, at the age of 13 years 104 days, making him the youngest ever male winner of an international diving event. The youngest female winner was Fu Mingxia (China), who took the women's world platform title in Australia in 1991, aged 12 years 141 days.

combat sports

MOST SUCCESSFUL SUMO WRESTLERS
Yokozuna (grand champion) Sadaji Akiyoshi, alias Futabayama, set the all-time record of 69 consecutive bout wins (1937–39).

Yokozuna Koki Naya, alias Taiho ('Great Bird'), had won the Emperor's Cup a record 32 times by the time he retired in 1971.

The *ozeki* (second highest rank) Tameemon Torokichi, alias Raiden, won 254 bouts and lost only 10 in 21 years, giving him the highest ever winning rate of 96.2%.

MOST SUCCESSFUL SUMO BROTHERS
Ozeki Wakanohana was promoted to the rank of *yokozuna*, a rank held by his younger brother Takanohana since 1994, after winning the *Natsu* (summer) *Basho* in 1998. This is the first time in the 1,500-year history of the sport that two brothers have attained the rank of *yokozuna*.

MOST SUMO TOURNAMENT WINS
Yokozuna Mitsugu Akimoto, alias Chiyonofuji, won the *Kyushu Basho* (one of the six annual tournaments) for a record eight successive years (1981–88). He also holds the record for the most career wins (1,045) and the most *Makunouchi* (top-division) wins (807).

LONGEST-RUNNING KUNG FU TV SERIES
The Warner Bros series Kung Fu *ran for 62 episodes from 1972 to 1975, starring David Carradine as Kwai Chang Caine. A new series was produced between 1992 and 1996, with Carradine as the grandson of the original Caine. It ran for four series and 88 episodes.*

MOST TOP-DIVISION SUMO BOUTS
Jesse Kuhaulua (USA) fought 1,231 consecutive bouts. He was also the first non-Japanese wrestler to win a top-division sumo tournament, in 1972.

The most bouts in all divisions is 1,631, by Yukio Shoji from 1964 to 1986.

The most bouts contested in a career is 1,891, by Kenji Hatano (alias Oshio) from 1962 to 1988.

MOST OLYMPIC WRESTLING TITLES
Three titles were won by: Carl Westergren (Sweden) in 1920, 1924 and 1932; Ivar Johansson (Sweden) in 1932 (two) and 1936; Aleksandr Medved (USSR) in 1964, 1968 and 1972; and Aleksandr Karelin (Russia) in 1988, 1992 and 1996.

MOST OLYMPIC WRESTLING MEDALS
Four Olympic medals were won by: Eino Leino (Finland) at freestyle from 1920 to 1932; Imre Polyák (Hungary) at Greco-Roman from 1952 to 1964; and Bruce Baumgartner (USA) at freestyle from 1984 to 1996.

MOST GRECO-ROMAN WORLD WRESTLING TITLES
Aleksandr Karelin (Russia) won 11 titles in the 30 kg class between 1988 and 1998.

LONGEST WRESTLING BOUT
The longest recorded bout lasted 11 hr 40 min, when Martin Klein (Estonia representing Russia) beat Alfred Asikáinen (Finland) in the Greco-Roman 75 kg 'A' event in the 1912 Olympics.

TALLEST WRESTLER

Jorge Gonzalez from Argentina is 2.29 m (7 ft 6 in) tall and weighs 195 kg (30 st 10 lb). Originally a basketball player, Gonzalez made a career as a professional wrestler in the USA between 1990 and 1994, performing under the name 'El Gigante' (the giant) in WWF, WCW and New Japan Pro Wrestling bouts during the boom years of celebrity wrestling. He also appeared in the TV movie *Hercules in the Underworld* (USA, 1994), playing the role of Eryz the boxer.

LONGEST REIGNS AS BOXING CHAMPION
Joe Louis (USA) was world heavyweight champion for 11 years 252 days, from 1937 to his retirement in 1949.

Heavyweight Rocky Marciano (USA) is the only world champion at any weight to have won every fight of his entire professional career (49 fights from 1947 to 1955).

LONGEST BOXING MATCH
The longest world title fight under Queensberry Rules was between lightweights Joe Gans and Oscar Nelson (both USA) at Goldfield, Nevada, USA, on 3 Sept 1906. Gans won in the 42nd round on a foul.

SHORTEST BOXING MATCH
The shortest world title fight lasted 20 seconds, when Gerald McClellan (USA) beat Jay Bell in a WBC middleweight bout in Puerto Rico on 7 Aug 1993.

LONGEST BOXING CAREER WITHOUT A DEFEAT
On 13 Nov 1998 Ricardo Lopez (Mexico) outpointed Rosendo Alvarez in Las Vegas, Nevada, USA, to retain his WBA Strawweight title. Lopez has remained unbeaten throughout his professional career, which has lasted 48 fights over 13 years 11 months.

MOST JUDO TITLES
Yasuhiro Yamashita (Japan) won one Olympic and four world titles: the Over 95 kg in 1979, 1981 and 1983, the Open in 1981 and the Olympic Open in 1984. He retired undefeated after a total of 203 successive wins (1977–85).

Four world titles were also won by Shozo Fujii (Japan) at Under 80 kg in 1971, 1973 and 1975 and the Under 78 kg in 1979, and by Naoya Ogawa (Japan) in the Open in 1987, 1989 and 1991 and the Over 95 kg in 1989.

Ingrid Berghmans (Belgium) won six women's world titles: the Open in 1980, 1982, 1984 and 1986 and the Under 72 kg in 1984 and 1989. She won the Olympic 72 kg title in 1988, when women's judo was introduced as a demonstration sport.

MOST SUCCESSFUL TAE KWON DO PRACTITIONERS
Juan Moreno (USA) won a silver medal in the finweight (lightest) class at the Olympics in Seoul, South Korea, in

HEAVIEST SUMO WRESTLER

Hawaiian-born Salevaa Atisance, known as Konishiki, tipped the scales at 274 kg (43 st 3 lb) in his prime. He retired in May 1998 and now works as an oyakata (stablemaster) under the name Sanoyama.

TAMASHIWARI CHAMPION

Bruce Haynes broke 15 cement slabs, with a combined weight of 310 kg (48 st 11 lb) on 22 March 1998 in Sydney, NSW, Australia. Haynes, the undisputed tamashiwari (breaking objects with a blow from a bare hand) champion of the world, is a seventh-dan karate black belt and has been International Sports Karate Association World Champion eight times.

1988 and took the silver again in Barcelona, Spain, in 1992, making him the most successful male tae kwon do contestant. Tae kwon do was a demonstration sport during these two Olympics, but will be an official event at the 2000 Olympics in Sydney, NSW, Australia.

Chen Yi-an (Taiwan) is the most successful female tae kwon do contestant, having won gold in the 51 kg class at Seoul in 1988 and the 60 kg class in Barcelona in 1992.

MOST WORLD KARATE TITLES
Great Britain has won a record six world titles at the Kumite team event (1975, 1982, 1984, 1986, 1988 and 1990).

The record for the most men's individual Kumite titles is two, shared by four competitors: Pat McKay (GB) at the Under 80 kg in 1982 and 1984; Emmanuel Pinda (France) at the Open in 1984 and the Over 80 kg in 1988; Thierry Masci (France) at the Under 70 kg in 1986 and 1988; and José Manuel Egea (Spain) at the Under 80 kg in 1990 and 1992.

MOST SUCCESSFUL ARM-WRESTLER
John Brzenk (USA), a middleweight, has dominated many weight classes in arm-wrestling over the past 17 years. During the 1998 World Championships in Petaluma, California, USA, Brzenk won championships at five different weights, three with his right arm, two with his left. In the same year he was named the greatest arm-wrestler in the history of the sport during the World Wristwrestling Championship.

marathons & endurance

LONGEST RUNNING RACE
The world's longest ever race covered a distance of 5,898 km (3,665 miles) from New York City to Los Angeles, USA, in 1929. Finnish-born Johnny Salo won in 79 days and an elapsed time of 525 hr 57 min 20 sec, averaging 11.21 km/h (6.97 mph).

MOST MARATHON FINISHERS
The record number of confirmed finishers in a marathon is 38,706, at the centennial race in Boston, Massachusetts, USA, on 15 April 1996.

HIGHEST-ALTITUDE MARATHON
The biennial Everest Marathon, first run on 27 Nov 1987, is the highest-altitude marathon. It begins at 5,212 m (17,100 ft) at Gorak Shep, and ends at Namche Bazar, at an altitude of 3,444 m (11,300 ft).

MOST MARATHONS RUN
Horst Preisler (Germany) ran 631 races of 42.195 km (26 miles 385 yd) or longer from 1974 to 29 May 1996.

Henri Girault (France) ran a total of 330 100-km races from 1979 to June 1996 and has completed a run on every continent except Antarctica.

FASTEST THREE MARATHONS IN THREE DAYS
The fastest combined time for three marathons in three days is 8 hr 22 min 31 sec, by Raymond Hubbard (Belfast 2 hr 45 min 55 sec, London 2 hr 48 min 45 sec and Boston 2 hr 47 min 51 sec) from 16 to 18 April 1988.

FASTEST BACKWARDS MARATHON
Timothy 'Bud' Badyna (USA) ran a marathon backwards in 3 hr 53 min 17 sec at Toledo, Ohio, USA, on 24 April 1994.

FASTEST THREE-LEGGED MARATHON
Identical twins Nick and Alastair Benbow (UK) set a three-legged running record of 3 hr 40 min 16 sec in the London Marathon, UK, on 26 April, 1998. They were tied together at the wrist and shared a three-legged pair of running trousers.

OLDEST MARATHON FINISHERS
Dimitrion Yordanidis (Greece) was 98 years old when he raced in Athens, Greece, in Oct 1976. His time was 7 hr 33 min.

The oldest woman to complete a marathon was Thelma Pitt-Turner (New Zealand), who was 82 when she raced in New Zealand in Aug 1985. Her time was 7 hr 58 min.

MOST MODERN PENTATHLON WORLD TITLES
András Balczó (Hungary) won six individual and seven team titles in the modern pentathlon World Championships from 1960 to 1972.

The USSR holds the record for team titles, with 18.

The most women's titles is four, by Eva Fjellerup (Denmark), who won the individual World Championship titles in 1990, 1991, 1993 and 1994.

FASTEST HALF-MARATHON
The world best time for a half-marathon course is 59 min 17 sec, by Paul Tergat (above) of Kenya at Milan, Italy, on 4 April 1998. The official women's record is 66 min 43 sec, set by Masako Chika (Japan) at Tokyo, Japan, on 19 April 1997. Ingrid Kristiansen (Norway) ran a half-marathon in 66 min 40 sec at Sandnes, Norway, on 5 April 1987 but the course measurement was not confirmed.

Poland has won a record eight women's world team titles (1985, 1988–92, 1995 and 1998).

MOST PENTATHLON OLYMPIC TITLES
The record for the most Olympic gold medals won is three, by András Balczó of Hungary, who took the team title in 1960 and 1968 and the individual title in 1972.

The record for individual Olympic titles is two, by Lars Hall (Sweden) in 1952 and 1956.

FASTEST MARATHONS

The fastest ever marathon by a man was 2 hr 6 min 5 sec, run by Ronaldo da Costa of Brazil (pictured right) at Berlin, Germany, on 20 Sept 1998. The women's record was set by Tegla Loroupe (Kenya) at Rotterdam, Netherlands, on 19 April 1998, with a time of 2 hr 20 min 7 sec. The marathon is supposedly based on the legendary run by the Greek messenger Pheidippides, bringing news of a Persian attack in 490 BC. The race was run at the first modern Olympic Games in Athens, Greece, in 1896, but the distance of the race varied until 1924, when it was set at 42.195 km (26 miles 385 yd). It is widely expected that a marathon time of under 2 hr 5 min will be set in the next decade. Because of problems in measuring the road courses precisely, the fastest times for marathons are officially referred to as 'world bests' rather than records.

FASTEST IRON MAN TIMES

The fastest ever time in an Iron Man race — a 3.8-km (2-mile 634-yd) swim, a 180-km (112-mile) cycle ride and a full marathon of 42.195 km (26 miles 385 yd) — is 7 hr 50 min 27 sec, by Luc van Lierde of Belgium (left) at Roth, Germany, on 13 July 1997.

Pavel Lednev (USSR) won a record seven medals (two team gold, one team silver, one individual silver and three individual bronze) from 1968 to 1980.

MOST WORLD BIATHLON TITLES
Frank Ullrich (GDR) won six individual titles: four at 10 km from 1978 to 1981 and two at 20 km in 1982 and 1983.

Aleksandr Tikhonov was a member of a record 10 winning Soviet relay teams from 1968 to 1980 and won four individual titles.

The women's record is four, set by Petra Schaaf (Germany): 5 km in 1988 and 15 km in 1989, 1991 and 1993.

LONGEST TRIATHLON
David Holleran (Australia) completed a 2,542-km (1,578-mile) triathlon, consisting of a 42-km (26-mile) swim, 2,000-km (1,242-mile) cycle ride and 500-km (310-mile) run, in 17 days 22 hr 50 min, from 21 March to 8 April 1998.

BEST WORLD TRIATHLON CHAMPIONSHIP TIMES
The best time in the men's championship is 1 hr 48 min 20 sec, set by Miles Stewart (Australia) in 1991.

The best women's time in a triathlon is 1 hr 59 min 22 sec, by Emma Carney (Australia) in 1997.

MOST WORLD TRIATHLON CHAMPIONSHIP WINS
The World Championship consists of a 1.5-km (4,921-ft 3-in) swim, a 40-km (24-mile 1,496-yd) cycle ride and a 10-km (6-mile 370-yd) run. Simon Lessing (GB) has won a record four times (1992, 1995, 1996 and 1998).

The most wins in the women's event is two, by Michelle Jones (Australia) in 1992 and 1993 and Karen Smyers (USA) in 1990 and 1995.

Prior to 1989 a race held annually in Nice, France, was regarded as the unofficial World Championship. Mark Allen (USA) won 10 titles, from 1982 to 1986 and from 1989 to 1993.

GREATEST DISTANCE RUN IN 24 HOURS
Yiannis Kouros (Australia) ran a record 303.506 km (188 miles 1031 yd) at Adelaide, South Australia, from 4 to 5 Oct 1997.

The women's record is 248.9 km (154 miles 1161 yd) by Yelena Siderenkova (Russia) in Feb 1996, on an indoor track.

MOST PENTATHLON WINS

Sweden has won a record nine gold medals at the modern pentathlon. Swedish athletes have also won seven silvers and five bronzes. Aleksandr Parygin of Kazakhstan (below left) is the current Olympic champion.

gymnastics & weightlifting

MOST MEN'S WORLD GYMNASTICS TITLES

The most individual men's titles won is 13, by Vitaliy Scherbo (Belarus) between 1992 and 1995. Scherbo also won a team gold medal in 1992.

The USSR won a record 13 team titles (eight World Championships and five Olympics) between 1952 and 1992.

MOST WOMEN'S WORLD GYMNASTICS TITLES

The most women's titles won is 18 (12 individual and six team), by Larisa Semyonovna Latynina (USSR) between 1954 and 1964.

The USSR won the women's team title on a record 21 occasions (11 World Championships and 10 Olympics).

YOUNGEST WORLD GYMNASTICS TITLE WINNERS

Aurelia Dobre (Romania) won the women's overall world title at the age of 14 years 352 days at Rotterdam, Netherlands, on 23 Oct 1987.

In 1990 Daniela Silivas (Romania) revealed that she was born a year later than she had previously claimed and had in fact been 14 years 185 days old when she won the gold medal for balance beam in 1985.

The youngest male world champion was Dmitriy Bilozerchev (USSR), who was 16 years 315 days old when he won the men's overall world title in Budapest, Hungary, on 28 Oct 1983.

MOST MEN'S OLYMPIC GYMNASTICS TITLES

The most men's individual gold medals won is six, by Boris Shakhlin (USSR) — one in 1956, four (two shared) in 1960 and one in 1964 — and by Nikolay Andrianov (USSR) — one in 1972, four in 1976 and one in 1980.

The men's team title has been won five times by Japan (1960, 1964, 1968, 1972 and 1976) and the USSR (1952, 1956, 1980, 1988 and 1992 — the last as the Unified team).

MOST MEN'S OLYMPIC GYMNASTICS MEDALS

Nikolay Andrianov (USSR) won a record 15 Olympic medals (seven gold, five silver and three bronze) from 1972 to 1980.

Aleksandr Dityatin (USSR) won a record eight medals (three gold, four silver and one bronze) at one Games, in Moscow, Russia (then USSR), in 1980.

MOST WOMEN'S OLYMPIC GYMNASTICS TITLES

Vera Caslavska-Odlozil (Czechoslovakia) holds the record for the most individual women's titles, with seven: three in 1964 and four (one shared) in 1968.

MOST WOMEN'S OLYMPIC GYMNASTICS MEDALS

Larisa Latynina (USSR) won six individual gold medals and three team golds from 1956 to 1964. She also won five silver and four bronze medals, making an Olympic record total of 18.

MOST WOMEN'S TEAM OLYMPIC GYMNASTICS TITLES

The USSR has won the Olympic women's title a record 10 times (from 1952 to 1980 and in 1988 and 1992). The last title was won by the Unified team from the republics of the former USSR. Pictured is Svetlana Khorkina, a member of the Russian team that took the gold medal at the 1998 World Cup in Sabae, Japan.

MOST WORLD CUP GYMNASTICS TITLES

Li Ning (China), Nikolay Andrianov, Aleksandr Dityatin and Maria Yevgenyevna Filatova (all USSR) have each won two World Cup overall titles.

MOST WORLD TEAM RHYTHMIC GYMNASTICS TITLES

Bulgaria has won a record nine team titles: 1969, 1971, 1981, 1983, 1985, 1987, 1989 (shared), 1993 and 1995.

MOST RHYTHMIC DISCIPLINES IN WHICH PERFECT SCORES ACHIEVED

At the 1988 Olympics in Seoul, South Korea, Marina Lobach (USSR) won the rhythmic gymnastics title with perfect scores in all six disciplines.

YOUNGEST INTERNATIONAL GYMNAST

Pasakevi 'Voula' Kouna (Greece) was just 9 years 299 days old at the start of the Balkan Games held at Serres, Greece, in 1981.

MOST TRAMPOLINING TITLES

The most men's trampolining titles won is five, by Aleksandr Moskalenko of Russia (three individual from 1990 to 1994 and pairs in 1992 and 1994); and Brett Austine of Australia (five individual from 1982 to 1986).

Judy Wills (USA) has won a record nine women's titles: five individual from

MOST MEN'S WEIGHTLIFTING TITLES

Naim Suleymanoglü (Turkey; pictured right) won 10 world titles (including Olympic titles): in 1985, 1986, 1988, 1989 and from 1991 to 1996. He was just 16 years 62 days old when he set world records for clean and jerk (160 kg or 352 lb 8 oz) and total (285 kg or 628 lb 8 oz) in the 56-kg class at Allentown, New Jersey, USA, on 26 March 1983. Born to a Turkish family in Bulgaria, Suleymanoglü was forced to take a Bulgarian version of his surname and competed as Suleimanov until he defected to Turkey in 1986. Suleymanoglü was banned from international competitions for a year after his defection, but subsequently competed for Turkey before retiring in 1997.

1964 to 1968, two pairs in 1966 and 1967 and two tumbling in 1965 and 1966.

FASTEST SOMERSAULTS
On 30 April 1986 Ashrita Furman (USA) performed 8,341 forward rolls in 10 hr 30 min over 19.67 km (12 miles 390 yd) from Lexington to Charleston, Massachusetts, USA.

On 21 July 1996 Ashrita Furman somersaulted 1.6 km (1 mile) in 19 min 38 sec at Edgewater Park, Cleveland, Ohio, USA.

On 31 Aug 1995 Vitaliy Scherbo (Belarus) somersaulted 50 m (54 yd) backwards in 10.22 seconds in Chiba, Japan.

MOST MEN'S WEIGHTLIFTING MEDALS
Norbert Schemansky (USA) has won a record four Olympic medals: gold in the middle-heavyweight class in 1952, silver heavyweight in 1948 and bronze heavyweight in 1960 and 1964.

MOST WOMEN'S WEIGHTLIFTING MEDALS
Li Hongyun (China) won 13 medals in the 60/64-kg class from 1992 to 1996.

OLDEST WEIGHTLIFTING WORLD RECORD BREAKER
Norbert Schemansky (USA) was 37 years 333 days old when he snatched a record 164.2 kg (362 lb) in the then unlimited heavyweight class in Detroit, Michigan, USA, in 1962.

MOST WORLD POWERLIFTING TITLES
The most men's world titles won is 17, by Hideaki Inaba (Japan) in the 52-kg class from 1974 to 1983 and 1985 to 1991.

The most women's powerlifting titles is six, by Beverley Francis of Australia (in the 75-kg class in 1980 and 1982 and the 82.5-kg class in 1981 and from 1983 to 1985); Sisi Dolman of the Netherlands (in the 52-kg class in 1985 and 1986 and from 1988 to 1991); and Natalia Rumyantseva of Russia (in the 82.5-kg class from 1993 to 1998).

BEST TIMED LIFTS
A world 24-hour deadlifting record of 3,137,904 kg (6,917,886 lb) was set by a team of 10 people at the Pontefract Sports and Leisure Centre, W Yorkshire, UK, from 3 to 4 May 1997.

The individual 24-hour deadlift record is held by Steph Smit (South Africa), who lifted 456,677.5 kg (1,004,595 lb) at Warren's Health Club, Pietermaritzburg, South Africa, from 13 to 14 Sept 1997.

A 24-hour bench press record of 4,748,283 kg (10,468,160 lb) was set by a team of nine men at the Pontefract Sports and Leisure Centre, W Yorkshire, UK, from 11 to 12 April 1998.

An individual bench press record of 815,434 kg (1,797,724 lb) was set by Glen Tenove (USA) in 12 hours at Irvine, California, USA, on 17 Dec 1994.

MOST WORLD RHYTHMIC GYMNASTICS TITLES
The most overall individual world titles won in rhythmic gymnastics is three, by two Bulgarian gymnasts: Maria Gigova in 1969, 1971 and 1973 and Maria Petrova (pictured right) in 1993, 1994 and 1995.

sports reference

NFL Records
MOST POINTS
Career: 2,002
George Blanda, Chicago Bears, Baltimore Colts, Houston Oilers, Oakland Raiders, 1949–75
Season: 176
Paul Hornung, Green Bay Packers, 1960
Game: 40
Ernie Nevers, Chicago Cardinals v. Chicago Bears, 28 Nov 1929
MOST TOUCHDOWNS
Career: 175
Jerry Rice, San Francisco 49ers, 1985–98
Season: 25
Emmitt Smith, Dallas Cowboys, 1995
Game: 6
Ernie Nevers, Chicago Cardinals v. Chicago Bears, 28 Nov 1929
Dub Jones, Cleveland Browns v. Chicago Bears, 25 Nov 1951
Gale Sayers, Chicago Bears v. San Francisco 49ers, 12 Dec 1965
MOST YARDS GAINED RUSHING
Career: 16,726
Walter Payton, Chicago Bears, 1975–87
Season: 2,105
Eric Dickerson, Los Angeles Rams, 1984
Game: 275
Walter Payton, Chicago Bears v. Minnesota Vikings, 20 Nov 1977
MOST YARDS GAINED RECEIVING
Career: 17,612
Jerry Rice, San Francisco 49ers, 1985–98
Season: 1,848
Jerry Rice, San Francisco 49ers, 1995
Game: 336
Willie Anderson, Los Angeles Rams v. New Orleans Saints, 26 Nov 1989
MOST COMBINED NET YARDS GAINED
Career: 21,803
Walter Payton, Chicago Bears, 1975–87
Season: 2,535
Lionel James, San Diego Chargers, 1985
Game: 404
Glyn Milburn, Denver Broncos v. Seattle Seahawks, 10 Dec 1995

MOST YARDS GAINED PASSING
Career: 58,913
Dan Marino, Miami Dolphins, 1983–98
Season: 5,084
Dan Marino, Miami Dolphins, 1984
Game: 554
Norm Van Brocklin, Los Angeles Rams v. New York Yanks, 28 Sept 1951
MOST PASSES COMPLETED
Career: 4,763
Dan Marino, Miami Dolphins, 1983–98
Season: 404
Warren Moon, Houston Oilers, 1991
Game: 45
Drew Bledsoe, New England Patriots v. Minnesota Vikings, 13 Nov 1994
PASS RECEPTIONS
Career: 1,139
Jerry Rice, San Francisco 49ers, 1985–98
Season: 123
Herman Moore, Detroit Lions, 1995
Game: 18
Tom Fears, Los Angeles Rams v. Green Bay Packers, 3 Dec 1950
MOST TOUCHDOWN PASSES
Career: 408
Dan Marino, Miami Dolphins, 1983–98
Season: 48
Dan Marino, Miami Dolphins, 1984
Game: 7
Sid Luckman, Chicago Bears v. New York Giants, 14 Nov 1943
Adrian Burk, Philadelphia Eagles v. Washington Redskins, 17 Oct 1954
George Blanda, Houston Oilers v. New York Titans, 19 Nov 1961
Y.A. Tittle, New York Giants v. Washington Redskins, 28 Oct 1962
Joe Kapp, Minnesota Vikings v. Baltimore Colts, 28 Sept 1969
FIELD GOALS
Career: 420
Gary Anderson, Pittsburgh Steelers, Philadelphia Eagles, San Francisco 49ers, Minnesota Vikings, 1982–98
Season: 37
John Kasay, Carolina Panthers, 1996
Game: 7
Jim Bakken, St Louis Cardinals v. Pittsburgh Steelers, 24 Sept 1967
Rich Karlis, Minnesota Vikings v. Los Angeles Rams, 5 Nov 1989
Chris Boniol, Dallas Cowboys v. Green Bay Packers, 18 Nov 1996

Super Bowl Game & Career Records
POINTS
Game: 18
Roger Craig (San Francisco 49ers), 1985
Jerry Rice (San Francisco 49ers), 1990 and 1995
Ricky Watters (San Francisco 49ers), 1995
Terrell Davis (Denver Broncos), 1998
Career: 42
Jerry Rice, 1989–90, 1995
TOUCHDOWNS
Game: 3
Roger Craig, 1985
Jerry Rice, 1990 and 1995
Ricky Watters, 1990
Terrell Davis, 1998
Career: 7
Jerry Rice, 1989–90, 1995
TOUCHDOWN PASSES
Game: 6
Steve Young (San Francisco 49ers), 1995
Career: 11
Joe Montana (San Francisco 49ers), 1982, 1985, 1989–90
YARDS GAINED PASSING
Game: 357
Joe Montana, 1989
Career: 1,142
Joe Montana, 1982, 1985, 1989–90

Field goal kicker Gary Anderson scores for the Minnesota Vikings against the Tennessee Oilers.

Alfred C. Glassell Jr with his 707.61-kg (1,560-lb) black marlin.

YARDS GAINED RECEIVING
Game: 215
Jerry Rice, 1989
Career: 512
Jerry Rice, 1989–90, 1995
YARDS GAINED RUSHING
Game: 204
Timmy Smith (Washington Redskins), 1988
Career: 354
Franco Harris (Pittsburgh Steelers), 1975–76, 1979–80
PASSES COMPLETED
Game: 31
Jim Kelly (Buffalo Bills), 1994
Career: 83
Joe Montana, 1982, 1985, 1989–90
PASS RECEPTIONS
Game: 11
Dan Ross (Cincinnati Bengals), 1982
Jerry Rice, 1989
Career: 28
Jerry Rice, 1989–90, 1995
FIELD GOALS
Game: 4
Don Chandler (Green Bay Packers), 1968
Ray Wersching (San Francisco 49ers), 1982
Career: 5
Ray Wersching, 1982, 1985
MOST VALUABLE PLAYER
Joe Montana, 1982, 1985, 1990

angling

FRESHWATER AND SALTWATER
A selection of All-Tackle angling records ratified by the International Game Fish Association by Jan 1999.
Barracuda, Great: 38.55 kg (85 lb)
John W. Helfrich
Christmas Island, Kiribati, 11 April 1992
Bass, Striped: 35.60 kg (78 lb 8 oz)
Albert R. McReynolds
Atlantic City, New Jersey, USA, 21 Sept 1982
Catfish, Flathead: 55.79 kg (123 lb 9 oz)
Ken Paulie
Elk City Reservoir, Independence, Kansas, USA, 14 May 1998
Cod, Atlantic: 44.79 kg (98 lb 2 oz)
Alphonse J. Bielevich
Isle of Shoals, New Hampshire, USA, 8 June 1969
Conger: 60.44 kg (133 lb 6 oz)
Vic Evans
Berry Head, Devon, UK, 5 June 1995
Halibut, Pacific: 208.2 kg (459 lb)
Jack Tragis
Dutch Harbor, Alaska, USA, 11 June 1996
Mackerel, King: 40.82 kg (90 lb)
Norton I. Thomton
Key West, Florida, USA, 16 Feb 1976
Marlin, Black: 707.61 kg (1,560 lb)
Alfred C. Glassell Jr
Cabo Blanco, Peru, 4 Aug 1953
Pike, Northern: 25 kg (55 lb 1 oz)
Lothar Louis
Grefeern Lake, Germany, 16 Oct 1986
Sailfish, Pacific: 100.24 kg (221 lb)
C. W. Stewart
Santa Cruz Island, Ecuador, 12 Feb 1947
Salmon, Atlantic: 35.89 kg (79 lb 3 oz)
Henrik Henriksen
Tana River, Norway, 1928
Shark, Hammerhead: 449.5 kg (991 lb)
Allen Ogle
Sarasota, Florida, USA, 30 May 1982
Shark, Porbeagle: 230 kg (507 lb)
Christopher Bennett
Pentland Firth, Caithness, UK, 9 March 1993
Shark, Thresher: 363.8 kg (802 lb)
Dianne North
Tutukaka, New Zealand, 8 Feb 1981
Shark, White: 1,208.38 kg (2,664 lb)
Alfred Dean
Ceduna, South Australia, 21 April 1959
Sturgeon, White: 212.28 kg (468 lb)
Joey Pallotta III
Benicia, California, USA, 9 July 1983
Swordfish: 536.15 kg (1,182 lb)
L. Marrón
Iquique, Chile, 7 May 1953
Trout, Brook: 6.58 kg (14 lb 8 oz)
Dr W. J. Cook
Nipigon River, Ontario, Canada, July 1916
Trout, Brown: 18.26 kg (40 lb 4 oz)
Howard L. Collins
Heber Springs, Arkansas, USA, 9 May 1992
Trout, Lake: 30.16 kg (66 lb 8 oz)
Rodney Harback
Great Bear Lake, NWT, Canada, 19 July 1991
Trout, Rainbow: 19.10 kg (42 lb 3 oz)
David Robert White
Bell Island, Alaska, USA, 22 June 1970
Tuna, Bluefin: 679 kg (1,496 lb)
Ken Fraser
Aulds Cove, Nova Scotia, Canada, 26 Oct 1979
Tuna, Yellowfin: 176.35 kg (388 lb 2 oz)
Curt Wiesenhutter
San Benedicto Island, Mexico, 1 April 1977
Wahoo: 71.9 kg (158 lb 8 oz)
Keith Winter
Loreto, Baja California, Mexico, 10 June 1996

archery

MEN (SINGLE FITA ROUNDS)
FITA: Oh Kyo-moon (South Korea) scored 1,368 points from a possible 1,440 in 1995.
90 m: Jang Yong-ho (South Korea) scored 331 points from a possible 360 in 1999.
70 m: Jackson Fear (Australia) scored 345 points from a possible 360 in 1997.
50 m: Kim Kyung-ho (South Korea) scored 351 points from a possible 360 in 1997.
30 m: Han Seuong-hoon (South Korea) scored 360 points from a possible 360 in 1994.
Team: South Korea (Oh Kyo-moon, Lee Kyung-chul, Kim Jae-pak) scored 4,053 points from a possible 4,320 in 1995.
WOMEN (SINGLE FITA ROUNDS)
FITA: Kim Jung-rye (South Korea) scored 1,377 points from a possible 1,440 in 1995.
70 m: Chung Chang-sook (South Korea) scored 341 points from a possible 360 in 1997.
60 m: Kim Jo-sun (South Korea) scored 350 points from a possible 360 in 1998.
50 m: Kim Moon-sun (South Korea) scored 345 points from a possible 360 in 1996.
30 m: Ha Na-young (South Korea) scored 360 points from a possible 360 in 1998.
Team: South Korea (Kim Soo-nyung, Lee Eun-kyung, Cho Yuon-jeong) scored 4,094 points from a possible 4,320 in 1992.
INDOOR (18 M)
Men
Magnus Pettersson (Sweden) scored 596 points from a possible 600 in 1995.
Women
Lina Herasymenko (Ukraine) scored 591 points from a possible 600 in 1996.
INDOOR (25 M)
Men
Magnus Pettersson (Sweden) scored 593 points from a possible 600 in 1993.
Women
Petra Ericsson (Sweden) scored 592 points from a possible 600 in 1991.

Oh Kyo-moon, a member of the 1995 South Korean archery team.

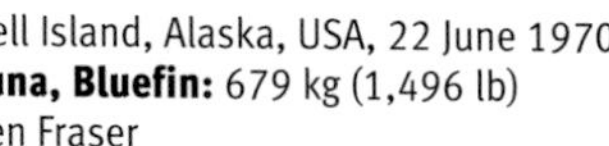

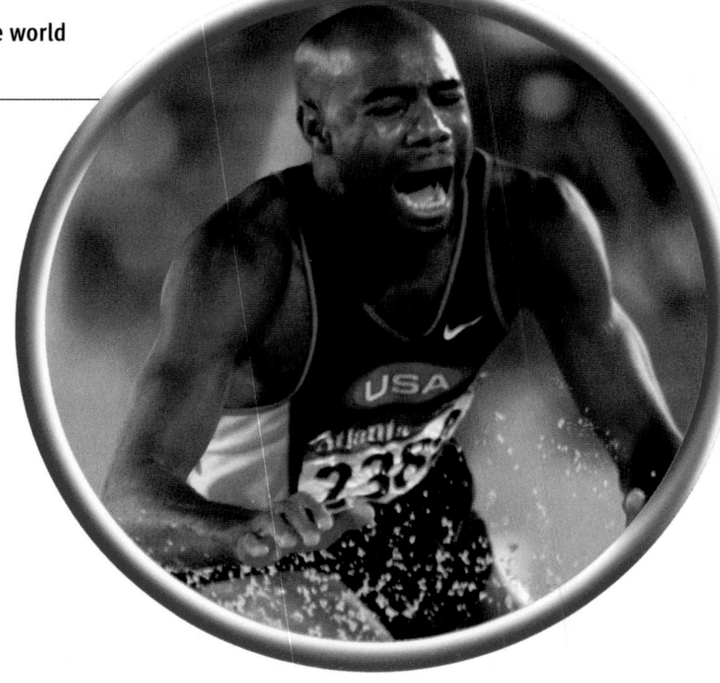

Mike Powell (USA) has held the world long-jump record since 1991.

MEN'S OUTDOOR RECORDS

World outdoor records for the men's events scheduled by the International Amateur Athletic Federation. Fully automatic electric timing is mandatory for events up to 400 m.

Running

100 m: 9.79
Maurice Greene (USA)
Athens, Greece, 16 June 1999

200 m: 19.32
Michael Johnson (USA)
Atlanta, USA, 1 Aug 1996

400 m: 43.29
Harry Lee 'Butch' Reynolds Jr (USA)
Zürich, Switzerland, 17 Aug 1988

800 m: 1:41.11
Wilson Kipketer (Denmark)
Cologne, Germany, 24 Aug 1997

1,000 m: 2:12.18
Sebastian Coe (GB)
Oslo, Norway, 11 July 1981

1,500 m: 3:26.00
Hicham El Guerrouj (Morocco)
Rome, Italy, 14 July 1998

1 mile: 3:44.39
Noureddine Morceli (Algeria)
Rieti, Italy, 5 Sept 1993

2,000 m: 4:47.88
Noureddine Morceli (Algeria)
Paris, France, 3 July 1995

3,000 m: 7:20.67
Daniel Komen (Kenya)
Rieti, Italy, 1 Sept 1996

5,000 m: 12:39.36
Haile Gebreselassie (Ethiopia)
Helsinki, Finland, 13 June 1998

10,000 m: 26:22.75
Haile Gebreselassie (Ethiopia)
Hengelo, Netherlands, 1 June 1998

20,000 m: 56:55.6
Arturo Barrios (Mexico, now USA)
La Flèche, France, 30 March 1991

25,000 m: 1:13:55.8
Toshihiko Seko (Japan)
Christchurch, New Zealand, 22 March 1981

30,000 m: 1:29:18.8
Toshihiko Seko (Japan)
Christchurch, New Zealand, 22 March 1981

1 hour: 21,101 m
Arturo Barrios (Mexico, now USA)
La Flèche, France, 30 March 1991

110-m hurdles: 12.91
Colin Jackson (GB)
Stuttgart, Germany, 20 Aug 1993

400-m hurdles: 46.78
Kevin Young (USA)
Barcelona, Spain, 6 Aug 1992

3,000-m steeplechase: 7:55.72
Bernard Barmasai (Kenya)
Cologne, Germany, 24 Aug 1997

4 x 100-m: 37.40
USA (Michael Marsh, Leroy Burrell, Dennis A. Mitchell, Carl Lewis)
Barcelona, Spain, 8 Aug 1992
and: USA (John A. Drummond Jr, André Cason, Dennis A. Mitchell, Leroy Burrell)
Stuttgart, Germany, 21 Aug 1993

4 x 200-m: 1:18.68
Santa Monica Track Club (USA) (Michael Marsh, Leroy Burrell, Floyd Wayne Heard, Carl Lewis)
Walnut, California, USA, 17 April 1994

4 x 400-m: 2:54.20
USA (Jerome Young, Antonio Pettigrew, Tyree Washington, Michael Johnson)
New York, USA, 22 July 1998

4 x 800-m: 7:03.89
Great Britain (Peter Elliott, Garry Cook, Steve Cram, Sebastian Coe)
London, UK, 30 Aug 1982

4 x 1,500-m: 14:38.8
West Germany (Thomas Wessinghage, Harald Hudak, Michael Lederer, Karl Fleschen)
Cologne, Germany, 17 Aug 1977

Field Events

High Jump: 2.45 m (8 ft 1/2 in)
Javier Sotomayor (Cuba)
Salamanca, Spain, 27 July 1993

Pole Vault: 6.14 m (20 ft 1 in)
Sergey Nazarovich Bubka (Ukraine)
Sestriere, Italy, 1 July 1994

Long Jump: 8.95 m (29 ft 4 1/2 in)
Mike Powell (USA)
Tokyo, Japan, 30 Aug 1991

Triple Jump: 18.29 m (60 ft 1/4 in)
Jonathan Edwards (GB)
Gothenburg, Sweden, 7 Aug 1995

Shot: 23.12 m (75 ft 10 1/4 in)
Randy Barnes (USA)
Los Angeles, California, USA, 20 May 1990

Discus: 74.08 m (243 ft)
Jürgen Schult (GDR)
Neubrandenburg, Germany, 6 June 1986

Hammer: 86.74 m (284 ft 7 in)
Yuriy Georgiyevich Sedykh (USSR, now Russia), Stuttgart, Germany, 30 Aug 1986

Javelin: 98.48 m (323 ft 1 in)
Jan Zelezny (Czech Republic)
Jena, Germany, 25 May 1996

Decathlon: 8,891 points
Dan Dion O'Brien (USA)
Talence, France, 4-5 Sept 1992
Day 1: 100 m: 10.43 sec; long jump: 8.08 m (26 ft 6 1/4 in); shot: 16.69 m (54 ft 9 1/4 in); high jump: 2.07 m (6ft 9 1/2 in); 400 m: 48.51 sec
Day 2: 110-m hurdles: 13.98 sec; discus: 48.56 m (159 ft 4 in); pole vault: 5.00 m (16 ft 4 1/4 in); javelin 62.58 m (205 ft 4 in); 1,500 m: 4:42.10

WOMEN'S OUTDOOR RECORDS

World outdoor records for the women's events scheduled by the International Amateur Athletic Federation. Fully automatic electric timing is mandatory for all events up to 400 m.

Running

100 m: 10.49
Florence Griffith Joyner (USA)
Indianapolis, Indiana, USA, 16 July 1988

200 m: 21.34
Florence Griffith Joyner (USA)
Seoul, South Korea, 29 Sept 1988

400 m: 47.60
Marita Koch (GDR)
Canberra, Australia, 6 Oct 1985

800 m: 1:53.28
Jarmila Kratochvílová (Czechoslovakia)
Munich, Germany, 26 July 1983

1,000 m: 2:28.98
Svetlana Masterkova (Russia)
Brussels, Belgium, 23 Aug 1996

1,500 m: 3:50.46
Qu Yunxia (China)
Beijing, China, 11 Sept 1993

1 mile: 4:12.56
Svetlana Masterkova (Russia)
Zürich, Switzerland, 14 Aug 1996

2,000 m: 5:25.36
Sonia O'Sullivan (Ireland)
Edinburgh, UK, 8 July 1994

3,000 m: 8:06.11
Wang Junxia (China)
Beijing, China, 13 Sept 1993

5,000 m: 14:28.09
Jiang Bo (China)
Beijing, China, 23 Oct 1997

10,000 m: 29:31.78
Wang Junxia (China)
Beijing, China, 8 Sept 1993

20,000 m: 1:06:48.8
Isumi Maki (Japan)
Amagasaki, Japan, 20 Sept 1993

25,000 m: 1:29:29.2
Karolina Szabo (Hungary)
Budapest, Hungary, 23 April 1988

30,000 m: 1:47:05.6
Karolina Szabo (Hungary)
Budapest, Hungary, 23 April 1988

Gabriela Szabo is pictured after setting a new indoor 5,000-m record.

1 hour: 18,340 m
Tegla Loroupe (Kenya)
Borgholzhausen, Germany, 7 Aug 1998
100-m hurdles: 12.21
Yordanka Donkova (Bulgaria)
Stara Zagora, Bulgaria, 20 Aug 1988
400-m hurdles: 52.61
Kim Batten (USA)
Gothenburg, Sweden, 11 Aug 1995
4 x 100-m: 41.37
GDR (Silke Gladisch, Sabine Rieger, Ingrid Auerswald, Marlies Göhr)
Canberra, Australia, 6 Oct 1985
4 x 200-m: 1:28.15
GDR (Marlies Göhr, Romy Müller, Bärbel Wöckel, Marita Koch)
Jena, Germany, 9 Aug 1980
4 x 400-m: 3:15.17
USSR (Tatyana Ledovskaya, Olga Nazarova, Maria Pinigina, Olga Bryzgina)
Seoul, South Korea, 1 Oct 1988
4 x 800-m: 7:50.17
USSR (Nadezhda Olizarenko, Gurina Lyubova, Lyudmila Borisova, Irina Podyalovskaya)
Moscow, USSR, 5 Aug 1984

Field Events

High Jump: 2.09 m (6 ft 10¼ in)
Stefka Kostadinova (Bulgaria)
Rome, Italy, 30 Aug 1987
Pole Vault: 4.60 m (15 ft 1 in)
Emma George (Australia)
Sydney, Australia, 20 Feb 1999
Long Jump: 7.52 m (24 ft 8 in)
Galina Chistyakova (USSR)
Leningrad, USSR, 11 June 1988
Triple Jump: 15.50 m (50 ft 10 in)
Inessa Kravets (Ukraine)
Gothenburg, Sweden, 10 Aug 1995
Shot: 22.63 m (74 ft 3 in)
Natalya Venedictovna Lisovskaya (USSR) Moscow, USSR, 7 June 1987
Discus: 76.80 m (252 ft)
Gabriele Reinsch (GDR)
Neubrandenburg, Germany, 9 July 1988
Hammer: 73.14 m (239 ft 11 in)
Mihaela Melinte (Romania)
Poiana Brasov, Romania, 16 July 1998
Javelin: 80.00 m (262 ft 5 in)
Petra Felke (GDR)
Potsdam, Germany, 9 Sept 1988
Heptathlon: 7,291 points
Jackie Joyner-Kersee (USA)
Seoul, South Korea, 23–24 Sept 1988
100-m hurdles: 12.69 sec; high jump: 1.86 m (6 ft 1¼ in); shot: 15.80 m (51 ft 10 in); 200 m: 22.56 sec; long jump: 7.27 m (23 ft 10¼ in); javelin: 45.66 m (149 ft 10 in); 800 m: 2:08.51

MEN'S INDOOR RECORDS

Running

Track performances around a turn must be made on a track of circumference no longer than 200 m.

50 m: 5.56*
Donovan Bailey (Canada)
Reno, Nevada, USA, 9 Feb 1996
and: Maurice Greene (USA)
Los Angeles, USA, 13 Feb 1999
60 m: 6.39
Maurice Greene (USA)
Madrid, Spain, 3 Feb 1998
200 m: 19.92
Frankie Fredericks (Namibia)
Liévin, France, 18 Feb 1996
400 m: 44.63
Michael Johnson (USA)
Atlanta, Georgia, USA, 4 March 1995
800 m: 1:42.67
Wilson Kipketer (Denmark)
Paris, France, 9 March 1997
1,000 m: 2:15.26
Noureddine Morceli (Algeria)
Birmingham, W Mids, UK, 22 Feb 1992
1,500 m: 3:31.18
Hicham El Gerrouj (Morocco)
Stuttgart, Germany, 2 Feb 1997
1 mile: 3:48.45
Hicham El Gerrouj (Morocco)
Ghent, Belgium, 12 Feb 1997
3,000 m: 7:24.90
Daniel Komen (Kenya)
Budapest, Hungary, 6 Feb 1998
5,000 m: 12:50.38
Haile Gebreselassie (Ethiopia)
Birmingham, UK, 14 Feb 1999
50-m hurdles: 6.25
Mark McKoy (Canada)
Kobe, Japan, 5 March 1986
60-m hurdles: 7.30
Colin Jackson (GB)
Sindelfingen, Germany, 6 March 1994
4 x 200-m: 1:22.11
Great Britain (Linford Christie, Darren Braithwaite, Ade Mafe, John Regis)
Glasgow, UK, 3 March 1991
4 x 400-m: 3:03.05
Germany (Rico Lieder, Jens Carlowitz, Karsten Just, Thomas Schönlebe)
Seville, Spain, 10 March 1991
5,000-m walk: 18:07.08
Mikhail Shchennikov (Russia)
Moscow, Russia, 14 Feb 1995

** Ben Johnson (Canada) ran 50 m in 5.55 seconds at Ottawa, Canada, on 31 Jan 1987 but this was invalidated after he admitted taking drugs, following his disqualification at the 1988 Olympics.*

Field Events

High Jump: 2.43 m (7 ft 11½ in)
Javier Sotomayor (Cuba)
Budapest, Hungary, 4 March 1989
Pole Vault: 6.15 m (20 ft 2¼ in)
Sergey Nazarovich Bubka (Ukraine)
Donetsk, Ukraine, 21 Feb 1993
Long Jump: 8.79 m (28 ft 10¼ in)
Carl Lewis (USA)
New York, USA, 27 Jan 1984
Triple Jump: 17.83 m (58 ft 6 in)
Alliacer Urrutia (Cuba)
Sindelfingen, Germany, 1 March 1997
Shot: 22.66 m (74 ft 4 in)
Randy Barnes (USA)
Los Angeles, California, USA, 20 Jan 1989
Heptathlon: 6,476 points
Dan Dion O'Brien (USA)
Toronto, Canada, 13–14 March 1993
60 m: 6.67 sec; long jump: 7.84 m (25 ft 8½ in); shot: 16.02 m (52 ft 6¾ in); high jump: 2.13 m (6 ft 11¾ in); 60-m hurdles: 7.85 sec; pole vault 5.20 m (17 ft ¾ in); 1,000 m: 2:57.96

WOMEN'S INDOOR RECORDS

Running

50 m: 5.96
Irina Privalova (Russia)
Madrid, Spain, 9 Feb 1995
60 m: 6.92
Irina Privalova (Russia)
Madrid, Spain, 11 Feb 1993
200 m: 21.87
Merlene Ottey (Jamaica) Liévin, France, 13 Feb 1993

400 m: 49.59
Jarmila Kratochvílová (Czechoslovakia)
Milan, Italy, 7 March 1982
800 m: 1:56.36
Maria Lurdes Mutola (Mozambique)
Liévin, France, 22 Feb 1998
1,000 m: 2:30.94
Maria Lurdes Mutola (Mozambique)
Stockholm, Sweden, 25 Feb 1999
1,500 m: 4:00.27
Doina Melinte (Romania)
East Rutherford, NJ, USA, 9 Feb 1990
1 mile: 4:17.14
Doina Melinte (Romania)
East Rutherford, New Jersey, USA, 9 Feb 1990
3,000 m: 8:33.82
Elly van Hulst (Netherlands)
Budapest, Hungary, 4 March 1989
5,000 m: 14:47.35
Gabriela Szabo (Romania)
Dortmund, Germany, 13 Feb 1999
50-m hurdles: 6.58
Cornelia Oschkenat (GDR)
Berlin, Germany, 20 Feb 1988
60-m hurdles: 7.69*
Lyudmila Narozhilenko (Russia)
Chelyabinsk, Russia, 4 Feb 1993
4 x 200-m: 1:32.55
S.C. Eintracht Hamm (West Germany) (Helga Arendt, Silke-Beate Knoll, Mechthild Kluth, Gisela Kinzel)
Dortmund, Germany, 19 Feb 1988
1:32.55
LG Olympic Dortmund (Germany) (Esther Moller, Gabi Rockmeier, Birgit Rockmeier, Andrea Phillip)
Karlsruhe, Germany, 21 Feb 1999
4 x 400-m: 3:26.84
Russia (Tatyana Chebykina, Olga Goncharenko, Olga Kotlyarova, Tatyana Alekseyeva)
Paris, France, 9 March 1997
3,000-m walk: 11:40.33
Claudia Iovan (Romania)
Bucharest, Romania, 30 Jan 1999

Field Events

High Jump: 2.07 m (6 ft 9½ in)
Heike Henkel (Germany)
Karlsruhe, Germany, 9 Feb 1992
Pole vault: 4.55 m (14 ft 11 in)
Emma George (Australia)
Adelaide, Australia, 26 March 1998

Australia's Emma George was a circus performer before she became a pole vaulter.

Long Jump: 7.37 m (24 ft 2½ in)
Heike Drechsler (GDR)
Vienna, Austria, 13 Feb 1988
Triple jump: 15.16 m (49 ft 8¾ in)
Ashia Hansen (GB)
Valencia, Spain, 28 Feb 1998
Shot: 22.5 m (73 ft 10 in)
Helena Fibingerová (Czechoslovakia)
Jablonec, Czechoslovakia, 19 Feb 1977
Pentathlon: 4,991 points
Irina Belova (Russia)
Berlin, Germany, 14–15 Feb 1992
60-m hurdles: 8.22 sec; high jump: 1.93 m (6 ft 4 in); shot: 13.25 m (43 ft 5¾ in); long jump: 6.67 m (21 ft 10 in); 800 m: 2:10.26

** Narozhilenko recorded a time of 7.63 seconds at Seville, Spain, on 4 Nov 1993, but was disqualified after a positive drugs test.*

badminton

Most World Championships
The most wins at the men's World Team Badminton Championships for the Thomas Cup (instituted in 1948) is 11, by Indonesia (1958, 61, 64, 70, 73, 76, 79, 84, 94, 96 and 98).

The most wins at the women's World Team Badminton Championships for the Uber Cup (instituted in 1956) is six, by China (1984, 86, 88, 90, 92 and 98).

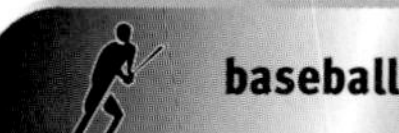

baseball

AL = American League
NL = National League

US MAJOR LEAGUE
Batting records
Average
Career: .367
Ty Cobb (Detroit AL, Philadelphia AL), 1905–28.
Season: .438
Hugh Duffy (Boston NL), 1894.
Runs
Career: 2,245
Ty Cobb, 1905–28.
Season: 196
Billy Hamilton (Philadelphia NL), 1894.

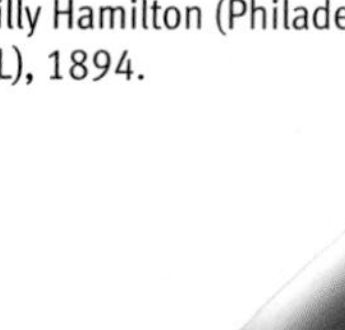

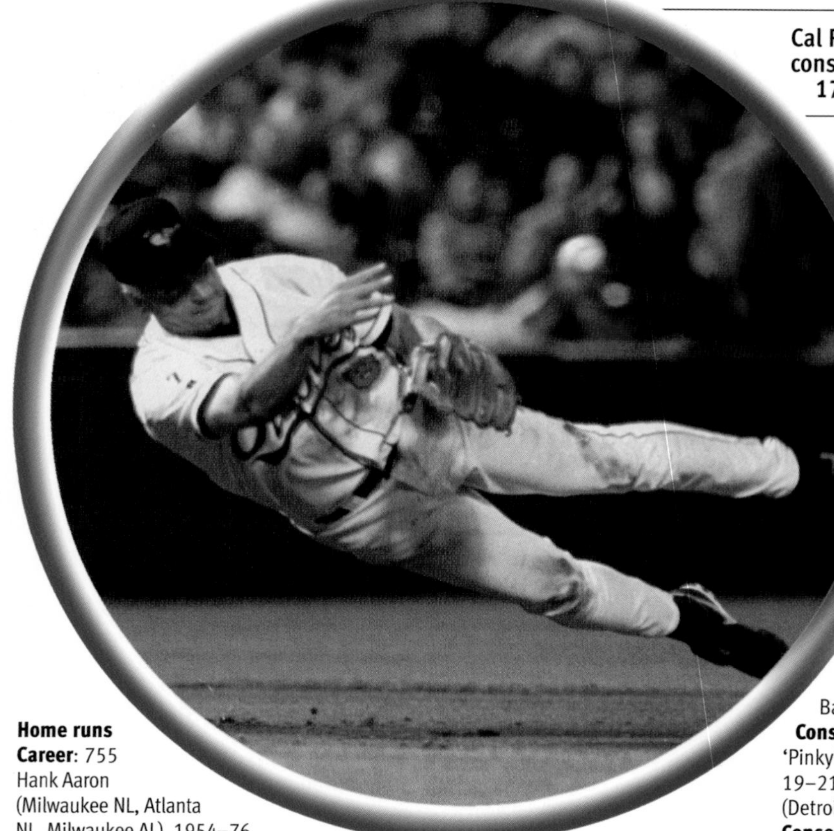

Home runs
Career: 755
Hank Aaron (Milwaukee NL, Atlanta NL, Milwaukee AL), 1954–76.
Season: 70
Mark McGwire (St Louis NL), 1998.

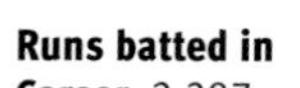

Runs batted in
Career: 2,297
Hank Aaron, 1954–76.
Season: 191
Hack Wilson (Chicago NL), 1930.
Game: 12
Jim Bottomley (St Louis NL), 16 Sept 1924; Mark Whiten (St Louis NL), 7 Sept 1993.
Innings: 7
Edward Cartwright (St Louis AL), 23 Sept 1890.
Base hits
Career: 4,256
Pete Rose (Cincinnati NL, Philadelphia NL, Montreal NL, Cincinnati NL), 1963–86.
Season: 257
George Sisler (St Louis AL), 1920.
Total bases
Career: 6,856
Hank Aaron, 1954–76.
Season: 457
Babe Ruth (New York AL), 1921.
Consecutive hits: 12
'Pinky' Higgins (Boston AL), 19–21 June 1938; Moose Dropo (Detroit AL), 14–15 July 1952.
Consecutive games batted safely: 56
Joe DiMaggio (New York AL), 15 May–16 July 1941.
Stolen bases
Career: 1,315
Rickey Henderson (Oakland AL, New York AL, Oakland AL, Toronto AL, Oakland AL, San Diego NL, Anaheim AL, Oakland AL, New York NL), 1979–99.
Season: 130
Rickey Henderson, (Oakland AL), 1982.
Consecutive games played: 2,632
Cal Ripken Jr (Baltimore AL), 30 May 1982–19 Sept 1998.
Pitching records
Games won
Career: 511
Cy Young (Cleveland NL, St Louis NL, Boston AL, Cleveland AL, Boston NL), 1890–1911.
Season: 60
'Hoss' Radbourn (Providence NL), 1884.
Consecutive games won: 24
Carl Hubbell (New York NL), 1936–37.
Shutouts
Career: 110
Walter Johnson (Washington AL), 1907–27.
Season: 16
George Bradley (St Louis NL), 1876; Grover Alexander (Philadelphia NL), 1916.
Strikeouts
Career: 5,714
Nolan Ryan (New York NL, California AL, Houston NL, Texas AL), 1966–93.
Season: 383
Nolan Ryan (California AL), 1973.
Game (9 innings): 20

Cal Ripken played 2,632 consecutive games over 17 seasons.

Rickey Henderson, currently of the New York Mets, holds career and season records for stolen bases.

Roger Clemens (Boston AL) v. Seattle, 29 April 1986 and v. Detroit, 18 Sept 1996; Kerry Wood (Chicago NL) v. Houston, 6 May 1998.

No-hit games
Career: 7
Nolan Ryan, 1973–91.

Earned run average
Season: .90 Ferdinand Schupp (140 inns) (New York NL), 1916; 0.96 Dutch Leonard (222 inns) (Boston AL), 1914; 1.12 Bob Gibson (305 inns) (St Louis NL), 1968.

WORLD SERIES RECORDS
Most series played: 14
Yogi Berra (New York AL), 1947–63
Most series played by pitcher: 11
'Whitey' Ford (New York AL), 1950–64
Most home runs in a game: 3
Babe Ruth (New York AL), 6 Oct 1926 and 9 Oct 1928; and Reggie Jackson (New York AL), 18 Oct 1977
Runs batted in: 6
Bobby Richardson (New York AL), 8 Oct 1960
Strikeouts: 17
Bob Gibson (St Louis NL), 2 Oct 1968
Perfect game: (9 innings)
Don Larsen (New York AL) v. Brooklyn, 8 Oct 1956

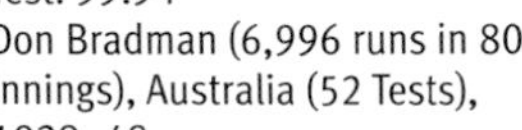

Highest average: FC: 95.14
Don Bradman, NSW/South Australia/Australia, 1927–49 (28,067 runs in 338 innings, including 43 not outs)
Test: 99.94
Don Bradman (6,996 runs in 80 innings), Australia (52 Tests), 1928–48

Mark Taylor made 157 catches in his Test career.

cricket

FIRST-CLASS (FC) AND TEST CAREER

Batting
Most runs: FC: 61,237
Sir Jack Hobbs (1882–1963) (av. 50.65) Surrey/England, 1905–34
Test: 11,174 Allan Border (av. 50.56) Australia (156 Tests), 1978–94

Most centuries: FC: 197
Sir Jack Hobbs (in 1,315 innings), Surrey/England, 1905–34
Test: 34 Sunil Gavaskar (in 214 innings), India, 1971–87

Bowling
Most wickets:
FC: 4,187
Wilfred Rhodes (av. 16.71), Yorkshire/England, 1898–1930
Test: 434
Kapil Dev (av. 29.62), India (131 Tests), 1978–94
Lowest average: Test 10.75
George Lohmann (112 wkts), England (18 Tests), 1886–96 (min 25 wkts)

Wicket-keeping
Most dismissals: FC: 1,649
Bob Taylor, Derbys/England, 1960–88
Test: 389
Ian Healy, Australia (115 Tests), 1988–99
Most catches: FC: 1,473
Bob Taylor, Derbys/England, 1960–88
Test: 360
Ian Healy, Australia (115 Tests), 1988–99
Most stumpings: FC: 418
Leslie Ames, Kent/England, 1926–51
Test: 52
William Oldfield, Australia, 1920–37

Fielding
Most catches: FC: 1,018
Frank Woolley, Kent/England, 1906–38
Test: 157
Mark Taylor, Australia (104 Tests), 1989–99

Ian Healy's 389 Test victims have included England's Mark Ramprakash, in 1997.

TEST SERIES

Batting
Most runs: 974
Don Bradman (av. 139.14), Australia v. England (5), 1930
Most centuries: 5
Clyde Walcott, West Indies v. Australia (5), 1954/55
Highest average: 563.00
Walter Hammond, England v. New Zealand (2), 1932/33 (563 runs, 2 inns, 1 not out)

Bowling
Most wickets: 49
Sydney Barnes (av. 10.93), England v. South Africa (4), 1913/14
Lowest average: 5.80
George Lohmann (35 wkts), England v. South Africa (3), 1895/96 (min 20 wkts)

Wicket-keeping
Most dismissals: 28
Rodney Marsh (all caught), Australia v. England (5), 1982/83
Most stumpings: 9
Percy Sherwell, South Africa v. Australia (5), 1910/11

Fielding
Most catches: 15
Jack Gregory, Australia v. England (5), 1920/21

All-round
400 runs/30 wkts 475/34, George Giffen (1859–1927), Australia v. England (5), 1894/95

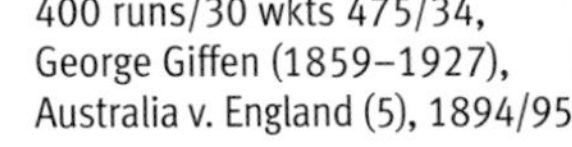

darts

24-HOUR

Men

(8 players): 1,722,249 by Broken Hill Darts Club at Broken Hill, NSW, Australia, 28–29 Sept 1985.

Women

(8 players): 830,737 by a team at the Cornwall Inn, Killurin, Co. Wexford, Ireland, 1–2 Aug 1997.

Individual: 567,145 by Kenny Fellowes at The Prince of Wales, Cashes Green, Glos, UK, 28–29 Sept 1996.

Bulls and 25s: (8 players) 526,750 by a team at the George Inn, Morden, Surrey, UK, 1–2 July 1994.

10-HOUR

Most trebles: 3,056 (from 7,992 darts) by Paul Taylor at the Woodhouse Tavern, London, UK, 19 Oct 1985.

Most doubles: 3,265 (from 8,451 darts) by Paul Taylor at the Lord Brooke, London, UK, 5 Sept 1987.

Highest score: 465,919 (retrieving own darts) by Jon Archer and Neil Rankin at the Royal Oak, Cossington, Leics, UK, 17 Nov 1990.

Bulls (individual): 1,321 by Jim Damore (USA) at the Parkside Pub, Chicago, Illinois, USA, 29 June 1996.

6-HOUR

Men: 210,172 by Russell Locke at the Hugglescote Working Men's Club, Coalville, Leics, UK, 10 Sept 1989.

Women: 99,725 by Karen Knightly at the Lord Clyde, London, UK, 17 March 1991.

Million and One Up

Men: (8 players) 36,583 by a team at Buzzy's Pub and Grub, Lynn, Massachusetts, USA, 19–20 Oct 1991.

Chris Boardman,
4-km record-holder

cycling

These records are those recognized by the Union Cycliste Internationale (UCI). From 1 Jan 1993 their list no longer distinguishes between those set by professionals and amateurs, indoor and outdoor records, or records set at altitude and sea level.

Men

Unpaced standing start

1 km: 1:00.613
Shane Kelly (Australia)
Bogotá, Colombia, 26 Sept 1995

4 km: 4:11.114
Chris Boardman (GB)
Manchester, UK, 29 Aug 1996

4 km team: 4:00.958
Italy
Manchester, UK, 31 Aug 1996

1 hour : 56.3759 km
Chris Boardman (GB)
Manchester, UK, 6 Sept 1996

Unpaced flying start

200 m: 9.865
Curtis Harnett (Canada)
Bogotá, Colombia, 28 Sept 1995

500 m: 26.649
Aleksandr Kiritchenko (USSR)
Moscow, USSR, 29 Oct 1988

Women

Unpaced standing start

500 m: 34.017
Felicia Ballanger (France)
Bogotá, Colombia,
29 Sept 1995

3 km: 3:30.974
Marion Clignet (France)
Manchester, UK, 31 Aug 1996

1 hour: 48.159 km
Jeanie Longo-Ciprelli (France)
Mexico City, Mexico, 26 Oct 1996

Unpaced flying start

200 m: 10.831
Olga Slyusareva (Russia)
Moscow, Russia, 25 April 1993

500 m: 29.655
Erika Salumäe (USSR)
Moscow, USSR, 6 Aug 1987

Felicia
Ballanger

Women: (8 players) 70,019 darts by the 'Delinquents' team at the Top George, Combe Martin, Devon, UK, 11–13 Sept 1987.

gliding

World Gliding Single-Seater Records
Straight Distance: 1,460.8 km (907 miles 1,232 yd)
Hans-Werner Grosse (West Germany)
Lübeck, Germany, to Biarritz, France, 25 April 1972
Declared Goal Distance: 1,383 km (859 miles 704 yd)
Jean Nöel Herbaud (France), Vinon, France, to Fes, Morocco, 14 April 1992
Gérard Herbaud (France), Vinon, France, to Fes, Morocco, 17 April 1992
Goal and Return: 1,646.68 km (1,023 miles 352 yd)
Thomas L. Knauff (USA)
Gliderport to Williamsport, Pennsylvania, USA, 25 April 1983
Absolute Altitude: 14,938 m (49,009 ft)
Robert R. Harris (USA)
California, USA, 17 Feb 1986
Height Gain: 12,894 m (42,303 ft)
Paul F. Bikle (USA)
Mojave, Lancaster, California, USA, 25 Feb 1961
SPEED OVER TRIANGULAR COURSE
100 km: 217.41 km/h (135.09 mph)
James Payne (USA)
California, USA, 4 March 1997
300 km: 176.99 km/h (109.97 mph)
Beat Bünzli (Switzerland)
Bitterwasser, Namibia, 14 Nov 1985
500 km: 171.7 km/h (106.7 mph)
Hans-Werner Grosse (West Germany)
Mount Newman, Australia, 31 Dec 1990
750 km: 161.33 km/h (100.24 mph)
Hans-Werner Grosse (West Germany)
Alice Springs, Australia, 10 Jan 1988
1,250 km: 143.46 km/h (89.14 mph)
Hans-Werner Grosse (West Germany)
Alice Springs, Australia, 10 Jan 1987

golf

Most Major Golf Titles
The Open: 6
Harry Vardon 1896, 1898–89, 1903, 11, 14
The Amateur: 8
John Ball 1888, 90, 92, 94, 99, 1907, 10, 12
US Open: 4
Willie Anderson 1901, 03–05
Bobby Jones Jr 1923, 26, 29–30
Ben Hogan 1948, 50–51, 53
Jack Nicklaus 1962, 67, 72, 80
US Amateur: 5
Robert Jones Jr 1924–25, 27–28, 30
US PGA: 5
Walter Hagen 1921, 24–27
Jack Nicklaus 1963, 71, 73, 75, 80
US Masters: 6
Jack Nicklaus 1963, 65–66, 72, 75, 86
US Women's Open: 4
Betsy Earle-Rawls 1951, 53, 57, 60
Mickey Wright 1958–59, 61, 64
US Women's Amateur: 6
Glenna Collett Vare 1922, 25, 28–30, 35
British Women's: 4
Charlotte Pitcairn Leitch 1914, 20–21, 26
Joyce Wethered 1922, 24–25, 29

The Netherlands have won more women's hockey World Cups than any other country.

Jack Nicklaus is the only golfer to have won five different major titles (The Open, US Open, Masters, PGA and US Amateur titles) twice and a record 20 all told (1959–86).
In 1930 Bobby Jones achieved a unique 'Grand Slam' of the US and British Open and Amateur titles.

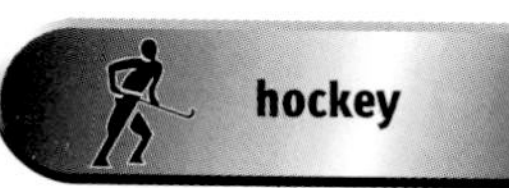

hockey

WORLD CUP
Women's wins: 5
Netherlands: 1974, 1978, 1983, 1986 and 1990.
Men's wins: 4
Pakistan: 1971, 1978, 1982 and 1994.

OLYMPIC GAMES
India was Olympic champion from the re-introduction of Olympic hockey in 1928 until 1960. They had their eighth win in 1980. Of the six Indians who have won three Olympic team gold medals, two have also won a silver medal — Leslie Walter Claudius, in 1948, 1952, 1956 and 1960 (silver), and Udham Singh, in 1952, 1956, 1964 and 1960 (silver).

A women's tournament was added in 1980, and Australia have won twice — in 1988 and 1996.

CHAMPIONS' TROPHY
The most wins is seven, by Germany, 1986–87 (as West Germany), 1991–92, 1995 and 1997.

The first women's Champions' Trophy was held in 1987. Australia has won four times: 1991, 1993, 1995 and 1997.

The legendary Jack Nicklaus has won a record 20 major titles.

horse racing

Major Race Records
1000 GUINEAS (UK)
Record time: 1:36.71
Las Meninas 1994
Most wins (jockey): 7
George Fordham 1859, 61, 65, 68, 69, 81, 83
Most wins (trainer): 9
Robert Robson 1818, 19, 20, 21, 22, 23, 25, 26, 27
Most wins (owner): 8
Duke of Grafton 1819, 20, 21, 22, 23, 25, 26, 27

2000 GUINEAS (UK)
Record time: 1:35.08
Mister Baileys 1994

Bart Cummings (pictured right) has trained 10 Melbourne Cup winners.

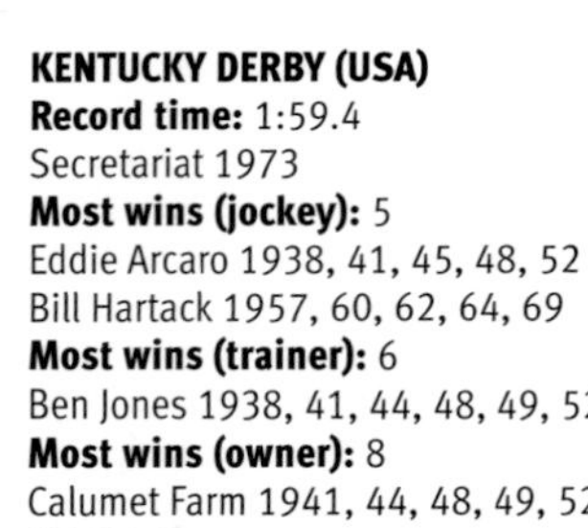

Most wins (jockey): 9
Jem Robinson 1825, 28, 31, 33, 34, 35, 36, 47, 48
Most wins (trainer): 7
John Scott 1842, 43, 49, 53, 56, 60, 62
Most wins (owner): 5
Duke of Grafton 1820, 21, 22, 26, 27
Earl of Jersey 1831, 34, 35, 36, 37

CHAMPION HURDLE (UK)
Record time: 3:48.4
Make A Stand 1997
Most wins (jockey): 4
Tim Molony 1951, 52, 53, 54
Most wins (trainer): 5
Peter Easterby 1967, 76, 77, 80, 81
Most wins (owner): 4
Dorothy Paget 1932, 33, 40, 46

CHELTENHAM GOLD CUP (UK)
Record time: 6:23.4
Silver Fame 1951
Most wins (jockey): 4
Pat Taaffe 1964, 65, 66, 68
Most wins (trainer): 5
Tom Dreaper 1946, 64, 65, 66, 68
Most wins (owner): 7
Dorothy Paget 1932, 33, 34, 35, 36, 40, 52

DERBY (UK)
Record time: 2:32.31
Lammtarra 1995
Most wins (jockey): 9
Lester Piggott 1954, 57, 60, 68, 70, 72, 76, 77, 83
Most wins (trainer): 7
Robert Robson 1793, 1802, 09, 10, 15, 17, 23
John Porter 1868, 82, 83, 86, 90, 91, 99
Fred Darling 1922, 25, 26, 31, 38, 40, 41
Most wins (owner): 5
Earl of Egremont 1782, 34, 1804, 05, 07, 26
Aga Khan III 1930, 35, 36, 48, 52

GRAND NATIONAL (UK)
Record time: 8:47.8
Mr Frisk 1990
Most wins (jockey): 5
George Stevens 1856, 63, 64, 69, 70
Most wins (trainer): 4
Fred Rimell 1956, 61, 70, 76
Most wins (owner): 3
James Machell 1873, 74, 76
Sir Charles Assheton-Smith 1893, 1912, 13
Noel Le Mare 1973, 74, 77

IRISH DERBY (REPUBLIC OF IRELAND)
Record time: 2:25.60
St Jovite 1992
Most wins (jockey): 6
Morny Wing 1921, 23, 30, 38, 42, 46
Most wins (trainer): 6
Vincent O'Brien 1953, 57, 70, 77, 84, 85
Most wins (owner): 5
Aga Khan III 1925, 32, 40, 48, 49

KENTUCKY DERBY (USA)
Record time: 1:59.4
Secretariat 1973
Most wins (jockey): 5
Eddie Arcaro 1938, 41, 45, 48, 52
Bill Hartack 1957, 60, 62, 64, 69
Most wins (trainer): 6
Ben Jones 1938, 41, 44, 48, 49, 52
Most wins (owner): 8
Calumet Farm 1941, 44, 48, 49, 52, 57, 58, 68

KING GEORGE VI AND QUEEN ELIZABETH DIAMOND STAKES (UK)
Record time: 2:26.98
Grundy 1975
Most wins (jockey): 7
Lester Piggott 1965, 66, 69, 70, 74, 77, 84
Most wins (trainer): 5
Dick Hern 1972, 79, 80, 85, 89
Most wins (owner): 3
Sheikh Mohammed 1990, 93, 94

OAKS (UK)
Record time: 2:34.19
Intrepidity 1993
Most wins (jockey): 9
Frank Buckle 1797, 98, 99, 1802, 03, 05, 17, 18, 23
Most wins (trainer): 12
Robert Robson 1802, 04, 05, 07, 08, 09, 13, 15, 18, 22, 23, 25
Most wins (owner): 6
Duke of Grafton 1813, 15, 22, 23, 28, 31

PRIX DE L'ARC DE TRIOMPHE (FRANCE)
Record time: 2:24.6
Peintre Célèbre 1997
Most wins (jockey): 4
Jacques Doyasbère 1942, 44, 50, 51
Frédéric Head 1966, 72, 76, 79
Yves St-Martin 1970, 74, 82, 84
Pat Eddery 1980, 85, 86, 87
Most wins (trainer): 4
Charles Semblat 1942, 44, 46, 49
Alec Head 1952, 59, 76, 81
François Mathet 1950, 51, 70, 82
Most wins (owner): 6
Marcel Boussac 1936, 37, 42, 44, 46, 49

ST LEGER (UK)
Record time: 3:01.6
Coronach 1926 and Windsor Lad 1934
Most wins (jockey): 9
Bill Scott 1821, 25, 28, 29, 38, 39, 40, 41, 46
Most wins (trainer): 16
John Scott 1827, 28, 29, 32, 34, 38, 39, 40, 41, 45, 51, 53, 56, 57, 59, 62
Most wins (owner): 7
9th Duke of Hamilton 1786, 87, 88, 92, 1808, 09, 14

VRC MELBOURNE CUP (AUSTRALIA)
Record time: 3:16.3
Kingston Rule 1990
Most wins (jockey): 4
Bobby Lewis 1902, 15, 19, 27
Harry White 1974, 75, 78, 79
Most wins (trainer): 10
Bart Cummings 1965, 66, 67, 74, 75, 77, 79, 90, 91, 96
Most wins (owner): 4
Etienne de Mestre 1861, 62, 67, 78

hurling

Most titles
The greatest number of All-Ireland Championships won by one team is 27, by Cork between 1890 and 1990.

Most appearances
The most appearances in All-Ireland finals is 10, by Christy Ring (Cork and Munster), John Doyle (Tipperary) and Frank Cummings (Kilkenny). Ring and Doyle also share the record of All-Ireland medals won, with eight each. Ring's appearances on the winning side were in 1941–44, 46 and 52–54, while Doyle's were in 1949–51, 58, 61–62 and 64–65. Ring also played in a record 22 inter-provincial finals (1942–63) and was on the winning side 18 times.

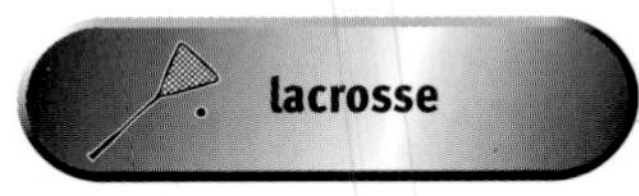

lacrosse

Men's World Titles
The USA has won seven of the eight World Championships, in 1967, 1974, 1982, 1986, 1990, 1994 and 1998. Canada won the other world title in 1978, beating the USA 17–16 after extra time — this was the first drawn international match.

Women's World Championships/ World Cup
The first World Cup was held in 1982, replacing the World Championships that had been held three times since 1969. The USA has won five times, in 1974, 1982, 1989, 1993 and 1997.

Highest scores (men)
The highest score in a World Cup match is Scotland's 34–3 win over Germany at Greater Manchester, UK, on 25 July 1994.

In the World Cup Premier Division, the record score is the USA's 33–2 win over Japan at Greater Manchester, UK, on 21 July 1994.

Highest score (women)
The highest score by any women's international team was by Great Britain and Ireland with their 40–0 defeat of Long Island during their 1967 tour of the USA.

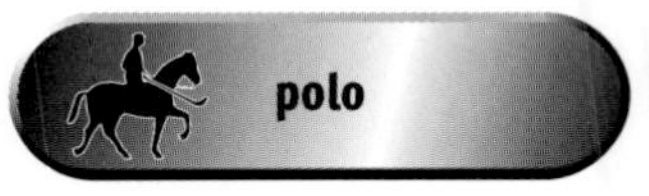

polo

Most Polo World Championships
Of the five world championships contested, three have been won by Argentina: in 1987 in Argentina, 1992 in Chile and 1998 in the USA. World Championships are held every three years under the auspices of the Federation of International Polo (FIP).

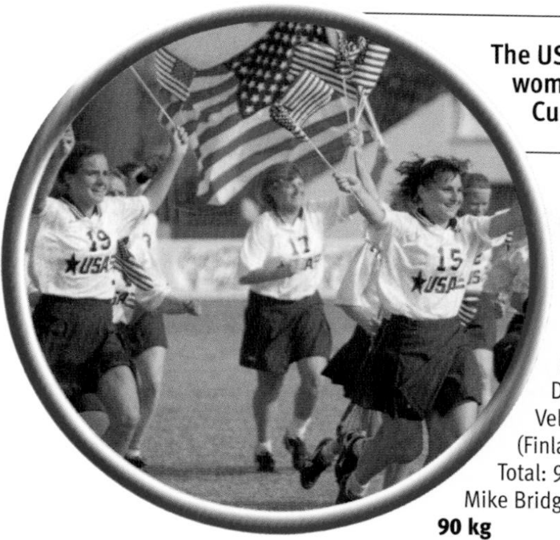
The USA won their fifth women's lacrosse World Cup in 1997.

Most goals in World Championships
Argentina have scored 35 goals during the finals of the FIP Polo World Championships. Brazil are second, with 19.

powerlifting

(All weights in kilograms)
MEN
52 kg
Squat: 277.5
Andrzej Stanaszek (Poland), 1997
Bench press: 177.5
Andrzej Stanaszek (Poland), 1994
Deadlift: 256
E. S. Bhaskaran (India), 1993
Total: 592.5
Andrzej Stanaszek (Poland), 1996
56 kg
Squat: 287.5
Magnus Carlsson (Sweden), 1996
Bench press: 187.5
Magnus Carlsson (Sweden), 1996
Deadlift: 289.5
Lamar Gant (USA), 1982
Total: 637.5
Hu Chun-hsing (Taiwan), 1997
60 kg
Squat: 315
Magnus Carlsson (Sweden), 1999
Bench press: 186.5
Magnus Carlsson (Sweden), 1999
Deadlift: 310
Lamar Gant, 1988
Total: 707.5
Joe Bradley (USA), 1982
67.5 kg
Squat: 305
Wade Hooper (USA), 1998
Bench press: 201
Aleksey Sivokon (Kazakhstan), 1998
Deadlift: 316.5
Aleksey Sivokon (Kazakhstan), 1998
Total: 800
Aleksey Sivokon (Kazakhstan), 1998
75 kg
Squat: 328
Ausby Alexander (USA), 1989
Bench press: 217.5
James Rouse (USA), 1980
Deadlift: 337.5
Daniel Austin (USA), 1994
Total: 850
Rick Gaugler (USA), 1982
82.5 kg
Squat: 379.5
Mike Bridges (USA), 1982
Bench press: 240
Mike Bridges, 1981
Deadlift: 357.5
Veli Kumpuniemi (Finland), 1980
Total: 952.5
Mike Bridges, 1982
90 kg
Squat: 375
Fred Hatfield (USA), 1980
Bench press: 255
Mike MacDonald (USA), 1980
Deadlift: 372.5
Walter Thomas (USA), 1982
Total: 937.5
Mike Bridges, 1980
100 kg
Squat: 423
Ed Coan (USA), 1994
Bench press: 261.5
Mike MacDonald (USA), 1977
Deadlift: 390
Ed Coan (USA), 1993
Total: 1035
Ed Coan (USA), 1994
110 kg
Squat: 415
Kirk Karwoski (USA), 1994
Bench press: 270
Jeffrey Magruder (USA), 1982
Deadlift: 395
John Kuc (USA), 1980
Total: 1,002.5
Aleksey Gankov (Russia), 1998
125 kg
Squat: 455
Kirk Karwoski, 1995
Bench press: 278.5
Tom Hardman (USA), 1982
Deadlift: 387.5
Lars Norén (Sweden), 1987
Total: 1,045
Kirk Karwoski, 1995
125+ kg
Squat: 447.5
Shane Hamman (USA), 1994
Bench press: 322.5
James Henderson (USA), 1997
Deadlift: 406
Lars Norén, 1988
Total: 1,100
Bill Kazmaier (USA), 1981

WOMEN
44 kg
Squat: 167.5
Raija Koskinen (Finland), 1998
Bench press: 87.5
Svetlana Tesleva (Russia), 1998
Deadlift: 166
Raija Koskinen (Finland), 1998
Total: 405
Raija Koskinen (Finland), 1998
48 kg
Squat: 175
Raija Koskinen (Finland), 1999
Bench press: 112.5
Irina Krylova (Russia), 1998
Deadlift: 182.5
Majik Jones (USA), 1984
Total: 420
Raija Koskinen (Finland), 1999
52 kg
Squat: 182.5
Oksana Belova (Russia), 1997
Bench press: 107.5
Anna Olsson (Sweden), 1997
Deadlift: 197.5
Diana Rowell (USA), 1984
Total: 475
Oksana Belova (Russia), 1997
56 kg
Squat: 191.5
Carrie Boudreau (USA), 1995
Bench press: 127.5
Valentina Nelubova (Russia), 1998
Deadlift: 222.5
Carrie Boudreau (USA), 1995
Total: 522.5
Carrie Boudreau (USA), 1995
60 kg
Squat: 210
Beate Amdahl (Norway), 1994
Bench press: 120
Yelena Fomina (Russia), 1998
Deadlift: 213.5
Ingeborg Marx (Belgium), 1997
Total: 525
Ingeborg Marx (Belgium), 1997
67.5 kg
Squat: 230
Ruthi Shafer (USA), 1984
Bench press: 142.5
Svetlana Miklazevich (Russia), 1998
Deadlift: 244
Ruthi Shafer, 1984
Total: 572.5
Lisa Sjöstrand (Sweden), 1997
75 kg
Squat: 245.5
Yelena Zhukova (Ukraine), 1998
Bench press: 147.5
Marina Zhguleva (Russia), 1998
Deadlift: 255
Yelena Zhukova (Ukraine), 1998
Total: 617.5
Yelena Zhukova (Ukraine), 1998
82.5 kg
Squat: 242.5
Anne Sigrid Stiklestad (Norway), 1997
Bench press: 151
Natalia Rumyantseva (Russia), 1997
Deadlift: 257.5
Cathy Millen (New Zealand), 1993
Total: 637.5
Cathy Millen (New Zealand), 1993
90 kg
Squat: 260
Cathy Millen (New Zealand), 1994
Bench press: 162.5
Cathy Millen (New Zealand), 1994
Deadlift: 260
Cathy Millen (New Zealand), 1994
Total: 682.5
Cathy Millen (New Zealand), 1994
90+ kg
Squat: 278.5
Chao Chen-yeh (China), 1999
Bench press: 178
Chao Chen-yeh (China), 1999
Deadlift: 263.5
Katrina Robertson (Australia), 1998
Total: 672.5
Chao Chen-yeh (China), 1999

Argentina have won three of the five World Polo Championships.

rowing

Most Olympic golds
The record for the most Olympic rowing golds is four by Steven Redgrave (GB): coxed fours (1984); and coxless pairs (1988, 92 and 96).

The women's record is three, by Canadian pair Kathleen Heddle and Marnie McBean: coxless pairs 1992; eights 1992; and double sculls 1996.

World Championships
World rowing championships — distinct from the Olympic Games — were first held in 1962, at first four-yearly, but from 1974 annually, except in Olympic years.
The most gold medals won at World Championships and Olympic Games is 12 by Steven Redgrave who, in addition to his four Olympic successes, won world titles at coxed pairs 1986, coxless pairs 1987, 91, 93–95, coxless fours, 1997–98.
Francesco Esposito (Italy) has won nine titles at lightweight events: coxless pairs, 1980–84, 88, 94; and coxless fours, 1990, 92.
At women's events Yelena Tereshina has won a record seven golds, all in eights for the USSR: 1978–79, 81–83, 85–86.
The most wins at single sculls is five by: Peter-Michael Kolbe (West Germany), 1975, 78, 81, 83 and 86; Pertti Karppinen, 1976, 79–80, 84–85; Thomas Lange (GDR/Germany), 1987–89, 91–92; and in the women's events by Christine Hahn (née Scheiblich) (GDR), 1974–78.
Highest speed
The record time for 2,000 m (1 mile 427 yd) on non-tidal water is 5:23.90 (22.22 km/h or 13.80 mph) by the Dutch National team (eight) at Duisburg, Germany, on 19 May 1996.
Highest speed
The women's record time for 2,000 m (1 mile 427 yd) on non-tidal water is 5:8.50 (20.08 km/h or 12.48 mph) by Romania at Duisburg, Germany, on 18 May 1996.
Highest speed
The single sculls record is 6:37.03 (18.13 km/h or 11.26 mph) by Juri Jaanson (Estonia) at Lucerne, Switzerland on 9 July 1995.
Highest speed
The single sculls record is 7:17.09 (16.47 km/h or 10.23 mph) by Silken Laumann (Canada) at Lucerne, Switzerland, on 17 July 1994.

Marnie McBean (left) and Kathleen Heddle (right) have won three Olympic rowing golds.

shooting

These are records recognized by the International Shooting Sport Federation (ISSF). The score for the number of shots specified is in brackets plus the score in the additional Final round.

MEN
Free Rifle 50 m 3 x 40 shots
1,287.9 (1,186+101.9)
Rajmond Debevec (Slovenia)
Munich, Germany, 29 Aug 1992
Free Rifle 50 m 60 Shots Prone
704.8 (600 + 104.8)
Christian Klees (Germany)
Atlanta, Georgia, USA, 25 July 1996
Air Rifle 10 m 60 shots
700.6 (598 + 102.6)
Jason Parker (USA)
Munich, Germany, 23 May 1998
Free Pistol 50 m 60 shots
675.3 (580 + 95.3)
Taniu Kiriakov (Bulgaria)
Hiroshima, Japan, 21 April 1995
Rapid-Fire Pistol 25 m 60 shots
699.7 (596 + 107.5)
Ralf Schumann (Germany)
Barcelona, Spain, 8 June 1994
Air Pistol 10 m 60 shots
695.1 (593 + 102.1)
Sergey Pyzhyanov (USSR)
Munich, Germany, 13 Oct 1989
Running Target 10 m 30/30 shots
687.9 (586 + 101.9)
Ling Yang (China)
Milan, Italy, 6 June 1996
Trap 125 targets
150 (125 + 25)
Marcello Tittarelli (Italy)
Suhl, Germany, 11 June 1996
Skeet 125 targets
150 (125 + 25)
Ennio Falco (Italy)
Lonato, Italy, 19 April 1997
Jan Henrik Heinrich (Germany)
Lonato, Italy, 5 June 1996
Andrea Benelli (Italy)
Suhl, Germany, 11 June 1996
Harald Jensen (Norway)
Kumamoto City, Japan, 1 June 1999
Double trap 150 targets
193 (145 + 48)
Richard Faulds (GB)
Atlanta, USA, 15 May 1998

WOMEN
Standard Rifle
50 m 3 x 20 shots
689.7 (591 + 98.7)
Wang Xian (China)
Milan, Italy, 29 May 1998
Air Rifle 10 m 40 shots
503.5 (398 + 105.5)
Gaby Bühlmann (Switzerland)
Munich, Germany, 24 May 1998
Sport Pistol 25 m 60 shots
696.2 (594 + 102.2)
Diana Jorgova (Bulgaria)
Milan, Italy, 31 May 1994
Air Pistol 10 m 40 shots
493.5 (390 + 103.5)
Ren Jie (China)
Munich, Germany, 22 May 1999
Skeet 100 targets
99 (75 + 24)
Svetlana Demina (Russia)
Kumamoto City, Japan, 1 June 1999
Trap 100 targets
95 (71 + 24)
Satu Pusila (Finland)
Nicosia, Cyprus, 13 June 1998
Double Trap 120 targets
149 (111 + 38)
Deborah Gelisio (Italy)
Munich, Germany,
3 Sept 1995

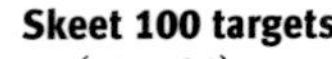

Norway's Ådne Søndrål holds the world 1,500-m speed skating record.

skating

World Speed Skating Records
Men
500 m: 34.76
Jeremy Wotherspoon (Canada)
Calgary, Canada, 20 Feb 1999
1,000 m: 1:08.55
Jan Bos (Netherlands)
Calgary, Canada, 21 Feb 1999
1,500 m: 1:46.43
Ådne Søndrål (Norway)
Calgary, Canada, 28 March 1998
3,000m: 3:45.23
Steven Elm (Canada)
Calgary, Canada, 19 March 1999
5,000 m: 6:21.49
Gianni Romme (Netherlands)
Calgary, Canada, 27 March 1998
10,000 m: 13:08.71
Gianni Romme (Netherlands)
Calgary, Canada, 29 March 1998

Women
500 m: 37.55
Catriona Le May Doan (Canada)
Calgary, Canada, 29 Dec 1997
1,000 m: 1:14.61
Monique Gabrecht (Germany)
Calgary, Canada, 21 Feb 1999
1,500 m: 1:55.50
Annamarie Thomas (Netherlands)
Calgary, Canada, 20 March 1999

3,000 m: 4:01.67
Gunda Niemann-Stirnemann (Germany)
Calgary, Canada, 27 March 1998
5,000 m: 6:57.24
Gunda Niemann-Stirnemann (Germany)
Hamar, Norway, 7 Feb 1999

WORLD RECORDS – SHORT TRACK
Men
500 m: 41.938
Nicola Franceschina (Italy)
Bormio, Italy, 29 March 1998
1,000 m: 1:28.23
Marc Gagnon (Canada)
Seoul, South Korea, 4 April 1997
1,500 m: 2:15.50
Kai Feng (China)
Habin, China, 11 Nov 1997
3,000 m: 4:53.23
Kim Dong-sung (South Korea)
Szekesfehervar, Hungary, 8 Nov 1998
5,000 m relay: 7:00.042
South Korea
Nagano, Japan, 30 March 1997

Women
500 m: 44.690
Yevgenia Radanova (Bulgaria)
Szekesfehervar, Hungary, 7 Nov 1998
1,000 m: 1:31.991
Yang Yang (China)
Nagano, Japan, 21 Feb 1998
1,500 m: 2:25.146
Yevgenia Radanova (Bulgaria)
Szekesfehervar, Hungary, 6 Nov 1998
3,000-m relay: 4:16.26
South Korea
Nagano, Japan, 17 Feb 1998

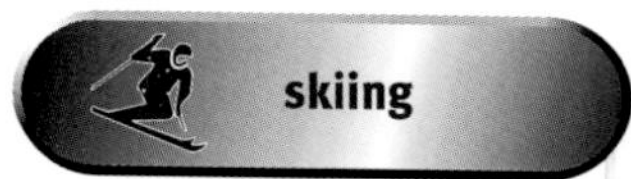

skiing

Most Olympic Skiing Titles
MEN
Alpine: 3
Toni Sailer (Austria)
Downhill, slalom, giant slalom 1956
Jean-Claude Killy (France)
Downhill, slalom, giant slalom 1968
Alberto Tomba (Italy)
Slalom, giant slalom 1988; giant slalom 1992
Nordic: 8
Bjørn Dæhlie (Norway)
15 km, 50 km, 4 x 10-km 1992;
10 km, 15 km 1994;
10 km, 50 km, 4 x 10-km 1998
Jumping: 4
Matti Nykänen (Finland) 70-m hill 1988; 90-m hill 1984, 88; Team 1988

WOMEN
Alpine: 3
Vreni Schneider (Switzerland)
Giant slalom, slalom 1988; slalom 1994
Katja Seizinger (Germany)
Downhill 1994; combined, downhill 1998
Deborah Campagnoni (Italy)
Super giant slalom 1992; giant slalom 1994; giant slalom 1998

Nordic: 6
Lyubov Yegorova (Russia)
10 km, 15 km, 4 x 5-km 1992; 5 km, 10 km, 4 x 5-km 1994

Most medals
12 (men): Bjørn Dæhlie (Norway) won eight gold and four silver in Nordic events, 1992–98.
10 (women): Raisa Smetanina (USSR/CIS), four gold, five silver and one bronze in Nordic events, 1976–92.
In Alpine skiing, the record is five: Alberto Tomba won three golds, plus silver in the 1992 and 94 slalom; Vreni Schneider won silver in the combined and bronze in the giant slalom in 1994; Katja Seizinger won bronze in the 1992 and 98 super giant slalom; and Kjetil André Aamodt (Norway) won one gold (super giant slalom 1992), two silver (downhill, combined 1994) and two bronze (giant slalom 1992, super giant slalom 1994).

Most World Cup Titles
MEN
Alpine
Overall: 5
Marc Girardelli (Luxembourg), 1985–86, 89, 91, 93
Downhill: 5
Franz Klammer (Austria), 1975–78, 83
Slalom: 8
Ingemar Stenmark (Sweden), 1975–81, 83
Giant Slalom: 7
Ingemar Stenmark (Sweden), 1975–76, 78–81, 84
Super Giant Slalom: 4
Pirmin Zurbriggen (Switzerland) 1987–90
Two men have won four titles in one year: Jean-Claude Killy (France) won all four possible disciplines (downhill, slalom, giant slalom and overall) in 1967; and Pirmin Zurbriggen (Switzerland) won four of the five possible disciplines (downhill, giant slalom, super giant slalom [added 1986] and overall) in 1987.
Nordic
Cross-country: 6
Bjørn Dæhlie (Norway), 1992–93, 95–97, 99
Jumping: 4
Matti Nykänen (Finland), 1983, 85–86, 88

WOMEN
Overall: 6
Annemarie Moser-Pröll (Austria), 1971–75, 79
Downhill: 7
Annemarie Moser-Pröll, 1971–75, 78–79
Slalom: 6
Vreni Schneider (Switzerland) 1989–90, 92–5
Giant Slalom: 5
Vreni Schneider (Switzerland), 1986–87, 89, 91, 95
Super Giant Slalom: 5
Katja Seizinger (Germany), 1993–96, 98
Nordic
Cross Country: 4
Yelena Välbe (USSR/Russia), 1989, 91–92, 95

squash

World Championships
The most men's world team titles is six by: Australia 1967, 69, 71, 73, 89 and 91; and Pakistan 1977, 81, 83, 85, 87 and 93.

The women's title has been won six times by Australia, 1981, 83, 92, 94, 96 and 98.

Jansher Khan (Pakistan) has won eight World Open (instituted 1976) titles, 87, 89–90, 92–96.

Jahangir Khan (Pakistan) won six World Open titles, 1981–85 and 88, and the International Squash Rackets Federation world individual title (formerly World Amateur, instituted in 1967) in 1979, 83 and 85.

Geoffrey B. Hunt (Australia) won four World Open titles, 1976–77 and 79–80 and three World Amateur, 1967, 69 and 71.

The most women's World Open titles is four by Susan Devoy (New Zealand), 1985, 87, 90 and 92.

Deborah Campagnoni has won three Olympic Alpine titles — a record she shares with two other women.

Frédéric Deburghgraeve won the 100-m breaststroke at the 1996 Olympics, and set a new world record as well.

World Records (50-m pools)
MEN
Freestyle
50 m: 21.81
Tom Jager (USA)
Nashville, Tennessee, USA, 24 March 1990
100 m: 48.21
Aleksandr Popov (Russia)
Monte Carlo, Monaco, 18 June 1994
200 m: 1:46.67
Grant Hackett (Australia)
Brisbane, Australia, 23 March 1999
400 m: 3:43.80
Kieren John Perkins (Australia)
Rome, Italy, 9 Sept 1994
800 m: 7:46.00
Kieren John Perkins (Australia)
Victoria, Canada, 24 Aug 1994
1,500 m: 14:41.66
Kieren John Perkins (Australia)
Victoria, Canada, 24 Aug 1994
4 x 100 m: 3:15.11
USA (David Fox, Joe Hudepohl, Jon Olsen, Gary Hall)
Atlanta, Georgia, USA, 12 Aug 1995
4 x 200-m: 7:11.86
Australia (Ian Thorpe, Daniel Kowlaski, Matthew Dunn, Michael Klim)

Kuala Lumpur, Malaysia, 13 Sept 1998
Breaststroke
100 m: 1:00.60
Frédéric Deburghgraeve (Belgium)
Atlanta, Georgia, USA, 20, July 1996
200 m: 2:10.16
Michael Ray Barrowman (USA)
Barcelona, Spain, 29 July 1992
Butterfly
100 m: 52.15
Michael Klim (Australia)
Brisbane, Australia, 9 Oct 1997
200 m: 1:55.22
Denis Pankratov (Russia)
Paris, France, 14 June 1995
Backstroke
100 m: 53.86
Jeff Rouse (USA)
Barcelona, Spain, 31 July 1992
200 m: 1:56.57
Martin López-Zubero (Spain)
Tuscaloosa, Alabama, USA, 23 Nov 1991
Medley
200 m: 1:58.16
Jani Nikanor Sievinen (Finland)
Rome, Italy, 11 Sept 1994
400 m: 4:12.30
Tom Dolan (USA) Rome, Italy, 6 Sept 1994
4 x 100-m: 3:34.84
USA (Gary Hall Jr, Mark Henderson, Jeremy Linn, Jeff Rouse)
Atlanta, Georgia, USA, 26 July 1996

WOMEN
Freestyle
50 m: 24.51
Le Jingyi (China)
Rome, Italy, 11 Sept 1994
100 m: 54.01
Le Jingyi (China)
Rome, Italy, 5 Sept 1994
200 m: 1:56.78
Franziska van Almsick (Germany)
Rome, Italy, 6 Sept 1994
400 m: 4:03.8
Janet Evans (USA)
Seoul, South Korea, 22 Sept 1988
800 m: 8:16.22
Janet Evans (USA)
Tokyo, Japan, 20 Aug 1989
1,500 m: 15:52.10
Janet Evans (USA)
Orlando, Florida, USA, 26 March 1988
4 x 100-m: 3:37.91
China (Le Jingyi, Shan Ying, Le Ying, Lu Bin)
Rome, Italy, 7 Sept 1994
4 x 200-m: 7:55.47
GDR (Manuela Stellmach, Astrid Strauss, Anke Möhring, Heike Friedrich)
Strasbourg, France, 18 Aug 1987
Breaststroke
100 m: 1:07.02
Penelope Heyns (South Africa)
Atlanta, Georgia, USA, 21 July 1996
200 m: 2:24.76
Rebecca Brown (Australia)
Brisbane, Australia, 16 March 1994
Butterfly
100 m: 57.93
Mary Terstegge Meagher (USA)
Brown Deer, Wisconsin, USA, 16 Aug 1981
200 m: 2:05.96
Mary Terstegge Meagher (USA)
Brown Deer, Wisconsin, USA, 13 Aug 1981
Backstroke
100 m: 1:00.16
He Cihong (China)
Rome, Italy, 10 Sept 1994
200 m: 2:06.62
Krisztina Egerszegi (Hungary)
Athens, Greece, 25 Aug 1991
Medley
200 m: 2:09.72
Wu Yanyan (China)
Shanghai, China, 17 Oct 1997
400 m: 4:34.79
Chen Yan (China)
Shanghai, China, 17 Oct 1997

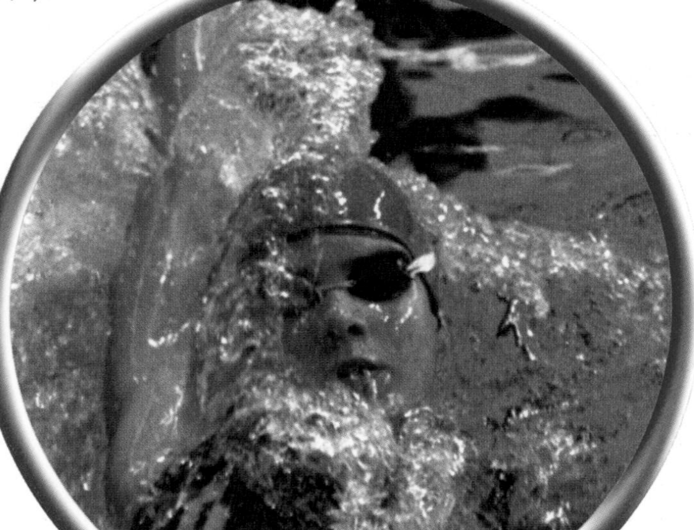

Krisztina Egerszegi holds the women's 200-m backstroke record.

Jenny Thompson holds the 100-m individual medley short-course record.

4 x 100-m: 4:01.67
China (He Cihong, Dai Guohong, Liu Limin, Le Jingyi)
Rome, Italy, 10 Sept 1994

Short-Course Records (25-m pools)

MEN

Freestyle

50 m: 21.31
Mark Foster (GB)
Sheffield, S Yorks, UK, 13 Dec 1998

100 m: 46.74
Aleksandr Popov (Russia)
Gelsenkirchen, Germany, 19 March 1994

200 m: 1:43.28
Ian Thorpe (Australia)
Hong Kong, China, 1 April 1999

400 m: 3:35.01
Grant Hackett (Australia)
Hong Kong, China, 2 April 1999

800 m: 7:34.90
Kieren Perkins (Australia)
Sydney, NSW, Australia, 25 July 1993

1,500 m: 14:19.55
Grant Hackett (Australia)
Perth, Australia, 27 Sept 1998

4 x 50-m: 1:26.99
Netherlands
Sheffield, S Yorks, UK, 13 Dec 1998

4 x 100-m: 3:10.45
Brazil
Rio de Janeiro, Brazil, 20 Dec 1998

4 x 200-m: 7:02.74
Australia
Gothenburg, Sweden, 18 April 1997

Backstroke

50 m: 24.13
Thomas Rupprath (Germany)
Sheffield, S Yorks, UK, 11 Dec 1998

100 m: 51.43
Jeff Rouse (USA)
Sheffield, S Yorks, UK, 12 April 1993

200 m: 1:52.51
Martin Lopez-Zubero (Spain)
Gainesville, Florida, USA, 10 April 1991

Breaststroke

50 m: 26.70
Mark Warnecke (Germany)
Sheffield, S Yorks, UK, 11 Dec 1998

100 m: 58.79
Frédéric Deburghgraeve (Belgium)
College Station, Texas, USA, 3 Dec 1998

200 m: 2:07.79
Andrey Korneev (Russia)
Paris, France, 28 March 1998

Butterfly

50 m: 23.35
Denis Pankratov (Russia)
Paris, France, 8 Feb 1997

100 m: 51.02
James Hickman (GB)
Sheffield, S Yorks, UK, 13 Dec 1998

200 m: 1:51.76
James Hickman (GB)
Paris, France, 28 March 1998

Medley

100 m: 53.10
Jani Nikanor Sievinen (Finland)
Malmö, Sweden, 30 Jan 1996

200 m: 1:54.65
Jani Sievinen (Finland)
Kuopio, Finland, 21 Jan 1994

400 m: 4:05.41
Marcel Wouda (Netherlands)
Paris, France, 8 Feb 1997

4 x 50-m: 1:35.51
Germany
Sheffield, S Yorks, UK, 13 Dec 1998

4 x 100-m: 3:28.88
Australia
Hong Kong, China, 4 April 1999

Grant Hackett holds three individual world swimming records.

WOMEN

Freestyle

50 m: 24.23
Le Jingyi (China)
Palma de Mallorca, Spain, 3 Dec 1993

100 m: 53.01
Le Jingyi (China)
Palma de Mallorca, Spain, 2 Dec 1993

200 m: 1:54.17
Claudia Poll (Costa Rica)
Gothenburg, Sweden, 18 April 1997

400 m: 4:00.03
Claudia Poll (Costa Rica)
Gothenburg, Sweden, 19 April 1997

800 m: 8:15.34
Astrid Strauss (GDR)
Bonn, Germany, 6 Feb 1987

1,500 m: 15:43.31
Petra Schneider (GDR)
Gainesville, Florida, USA, 10 Jan 1982

4 x 50-m: 1:39.56
Germany
Sheffield, S Yorks, UK, 13 Dec 1998

4 x 100-m: 3:34.55
China
Gothenburg, Sweden, 19 April 1997

4 x 200-m: 7:51.70
Sweden
Hong Kong, China, 1 April 1999

Backstroke

50 m: 27.27
Sandra Volker (Germany)
Sheffield, S Yorks, UK, 13 Dec 1998

100 m: 58.50
Angel Martino (USA)
Palma de Mallorca, Spain, 3 Dec 1993

200 m: 2:06.09
He Cihong (China)
Palma de Mallorca, Spain, 5 Dec 1993

Breaststroke 50 m: 30.77
Han Xue (China)
Gelsenkirchen, Germany, 2 Feb 1997

100 m: 1:05.70
Samantha Riley (Australia)
Rio de Janeiro, Brazil, 2 Dec 1995

200 m: 2:20.22
Masami Tanaka (Japan)
Hong Kong, China, 2 April 1999

Butterfly

50 m: 26.05
Jenny Thompson (USA)
College Station, Texas, USA, 2 Dec 1998

100 m: 56.90
Jenny Thompson (USA)
College Station, Texas, USA, 1 Dec 1998

200 m: 2:05.65
Susan O'Neill (Australia)
Malmö, Sweden, 17 Feb 1999

Medley

100 m: 59.30
Jenny Thompson (USA)
Hong Kong, China, 2 April 1999

200 m: 2:07.79
Allison Wagner (USA)
Palma de Mallorca, Spain, 5 Dec 1993

400 m: 4:29.00
Dai Gouhong (China)
Palma de Mallorca, Spain, 2 Dec 1993

4 x 50-m: 1:52.13
Germany
Sheffield, S Yorks, UK, 13 Dec 1998

4 x 100-m: 3:57.62
Japan
Hong Kong, China, 3 April 1999

waterskiing

SLALOM
Men: 1 buoy on 9.75-m (32-ft) line
Jeff Rogers (USA)
Charleston, South Carolina, USA,
31 Aug 1997
Andy Mapple (GB)
Miami, Florida, USA,
4 Oct 1998
Women: 1 buoy on 10.25-m (34-ft) line
Kristi Overton Johnson (USA)
West Palm Beach, Florida, USA,
14 Sept 1996

TRICKS
Men: 11,680 points
Cory Pickos (USA)
Zachary, Louisiana, USA, 10 May 1997
Women: 8,580 points
Tawn Larsen (USA)
Groveland, Florida, USA, 4 July 1992

JUMPING
Men: 67.8 m (222 ft)
Bruce Neville (Australia)
Orangeville, Canada, 27 July 1997
John Swanson (USA)
Bow Hill, Washington, USA,
13 Sept 1997
Women: 50.5 m (165 ft)
Brenda Nichols Baldwin (USA)
Okahumpka, Florida, USA,
27 April 1997

Andy Mapple, slalom joint record-holder

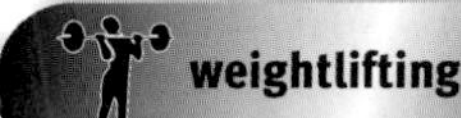

weightlifting

On 1 Jan 1998 the International Weightlifting Federation (IWF) introduced modified bodyweight categories, thereby making the then-world records redundant. This is the current list, with world standards where no record has yet been set.

Records achieved at IWF-approved events, exceeding the world standard/record by 0.5 kg for snatch or clean and jerk, or by 2.5 kg for the total, are acceptable as records.

MEN
Bodyweight 56 kg
Snatch: 135.5 kg
Halil Mutulu (Turkey) La Coruna, Spain,
14 April 1999
Jerk: 165.5 kg
Lan Shizang (China)
Szekszárd, Hungary, 9 May 1998
Total: 300 kg
World Standard

Bodyweight 62 kg
Snatch: 147.5 kg
Leonidas Sabanis (Greece)
Lahti, Finland, 11 Nov 1998
Jerk: 180 kg
World Standard
Total: 325 kg
World Standard
Bodyweight 69 kg
Snatch: 160 kg
Plamen Jeliazkov (Bulgaria)
Lahti, Finland, 12 Nov 1998
Jerk: 187.5 kg
Zhang Guozheng (China)
Chiba, Japan, May 1999
Total: 352.5 kg
Galabin Boevski (Bulgaria)
La Coruna, Spain, 16 April 1999
Bodyweight 77 kg
Snatch: 168 kg
Georgi Asanidze (Georgia)
Lahti, Finland, 12 Nov 1998
Jerk: 205 kg
World Standard
Total: 372.5 kg
World Standard
Bodyweight 85 kg
Snatch: 180 kg
Georgi Gardev (Bulgaria)
La Coruna, Spain,
17 April 1999
Jerk: 218 kg
Zhang Yong (China)
Tel Aviv, Israel, 24 Apr 1998
Total: 395 kg
World Standard
Bodyweight 94 kg
Snatch: 187.5 kg
World Standard
Jerk: 230 kg
World Standard
Total: 417.5 kg
World Standard
Bodyweight 105 kg
Snatch: 197.5 kg
World Standard
Jerk: 242.5 kg
World Standard
Total: 440 kg
World Standard
Bodyweight +105 kg
Snatch: 205.5 kg
Ronny Weller (Germany)
Riesa, Germany, 3 May 1998
Jerk: 262.5 kg
World Standard
Total: 465 kg
Ronny Weller (Germany)
Riesa, Germany, 3 May 1998

WOMEN
Bodyweight 48 kg
Snatch: 83.5 kg
Liu Xiuhua (China)
Bangkok, Thailand, 7 Dec 1998
Jerk: 112.5 kg
Li Xuezhao (China)
Tel Aviv, Israel, 24 April 1998
Total: 192.5 kg
Li Xuezhao (China)
Tel Aviv, Israel, 24 April 1998

Ronny Weller holds two weightlifting world records in the bodyweight +105 kg class.

Dennis Conner, America's Cup veteran

Bodyweight 53 kg
Snatch: 97.5 kg
Meng Xianjuan (China)
Chiba, Japan, 1 May 1999
Jerk: 120 kg
Yang Xia (China)
Bangkok, Thailand, 8 Dec 1998
Meng Xianjuan (China)
Chiba, Japan, 1 May 1999
Total: 217.5 kg
Meng Xianjuan (China)
Chiba, Japan, 1 May 1999
Bodyweight 58 kg
Snatch: 97.5 kg
Zhijuan Song (China)
Chiba, Japan, 1 May 1999
Jerk: 125 kg
Ri Song-hui (North Korea)
Bangkok, Thailand, 9 Dec 1998
Zhijuan Song (China)
Chiba, Japan, 1 May 1999
Total: 222.5 kg
Zhijuan Song (China)
Chiba, Japan, 1 May 1999
Bodyweight 63 kg
Snatch: 110 kg
Lei Li (China)
Chiba, Japan, 2 May 1999
Jerk: 128.5 kg
Hou Kang-feng (China)
Sofia, Bulgaria, 21 May 1998
Total: 237.5 kg
Lei Li (China)
Chiba, Japan, 2 May 1999
Bodyweight 69 kg
Snatch: 111 kg
Sun Tianni (China)
Bangkok, Thailand, 11 Dec 1998
Jerk: 135.5 kg
Milena Trendafilova (Bulgaria)
La Coruna, Spain, 16 April 1999
Total: 245 kg
Sun Tianni (China)
Bangkok, Thailand,
11 Dec 1998

Bodyweight 75 kg
Snatch: 115 kg
Wai Xiangying (China)
Bangkok, Thailand, 12 Dec 1998
Jerk: 140 kg
Tang Weifang (China)
Chiba, Japan, 3 May 1999
Total: 250 kg
World Standard
Bodyweight +75 kg
Snatch: 120.5 kg
Agata Wrobel (Poland)
La Coruña, Spain,
18 April 1999
Jerk: 155.5 kg
Tang Gonghong (China)
Tel Aviv, Israel,
24 April 1998
Total: 275 kg
Ding Meiyuan (China)
Chiba, Japan, May 1999

yachting

Olympic titles
The first sportsman ever to win individual gold medals in four successive Olympic Games was Paul Elvstrøm (Denmark), in the Firefly class in 1948 and the Finn class in 1952, 1956 and 1960.

Paul Elvstrøm also won eight other world titles in a total of six classes.

America's Cup
There have been 29 challenges since 1870, with the USA winning on every occasion except 1983 (to Australia) and 1995 (to New Zealand). In individual races sailed, US boats have won 81 races and challengers have won 13.

Most appearances in the America's Cup
Dennis Conner (USA) has made six appearances since 1974.

Admiral's Cup
The ocean racing team series to have had the most participating nations (three boats allowed to each nation) is the Admiral's Cup, organized by the Royal Ocean Racing Club.

A record 19 nations competed in 1975, 1977 and 1979.

Britain has had a record nine wins.

Highest speeds
MEN
The highest speed reached under sail on water by any craft over a 500-m (547-yd) timed run is 46.52 knots (86.21 km/h or 53.57 mph), by trifoiler *Yellow Pages Endeavour* piloted by Simon McKeon and Tim Daddo, both of Australia, at Sandy Point near Melbourne, Australia, on 26 Oct 1993.

WOMEN
The highest speed reached under sail on water by any craft over a 500-m (547-yd) timed run is by Elisabeth Coquelle (France), with 40.38 knots (74.83 km/h or 46.5 mph) at Tarifa, Spain, on 7 July 1995.

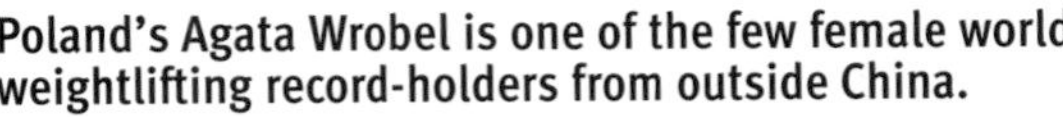

Poland's Agata Wrobel is one of the few female world weightlifting record-holders from outside China.

becoming a record breaker

The Guinness Book of Records features many people who have accomplished extraordinary feats. Do you think you have what it takes to become one of those extraordinary people? If you think you would like to break, or establish, a record, you are on the way to getting into the book.

'I CAN DO THAT!'
Not everyone can break the 100-m track record, walk the high wire at a record altitude or become the world's youngest supermodel. But everyone can break or set a record, as an individual or as part of a team.

One option might be to start a large and unusual collection. This need not entail great expense: among current record-breaking collections are four-leaf clovers and lightbulbs. Nor would you have to be a professional dancer to take part in an attempt on the world line dance record.

Even the most sedentary could participate in a record-breaking event — by joining in the biggest gathering of couples kissing simultaneously, for instance. Another way of getting into the book could be to devise your own record category.

Every day brings innovative suggestions for new record categories and we try to find ways of accepting as many of these ideas as possible. What we are looking for in a new category is a challenge that is interesting, requires skill, is safe and — most importantly — is likely to attract subsequent challenges from other people.

One recent expansion of record categories has been the reintroduction of marathons, from DJ broadcasts and quizzes to musical and sporting feats. These were temporarily rested in 1990–91 owing to increasing concerns about safety. We have found ways to reintroduce marathons in a new form, with strict guidelines emphasising the safety of the competitor. A line has been drawn under the marathon records of the past — those records will never be broken.

All record-breakers receive a certificate recognizing that they have become a member of an exclusive body — official *Guinness Book of Records* record holders. To receive that sought-after certificate you have not only to break a record, either as an individual or as part of a team, but also to prove that you have done so.

DOCUMENTATION
Dozens of people have attempted to break records in the most public way possible — in front of millions of viewers on the *Guinness® World Records* TV show. But any potential record-breaker must allow his or her attempt to be scrutinized.

A requirement for all record challenges is a clearly-labelled VHS video tape (with the official clock in view when appropriate to the record category). Reproducible colour photographs or transparencies should also be submitted with the record claim. Newspaper cuttings, usually local, are useful additional evidence. It is a good idea to get your local newspaper interested in your record challenge and persuade a reporter to be present.

Each and every record claim must be accompanied by detailed documentation. Two independent witness statements are the minimum requirement, and your witnesses should be people of some standing in the local community: a doctor, lawyer, councillor, police officer or an official of a professional or sporting body, for example. Certain records may also require the judgement of an expert, such as a surveyor or a public health official. Neither witness should be related to you. Witnesses should not only be able to confirm that they have seen the successful progress and completion of the record attempt, but also that the guidelines have been followed. *The Guinness Book of Records* is unable to supply personnel to invigilate attempts but reserves the right to do so.

Many record attempts also require a log book or some form of similar documentation. These requirements are specified in the guidelines.

MOST DOMINOS STACKED

Edwin Sirko (USA) stacked 545 dominos on top of a single vertical domino on 11 April 1998 in Irvine, California, USA. The stack remained standing for 1 hour. Could you do better?

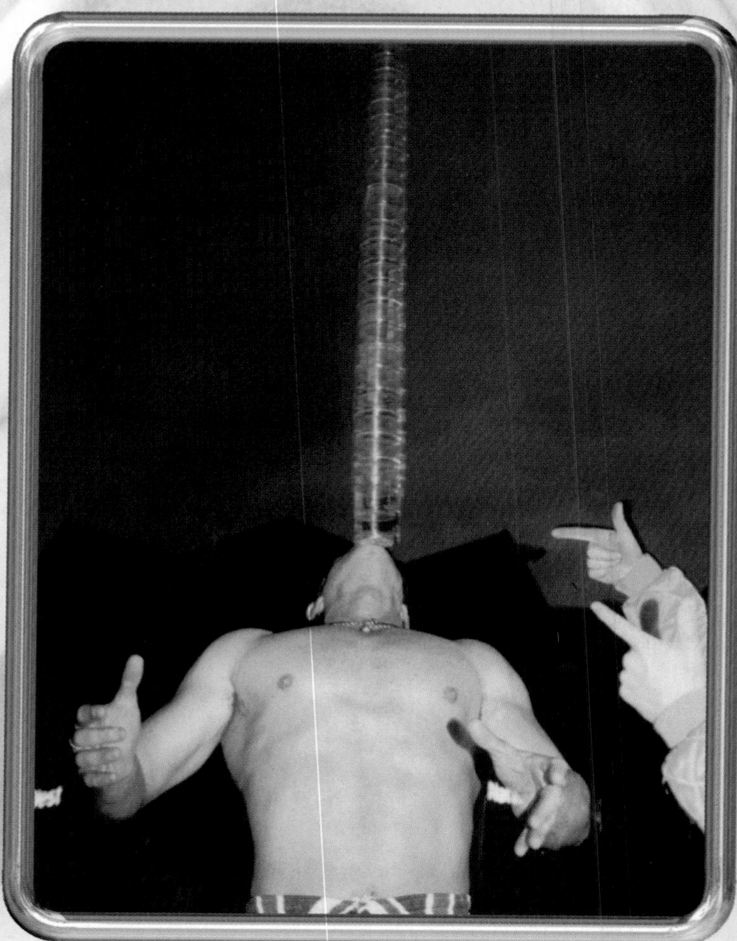

MOST GLASSES BALANCED ON THE CHIN

Terry Cole is pictured balancing 80 pint glasses on his chin in Walthamstow, London, UK. Before embarking upon a record attempt you must get in touch with us to find out what the relevant Guinness Book of Records *guidelines are.*

LONGEST CHEWING GUM WRAPPER CHAIN

Gary Duschl (Canada) began making a chain of chewing gum wrappers in 1965. By March 1999 it was 9.38 km (5 miles 1,458 yd) long. He provided full documentation to support his claim including articles from local newspapers and signed witness statements.

BIGGEST SWATCH WATCH COLLECTION

Fiorenzo Barindelli is pictured with his record-breaking collection of 3,524 Swatch watches — the biggest in the world. Interest in collections is evident from the many requests from collectors received by The Guinness Book of Records. *To be considered for inclusion, collections should be clearly 'themed' or contain broadly similar, but different, items. Duplicates do not count.*

APPLY EARLY
Whatever record category you decide to attempt, it is important to contact us early. If your proposal is accepted as a new category, we may have to draw up new guidelines with the assistance of experts. So please allow both us and you plenty of time for preparation. You should also check with us shortly before the attempt in order to make sure that the record has not recently been broken.

GETTING IN TOUCH
To contact *The Guinness Book of Records*, call: 0891 517607 (++ 44 891 517607 if calling from outside the UK). Calls currently cost no more than 50p per minute if dialling from within the UK.
Alternatively, you can e-mail us at:
infouk@guinnessrecords.com
fax us on:
020 7891 4504 (++ 44 20 7891 4504 if dialling from outside the UK)
or write to us at:
GUINNESS WORLD RECORDS LTD.,
338 EUSTON ROAD,
LONDON NW1 3BD,
UNITED KINGDOM

WILL IT BE IN THE BOOK?
Not all new records appear in the book. With tens of thousands of records on the *Guinness Book of Records* database, the book is a selection of the subjects and categories that we believe are of the most interest to our readers.

TAKING CARE
Safety precautions are an important factor in record guidelines. All record attempts are undertaken at the sole risk of the competitor. Guinness World Records Ltd. cannot be held responsible for any (potential) liability whatsoever arising out of any such attempt, whether to the claimant or any third party.

GUIDELINES
For most human endeavour categories *The Guinness Book of Records* has specific guidelines to ensure that all contestants are attempting a record under exactly the same conditions as previous and subsequent challengers. Only in this way will we be able to compare achievements.

Guinness World Records **was first shown on 14 May 1999. Hosted by West Ham and former England striker Ian Wright and former model and actress Kate Charman, the show was produced by London Weekend Television for the ITV Network. Here's a reminder of some of the amazing people featured on the show.**

STRETCHIEST SKIN
Gary Turner of Caistor, Lincs, UK, has a mild case of Ehlers Danlos Syndrome enabling his skin to stretch out 15.24 cm (6 in).

MOST MOVING CARS JUMPED
Jake Semtex of Ripley, Derbys, UK, completed a head-on motorcycle jump over four saloon cars from a ramp mounted on the lead car.

MOST SWORDS SWALLOWED BY A WOMAN
Amy Saunders of London, UK, swallowed five 35.56–53.34-cm (14–21-in) swords.

MOST INVERTED SPINS
Chris Gauge of St Agnes, Cornwall, UK, completed 64 complete rotations while in helicopter spin skysurfing position in 20 seconds.

MOST BENCHPRESSES OF A PERSON
Layne Snook benchpressed Ian Wright and a specially designed bench — a combined weight of 106.28 kg (234 lb 5 oz) — 56 times in one minute.

FASTEST MOTORBIKE SKIER
Gary Rothwell from Liverpool, UK, reached a record speed of 251.5 km/h (156.3 mph) while being pulled by a motorcycle on 2-mm-thick ($^2/_{25}$-in) titanium-soled boots.

NARROWEST J-TURN & TIGHTEST PARALLEL PARKING
Russ Swift of Darlington, UK, made a J-turn in a 1.72-m (5-ft $7^1/_2$-in) gap. He turned a Ford Escort Estate through 180° from reversing in a straight line to driving forwards in a straight line. The car was 4.26 m (14 ft) long and the turning area was 5.98 m (19 ft $7^1/_2$ in) wide. He also performed a parallel parking manoeuvre (parking with a handbrake turn into the tightest possible space without touching the kerb or other cars) in a space measuring 33.5 cm (1 ft $1^2/_5$ in).

HEAVIEST DOG
Murphy, an English Mastiff owned by Martin and Julie Barker, weighs 110 kg (17 st 4 lb).

MOST MARTIAL ARTS BOARDS BROKEN
Trish Chang of Wembley, Middx, UK, broke 185 standard martial arts wooden pine boards measuring 25.4 x 20.32 x 2.54 cm (10 x 8 x 1 in) in two minutes.

MOST SUCCESSFUL BIONIC ARM
Campbell Aird of Moffatt, UK, has learnt to control his artificial arm by training the muscles in his shoulder to activate pressure sensors.

FASTEST WHEELIE
Patrick Furstenhoff (Sweden) reached a speed of 307.9 km/h (191.3 mph).

GREATEST GLUTTON
Peter Dowdeswell of Earlsbarton, Northants, UK, ate 0.47 litres (1 pint) of strained oxtail soup, 454 g (1 lb) of mashed potato, 227 g (8 oz) of tinned sausages and baked beans and 50 prunes in 45 seconds.

MOST CONCRETE BLOCKS SMASHED
Austin Goh of London, UK, broke a total of 15 concrete blocks measuring 43.5 x 21 x 7.5-cm (17 x $8^1/_4$ x 3 in) in one minute. He then had 16 blocks smashed on his chest.

MOST BEES IN MOUTH
Dr Norman Gary held 109 venomous bees his mouth for 10 seconds.

BUS PULLED FURTHEST WITH HAIR
Letchemanah Ramasamy (Malaysia) pulled a double-decker bus weighing 7.874 tonnes a record distance of 32.85 m (107 ft 9 in).

TALLEST MAN IN THE UK
Christopher Greener, who comes from Hayes, Middlesex, UK, is 2.29 m (7 ft $6^3/_4$ in) tall.

MOST TATTOOED HUMAN
Tom Leppard of Skye, UK, has 99.9% of his body covered.

MOST TATTOOED SENIOR CITIZEN
Isobel Varley of Stevenage, Herts, UK, has 76% body coverage.

HEAVIEST CAR BALANCED
John Evans of Heanor, Derbys, UK, balanced a Mini weighing 159.67 kg (352 lb) on his head for 33 seconds.

TOP SPEED AND DISTANCE IN A ZORB BALL
Rich Eley of Telford, Salop, UK, reached a speed of 49.9 km/h (31 mph) in a standard Zorb ball. He also achieved a distance record of 323 m (1,060 ft).

MOST CRABWALK DUNKS
Gavin Chiu of Ruislip, Middx, UK, made eight dunks into a 48.26-cm-high (19-in) basketball hoop while walking on his hands. He was wearing a helmet with a 17.78-cm (7-in) colander attached to it, from which he dropped a standard volleyball.

MOST RATTLESNAKES IN BATH
Jackie Bibby sat in a tub with 35 western diamondback rattlesnakes.

MOST CONTINUOUS HEADSPINS
Jason 'EZ Rock' Geoffrey of Chicago, Illinois, USA, made 28 headspins.

MOST STRAWS STUFFED IN MOUTH
Jim Purol (USA) crammed 151 drinking straws into his mouth.

MOST PEGS ON FACE
Timo Heitala (Sweden) put 86 ordinary wooden clothes pegs on his face, beating his old record of 81.

MOST BARANIS
Dominic Swaffer of Maidstone, Kent, UK, did 84 baranis in one minute using a standard trampoline. A barani is a somersault with a half-twist.

BIGGEST MANTLE OF BEES
Mark Biancaniello (USA) 'wore' 353,150 bees weighing 39.69 kg (87 lb 8 oz).

HIGHEST MARTIAL ARTS KICK
Paul Ingleton of Wembley, Middx, UK, kicked a target at a height of 2.667 m (8 ft 9 in). The target had a pin attached, which burst a balloon.

MOST ITEMS MEMORIZED
Dominic O'Brien of Barley, Herts, UK, memorized and then recalled 51 random items in the order they were read to him, beating his existing record of 50 set on the US TV show *Guinness World Records: Primetime.*

MOST TRAMPOLINE SOMERSAULTS
Ken Kovatch (USA) made 122 somersaults through a standard 91-cm (3-ft) hula hoop while trampolining, breaking his own record of 101 set on the US TV show *Guinness World Records: Primetime.*

HIGHEST BALLOON SKYWALK
Mike Howard (USA) walked between two balloons at a height of 5.76 km (3 miles 1,017 yd).

MOST BASKETBALLS SPUN
Michael Kettman (USA) simultaneously spun 28 regulation Franklin Hardcourt No. 1 basketballs on a specially designed frame, beating his own record of 25, set on the US TV show *Guinness® World Records: Primetime.*

GREATEST WEIGHT BALANCED ON TEETH

Frank Simon (USA) balanced a 61.236-kg (135-lb) motorcycle on his teeth for 14.5 seconds. The feat was shown on the first edition of Guinness World Records, *shown on 14 May 1999.*

WORLD'S TALLEST MAN

Radhouane Charbib of Tunisia, who measures 2.359 m (7 ft 8⁹⁄₁₀ in) in height, appeared on Guinness World Records *on 4 June 1999. He is pictured with Kate Charman and Ian Wright, the show's presenters.*

stop press

Records are being broken all the time and our thorough verification process at Guinness World Records means that sometimes we cannot include all of the latest records in the main body of the book. Our Stop Press page allows us to bring you the very latest developments in the world of record-breaking that were happening just as we went to press. Fuller details may appear in the 2001 edition.

MOST VALUABLE OSCAR
Pop star Michael Jackson paid a record $1.54 million (£910,470) at Sotheby's, New York City, USA, for the Best Film Oscar won by producer David O. Selznick for *Gone With The Wind* (USA, 1939).

The world's most valuable Oscar, now owned by pop legend Michael Jackson.

MOST VALUABLE GUITAR
The 1956 Fender Stratocaster 'Brownie' used by Eric Clapton (UK) on his classic song *Layla* fetched $497,500 (£301,972) at a charity auction at Christie's, New York City, USA. The auction raised a total of over $5 million (£3.03 million) for the Crossroads Centre in Antigua, a drug and alcohol treatment centre founded in 1997 by Clapton, a former member of the Yardbirds, Cream and Blind Faith.

OLDEST SHIPS
Dr Robert Ballard (USA), who located the *Titanic* in 1985 and the *Bismarck* in 1988, discovered two Phoenician vessels that have been sitting half-buried in the sea bed 304.8 m (1,000 ft) below the water's surface for 2,700 years, off the coast of Israel. The two vessels, which measure 17.7 m (58 ft) and 14.6 m (48 ft) in length, appear to have had a crew of six in addition to a team of oarsmen. The Phoenicians, who founded the city of Carthage on the coast of north Africa, were a sea-going people who lived on the eastern Mediterranean coast from 2,300 BC to 300 BC.

LONGEST STAY ON MT EVEREST
Babu Chhiri Sherpa from Nepal completed a stay of 21 hours at the summit of Mt Everest (8,848 m or 29,029 ft) without the use of bottled oxygen — other climbers who reach the summit usually stay for no longer than an hour. Chhiri climbed Mt Everest again just weeks later to become the first person to climb the mountain twice in the same season.

BIGGEST ART COMPETITION
The Winsor & Newton Millennium Painting Competition, held from 1997 to 1999, attracted a record total of 22,367 entries from amateur and professional artists in 51 countries.

LONGEST DJ MARATHON
Disc jockey Steve Harris of URN, Nottingham, UK, broadcast non-stop for 40 hours. Live coverage of the marathon was also provided on the internet.

LONGEST TAP DANCE (WOMAN)
The greatest distance tap danced by a woman was 32.24 km (20 miles 63 yd), by Angell Husted of Palmyra, Virginia, USA, who tapped for 8 hr 50 min on a 92.66-m (304-ft) plywood track at the Fluvanna County High School Gym in Palmyra.

MOST VALUABLE CEZANNE
Still Life With a Curtain, Pitcher and Bowl of Fruit by Paul Cézanne sold at Sotheby's, New York City, USA, for $58.2 million (£35.7 million), making it the most valuable picture by the artist and the fourth most expensive painting ever sold at auction.

Babu Chhiri, who stayed on Mt Everest for a record 21 hours.

STRONGEST COMMERCIALLY AVAILABLE BEER
The strongest beer currently available commercially is Samuel Adams Triple Bock. Brewed by the Boston Beer Company, Massachusetts, USA, its alcohol content is 18% by volume and 14.4% by weight.

LONGEST LAWNMOWER RIDE
Brad Hauter of Lake in the Hills, Illinois, USA, rode a lawnmower a record 6,501 km (4,039 miles 1,056 yd) from Atlanta, Georgia, to Blanding, Utah, USA.

MOST TENNIS GRAND SLAMS (MEN)
Pete Sampras (USA) won his 12th Grand Slam tournament at Wimbledon, equalling the record that had been set by Roy Emerson (Australia) in 1967.

MOST PENALTIES MISSED IN A FOOTBALL INTERNATIONAL
Martín Palermo (Argentina) missed three penalties during his team's 0–3 defeat by Colombia in the 1999 Copa América, played in Paraguay. His first shot hit the crossbar, his second went into the stands and his third was saved.

FASTEST MILE
Hicham el-Guerrouj (Morocco) set a new record for the mile in Rome, Italy, with a time of 3:43.13.

Eric Clapton with the world's most valuable guitar.

MEN'S DECATHLON
8,994 points: Tomas Dvorak (Czech Republic). Set at Prague, Czech Republic.
Day 1: 100 m 10.54 sec; long jump 7.90 m; shot 16.76 m; high jump 2.04 m; 400 m 48.08 sec.
Day 2: 110 m-hurdles 13.73 sec; discus 48.33 m; pole vault 4.90 m; javelin 72.32 m; 1,500 m 4:37.20 sec.

WOMEN'S 50-M BUTTERFLY
Inge de Bruijn (Netherlands) set a new women's swimming record of 26.54 seconds for the 50-m butterfly at Amersfoort, Netherlands.

LARGEST BUNNY HOP
The largest Bunny Hop took place at Walt Disney World, Orlando, Florida, USA, during the Happy Easter Parade. A record 1,241 participants formed a continuous line and hopped for the required time of five minutes.

TALLEST SNOWMAN
Residents of Bethel, Maine, USA, took 14 days to build the world's tallest snowman. It was 34.633 m (113 ft $7\frac{1}{2}$ in) tall and consisted of approximately 4,587 m^3 (162,000 ft^3) of snow.

index

Acknowledgements

Founder editor: Norris McWhirter • Guinness World Records Ltd would like to thank the following organizations and individuals: Eddie Anderson • John Arblaster • Dr Joseph Arditti at Department of Developmental and Cell Biology University of California, USA • Irvine Caroline Ashasian at Fox Television • Simon Baylis • Catherine Bonifassi • Stephen Booth • Richard Braddish • Ben Brandstätter • Nandita Choudhary • Eric Christin • Debra Clapson • Deborah Colin • Mike Davis • Andrew Durham • Nick Edser • Mark Elliott • Richard Fairbairn • Adrian Fisher • Charlotte Freemantle • Mike Flynn • Sean Geer • Simon Gold • Michelle Gupta • Kevin Hardy • Sue Harper • Martin Harvey • Liz Hawley • Tom Hibbert • Ron Hildebrant • Jennifer Jaffrey • Sir Peter Johnson • Bernardo Joselvich • Kathy Kanable • Dr Ludger Kappen at Christian-Albrechts-University, Kiel, Germany • Adam Kesek • Elizabeth Leicester • Claire Lieberman • Dave McAleer • Pamela McCroskery at the Audubon Society, Fort Worth, Texas, USA • Juliet MacDonald • Chris McHugh • Bruce McLaughlin • Alexandra Maier at Autodesk • Nisse Matti • Bill Morris • Liliana Najdorf • Charlene Nikolai • Barry Norman • Karen O'Brien • Stephanie Pain • Joseph J. Pankus • Ulrike Papin • Greg Parkinson • Dr Paul Parsons • Jayne Parsons • Dr Rod Peakall at Australian National University • Matthew Pettit • Roger Pfister • Dr Ronald Pine at Illinois Mathematics and Science Academy, USA • Sir Ghillean Prance at Royal Botanic Gardens, Kew, UK • Mariano Rao • Lois Reamy • Sir Martin Rees, Astronomer Royal, Cambridge University, UK • David Roberts • Dr Larry S. Roberts at Texas Technical University and University of Miami, USA • Adrián Roldán • Jim Schelberg • Henk Schiffmacher • Dr Mark Seaward at University of Bradford, UK • Dr Karl Shukur • Arvind Sikand at CineAsia Publications • Ingrid Sterner • Gary Still • Dan Stopczynski • Jackie Swanson • Paul Tidwell • Sharon Traer at Aardman Animation • Colin Uttley • Juhani Virola • Jonathan Wall • Lt Col Digby Willoughby

010 NASA
010 NASA
011 E. Lockwood/NASA
011 NASA
012 Giraffa News/Rex Features
012 Fabrice Coffrini/Keystone/AP
013 Rex Features
013 Masaharu Hatano/Reuters
014 Garry Sowerby/Odyssey International Ltd
014 Damian Dovarganes/AP
015 Y. Genvay/Sipa Press/Rex Features
016 Gopal Chitrakar/Reuters
016 Gopal Chitrakar/Reuters
017 Herwig Prammer/Reuters
018 Trippett/Sipa Press/Rex Features
018 The Cousteau Society/AP
019 Margot Nicol-Hathaway/AP
020 Tony Stone
020 Julian Makey/Rex Features
021 Michel Lethenet/DPPI/Rex Features
022 AP
023 Sidsel Jensen
023 Riky Ash
024 Antony Njuguna/Reuters
024 Villa/AP
025 Muzammil Pasha/Reuters
026 AP
026 Jim Rogash/AP
027 Reuters
030 Chuck Robinson/AP
030 Duane Burleson/AP
031 Susan Ragan/AP
032 Sakchai Lalit/AP
032 CERN
033 Charles Rex Arbogast/AP
034 Tim Ockenden/PA
034 Reuters
035 Elise Amendola/AP
035 Paul Brown/Rex Features
036 Swaminarayan Hindu Mission
036 J.Pierce/Photosport/Rex Features
037 Chris Harris/Rex Features
037 Michael Probst/AP
038 University Medical Center
038 Radu Sigheti/Reuters
039 Steven Senne/AP
040 Thierry Renavand/Sipa/Rex Features
040 Don Ryan/AP
041 Le Morvan/Kunda/Stills/Rex Features
041 Vic Thomasson/Rex Features
042 Daniel Heuclin/Sipa Press/Rex Features
042 Blondin/Sipa Press/Rex Features
043 Incredible Features/Rex Features
046 Dimitry Kinkladze
046 John Pryke/Reuters
047 Jeff Werner/Incredible Features/Rex Features
048 Ron Tom/Fox Television
048 Mike Jones/Fox Television
049 Mike Jones/Fox Television
050 Fox Television
050 Miguel Najdorf
051 Dan White
051 Simon Roberts/BBC Radio 1
052 Bristol Evening Post
052 Totally in Sand
053 David Rozing/CameraPress
054 Remy Bricka
054 Nils Jorgensen/Rex Features
055 Rex Features
056 Chris Drown/Sipa Press/Rex Features
056 Ron Rosenfeld/Rosenfeld Photography
057 Peter Brooker/Rex Features
057 Ian Sumner/Wessex Water
058 Gary Tramontina/AP
058 K.H. Wallis
059 Savita Kirloskar/Reuters
060 Santiago Lyon/AP
060 Joe Viles/Fox Television
061 Paul Chesley/Tony Stone
062 Azadour Guzelian/Rex Features
062 North of England Newspapers/Newsquest Northeast Ltd
063 Jiji Press/AFP/EPA/PA
063 Matija Kokovic/Sipa Press/Rex Features
064 Peter Brooker/Rex Features
065 Ken McKay
068 Charlotte Observer/AP
068 Rex Features
069 Clive Limpkin/Rex Features
069 Richard Young/Rex Features
070 Gerald Davis/Rex Features
070 Keystone/AP
071 Alexander Zemlianichenko/AP
071 Fabian Bimmer/AP
072 Eugene Hoshiko/AP
072 Lennox McLendon/AP
073 Kevin Wisniewski/Rex Features
074 Nils Jorgensen/Rex Features
074 Ken McKay/Rex Features
075 Werlitzer
075 Mathmos Ltd
076 Diamond Cutters International
076 Toby Melville/PA
077 Dufoto/Sipa Press/Rex Features
077 Pascal Volery/Reuters
078 Reuters
078 Michael Crabtree/Reuters
079 Russell Boyce/Reuters
079 Peter Brooker/Rex Features
080 John Lamb/Tony Stone
080 Jeff Scheid/AP
081 Rex Features
082 Lennox McLendon/AP
083 Richard Young/Rex Features
083 Rex Features
083 Bizuayehu Tesfaye/AP
086 U.S. Navy, PH2 Damon J. Moritz/AP
086 Rex Features
087 Joyce Silverstein/Rex Features
087 Lucasfilm Ltd
088 Rex Features
088 Brian Rasic/Rex Features
089 Brian Rasic/Rex Features
090 Renzo Gostoli/AP
090 Charles Ommanney/Rex Features
091 Munawar Hosain/Rex Features
092 Reuters
092 Bob Child/AP
093 Steve Holland/AP
093 Howard Burditt/Reuters
094 Barthelemy/Rex Features
094 Lionel Cironneau/AP
095 Rex Features
095 Barthelemy/Rex Features
096 Reed Saxon/AP
096 Brian Rasic/Rex Features
097 Sipa Press/Rex Features
097 Rex Features
098 Jose Goitia/AP
098 Reuters
099 Reuters
099 Eckehard Schulz/AP
100 PA
100 Jeff Christensen/Reuters
101 Alex Oliveira & Damian Dovarganes/AP
102 Kevork Djansezian/AP
102 Nils Jorgensen/Rex Features
103 Nils Jorgensen/Rex Features
103 Erik Pendzich/Rex Features
104 Rex Features
104 Neal Simpson/Empics
105 Greg Williams/Rex Features
106 Dragon News
106 Eva Magazine/Rex Features
107 Jeremy Young/Rex Features
107 Yoshikazu Tsuno/EPA/PA
108 Terry Schmitt/AP
108 Krishnan Guruswamy/AP
109 Plinio Lepri/AP
109 Adam Nadel/AP
110 Xinhua/AP
110 Peter Andrews/Reuters
111 Sintesi/Sipa Press/Rex Features
114 Miramax Films
114 MGM
115 LucasFilm Ltd
116 Gautam Rajadhyaksha/Cine Blitz
116 Gautam Rajadhyaksha/Cine Blitz
117 Gautam Rajadhyaksha/Cine Blitz
117 Gautam Rajadhyaksha/Cine Blitz
118 Rex Features
118 Spelling Entertainment/Columbia Television
119 Chris Pizzello/AP
119 Disney/AP
120 Kevork Djansezian/AP
120 Mychal Watts/East West Records/Warner Music
121 Hamish Brown/Chrysalis Records
122 Warren Johnson/Rex Features
122 Richard Young/Rex Features
123 Rex Features
123 Richard Young/Rex Features
124 Ian Waldie/Rex Features
124 Scarlet Page/Rex Features
124 John Rogers/Rex Features
125 Rex Features
126 Greg Brennan/Rex Features
126 Rex Features
127 Reed Saxon/AP
128 Dave Lewis/Rex Features
128 Mark Lennihan/AP
129 Dave Hogan/Rex Features
130 Suzanne Plunkett/AP
130 H.Kuehn/Fotex/Rex Features
131 Phil Rees/Rex Features
131 Geoff Wilkinson/Rex Features
132 Dreamworks SKG
132 Aardman Animations Ltd
133 Matt Groening/Fox Television
134 Rex Features
134 Seagaia Group
135 Reuters
136 Lucasfilm Ltd
136 Benetton/Rex Features
137 Fred Prouser/Reuters
137 Levis Strauss Ltd
138 Time/AP
138 Jim Cooper/AP
139 Michael C. York/AP
139 Mark Mawson/Rex Features
140 Reuters
140 Susan Sterner/AP
141 Jeff J. Mitchell/Reuters
142 Kathy Willens/AP
142 Rick Rycroft/AP
143 Juergen Schwarz/Reuters
144 Steve Wood/Rex Features
144 Mitch Jacobson/AP
145 Doug Mills/AP
145 Rex Features
146 Luc de Tienda/DPPI/Rex Features
146 Richard Drew/AP
147 Marks & Spencer
150 Barbara & Kalamandalam Vijayakumar
150 Nils Jorgensen/Rex Features
151 Rex Features
151 Jyoti Taglani
152 Scott McKernan/Incredible Features/Rex Features
152 Simon Kwong/Reuters
153 Rob Nelson/Fox Television
154 Joe Viles/Fox Television
154 Mike Jones/Fox Television
155 Joe Viles/Fox Television
156 AP
156 Julius Vitali/Sipa Press/Rex Features
157 Andy Whale/Tony Stone
158 Jennifer Bowles/AP
158 Frank Wiese/AP
159 RDR Productions/Rex Features
162 Cable News Network Inc/Time Warner
162 Nigel Marple/AP
163 Andy Pearlman/Shooting Star
163 The Alta Vista Company
164 Hewlett Packard
164 Origin
165 Autodesk
166 Mike Segar/Reuters
167 Rex Features
168 Sega of America/Court Mast/AP
168 Microsoft Corporation
169 Electronic Arts
169 Eidos Interactive
170 Sergio Perez/Reuters
170 Joe Brockert/AP
171 Sam Ogden/Science Photo Library
172 Reuters
172 Hughes Space and Communications
173 NASA
174 Sony Corporation
174 Koji Sasahara/AP
175 Diamond
175 Koji Sasahara/AP
175 Sony Corporation
176 McLaren Cars
177 Rex Features
177 Mercedes Benz
178 Peter Rosendahl
178 Morbidelli Motorcycles
179 Eriko Sugita/Reuters
179 Suzuki
180 Yellow Pages Endeavour
180 Donald Stits
181 Linda Radin/AP
181 Oxley/Rex Features
182 Jet Propulsion Laboratories/AP
182 ESA/Ducros/AP
183 NASA
183 NASA
185 Tony Larkin/Rex Features
185 U.S. Army
188 Gleb Garanich/Reuters
188 Itsuo Inouye/AP
189 AP
189 Zaheeruddin Abdullah/AP
190 John Gaps III/AP
190 George Mulala/Reuters
191 Al Jawad/Rex Features
191 Reuters
192 Felice Calabro/AP
192 Sergo Edisherashvilli/Reuters
193 Charles Daughty/AP
193 NASA/AP
194 Jacques Boissinot/AP
194 Austrian Defense Ministry/AP
195 Victor R. Caivano/AP
195 Toko Shimbun/AP
196 Humberto Pradera/Agencia Estado/AP
196 Dario Lopez Mills & Joe Cavaretta/AP
197 Sergei Karpukhin/AP
198 Corinne Dufka/Reuters
198 R.J. Kumar/AP
199 Tran Viet Duc/YNS/AP
200 Rex Features
200 Apichart Weerawong/Reuters
201 Peter Frey/Rex Features
202 Wellcome Trust
202 Wellcome Trust
203 Wellcome Trust
204 William Lesch/The Image Bank
204 F. Gohier/Jacana
205 Joseph van Os/The Image Bank
208 Phil Walter/Fotopress/AP
208 Michael Pissotte/DPPI/Rex Features
208 Bernd Kammerer/AP
209 Lehtikuva Oy/Rex Features
210 Stephane Compoint/DPPI/Rex Features
210 Matt York/AP
210 Rex Features
211 Eric Risberg/AP
212 Denis Poroy/AP
212 Rex Features
213 De Tienda/DPPI/Rex Features
213 Neale Hayes/Rex Features
214 Madonna di Campiglio/Reuters
214 Felice Calabro/AP
215 Rex Features
215 Beth A. Keiser/AP
216 Claudio Scaccini/AP
216 Armando Trovati/AP
217 Srdjan Zivulovic/Reuters
217 Steve Powell/Allsport
218 Rex Features
218 Eric Johansen/Scanpix/AP
219 Stephano Rellandini/Reuters
220 Shaun Best/Reuters
221 Robert Galbraith/AP
221 David Zalubowski/AP
222 Dieter Endlicher/AP
222 Michael Probst/AP
222 Viorgos Karahalis/Reuters
223 Domenico Stinellis/AP
224 Eric Gay/AP
224 Charles Knight/Rex Features
225 Sean Garnsworthy/AP
225 Jack Smith/AP
226 Blake Sell/Reuters
226 Pierre Virot/Reuters
227 Tony Marshall/Empics
227 Rick Stevens/AP
228 Neal Simpson/Empics
228 Clive Brunskill/Allsport
229 Tony Marshall/Empics
230 Marc Aspland/Rex Features
230 Rex Features
231 DPPI/Rex Features
232 Jack Dempsey/AP
232 Duane Burleson/AP
233 Tom Strattman/AP
233 Tony Gutierrez/AP
234 Matthew Ashton/Empics
234 Max Nash/AP
235 Saurabh Das/AP
235 Chris Turvey/Empics
236 Steve Morton/Empics
236 Mark Baker/Reuters
237 Neal Simpson/Empics
237 Paul Hackett/Reuters
238 Kevork Djansezian/AP
238 Alan Mothner/AP
238 Moliere/Rex Features
239 Damian Dovarganes/AP
240 Beth A. Keiser/AP
240 Fred Jewell/AP
240 Eric Draper/AP
241 Gene J. Puskar/AP
242 Mercedes-Benz
242 Eduardo Di Baia/AP
242 Lionel Cironneau/AP
243 Geoff Wilkinson/Rex Features
244 Tony Marshall/Empics
244 Michel Spingler/AP
245 Eric Gaillard/Reuters
245 Alejandro Pagni/AP
246 John Moran/Rex Features
246 Michel Euler/AP
247 Frank Gunn/ Canadian Press/AP
248 Vim Jethwa/Rex Features
248 Jeffrey Werner/Rex Features
249 Steve Christo/Sydney Morning Herald/AP
249 Paul Sakuma/AP
250 Hans Edinger/AP
250 ANSA/Reuters
251 Ronen Zilberman/AP
251 John Bazemore/AP
252 Chiaki Tsukumo/AP
252 Kang Hyungwon/AP
253 Laszlo Balogh/Reuters
254 Wade Payne/AP
255 International Game Fish Association
255 Jeff Yinnick/Reuters
256 Lynne Sladky/AP
257 Ina Fassbender/Reuters
257 Remy Steinegger/Reuters
258 Alan Diaz/AP
258 Nick Wass/AP
259 Adrian Dennis/AP
259 Rick Rycroft/AP
260 Michel Euler/AP
260 Fernando Llano/AP
261 Rusty Kennedy/AP
261 Frank Augstein/AP
262 Mark Baker/Reuters
263 Shizuo Kambayashi/AP
263 Andy Mettler/Reuters
264 Reuters
264 Bernhard Grossruck/AP
265 Steve Powell//Allsport
266 Denis Paquin/AP
266 Martin Cleaver/AP
267 Bobby Yip/Reuters
267 Mike Fiala/AP
268 Simon Bruty/Allsport
268 Garrige Ho/Reuters
269 Lehtikuya/Reuters
269 Stephen Munday/Allsport
270 Travis Carpenter
276 Fox Television
277 Della Batchelor
284 J.Gilroy

history of the book

 **CASTLEBRIDGE HOUSE**

Castlebridge House, Co. Wexford, Ireland, where Sir Hugh Beaver first put forward the idea of a book of records.

 **PARK ROYAL BREWERY**

A shot of Guinness' Park Royal Brewery, London, UK, taken in the 1960s.

In 1759 Arthur Guinness founded the Guinness Brewery at St James' Gate, Dublin, and by 1833 the brewery was the largest in Ireland. Arthur Guinness Son & Co. Ltd became a limited liability company in London in 1886, and by the 1930s Guinness had two breweries in Britain producing its special porter stout. The slogans 'Guinness is good for you', 'Guinness for strength' and 'My Goodness, My Guinness' appeared everywhere. Guinness was the only beer on sale in every public house, yet Guinness did not actually own any of the pubs — except for the Castle Inn on its hop farms at Bodiam, Sussex. Thus the company was always on the look-out for promotional ideas.

Whilst at a shooting party in Co. Wexford, Ireland, in 1951, Sir Hugh Beaver, the company's managing director, was involved in a dispute as to whether the golden plover was Europe's fastest game bird. In 1954, another argument arose as to whether grouse were faster than golden plover. Sir Hugh realized that such questions could arise among people in pubs and a book that provided answers for debates such as these would be of great use to licensees.

Chris Chataway, the record-breaking athlete, was then an underbrewer at Guinness' Park Royal Brewery in London. He recommended the ideal people to produce the book — the twins Norris and Ross McWhirter, whom he had met through athletics events, both having won their blues for sprinting at Oxford. The McWhirters were then running a fact-finding agency in Fleet Street. They were commissioned to compile what became *The Guinness Book of Records* and, after a busy year of research, the first copy of the 198-page book was bound on 27 August 1955. It was an instant success and became Britain's No. 1 best-seller before Christmas.

The *Guinness Book of Records* English edition is now distributed in 70 different countries with another 22 editions in foreign languages. Sales of all editions passed 50 million in 1984, 75 million in 1994 and will reach the 100 million mark early in the next decade.

THE GUINNESS TOUCAN

Pictured right is the first Guinness advertisement to feature the toucan — arguably Guinness advertising's most recognizable icon. The poster was produced by the advertising agency S.H. Benson of London, UK, in 1935. Crime writer Dorothy L. Sayers, then a Benson employee, provided the copy, while the design was by John Gilroy. The toucan went on to appear on countless Guinness print advertisements, animated commercials, promotional merchandise and show cards, often sporting two pints of Guinness on its beak.